STUDY GUIDE

STATISTICS FOR MANAGEMENT AND ECONOMICS

Sixth Edition

STUDY GUIDE

STATISTICS FOR MANAGEMENT AND ECONOMICS

Sixth Edition

William Mendenhall
Professor Emeritus, University of Florida

James E. Reinmuth
University of Oregon

Robert Beaver
University of California, Riverside

Prepared by

Barbara M. Beaver
Robert J. Beaver
University of California, Riverside

PWS-KENT Publishing Company
Boston

PWS Publishers is a division of Wadsworth, Inc.

ISBN 0-53491-659-7

Printed in the United States of America

90 91 92 93 — 10 9 8 7 6 5 4 3 2

PREFACE

The study of statistics differs from the study of many other college subjects. Not only must students absorb a set of basic concepts and applications, they must also acquire a new language.

Understanding the meaning of words employed in the study of a subject is a prerequisite to the mastery of concepts. Such understanding offers little difficulty in many branches of the physical, social, and biological sciences; many terms related to these disciplines occur in the curricula of the public schools, in the news media, in periodicals, and in everyday conversation. In contrast, few students encounter the language of probability and statistical inference before embarking on an introductory college-level study of the subject. However, for a student of business and economics, familiarization with this language and a working knowledge of the methods of probability and statistical inference are minimal requirements for mastering the complexities of economic forecasting, production control, and marketing research.

This study guide attempts to lead the student through the language and concepts necessary for a mastery of the material in *Statistics for Management and Economics* by Mendenhall, Reinmuth, and Beaver (Duxbury Press, 1989). The intent of both the study guide and the textbook it accompanies is to present a study of probability and statistical inference, relate the information given to problems in business and economics through examples and exercises, and supplement the material with some statistical methods of special interest within the fields of business and economics.

Although the study guide is intended to be a supplement to the textbook, *Statistics for Management and Economics* by Mendenhall, Reinmuth, and Beaver, it can be used effectively by itself in certain instances. For the graduate student or individual seeking a quick but thorough review of the elements of business and economic statistics, the study guide alone provides a valuable aid.

A study guide with answers is intended to be an individual student study aid. The subject matter is presented in an organized manner that incorporates continuity with repetition. For the most part, the chapters bear the same titles and order as the textbook chapters. Within each chapter, the material both summarizes and reexplains the essential concepts from the corresponding textbook chapter. This gives the student more than one perspective on each topic and, hopefully, enhances his understanding of the material.

At appropriate points in each chapter, the student will encounter a set of Self-Correcting Exercises in which problems relating to new material are presented. Terse, stepwise solutions to these problems are found at the back of the study guide and can be referenced by the student at any intermediate point in the solution of each problem, or used as a stepwise check on any final answer. These exercises not only provide the student with the answers to specific problems, but also reinforce the stepwise logic required to arrive at a correct solution to each problem.

With the exception of Chapter 14, further sets of exercises can be found at the end of each chapter. These exercises are provided for the student who feels that additional individual practice is needed in solving the kinds of problems found within each chapter. At this point, having been given stepwise solutions to the Self-Correcting Exercises, the student is now presented only with final answers to these problems. Hopefully, when the student's answer disagrees with that given in the study guide, the solutions to similar Self-Correcting Exercises can be recalculated and compared and then the error can be found. If the answer given disagrees with the student's only in decimal accuracy, this difference can be taken to be due only to rounding error at various stages in the calculations.

When the study guide is used as a supplement, the textbook chapter should be read first. Then the student should study the corresponding chapter within the study guide. Key words, phrases, and numerical computations have been left blank for the student to insert a response. The answers are presented in the page margins. These should be covered until the student has supplied the response. One should bear in mind that in some instances, more than one answer may be appropriate for a given blank. It is left to the reader to determine whether the answer is synonymous with the answer given within the margin.

Since perfection is something to be desired, we ask that the reader who has located an error kindly bring it to our attention.

CONTENTS

Chapter 1

WHAT IS STATISTICS?

1.1 The Population and the Sample

Statistics most often involves sampling from a larger body of data called a ______. Consider the following examples of statistical problems. population

1. The opinions of stockholders in a large corporation are of interest to the board of directors of the corporation. Rather than poll the entire set of stockholders, questionnaires are sent only to a selected group.
2. An experiment was conducted by the owner of a taxi company to determine the tire wear after 10,000 miles of use of the tires of a particular manufacturer. Ten of the manufacturer's tires were placed on the right rear wheels of ten different taxis. The amount of tread on the manufacturer's ten tires after 10,000 miles of use is recorded.

The following characteristics are common to both of these statistical problems.

a. The measurements or observations obtained cannot be predicted in advance.
b. A sample is taken from a larger body of data.
c. From each element in the sample, one or more measurements or pieces of data are collected.
d. It is assumed that the conclusions drawn from the study apply to more than those elements within the sample. For example, opinions of all stockholders would comprise the larger set of measurements of interest to the experimenter. This larger set of measurements is called a population.

A population can exist conceptually or it can exist in fact. In example 2, given above, the measurements constitute a ______ population of measurements made on tires under the same experimental conditions. On the other hand, consider the problem of estimating the proportion of stockholders of a particular corporation who are in favor of a certain proposal. Here, each voting stockholder in favor of the proposal could be counted as a "1," and those opposed or conceptual

population

having no opinion as a "0." For this problem, the ______________ consists of a set of ones and zeros associated with the stockholders in the corporation.

sample

A ______________ is a subset of measurements selected from the population.

actual

1. One hundred businessmen, chosen as a cross-section of a given city, were polled regarding their opinion about the new city bond issue. These 100 businessmen represent a sample from the (actual, conceptual) population of businessmen of that city.

sample; conceptual

2. Examination scores are recorded for 5 business students who have been taught using a certain experimental method. These scores represent a ______________ from a(n) (actual, conceptual) population consisting of the large number of measurements that might have been obtained from other students placed under similar conditions.

In statistical terminology, we should make a distinction between the objects upon which measurements are taken and the measurements themselves. For the stockholder example, the set of "0"s and "1"s associated with the stockholders' opinion constituted the population, and not the stockholders themselves. Although the distinction is often not made in practice, the objects upon which measurements are taken are called experimental units or elements of the sample (or population). The sample (or population) consists of the measurements themselves.

1.2 Descriptive and Inferential Statistics

Statistical procedures are categorized as belonging to one of two types depending on the purpose of the experimenter.

Descriptive

1. (Descriptive, Inferential) statistics consist of procedures used to summarize the information in a set of measurements and describe its important characteristics.

Inferential

2. (Descriptive, Inferential) statistics consist of procedures used to make inferences about population characteristics from information contained in a sample.

population

sample

inferences

If the experimenter has collected measurements which represent the entire set of measurements in which he is interested, then the experimenter has enumerated the entire (population, sample). In this case, he need only use descriptive statistical techniques to summarize the pertinent information. On the other hand, if the experimenter has collected measurements which represent only a *subset* of the entire set in which he is interested, then the experimenter has collected a (population, sample). Although descriptive techniques can be used to summarize the information in the sample, the experimenter will more often be interested in using inferential statistical techniques. Inferential statistics is concerned with a theory of information and its application in making inferences based on sample information about populations in the sciences and industry. The objective of inferential statistics is to make ________ about a population from information contained in a sample.

1.3 The Parts of an Inferential Statistical Problem

We have noted that the objective of inferential statistics is to make inferences about a ______________ based on information contained in a ______________. Sampling implies the acquisition of data, so statistics is concerned with a theory of information. The attainment of the objective of statistics—inference making—is dependent upon five steps, which we will call the elements of a statistical problem.

population; sample

The first important task facing the experimenter is one which is many times ignored or performed only cursorily. In order to make inferences about a population, the experimenter must be able to clearly specify the ___________ of this population. Further, the experimenter must specify the ____________ to be answered about the population using statistical inference. If the population is improperly defined, it may be that the sample will be drawn from the wrong population. Moreover, if the questions to be answered are not accurately stated, inappropriate methods of inference might be used. Before any sampling is done, the problem must be clear in the mind of the experimenter.

nature

questions

The sample contains a quantity of information on which the inference about the population will be based. In fact, information can be quantified as easily as weight, heat, profit, or other quantities of interest. Consequently, the second step in a statistical problem is deciding upon the most economical procedure for buying a specified quantity of information. This is called the ___________ procedure or the _____________ of the experiment. The cost of the specified amount of information will vary greatly depending upon the method used for collecting the data in a sample.

sampling

design

The third step in a statistical problem involves the extraction of information contained in the ______________. By analogy, suppose that information was measured in units of pounds (which it is not). It is not unusual for an experimenter to extract only three pounds from a sample that contains ten pounds of information. Thus extracting information from a sample is equivalent to the problem of extracting juice from an orange. We wish to obtain the ______________ amount of information from a given set of data.

sample

maximum

The fourth step in a statistical problem involves the use of the information in a sample to make an ______________ about the population from which the sample was drawn. Some inferences, say, estimates of the characteristics of the population, are very accurate and consequently are good. Others are far from reality and bad. It is therefore necessary to clearly define a measure of goodness for an inference maker. Most people observe the world about them and make inferences daily. Some of these subjective inference makers are very good and accurate; others are very poor. Statistical inference makers are objective rather than subjective, but they vary in their goodness. The statistician wishes to obtain the best inference maker for a given situation.

inference

A measure of the goodness or reliability of an inference is the fifth step in a statistical problem and is always necessary in order to assess its practical value. Thus, inference making is regarded as a two-step procedure. First, we select

inference
reliability

the best method and use it to make an ______________. Second, we always give a measure of the goodness or ______________ of the inference.

population; design
analysis
population
sample
goodness

The five elements of a statistical problem are (1) the definition of the specific problem and the ______________ of interest, (2) the ______________ of the experiment, (3) the ______________ of the data, (4) the procedure for making inferences about the ______________ from information contained in the ______________, and (5) the provision of a measure of the ______________ of the inference.

EXERCISES

1. A market analyst wishes to determine which factors exert the most influence on a purchaser's decision process in selecting his or her new car. Describe the population of interest to the analyst, and indicate what kind of information the analyst might consider collecting.
2. A pharmaceutical company is interested in determining whether a new drug is more effective than those currently available for treating degenerative arthritis. Identify the population or populations of interest to the researcher. Should severity and time since onset of this disease enter into any proposed sampling plan? Why or why not?
3. An agricultural economist is interested in determining the revenue loss to cotton growers in the Imperial Valley of California due to crop infestation by the pink bollworm. Identify the population of interest to the economist. Would his findings apply equally well to cotton growers in Texas?
4. A market research analyst would like to demonstrate that when brand labels on containers of cola softdrinks are removed or hidden, the cola softdrink produced by his company will be preferred over its strongest competitor by people who drink cola softdrinks. Describe the population of interest to this analyst. In taste-testing experiments, the order in which a person samples the items under test may influence his/her ultimate choice. Could this be a potential problem in this research?

Chapter 2

DESCRIBING DISTRIBUTIONS OF MEASUREMENTS

2.1 Introduction

In Chapter 1, we considered the steps involved in achieving the objective of inferential statistics, which is making ____________ about a ____________ from information contained in a ____________. An obvious but often ignored requirement is that the sample be drawn from the population of interest to the experimenter.

inferences; population
sample

How are inferences made? First, we must be able to condense and describe data in a straightforward pictorial or graphical form. Second, we must be able to reconstruct this visual representation using numerical descriptive measures that describe the salient characteristics of the visual representation. For example, where is the middle of the distribution? Are the measurements tightly grouped or widely scattered? Whether the set of data under consideration comprises an entire population or is merely a sample from a population, we must be able to agree upon numerical measures that describe the data. Inferences about a population can then be made in terms of the population by using the relevant information contained in the sample. Hence, the tools of (*inferential*, *descriptive*) *statistics* are used before the methods of (*inferential*, *descriptive*) *statistics* can be used to make inferences about a ____________. The objective of this chapter will be to introduce the reader to some of the methods used in describing data.

descriptive
inferential
population

2.2 Frequency Distributions

Graphical methods attempt to present the set of measurements in pictorial form so as to give the reader an adequate visual description of the measurements. A simple and informative method for displaying a set of data graphically is called a frequency distribution. Consider the following example.

Example 2.1
The following data are the numbers of correct responses on a recognition test consisting of 30 items, recorded for 25 students:

25	29	23	27	25
23	22	25	22	28
28	24	17	24	30
19	17	23	21	24
15	20	26	19	23

30 1. First find the highest score, which is _____, and the lowest score,
15 which is _____. These two scores indicate that the measurements have a range of 15.

2. To determine how the scores are distributed between 15 and 30, we divide this interval into subintervals of equal length. The interval from 15 to 30 could be divided into from 5 to 20 subintervals, depending upon the number of measurements available. Wishing to obtain about 7 subintervals, a suitable width is determined by dividing 30 − 15 = 15 by 7. The integer
2 _____ would seem to provide a satisfactory subinterval width for these data.

18.50–20.49 3. Utilizing the subintervals 14.50–16.49, 16.50–18.49, _____,
22.50–24.49 20.50–22.49, _____, 24.50–26.49, 26.50–28.49, 28.50–30.49, we guarantee that none of the given measurements will fall on a boundary point. Thus, each measurement falls into only one of the subintervals or classes.

4. We now proceed to tally the given measurements and record the class frequencies in a table. Fill in the missing information.

Tabulation of Data for Histogram

	Class i	*Class Boundaries*	*Tally*	*Frequency*, f_i	*Relative Frequency*, f_i/n
	1	14.50–16.49	I	1	1/25
	2	16.50–18.49	II	2	2/25
III	3	18.50–20.49	_____	3	3/25
3/25	4	20.50–22.49	III	3	_____
7	5	22.50–24.49	~~IIII~~ II	_____	7/25
24.50–26.49	6	_____	IIII	4	4/25
III	7	26.50–28.49	_____	3	3/25
	8	28.50–30.49	II	2	2/25

5. The number of measurements falling in the ith class is called the ith class frequency and is designated by the symbol f_i. Of the total number of
relative measurements, the fraction falling in the ith class is called the _____ frequency in the ith class. Given n measurements, the relative frequency in the ith class is given as f_i/n. As a check on your tabulation, remember that for k classes,
   n a. the sum of the frequencies (f_i) over all k classes is _____.
   1 b. the sum of the relative frequencies (f_i/n) over all k classes is _____.

6. With the data so tabulated, we can now use a frequency histogram (plotting frequency against classes) or a relative frequency histogram (plotting rela-

tive frequency against classes) to describe the data. The two histograms are identical except for scale.

a. Study the following histogram based on the given data.

Frequency Histogram

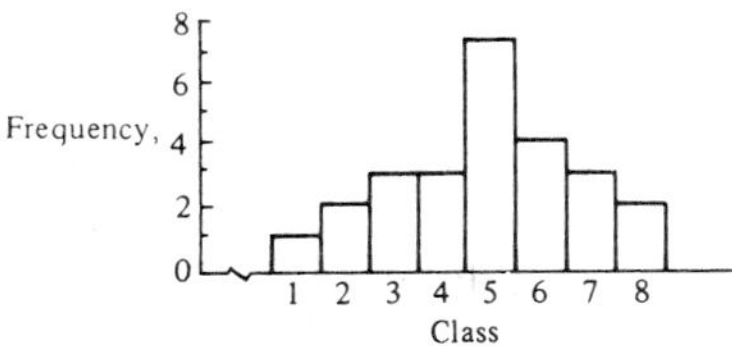

b. Complete the following relative frequency histogram for the same data:

Relative Frequency Histogram

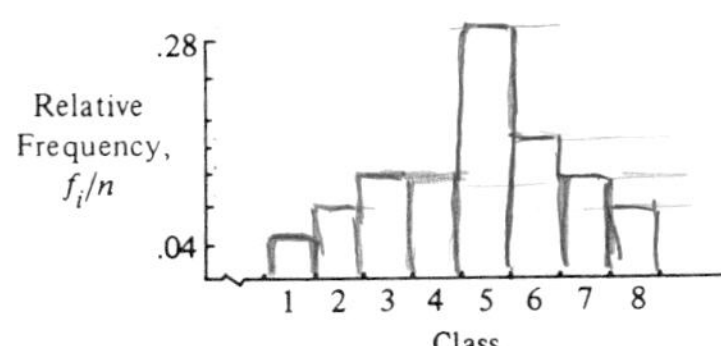

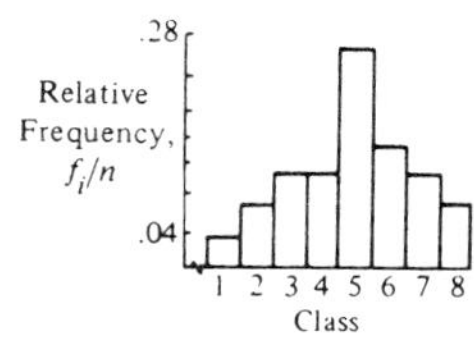

c. When completed, the histograms in parts a and b should appear identical except for scale.

7. By examining the tabulation found in step 4, answer the following questions:

a. What fraction of the respondents had scores less than 20.5? 6/25 (24%). — 6/25 or 24%

b. What fraction of the respondents had scores greater than 26.5? 5/25 (20%). — 5/25 or 20%

c. What fraction of the respondents had scores between 20.5 and 26.5? 14/25 (56%). — 14/25 or 56%

8. As the number of measurements in the sample increases, the sample histogram should resemble the population histogram more and more. Thus, to estimate the fraction of respondents in the entire population that would have scores greater than 26.5, we could use our sample histogram, estimating this fraction to be 5/25 or 20%. — 5/25; 20%

9. A relative frequency histogram is often called a relative frequency distribution because it displays the manner in which the data are distributed along the horizontal axis of the graph. The rectangular bars above the class intervals in the relative frequency histogram can be given two interpretations:

a. The height of the bar above the ith class represents the fraction of observations falling in the ith class.

b. The height of the bar above the *i*th class also represents the probability that a measurement drawn at random from this sample will belong to the *i*th class.

10. Complete the following statements based on the data tabulation in step 4.
    a. The probability that a measurement drawn at random from this data will fall in the interval 22.5 to 24.5 is ________.
    b. The probability that a measurement drawn at random from this data will be greater than 18.5 is ________.
    c. The probability that a measurement drawn at random from this data will be less than 24.5 is ________.

7/25
22/25
16/25

Example 2.2

The following data represent the burning times for an experimental lot of fuses, measured to the nearest tenth of a second:

5.2	3.8	5.7	3.9	3.7
4.2	4.1	4.3	4.7	4.3
3.1	2.5	3.0	4.4	4.8
3.6	3.9	4.8	5.3	4.2
4.7	3.3	4.2	3.8	5.4

Construct a relative frequency histogram for these data.

Solution

Fill in the missing entries in the table.

Tabulation of Data

Class	*Class Boundaries*	*Tally*	*Frequency*	*Relative Frequency*
1	2.45–2.95	I	1	.04
2	2.95–3.45	III	3	____
3	3.45–3.95	卌 I	____	.24
4	3.95–4.45	____	7	.28
5	4.45–4.95	IIII	4	____
6	____	III	3	.12
7	5.45–5.95	I	1	.04

.12
6
卌 II
.16
4.95–5.45

Relative Frequency Histogram

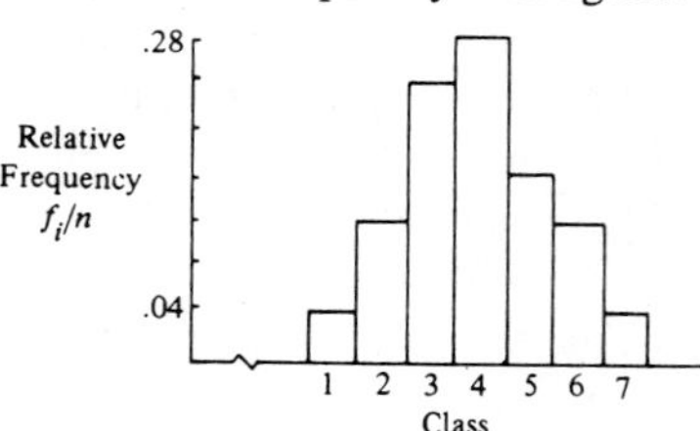

Complete the following statements based on the preceding tabulation.

1. The probability that a measurement drawn at random from this sample is greater than 4.45 is ____. 8/25
2. The probability that a measurement drawn at random from this sample is less than 3.45 is ____. 4/25
3. An estimate of the probability that a measurement drawn at random from the sampled population would be in the interval 3.45 to 4.45 is ____. 13/25

In conclusion, recall the steps necessary to construct a frequency distribution.

1. Determine the number of classes depending on the amount and uniformity of the data. It is usually best to have from ____ to ____ (give numbers) classes. 5; 20
2. Determine the class width, by dividing the range by the number of ____, and adjusting the resulting quotient to obtain a convenient figure. With the possible exception of the lowest and highest classes, all classes should be of ____ width. classes; equal
3. Locate the class ____. Class boundaries should be chosen so that it is (impossible, likely) that a measurement will fall on a boundary. boundaries; impossible

In recent years, computers and microcomputers have become much more accessible to the general public. In the field of statistics, this availability provides even the beginning student with an invaluable tool. It allows him to perform more complex types of analysis with a high degree of accuracy. Many excellent packaged programs for statistical analyses are available at most computer facilities. These programs, called *statistical* ____, differ in terms of the different types of analyses available, the options which are available within an analysis, and the form of the printed results (called ____). Some of the more common statistical packages available at computer facilities are MINITAB, SAS (Statistical Analysis Systems), SPSS (Statistical Package for the Social Sciences) and BMDP (Biomedical Package). *software*; *output*

In the text, the MINITAB and SAS software packages are most frequently used to illustrate the use of computers in implementing various statistical procedures. Even if you do not have access to these particular packages, a knowledge of the basic output generated by MINITAB and SAS will help you to interpret output generated by other *software systems*, since they are all quite similar. However, it is important that you use these statistical tools carefully. Inaccurate entry of data, improper procedure commands, or incorrect interpretation of output can result in erroneous inferences, even though the results *did* come from a computer!

The MINITAB software package can be used to generate relative frequency histograms for data which has been stored in the computer using the appropriate methods. The MINITAB system requires that the data be stored by column, using either the READ or SET commands.

The command HISTOGRAM followed by a column number will produce a histogram similar to those presented in this section. The MINITAB program and output which produce a histogram for the data in Example 2.2 are shown below.

```
MTB > HISTOGRAM C1
Histogram of C1     N = 25
Midpoint        Count
     2.5            1    *
     3.0            2    **
     3.5            3    ***
     4.0            8    ********
     4.5            5    *****
     5.0            3    ***
     5.5            3    ***
```

could
one

The first column in the HISTOGRAM output records the midpoints of the class intervals. Hence, the class intervals (could, could not) be reconstructed if needed. Each typed asterisk (*) represents ____________ (give number) observation, and the histogram is drawn vertically rather than horizontally as we have seen it previously in this section.

Self-Correcting Exercises 2A

1. The following data are the ages in years of the employees of a recently organized small manufacturing firm.

51	32	31	33	23	52
23	21	55	34	38	32
49	35	26	29	50	34
30	19	41	39	41	27
25	21	18	36	35	28
44	44	59	28	23	46
27	37	42	32	43	30

a. Find the range of these data.
b. Using about 10 intervals of equal width, set up class boundaries to be used in the construction of a frequency distribution and complete the tabulation of the data.
c. Construct a frequency histogram for these data.
d. For these same data construct a frequency histogram utilizing about 6 intervals.
e. Which histogram presents the data in the more meaningful way?

2. The following are the annual rates of profit on stockholders equity after taxes in percent for 32 industries.

10.6	10.8	14.8	10.8
12.5	6.0	10.7	11.0
14.6	6.0	12.8	10.1
7.9	5.9	10.0	10.6
10.8	16.2	18.4	10.7
10.6	13.3	8.7	15.4
6.5	10.1	8.7	7.5
11.9	9.0	12.0	9.1

a. Construct a relative frequency histogram for these data utilizing 7 intervals of length 2, beginning at 5.55.

Using your histogram (or tabulation) answer the following questions.

b. What is the probability that an industry drawn at random from this distribution has a rate of profit greater than 15.55%?
c. What is the probability that an industry drawn at random has a rate of profit less than 9.55%?
d. What is the probability that an industry drawn at random has a rate of profit greater than 9.55% but less than 15.55%?

2.3 Stem and Leaf Displays

Another method of graphical description for a set of measurements is called the *stem-and-leaf display*. It emerges from a new and quickly developing area of statistics called exploratory data analysis (EDA), whose chief proponent is John Tukey. The objective of EDA is to provide the experimenter with simple techniques which allow him to look more effectively at his data. In particular, the stem-and-leaf display represents a histogram-like picture of the data, while allowing the experimenter to retain the actual observed values of each data point. Since in the process of tabulating the data, we also create a histogram-like picture, the stem-and-leaf display is partly graphical and partly tabular in nature.

In creating a stem-and-leaf display, we must choose part of the original measurement as the *stem* and the remaining part as the *leaf*. Consider for example a set containing four measurements:

624, 538, 465, 552

We could use the digit in the "hundreds" place as the stem, and the remainder
(the digits at or to the right of the "tens" place) as the leaf. In this case, for the
stem — observation 624, the digit 6 would be the (stem, leaf) and the digits 24 would be
leaf — the (stem, leaf). We could also choose to use the digits at or to the left of the
"tens" place as the stem and the remainder as the leaf. Then for the observation
46; 5 — 465, the digit(s) __________ would be the stem and the digit(s) __________
would be the leaf. The choice of the stem-and-leaf coding depends upon the
nature of the observations at hand.

The stems and leaves are now used as follows:

1. List all the stem digits vertically, from lowest to highest.
2. Draw a vertical line to the right of the stem digits.
3. For each data point, place the leaf digit of that point in the row corresponding to the correct stem.
4. The stem-and-leaf display may be made more visually appealing by reordering the leaf digits from lowest to highest within each stem row.
5. Make sure that you provide a key to your stem-and-leaf coding, so that the reader can recreate the actual measurements from your display.

Example 2.3

The following data represent the state gasoline tax in cents per gallon for the 50 United States and the District of Columbia for a recent year.

AL	11.0	IN	11.1	NV	12.0	TN	9.0
AK	8.0	IA	13.0	NH	14.0	TX	5.0
AZ	12.0	KS	10.0	NJ	8.0	UT	11.0
AR	9.5	KY	10.0	NM	11.0	VT	11.0
CA	9.0	LA	8.0	NY	8.0	VA	11.0
CO	12.0	ME	14.0	NC	12.0	WA	16.0
CT	14.0	MD	13.5	ND	13.0	WV	15.3
DE	11.0	MA	11.0	OH	12.0	WI	15.0
DC	14.8	MI	13.0	OK	6.5	WY	8.0
FL	9.7	MN	13.0	OR	8.0		
GA	7.5	MS	9.0	PA	12.0		
HI	8.5	MO	7.0	RI	13.0		
ID	14.5	MT	15.0	SC	13.0		
IL	11.0	NE	15.5	SD	13.0		

Source: Federal Highway Adm: National Transportation Safety Board.

Construct a stem-and-leaf display for the data.

Solution

From an initial survey of the data, the largest observation is 16.0, while the smallest observation is 5.0. The data in this example are recorded in tenths of a cent. Suppose that we were to choose the leading digit, that is, the digit in the "tens" place as the stem. There would be only ______________ stems for the data, namely "0" and "1". This would not provide a very good visual description of the data. Therefore, we choose to use the digits at or to the left of the "ones" place as the stem. This is also called the "integer part" of the observation. The leaf will be the remaining digits, those falling to the (left, right) of the decimal point. two right

The stems, from 5 to 16 are listed vertically below, a vertical line is drawn, and the leaves are entered in the correct row. Fill in the missing entries in the stem-and-leaf display.

Stem	Leaves	
5	0	
6	5	
7	5 ___	0
___	0 5 0 0 0 0 0	8
9	5 0 ___ 0 0	7
10	0 0	
11	0 0 1 ___ 0 0 0 0 0	0
12	0 0 0 0 0 0	
13	0 5 0 0 0 0 0 0	
___	0 8 ___ 0 0	14; 5
15	0 5 3 0	
16	0	

As an aid to decoding the stem-and-leaf display, we write

leaf digit unit = 0.1

5 0 represents 5.0

This will allow the reader to recreate the original data from the stem-and-leaf display. The display can now be redone, with the leaves reordered from lowest to highest. Fill in the missing entries.

Stem	Leaves	
5	0	
6	5	
7	0 ___	5
8	0 0 0 0 0 0 5	
9	___ ___ 0 5 7	0; 0
10	0 0	
11	0 0 0 0 0 0 0 0 ___	1
12	___ ___ ___ 0 0 0	0; 0; 0
13	0 0 0 0 0 0 0 5	
14	0 0 0 ___ 8	5
15	0 ___ 3 5	0
16	0	

From the stem-and-leaf display, we may make the following observations:

5.0 1. The lowest state gasoline tax is __________ cents per gallon. The highest
16.0 gasoline tax is __________ cents per gallon.
no 2. There are (no, some) extreme values (values which are much higher or much lower than all the others).
are 3. The data (are, are not) approximately mound-shaped.
8.0 4. Most of the gasoline taxes fall between __________ cents per gallon and
15.5 __________ cents per gallon.

The stem-and-leaf procedure can be extended to accommodate data which do not fit easily into the structure described above. If the data consist of a large number of digits, as many as six or seven, the resulting steam-and-leaf display will have either an extremely large number of stems or an adequate number of stems with leaves consisting of four or five digit numbers. This will tend to destroy the clarity and hence the informativeness of the display. In this case, it may be more convenient to use the first one or two digits as the stem, the second one or two as the leaf, and to drop the remaining digits. Hence, we are sacrificing the ability to *exactly* recreate the data from the stem-and-leaf display in order to clarify the display.

Example 2.4

The following data represent the ultimate rated capacity in milliwatts for the world's 57 largest hydroelectric plants.

12600	4500	2700	2400	2100	1824
10080	4150	2700	2400	2069	1807
10060	4050	2700	2304	2031	1800
6480	3600	2680	2300	2030	1800
6400	3575	2650	2300	2000	1800
6000	3409	2637	2250	2000	1800
6096	3300	2610	2124	2000	1750
5328	3200	2560	2100	1979	
5225	2820	2500	2100	1950	
4600	2715	2416	2100	1890	

Construct a stem-and-leaf display for the data.

Solution

We will take the leading digit, (the digits at or to the left of the "thousands" place) to be the stem. Then to simplify the presentation, take the two digits in the "hundreds" and "tens" places as the leaf. For example, the observation 12600 will have stem 12 and leaf 60. The observation 2124 will have stem __________ and leaf __________. The stem-and-leaf plot is constructed below. As an aid to decoding the stem-and-leaf display, we write

leaf unit = 10.0

1 75 represents 1750

Fill in the missing entries.

Stem	Leaves	
1	___ ___ 80 80 80 80 82 89 95 97	75; 80
2	00 00 00 03 03 06 10 10 10 10 ___ 25 30 30 30 40	12
	40 ___ 50 56 61 63 65 68 70 70 71 ___	41; 82
___	20 30 40 57 60	3
4	40 41 50 60	
5	22 ___	32
6	09 00 40 ___	48
7		
8		
___		9
10	___ 08	06
11		
___	60	12

The stem-and-leaf display indicates a high concentration of capacities between 2000 and 3000 milliwatts, with almost all of the data falling between ________ 1000
and ________ milliwatts. There are three unusually large values. 7000

Sometimes the available stem choices result in a display containing too many stems (and very few leaves within a stem) or in too *few* stems (and many leaves within a stem). This was the case in Example 2.4, with stem 2 containing many leaves. In this situation, we may divide the too few stems by stretching them into two or more lines depending on the leaf values with which they will be associated. Two options are available.

1. The stem to be stretched is divided into two parts. The first, marked by the symbol (*) is associated with leaves having 0, 1, 2, 3 or 4 as a leading digit. The second, marked by the symbol (•), is associated with leaves having 5, 6, 7, 8 or 9 as a leading digit.
2. The stem to be stretched is divided into five parts as follows:

Stem Designation	*Leading digit of Leaf*
*	0 or 1
T	2 or 3 (Two or Three)
F	4 or 5 (Four or Five)
S	6 or 7 (Six or Seven)
•	8 or 9

Example 2.5

Construct a stem-and-leaf display for the data in Example 2.4 by dividing each of the stems given there into two parts.

Solution

Each stem will now become two, the first whose leaves have leading digits 0, 1,
________, ________, or 4 and the second whose leaves have leading digits 2; 3

5; 6

__________ , __________ , 7, 8 or 9. For example, the stem labelled 2 now becomes 2* and 2•. The stem-and-leaf display is shown below.

Margin	Stem	Leaves
80	1•	75 80 80 ___ 80 80 82 89 95 97
06	2*	00 00 00 03 03 ___ 10 10 10 10 12 25 30 30 30 40 40 41
56; 61	2•	50 ___ ___ 63 65 68 70 70 70 71 82
	3*	20 30 40
3•	___	57 60
	4*	40 41
60	4•	50 ___
22	5*	___ 32
	5•	
	6*	09 00 40 48

HI 10060, 10080, 12600

leaf unit = 10.0

1 75 represents 1750

Notice that we have chosen to indicate the three extreme values as "HI" rather than to extend the stem-and-leaf display to accommodate these values.

The MINITAB software package can be used to generate a stem-and-leaf display for data which has been stored by column in the computer. The command STEM (stem and leaf display) followed by a column number indicates the data for which we want to construct the stem-and-leaf display.

The MINITAB program and output which produce a stem and leaf display for the data in Example 2.4 are shown below.

```
MTB > STEM C1

Stem-and-leaf of C1     N = 57
Leaf Unit = 100

  10      1 7888888899
 (29)     2 00000011111233344455666677778
  18      3 23456
  13      4 0156
   9      5 23
   7      6 0044
   3      7
   3      8
   3      9
   3     10 00
   1     11
   1     12 6
```

The STEM-and-leaf output is quite similar to the stem-and-leaf display constructed in Example 2.5. Notice the following differences:

1. The MINITAB program uses a single digit as the stem. Hence, only the first digit of the two digit leaves given in Example 2.4 are recorded. Because of this difference, the decoding procedure is slightly different from the one used in Example 2.4, with

   leaf unit = 100

2. The MINITAB program does not display the stems divided into two parts. Moreover, the three high observations are displayed within the stem-and-leaf display.
3. The column on the far left of the output records the number of leaves on that stem, or on a stem closer to the nearer end of the display. This column can be ignored for the time being, but it will be useful in locating the *median*, which will be discussed in Section 2.5.

Self-Correcting Exercises 2B

1. The following data from Exercise 1, Self-Correcting Exercises 2A, are the ages in years of the employees of a recently organized small manufacturing firm.

51	32	31	33	23	52
23	21	55	34	38	32
49	35	26	29	50	34
30	19	41	39	41	27
25	21	18	36	35	28
44	44	59	28	23	46
27	37	42	32	43	30

   a. Construct a stem-and-leaf display of the data using the digit in the "tens" place as the stem and the digit in the "ones" place as the leaf.
   b. Construct a stem-and-leaf display as described in part a, this time dividing each stem into two parts, marked by (*) and (•).
   c. Which of the two stem-and-leaf displays seems to provide a better visual description of the data?
2. The following data represent the per capita taxes (state income and sales or gross receipts taxes and vehicle fees) in each of the 50 United States for a recent fiscal year, measured to the nearest tenth of a dollar.

AL	$563.90	HI	1104.90	MA	837.30	NM	941.30	SD	475.80
AK	6316.40	ID	612.90	MI	681.00	NY	879.30	TN	467.50
AZ	682.90	IL	650.20	MN	932.10	NC	644.30	TX	639.50
AR	552.80	IN	558.00	MS	580.00	ND	815.70	UT	650.80
CA	921.90	IA	685.30	MO	470.40	OH	538.90	VT	650.30
CO	584.80	KS	610.30	MT	672.40	OK	896.90	VA	605.20
CT	752.70	KY	680.60	NE	548.10	OR	589.60	WA	853.90
DE	1001.40	LA	743.50	NV	931.80	PA	690.00	WV	753.30
FL	570.00	ME	649.80	NH	353.40	RI	712.60	WI	836.10
GA	600.60	MD	757.20	NJ	757.30	SC	627.60	WY	1622.40

a. Construct a stem and leaf display using digits at or to the left of the "hundreds" place as the stem and the digits at or to the right of the "tens" place as the leaf.

b. Round the data to the nearest tens of dollars. Construct a stem and leaf display using the digits at or to the left of the "hundreds" place as the stem and the digit in the "tens" place as the leaf.

c. Which of the two stem and leaf displays provides a better visual description of the data?

2.4 Other Graphical Methods

frequency distributions
bar; pie

Bar charts, line charts, ratio charts, and pie charts are designed to serve as visual summarizations of a set or sets of data. Ratio charts and line charts are usually used to trace a firm's profits or productivity or their change over time. Bar charts and pie charts are pictorial ______________ ______________. The most commonly used statistical charts are the ______________ chart and the ______________ chart.

nonoverlapping; all-inclusive

In many instances, experimental data is such that the observations fall naturally into several different categories. The experimenter may define these several categories, which are ______________ and ______________, and then classify each observation as belonging to one of these categories or classes.

Example 2.6

1. If we wish to categorize stockholders with respect to political affiliation, we might use the categories: Republican, Democrat, Socialist, Independent, Other.
2. We could classify people according to whether they were employed or unemployed during a certain time period.
3. Individuals could be classified as belonging to a high, medium, or low income group.
4. Cars could be classified according to manufacturer, or according to the year in which they were made.

The *bar chart* is a method of graphical description in which the horizontal axis of a graph is used to locate the categories of interest. Rectangles are then constructed over each category, with a height corresponding to the number of observations in the category. This number is called the *frequency* or *group frequency* for the particular category of interest.

Example 2.7

The following data represent the total sales and the domestic sales for an electronics firm over the years 1984–1988.

	Sales (thousands of dollars)				
	1984	*1985*	*1986*	*1987*	*1988*
Domestic	550	600	650	690	700
Total	600	650	800	820	900

Construct a bar chart to depict these data.

Solution

1. The horizontal axis of the graph is used to locate the ____________ of interest to the experimenter. years
2. In order to incorporate domestic and total sales into one graph, the height of the bar for a particular year is taken to be the ____________ sales for this year. The bar is then subdivided, with a shaded area equal to the ____________ of that year's sales that were domestic. total proportion
3. The bar chart can now be constructed on the axes given below.

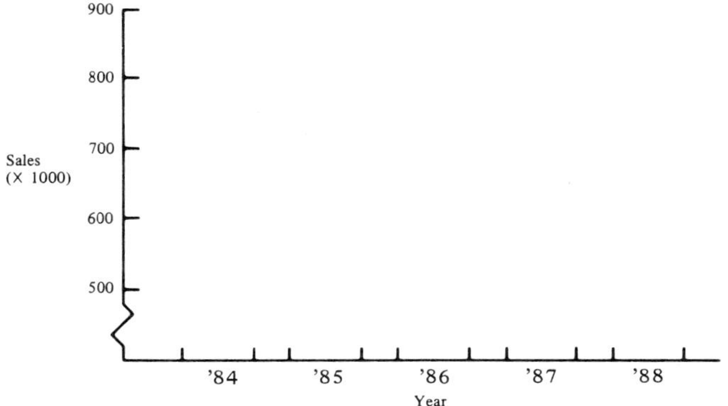

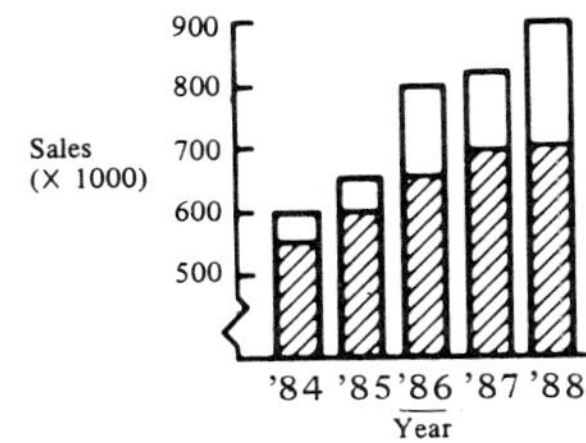

4. Using the bar chart, complete the following statements about the company's sales.
   a. Since the total sales for 1988 were $900,000 as compared to 1985 sales of $650,000, the 1988 bar is __________ times as high as the 1985 bar. 1.71
   b. Since domestic sales for 1987 were $690,000 while total sales were $820,000, the proportion of the 1987 bar that is shaded (indicating domestic sales) is __________%. 75

A *circle chart* or *pie chart* is a method of graphical description in which a subdivided circle is used to represent the way in which a group of objects are distributed among a set of categories. The circle is subdivided into sectors, with each sector representing the percentage of the total contributed by a particular category.

Example 2.8

The following data represent the 1988 purchases by a local car rental company.

Car Make	*Frequency*
Ford Escort	45
Chevrolet Citation	30
Plymouth Horizon	60
Dodge Omni	15

Construct a pie chart to depict these data.

Solution

The percentages of the total falling in each of the four categories are obtained by
150 dividing each frequency by n = ________ and then multiplying by 100.
Calculate the necessary percentages in the table below.

	Car Make	*Frequency*	*Percentage*
	Ford Escort	45	30%
20%	Chevrolet Citation	30	________
40%	Plymouth Horizon	60	________
	Dodge Omni	15	10%

The total number of degrees in a circle is 360 and the number of degrees that will be apportioned to each category is computed as a percentage of 360°. For example, since Chevrolets comprise 20% of the total purchases, this category will be represented by a sector with a central angle of

$$(.20)(360) = 72 \text{ degrees}$$

The sector angles corresponding to the other three categories are found in the following table.

	Car Make	*Frequency*	*Percentage*	*Sector Angle*
	Ford Escort	45	30%	108°
72°	Chevrolet Citation	30	20%	________
144°	Plymouth Horizon	60	40%	________
36°	Dodge Omni	15	10%	________

The pie chart is now constructed by marking off the first three sector angles with a protractor. The remaining sector is allotted to the final category.

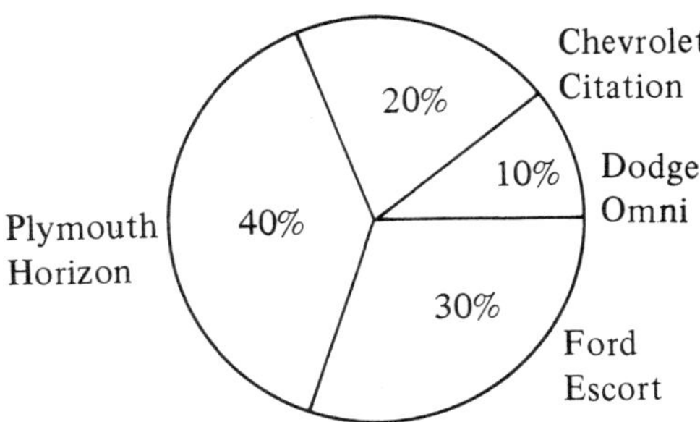

The charts produced by graphical descriptive techniques must be interpreted with care, or the wrong conclusions may result. It is especially easy to mislead a careless reader by breaking, shrinking, or stretching the AXES ______ of a graph. To protect oneself, always examine the SCALES ______ of measurement on graphs and charts carefully.

axes
scales

Self-Correcting Exercises 2C

1. The following data supplied by the Bureau of Labor Statistics gives the total civilian labor force and those employed during the years 1980–1986.

	Civilian Labor Force ($\times 10^6$)						
	1980	*1981*	*1982*	*1983*	*1984*	*1985*	*1986*
Employed	99.3	100.4	99.5	100.8	105.0	107.2	109.6
Total labor force	106.9	108.7	110.2	111.6	113.5	115.6	111.3

   a. Construct a bar chart to depict these data.
   b. Suppose that, for political reasons, you wanted to make the drop in employment in 1982 look as large and dramatic as possible. Construct a bar chart that distorts the information in order to achieve that goal.

2. The following data are the number of persons employed during 1986 according to the following occupational groups.

Group	*Millions Employed*
1. Managerial, professional	26.6
2. Technical, sales, administrative support	34.4
3. Service occupations	14.7
4. Precision production, craft, and repair	13.4
5. Operators, fabricators, laborers	17.2
6. Farming, forestry, fishing	3.4
Total	109.7

   Construct a pie chart to depict these data.

3. The following data show the production of crude oil by serveral nations for the years 1984–86. Figures shown are millions of barrels per day.

	1984	*1985*	*1986*
USSR	11.6	11.2	11.6
United States	8.9	9.0	8.7
OPEC Nations	17.5	16.1	18.4
Other	15.9	16.7	16.8

a. Construct pie charts representing the crude oil production for each of the years 1984, 1985, 1986.
b. Construct a bar graph comparing the crude oil production for the years 1984 and 1986 simultaneously.
c. Which of the two graphical methods is more effective in describing the data?

2.5 Numerical Descriptive Methods

The chief advantage to using a graphical method is its visual representation of the data. Many times, however, we are restricted to reporting our data verbally. In this case a graphical method of description cannot be used. The greatest disadvantage to a graphical method of describing data is its unsuitability for making inferences, since it is difficult to give a measure of goodness for a graphical inference. Therefore, we turn to *numerical descriptive measures.* We seek a set of numbers that characterizes the frequency distribution of the measurements and at the same time will be useful in making inferences.

We will distinguish between numerical descriptive measures for a population and those associated with a set of sample measurements. A numerical descriptive measure calculated from all the measurements in a population is called a (statistic, parameter). Those numerical descriptive measures calculated from sample measurements are called ______________ .

parameter
statistics

Numerical descriptive measures are classified into two important types.

1. Measures of *central tendency* locate in some way the "center" of the data or frequency distribution.
2. Measures of *variability* measure the "spread" or dispersion of the data or frequency distribution.

Using measures of both types, the experimenter is able to create a concise numerical summary of the data.

2.6 Measures of Central Tendency

We will consider three of the more important measures of central tendency that attempt to locate the center of the frequency distribution.

The arithmetic *mean* of a set of n measurements $x_1, x_2, \ldots, x_n$ is defined to be the sum of the measurements divided by n. The symbol $\bar{x}$ is used to designate the sample mean while the Greek letter μ is used to designate the population mean.

The sample mean can be shown to have very desirable properties as an inference maker. In fact, we will use $\bar{x}$ to estimate the population mean, μ. To indicate the sum of the measurements, we will use the Greek letter Σ (sigma). Then Σx_i will indicate the sum of all the measurements that have been denoted by the symbol x. Using this summation notation, we can define the sample mean by formula as

$$\bar{x} = \frac{\Sigma x_i}{n}$$

$\frac{\Sigma x_i}{n}$

Example 2.9
Find the mean of the following measurements:

2, 5, 7, 10, 11, 13

Solution

$$\Sigma x_i = 48$$

$$\bar{x} = \frac{\Sigma x_i}{n} = \frac{48}{6}$$

$$\bar{x} = 8.00$$

48

48

8

In addition to being an easily calculated measure of central tendency, the mean is also easily understood by all users. The calculation of the mean utilizes all the measurements and can always be carried out exactly.

One disadvantage of using the mean to measure central tendency is well known to any student who has had to pull up one low test score: the mean (is, is not) greatly affected by extreme values. For example, you might be unwilling to accept, say, an average property value of $105,000 for a given area as an acceptable measure of the middle property value if you knew that (a) the property value of a residence owned by a millionaire was included in the calculation and (b) excluding this residence, the property values ranged from $45,000 to $60,000. A more realistic measure of central tendency in this situation might be the property value such that 50% of the property values are less than this value and 50% are greater.

is

The *median* of a set of measurements is that value of x such that at most 1/2 of the measurements are less than x and at most 1/2 are greater than x.

In order to find the median for a finite sample of size n, the definition of the median will be used in the following way.

The *median* of a sample of n measurements $x_1, x_2, \ldots, x_n$ is the value of x that falls in the $.5(n + 1)^{st}$ position when the measurements are arranged in order of magnitude. When n is even and $.5(n + 1)$ ends in .5, the median is taken to be the simple average of the two values in the positions adjacent to the median position.

Example 2.10

Find the median of the following set of measurements:

5, 3, 2, 7, 4

Solution

1. Arranging the measurements in order of magnitude, we have

   2, 3, 4, 5, 7

third 2. The median will be the ________ ordered value, since $.5(n + 1) =$

4; 2/5 $.5(6) = 3$. Hence, the median is ________. Notice that ________ of the

2/5 measurements (which is at most 1/2) are less than 4 and ________ of the

is measurements (which is at most 1/2) are greater than 4. This (is, is not) consistent with the first definition of the median.

Example 2.11

Find the median of the following set of measurements:

10, 8, 13, 14, 9, 8

Solution

1. Arranging the measurements in order of magnitude, we have

   8, 8, 9, 10, 13, 14

2. Since $n = 6$ is even and $.5(n + 1) = .5(7) = 3.5$, the median will be the average

third; fourth of the ________ and ________ ordered values. Hence

9; 10

$$\text{median} = \frac{\_\_\_\_ + \_\_\_\_}{2}$$

9.5

$$= \_\_\_\_\_\_$$

Example 2.12

Find the mean and median of the following data:

5, 7, 8, 10, 10, 11, 13, 14

Solution

1. $\Sigma x_i =$ ________ 78

$$\bar{x} = \frac{\Sigma x_i}{n} = \frac{\_\_\_\_\_\_}{8} = \_\_\_\_\_\_$$ 78; 9.75

2. To find the median, we note that the measurements are already arranged in order of magnitude and that $n = 8$ is even. Therefore, the median will be the average of the fourth and fifth ordered values.

$$\text{median} = \frac{10 + 10}{2} = \_\_\_\_\_\_$$ 10

In the last example, the mean and median gave reasonably close numerical values as measures of central tendency. However, if the measurement $y_9 = 30$ were added to the eight measurements given, the recalculated mean would be $\bar{x} =$ ________, but the median would remain at 10, reflecting the fact that the median is a positional average unaffected by extreme values. 12

The *mode* of a set of n measurements $x_1, x_2, x_3, \ldots, x_n$, is the value of x occurring with the greatest frequency. If there are two such values, the set is said to be *bimodal.*

Example 2.13

Find the mode of the following measurements:

1, 2, 3, 3, 5, 6, 8

Solution

The measurement that occurs with the greatest frequency is ________; 3
therefore, the mode is ________. 3

The mode is generally not a good measure of central tendency, since data may be grouped in such a way that the greatest frequencies occur nowhere near the central area of the distribution. The mode may not even be unique because the greatest frequency can occur at more than one value. However, there are situations in which the mode might be a desirable measure. For example, the ________ is important for studies of demand for a product. A purchasing agent is concerned about the modal sizes and styles of his product before placing a purchase order, while the ________ size or the ________ ________ of sizes may be meaningless. mode; median; arithmetic mean

In summary, the ________ is the statistic describing the most frequent outcome; the ________ is the center measurement of a group of measurements arranged in order of magnitude; the ________ ________ is, in a physical sense, the "weighted average" of a group of measurements. If the values of a measured variable equidistant from the mean occur with equal frequency, the resulting frequency distribution is said to be ________. When the distribution of a group of measurements is ________, the mean, mode; median; arithmetic mean; symmetric; symmetric

median, and mode are equal. A distribution which is not symmetric is said to be
skewed ______ and has at least two different values of the mean, median, and mode.

2.7 Measures of Variability

Having found measures of central tendency, we next consider measures of the variability or dispersion of the data. A measure of variability is necessary since a measure of central tendency alone does not adequately describe the data. Consider these two sets of data:

Set I. $x_1 = 9$ Set II. $y_1 = 1$

10; 10 $x_2 = 10$ $\bar{x} =$ ______ $y_2 = 10$ $\bar{y} =$ ______

$x_3 = 11$ $y_3 = 19$

10 Both sets of data have a mean equal to ______. However, the second set of measurements displays much more variability about the mean than does the first set.

In addition to a measure of central tendency, a measure of variability is indispensable as a descriptive measure for a set of data. A manufacturer of
little machine parts would want very (little, much) variability in her product in order to control oversized or undersized parts, while an educational testing
large service would be satisfied only if the test scores showed a (large, small) amount of variability in order to discriminate among people taking the examination.

We have already used the simplest measure of variability, the range.

The *range* of a set of measurements is the difference between the largest and smallest measurements.

Example 2.14

Find the range for each of the following sets of data:

Set I.				
	23	73	34	74
	28	29	26	17
	88	8	52	49
	37	96	32	45
	81	62	23	62

8; 88 Range = 96 − ______ = ______

Set II.				
	8.8	6.7	7.1	2.9
	9.0	0.2	1.2	8.6
	6.3	6.4	2.1	8.8

0.2; 8.8 Range = 9.0 − ______ = ______

By examining the following distributions, it is apparent that although the range is a simply calculated measure of variation, it alone is not adequate. Both distributions have the same range, but display different variability.

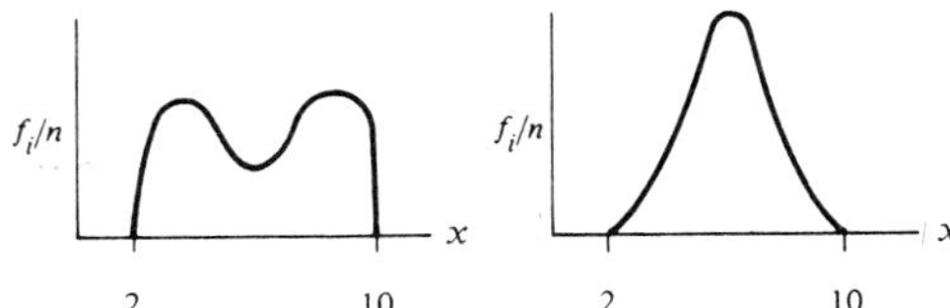

In looking for a more sensitive measure of variability, we can extend the concept of the median as follows:

Let $x_1, x_2, \ldots, x_n$ be a set of n measurements, arranged in order of increasing magnitude. The *lower quartile*, Q_1, is a value of x such that at most 1/4 of the measurements are less than x and at most 3/4 are greater than x. The *upper quartile*, Q_3, is a value of x such that at most 3/4 of the measurements are less than x and at most 1/4 are greater.

The upper and lower quartiles, when located along with the median on the horizontal axis of a frequency distribution representing the measurements of interest, divide that frequency distribution into Four parts, each containing an equal number of measurements.

four

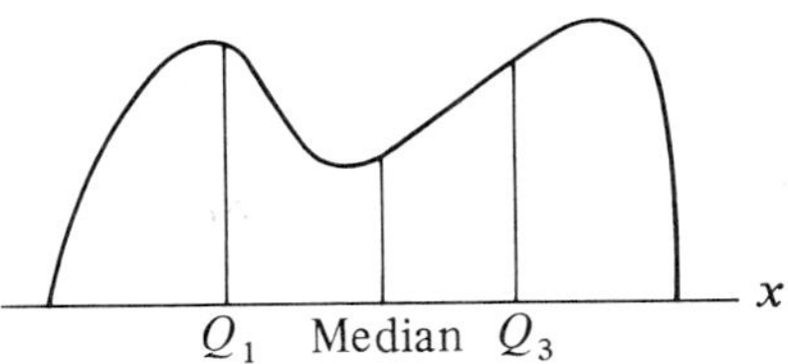

When working with a small set of data, the above definition sometimes admits many numbers which would satisfy the criteria necessary for Q_1 and Q_3. For this reason, we will avoid this inconsistency by calculating quartiles in the following way.

Let $x_1, x_2, \ldots, x_n$ be a set of n measurements arranged in order of increasing magnitude. The lower quartile, Q_1, is the value of x in the $.25(n + 1)$ position and the upper quartile, Q_3, is the value of x in the $.75(n + 1)$ position.

When $.25(n + 1)$ and/or $.75(n + 1)$ are not integers, Q_1 and Q_3 are found by using a weighted average of the values of x found in the positions adjacent to the quartile position.

Example 2.15
Find the upper and lower quartiles for the following set of measurements:

3, 8, 7, 1, 1, 12, 13, 9, 3, 2, 10

Solution
The measurements are first arranged in order of increasing magnitude.

2; 10 1, 1, ______, 3, 3, 7, 8, 9, ______, 12, 13

Since $n = 11$, the lower quartile, Q_1, will be in position

11; 3 $.25(n + 1) = .25($______ $+ 1) =$ ______

and the upper quartile, Q_3, will be in position

12; 9 $.75(n + 1) = .75($______$) =$ ______

are Since the quartile positions (are, are not) both integer valued, the quartiles can be read directly as

10 $Q_1 =$ 3 and $Q_3 =$ ______

Example 2.16
Find the upper and lower quartiles for the following set of prices:

$2.15, 3.50, 6.80, 4.29, 1.67, 2.20, 1.59, 2.98

Solution
The measurements are first arranged in order of increasing magnitude.

2.20; 4.29 $1.59, 1.67, 2.15, ______, 2.98, 3.50, ______, 6.80

Since $n = 8$, the lower quartrile, Q_1, is found in position

$.25(n+1) = .25\,(\_\_\_\_\_\_) = 2.25$ 9

and the upper quartile, Q_3, is found in position

$\_\_\_\_\_\_\,(n+1) = \_\_\_\_\_\_\,(9) = \_\_\_\_\_\_$ .75; .75; 6.75

Since Q_1 and Q_3 (are, are not) integer valued, the quartile values (can, cannot) be taken directly from the set eight prices given in the example. The lower quartile must be a value of x between the second and third ordered price. In order to be consistent with the calculations used in the MINITAB software, and since the lower quartile position is ______, we choose to locate the lower quartile 1/4 of the distance between the ______ and third ordered price. That is,

are not; cannot

2.25

second

$$Q_1 = 1.67 + .25(2.15 - 1.67)$$

$$= 1.67 + \_\_\_\_\_\_$$ .12

$$= \_\_\_\_\_\_$$ 1.79

Similarly, the upper quartile, Q_3, is taken to be the price value 3/4 of the distance between the sixth and ______ ordered price. That is,

seventh

$$Q_3 = 3.50 + .75(4.29 - 3.50)$$

$$= 3.50 + \_\_\_\_\_\_$$ .5925

$$= \_\_\_\_\_\_$$ 4.0925

The student should note that there are many possible values which will satisfy the definition of a quartile. The author chooses to use the above convention in order to be consistent with the calculations used in the MINITAB software package. The student should not be surprised to find that other references may choose to calculate quartiles in a different way.

The concept of median and quartile can be further extended by defining a *percentile*. Percentiles are often used to describe the variability of large sets of data, and their definition follows directly from the definition of a quartile.

Let $x_1, x_2, \ldots, x_n$ be a set of measurements arranged in order of increasing magnitude. The $100p$-th percentile is a value of x such that at most $100p$ percent of the measurements are less than x and at most $100(1 - p)$ percent are greater.

The procedure for calculating a percentile for a set of n measurements is as follows:

When the n measurements are arranged in ascending order, the $100p$-th percentile is the value in position $p(n + 1)$. If this position is not integer valued, the $100p$-th percentile is taken to be the appropriate interpolated value lying between the values in the two positions adjacent to the percentile position.

Example 2.17

A set of aptitude scores consists of $n = 200$ measurements. Describe how the experimenter would proceed in attempting to find the 90th percentile for the scores.

Solution

The experimenter should first arrange the scores in order of their increasing
200 magnitude. Then, since $n =$ ________, the 90th percentile implies that $p =$
.90 ________. The percentile position is

201; 180.9 $$.90\,(n + 1) = .90(\_\_\_\_\_\_) = \_\_\_\_\_\_$$

Thus, the 90th percentile lies somewhere between the 180th and 181st ordered
9/10 scores. By convention, we choose to locate the 90th percentile ________
of the distance between the 180th and 181st ordered scores.

25th Notice that the lower quartile, Q_1, is also the ________ percentile, while the
75th upper quartile, Q_3, is the ________ percentile. Percentiles are more sensitive than the range in measuring variability, but have the disadvantage that several percentiles must be calculated to provide an adequate description of the data.

We base the next important measure of variability on the dispersion of the data about their mean. Consider two sets of measurements. The first set consists of N measurements and represents the entire population of interest to the experimenter. The second set is a sample of n measurements taken from this population. Define μ to be the population mean. For a finite population consisting of N measurements,

$$\mu = \sum_{i=1}^{N} x_i / N$$

The indices above and below the summation sign indicate the values that the subscript i may take on as the summation is performed. That is,

$$\sum_{i=1}^{N} x_i = x_1 + x_2 + \ldots + x_N$$

Similarly, define

$$\bar{x} = \sum_{i=1}^{n} x_i/n = \frac{x_1 + x_2 + \ldots + x_n}{n}$$

to be the sample mean. Finally, we define the quantity $(x_i - \mu)$, or $(x_i - \bar{x})$ (depending upon whether the set of measurements is a population or a sample), as the *i*th deviation from the mean. Large deviations indicate (more, less) variability of the data than do small deviations. We could utilize these deviations in different ways.

more

1. If we attempt to use the average of the N (or n) deviations, we find that the sum of the deviations is zero. To avoid a zero sum, we could use the average of the absolute values of the deviations. This measure, called the *mean deviation,* is difficult to calculate, and we cannot easily give a measure of its goodness as an inference maker.
2. A more efficient use of data is achieved by averaging the sum of squares of the deviations. For a finite population of N measurements, this measure, called the *population variance,* is given by

$$\sigma^2 = \sum_{i=1}^{n} (x_i - \mu)^2/N$$

Large values of σ^2 indicate (large, small) variability, while (large, small) values indicate small variability.

large; small

Since the units of σ^2 are not in the original units of measurement, we can return to these units by defining the standard deviation.

The *standard deviation* σ is the positive square root of the variance. That is,

$$\sigma = \sqrt{\sigma^2} = \sqrt{\Sigma(x_i - \mu)^2/N}$$

For a sample of size n, it would seem reasonable to define the sample variance in a similar way, using $\bar{x}$ in place of μ and n in place of N. However, we choose to modify this definition slightly.

Since our objective is to make inferences about the population based on sample data, it is appropriate to ask if the sample mean and variance are good estimators of their population counterparts, μ and σ^2. The fact is that $\bar{x}$ is a good estimator of μ, but the quantity

$$\Sigma(x_i - \bar{x})^2/n$$

underestimate appears to (underestimate, overestimate) the population variance σ^2 when the sample size is small.

The problem of underestimating σ^2 can be solved by dividing the sum of squares of deviations by $n - 1$ rather than n. We then define

$$s^2 = \Sigma(x_i - \bar{x})^2/(n - 1)$$

as the sample variance. The sample standard deviation is then

$$s = \sqrt{s^2} = \sqrt{\Sigma(x_i - \bar{x})^2/(n - 1)}$$

Example 2.18

Calculate the sample mean, variance, and standard deviation for the following data:

4, 2, 3, 5, 6

Solution

Arrange the measurements in the following way, first finding the mean,
4 $\bar{x}$ = 4.00.

x_i	$x_i - \bar{x}$	$(x_i - \bar{x})^2$
4	0	0
2	-2	4
3	-1	1
5	1	1
6	2	4
0; 10 $\Sigma x_i = 20$	$\Sigma(x_i - \bar{x}) =$ 0	$\Sigma(x_i - \bar{x})^2 =$ 10

After finding the mean, complete the second column and note that its sum is zero. The variance is

10; 2.5 $$s^2 = \Sigma(x_i - \bar{x})^2/(n - 1) = 10/4 = 2.5$$

while the standard deviation is

1.581 $$s = \sqrt{2.5} = 1.581$$

Note: We will introduce a shortcut formula for calculating

$$\sum_{i=1}^{n} (x_i - \bar{x})^2$$

more examples will be given then.

Self-Correcting Exercises 2D

1. Fifteen brands of breakfast cereal were judged by nutritionists according to four criteria: taste, texture, nutritional value and popularity with the buying public. Each brand was rated on a 0–5 scale for each criterion and the sum of the four ratings reported. (A high score with respect to the maximum of 20 points indicates a good evaluation of the brand.)

9	8	16	17	10
15	12	6	12	13
10	13	19	11	9

   a. Find the mean and the median scores for these data. Compare their values.
   b. Why would the mode be inappropriate in describing these data?
   c. Calculate the range of these scores.
   d. Calculate the standard deviation of these scores. (As an intermediate check on your calculations, remember that the sum of the deviations must be zero.)

2. The number of daily arrivals of cargo vessels at a west coast port during an 11-day period are given below.

3	2	0
5	4	4
2	3	2
7	1	

   a. Calculate the mean and standard deviation of the number of arrivals per day during this 11-day period.
   b. Compare the mean and the median for these data.

2.8 On the Practical Significance of the Standard Deviation

Having defined the mean and standard deviation, we now introduce two theorems that will use both these quantities in more fully describing a set of data.

Tchebysheff's Theorem: Given a number k greater than or equal to one and a set of n measurements $x_1, x_2, \ldots, x_n$, at least $(1 - 1/k^2)$ of the measurements will lie within k standard deviations of their mean.

The importance of this theorem is due to the fact that it applies to any set of measurements. It applies to a population using the population mean μ and the population standard deviation σ, and it applies to a sample from a given population using $\bar{x}$ and s, the sample mean and sample standard deviation.
any Since this theorem applies to ______________ set of measurements, it is of necessity a conservative theorem. It is therefore very important to stipulate
at least that ______________ ______________ $(1 - 1/k^2)$ of the measurements will lie within k standard deviations of their mean.

Complete the following chart for the values of k given.

	k	Interval $\bar{x} \pm ks$	Interval Contains at Least the Fraction $(1 - 1/k^2)$
0	1	$\bar{x} \pm s$	________
3/4	2	$\bar{x} \pm 2s$	________
8/9	3	$\bar{x} \pm 3s$	________
99/100	10	$\bar{x} \pm 10s$	________

Example 2.19

The mean and variance of a set of $n = 20$ measurements are 35 and 25, respectively. Use Tchebysheff's Theorem to describe the distribution of these measurements.

Solution

Collecting pertinent information we have

$$\bar{x} = 35, \quad s^2 = 25, \quad s = \sqrt{25} = 5$$

1. At least 3/4 of the measurements lie in the interval $35 \pm 2(5)$ or from
25; 45 ________ to ________.
2. At least 8/9 of the measurements lie in the interval $35 \pm 3(5)$ or from
20; 50 ________ to ________.
3. At least 15/16 of the measurements lie in the interval $35 \pm 4(5)$ or from
15; 55 ________ to ________.

Example 2.20

If the mean and variance of a set of $n = 50$ measurements are 42 and 36, respectively, describe these measurements using Tchebysheff's Theorem.

Solution

Pertinent information: $\bar{x} = 42$, $s^2 = 36$, and $s = 6$.

1. At least 3/4 of the measurements lie in the interval $42 \pm 2(6)$ or from
30; 54 ________ to ________.

2. At least 8/9 of the measurements lie in the interval 42 ± 3(6) or from __________ to __________. 24; 60
3. At least 15/16 of the measurements lie in the interval 42 ± 4(6) or from __________ to __________. 18; 66

A second theorem can be used if the distribution of measurements is known to be of a particular form.

Empirical Rule: Given a distribution of measurements that is approximately bell-shaped, the interval

a. $\mu \pm \sigma$ contains approximately 68% of the measurements.
b. $\mu \pm 2\sigma$ contains approximately 95% of the measurements.
c. $\mu \pm 3\sigma$ contains almost all (approximately 99.7%) of the measurements.

This rule holds reasonably well for any set of measurements that possesses a distribution that is mound-shaped. Bell-shaped or mound-shaped is taken to mean that the distribution has the properties associated with the normal distribution, whose graph is given in your text and elsewhere in this study guide.

Example 2.21

A random sample of 100 oranges was taken from a grove and individual weights measured. The mean and variance of these measurements were 7.8 ounces and 0.36 (ounces)^2, respectively. Assuming the measurements produced a mound-shaped distribution, describe these measurements using the Empirical Rule.

Solution

First find the intervals needed.

k	$\bar{x} \pm ks$	$\bar{x} - ks$	to	$\bar{x} + ks$	
1	$\bar{x} \pm s$	7.2	to	8.4	7.2; 8.4
2	$\bar{x} \pm 2s$	6.6	to	9.0	6.6; 9.0
3	$\bar{x} \pm 3s$	6.0	to	9.6	6.0; 9.6

Then approximately

1. __________% of the measurements lie in the interval from __________ to __________. 68; 7.2 8.4
2. __________% of the measurements lie in the interval from __________ to __________. 95; 6.6 9.0
3. __________% of the measurements lie in the interval from __________ to __________. 100 (or 99.7); 6.0 9.6

would not
would not

When n is small, the distribution of measurements (would, would not) be mound-shaped and as such the Empirical Rule (would, would not) be appropriate in describing these data. Since Tchebysheff's Theorem applies to any set of measurements, it can be used regardless of the size of n.

2.9 A Short Method for Calculating the Variance

The calculation of $s^2 = \Sigma(x_i - \bar{x})^2/(n - 1)$ requires the calculation of the quantity $\sum_{i=1}^{n} (x_i - \bar{x})^2$. To facilitate this calculation, we introduce the identity

$$\sum_{i=1}^{n} (x_i - \bar{x})^2 = \sum_{i=1}^{n} x_i^2 - \frac{\left(\sum_{i=1}^{n} x_i\right)^2}{n}$$

the proof of which is omitted. This computation requires the following:

1. The ordinary arithmetic sum of the measurements, $\sum_{i=1}^{n} x_i$.

2. The sum of the squares of the measurements, $\sum_{i=1}^{n} x_i^2$.

Note the distinction between $\sum_{i=1}^{n} x_i^2$ and $\left(\sum_{i=1}^{n} x_i\right)^2$ used in the identity given above.

1. To calculate $\sum_{i=1}^{n} x_i^2$, we *first square* each measurement and *then sum* these squares.

2. To calculate $\left(\sum_{i=1}^{n} x_i\right)^2$, we *first sum* the measurements and *then square* this sum.

Example 2.22
Calculate s^2 for Example 2.18.

Solution
Display the data in the following way, finding Σx_i and Σx_i^2:

x_i	x_i^2
4	16
2	4
3	9
5	25
6	36

Σx_i = ________ Σx_i^2 = ________ 20; 90

1. We first calculate

$$\Sigma(x_i - \bar{x})^2 = \Sigma x_i^2 - (\Sigma x_i)^2/n$$

$$= 90 - (20)^2/5$$

$$= 90 - \text{\_\_\_\_\_\_\_\_}$$ 80

$$= \text{\_\_\_\_\_\_\_\_}$$ 10

2. Then

$$s^2 = \Sigma(x_i - \bar{x})^2/(n-1) = \text{\_\_\_\_\_\_\_\_}/(5-1) = \text{\_\_\_\_\_\_\_\_}$$ 10; 2.5

Example 2.23
Calculate the mean and variance of the following data: 5, 6, 7, 5, 2, 3.

Solution
Display the data in a table.

x_i	x_i^2
5	25
6	36
7	49
5	25
2	4
3	9

Σx_i = ________ Σx_i^2 = ________ 28; 148

4.67 $\bar{x} = \Sigma x_i/n = 28/6 =$ _________

$\Sigma(x_i - \bar{x})^2 = \Sigma x_i^2 - (\Sigma x_i)^2/n$

$= 148 - (28)^2/6$

$= 148 - 130.67$

17.33 $=$ _________

17.33; 3.467 $s^2 = \Sigma(x_i - \bar{x})^2/(n-1) =$ _________ $/(6-1) =$ _________

The MINITAB system provides a command which allows the user to compute various numerical descriptive measures for a set of data stored in some column in the computer. In MINITAB, the command DESCRIBE (describe) followed by a column number will generate a set of ten measures based on the data stored in the designated column. Consider for example the output generated by DESCRIBE for the data in Example 2.4.

```
MTB > DESCRIBE C1

          N     MEAN     MEDIAN    TRMEAN    STDEV    SEMEAN
C1       57     3322       2500      2966     2215       293

        MIN      MAX         Q1        Q3
C1     1750    12600       2030      3588
```

Of the ten measures given in the printout, we have discussed all but two. The quantity TMEAN (trimmed mean) is an average calculated after having eliminated some of the lowest and highest measurements in the set (in particular, the lowest 5% and the highest 5%). The quantity SEMEAN (standard error of the mean) is calculated as $s/\sqrt{n}$. We will discuss this measure later in the text.

Self-Correcting Exercises 2E

1. Using the breakfast cereal data from Self-Correcting Exercises 2D, problem 1, calculate the sample variance utilizing the shortcut formula to calculate the required sum of squared deviations. Verify that the values of the

variance (and hence the standard deviation) found using both calculational forms are identical. The data are reproduced below.

9	8	16	17	10
15	12	6	12	13
10	13	19	11	9

s = 3,5857
s^2 = 12,8571

2. Follow the instructions in Exercise 1 using the data from Exercise 2, Self-Correcting Exercises 2D, which are reproduced below.

3	2	0
5	4	4
2	3	2
7	1	

s = 1,9494
s^2 = 3,800

3. A MINTAB software package was used to analyze the data of Exercise 2, Self-Correcting Exercises 2B, using the DESCRIBE command. The following output was obtained.

```
MTB > DESCRIBE C3

           N     MEAN    MEDIAN    TRMEAN    STDEV    SEMEAN
C3        50      825       677       703      817       116

         MIN      MAX        Q1        Q3
C3       353     6316       588       836
```

a. Discuss the ten measures given in the output and describe how they are calculated.
b. Use the Empirical Rule to describe the data.

4. If a person were concerned about accuracy due to rounding of numbers at various stages in computation, which formula for calculating

$$\sum_{i=1}^{n} (x_i - \bar{x}) \text{ would be preferred?}$$

a. $$\sum_{i=1}^{n} (x_i - \bar{x})^2 \quad \text{or}$$

b. $$\sum_{i=1}^{n} x_i^2 - \frac{\left(\sum_{i=1}^{n} x_i\right)^2}{n}$$

Defend your choice of either part a or b.

2.10 Estimating the Mean and Variance for Grouped Data (Optional)

When published data are listed only in terms of the frequency of measurements within various classes, the usual formulas cannot be used to compute the mean and variance of the data. Nevertheless, the mean $\bar{x}$ and variance s^2 for grouped data can be approximated by using the grouped formulas

$$\bar{x}_g = \sum_{i=1}^{k} \frac{f_i m_i}{n}$$

and

$$s_g^2 = \frac{\sum_{i=1}^{k} f_i m_i^2 - \left(\sum_{i=1}^{k} f_i m_i\right)^2 \Big/ n}{n - 1}$$

midpoint; frequency
classes
measurements

where m_i is the ______________ of class i, f_i is the ______________ of measurements within class i, k is the number of ______________, and n is the total number of ______________.

Example 2.24
The number of defective electrical components produced in an assembly operation has been recorded for each of the past 30 days. The results are summarized in the following frequency histogram.

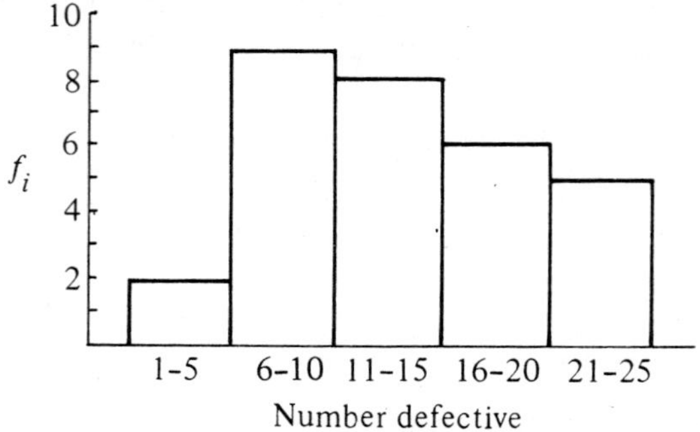

Estimate $\bar{x}$ and s^2, the mean and variance of the number of defectives produced each day by the assembly operation.

Solution

Complete the following table.

Class	Class Boundaries	f_i	m_i	$f_i m_i$	$f_i m_i^2$
1	1-5	2	3	6	18
2	6-10	______	8	______	______
3	11-15	8	______	______	______
4	16-20	______	18	______	______
5	21-25	5	23	115	______
	Totals	______		______	6015

9; 72; 576
13; 104; 832
6; 108; 1944
2645

30; 405

The mean of the grouped data can be approximated by

$$\bar{x}_g = \frac{\sum_{i=1}^{5} f_i m_i}{30} = \frac{\_\_\_\_\_\_}{30}$$

405

$$= \_\_\_\_\_\_$$

13.5

while the variance is approximated by

$$s_g^2 = \frac{\sum_{i=1}^{5} f_i m_i^2 - \left(\sum_{i=1}^{5} f_i m_i\right)^2 \Big/ 30}{29}$$

$$= \frac{6015 - (\_\_\_\_\_\_)^2/30}{29}$$

405

$$= \frac{6015 - \_\_\_\_\_\_}{29}$$

5467.5

$$= \frac{\_\_\_\_\_\_}{29}$$

547.5

$$= \_\_\_\_\_\_$$

18.879

In order to apply the formulas for approximating the mean and variance of

do not
midpoints
arithmetic mean

grouped data, we (do, do not) need to assume that classes are of equal width. The approximations obtained are reliable only if the class ________ are approximately equal to the ________________________ of the measurements within each class. Using the class midpoints to represent the average value within a class tacitly implies that no class should be open-ended since the midpoint of such a class would not be defined.

Self-Correcting Exercises 2F (Optional)

1. The following frequency distribution has been published by an airline to indicate the number of separate air journeys taken during the past year by 20 randomly selected passengers.

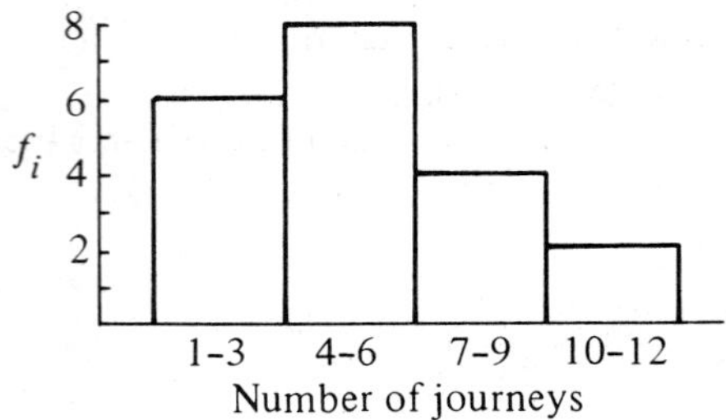

   Approximate the average, $\bar{x}$, and the standard deviation, s, of the number of journeys during the past year for the passengers of the airline using the formulas for grouped data.

2. The number of traffic accidents during a one-week period at a dangerous intersection was recorded for 50 weeks. The following tabulation has resulted.

Number of accidents /wk	*Frequency*
0	10
1	18
2	13
3	6
4	2
5	1

   a. Find the mean and standard deviation of the number of accidents per week during this 50-week period.
   b. In this particular case will the mean and standard deviation found in a. be approximations or exact values of $\bar{x}$ and s?

2.11 Boxplots for Detecting Outliers (Optional)

In Section 2.3 we discussed a technique used in the field of exploratory data analysis (EDA) called the stem-and-leaf plot. Using this graphical technique we were able to examine the shape of the distribution, the range of its measurements and to ascertain within what intervals the measurements were most highly concentrated. In Sections 2.6 and 2.7, several numerical measures were presented which allowed us to describe the central location of the measurements and their spread from the center. The *boxplot* is a technique which was also introduced in the field of exploratory data analysis (EDA). It utilizes several of the numerical descriptive measures we have already discussed, and it allows us to examine the symmetry or asymmetry of the data as well as the behavior of the data in the tails of the distribution. Let us consider these two concepts in more detail.

For a given set of measurements, the frequency distribution is symmetric if, when a vertical line is drawn through the distribution at some point, the portions of the distribution to the right and left of this line appear as mirror images. (This point of symmetry is both the mean and the median.) Indicate whether the following distributions are symmetric or asymmetric:

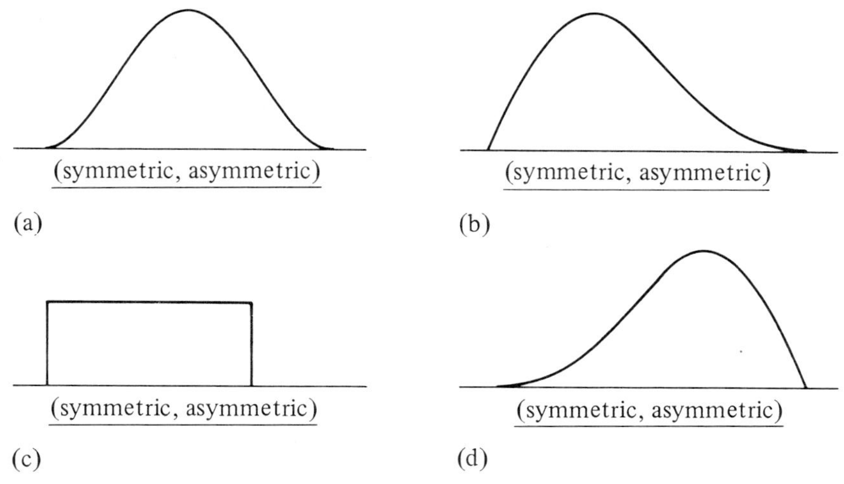

symmetric; asymmetric

symmetric; asymmetric

The boxplot technique will allow us to determine whether a distribution is symmetric (a or c above), skewed to the right (b) or skewed to the left (d).

Further, a set of measurements may contain values which for some reason lie very far from the middle of the distribution in either direction. These values lie in the tails of the distribution and are called *outliers*. Sometimes outliers are generated when a mistake is made in the recording of the data. A number may be misread or mistyped. Perhaps the environmental conditions under which an experiment is performed changed drastically for a short time. Sometimes outliers simply occur naturally, without having been caused by human error.

In any event, the boxplot is expressly designed to detect these outliers which may be of great importance to the experimenter.

Recall from Sections 2.6 and 2.7 that the *median* of a set of measurements is a value such that ______________ of the measurements are less than the median and half of the measurements are greater. That is, the median is a value which divides the ordered data into two halves. The *lower quartile*, Q_1, is a value, say x, such that __________ of the measurements are (less, greater) than x and __________ of the measurements are greater. The *upper quartile*, Q_3, is a value x such that 3/4 of the measurements are (less, greater) than x and __________ are greater. The *boxplot* uses the median and two measures called *hinges*. These hinges are very similar to quartiles and serve essentially the same purpose, as described above. As the number of observations in the data set increases, the hinges and quartiles become almost identical.

half

1/4; less

3/4

less; 1/4

The procedure used in creating a *boxplot* for a set of n measurements is as follows:

1. a. Find the *median position*, which is ______________.
   b. Find the *"depth" of the median*, $d(M)$, which is the median position with the decimal .5 omitted if it is present.
   c. Find the *"depth" of the hinges* as given by

$$d(H) = \underline{\qquad\qquad}$$

.5(n + 1)

$\frac{d(M) + 1}{2}$

2. Find the median, the lower hinge and the upper hinge using the "depths" given in part 1. The hinges are the values in position $d(H)$ as measured from each end of the ordered set. If either the median position or $d(H)$ is not an integer, the value is taken to be the ______________ of the two ordered observations on either side of the particular position.
3. Calculate the H-spread as

$$H\text{-spread} = \text{upper hinge} - \text{lower hinge}$$

average

The H-spread can now be used as a yardstick to detect outliers. Define the *inner fences* as

$$\text{lower inner fence} = \text{lower hinge} - 1.5\ (H\text{-spread})$$

$$\text{upper inner fence} = \text{upper hinge} + 1.5\ (\underline{\qquad\qquad})$$

H-spread

4. Define the *outer fences* as

$$\text{lower outer fence} = \text{lower hinge} - 3\ (H\text{-spread})$$

$$\text{upper outer fence} = \underline{\qquad\qquad} + 3(\underline{\qquad\qquad})$$

upper hinge; H-spread

If a measurement lies between the inner and outer fences, it is considered a mild outlier. If a measurement lies outside the outer fences, it is considered a (mild, extreme) outlier. — extreme

5. The data points in the set closest to the lower inner fence (but still inside them) are called the _____________ _____________. — adjacent values
6. The boxplot is constructed by drawing a box between the upper and lower hinges, with a solid line drawn vertically across the box to locate the median. A dotted line is then drawn from either side of the box to the points representing the adjacent values. Mild outliers are plotted using (*) while extreme outliers are plotted using zero.

Example 2.25

Construct a boxplot for the hydroelectric plant capacities, given in Example 2.4. The data are reproduced below, but they have been put in ascending numerical order.

1750	2000	2124	2610	3300	6000
1800	2000	2250	2637	3409	6096
1800	2000	2300	2650	3575	6400
1800	2030	2300	2680	3600	6480
1800	2031	2304	2700	4050	10060
1807	2069	2400	2700	4150	10080
1824	2100	2400	2700	4500	12600
1890	2100	2416	2715	4600	
1950	2100	2500	2820	5225	
1979	2100	2560	3200	5328	

Solution

1. The median position for $n =$ _________ is — 57

$$.5(n+1) = .5(\_\_\_\_\_\_) = \_\_\_\_\_\_$$ — 58; 29

The "depth" of the median is also 29, and the "depth" of the hinges is

$$d(H) = \frac{d(M)+1}{2} = \frac{\_\_\_\_\_\_}{2} = \_\_\_\_\_\_$$ — 30; 15

2. The median is the 29th ordered observation or _____________. The lower hinge is the 15th ordered observation from the bottom or _____________. The upper hinge is the _____________ ordered observation from the top or _____________. — 2500; 2031; 15th; 3575
3. The H-spread is

$$3575 - 2031 = \_\_\_\_\_\_.$$ — 1544

4. Calculate the inner and outer fences:
   The inner fences are

-285 $\quad 2031 - 1.5(1544) = 2031 - 2316 =$ ________

5891 $\quad$ and $\quad 3575 + 1.5(1544) = 3575 + 2316 =$ ________

   The outer fences are

4632 $\quad 2031 - 3(1544) = 2031 -$ ________ $= -2601$

4632 $\quad$ and $\quad 3575 + 3(1544) = 3575 +$ ________ $= 8207$

1750; 5329 — 5. The adjacent values are then ________ and ________, since they are closest to, but do not fall outside the inner fences.

Mild — 6. (Mild, extreme) outliers lie between −2601 and −285 or between 8207 and
-2601; 8207 — 5891. Extreme outliers are less than ________ or greater than ________. From the original data, the observed values 6000, 6096, 6400, and 6480 are
mild — judged to be (mild, extreme) outliers, while the observed values 10060,
12600; extreme — 10080 and ________ are (mild, extreme) outliers.

7. The boxplot is shown below, with the ends of the box located at 2031 and 3575. The length of the lines on either side of the box extends to the adjacent values. We use an asterisk (*) to designate mild outliers and a (0) to designate extreme outliers.

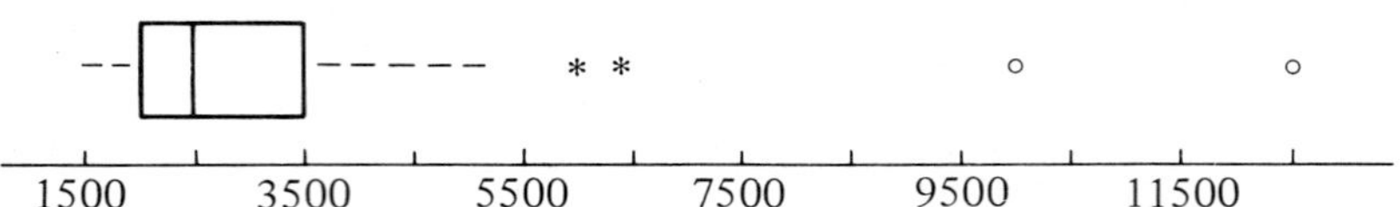

There are a number of outliers in this data set. Notice that the median
is not; left — (is, is not) in the middle of the box, but is to the (right, left) of middle. This indicates that the distribution is skewed to the right. Examination of the stem-and-leaf display constructed in Example 2.4 will confirm this conclusion.

The MINITAB command BOXPLOT followed by a column number generates a boxplot of the data in the designated column. The output generated by BOXPLOT is shown below for the data of Example 2.4.

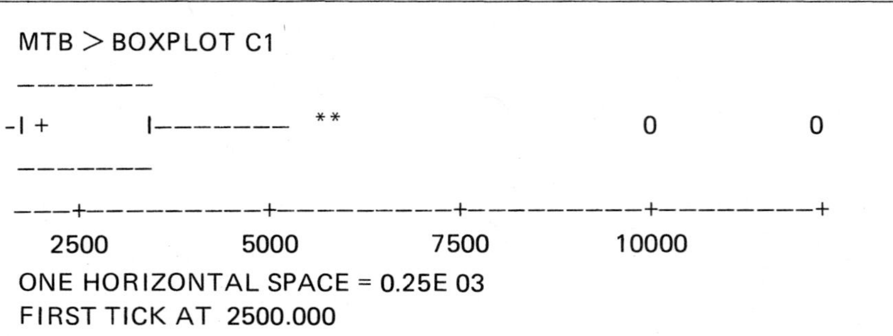

```
MTB > BOXPLOT C1

      --------
  -I +        I-------     **                    0            0
      --------
 ---+---------+---------+---------+--------+
   2500      5000      7500     10000
ONE HORIZONTAL SPACE = 0.25E 03
FIRST TICK AT  2500.000
```

The decoding message below the boxplot allows us to mark the scale of measurement on the horizontal line. The first tick (+) is at 2500.000. Since each horizontal space equals 0.25E 03, each space equals __________, and four spaces equals __________. The horizontal scale has been superimposed on the computer printout above. The boxplot is identical to the one drawn in Example 2.25. Notice that if two outliers lie very close together, the computer may only type one character to represent several outliers.

250
1000.000

Self-Correcting Exercises 2G

1. Use the data given in Exercise 1, Self-Correcting Exercises 2A to construct a boxplot. Are there any outliers? The data are reproduced below in order of ascending magnitude.

18	25	30	34	39	46
19	26	30	34	41	49
21	27	31	35	41	50
21	27	32	35	42	51
23	28	32	36	43	52
23	28	32	37	44	55
23	29	33	38	44	59

2. Construct a boxplot for the data given in Exercise 2, Self-Correcting Exercises 2B. The data have been reproduced below in order of ascending magnitude. Are there any outliers?

NH	353.40	MS	580.00	ME	649.80	RI	712.60	NY	879.30
TN	467.50	CO	584.80	IL	650.20	LA	743.50	OK	896.90
MO	470.40	OR	589.60	VT	650.30	CT	752.70	CA	921.90
SD	475.80	GA	600.60	UT	650.80	WV	753.30	NV	931.80
OH	538.90	VA	605.20	MT	672.40	MD	757.20	MN	932.10
NE	548.10	KS	610.30	KY	680.60	NJ	757.30	NM	941.30
AR	552.80	ID	612.90	MI	681.00	ND	815.70	DE	1001.40
IN	558.00	SC	627.60	AZ	682.90	WI	836.10	HI	1104.90
AL	563.90	TX	639.50	IA	685.30	MA	837.30	WY	1622.40
FL	570.00	NC	644.30	PA	690.00	WA	853.90	AK	6316.40

EXERCISES

1. The following set of data represents the gas mileage for each of 20 cars selected randomly from a production line during the first week in March.

18.1	16.3	18.6	18.7
15.2	19.9	20.3	22.0
19.7	17.7	21.2	18.2
20.9	19.7	19.4	20.2
19.8	17.2	17.9	19.6

a. What is the range of these data?

b. Construct a relative frequency histogram for these data using subintervals of width 1.0. (You might begin with 15.15.)
c. Based on the histogram in part b:
   i. What is the probability that a measurement selected at random from these data will fall in the interval 17.15 to 21.15?
   ii. What is the estimated probability that a measurement taken from the population would be greater than 19.15?
d. Arrange the measurements in order of magnitude beginning with 15.2.
e. What is the median of these data?
f. The ________th percentile would be any number lying between 16.3 and 17.2.
g. The ________th percentile would be any number lying between 19.9 and 20.2.
h. Calculate $\bar{x}$, s^2, and s for these data. (Remember to use the shortcut method.)
i. Do these data conform to Tchebysheff's Theorem? Support your answer by calculating the fractions of the measurements lying in the intervals $\bar{x} \pm ks$ for $k = 1, 2, 3$.
j. Does the Empirical Rule adequately describe these data?

2. Refer to Exercise 1. Construct a boxplot for the data. Are there any outliers? Is the distribution roughly symmetric or is it skewed?
3. A life insurance company randomly sampled 25 new policy holders and for each recorded the number of children claimed by the policy holder. The data are shown below.

2	0	2	1	3
3	1	1	3	2
1	0	7	0	2
0	0	0	4	1
4	3	2	2	5

a. What is the range of these data?
b. Calculate the median.
c. What is the mode?
d. Calculate $\bar{x}$, s^2, and s for these data.
e. Construct a relative frequency histogram for these data using classes of width 1.0. (You might begin with −0.5.)
f. Assuming the above sample is representative of all the company's policy holders,
   i. what is the probability a policy holder has no more than 1 child?
   ii. what is the probability a policy holder has 3 or more children?
g. Can the Empirical Rule be applied to these data? Explain.

4. The annual sales for a small variety store for the years 1984 through 1988 are listed below.

	1984	*1985*	*1986*	*1987*	*1988*
Cash	31,000	35,000	42,000	50,000	38,000
Credit	44,000	46,000	55,000	58,000	44,000

a. Construct a bar graph to depict the store's total sales volume for the five-year period.
b. Construct a bar graph to depict simultaneously the store's cash sales and credit sales over the five-year period.

5. The 1988 federal budget dollar in terms of receipts and expenditures was presented using the following figures.

Receipts	
Individual income taxes	$.38
Corporation income taxes	.11
Social insurance taxes and contributions	.33
Excise taxes	.03
Other	.15
Total	$1.00

Expenditures	
Income Security	$.42
National defense	.29
Net interest	.14
Other federal operations	.15
Total	$1.00

Depict the proposed budget using two separate pie charts.

6. The investment portfolio of pension funds of the employees of a particular company for 1978 and 1988 are listed below.

Type of Asset	*1978*	*1988*
Common stocks	$600,000	$690,000
Preferred stocks	120,000	115,000
Industrial bonds	120,000	345,000
Government bonds	300,000	690,000
Real estate mortgages	60,000	460,000

Construct two separate pie charts to depict the company's portfolio composition, one to depict the composition in 1978, the other to depict the composition in 1988.

7. A small manufacturer sells men's and women's clothing on the export market. Their primary export business is with Australia, Great Britain, and West Germany. Over the past five years, the dollar volume of their business with these three countries has been:

Year	*Australia*	*Great Britain*	*West Germany*
1984	$200,000	$250,000	$150,000
1985	210,000	240,000	130,000
1986	210,000	250,000	170,000
1987	270,000	250,000	220,000
1988	310,000	230,000	250,000

Construct a bar graph to depict simultaneously the sales in these three countries over the past five years.

8. The carrying capacities of 100 barrels of crude oil designed to hold 42 gallons, are measured and found to have a mean of 42.5 gallons and a variance of .66, respectively.
   a. Use Tchebysheff's Theorem to describe these measurements.
   b. Assuming that the capacities have approximately a normal distribution, use the Empirical Rule to describe the data.
9. The lifetime of a particular television tube is known to be approximately mound-shaped with mean 900 hours and standard deviation 90.
   a. If one classifies as "substandard" any tube whose length of life is less than 810 hours, what percentage of tubes will be "substandard"?
   b. What percentage of tubes will have lifetimes between 810 and 1080 hours? Hint: Use the symmetry of the normal distribution; ½ of 68% of the measurements lie within one standard deviation to the left *or* to the right of the mean, and ½ of 95% of the measurements lie within two standard deviations to the left or to the right of the mean.
10. For mound-shaped or approximately normal data, one can use the range as a check on the computation of s, the standard deviation.
    a. Since 95% of the measurements are expected to fall within two standard deviations of their mean, the range should equal approximately how many standard deviations?
    b. Therefore to check the calculation of s, one can divide the range by ______________ and compare this quantity with s.
    c. Use this method to check the calculation of s in the following:
       i. Exercise 1
       ii. Example 2.18
       iii. Example 2.23
    d. Since extreme measurements are more likely to be observed in large samples, we can adjust this approximation to s by dividing the range by a divisor that depends on sample size, n. A rule of thumb to use in approximating s by using the range is presented in the following table:

n	*Divide Range by*
5	2.5
10	3
25	4
100	5

e. Compute s for the data in Example 2.18. Approximate s as in d and compare these two values.

11. A certain company operates a fleet of 40 cars to be used for executive business trips. The fuel consumptions in miles per gallon range from 8.5 to 12.3. In presenting this data in the form of a histogram, suppose you had decided to use 0.5 m.p.g. as the width of your class interval.
    a. How many intervals would you use?
    b. Give the class boundaries for the first and the last classes.
12. A machine designed to dispense cups of instant coffee will dispense on the average μ oz., with standard deviation $\sigma = .7$ oz. Assume that the amount of coffee dispensed per cup is approximately mound-shaped. If 8 oz. cups are to be used, at what value should μ be set so that approximately 97.5% of the cups filled will not overflow?
13. A pharmaceutical company wishes to know whether an experimental drug being tested in its laboratories has any effect on systolic blood pressure. Fifteen subjects, randomly selected, were given the drug and the systolic blood pressures in millimeters recorded.

115	161	142
172	148	123
140	108	152
123	129	133
130	137	128

    a. Approximate s using the method described in Exercise 10d.
    b. Calculate $\bar{x}$ and s for the data.
    c. Find values for the points a and b such that at least 75% of the measurements fall between a and b.
    d. Would Tchebysheff's Theorem be valid if the approximated s (part a) were used in place of the calculated s (part b)?
    e. Would the Empirical Rule apply to this data?
14. Approximate s using the rule in Exercise 10d, and then calculate $\bar{x}$, s^2, and s for the following data: 5, 4, 6, 5, 5. Compare the estimated value of s with the computed value of s.
15. Construct a stem and leaf display for the data in Exercise 13.
16. Construct a boxplot for the data in Exercise 13. Are there any outliers? Are the data roughly symmetric or are they skewed?
17. Calculate $\bar{x}$, s^2, and s and use Tchebysheff's Theorem to describe the following data:

$$-1,\ 4,\ 0,\ 2,\ 3,\ 2,\ 1,\ 2,\ 0,\ 1$$

18. It is known that a population has a mean and standard deviation of 50 and 7, respectively.
    a. What fraction of the measurements would lie in the interval 43 to 57?
    b. If the population is mound-shaped, approximately what fraction of the measurements would lie in the interval 36 to 64?

19. A lumbering company interested in the lumbering rights for a certain tract of slash pine trees is told that the mean diameter of these trees is 14 inches with a standard deviation of 2.8 inches. Assume the distribution of diameters is approximately normal.
    a. What fraction of the trees will have diameters between 8.4 inches and 22.4 inches?
    b. What fraction of the trees will have diameters greater than 16.8 inches?
20. If the mean duration of television commercials on a given network is one minute, 15 seconds, with a standard deviation of 25 seconds, what fraction of these commercials would run longer than two minutes, five seconds? Assume that duration times are approximately normally distributed.
21. Calculate $\bar{x}$, s^2, and s for the following data.

12	16
15	18
14	15
11	14
19	15

Chapter 3

PROBABILITY

3.1 Introduction

We have already stated that our aim is to make inferences about a population based upon sample information. However, in addition to making the inference, we also need to assess how good the inference will be.

Suppose that an experimenter is interested in estimating the unknown mean of a population of observations to within two units of its actual value. If an estimate is produced based upon the sample observations, what is the chance that the estimate is no further than two units away from the true but unknown value of the mean?

If an investigator has formulated two possible hypotheses about a population and only one of these hypotheses can be true, when the sample data are collected she must decide which hypothesis to accept and which to reject. What is the chance that she will make the correct decision?

In both these situations, we have used the term "chance" in assessing the goodness of an inference. But chance is just the everyday term for the concept statisticians refer to as ______________. Therefore, some elementary results from the theory of probability are necessary in order to understand how the accuracy of an inference can be assessed. probability

In the broadest sense, the probability of the occurrence of an event A is a measure of one's belief that the event A will occur in a single repetition of an experiment. One interpretation of this definition that finds widespread acceptance is based upon empirically assessing the probability of the event A by repeating an experiment N times and observing n_A/N, the relative frequency of the occurrence of event A. When N, the number of repetitions, becomes very large, the fraction n_A/N will approach a number we will call $P(A)$, the probability of the occurrence of the event A.

3.2 The Sample Space

When the probability of an event must be assessed, it is important that we be able to visualize under what conditions that event will be realized.

experiment
population
sample

An ______________ is the process by which an observation or measurement is obtained. When an experiment is run repeatedly, a ______________ of observations results. A ______________ would consist of any set of observations taken from this population.

A simple event is defined as one of the possible outcomes of a single repetition of the experiment. *One and only one* simple event can occur on a single repetition of an experiment. Simple events are denoted by the letter E with a subscript. Any collection of simple events is called a compound event. Compound events are denoted by capital letters such as A, B, G, and so on.

Example 3.1

An experiment involves ranking three applicants, X, Y, and Z, in order of their ability to perform in a given position. List the possible simple events associated with this experiment.

Solution

Using the notation (X, Y, Z) to denote the outcome that X is ranked first, Y is ranked second, and Z is ranked third, the six possible outcomes or simple events associated with this experiment are

X, Y

$$E_1: (X, Y, Z),\quad E_2: (Y, X, Z),\quad E_3: (Z, \underline{\qquad\qquad})$$

Z, Y, X

$$E_4: (X, Z, Y),\quad E_5: (Y, Z, X),\quad E_6: (\underline{\qquad\qquad})$$

$E_1; E_4$

If A is the event that applicant X is ranked first, then A will occur if simple event __________ or __________ occurs.

Example 3.2

The financial records of two companies are examined to determine whether each company showed a profit (P) or not (N) during the last quarter.

1. List the simple events associated with this experiment.
2. List the simple events comprising the event B, "exactly one company showed a profit."

Solution

1. The simple events consist of the *ordered* pairs

$$E_1: (P, P),\quad E_2: (P, N)$$

N, N

$$E_3: (N, P),\quad E_4: (\underline{\qquad\qquad})$$

2. Event B consists of the simple events ________ and ________. | E_2; E_3

A Venn diagram is a pictorial representation of the possible outcomes of an experiment in which each simple event is associated with a point called a sample point, and all the sample points are enclosed by a closed curve. The totality of the sample points enclosed by the curve is called the ________ ________ and is denoted by S. | sample space

Example 3.3

Three coins are tossed. Let H denote a head and T denote a tail. There are ________ (give number) simple events. Complete the following table of the simple events E_1, E_2, etc. generated by this experiment. | 8

Event	*Coin 1*	*Coin 2*	*Coin 3*
E_1	H	H	H
E_2	H	H	T

E_3; HTH
E_4; HTT
E_5; THH
E_6; THT
E_7; TTH
E_8; TTT

1. In this experiment, the event "observe exactly two tails" is a (simple, compound) event because it is composed of the simple events ________, ________, and ________. On the other hand, the event "observe no tails" is a (simple, compound) because it is composed of exactly one simple event, namely ________. | compound; E_4, E_6, E_7; simple; E_1
2. In the space below, complete the Venn diagram corresponding to this experiment by assigning the eight simple events to eight points enclosed by the closed curve.

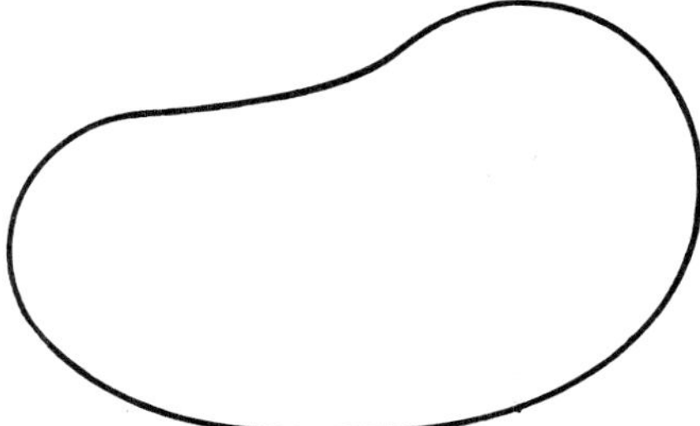

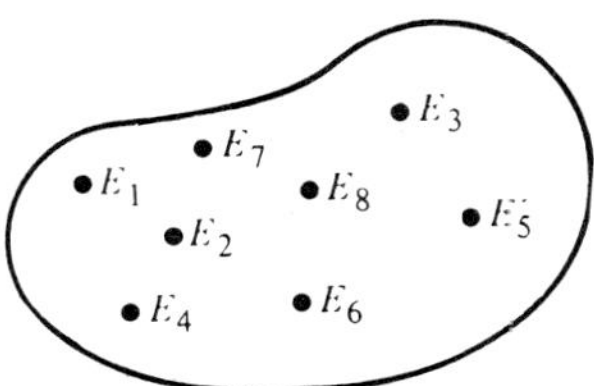

3. Let A be the event "observe no tails," B be the event "observe at least two tails," and C be the event "observe an odd number of tails" in the

three-coin-toss experiment. Represent A, B, C in a Venn diagram in the space below.

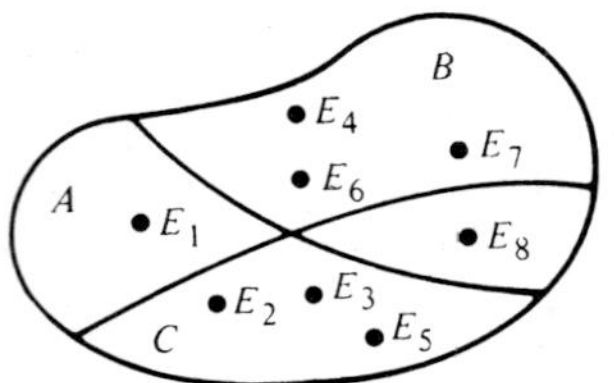

3.3 The Probability of an Event

The Assignment of Probabilities

When the sample space has been defined, the next step is to assign probabilities to each of the simple events. Recall the relative frequency interpretation of probability given in the introduction to this chapter. If an experiment is repeated a large number of times, N, and the event A is observed n_A times, then the probabilitiy of A, denoted by $P(A)$, is approximated by $P(A) \approx$ ________.

n_A/N

Using the relative frequency interpretation of the probability of an event imposes two restrictions on the assignment of probabilities to the simple events. These are as follows:

0; 1

1. ________ $\leqslant P(E_i) \leqslant$ ________

1

2. $\sum_{\text{all } i} P(E_i) =$ ________

After the probabilities have been assigned to the simple events $E_1, E_2, \ldots,$ then the probability associated with any compound event A is found by summing the probabilities of all the simple events that comprise the event A:

$$P(A) = \sum_{\text{all } E_i \text{ in } A} P(E_i)$$

If an experiment has N possible equally likely outcomes, then the condition

$$\sum_{i=1}^{N} P(E_i) = 1$$

requires that $P(E_i) =$ __________ for $i = 1, 2, \ldots, N$. In this case, if the event A contains n_A sample points, then | $1/N$

$$P(A) = \frac{n_A}{N}$$

Remember that this is a special case and that the probabilities assigned to the sample points will not in general be equal.

Example 3.4

Suppose that two coins are tossed and the upper faces recorded. Suppose further that the coins are not fair and the probability that a head results on either coin is greater than a half. The following probabilities are assigned to the sample points:

Sample Point	*Outcome*	*Probability*
E_1	*HH*	.42
E_2	*HT*	.18
E_3	*TH*	.28
E_4	*TT*	.12

1. Verify that this assignment of probabilities satisfies the conditions

$$0 \leqslant P(E_i) \leqslant 1 \quad \text{and} \quad \sum_{i=1}^{4} P(E_i) = 1$$

2. Find the probability of the event A, "the toss results in exactly one head and one tail."
3. Find the probability of the event B, "the toss results in at least one head."

Solution

1. We need but verify the second condition since observation shows that the assigned probabilities satisfy the first condition. Hence,

$$\sum_{i=1}^{4} P(E_i) = P(E_1) + P(E_2) + P(E_3) + P(E_4)$$

$= .42 + .18 +$ __________ $+$ __________ | .28; .12

$=$ __________ | 1

and the second condition (is, is not) satisfied. | is

2. The event A, "exactly one head and one tail," consists of the sample points E_2 and E_3. Therefore,

$$P(A) = P(E_2) + P(E_3)$$

.18; .28 $= \_\_\_\_\_\_\_\_ + \_\_\_\_\_\_\_\_$

.46 $= \_\_\_\_\_\_\_\_$

3. The event B, "at least one head," consists of the sample points E_1, E_2, and E_3. Therefore,

$$P(B) = P(E_1) + P(E_2) + P(E_3)$$

.42 $= \_\_\_\_\_\_\_\_ + .18 + .28$

.88 $= \_\_\_\_\_\_\_\_$

Example 3.5

In a shipment of four radios, R_1, R_2, R_3, and R_4, one radio is defective (say R_3). If a dealer selects two radios at random to display in his store, what is the probability that exactly one of the radios is defective?

Solution

If we disregard the order of selection of the two radios to be displayed, the possible outcomes are

E_1: (R_1, R_2), E_4: (R_2, R_3)

R_4 — E_2: (R_1, R_3), E_5: $(R_2, \_\_\_\_\_\_\_\_)$

R_3, R_4 — E_3: (R_1, R_4), E_6: $(\_\_\_\_\_\_\_\_)$

1/6 — If the radios are selected at random, all combinations should have the same chance of being drawn. Therefore, we assign $P(E_i) = \_\_\_\_\_\_\_\_$ to each of the six sample points.

E_6 — The event D, "exactly one of the two radios selected is defective," consists of the sample points E_2, E_4, and $\_\_\_\_\_\_\_\_$. Therefore,

$$P(D) = P(E_2) + P(E_4) + P(E_6)$$

$$= 1/6 + 1/6 + 1/6$$

1/2 $= \_\_\_\_\_\_\_\_$

Calculating the Probability of an Event: Sample Point Approach

The sample point approach to finding $P(A)$ comprises five steps.

Step 1. Define the experiment.

Step 2. List all the sample points. Test to make certain that none can be decomposed.

Step 3. Specify which sample points lie in A.

Step 4. Assign appropriate probabilities to the sample points. Make sure that

$$\sum_{\text{all } i} P(E_i) = 1$$

Step 5. Find $P(A)$ by summing the probabilities for all points in A.

Example 3.6

A taste-testing experiment is conducted in a local grocery store. Two brands of soft drinks are tasted by a passing shopper, who is then asked to state a preference for brand C or brand P. Suppose that four shoppers are asked to participate in the experiment and that all four choose brand P. Under the assumption that there is no difference between the two brands, what is the probability of the event A, "all four shoppers choose brand P"?

Solution

Step 1. The experiment consists of observing the preferences of each of the four shoppers for either brand P or brand C.

Step 2. The sample space contains the following __________ sample points. 16

E_1: (_____), E_5: (_____), E_9: ($CPPC$), E_{13}: ($CCPC$), *PPPP; PPPC*

E_2: ($CPPP$), E_6: ($PPCC$), E_{10}: ($PCCP$), E_{14}: ($CPCC$),

E_3: ($PCPP$), E_7: ($CCPP$), E_{11}: (_____), E_{15}: ($PCCC$), *PCPC*

E_4: ($PPCP$), E_8: ($CPCP$), E_{12}: ($CCCP$), E_{16}: (_____). *CCCC*

Step 3. $A = \{$(__________)$\}$. *PPPP*

Step 4. The requirement that there be no difference between the two brands implies that a probability of __________ should be assigned to each sample point. 1/16

Step 5. There is (are) __________ sample point(s) in A. Hence, $P(A)$ one
= __________. 1/16

Modified Sample Point Approach

It may be that the list of sample points is quite long. But if equal probabilities are assigned to the sample points, all that is actually required is that you know precisely the number N of points in S and the number n_A of points in the event A. Then $P(A) = n_A/N$. If, however, a list is not made of the sample points, you must take care that no sample point in A is overlooked.

Example 3.7

A dealer who buys items in lots of ten selects two of the ten items at random and inspects them thoroughly. He accepts all ten if there are no defectives among the two inspected. Suppose that a lot contains two defective items.

1. What is the probability that the dealer will nonetheless accept all ten?
2. What is the probability that he will find both of the defectives?

Solution

1. Let A be the event that the dealer accepts the lot.

Step 1. The experiment consists of selecting two items at random from ten items.

Step 2. The sample space consists of *unordered* pairs of the form $(G_1 G_2)$ or $(G_7 D_1)$. The number of sample points is $N = 45$; the sample points are listed below.

$(G_1 G_2)$ $(G_2 G_3)$ $(G_3 G_5)$ $(G_4 G_8)$ $(G_6 G_8)$
$(G_1 G_3)$ $(G_2 G_4)$ $(G_3 G_6)$ $(G_4 D_1)$ $(G_6 D_1)$
$(G_1 G_4)$ $(G_2 G_5)$ $(G_3 G_7)$ $(G_4 D_2)$ $(G_6 D_2)$
$(G_1 G_5)$ $(G_2 G_6)$ $(G_3 G_8)$ $(G_5 G_6)$ $(G_7 G_8)$
$(G_1 G_6)$ $(G_2 G_7)$ $(G_3 D_1)$ $(G_5 G_7)$ $(G_7 D_1)$
$(G_1 G_7)$ $(G_2 G_8)$ $(G_3 D_2)$ $(G_5 G_8)$ $(G_7 D_2)$
$(G_1 G_8)$ $(G_2 D_1)$ $(G_4 G_5)$ $(G_5 D_1)$ $(G_8 D_1)$
$(G_1 D_1)$ $(G_2 D_2)$ $(G_4 G_6)$ $(G_5 D_2)$ $(G_8 D_2)$
$(G_1 D_2)$ $(G_3 G_4)$ $(G_4 G_7)$ $(G_6 G_7)$ $(D_1 D_2)$

Step 3. The event A consists of the sample points containing two good items. In this case, $n_A = 28$.

Step 4. Since the selection is made at random, each sample point should
1/45 be assigned the same probability, equal to ________.

28/45 Step 5. There are 28 sample points in A. Hence $P(A) =$ ________.

2. Let B be the event that the dealer finds both defective items in the random selection.

$D_1 D_2$ Step 3. The event B consists of the single sample point (________).
1 Hence $n_B =$ ________.

Step 5. Therefore, $P(B) = n_B/N = 1/45$.

Notice that it was very tedious to list the $N = 45$ sample points in this situation. Moreover, it is easy to overlook sample points when their number becomes large. In many instances the counting rules presented in Section 3.8 can be used to find N and n_A without listing the individual sample points. The interested reader is referred to that section.

Self-Correcting Exercises 3A

1. A lot containing six items is comprised of four good items and two defective items. Two items are selected at random from the lot for testing purposes.
   a. List the sample points for this experiment.
   b. List the sample points in each of the three following events:
      A: at least one item is defective.
      B: exactly one item is defective.
      C: no more than one item is defective.
   c. Suppose that each item in the six has an equal chance of being selected. Find $P(A)$, $P(B)$, and $P(C)$.
2. A hospital spokesperson reported that four births had taken place at the hospital during the last twenty-four hours. If we consider only the sex of these four children, recording M for a male child and F for a female child, there are 16 sex combinations possible.
   a. List these 16 outcomes in terms of sample points, beginning with E_1 as the outcome $(FFFF)$.
   b. Define the following events in terms of the sample points $E_1, \ldots, E_{16}$:
      A: two boys and two girls are born.
      B: no boys are born.
      C: at least one boy is born.
      D: either A or B occurs.
      E: both B and C occur.
      F: either A or C or both A and C occur.
   c. If the sex of a newborn baby is just as likely to be male as female, find the probabilities associated with the six events defined in b.

3.4 Compound Events

When attempting to find the probability of an event A, it is often useful and convenient to express A in terms of other events whose probabilities are known or perhaps easily calculated. Composition of events occurs in one of the two following ways or a combination of these two:

Intersections. The intersection of two events A and B is the event consisting of those sample points that are in both A and B. The intersection of A and B is denoted by AB.

Unions. The union of two events A and B is the event consisting of those sample points that are in either A or B or both A and B. The union of A and B is denoted by $A \cup B$.

Example 3.8

In each of the Venn diagrams that follow, express symbolically the event represented by the shaded area. In each case the sample space S comprises all sample points within the rectangle.

1.

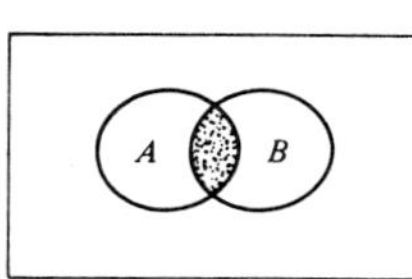

Symbol__________

AB

2.

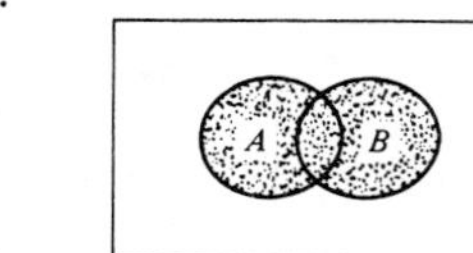

Symbol__________

$A \cup B$

3.

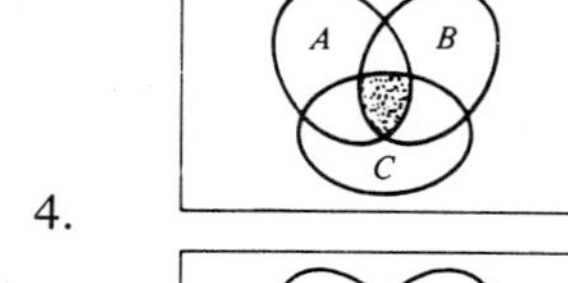

Symbol__________

ABC

4.

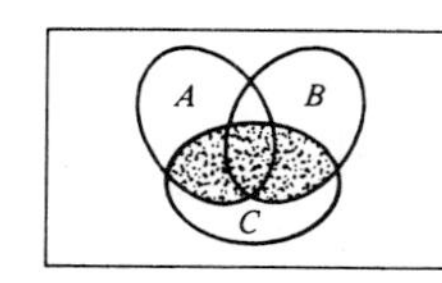

Symbol__________

$AC \cup BC$

Example 3.9

In each of the Venn diagrams below, shade in the event symbolized.

1. Symbol: $A \cup B$.

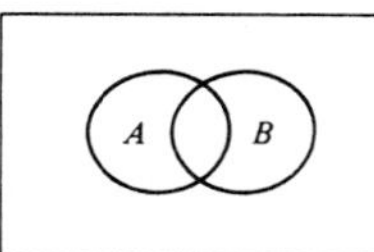

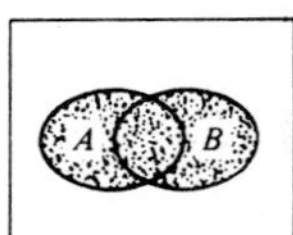

2. Symbol: BC.

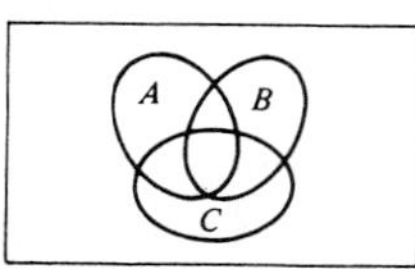

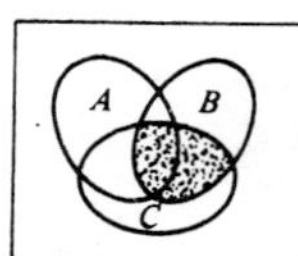

3. Symbol: $AE_1 \cup AE_2$.

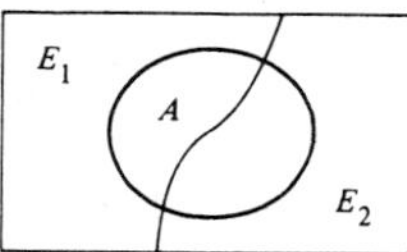

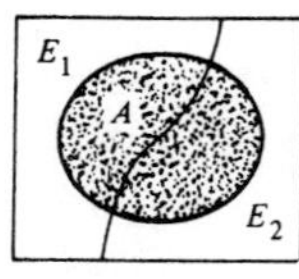

4. Note that $E_1 \cup E_2 = S$ and $AE_1 \cup AE_2 =$ __________.

A

Example 3.10

Refer to example 3.3, where events A, B and C are defined. For each of the compound events listed below, indicate which simple events $E_1, E_2, \ldots, E_8$ are included, and shade in the event on the Venn diagram.

1. $A \cup B$ includes the simple events ______________.

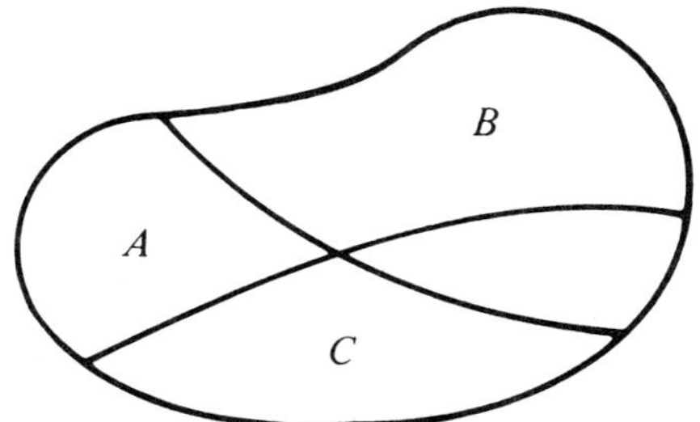

E_1, E_4, E_6, E_7, E_8

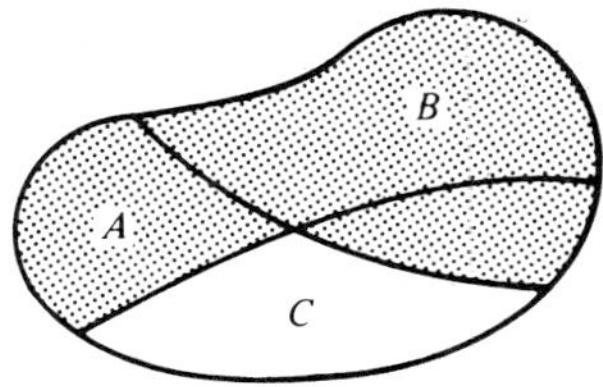

2. BC (or $B \cap C$) includes the simple events __________.

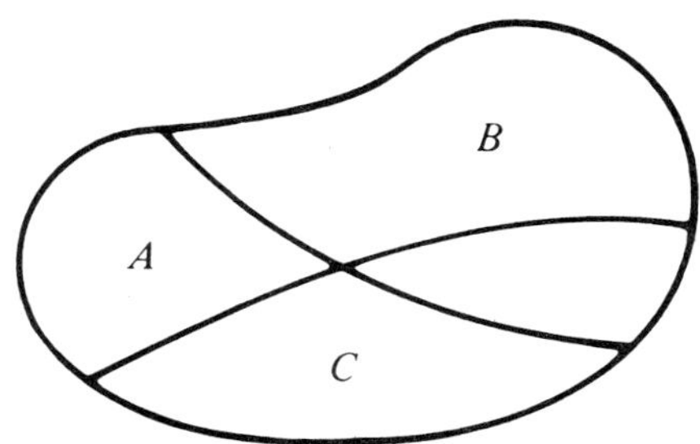

E_8

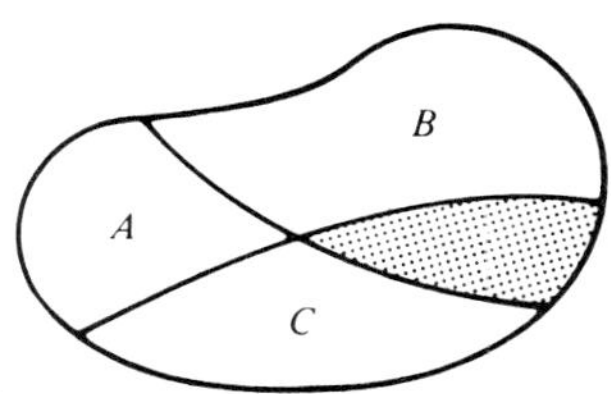

3. AC (or $A \cap C$) includes the simple events ______________.

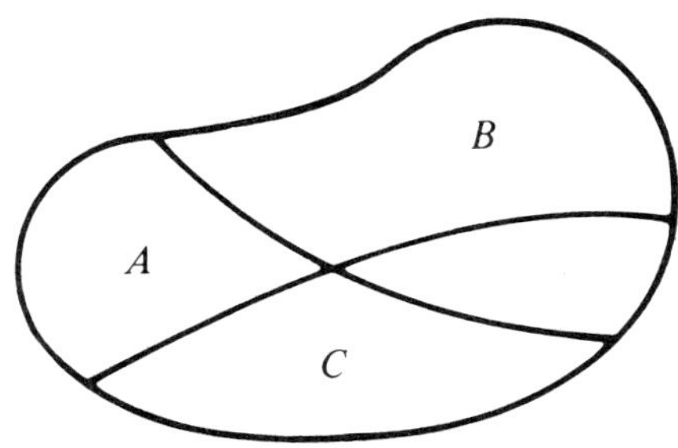

none of E_i are in both A and C

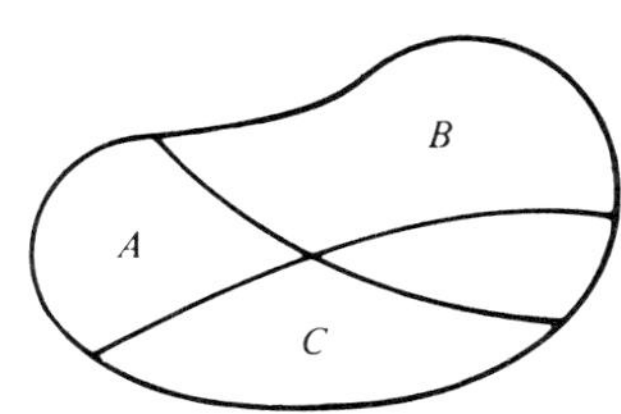

Example 3.11

A researcher proposed the following experiment to assess public attitudes toward racial minorities. In the experiment, a person is shown four photographs—1, 2, 3 and 4—of armed robberies that have been committed and is asked to select what he considers to be the two worst crimes. All four robberies have essentially the same features and involve the same amount of money. However, 1 and 2 are robberies committed against nonwhite victims. In 3 and 4, the victims are white. If the person shows no bias in his selection, find the probabilities associated with the following events:

> A: the selection includes pictures 1 and 2.
> B: the selection includes picture 3.
> C: both A and B occur.
> D: either A or B or both occur.

Solution

The experiment consists of selecting two pictures out of four. Listing the possible outcomes, we have the following distinct pairs.

	Sample point	E_1	E_2	E_3	E_4	E_5	E_6
3,4	Pair	(1,2)	(1,3)	(1,4)	(2,3)	(2,4)	(__)

If there is no bias in selection, each sample point would be assigned
1/6 probability equal to __________ .
E_1 1. The event A consists of the sample point __________. Hence,

E_1; 1/6 $P(A) = P($________$) =$ ________

2. The event B consists of the sample points E_2, E_4, and E_6. Then

3/6 $P(B) =$ ________

3. The event C is the intersection of A and B and consists of the sample point that includes pictures 1 and 2 and at the same time includes picture 3. Since no sample points satisfy these conditions,

0 $P(C) = P(AB) =$ ________

4. The event D is the union of the events A and B and consists of those sample points which include picture 3 and the sample point that includes pictures 1 and 2. Hence $A \cup B$ consists of the sample points E_1, E_2, E_4 and E_6 and

4/6 $P(D) = P(A \cup B) =$ ________

Self-Correcting Exercises 3B

1. Imagine a coin that is so thick that one is just as likely to obtain a toss that lands on edge (G) as it is a head (H) or tail (T). That is, G, H, and T each occur one-third of the time. Suppose that two such coins are tossed.
   a. List the sample points for this experiment.
   b. Define the following events in terms of sample points:
      A: no edges (G's) are observed.
      B: at least one head (H) is observed.
      C: both coins show the same result (i.e., TT, HH, or GG).
   c. Find the probabilities of A, B, C, $A \cup C$, BC.
   d. Draw a Venn diagram of the sample space. Show events A, B, and C in the diagram. Shade in the space corresponding to $B \cup C$.
2. In quality control on taste and texture, it is common to have a taster compare a new batch of a food product with one having the desired properties. Three new batches are independently tested against the standard and classified as having the desired properties H or not having the desired properties N.
   a. List the sample points for this experiment.
   b. If in fact all three new batches are no different from the standard, all sample points in part a should be equally likely. If this is the case, find the probabilities associated with the following events:
      A: exactly one batch is declared as not having the desired properties.
      B: batch number one is declared to have the desired property.
      C: all three batches are declared to have the desired property.
      D: at least two batches are declared to have the desired property.
   c. Using the information in parts a and b, find the probabilities for $A \cup D$ and BD.

3.5 Event Relations

Events may be related to other events in several ways. Relations between events can often be used to simplify calculations involved when finding the probability of an event.

The event consisting of all those sample points in the sample space S that are not in the event A is defined as the *complement of A* and is denoted by $\bar{A}$.

It is always true that $P(A) + P(\bar{A}) =$ __________. Therefore, $P(A) = 1 - P(\bar{A})$. 1
If $P(\bar{A})$ can be found more easily than $P(A)$, this relationship greatly simplifies finding $P(A)$.

Example 3.12
Suppose that 10% of the fuses in a large lot of electrical fuses are defective. A packet of three fuses will be obtained by packaging three fuses selected at random from the lot. Let A be the event that at least two of the three fuses will be defective. It can be shown that the probability that at most one of the fuses will be defective is .972. Find $P(A)$.

Solution

one — $\bar{A}$ is the event that at most ____________ of the fuses will be defec-
.972; .028 — tive. Thus $P(\bar{A})$ = __________ and $P(A)$ = __________.

Events A and B which have no common sample points are said to be *mutually exclusive.*

When A and B are mutually exclusive, their intersection AB contains no
0 — sample points and $P(AB)$ = __________. Notice that the events A and $\bar{A}$
are — (are, are not) mutually exclusive.

To introduce the concept of independence of two events, it is first necessary to define a conditional probability.

The probability that event A has occurred, *given that* the event B has occurred, is given by

$$P(A|B) = \frac{P(AB)}{P(B)}$$

for $P(B) > 0$.

Use a Venn diagram with events A and B to see that by knowing the event B has occurred, you effectively exclude any sample points lying outside the event B from further consideration. Since $P(B)$ and $P(AB)$ represent the amounts of probability associated with events B and AB, then

$$P(A|B) = \frac{P(AB)}{P(B)}$$

merely represents the proportion of $P(B)$ that will give rise to the event A.

When $P(A|B) = P(A)$, the events A and B are said to be (probabilistically) independent, since the probability of the occurrence of A is not affected by knowledge of the occurrence of B. If $P(A|B) \neq P(A)$, the events A and B are said to be dependent.

Example 3.13
Five applicants, all equally qualified, are being considered for a mana-

gerial position. There are three males and two females among the applicants. Define the following events:

A: female number one is selected.
B: a female is selected.

If the selection is done at random, find $P(A)$ and $P(A|B)$. Are A and B independent? Are A and B mutually exclusive?

Solution

The unconditional probability, $P(A)$ = ________ and $P(AB) = P(A)$ = ________. Hence, A and B (are, are not) mutually exclusive. We can find $P(A|B)$ in one of two ways.

1/5
1/5; are not

1. *Direct enumeration.* If B has occurred, then we need only consider the two female applicants as comprising the new restricted sample space. Hence, $P(A|B)$ = ________.

1/2

2. *Calculation.* By definition,

$$P(A|B) = P(AB)/P(B)$$

$$= \frac{1/5}{\_\_\_} = \_\_\_\_\_\_\_\_$$

2/5; 1/2

Example 3.14

You hold ticket number 7 in an office lottery in which ten tickets numbered 1 through 10 were sold. The winning ticket is drawn at random from those sold. You are told that an odd number was drawn. Does this information increase the probability that you have won?

Solution

Define the events.

A: number 7 is drawn.
B: an odd number is drawn.

Then $P(A)$ = ________ and $P(A|B)$ = ________. The events A and B are ____________ and the probability that you have won is now doubled.

1/10; 1/5
dependent

Example 3.15

In a marketing research survey an individual is first classified as belonging to one of the following age groups:

G_1: 25 years of age or younger.
G_2: older than 25 but not older than 40.
G_3: older than 40 but not older than 60.
G_4: over 60 years of age.

are — These groups (are, are not) mutually exclusive. Hence the probability that a person will be categorized as simultaneously belonging to two groups will be ______________.

zero

3.6 Two Probability Laws and Their Use

Many events can be viewed as the union or intersection, or both, of simpler events whose probabilities may be known or easily calculated. In such cases the Additive and Multiplicative Laws of Probability can be used in assessing the probability of the event.

The Additive Law of Probability: The probability of the union of events A and B is given by

$$P(A \cup B) = P(A) + P(B) - P(AB)$$

---

0 — When the events A and B are mutually exclusive, $P(AB) =$ __________ and

$$P(A \cup B) = P(A) + P(B)$$

$P(B)$ — If the event A is contained in the event B, then $P(A \cup B) =$ __________.

The Multiplicative Law of Probability: The probability of the intersection of events A and B is given by

$$P(AB) = P(A)P(B|A)$$

or, equivalently, by

$$P(AB) = P(B)P(A|B)$$

If the events A and B are independent,

$$P(AB) = P(A)P(B)$$

Example 3.16

In the following Venn diagram the ten sample points shown are equally likely. Thus to each sample point is assigned the probability __________.

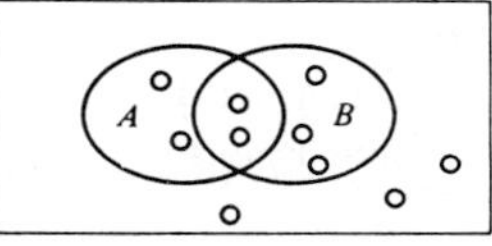

1. $P(A \cup B)$ = ________. — 7/10
2. $P(AB)$ = ________. — 2/10
3. $P(B)$ = ________. — 5/10
4. $P(A|B)$ = ________. — 2/5
5. $P(\bar{B})$ = ________. — 5/10
6. A and B are (independent, dependent). — independent

The information provided by the Venn diagram for Example 3.16 can also be presented using a two-way *probability table*. When considering two events A and B, the entries in the body of the table are the four intersection probabilities AB, $A\bar{B}$, $\bar{A}B$ and $\bar{A}\bar{B}$. Furthermore, the marginal row or column sums are the unconditional probabilities $P(A)$, $P(\bar{A})$, $P(B)$ and $P(\bar{B})$. Use Example 3.16 to fill in the missing entries in the probability table which follows:

	B	$\bar{B}$		
A	.2	________	.4	.2
$\bar{A}$	________	.3	.6	.3
	.5	________		.5

Notice that $P(AB) = .2$, $P(B) = .5$ and $P(\bar{B})$ = ________ are found directly as either table entries (intersections) or marginal sums (unconditional probabilities). — .5
Furthermore, the information needed to find the conditional probability $P(A|B)$ is also readily available, since $P(A|B) = P(AB)/P(B) = (.2)/($________$)$ = — .5
________. — .4

Example 3.17

The personnel files for a large real estate agency lists its 150 employees as follows:

	Years Employed with the Agency		
	0–5 (*A*)	*6–10* (*B*)	*11 or More* (*C*)
Not a college graduate (D)	10	20	20
College graduate (E)	40	50	10

If *one* personnel file is drawn at random from the agency's personnel files, calculate the probabilities requested below.

1. $P(A)$ = ________. — 1/3
2. $P(E)$ = ________. — 2/3
3. $P(BD)$ = ________. — 2/15
4. $P(C|E)$ = ________. — 1/10
5. $P(A \cup E)$ = ________. — 11/15
6. $P(A|C)$ = ________. — 0
7. A and E are (independent, dependent). — dependent

Self-Correcting Exercises 3C

1. Refer to Exercise 2, Self-Correcting Exercises 3A.
   a. Rewrite events D, E, and F in terms of the events A, B and C.
   b. List the sample points in the following events: AB, $B \cup C$, $AC \cup BC$, $\bar{C}$, $\overline{AC}$.
   c. Using the results of part c in Exercise 2, Self-Correcting Exercises 3A, calculate $P(A \cup B)$, $P(\bar{C})$, $P(\overline{BC})$.
   d. Calculate $P(A|C)$. Are A and C mutually exclusive? Are A and C independent?
   e. Calculate $P(B|C)$. Are B and C independent? Mutually exclusive?
2. Two hundred corporate executives in the Los Angeles area were interviewed. They were classified according to the size of the corporation they represented and their choice as to the most effective method for reducing air pollution in the Los Angeles basin. (Data are fictitious.)

	Corporation Size		
	A (*Small*)	*B* (*Medium*)	*C* (*Large*)
D: Car pooling	20	15	20
E: Bus expansion	30	25	11
F: Gas rationing	3	8	4
G: Conversion to natural gas	10	7	5
H: Anti-pollution devices	12	20	10

   Suppose that one executive is chosen at random to be interviewed on a television broadcast.
   a. Calculate the following probabilities and describe each probability in terms of the above problem: $P(A)$, $P(F)$, $P(AF)$, $P(A \cup G)$, $P(AD)$, $P(\bar{F})$.
   b. Calculate $P(A|F)$, $P(A|D)$. Are A and F independent? Mutually exclusive? Are A and D independent? Mutually exclusive?
3. The selling style of a temperamental salesman is strongly affected by his success or failure in his preceding attempt to sell. If he has just made a sale his confidence and effectiveness rise and the probability of selling to his next prospect is 3/4. When he fails to sell, his manner is fearful and the probability of his selling to his next prospect is only 1/3. Suppose that the probability that he will sell to his first contact on a given day is 1/2. Find the probability of the event A, that he makes at least two sales on his first three contacts on a given day.
4. An investor holds shares in three independent companies which, according to his business analyst, should show an increase in profit per share with probabilities .4, .6 and .7 respectively. Assume that the analyst's estimates for the probabilities of profit increases are correct.
   a. Find the probability that all three companies show increases for the coming year.
   b. Find the probability that none of the companies show a profit.
   c. Find the probability that at least one company shows a profit.

3.7 Bayes' Law

Bayes' Law gives a formula for the computation of a ______________ probability, $P(B|A)$, when the conditional probabilities __________ and __________ and the marginal probabilities $P(B)$ and __________ are known. The computational formula for Bayes' Law is

conditional
$P(A|B)$
$P(A|\bar{B}); P(\bar{B})$

$$P(B|A) = \frac{P(A|B)\,P(B)}{P(A|B)\,P(B) + P(A|\bar{B})\,P(\bar{B})}$$

The probability $P(B|A)$ is called the ______________ probability of event B given ______________. The simple or marginal probabilities $P(B)$ and $P(\bar{B})$ are called the ______________ probabilites of events B and $\bar{B}$, respectively.

posterior
event A
prior

Example 3.18

An oil wildcatter must decide whether or not to hire a seismic survey before deciding whether or not to drill for oil on a plot of land. Given that oil is present, the survey will indicate a favorable result with probability .8; if oil is not present, a favorable result will occur with probability .3. The wildcatter figures the probability is .5 that oil is present on the plot of land. Determine the effectiveness of the survey by computing the probability that oil is present given a favorable seismic survey outcome.

Solution

Define the events. F: a favorable seismic outcome results.
O: oil is actually present.
$\bar{O}$: oil is not present.

1. We want to find
   $P(O|F) =$ ______________ / ______________
2. $P(F|O) =$ __________, $P(F|\bar{O}) =$ __________
3. Since $P(O) =$ __________, then $P(\bar{O}) = 1 - P(O) =$ __________
4. Thus, $P(O|F) =$ __________

$P(F|O)P(O); P(F|O)P(O) + P(F|\bar{O})P(\bar{O})$.
.8; .3
.5; .5
8/11

The information available in Example 3.18 can easily be depicted using a *tree diagram* in which probabilities along each branching of the tree are the *conditional* probabilities associated with this step on the tree, given the preceding steps along the path. Probabilities associated with experimental outcomes are found as the product of the probabilities along the path leading to that outcome. The information in Example 3.18 can be depicted as follows.

Step 1	*Step 2*	*Outcome*	*Probability*
O (.5)	F (.8)	OF	.40
	$\bar{F}$ (.2)	$O\bar{F}$	.10
$\bar{O}$ (.5)	F (.3)	$\bar{O}F$	.15
	$\bar{F}$ (.7)	$\overline{OF}$	.35

With this information, calculating the desired probability $P(O|F)$ requires that we know $P(OF)$ which is .40 and $P(F) = P(OF) + P(\bar{O}F)$ found as .40 + .15 = .55. Thus, $P(O|F) = .40/.55$ or 8/11.

Example 3.19
Each item coming off a given production line is inspected by either Inspector 1 or Inspector 2. Inspector 1 inspects about 60% of the production items while Inspector 2 inspects the rest. Inspector 1, who has been at his present job for some time, will not find 1% of the defective items he inspects. Inspector 2, who is newer on the job, misses about 5% of the defective items he inspects. If an item which has passed an inspector is found to be defective, what is the probability that it was inspected by Inspector 1?

Solution
Define the following events.

> D: a defective item is passed by an inspector.
> A: Inspector 1 inspected the item.
> $\bar{A}$: Inspector 2 inspected the item.

1. The following information is available.

.4 $P(A) = .6$ $\qquad P(\bar{A}) =$ ________
.01; .05 $P(D|A) =$ ________ $\qquad P(D|\bar{A}) =$ ________

2. We want to find

$$P(A|D) = \frac{P(A)\,P(D|A)}{P(A)\,P(D|A) + P(\bar{A})\,P(D|\bar{A})}$$

.006 3. $P(A)\,P(D|A) = (.6)\,(.01) =$ ________
.020 $P(\bar{A})\,P(D|\bar{A}) = (.4)\,(.05) =$ ________
.23 4. Then $P(A|D) = .006/(.006 + .020) =$ ________

Alternately, a *tree diagram* can be used to find $P(A|D)$. Fill in the missing entries.

Step 1	*Step 2*	*Outcome*	*Probability*
A (.60)	D (.01)	AD	______
	$\bar{D}$ (.99)	$A\bar{D}$	.594
$\bar{A}$ (.40)	D	$\bar{A}D$	______
	$\bar{D}$ (.95)	$\overline{AD}$	.380

.006

(.05); .020

Since $P(A|D) = P(AD)/P(D)$ and $P(D) = P(AD) + P(\bar{A}D)$, then

$$P(A|D) = .006/(.006 + .020) = .2307$$

which when rounded to two-decimal accuracy agrees with our previous answer.

Self-Correcting Exercises 3D

1. A manufacturer of air-conditioning units purchases 70% of its thermostats from company A, 20% from company B, and the rest from company C. Past experience shows that .5% of company A's thermostats, 1% of company B's thermostats, and 1.5% of company C's thermostats are likely to be defective. An air-conditioning unit randomly selected from this manufacturer's production line was found to have a defective thermostat.
   a. Find the probability that the defective thermostat was supplied by company A.
   b. Find the probability that the defective thermostat was supplied by company B.
2. Suppose that on the basis of past experience it is known that a lie detector test will indicate that an innocent person is guilty with probability .08, while the test will indicate that a guilty person is innocent with probability .15. Suppose further that 10% of the population under study has committed a traffic violation. If a lie detector test indicates that a randomly chosen individual from this population has committed a traffic violation, what is the probability that this person is innocent of committing a traffic violation?

3.8 Results Useful in Counting Sample Points (Optional)

There are three basic counting rules that are useful in counting the number of sample points N arising in many experiments. When all the N sample points are equally likely, the probability of an event A can be found without listing the sample points if N, the number of points in S, and n_A, the number of points in A, can be counted, since in this case $P(A) = n_A/N$. This is often important, since N and n_A can become quite large.

The mn Rule. Suppose a procedure can be completed in two stages. If the first stage can be done in m ways and the second stage in n ways after the first stage has been completed, then the number of ways of completing the procedure is mn (m times n).

Example 3.20

An experiment involves ranking three applicants in order of merit. In how many ways can the three applicants be ranked?

Solution

The process of ranking three applicants can be accomplished in two stages.
Stage 1: Select the best applicant from the three.
Stage 2: Having selected the best, select the next best from the remaining two applicants.

The ranking of the remaining applicant will automatically be third. The num-
3 ber of ways of accomplishing stage 1 is __________. When stage 1 is com-
2 pleted, there are __________ ways of accomplishing stage 2. Hence there are
6 (3)(2) = __________ ways of ranking three applicants.

Example 3.21

A lot of items consists of four good items (G_1, G_2, G_3, and G_4) and two defective items (D_1 and D_2).

1. How many different samples of size two can be formed by selecting two items from these six?
2. How many different samples will consist of exactly one good and one defective item?
3. What is the probability that exactly one good and one defective will be drawn?

Solution

1. Selecting two items from six items corresponds to the two-step procedure of (1) picking the first item and (2) picking the second item after picking
6; 5 the first. Hence m = __________, n = __________, and the number of
30 ordered pairs is $N = mn = (6)(5)$ = __________.
2. Selecting one good and one defective item can be done in either of two ways.

a. The *defective* item can be drawn *first* in m = __________ ways and the *good* item drawn *second* in n = __________ ways. Hence there are mn = __________ ways of selecting a defective item on the first draw and a good item on the second draw. — 2; 4; 8

b. However, the *good* item can be drawn *first* in m = __________ ways and the *defective* item drawn second in n = __________ ways, so that there are mn = __________ ways in which a good item is drawn first and a defective item is drawn second. — 4; 2; 8

c. Combining the results of Steps a and b, there are exactly $8 + 8$ = ______ samples that will contain exactly one defective and one good item. — 16

3. Let A be the event that exactly one good and one defective item are drawn. From part 1, N = ________ , and from part 2, n_A = ________ . Hence — 30; 16

$$P(A) = n_A/N = 16/30 = \text{\_\_\_\_\_\_\_\_\_\_}$$

8/15

An ordered arrangement of r distinct objects is called a *permutation.* The number of permutations consisting of r objects selected from n objects is given by the formula

$$P_r^n = n!/(n-r)! = n(n-1)(n-2)\ldots(n-r+1)$$

where $n! = n(n-1)\ldots(3)(2)(1)$ and $0! = 1$.

Example 3.22

In how many ways can three different office positions be filled if there are seven applicants who are qualified for all three positions?

Solution

Notice that assigning the same three people to different office positions would produce different ways of filling the three positions. Hence we need to find the number of permutations (*ordered arrangements*) of three people selected from seven. Therefore,

$$P_3^7 = 7!/4! = (7)(6)(\text{\_\_\_\_\_\_\_\_\_\_}) = \text{\_\_\_\_\_\_\_\_\_\_}$$

5; 210

Example 3.23

A corporation will select two sites from ten available sites under consideration for building two manufacturing plants. If one plant will produce flashbulbs and the other cameras, in how many ways can the selection be made?

Solution

We are interested in the number of permutations of two sites selected from ten sites, since if two sites, say 6 and 8, were chosen, and the flashbulb plant was built at site 6 while the camera plant was built at site 8, this would result in a different selection than would occur if the camera plant was built at site 6 and the flashbulb plant at site 8. Therefore, the number of selections is

9; 90

$$P_2^{10} = (10)(\_\_\_\_\_\_) = \_\_\_\_\_\_$$

A selection of r objects from n distinct objects without regard to their ordering is called a *combination.* The number of combinations that can be formed when selecting r objects from n objects is given as

$$C_r^n = \frac{n!}{r!\,(n-r)!}$$

Example 3.24
Thirteen company employees have been found equally qualified for promotion to a particular job. It has been decided to choose five of the employees at random for immediate promotion. How many different groups of five employees are possible?

Solution
Since it is the names of the five employees, and not the order in which they are chosen, which is important, the number of distinct groups is

1287

$$C_5^{13} = \frac{13!}{5!\,8!} = \frac{13(12)(11)(10)(9)}{5(4)(3)(2)(1)} = \_\_\_\_\_\_$$

Example 3.25
Refer to Example 3.7. A dealer tests two items randomly chosen from a lot of ten items and accepts the lot if the two items are not defective. Use the counting rules to find the following probabilities if a lot contains two defective items:

1. The probability that the dealer accepts the lot.
2. The probability that both defectives are found.

A: no defectives are found.
B: two defectives are found.

Solution
In order to calculate $P(A)$ and $P(B)$ it is necessary to find N, n_A, and n_B.

1. Since a sample point is an unordered pair of the form (G_1G_2) or (G_1D_1), the total number of sample points is

$$N = C_2^{10} = \frac{10!}{2!\,8!} = \frac{(10)(9)}{(2)(1)} = 45$$

2. The number of ways to draw no defectives is the same as the number of ways of drawing ______ good items (from a total of ______ good items). Hence

two; eight

$$n_A = C_2^8 = \frac{8!}{2!\,6!} = \frac{(8)(7)}{(2)(1)} = \_\_\_\_\_\_$$

28

3. The number of ways to draw two defective items (from a total of two defective items) is

$$n_B = C_2^2 = \frac{2!}{0!\,2!} = \_\_\_\_\_\_$$

1

4. Using the results of steps 1, 2, and 3,

$$P(A) = n_A/N = 28/45$$

$$P(B) = n_B/N = 1/45$$

Notice that this method of solution is much less tedious than the solution used in Example 3.7.

Self-Correcting Exercises 3E (Optional)

1. Refer to Example 3.24. Suppose that only one vacancy will occur at a time, and that five employees must be chosen for assignment sequentially. These five will then be promoted as vacancies occur in the order they are listed. How many different promotional lists are possible?
2. A stereo components retailer is advertising a sale plan which allows a customer to build a high-fidelity system for $500 by choosing one of four receivers, one of five turntables, one of three cassette decks, and one of six sets of speakers. The dealer's cost of one model within each category of equipment is such that he will lose money if a customer includes that model in his system selection. That is, there is one brand of receiver, one brand of turntable, etc., that will cause a loss to the store if a customer selects it. Assume that customers choose components at random. What is the probability that the dealer will make a profit on any particular sale?
3. There are six new advertising accounts that the manager of an advertising agency must assign to his six new account executives. In how many different ways can the six accounts be assigned?
4. A company makes six different models of camp stoves. A magazine advertisement is being prepared, and the layout provides space for displaying only four of the camp stoves. It has already been decided that two particular models, the most expensive one and a medium-

priced model whose sales have been lagging, will definitely appear in the layout. If the other stove models are selected at random, how many different layouts are possible?

EXERCISES

1. Assume that probabilities have been assigned to all the points in a sample space; tell how you would find the probability of an event A.
2. The probabilities associated with a sample space must satisfy two requirements. State these requirements.
3. a. How would you tell whether two events A and B are independent?
   b. How would you tell whether events A and B are mutually exclusive?
4. Suppose that an experiment requires the ranking of three applicants A, B, and C in order of their abilities to do a certain job. The sample points could then be symbolized by the ordered triplets ABC, BAC, etc.
   a. The event A that applicant A will be ranked first comprises which of the sample points?
   b. The event B that applicant B will be ranked third comprises which of the sample points?
   c. List the points in $A \cup B$.
   d. List the points in AB.
   e. If equal probabilities are assigned to the sample points show whether or not events A and B are independent.
5. An investor is considering investing in three investment opportunities A, B, and C. The probability each investment "pays off" is $P(A) = .5$, $P(B) = .4$, and $P(C) = .6$. Assuming the performances of the investments are independent of one another, find:
   a. The probability all investments will pay off.
   b. The probability two of the three investments will pay off.
   c. The probability at least one of the investments pays off.
6. The owner of a camera shop knows from experience that 5% of all cameras produced by a particular company prove to be defective. If the owner purchases five cameras from this company, find the probability none are defective.
7. The owner of the camera shop mentioned in Exercise 6 has been sent five cameras by this company, but, unknown to the owner, one of the cameras is defective. Suppose the store owner tests the cameras one at a time.
   a. What is the probability he discovers the defective camera on the first test?
   b. As a time saving measure, suppose the store owner tests only 40% of the cameras in shipments sent to him by manufacturers. If he adopts this rule with this shipment, what is the probability the defective camera is found in testing?

c. Is the fact that 5% of all cameras produced by this company are defective of any assistance in solving parts a and b? Explain.

8. Suppose $P(A) = 1/2$ and $P(B) = 1/4$. Find $P(AB)$ if:
   a. A and B are independent.
   b. A and B are mutually exclusive.
9. Suppose $P(A) = 1/3$, $P(B) = 1/4$ and $P(A|B) = 1/2$. Find $P(A \cup B)$.
10. Suppose that independent events A and B have nonzero probabilities. Show that A and B cannot be mutually exclusive.
11. An antique dealer had accumulated a number of small items including a valuable stamp collection and a solid gold vase. To make room for new stock he distributed these small items among four boxes. Without revealing which items were placed in which box, the dealer stated that the stamp collection was included in one box and the gold vase in another. The four boxes were sealed and placed on sale, each at the same price. A certain customer purchased two boxes selected at random from the four boxes. What is the probability that he acquired
    a. the stamp collection?
    b. the vase?
    c. at least one of these bonus items?
12. The sample space for a given experiment is comprised of the simple events E_1, E_2, E_3, and E_4. Let the compound events A, B, and C be defined by the relationships

$$A = E_1 \cup E_2, \quad B = E_1 \cup E_4, \quad C = E_2 \cup E_3$$

    Construct a Venn diagram showing the events E_1, E_2, E_3, E_4, A, B, and C.
13. Refer to Exercise 12. Probabilities are assigned to the simple events as indicated in the following table.

Simple event	E_1	E_2	E_3	E_4
Assigned probability	1/3	1/3	1/6	—

    a. Supply the missing entry in the table.
    b. Find $P(A)$ and $P(AB)$.
    c. Find $P(A|B)$ and $P(A|C)$.
    d. Find $P(A \cup B)$ and $P(A \cup C)$.
14. Refer to Exercise 12.
    a. Which pairs of the events A, B, and C are mutually exclusive?
    b. Which pairs of the events A, B, and C are independent?
15. A large commercial bank has branch banks located throughout five western states. The 120 branch banks are categorized below according to the state in which they are located and the number of years they have been in operation.

	State				
	Washington	*Oregon*	*California*	*Nevada*	*Idaho*
Under 5	11	9	17	3	6
5–10	12	5	23	4	3
Over 10	7	6	10	3	1

A bank is selected at random from among the 120 branch banks.

a. Find the probability that the bank is located in Washington.
b. Find the probability that the bank has been in operation less than five years.
c. Find the probability that the bank has been in operation at least five years.
d. Find the probability that the bank is in California or has been in operation over 10 years, or both.
e. Find the probability that the bank has been in operation at least five years or is located in Oregon or both.
f. Find the probability that the bank is located in Washington and has been in operation at least 10 years.
g. Given that the bank has been in operation less than five years, find the probability that it is located in Idaho.
h. Given that the bank is located in California, find the probability that it has been in operation 10 years or less.
i. Find the probability that the bank is located outside of California.

16. A random sample of size five is drawn from a large production lot with fraction defective 10%. The probability that this sample will contain no defectives is .59. What is the probability that this sample will contain at least one defective?
17. In an article in a local newspaper it was stated that if the probability of destroying an attacking plane were .15 at each of five defense barriers, and if an attacking plane had to pass all five barriers to get to the target, then the probability of destroying the plane before it passed all five barriers would be .75. Is the newspaper correct in its conclusion? Explain.
18. To test the competence of a diamond salesman, a dealer requires the salesman to select the three most valuable gems from a collection of ten gems, and to specify which of these is first, which is second, and which is third in order of value. Suppose that the salesman is totally lacking in ability to rank gems in order of value.
    a. What is the probability that the salesman will achieve total success?
    b. What is the probability that at least one of the three most valuable gems will be included among the three selected by the salesman?

19. A factory operates an eight-hour day shift. Five machines of a certain type are used. If one of these machines breaks down, it is set aside and repaired by a crew operating at night. Suppose the probability that a given machine suffers a breakdown during a day's operation is 1/5.
    a. What is the probability that no machine breakdown will occur on a given day?
    b. What is the probability that two or more machine breakdowns will occur on a given day?
20. Income in a neighborhood is approximately normally distributed (bell-shaped) with mean and standard deviation equal to \$4600 and \$500, respectively. If two wage earners are selected randomly from the neighborhood, give the probability that both will have incomes in excess of \$5100 per year.
21. An oil prospector will drill a succession of holes in a given area to find a productive well. The probability that he is successful on a given trial is .2.
    a. What is the probability that the third hole drilled is the first which locates a productive well?
    b. If his total resources allow the drilling of no more than three holes, what is the probability that he locates at least one productive well?
22. Suppose that two defective refrigerators have been included in a shipment of six refrigerators. The buyer begins to test the six refrigerators one at a time.
    a. What is the probability that the last defective refrigerator is found on the fourth test?
    b. What is the probability that no more than four refrigerators must be tested before locating both of the defective refrigerators?
23. An individual is to be selected at random from a given population. Let T be the event that this individual has tuberculosis and E be the event that his X-ray examination indicates (rightly or wrongly) that he has tuberculosis. Suppose that we know the following probabilities:

$$P(T) = .001, \quad P(E|T) = .90, \quad P(E|\bar{T}) = .01$$

    a. State in words what is meant by $P(E|\bar{T})$.
    b. Noting that $E = ET \cup E\bar{T}$, calculate $P(E)$.
    c. Calculate $P(T|E)$, and state in words what is implied about the proper interpretation of the X-ray examination.
24. Construction firm A must be awarded at least two jobs within a week to maintain employment for its basic personnel. It has submitted bids for each of three jobs of type I and for each of two jobs of type II. The winning firms will be announced within the crucial week. Suppose that firm

A has probability 1/2 of being awarded a given job of type I and probability 3/4 of being awarded a given job of type II. The decisions will be made independently. What is the probability that firm A will be able to continue the employment of its basic personnel?

25. Construction firm B is considering bidding on a construction job to build an apartment building. They feel they will win the contract to build the apartment with probability 3/4 if construction firm C does not submit a bid, but the probability that they will win the contract if C does submit a bid on the job is 1/3. What is the probability that firm B will win the contract, given that C bids on 30% of the construction jobs?

Chapter 4

RANDOM VARIABLES AND PROBABILITY DISTRIBUTIONS

4.1 Random Variables: How They Relate to Statistical Inference

Sets of measurements can be classified as either *quantitative* or *qualitative*, according to whether the measurement is a numerical quantity or a descriptive quantity.

Example 4.1
The selling price of 50 homes represents a quantitative set of data, since each measurement is numerical.

Example 4.2
A particular brand of microwave oven is rated by 25 consumers according to overall performance as either excellent, very good, good, fair, or poor. The set of 25 measurements represents a qualitative set of data, since each measurement is one of the five "qualities" given above.

Example 4.3
Identify each of the following sets of data as either quantitative or qualitative.

1. The cost of identical models of a Toyota station wagon was recorded at each of 12 Toyota dealers in Southern California. (quantitative, qualitative) quantitative
2. In the process of applying for credit, 25 applicants are asked whether or not they currently have an outstanding bank loan. (quantitative, qualitative) qualitative
3. In 1988, 150 cars were purchased by a local taxi company, and the make of car was recorded for each. There were 45 Fords, 30 Chevrolets, 60 Plymouths, and 15 Dodges. (quantitative, qualitative) qualitative
4. The total sales and the domestic sales were recorded for an electronics firm over the five years 1984 to 1988. (quantitative, qualitative) quantitative

Recall from Chapter 3 that an experiment is the process by which an observation (or measurement) is obtained. Most experiments result in numerical outcomes or events. The outcome itself may be a numerical quantity such as height, weight, time, or some rank ordering of a response. That is, the data is (quantitative, qualitative). If the data is qualitative, many times the observations will fall into one of several categories. When categorical observations are made – such as good or defective, color of eyes, income bracket, and so on – we are usually concerned with the number of observations falling into a specified category. Again, the experiment results in a numerical outcome. Each time we observe the outcome of an experiment and assign a numerical value to the event that occurs, we are observing one particular value of a variable of interest. Since the value of this variable is determined by the outcome of a random experiment, we call the variable a *random variable*, and designate it symbolically by the letter x.

quantitative

> A variable x is a *random variable* if the value that it assumes, corresponding to the outcome of an experiment, is a random or chance event.

When an experiment is repeated many times and a large body of data is obtained, a ______________ is generated. We seldom ever measure every member of the population. Instead, we obtain a small set of measurements called a ______________, and use the information therein to describe or make inferences about the ______________.

population

sample
population

Suppose that a sample of 100 people was randomly drawn from a population of voters and the number favoring candidate Jones was recorded. This process defines an experiment. The number of voters in the sample favoring candidate Jones is an example of a ______________ ______________.

random variable

Further, suppose that of the 100 voters in the sample, 60 favored Jones. This would not necessarily imply that Jones will win because one could obtain 60 or more in the *sample* favorable to Jones even though only half of the voting *population* favor him. In fact, the crucial question is, "What is the probability that 60 or more of the 100 voters in the sample are favorable to Jones when actually just 50% of the voting population will vote for him?" To answer this question, we need to investigate the probabilistic behavior of the random variable x, the number of favorable voters in a sample of 100 voters. The set of values that the random variable x may assume and the probability $p(x)$ associated with each value of x define a probability distribution. Hence before we can use a random variable to make inferences about a population, we must study some basic characteristics of probability distributions.

4.2 Classification of Random Variables

Random variables are divided into two classes according to the values that the random variable can assume. If a random variable x can take on only a finite or a countable infinity of distinct values, it is classified as a *discrete random variable.* If a random variable x can take on all the values associated with the points on a line interval, then x is called a *continuous random variable*. It is necessary to make the preceding distinction between the discrete and continuous cases because the probability distributions require different mathematical treatment. In fact, calculus is a prerequisite to any complete discussion of continuous random variables. Arithmetic and elementary algebra are all we need to develop discrete probability distributions.

The following would be examples of discrete random variables:

1. The number of voters favoring a political candidate in a given precinct.
2. The number of defective bulbs in a package of twenty bulbs.
3. The number of errors in an income tax return.

Notice that discrete random variables are basically counts and the phrase "the number of" can be used to identify a discrete random variable. The following would be examples of continuous random variables:

1. The time required to complete a clerical operation.
2. The height of a tree on a tree farm.
3. The amount of ore produced by a given mining operation.

Classify the following random variables as discrete or continuous:

1. The number of psychological subjects responding to stimuli in a group of thirty. (______________) discrete
2. The number of building permits issued in a community during a given month. (______________) discrete
3. The number of amoebae in 1 cubic centimeter of water. (______________) discrete
4. The juice content of six Valencia oranges. (______________) continuous
5. The time to failure for an electronic system. (______________) continuous
6. The amount of radioactive iodine excreted by rats in a medical experiment. (______________) continuous
7. The number of defects in 1 square yard of carpeting. (______________) discrete

4.3 Probability Distributions for Discrete Random Variables

The probability distribution for a discrete random variable x consists of the pairs $(x, p(x))$ where x is one of the possible values of the random variable x and $p(x)$ is its corresponding probability. This probability distribution must satisfy two requirements:

1. $\sum_x p(x) =$ __________ 1

2. __________ $\leqslant p(x) \leqslant$ __________ 0; 1

One can express the probability distribution for a discrete random variable x in any one of the three ways:

1. By listing, opposite each possible value of x, its probability $p(x)$ in a table.
2. Graphically as a probability histogram.
3. By supplying a formula together with a list of the possible values of x.

Example 4.4

Suppose an investor records whether the value per share of a stock rises R or drops D over a three-day period. If the stock is just as likely to rise as it is to drop, let us find the probability distribution for x, the number of days that the stock shows a rise. Let us list the sample points associated with this experiment as follows:

Simple event	*Day* 1	2	3
E_1	R	R	R
E_2	D	R	R
E_3	R	D	R
E_4	R	R	D
E_5	D	D	R
E_6	______	______	______
E_7	R	D	D
E_8	D	D	D

(margin: $D; R; D$)

1. Since the stock is just as likely to rise as it is to drop for any given day, each of the 8 sample points is equally likely. Therefore we assign $P(E_i)$ = __________.
2. There are four possible values x can assume, namely x = __________, __________, __________, __________. The value $x = 0$ will occur only if the simple event __________ occurs, so that the probability that x equals zero is

(margin: 1/8; 0; 1; 2; 3; E_8)

$$p(0) = P(\_\_\_\_\_\_\_\_\_\_) = \_\_\_\_\_\_\_\_\_\_$$

(margin: E_8; 1/8)

The value $x = 1$ will occur only if one of the simple events E_5, E_6 or __________ occurs. Then,

(margin: E_7)

$$p(1) = P(E_5) + P(E_6) + P(\_\_\_\_\_\_\_\_\_\_) = \_\_\_\_\_\_\_\_\_\_$$

(margin: E_7; 3/8)

In like manner we find $p(2)$ = __________ and $p(3)$ = __________.
For this example, the tabular presentation would be:

(margin: 3/8; 1/8)

x	$p(x)$
0	__________
1	__________
2	__________
3	__________

(margin: 1/8; 3/8; 3/8; 1/8)

while the probability histogram would be:

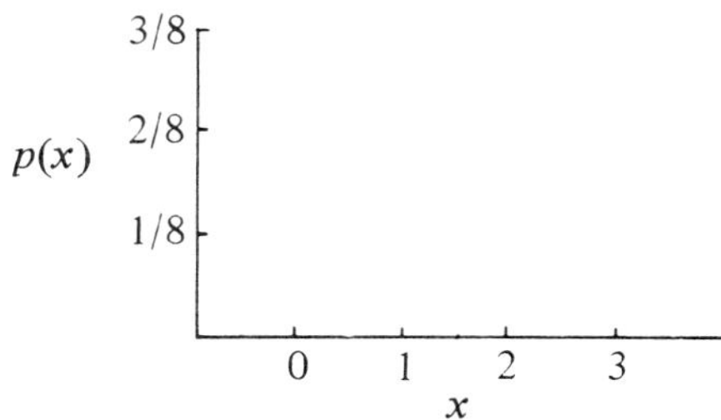

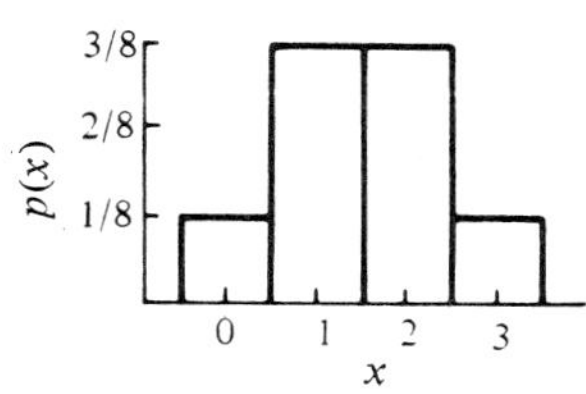

Note that the two requirements for a discrete probability distribution are satisfied in this example. These are:

1. ______________ $\sum_x p(x) = 1$

2. ______________ $0 \leqslant p(x) \leqslant 1$

Finally, a formula appropriate for this probability distribution is

$$p(x) = \frac{3!}{x!\,(3-x)!}\left(\frac{1}{2}\right)^3 \quad \text{for } x = 0, 1, 2, 3$$

You may verify that the formula does indeed give the correct values for $p(x)$.

Example 4.5

A product recognition experiment required a subject to classify a set of prints according to whether he did or did not recognize the product described in an advertising layout. Suppose that a subject can correctly identify each print with probability $p = .7$, that sequential classifications are independent events, and that he is presented with $n = 3$ prints to classify. We are interested in x, the number of correct classifications for the three prints.

Solution

1. This experiment is analogous to tossing three unbalanced coins where correctly classifying a print corresponds to the observation of a head in the toss of a single coin. Each classification results in one of two outcomes, correct or incorrect. The total number of sample points in the sample space is __________. 8
2. Let *IIC* represent the sample point for which the classification of the first and second prints is incorrect and the third is correct. Complete the listing of all sample points in the sample space.

	Sample Points		Sample Points	
	E_1	III	E_5	CII
	E_2	IIC	E_6	CCI
CIC	E_3	ICI	E_7	________
	E_4	ICC	E_8	CCC

3. The sample point E_2 is an *intersection* of three independent events. That is,

$$E_2 = IIC$$

Applying the Multiplicative Law of Probability,

$$P(E_2) = P(IIC) = P(I)P(I)P(C) = (.3)(.3)(.7)$$
$$= .063$$

.027; .063 Similarly, $P(E_1) =$ ________; $P(E_3) =$ ________. Calculate the probabilities for all sample points in the sample space.

.027; .063	$P(E_1) =$ ________	$P(E_5) =$ ________
.147	$P(E_2) = .063$	$P(E_6) =$ ________
.063; .147	$P(E_3) =$ ________	$P(E_7) =$ ________
.147; .343	$P(E_4) =$ ________	$P(E_8) =$ ________

4. The random variable x, the number of correct classifications for the set of three prints, takes the value $x = 1$ for sample point E_2. Similarly,
0 we would assign the value $x =$ ________ to E_1. Assign a value of x to each sample point in the sample space.

	Sample Points	Value of x
E_1	________	0
	E_2, E_3, E_5	1
E_4, E_6, E_7	________	2
E_8	________	3

5. The numerical event $x = 0$ contains only the sample point E_1. Summing the probabilities of the sample points in the event $x = 0$, we have
.027 $P[x = 0] = P(E_1) =$ ________. Similarly, the numerical event $x = 1$ contains three sample points. Summing the probabilities of these
.189 sample points, we have $P[x = 1] = p(1) =$ ________.

6. The probability distribution, $p(x)$, presented in tabular form is

x	$p(x)$
0	.027
1	______
2	______
3	______

.189
.441
.343

Calculate the probabilities $p(2)$ and $p(3)$ and complete the table.

7. Present $p(x)$ graphically in the form of a probability histogram.

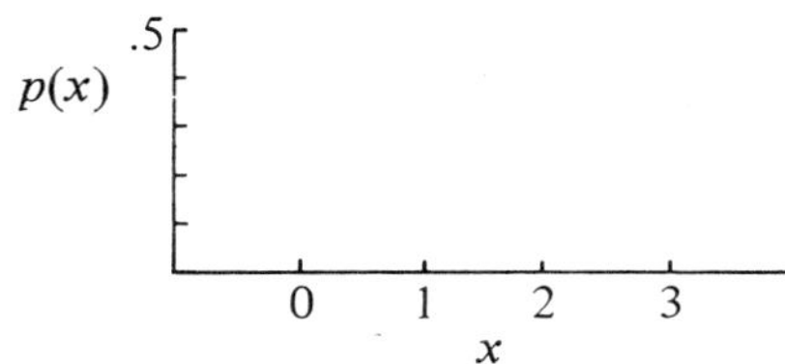

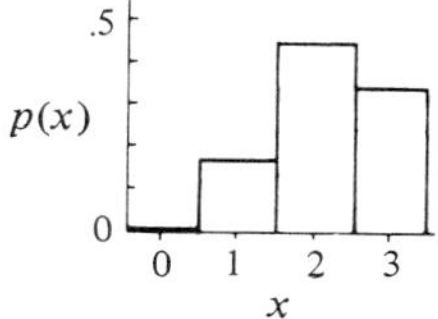

8. After studying Chapter 5, you will be able to express this probability distribution as a formula.

Self-Correcting Exercises 4A

1. An electronic system involves four components. If each component has a reliability of .99 and the components act independently, find the probability distribution for y, the number of components that have failed. Note that reliability is measured as the probability that an item will not fail.
   a. What is the reliability for the total system?
   b. What would the reliability of the system be if the requirement for successful operation was that at least three components in the system had not failed?
2. Five equally qualified applicants for a managerial position were ranked in order of preference by a personnel manager. If two of the applicants hold master's degrees in business administration, find the probability distribution for x, the number of applicants holding a master's in business administration ranked as the first or second applicant.
3. A car rental agency has three Ford Escorts and two Chevrolet Citations left in its car pool. If two cars are needed and the keys are randomly selected from the keyboard, find the probability distribution for x, the number of Fords in the selection.
4. Someone claims that the following is the probability distribution for a random variable x:

x	-1	0	1	2
$p(x)$	1/10	$-2/10$	5/10	3/10

Give two reasons why this is not a valid probability distribution.

5. Suppose that the unemployment rate in a given community is 7%. Four households are randomly selected to be interviewed. In each household, it is determined whether or not the primary wage earner is unemployed. If the 7% rate is correct, find the probability distribution for x, the number of primary wage earners who are unemployed.

4.4 Probability Distributions for Continuous Random Variables

continuous

A ______________ random variable can assume a noncountable infinity of values corresponding to points on a line interval. Since the mathematical treatment of continuous random variables requires the use of calculus, we will do no mathematics here, but merely state some basic concepts. The probability distribution for a continuous random variable can be thought of as the limiting histogram for a very large set of measurements utilizing the smallest possible interval width. In such a case, the outline of the histogram would appear as a continuous curve.

Let us illustrate what happens if we begin with a histogram and allow the interval width to get smaller and smaller while the number of measurements gets larger and larger.

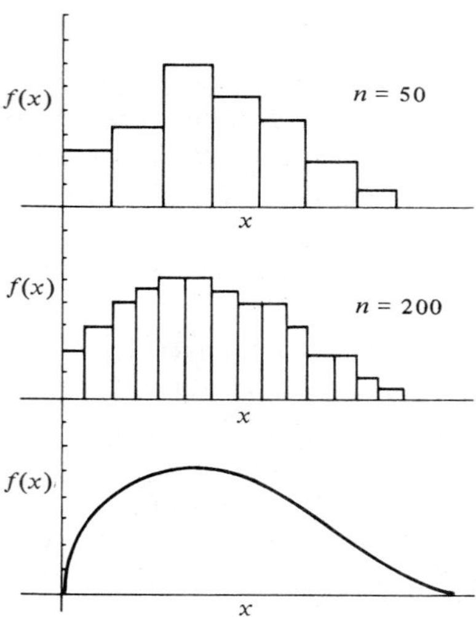

probability

one

one

probability

The mathematical function $f(x)$ that traces this curve with varying values of x is called the ______________ distribution or the probability density for the random variable x. In the same way that the area under a relative frequency histogram is __________, the area under the curve $f(x)$ is also equal to __________. The area under the curve between two points, say a and b, represents the ______________ that the random variable x will fall into the interval from a to b.

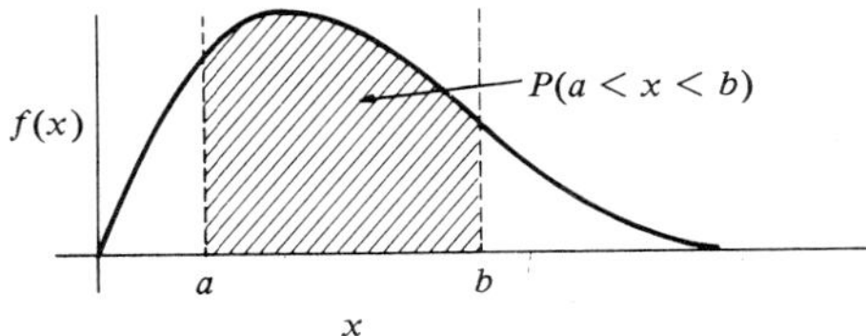

When choosing a model to describe the population of measurements of interest, we must choose $f(x)$ appropriate to our data. Any inferences we may make will only be as valid as the model we are using. It is therefore very important to know as much as possible about the phenomenon under study that will give rise to the measurements that we record.

The idea of modeling the responses that we will record for an experiment may seem strange to you, but you have probably seen models before, though in a different context. For example, when a physicist says, "The distance (s) traversed by a free-falling body is equal to one-half the force of gravity (g) multiplied by the time (t) squared," and writes $s = (1/2)gt^2$, he is merely _______________ a physical phenomenon with a mathematical formula. These mathematical models merely provide _______________ to reality which further need to be verified by experimental techniques.

modeling
approximations

4.5 Mathematical Expectation

When we develop a probability distribution for a random variable, we are actually proposing a model that will describe the behavior of the random variable in repeated trials of an experiment. For example, when we propose the model for describing the distribution of x, the number of heads in the toss of 2 fair coins, given by

x	$p(x)$
0	1/4
1	1/2
2	1/4

we mean that if the two coins were tossed a large number of times, about one-fourth of the outcomes would result in the outcome "zero heads," one-half would result in the outcome "one head," and the remaining fourth would result in "two heads." A probability distribution is not only a measure of belief that a specific outcome will occur on a single trial but, more important, it actually describes a population of observations on the random variable x. It is reasonable then to talk about and calculate the mean and the standard deviation of a random variable by using the probability distribution as a population model.

The expected value of a random quantity is its average value in the population. In particular, the expected value of x is simply the population mean. The expected value of $(x - \mu)^2$ describes the population variance.

If x is a discrete random variable with probability distribution $p(x)$, then the *mean* or *expected value* of x is given by the formula

$$\mu = E(x) = \sum_x xp(x)$$

Example 4.6

The manager of an automobile parts supply store has recorded the daily demand for a certain part over a long period of time. From his records, he has developed the following probability distribution for x, the daily demand for the part.

x	$p(x)$
0	.30
1	.25
2	.20
3	.15
4	.08
5	.02

Find the expected daily demand.

Solution

is

Before calculating the mean of x, we see that this (is, is not) a valid probability distribution since

1; 0; 1

$$\sum_x p(x) = \_\_\_\_\_\_ \text{ and } \_\_\_\_\_\_ \leqslant p(x) \leqslant \_\_\_\_\_\_$$

The expected daily demand, $E(x)$, is calculated as

$$\mu = E(x) = \sum_x xp(x)$$

.25; .20; .15
.08; .02

$$= 0(.30) + 1(\_\_\_\_) + 2(\_\_\_\_) + 3(\_\_\_\_) + 4(\_\_\_\_) + 5(\_\_\_\_)$$

1.52

$$= \_\_\_\_\_\_$$

Example 4.7

Construct the probability histogram for the distribution of daily demand given in Example 4.6. Visually locate the mean and compare it with the computed value, $\mu = 1.52$.

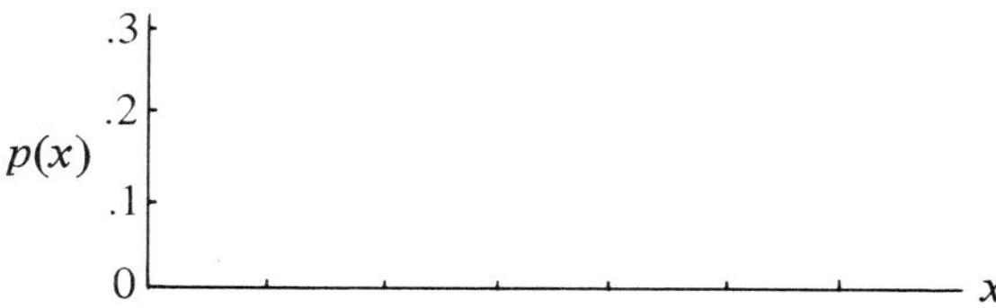

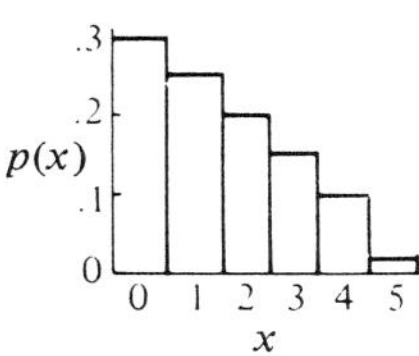

Example 4.8

A corporation has four investment possibilities A, B and C with respective gains of 10, 20 and 50 million dollars and investment possibility D with a loss of 30 million dollars. If one investment will be made and the probabilities of choosing A, B, C or D are .1, .4, .2 and .3, respectively, find the expected gain for the corporation.

Solution

The random variable is x, the corporation's gain, with possible values 10, 20, 50 and -30 million dollars. The probability distribution for x is given as

x (in millions)	$p(x)$
10	.1
20	.4
50	.2
-30	.3

The expected gain, $E(x)$ = __________ million dollars. 10

Example 4.9

A parcel post service which insures packages against loss up to $200 wishes to re-evaluate their insurance rates. If one in a thousand packages had been reported lost during the last several years, what rate should be charged on a package insured for $200 if the postal service's expected gain is zero? Administrative costs will be added to this rate.

Solution

Let x be the gain to the parcel post service and let r be the charge for insuring a package for $200.

1. In this example, the "experiment" has two possible outcomes:
   a. The parcel post service receives r dollars in insurance charges and pays out nothing in insurance claims. In this case, the value of x (the parcel post service's gain) is ______________. r
   b. It receives r dollars in insurance charges but must pay a $200 claim because a package has been reported lost. In this case the value of x is ______________ . $r - 200$
2. Complete the probability distribution for x.

	x	$p(x)$
.999	r	______
.001	$r - 200$	______

3. If $E(x)$ is to be zero, we need to solve the equation

$$\sum_x xp(x) = 0$$

Hence, for our problem

$$r(.999) + (r - 200)(.001) = 0$$

$ .20 $r =$ ________

4.6 The Variance of a Random Variable

The expected value of a random variable gives no information on how the random variable is distributed about its expected value. In many situations, such as in using Tchebysheff's Theorem or the ____________ ____________, for example, we also need a measure of the spread of the probability distribution $p(x)$ of the random variable x. It is natural to use the ____________ and ____________ ____________ of x to measure the variability of $p(x)$.

Empirical Rule

variance; standard deviation

We have seen in the previous section how the mean of a random variable can be thought of as an "expected value." The same is true for the variance of a random variable.

If x is a discrete random variable with probability distribution $p(x)$ and expected value $E(x) = \mu$, then the *variance* of the random variable x is

$$\sigma^2 = E(x - \mu)^2 = \sum_x (x - \mu)^2 p(x)$$

The *standard deviation* of x is given as $\sigma = \sqrt{\sigma^2}$.

Example 4.10

Refer to Example 4.6 and calculate the variance and standard deviation of the daily demand in the auto parts store.

Solution

1.52 Recall that $\mu = E(x) =$ ________. Then

$$\sigma^2 = E(x-\mu)^2 = (0-1.52)^2(.30) + (1-1.52)^2(\_\_\_\_\_\_\_\_) + (2-1.52)^2(.20) + (\_\_\_\_\_\_\_\_)^2(.15) + (4-1.52)^2(.08) + (5-\_\_\_\_\_\_\_\_)^2(\_\_\_\_\_\_\_\_) = \_\_\_\_\_\_\_\_$$

.25

3 - 1.52

1.52; .02

1.8696

and $\sigma = \sqrt{\_\_\_\_\_\_\_\_} = \_\_\_\_\_\_\_\_$

1.8696; 1.37

If x is a random variable, continuous or discrete, it can be shown that

$$E(x-\mu)^2 = E(x^2) - \mu^2$$

This result can be used as a shortcut computational formula to calculate the variance, σ^2.

Example 4.11
Use the computational formula to calculate σ^2 for Example 4.6.

Solution
For a discrete random variable x,

$$E(x^2) = \sum_x x^2 p(x)$$

which is the average value of x^2 over all its possible values. For this example,

$$E(x^2) = 0^2(.30) + 1^2(.25) + 2^2(\_\_\_\_\_\_\_\_) + \_\_\_\_\_\_\_\_(.15) + 4^2(\_\_\_\_\_\_\_\_) + 5^2(.02) = \_\_\_\_\_\_\_\_$$

.20; 3^2

.08

4.18

Then $\sigma^2 = E(x^2) - \mu^2$

$$= \_\_\_\_\_\_\_\_ - (\_\_\_\_\_\_\_\_)^2 = \_\_\_\_\_\_\_\_$$

4.18; 1.52; 1.8696

Example 4.12
Find the variance and standard deviation of x in Example 4.9 when $r = \$.20$.

Solution
The probability distribution for x is

x	$p(x)$
.20	.999
-199.80	.001

Then $$E(x^2) = \sum_x x^2 p(x) = (.20)^2(.999) + (-199.80)^2(.001)$$

$$= .03996 + 39.92004$$

$$= 39.96$$

0; 39.96; 39.96
6.32

Since $\mu = E(x) =$ ________, $\sigma^2 = E(x^2) - \mu^2 =$ ________ and $\sigma = \sqrt{\_\_\_\_\_\_\_\_}$ = ________.

Self-Correcting Exercises 4B

1. A publishing company is considering the introduction of a monthly gardening magazine. Advance surveys show the initial market for the magazine will be approximated by the following distribution for x, the number of subscribers.

x	$p(x)$
5,000	.30
10,000	.35
15,000	.20
20,000	.10
25,000	.05

   Find the expected number of subscribers and the standard deviation of the number of subscribers.
2. Refer to Exercise 1. Suppose the company expects to charge $20 for an annual subscription. Find the mean and standard deviation of the revenue the company can expect from the annual subscriptions of the initial subscribers.
3. Refer to Exercise 2. Production and distribution costs for the gardening magazine are expected to amount to slightly over $200,000. What is the probability that revenue from initial subscriptions will fail to cover these costs?
4. You are given the following information. An insurance company wants to insure an $80,000 home against fire. One in every hundred of such homes is likely to have a fire; 75% of the homes having fires suffered damages amounting to $40,000, while the remaining 25% suffered total loss. Ignoring all other partial losses, what premium should the company charge in order to break even?

4.7 Random Sampling

sample

The objective of the study of statistics is to allow the experimenter to make inferences about a population from information contained in a ________. Since it is the sample that provides the information that is used in inference making, we must be duly careful about the selection of the elements in the sample so that we do not systematically exclude or include certain elements of the population in our sampling plan. The sample should be representative of the population being sampled.

We call a sample that has been drawn without bias a *random sample.* This is a shortened way of saying that the sample has been drawn in a random manner. Several types of random samples are available for use in a particular situation, depending on the scope of the experiment and the objectives of the experimenter. A commonly employed and uncomplicated sampling plan is called the *simple random sample.*

A *simple random sample* of size n is said to have been drawn if each possible sample of size n in the population has the same chance of being selected.

If a population consists of N elements and we wish to draw a sample of size n from this population, there are

$$C_n^N = \frac{N!}{n!\,(N-n)!}$$

samples to choose from. A random sample in this situation would be one drawn in such a manner that each sample of size n had the same chance of being drawn, namely, $(C_n^N)^{-1}$ or $1/C_n^N$.

Example 4.13

A medical technician at a major pharmaceutical corporation needs to choose four animals for testing from a cage containing six animals. How many samples are available to the technician? List these samples.

Solution

The number of ways to choose four animals from a total of six is

$$C_4^6 = \frac{6!}{4!\,2!} = 15$$

Designating each animal by a number from 1 to 6, the samples are

(1234) (1256) (____) 2345

(1235) (1345) (2346)

(1236) (1346) (2356)

(1245) (1356) (2456)

(____) (1456) (____) 1246; 3456

A simple random sampling plan for this experiment would allow each of these 15 possible samples an equal chance of being selected, namely, 1/15.

Although perfect random sampling is difficult to achieve in practice, there are several methods available for selecting a sample that will satisfy the conditions of random sampling when N, the population size, is not too large.

1. *Method A.* List all the possible samples and assign them numbers. Place each of these numbers on a chip or piece of paper and place them in a bowl. Drawing one number from the bowl will select the random sample to be used.
2. *Method B.* Number each of the N members of the population. Write each of these numbers on a chip or slip of paper and place them in a bowl. Now draw n numbers from the bowl and use the members of the population having these numbers as elements to be included in the sample.
3. *Method C.* A useful technique for selecting random samples is one in which a table of random numbers is used to replace the chance device of drawing chips from a bowl.

Why is it so important that the sample be randomly drawn? From the practical point of view, one would want to keep the experimenter's biases out of the selection and, at the same time, keep the sample as representative of the

population
______________ as possible. From the statistical point of view, we can assess the probability of observing a random sample and hence make valid

inferences
______________ about the parent population. If the sample is nonrandom,

cannot
its probability (can, cannot) in general be determined and hence no valid inferences can be made from it.

There are several different types of random samples. A more detailed discussion of sampling will be presented in Chapter 16.

EXERCISES

1. Suppose it is known that two out of four given stocks will show a rapid and profitable rise in price during the coming year. If a person holding shares of these four stocks randomly decides to sell two of the stocks, what is the probability distribution for x, the number of "profitable" stocks he still owns?
2. Graph $p(x)$ for Exercise 1.
3. Let two pennies and two nickels represent the two poor and two good stocks, respectively, for Exercise 1. Randomly draw two of the coins and record y, the number of good stocks in the selection. Repeat this experiment 50 times and construct a relative frequency histogram. Compare with $p(x)$ in Exercise 2. What would happen to the histogram if the number of repetitions of the experiment were allowed to become infinitely large?
4. Show that $p(x)$, Exercise 1, satisfies the two requirements for a probability distribution.
5. A manufacturing organization believes that the chances are 2/3 they will win each of three contracts on which they have submitted bids. Let x be the number (out of three) of contracts which they win. Find the probability distribution for x. Construct a probability histogram for $p(x)$.

6. Show that $p(x)$, Exercise 5, satisfies the two requirements for a probability distribution.
7. Suppose that a radio contains six transistors, two of which are defective. Three transistors are selected at random, removed from the radio, and inspected. Let x be the number of defective transistors observed. Find the probability distribution for x in tabular form with all calculations performed. That is, express each of the probabilities in decimal form correct to the nearest hundredth.
8. The probability of hitting oil in a single drilling operation is 1/4. If drillings represent independent events, find the probability distribution for x, the number of drillings until the first success ($x = 1, 2, 3, \ldots$). Proceed as follows:

   a. Find $p(1)$.
   b. Find $p(2)$.
   c. Find $p(3)$.
   d. Give a formula for $p(x)$.
   Note that x can become infinitely large.

   e. Will $\sum_{x=1}^{\infty} p(x) = 1$?

9. Given a random variable x with the probability distribution

x	$p(x)$
1	1/8
2	5/8
3	1/4

   graph $p(x)$ and make a visual approximation to the mean and standard deviation. (Use your knowledge of Tchebysheff's Theorem to assist in approximating σ.)
10. Refer to Exercise 9 and find the expected value and standard deviation of x. Compare with the answers to Exercise 9.
11. Given the following probability distribution, find the expected value and variance of x.

x	$p(x)$
0	1/2
3	1/3
6	1/6

12. The following is the probability function for a discrete random variable, x.

$$p(x) = (.1)(x + 1) \qquad x = 0, 1, 2, 3$$

   Find $E(x)$, the expected value of x.

13. In a marketing experiment, a subject can make one of three decisions with equal probability, 1/3. If three subjects perform the experiment, let x be the number that select decision number one. Find $p(x)$.
14. Refer to Exercise 13 and find the expected value and variance of x.
15. An investment can result in one of the three outcomes: a $10,000 gain, a $6,000 gain, or a $5,000 loss, with probabilities .3, .3, and .4, respectively. Find the expected gain for the investor.
16. History has shown that buildings of a certain type of construction suffer fire damage during a given year with probability .01. If a building suffers fire damage, it will result in either a 50% or a 100% loss with probabilities of .7 and .3, respectively. Find the premium required per $1,000 coverage in order that the expected gain for the insurance company will equal zero (break-even point).
17. Let x be a discrete random variable with probability distribution given by

x	$p(x)$
0	1/6
1	4/6
2	1/6

a. Construct a probability histogram for $p(x)$.
b. Use the histogram to obtain a visual approximation to the expected value and standard deviation of x.

18. Refer to Exercise 17. Find the expected value and standard deviation of x. Compare with the visual approximations obtained in Exercise 17.
19. A police car visits a given neighborhood a random number of times, x, per evening. If $p(x)$ is given by

x	$p(x)$
0	.1
1	.6
2	.2
3	.1

a. Find $E(x)$.
b. Find σ^2.

20. Refer to Exercise 19. What is the probability that the patrol will visit the neighborhood at least twice in a given evening?
21. Experience has shown that a rare disease will cause partial disability with probability .6, complete disability with probability .3 and no disability with probability .1. Only one in ten thousand will become afflicted with the disease in a given year. If an insurance policy pays $20,000 for partial disability and $50,000 for complete disability, what premium should be charged in order that the insurance company break even (i.e., in order that the expected loss to the insurance company will be zero)?
22. Consider the following situation: A man has an urn containing 20 white and 3 red balls. He asks a little boy to close his eyes and pick 3 balls from

the urn. For each red ball selected by the youngster, the man promises him a candy bar. Just as the boy is ready to pick the first ball, the doorbell rings. The man instructs the boy to continue and leaves the room to answer the door. Upon his return he finds the lad has picked 3 red balls. Would you consider this random sampling on the part of the boy?

23. A sidewalk interviewer stopped three men who were walking together, asked their opinions on some topical subjects, and found their answers quite similar. Would you consider the interviewer's selection to be random in this case? Is it surprising that similar answers were given by these three men?

Chapter 5

THREE USEFUL DISCRETE PROBABILITY DISTRIBUTIONS

5.1 Introduction

Having discussed probability and its role in inference making, we now turn our attention in particular to three discrete random variables. The binomial, Poisson and hypergeometric random variables and their probability distributions provide three models which are very useful for modeling a wide variety of business and economic phenomena.

5.2 The Binomial Experiment

coin tosses

Many experiments in business and economics are analogous to a series of ______________ ______________ in which the outcome on each trial is either a head or a tail. Consider the following situations:

1. The closing price of a stock will either rise (head) or not rise (tail) above the previous day's price.
2. A consumer identifies either correctly (head) or incorrectly (tail) a given product by its advertising slogan.
3. A voter cases his ballot either for candidate A (head) or against him (tail).
4. An executive makes either a correct decision (head) or an incorrect one (tail).
5. A house insured against fire either has a fire (head) or does not have a fire (tail) during the term of the policy.
6. A licensed driver either has an accident (head) or does not have an accident (tail) during the period his license is valid.
7. An item from a production line is inspected and classified as either defective (head) or not defective (tail).

Notice, however, that the analogy to a coin toss is not perfect, in that we tend to regard a head or a tail on a real coin as equiprobable. Such is not generally the case with the examples above.

If any of the above situations were repeated n times and we counted the number of *heads* that occurred in the n trials, the resulting random variable would behave approximately as a ______________ random variable. Let us examine the characteristics that these experiments have in common. We shall call a head a success (S) and a tail a failure (F). Note well that the designation *success* does not necessarily denote a desirable outcome, but rather identifies the event of interest. — binomial

---

The five defining characteristics of a binomial experiment are:

1. The experiment consists of __________ identical trials. — n
2. Each trial results in one of __________ outcomes, success (S) or failure (F). — two
3. The probability of success on a single trial is equal to __________ and remains constant from trial to trial. The probability of failure is equal to q = ______________ . Note that, in general, q is (equal, not equal) to p. — p; $1 - p$; not equal
4. The n trials are ______________ . — independent
5. Attention is directed to the random variable x, the total number of ______________ observed in n trials. — successes

---

Although very few real-life situations perfectly satisfy all five characteristics, this model can be used with fairly good results provided the violations are moderate. The next several examples will illustrate binomial experiments.

Example 5.1

The "triangle test," a procedure often used to control the quality of name-brand food products, utilizes a panel of n "tasters." Each member of the panel is presented three specimens, two of which are from batches of product known to possess the desired taste while the other is a specimen from the latest batch. Each panelist is asked to select the specimen which is different from the other two. If the latest batch does possess the desired taste, then the probability that a given taster will be "successful" in selecting the specimen from the latest batch is __________. If there is no communication among the panelists their responses will comprise n independent ______________ with probability of success on a given trial equal to __________. — 1/3; trials; 1/3

Example 5.2

Almost all auditing of accounts is done on a sampling basis. Thus, an auditor might check a random sample of n items from a ledger or inventory list comprising a large number of items. If 1% of the items in the ledger are erroneous, then the number of erroneous items in the sample is essentially a ______________ random variable with __________ (give number) trials and probability of "success" (finding an erroneous item) on a given trial equal to __________. — binomial; n; .01

Example 5.3

No treatment has been known for a certain serious disease for which the mortality rate in the United States is 70%. If a random selection is made of 100 past victims of this disease in the United States, the number, x_1, of those in the sample who died of the disease is essentially a binomial ran-
100; .70 — dom variable with $n =$ __________ and $p =$ __________. More importantly, if observation is made of the next 100 persons in the United States who will in the future become victims of this disease, the number, x_2, of these who will die from the disease has a distribution approximately the same as that of x_1 if conditions affecting this disease remain essentially constant for the time period considered.

Example 5.4

The continued operation (reliability) of a complex assembly often depends on the joint survival of all or nearly all of a number of similar components. Thus, a radio may give at least 100 hours of continuous service if no more than two of its ten transistors fail during the first 100 hours of operation. If the ten transistors in a given radio were selected at random from a large lot of transistors, then each of these (ten) transistors would have the same probability, p, of failing within 100 hours. The number of transistors in
binomial — the radio which will fail within 100 hours is a ______________ random
10 — variable for __________ trials with probability of "success" on each trial
p — equal to __________. ("Success" is a word that denotes one of the two outcomes of a single trial and does not necessarily represent a desired outcome.)

Three experiments are described below. In each case state whether or not the experiment is a binomial experiment. If the experiment is binomial, specify the number, n, of trials and the probability, p, of success on a given trial. If the experiment is not binomial, state which characteristics of a binomial experiment are not met.

not binomial — 1. A fair coin is tossed until a head appears. The number of tosses, x, is observed. If binomial, $n =$ ______________ and $p =$ ______________.
1, 5 — If not binomial, list characteristic(s) (1, 2, 3, 4 or 5) violated.

2. The probability that an applicant scores above the 90th percentile on a qualifying examination is .10. The examiner is interested in x, the number of applicants out of 25 taking the examination that score above
25; .10 — the 90th percentile. If binomial, $n =$ __________ and $p =$ __________.
none — If not binomial, list characteristic(s) (1, 2, 3, 4 or 5) violated.

3. A sample of five transistors will be selected at random from a box of twenty transistors of which ten are defective. The experimenter will observe the number, x, of defective transistors appearing in the sample.
not binomial — If binomial, $n =$ ______________ and $p =$ ______________. If not
3, 4 — binomial, list characteristic(s) (1, 2, 3, 4 or 5) violated. __________

5.3 Review: The Binomial Theorem (Optional)

1. The following identity is proved in most high school algebra books.

$$(a+b)^n = \sum_{x=0}^{n} \frac{n!}{x!\,(n-x)!} a^x b^{n-x}$$

where a and b are any real numbers and n is a positive integer. This identity is known as the binomial theorem. The coefficients in the sum are known as binomial coefficients and we can write

$$\frac{n!}{x!\,(n-x)!} = C_x^n$$

to represent the coefficient of $a^x b^{n-x}$ in the expansion of $(a+b)^n$. Recall from Chapter 3 that $n! = n(n-1)(n-2)\ldots(3)(2)(1)$ and $0! = 1$.

2. For the special case when $n = 2$ we find

$$(a+b)^2 = \sum_{x=0}^{2} C_x^2 a^x b^{2-x}$$

$$= \underline{\qquad\qquad}$$ $a^2 + 2ab + b^2$

When $n = 3$, we have

$$(a+b)^3 = \sum_{x=0}^{3} C_x^3 a^x b^{3-x}$$

$$= a^3 + 3a^2b + \underline{\qquad\qquad}$$ $3ab^2 + b^3$

3. If a is replaced by a probability, p, and b is replaced by the probability, $q = 1 - p$, then the binomial theorem implies that

$$\sum_{x=0}^{n} C_x^n p^x q^{n-x} = (p+q)^n$$

Note the following points about this binomial identity involving p and q when $0 < p < 1$.

a. The terms $C_x^n p^x q^{n-x}$ are each positive.

1 b. The sum of the terms is $(p + q)^n =$ __________.

c. Since the total can be no greater than any of its parts

0; 1 $$\_\_\_\_\_\_ \leqslant C_x^n p^x q^{n-x} \leqslant \_\_\_\_\_\_$$

Thus the function

$$p(x) = C_x^n p^x q^{n-x}, \qquad x = 0, 1, 2, \ldots, n$$

satisfies the two requirements of a probability function for a discrete random variable, namely

0; 1 $$\_\_\_\_\_\_ \leqslant p(x) \leqslant \_\_\_\_\_\_$$

and

1 $$\sum_x p(x) = \_\_\_\_\_\_$$

5.4 The Binomial Probability Distribution

The probability distribution for x, the number of successes in n trials where p is the probability of a success on a given trial, is given by the formula

$$p(x) = \frac{n!}{x!(n-x)!} p^x q^{n-x}$$

for the values $x = 0, 1, 2, \ldots, n$ with $q = 1 - p$.

To illustrate the use of the formula for the binomial distribution, consider the next example.

Example 5.5

Suppose that the probability that an electronic component fails before 1000 hours of use is .7. Four such components are put on test. Let x be the number of components out of the four on test that fail before 1000 hours of use. Then x is a binomial random variable with $p = .7$ and $n = 4$.

1. The probability that no component fails before 1000 hours is

$$p(0) = \frac{4!}{0!\,4!}(.7)^0(.3)^4$$

.0081 $$= (.3)^4 = \_\_\_\_\_\_$$

2. The probability that exactly three components fail before 1000 hours is

$$p(3) = \frac{4!}{3!\,1!}(.7)^3(.3)^1$$

$$= 4\,(\underline{\qquad\qquad})\,(.3)$$ .343

$$= \underline{\qquad\qquad}$$ .4116

3. The probability that at least three components fail before 1000 hours is

$$P[x \geqslant 3] = p(3) + p(4)$$

$$= p(3) + \frac{4!}{4!\,0!}(.7)^4(.3)^0$$

$$= .4116 + \underline{\qquad\qquad}$$ .2401

$$= \underline{\qquad\qquad}$$ .6517

4. To check that $p(x)$ is a properly defined probability distribution, complete the following table and find $\sum_x p(x)$.

x	$p(x)$	
0	______	.0081
1	______	.0756
2	______	.2646
3	______	.4116
4	______	.2401
	$\sum_{x=0}^{4} p(x) =$ ______	1.0000

Example 5.6
A marketing research survey shows that approximately 80% of the car owners surveyed indicated that their next car purchase would be either a compact or an economy car. If the 80% figure is taken to be correct, and five prospective buyers are interviewed,

1. find the probability that all five indicate that their next car purchase would be either a compact or an economy car.
2. find the probability that at most one indicates that his next purchase will be either a compact or an economy car.

Solution
Let x be the number of car owners who indicate that their next pur-

5 chase will be a compact or an economy car. Then $n =$ __________ and
.8 $p =$ __________ and the distribution for x is given by

$$p(x) = \frac{5!}{x!\,(5-x)!}(.8)^x(.2)^{5-x} \qquad x = 0, 1, 2, \ldots, 5$$

1. The required probability is $p(5)$ which is given by

$$p(5) = \frac{5!}{5!\,0!}(.8)^5(.2)^0$$

$$= (.8)^5$$

.32768 $=$ __________

2. The probability that at most one car owner indicates that his next purchase will be either a compact or an economy car will be

$$P[x \leqslant 1] = p(0) + p(1)$$

For $x = 0$,

$$p(0) = \frac{5!}{0!\,5!}(.8)^0(.2)^5$$

$$= (.2)^5$$

.00032 $=$ __________

For $x = 1$,

.0064 $p(1) = \frac{5!}{1!\,4!}(.8)^1(.2)^4 = 5(.8)(.0016) =$ __________

Hence $P[x \leqslant 1] = .0064 + .00032$

.00672 $=$ __________

As you might expect, the calculation of the binomial probabilities becomes quite tiresome as n, the number of trials, increases. Table 1 of binomial probabilities in the Appendix of your text, can be used to find binomial probabilities for values of $p = .01, .05, .10, .20, \ldots, .90, .95, .99$ when

$n = 5, 10, 15, 20, 25$. These tables have been reproduced as Table 1 in the Appendix to this Study Guide for your convenience.

1. The tabled entries are not the individual terms for binomial probabilities, but rather cumulative sums of probabilities, beginning with $x = 0$ up to and including the value $x = a$. By formula, the entries for n, p, and a are

$$\sum_{x=0}^{x=a} p(x) = p(0) + p(1) + \ldots + p(a)$$

2. By using a tabled entry, which is $\sum_{x=0}^{a} p(x)$, these tables allow the user to find
   a. left-tailed cumulative sums (so-called because they are sums of probabilities beginning with the left end or tail of the probability distribution),

$$P[x \leqslant a] = \sum_{x=0}^{a} p(x)$$

   b. right-tail cumulative sums,

$$P[x \geqslant a] = 1 - \sum_{x=0}^{a-1} p(x)$$

   c. or individual terms such as

$$P[x = a] = \sum_{x=0}^{a} p(x) - \sum_{x=0}^{a-1} p(x)$$

Example 5.7

Refer to Example 5.6. Find the probabilities asked for by using Table 1.

Solution

For this problem, we shall use the table with $n = 5$ and $p = .8$.

1. To find the probability that $x = 5$ we proceed as follows.

$$p(5) = [p(0) + p(1) + p(2) + p(3) + p(4) + p(5)]$$
$$- [p(0) + p(1) + p(2) + p(3) + p(4)]$$

$$= \sum_{x=0}^{5} p(x) - \sum_{x=0}^{4} p(x)$$

$$= 1 - .672$$

$$= .328$$

2. To find the probability that $x \leqslant 1$, we need

$$P[x \leqslant 1] = p(0) + p(1)$$

$$= \sum_{x=0}^{1} p(x)$$

.007 $= \_\_\_\_\_\_\_\_$

3. Let us extend the problem and find the probabilities associated with the terms, $x = 2$ and $x = 3$.
For $x = 2$,

$$p(2) = \sum_{x=0}^{2} p(x) - \sum_{x=0}^{1} p(x)$$

.058 $= \_\_\_\_\_\_\_\_ - .007$

.051 $= \_\_\_\_\_\_\_\_$

For $x = 3$,

$$p(3) = \sum_{x=0}^{3} p(x) - \sum_{x=0}^{2} p(x)$$

.263 $= \_\_\_\_\_\_\_\_ - .058$

.205 $= \_\_\_\_\_\_\_\_$

4. Complete the following table.

x	$p(x)$	
0	______	.000
1	______	.007
2	______	.051
3	______	.205
4	______	.409
5	______	.328

with $\sum_{x=0}^{5} p(x) =$ ______ 1

5. Graph this distribution as a probability histogram.

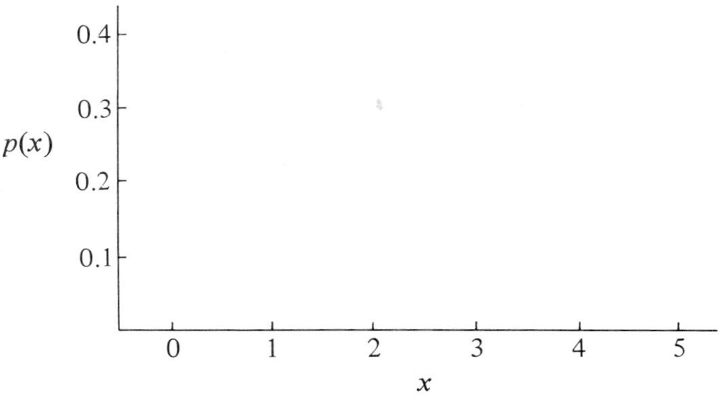

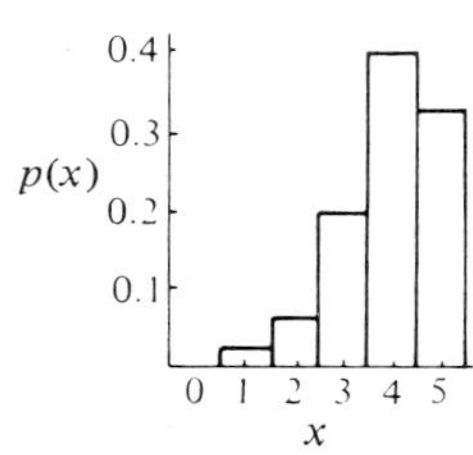

Example 5.8
Using Table 1, find the probability distribution for x if $n = 5$ and $p = ½$, and graph the resulting probability histogram.

Solution

1. To find the individual probabilities for $x = 0, 1, 2, \ldots, 5$, we need but subtract successive entries in the table for $n = 5$, $p = .5$.

$$p(0) = \sum_{x=0}^{0} p(x) = \text{\_\_\_\_\_\_} \qquad .031$$

$$p(1) = \sum_{x=0}^{1} p(x) - \sum_{x=0}^{0} p(x) = .188 - .031 = \text{\_\_\_\_\_\_} \qquad .157$$

.312 $p(2) = \sum_{x=0}^{2} p(x) - \sum_{x=0}^{1} p(x) = .500 - .188 =$ ________

.812; .312 $p(3) =$ ________ $- .500 =$ ________

.969; .157 $p(4) =$ ________ $- .812 =$ ________

.969; .031 $p(5) = 1.000 -$ ________ $=$ ________

2.5 2. Using the results of part a we find the probability histogram to be symmetric about the value $x =$ ________.

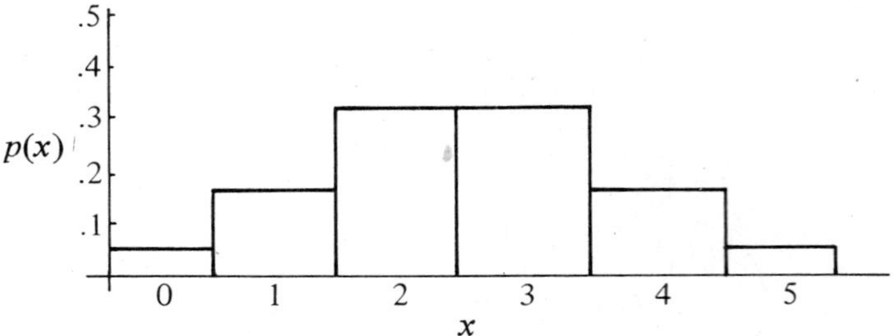

Example 5.9
Find the probability distribution for x if $n = 5$ and $p = .3$, and graph the probability histogram in this case.

Solution
Again, subtracting successive entries for $n = 5, p = .3$, we have

.168 $p(0) =$ ________

.360 $p(1) = .528 - .168 =$ ________

.309 $p(2) = .837 - .528 =$ ________

.132 $p(3) = .969 - .837 =$ ________

.029 $p(4) = .998 - .969 =$ ________

.002 $p(5) = 1 - .998 =$ ________

Graph the resulting histogram using these probabilities.

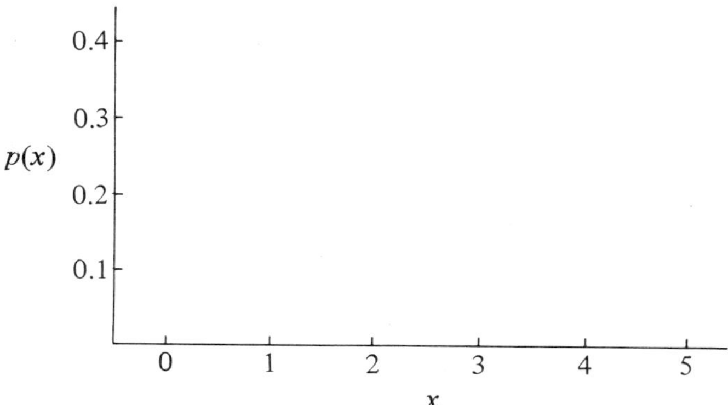

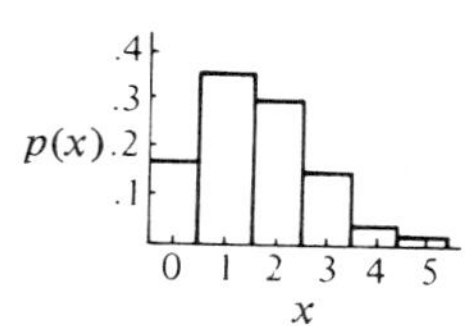

In comparing the histograms in Examples 5.7, 5.8 and 5.9 notice that when $p = \frac{1}{2}$, the histogram is ____________. However, if $p = .8$, which is greater than ½, the mass of the probability moves to the ____________ with p; and for $p = .3$, which is less than ½, the mass of the probability distribution moves to the ____________ with p. Locating the center of the distribution by eye, we see that the mean of the binomial distribution varies directly as __________, the probability of success.

symmetric
right

left

p

The MINITAB software package contains two commands called PDF and CDF which are extremely useful. The command PDF (probability density function) with the subcommand BINOMIAL followed by a value for n and a value for p will generate individual binomial probabilities, $P(X = K)$. The command CDF (cumulative density function) with the subcommand BINOMIAL followed by n and p generates the cumulative probabilities, $P(X$ LESS OR $= K)$.

For the binomial random variable x, the probability $P(X = K)$ is equivalent to

$$P(x = K) = \_\_\_\_\_\_\_\_\_\_\_\_$$

$C_K^n \, p^K \, q^{n-K}$

while the cumulative probability $P(X$ LESS OR $= K)$ is equivalent to

$$P(\_\_\_\_\_\_\_\_\_\_) = \sum_{x=1}^{K} C_x^n p^x q^{n-x}$$

$(y \leqslant K)$

These cumulative probabilities (will, will not) be identical to those given in Table 1 for identical values of n and p. The advantage of the MINITAB program lies in the fact that the user (is, is not) restricted to only 5 values of n and 13 values of p, as he was using Table 1.

will

is not

Example 5.10
Use the following MINITAB output to verify the solution to Example 5.9.

```
MTB > PDF;
SUBC > BINOMIAL 5  .3.

BINOMIAL WITH N = 5
                    P = 0.300000
     K              P(X = K)
     0               0.1681
     1               0.3601
     2               0.3087
     3               0.1323
     4               0.0284
     5               0.0024
```

```
MTB > CDF;
SUBC > BINOMIAL 5  .3.

BINOMIAL WITH N = 5
                    P = 0.300000
     K     P(X LESS OR = K)
     0               0.1681
     1               0.5282
     2               0.8369
     3               0.9692
     4               0.9976
     5               1.0000
```

Solution

1. The output given above was generated by computer using the MINITAB commands CDF and PDF followed by the subcommand

5; .3 BINOMIAL __________ (give number) __________ (give number)

2 2. Column __________ (give number) of the output gives the exact probabilities needed to graph the probability histogram. This column, in fact, directly displays the probability distribution for x with $n = 5$ and $p = .3$. The probabilities agree with those found in Example 5.9, correct to three decimal places.

4 3. Column __________ (give number) of the output, when rounded to 3 decimal places, exactly duplicates the column labeled $p = .3$ in Table 1 with $n = 5$.

Let us consider two more examples. You are now free to either calculate the probabilities by hand, to use a MINITAB program if available, or to use the tables when appropriate.

Example 5.11

To test two alloys for resistance to corrosion, 10 pairs each consisting of a strip of alloy 1 and a strip of alloy 2 were subjected to artificial weathering and wear. At the end of the test, each pair was examined and the member of each pair exhibiting the most corrosion was recorded. If the two alloys are actually equally resistant to corrosion, then the probability that alloy 1 exhibits more corrosion than alloy 2 can be taken to be $p = .5$. If the alloys are equally resistant,

1. what is the probability that alloy 1 exhibited more corrosion than alloy 2 in 8 or more of the ten pairs?
2. what is the probability that alloy 2 exhibited more corrosion than alloy 1 in 6 or more pairs?

Solution

Let x be the number of times that alloy 1 exhibited more corrosion. If the alloys are equally resistant we can take $p = .5$. Then

$$p(x) = \frac{10!}{x!\,(10-x)!}(.5)^x(.5)^{10-x}$$

for $x = 0, 1, 2, \ldots, 10$.

1. Using Table 1,

$$P[x \geqslant 8] = \sum_{x=8}^{10} p(x)$$

$$= 1 - \sum_{x=0}^{7} p(x)$$

$$= 1 - \underline{\qquad\qquad}$$ .945

$$= \underline{\qquad\qquad}$$ .055

2. If 6 or more pairs listed alloy 2 as more corroded, then 4 or less pairs listed alloy 1 as more corroded. Hence

$$P[x \leqslant 4] = \sum_{x=0}^{4} p(x) = \underline{\qquad\qquad}$$ .377

Example 5.12

Suppose that a trainee is taught to do a task in two different ways. Studies have shown that, when subjected to mental strain and asked to perform the task, the trainee most often reverts to the method first learned, regardless of whether it was more difficult or easier than the second. If the probability that a trainee returns to the first method learned is .8 and six trainees are tested, what is the probability that at least 5 of the trainees revert to their first learned method when asked to perform their task under mental strain?

Solution

1. Letting x equal the number of trainees who revert to the first method, we have a binomial random variable with $n = 6$ and $p = .8$. There is no table of binomial probabilities for $n = 6$, so we must calculate $P[x \geqslant 5]$.

2. In this case

$$p(x) = \frac{6!}{x!(6-x)!}(.8)^x(.2)^{6-x} \qquad x = 0, 1, 2, \ldots, 6$$

Since

$$P[x \geqslant 5] = p(5) + p(6)$$

we need to calculate $p(5)$ and $p(6)$.

3. $$p(5) = \frac{6!}{5!\,1!}(.8)^5(.2)^1$$

$$= (6)(.32768)(.2)$$

.393216 $$= \_\_\_\_\_\_\_\_$$

4. $$p(6) = \frac{6!}{6!\,0!}(.8)^6(.2)^0$$

$$= (.8)^6$$

.262144 $$= \_\_\_\_\_\_\_\_$$

5. Collecting results we have

$$P[x \geqslant 5] = .393216 + .262144$$

.655360 $$= \_\_\_\_\_\_\_\_$$

6; .8

6. If the student has access to a MINITAB software package, the command PDF followed by the subcommand BINOMIAL ________ (give number) ________ (give number) can be used to generate the probability distribution for x. The output is shown below.

```
 MTB > PDF;
SUBC > BINOMIAL 6  .8.
    BINOMIAL WITH N = 6   P = 0.800000
           K              P(X = K)
           0                0.0001
           1                0.0015
           2                0.0154
           3                0.0819
           4                0.2458
           5                0.3932
           6                0.2621
```

From column 2, with $K = 5$ and $K = 6$, we have

$p(5) =$ ________ .3932

$p(6) =$ ________ .2621

so that

$P(x \geqslant 5) =$ ________ .6553

which agrees with the results obtained by hand calculation.

Self-Correcting Exercises 5A

1. A city planner claims that 20% of all apartment dwellers move from their apartments within a year from the time they first moved in. In a particular city, 7 apartment dwellers who had given notice of termination to their landlords are to be interviewed.
   a. If the city planner is correct, what is the probability that 2 of the 7 had lived in the apartment for less than one year?
   b. What is the probability that at least 6 had lived in their apartment for at least one year?
2. Suppose that 70% of the first class mail from New York to California is delivered within four days of being mailed. If twenty pieces of first class mail are mailed from New York to California,
   a. find the probability that at least 15 pieces of mail arrive within 4 days of the mailing date.
   b. find the probability that 10 or fewer pieces of mail arrive later than four days after the mailing date.
3. On the average, a contractor has been awarded three out of every five contracts for which he has submitted bids. If this contractor plans to submit five bids in the near future,
   a. what is the probability that he will be awarded all five contracts?
   b. what is the probability that he will be awarded at least three contracts?
4. A builder has found that 60% of the grade 2 lumber is satisfactory for a specific purpose. Ten pieces of grade 2 lumber are brought to a building site for use by a workman.
   a. What is the probability that at most three pieces will be satisfactory?
   b. What is the probability that at least eight pieces will be usable?
   c. If the workman needs seven usable pieces of lumber to complete the job, what is the probability that he gets the required number of satisfactory pieces of lumber?

5.5 The Mean and Variance for the Binomial Random Variable

The mean and standard deviation of a probability distribution are important summary measures that are used to locate the center of the distribution and to describe the dispersion of the measurements about the mean. We noted in the last section that the mass of the probability distribution for a binomial variable with $n = 5$ shifted with the value of p. Further calculations with various values for n and p will show that the mean varies directly with p.

The mean and variance (and hence the standard deviation) can be found using the expectation definitions of Chapter 4 together with

$$p(x) = C_x^n \, p^x \, q^{n-x}, \quad x = 0, 1, 2, \ldots, n$$

It can be shown by those willing to tackle the algebra (and can be *used* by those not so willing) that for a binomial experiment consisting of n trials with the probability of success equal to p,

1. $\mu = E(x) = np$

2. $\sigma^2 = E(x - \mu)^2 = npq$

3. $\sigma = \sqrt{npq}$

Tchebysheff's Theorem can be used in conjunction with the distribution of a binomial random variable since *at least* $(1 - 1/k^2)$ of *any* distribution lies within k standard deviations of the mean. However, when the number of trials n becomes large and p is not too close to zero or one, the Empirical Rule can be used with fairly accurate results. The interval $np \pm 2\sqrt{npq}$ should contain approximately 95% of the distribution, while the interval $np \pm 3\sqrt{npq}$ should contain almost all (approximately 99.7%) of the distribution.

Example 5.13

Suppose it is known that about 10% of new small business enterprises close in less then six months. A random sample of 100 such enterprises is taken and the number that closed in less than six months recorded.

1. Find the mean and standard deviation of x, the number of small business closures in less than six months.
2. Within what limits would we expect to find the number of small business closures?

Solution

1. With $n = 100$ and $p = .1$

10 $\mu = np = 100(.1) =$ ________

9 $\sigma^2 = npq = 100(.1)(.9) =$ ________

9; 3 $\sigma = \sqrt{npq} = \sqrt{\_\_\_\_\_\_} =$ ________

2. From part a, $\mu = 10$ and $\sigma = 3$. Using two standard deviations we find the interval $\mu \pm 2\sigma$ to be $10 \pm 2(3)$ or 10 ± 6. Since approximately 95% of the distribution lies within this interval, we would expect the number of small business closures to lie between __________ and __________ if, in fact, $p = .1$. 4; 16

Example 5.14
Each person in a random sample of 64 people was asked to state a preference for Brand A or Brand B. If there is no underlying preference for either brand, then the probability that an individual chooses Brand A will be $p =$ __________. .5

1. What will be the expected number and standard deviation of preferences for Brand A?
2. Within what limits would you expect the number of stated preferences for Brand A to lie?

Solution
Let x be the number of people stating a preference for Brand A. If there really is no preference for either brand (that is, the person chooses a brand at random), then x has a binomial distribution with $n = 64$ and $p =$ __________. .5

1. $\mu = np = 64(.5) =$ __________ 32

   $\sigma^2 = npq = 64(.5)(.5) =$ __________ 16

   $\sigma = \sqrt{npq} =$ __________ 4

2. From part a, $\mu = 32$ and $\sigma = 4$. Hence $\mu \pm 2\sigma = 32 \pm 8$. We would expect the number of preferences for Brand A to lie between __________ and 24
   __________ if, in fact, $p = .5$. 40

Self-Correcting Exercises 5B

1. Assume that 30% of the voting stockholders of a company favor a proposal put forth by the board of directors. If 100 stockholders are randomly selected and interviewed, find the mean and standard deviation of the sample number of stockholders that agree with the proposal. Within what limits would you expect the number of agreements to lie with approximately 95% chance?
2. If 20% of the registered voters in a given city belong to a minority group and voter registration lists are used in selecting potential jurors, within what limits would you expect the number of minority members on a list of 80 potential jurors to lie if the 80 persons were randomly selected from the voter registration lists?
3. A television network claims that its Wednesday evening prime time program attracts 40% of the television audience. If 400 randomly sampled television viewers were asked whether they had seen the previous show, within what limits would you expect the number of viewers who had seen the previous show to lie if the 40% figure is correct? What would you con-

clude if the interviews revealed that 96 of the 400 had actually seen the previous show?

5.6 The Poisson Probability Distribution (Optional)

The Poisson probability distribution is a discrete distribution which is given by the formula

$$p(x) = \frac{\mu^x e^{-\mu}}{x!}$$

for $x = 0, 1, 2, \ldots$. the constant μ is the mean or expected value of x. This distribution provides an excellent model for the probability distribution of "rare" events occurring in a given unit of time or space. For example, the number of calls received at a telephone switchboard or the number of ships arriving in a harbor during a given period of time might be modeled by the Poisson distribution. In such applications, x represents the number of rare events during a period
average of time over which an ______________ of μ such events can be expected to occur. Remember that in order to use the Poisson distribution, one must be able
randomly; independently to assume that the rare events occur ______________ and ______________ .

Example 5.15

In a food processing and packaging plant, there are, on the average, two packaging machine breakdowns per week. Assuming the weekly machine breakdowns follow a Poisson distribution, what is

1. the probability that there are no machine breakdowns in a given week?
2. the probability that there are no more than two machine breakdowns in a given week?

Solution

2 Machine breakdowns occur at the average rate of $\mu =$ __________ breakdowns per week. If the number of breakdowns follows a Poisson distribution, then

$$p(x) = \frac{2^x e^{-2}}{x!} \qquad \text{for } x = 0, 1, 2, \ldots$$

1. $$P[x = 0] = p(0) = \frac{2^0 e^{-2}}{0!}$$

$$= \frac{e^{-2}}{1}$$

.135335 $= $ __________

2. The probability that no more than two machine breakdowns occur in a given week is

$$P[x \leqslant 2] = p(0) + p(1) + p(2)$$

From part a, we know that $p(0) =$ ________. We need to evaluate $p(1)$ and $p(2)$. .135335

$$p(1) = \frac{2^1 e^{-2}}{1!} = 2(.135335) = \text{________}$$ .270670

$$p(2) = \frac{2^2 e^{-2}}{2!} = 2(.135335) = \text{________}$$ .270670

Hence

$$P[x \leqslant 2] = \text{________}$$ .676675

As in the case of the binomial probability distribution, it becomes tedious to calculate individual probabilities by hand. The MINITAB commands CDF and PDF with the subcommand POISSON followed by the appropriate value for μ will generate the individual Poisson probabilities and the cumulative Poisson probabilities, respectively. The MINITAB output generated by the commands PDF; POISSON 2. and CDF; POISSON 2. are shown below.

```
MTB > PDF;
SUBC > POISSON 2.

 POISSON WITH MEAN = 2.000
     K        P(X = K)
     0         0.1353
     1         0.2707
     2         0.2707
     3         0.1804
     4         0.0902
     5         0.0361
     6         0.0120
     7         0.0034
     8         0.0009
     9         0.0002
    10         0.0000
```

```
MTB > CDF;
SUBC > POISSON 2.

 POISSON WITH MEAN = 2.000
     K     P(X LESS OR = K)
     0              0.1353
     1              0.4060
     2              0.6767
     3              0.8571
     4              0.9473
     5              0.9834
     6              0.9955
     7              0.9989
     8              0.9998
     9              1.0000
```

2 From column ________ (give number), indexing $K = 0, 1$, and 2, we have

$$p(0) = .1353$$

.2707 $p(1) =$ ________

$$p(2) = .2707$$

so that

.6767 $P(x \leqslant 2) =$ ________

which confirms the results of Example 5.15. Alternatively, from column 3, indexing $K = 2$, we have the result directly:

.6767 $P(x \leqslant 2) =$ ________

It is important to keep in mind that the Poisson distribution is fixed in time or space. In the last example, the mean number of breakdowns per week was two. The mean number of breakdowns in a three-week period would be 6. The parameter μ in a Poisson distribution is always equal to the *mean* number of rare events observed occurring in a *given unit* of time or space.

The Poisson probability distribution is often used to approximate binomial
large; small probabilities in cases where n is ____________ and p or q is ____________.
Generally, the Poisson approximation to binomial probabilities is adequate
seven when the binomial mean, $\mu = np$, is less than or equal to ____________.

Example 5.16

Evidence shows that the probability that a driver will be involved in a serious automobile accident during a given year is .01. A particular corporation employs 100 full-time traveling salesmen. Based upon the above evidence, what is the probability that exactly two of the salesmen will be involved in a serious automobile accident during the coming year?

Solution

100 This is an example of a binomial experiment with $n =$ ________ trials and
.01 $p =$ ________. The exact probability distribution for the number of
serious automobile accidents in $n = 100$ trials is

$$p(x) = \frac{100!}{x!\,(100 - x)!}(.01)^x(.99)^{100-x} \qquad x = 0, 1, 2, \ldots, 100$$

Since we do not have binomial tables for $n = 100$, we note that the binomial mean $\mu = np = 1$. The Poisson approximation to binomial probabili-

ties can be used in this case with the Poisson mean taken to be μ = _______. 1
Therefore,

$$p(2) \approx \frac{(1)^2 e^{-1}}{2!}$$

$$= \frac{.367879}{2}$$

$$= \_\_\_\_\_\_\_\_\_\_$$ .1839

Example 5.17
Suppose that past records show that the probability of default on an FHA loan is about .01. If 25 homes in a given area are financed by FHA, use the Poisson approximation to binomial probabilities to find
a. the probability that there will be no defaults among these 25 loans.
b. the probability that there will be two or more defaults.
Compare the values found in parts a and b with the actual binomial probabilities found using Table 1 of the Appendix.

Solution
Although a sample of size n = 25 is not usually considered to be large, the value of p = .01 is small and $\mu = np$ = .25 is less than 7. We will in any case assess the accuracy of the Poisson approximation compared to the actual binomial probabilities. We shall use

$$p(x) = \frac{(.25)^x e^{-.25}}{x!}$$

with $e^{-.25}$ = .778801.

1. The probability of x = 0 defaults is approximated to be

$$p(0) \approx \frac{(.25)^0 e^{-.25}}{0!}$$

$$= \_\_\_\_\_\_\_\_\_\_$$ .778801

The actual probability from Table 1 is __________. .778

2. The probability of two or more defaults can be found by using

$$P[x \geqslant 2] = 1 - P[x \leqslant 1]$$

$$= 1 - [p(\_\_\_\_\_\_\_\_\_\_) + p(\_\_\_\_\_\_\_\_\_\_)]$$ 0; 1

We need

$$p(1) \approx \frac{(.25)^1 e^{-.25}}{1!}$$

.778801 $= (.25)(\_\_\_\_\_\_\_\_)$

.194700 $= \_\_\_\_\_\_\_\_$

Hence

$$P[x \geqslant 2] \approx 1 - (.778801 + .194700)$$

.973501 $= 1 - \_\_\_\_\_\_\_\_$

.026499 $= \_\_\_\_\_\_\_\_$

The actual value from Table 1 is

.974 $P[x \geqslant 2] = 1 - \_\_\_\_\_\_\_\_$

.026 $= \_\_\_\_\_\_\_\_$

Notice that for this problem there is fairly good agreement between the Poisson approximations and the actual binomial probabilities even though
.25 n is not large. This is due mainly to the small value of $\mu = np =$ ________.

5.7 The Hypergeometric Probability Distribution (Optional)

Suppose that we are selecting a sample of n elements from a population containing N elements, some of which are of one type, and the rest of which are of another type. If we designate one type of element as a "success" and the other as "failure", the situation is similar to the binomial experiment described in Section 5.2. However, one of the assumptions required for the application of the binomial probability distribution is that the probability of a success
constant remains ____________ from trial to trial. This assumption is violated when-
without ever the sampling is done (with, without) replacement (that is, once an element has been chosen, it cannot be chosen again).

This departure from the conditions required of the ideal binomial experi-
large ment is not important when the population is (small, large) relative to the
sample ____________ size. In such circumstances, the probability p of a success
constant is approximately ____________ for each trial or selection.
However, if the number of elements in the population is small in relation to the number of elements in the sample, the probability of a success for a
dependent on given trial is (dependent on, independent of) the outcomes of preceding trials. In this case, the number x of successes follows the hypergeometric probability distribution.

The probability distribution of a random variable x having the *hypergeometric distribution* is given by the formula

$$p(x) = \frac{C_x^k C_{n-x}^{N-k}}{C_n^N}$$

for $x = 0, 1, 2, \ldots,$ ________ if $n < k$ — n

$x = 0, 1, 2, \ldots,$ ________ if $n \geqslant k$ — k

where

N = number of elements in the population

k = number of elements in the population that are successes

n = number of elements in the sample which are selected from the population

x = number of successes in the sample

C_b^a defined in Section 3.8 is taken to be zero if $b > a$.
The hypergeometric probability distribution is applicable when one is selecting a sample of elements from a population without __________ and one records whether or not each element does or does not possess a certain characteristic. — replacement

Example 5.18
An auditor is checking the records of an accountant who is responsible for ten clients. The accounts of two of the clients contain major errors, and the accountant will fail the inspection if the auditor finds even a single erroneous account. What is the probability that the accountant will fail the inspection if the auditor inspects the records of three clients chosen at random?

Solution
Let x be the number of erroneous accounts found in the (population, sample). Then — sample

$N =$ ________ — 10

$k =$ ________ — 2

8 | $N - k =$ ________

3 | $n =$ ________

1; 2 | The accountant will fail the inspection if $x =$ ________ or ________.

1; 1; 2 | So $P(\text{accountant fails}) = P(x \geqslant$ ________$) = p($________$) + p($________$)$

$\frac{8!}{2!\,6!}$; $\frac{10!}{3!\,7!}$

$$P(x = 1) = \frac{\left(\frac{2!}{1!\,1!}\right)\left(\rule{2em}{0.4pt}\right)}{\left(\rule{2em}{0.4pt}\right)}$$

.467

$$= \rule{3em}{0.4pt}$$

$\frac{2!}{2!\,0!}$; $\frac{8!}{1!\,7!}$

$$P(x = 2) = \frac{\left(\rule{2em}{0.4pt}\right)\left(\rule{2em}{0.4pt}\right)}{\left(\frac{10!}{3!\,7!}\right)}$$

.067

$$= \rule{3em}{0.4pt}$$

.467; .067; .534

Therefore, the probability that the accountant will fail the inspection is ________ + ________ = ________.

Self-Correcting Exercises 5C (Optional)

1. The probability of a serious fire during a given year to any one house in a particular city is believed to be .005. A particular insurance company holds fire insurance policies on 1000 homes in this city.
   a. Find the probability that the company will not have any serious fire damage claims by the owners of these homes during the next year.
   b. Find the probability they will have no more than three claims.
2. In a certain manufacturing plant, wood-grain printed 4′ × 8′ wall board panels are mass produced and packaged in lots of 100. Past evidence indicates that the number of damaged or imperfect panels per bundle follows a Poisson distribution with mean $\mu = 2$.
   a. Find the probability that there are exactly three damaged or imperfect panels in a bundle of 100.
   b. Find the probability that there are at least two damaged or imperfect panels in a bundle of 100.
3. A home improvement store has purchased two bundles (2 bundles of 100 each) of panels from the manufacturer described in Exercise 2. Find the probability his lot contains no more than four damaged or imperfect panels.
4. The board of directors of a company has voted to create an employee

council for the purpose of handling employee complaints. The council will consist of the company president, the vice-president for personnel, and four employee representatives. The four employees will be randomly selected from a list of 15 volunteers. This list consists of nine men and six women.

a. What is the probability that two or more men will be selected from the list of volunteers?
b. What is the probability that exactly three women will be selected from the list of volunteers?

5. A bin of 50 parts contains three defective units. A sample of five units is drawn randomly from the bin. What is the probability that no defective units will be selected?

5.8 The Role of the Probability Distribution in Making Inferences: A Test of a Researcher's Theory

We have described binomial populations in the first four sections of this chapter using the viewpoint that if we know the values of n and p, the population distribution can be found and the mean and variance of the population can be calculated. In short, we are able to calculate the probability of our sample outcome. Let us now look at the same problem in a different light. Given that we have a sample of n measurements from a dichotomous population with x of these outcomes designated as "successes," what information about the value of p can be gleaned from the sample? As we have seen, the mass of the probability distribution shifts with the value of ________, the probability of success, so that certain values of x are highly probable for one value of p and highly improbable for other values of p.

p

Our approach will be to draw a random sample from a dichotomous population and decide whether we will accept or reject an hypothesized value for p. The decision will be made on the basis of whether the sample results are highly ______________ and support the hypothesized value or are ______________ and fail to support the hypothesized value. Our procedure is very similar to a court trial in which the accused is assumed innocent until proved guilty. In fact, our sample acts as the __________ for or against the accused. What we do is to compare the hypothesized value with reality. Let us illustrate how a test of an hypothesis is conducted.

probable
improbable

evidence

Example 5.19

In an initial experiment to assess the merits of using a newly developed filling material in bed pillows, 10 persons randomly selected from a group of volunteers agreed to test the new filling by actually using both the standard pillow and one made with the new filling in their homes. To avoid biases that might influence the volunteer's decision, both pillows were covered with the same material. One pillow carried the number "one" and the other the number "two." Only the experimenter knew which number represented the standard and which represented the new material. After one week's use, each volunteer stated his or her preference for one of the two pillows. If there is no underlying difference between the new and standard pillow, then the probability that a volunteer would prefer the new pillow to the standard would be $p = 1/2$. If, on the other hand, this is not true and the new pillow has more desirable properties than the standard, then p, the probability that a volunteer prefers the new pillow, would be greater than 1/2.

Assuming that there is no difference between the pillows ($p = 1/2$), it would be extremely unlikely that in a sample of $n = 10$ trials we would observe 9 or more people preferring the new pillow. From the table of binomial probabilities, this probability, $p(9) + p(10)$, is .011. Therefore, more than 8 preferences for the new pillow would be sufficient evidence to reject the value $p = 1/2$. Since x, the number of preferences, is a binomial random variable with possible values 0, 1, 2, . . . , 10, the possible outcomes can be divided into

reject
accept

those (9 and 10) for which we agree to ______________ the null hypothesis and those (0, 1, 2, . . . , 8) for which we ______________ the null hypothesis.

Possible Values for x

0 1 2 3 4 5 6 7 8 | 9 10

Acceptance Region | Rejection Region

The decision to reject the null hypothesis will be made if the observed value of x lies in the rejection region.

A statistical test of a theory possesses four elements:

null
hypothesis

1. There must be a theory to be tested, which we call the ______________ ______________, H_0. In our problem, H_0 declares that $p = 1/2$. The objective of the test is to give the facts (data) a chance to refute H_0.

alternative

2. There must be an ______________ hypothesis, H_a. If H_0 is false, then some alternative hypothesis is true. H_a generally expresses the experimenter's intuitive feeling about the true state of nature. In our example, if the new filling is better than the standard, then H_a would appropriately be $H_a: p > 1/2$.

preferences

3. *The test statistic.* What information supplied by the data is relevant to a test of H_0? The statistic that reflects the true value of p is x, the number of ______________ in 10 trials.

rejection
reject

4. *The rejection region.* Certain values of the test statistic are more likely if H_a is true than if H_0 is true. A set of such values may be used as the ______________ region for the test. Hence, if x takes on a value in the rejection region, we agree to (accept, reject) H_0. In our example, the expected number of preferences would be 5 if H_0 is true. However, if H_a is true and $p = .8$, then the expected number of preferences would be $np = 10(.8) = 8$. Thus when $H_a: p > 1/2$ is true, we would expect to obtain larger values of x, and the rejection region $x = 9, 10$ would be appropriate for our alternative.

The rejection region given as $x = 9, 10$ is not the only possible choice available to the experimenter. Someone requiring stronger evidence before rejecting H_0 as false might prefer the following assignment:

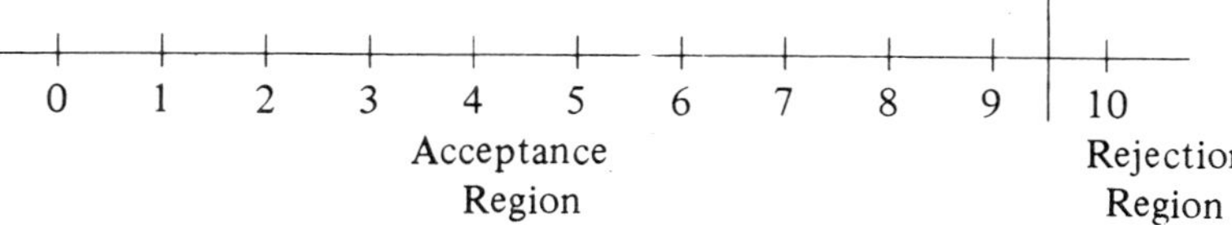

Another person might be particularly interested in protecting herself against accepting H_0 when in fact p is greater than 1/2 and could argue for the following assignment:

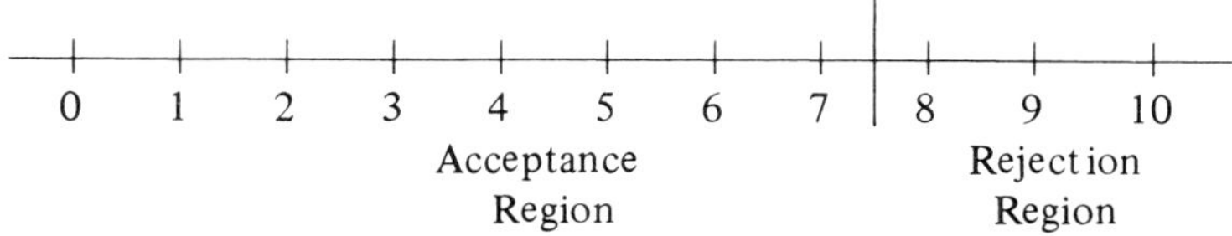

A sound choice among various reasonable rejection regions can be made after considering the possible errors that can be made in a test of an hypothesis.

The following table is called a *decision table* and looks at the two possible states of nature (H_0 and H_a) and the two possible decisions in a test of an hypothesis. Fill in the missing entries as either "correct" or "error":

	Decision	
Null Hypothesis	*Reject H_0*	*Accept H_0*
True	______	correct
False	correct	______

error
error

An error of type I is made when we reject H_0 when H_0 is (true, false). An error of type II is made when we fail to reject H_0 when H_a is (true, false). In considering a statistical test of an hypothesis, it is essential to know the probabilities of committing errors of type I and type II when the test is used. We define

true
true

$$\alpha = P(\text{type I error}) = P(\text{reject } H_0 \text{ when } H_0 \text{ true})$$

$$\beta = P(\text{type II error}) = P(\text{accept } H_0 \text{ when } H_a \text{ true})$$

For our example, let us look at α and β for the three rejection regions discussed above, using the tables of binomial probabilities, Table 1.

1. For the rejection region given as $x = 9, 10$,

$$\alpha = P(\text{reject } H_0 \text{ when } H_0 \text{ true})$$

$$= P(x = 9 \text{ or } 10 \text{ when } p = 1/2)$$

$= 1 - P(x \leqslant 8 \text{ when } p = 1/2)$

.989 $= 1 -$ __________

.011 $=$ __________

If H_0 is false and if $p = .8$, then

$\beta = P(\text{accept } H_0 \text{ when } H_a \text{ true})$

$= P(x \leqslant 8 \text{ when } p = .8)$

.624 $=$ __________

2. For the second rejection region, $x = 10$,

$\alpha = P(x = 10 \text{ when } p = 1/2)$

$= 1 - P(x \leqslant 9 \text{ when } p = 1/2)$

.999 $= 1 -$ __________

.001 $=$ __________

while if H_0 is false and if $p = .8$,

$\beta = P(x \leqslant 9 \text{ when } p = .8)$

.893 $=$ __________

3. For the third rejection region, $x = 8, 9, 10$,

$\alpha = P(x \geqslant 8 \text{ when } p = 1/2)$

$= 1 - P(x \leqslant 7 \text{ when } p = 1/2)$

.945 $= 1 -$ __________

.055 $=$ __________

If H_0 is false and if $p = .8$, then

$$\beta = P(x \leqslant 7 \text{ when } p = .8)$$

$$= \_\_\_\_\_\_\_\_$$

.322

Notice that both α and β depend on the rejection region employed and that when the sample size n is fixed, α and β are inversely related: as one increases, the other ________. Increasing the sample size provides more information on which to make the decision and will reduce the probability of a type II error. Since these two quantities measure the risk of making an incorrect decision, the experimenter chooses reasonable values for α and β and then chooses the rejection region and sample size accordingly. Since experimenters have found that a 1-in-20 chance of a type I error is usually tolerable, common practice is to choose $\alpha \leqslant$ ________ and a sample size n large enough to provide the desired control of the type II error.

decreases

.05

Example 5.20

Twenty office workers were tested for reaction time before and after lunch. Seventeen of the workers showed increased reaction time after lunch. Is this sufficient evidence to indicate that reaction times are increased after lunch?

Solution

We begin by putting this problem into the context of a test of an hypothesis concerning p, the probability that reaction time has increased after lunch. The 20 workers will be considered as $n = 20$ trials in a binomial experiment with $x = 17$. If eating lunch does not affect reaction time, then $p =$ ________; but if eating lunch causes reaction time to increase, then p ________.

1/2
$> 1/2$

1. The *hypotheses* to be tested are

$$H_0: p = 1/2 \quad \text{versus} \quad H_a: p > 1/2$$

2. The *test statistic* will be x, the number of workers exhibiting increased reaction time after lunch.
3. To choose a *rejection region*, we note that if H_0 is true, $\mu = np = 20(1/2)$ $=$ ________, while if H_a is true, and say $p = .7$, then $\mu = np = 20(.7)$ $=$ ________. If $p = .9$, $\mu = np = 20(.9) =$ ________. If H_a is true, we should expect to obtain ________ values of x. Using the table of

10
14; 18
larger

binomial probabilities with $n = 20$ and $p = 1/2$, we need to find a cutoff number, a, such that

$$\alpha = P(x \geqslant a \text{ when } p = 1/2) \leqslant .05$$

Complete the entries below:

	a	$P(x \geqslant a$ when $p = 1/2)$
	20	.000
	19	.000
	18	.000
	17	.001
.006	16	______
.021	15	______
.058	14	______
.132	13	______

The largest rejection region with $\alpha \leqslant .05$ would consist of the values
15; 16 $x =$ __________, __________, . . . , 20. (Note that an experimenter might be willing to include $x = 14$ in the rejection region and use $\alpha = .058$.)

4. Since the observed value of $x = 17$ lies in the rejection region, we reject
null hypothesis the ______________ ______________ and conclude that eating lunch
does (does, does not) significantly increase reaction time.

5. It is worthwhile to note that both types of errors cannot be made at the same time. If we decide to reject H_0, the only error applicable is the
type I ______________ error. If we decide to accept H_0, the only possible error
type II is ______________. For this problem, we could then put a measure of
.021 goodness on our inference by noting that with probability __________ of being incorrect, we conclude that eating lunch increases reaction time.

Self-Correcting Exercises 5D

1. While ordering a new shipment of shirts, the owner of a men's shop was told that the demand for a new color was anticipated to comprise about 40% of sales during the next season. The owner ordered his shipment in line with this 40% figure. If a random inspection of 25 sales slips involving the sale of a shirt revealed that 6 of these sales involved shirts of the new color, could the owner conclude that the 40% figure was actually too high?
2. A manufacturer has claimed that the proportion of defective items in lots supplied by him is at most 5%. To verify his claim, a random sample of 20 items produced by this manufacturer were examined and 4 items found to

be defective. Is this sufficient evidence to reject the manufacturer's claim at the 5% level of significance?

3. A comparison of the color quality of two brands of television sets, A and B, was of interest to manufacturer A, since B was his strongest competitor. Fifteen subjects, who had ample opportunity to view both brands of television, were asked to state a preference for Brand A or Brand B solely on the basis of the color of the television picture. If 12 of the 15 subjects stated a preference for Brand A, would this be sufficient evidence to conclude that the sets are not equally preferred when compared on the basis of picture color?

EXERCISES

1. Give the five defining characteristics of a binomial experiment.
2. Let x denote a binomial random variable for n trials. Give the probability function for x and list its possible values.
3. Four experiments are described below. Identify which of these might reasonably be treated as a binomial experiment. If a given experiment is clearly not binomial, state what feature disqualifies it. If it is a binomial experiment, write down the probability function for x.
   a. Five percent of the stamps in a large collection are extremely valuable. The stamps are withdrawn one at a time until ten extremely valuable stamps are located. The observed random variable is x, the total number of stamps withdrawn.
   b. There are 15 students in a particular economics class. The names of these students are written on tags placed in a box. Periodically, a tag is drawn at random from the box and the student with that name is asked to recite. The tag is returned to the box and the proceedings continued. Let x denote the number of times a particular student will be called upon to recite when the teacher draws from the box five times.
   c. This example is conducted in the manner prescribed for part b except that a tag drawn from the box is not returned. Let x denote the number of times the particular student will be called upon to recite when the teacher draws from the box five times.
   d. Sixty percent of the homes in a given county carry fire insurance. A sample of five homes is drawn at random from this county. Let x denote the number of insured homes among the five selected.
4. Let x denote the number of successes in a single trial given that the probability of success is p.
   a. Construct the probability distribution for x in tabular form.

b. Use the definitions of mean and variance to determine the mean and variance of x.

5. A binomial experiment consists of four independent trials in which the probability of success on a given trial is 1/2. Let x denote the number of successes in the four trials.
   a. Write down the probability function for x as a formula.
   b. Construct the probability distribution of x in tabular form.
   c. Use the table constructed in part b and the definition of $E(x)$ to find the expected value of x.
   d. Use the table constructed in part b and the definition of σ^2 to find the variance of x.
   e. Use the formula for the mean and variance of a binomial random variable to check the values determined in parts c and d.
6. If x is binomial for $n = 100$ trials and $p = .9$, find limits A and B such that $P[A < x < B] \geqslant 8/9$. Hint: Use Tchebysheff's Theorem.
7. If a TV program cannot attract about a third of the available viewers it is apt to be tabbed as unequal to competing programs in the same time slot. Suppose a certain program is preferred in its time slot by 1/3 of the viewers. In a random sample of 450 viewers, within what limits would you expect to find the number preferring this program?
8. Eastern University has found that about 90% of its accepted applicants for enrollment in the freshman class will actually take a place in that class. In 1980, 1360 applicants to Eastern were accepted. Within what limits would you expect to find the size of the freshman class at Eastern in the fall of 1988?
9. In the past history of a certain serious disease it has been found that about 1/2 of its victims recover.
   a. Find the probability that exactly one of the next five patients suffering from this disease will recover.
   b. Find the probability that at least one of the next five patients afflicted with this disease will recover.
10. The length of life of a certain type of battery is at least 15 hours with probability $p = .80$. Suppose that five of these batteries are put into service.
    a. What is the probability that all five of these batteries will serve for at least 15 hours?
    b. What is the probability that at least three of these batteries will serve for at least 15 hours?
11. The probability of rain is 1/2 for each of the next five days. For the purpose of this problem, assume that the five days comprise independent trials.
    a. What is the probability of no rain at all during the next five days?
    b. What is the probability of rain on at least two of the next five days?
12. On a certain university campus a student is fined \$1.00 for the first parking violation of the academic year. The fine is doubled for each subsequent offense, so that the second violation costs \$2.00, the third \$4.00, etc. The

probability that a parking violation on a given day is detected is .10. Suppose that a certain student will park illegally on each of 20 days during a given academic year.

a. What is the probability he will not be fined?

b. What is the probability that his fines will total no more than \$15.00?

13. A multiple-choice test offers four alternative answers to each of 100 questions. In every case there is but one correct answer. A particular student responded correctly to each of the first 76 questions when he noted that just 20 seconds remained in the test period. He quickly checked an answer at random for each of the remaining 24 questions without reading them.

    a. What is the student's expected number of correct answers?

    b. If the instructor assigns a grade by taking 1/3 of the wrong from the number marked correctly, what is the student's expected grade?

14. Consider 10 management trainees in a firm's rotation program where three of the 10 are members of minority groups. If five of the trainees are randomly assigned to the marketing division, what is the probability that there will be three minority trainees in the group assigned to marketing?

15. Improperly wired control panels were mistakenly installed on two of eight large automated machine tools. It is uncertain which of the machine tools have the defective panels, and a sample of four tools is randomly chosen for inspection.

    a. What is the probability that the sample will include no defective panels? Both defective panels?

    b. Find the binomial approximations for part a.

16. A coroner's null hypothesis is H_0: "This man is alive." If you were "this man" would you prefer a test with $\alpha = .05$ and $\beta = .001$ or a test with $\alpha = .001$ and $\beta = .05$? Explain your preference.

17. A new method of packaging Brand A candy has been proposed as a means of increasing sales. It is known that approximately 40% of the potential customers now purchase Brand A. If at least six of the next ten customers (each of whom is given a choice of Brand A in the new package or one of its competitors) select Brand A, we shall conclude that the new packaging method is effective in increasing sales.

    a. State H_0 in terms of p, the probability that a given customer will select Brand A.

    b. Find α for this experiment. (Use Table 1 in the text or Study Guide).

    c. State H_a in terms of p.

    d. Find β for $H_a: p = .6$. (Use Table 1 in the text or Study Guide).

18. It is thought that cottage cheese batches in two tanks (Tank A and Tank B) are equally desirable. Let p denote the probability that a given taster will express a preference for the cottage cheese in Tank A. To test the null hypothesis, $H_0: p = 1/2$, against the alternative, $H_a: p \neq 1/2$, each member of a panel of ten tasters is asked to judge which cottage cheese is the more desirable. Let x denote the number of tasters who will state a preference

for the product in Tank A. Suppose that the rejection region consists of the values $x = 0, 1, 9$ and 10.

a. Describe the Type I error in terms of the cheeses.
b. Describe the Type II error in terms of the cheeses.
c. Find α for the above test.
d. Find β if indeed $p = .60$.
e. Find β if indeed $p = .90$.
f. Find β if indeed $p = .99$.
g. From the answers recorded for parts d, e, and f state whether β is larger when p is close to the value specified in H_0 or when p is grossly different from the value specified in H_0.

19. A delicatessen has found that the weekly demand for caviar follows a Poisson distribution with a mean of four tins (each tin contains 8 ounces of caviar).
    a. Find the probability that no more than 4 tins are requested during a given week.
    b. As caviar spoils with time, it must be replenished weekly by the delicatessen's owner. How many tins should he buy if it is desired that the probability not exceed .10 that demand cannot be met during a given week?
20. A manufacturer of a small mini-computer has found that the average number of service calls per computer each year is 2.2. Assume the number of service calls follows a Poisson distribution.
    a. Find the probability that a particular mini-computer requires no service during a given year.
    b. A small firm has purchased two mini-computers from the manufacturer. Find the probability that the firm requires no service calls during a given year.
    c. Find the probability that the firm requires exactly two service calls during a given year.
21. Refer to Exercise 20. Suppose service calls cost the computer manufacturer an average of \$20 each.
    a. What is the expected cost per computer each year?
    b. If the manufacturer has sold 50 mini-computers in the Seattle area, what is the expected annual cost of service in this area?
22. Customers arrive at a certain gasoline filling station at the average rate of one every ten minutes. Assume the arrivals follow a Poisson distribution. The station has only one attendant and he takes an average of five minutes to service each arrival. What is the probability that two customers arrive while the attendant is servicing an earlier arrival?
23. Suppose that the national unemployment rate for a particular year is 7.1%. A sample of $n = 100$ persons is taken in the Los Angeles area and the number of unemployed persons is recorded.

a. If the unemployment rate for the Los Angeles area is the same as the national rate, within what limits would you expect the number of unemployed to fall?
b. If 15 of the 100 persons interviewed said that they were unemployed, what would you conclude about the unemployment rate in the Los Angeles area?

24. Suppose that 1 out of 10 homeowners in the state of California have invested in earthquake insurance. If 15 homeowners are randomly chosen to be interviewed,
    a. What is the probability that at least 1 has earthquake insurance?
    b. What is the probability that 4 or more have earthquake insurance?

Chapter 6

THE NORMAL AND OTHER CONTINUOUS PROBABILITY DISTRIBUTIONS

6.1 Introduction

discrete
continuous
finite
infinity; continuous

Recall that a random variable was defined to be a numerically valued variable resulting from the outcome of a random experiment. Random variables are divided into two categories, (1) ______________ random variables and (2) ______________ random variables. We have confined our discussion to problems concerning discrete random variables, which can take a ______________ or countable ______________ of values. In contrast, a ______________ random variable can assume any of the values associated with an interval on the real line.

discrete
continuous

While the probability distribution or frequency distribution of a ______________ random variable can be represented by a relative frequency histogram, the probability distribution for a ______________ random variable is represented by a smooth curve. The probability distribution for the normal random variable y is

$$f(x) = \frac{1}{\sigma\sqrt{2\pi}} e^{-\frac{1}{2}\left(\frac{x-\mu}{\sigma}\right)^2}, \quad -\infty < x < \infty$$

bell

which produces the ______________-shaped curve shown below.

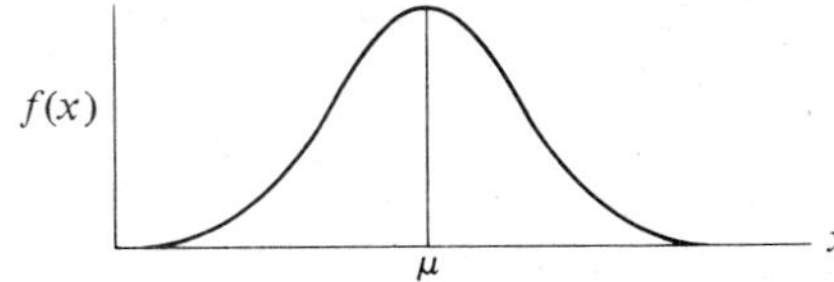

The symbols used in the function $f(x)$ are defined as follows:

1. π and e are irrational numbers whose approximate values are 3.1416 and 2.7183, respectively.
2. μ and σ are constants which represent the population __mean__ and __standard__ __deviation__, respectively.

mean
standard deviation

Encountering a random variable whose values can be extremely small (a large negative value) or extremely large might at first be disconcerting to the student who has heard that heights, weights, response times, and errors of measurements are approximately normally distributed. Surely we do not have heights, weights, or times that are less than zero! Certainly not, but almost all of the distribution of a normally distributed random variable lies within the interval $\mu \pm 3\sigma$. In the case of heights or weights, this interval almost always encompasses positive values. Keep in mind this curve is merely a *model* that approximates an actual distribution of measurements. Its great utility lies in the fact that it *can* be used effectively as a model for so many types of measurements.

6.2 The Standard Normal Probability Distribution

Probability is the vehicle through which we are able to make inferences about a population in the form of either estimation or decisions. To make inferences about a normal population, we must be able to compute or otherwise find the probabilities associated with a normal random variable. As explained in Section 4.4, the probability that the normal random variable x lies between two points a and b is equivalent to the area under the normal curve between a and b. However, since the probability distribution for a normal random variable x depends on the population parameters ________ and ________, we would be required to recalculate the probabilities associated with x each time a new value for μ or σ was encountered. We resort to a standardization process whereby we convert a normal random variable x to a ________ normal random variable z, which represents the distance of x from its mean μ in units of the standard deviation σ. To standardize a normal random variable x, we use the following procedure:

μ; σ

standard

1. From x, subtract its mean μ:

   $$x - \mu$$

   This results in the signed distance of x from its mean, a negative sign indicating that x is to the left of μ while a positive sign indicates x is to the right of μ.

   right

2. Now divide by σ:

   $$\frac{x - \mu}{\sigma}$$

Dividing by σ converts the signed distance from the mean to the number of standard deviations to the right or left of μ.

3. Define

$$z = \frac{x - \mu}{\sigma}$$

z is the standard normal variable having the standardized normal distribution with mean 0 and standard deviation 1.

Given the curve representing the distribution of a continuous random variable
area — x, the probability that $a \leqslant x \leqslant b$ is represented by the ______
a; b — under the curve between the points ______ and ______. Hence in finding probabilities associated with a standardized normal variable z, we could refer directly to the areas under the curve. These areas are tabulated in Table 3 of the Appendix to your text. They have been reproduced as Table 3 in the Appendix to this Study Guide for your convenience.

symmetric — Since the standardized normal distribution is ______ about the mean 0, half of the area lies to the left of 0 and half to the right of 0. Further, the areas to the left of the mean $z = 0$ can be calculated by using the corresponding and equal area to the right of $z = 0$. Hence Table 3 exhibits areas only for positive values of z correct to the nearest hundredth. Table 3 gives the area between $z = 0$ and a specified value of z, say z_0. A convenient notation used to designate the area between $z = 0$ and z_0 is $A(z_0)$.

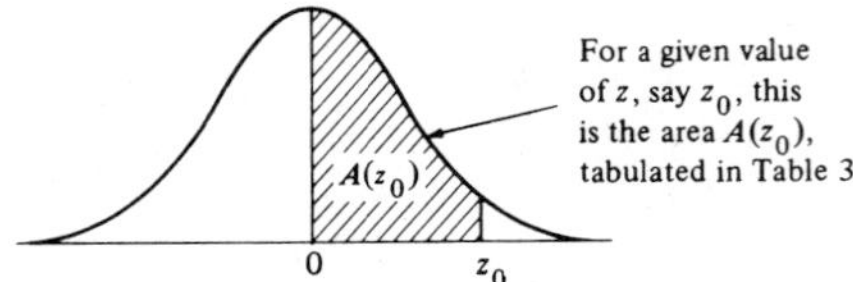

a. For $z = 1$, the area between $z = 0$ and $z = 1$ is $A(z = 1) = A(1) = .3413$.
.4772 — b. For $z = 2$, $A(z = 2) = A(2) =$ ______.
.4452 — c. For $z = 1.6$, $A(1.6) =$ ______.
.4918 — d. For $z = 2.4$, $A(2.4) =$ ______.

Now try reading the table for values of z given to two decimal places.

.4951 — e. For $z = 2.58$, $A(2.58) =$ ______.
.2734 — f. For $z = .75$, $A(.75) =$ ______.
.4545 — g. For $z = 1.69$, $A(1.69) =$ ______.
.4979 — h. For $z = 2.87$, $A(2.87) =$ ______.

We will now find probabilities associated with the standard normal random variable z by using Table 3.

Example 6.1

Find the probability that z is greater than 1.86, that is, $P(z > 1.86)$.

Solution
Illustrate the problem with a diagram as follows:

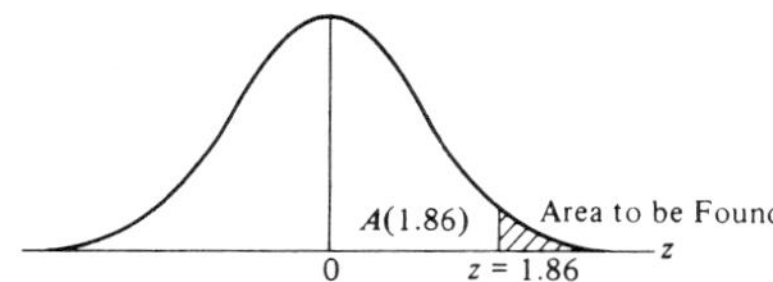

1. The total area to the right of $z = 0$ is equal to .5000.
2. From Table 3, $A(1.86)$ = __________. .4686
3. Therefore, the shaded area is found by subtracting $A(1.86)$ from ________. .5000
4. Hence

$$P(z > 1.86) = .5000 - A(1.86)$$

$$= .5000 - \underline{\hspace{2cm}}$$ .4686

$$= \underline{\hspace{2cm}}$$ .0314

Example 6.2
Find $P(z < -2.22)$.

Solution
Illustrate the problem with a diagram.

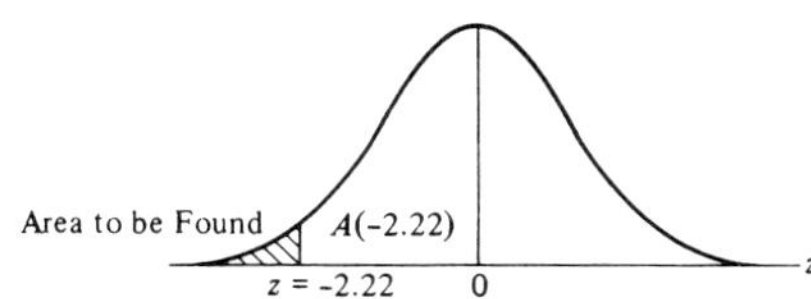

1. Using the symmetry of the normal distribution, $A(-2.22) = A(2.22)$ = __________. The negative value of z indicates that you are to the (left, right) of the mean, $z = 0$. .4868 left

2. $P(z < -2.22) = .5000 -$ __________ $=$ __________ .4868; .0132

Example 6.3
Find $P(-1.21 < z < 2.43)$.

Solution
Illustrate the problem with a diagram.

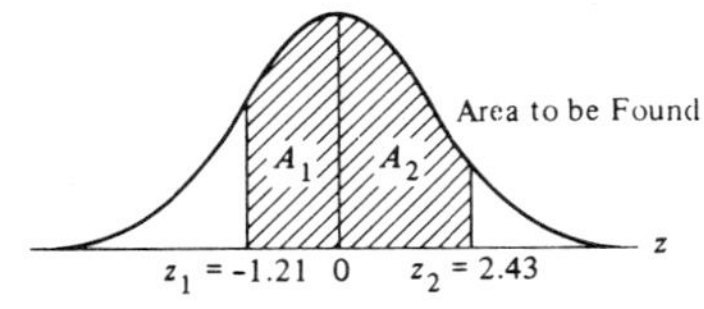

$$P(-1.21 < z < 2.43) = P(-1.21 < z < 0) + P(0 < z < 2.43)$$

.3869; .4925 $= \_\_\_\_\_\_\_\_ + \_\_\_\_\_\_\_\_$

.8794 $= \_\_\_\_\_\_\_\_$

A second type of problem that arises is that of finding a value of z, say z_0, such that a probability statement about z will be true. We explore this type of problem with examples.

Example 6.4
Find the value of z_0 such that

$$P(0 < z < z_0) = .3925$$

Solution
Once again, illustrate the problem with a diagram and list the pertinent information.

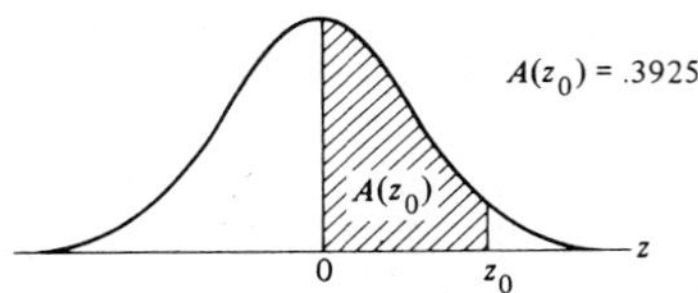

1. Search Table 3 until the area .3925 is found. The value such that

1.24 $A(z_0) = .3925$ is $z_0 = \_\_\_\_\_\_\_\_$

1.24 2. $P(0 < z < \_\_\_\_\_\_\_\_) = .3925$

Example 6.5
Find the value of z_0 such that $P(z > z_0) = .2643$.

Solution
Illustrate the problem and list the pertinent information.

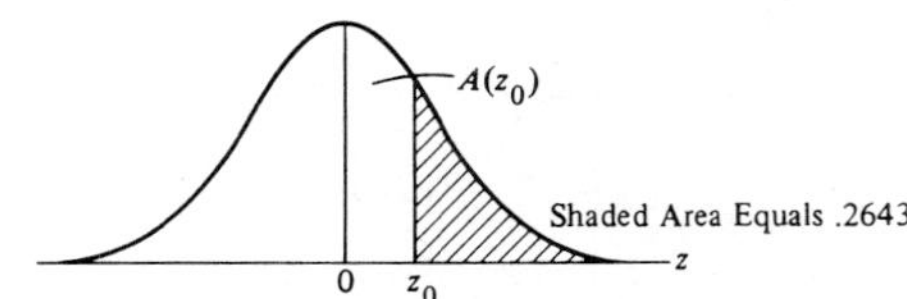

.2357 1. $A(z_0) = .5000 - .2643 = \_\_\_\_\_\_\_\_$

2. The value of z_0 such that

$A(z_0) =$ ________ is $z_0 =$ ________ .2357; .63

3. $P(z >$ ________ $) = .2643$ .63

Self-Correcting Exercises 6A

1. Find the following probabilities associated with the standard normal random variable z:

a.	$P(z > 2.1)$	d.	$P(-2.75 < z < -1.70)$
b.	$P(z < -1.2)$	e.	$P(-1.96 < z < 1.96)$
c.	$P(.5 < z < 1.5)$	f.	$P(z > 1.645)$

2. Find the value of z, say z_0, such that the following probability statements are true:

   a. $P(z > z_0) = .10$

   b. $P(z < z_0) = .01$

   c. $P(-z_0 < z < z_0) = .95$

   d. $P(-z_0 < z < z_0) = .99$

3. An auditor has reviewed the financial records of a hardware store and has found that its billing errors follow a normal distribution with mean and standard deviation equal to \$0 and \$1, respectively.
   a. What proportion of the store's billings are in error by more than \$1?
   b. What is the probability that a billing represents an overcharge of at least \$1.50?
   c. What is the probability that a customer has been undercharged from \$.50 to \$1.00?
   d. Within what range would 95% of the billing errors lie?
   e. Of the extreme undercharges, 5% would be at least what amount?

6.3 Use of the Table for the Normal Random Variable x

We can now proceed to find probabilities associated with any normal random variable x having mean μ and standard deviation σ. This is accomplished by converting the random variable x to the standard normal random variable z, and then working the problem in terms of z.

Since probability statements are written in the form of inequalities, you are reminded of two facts. A statement of inequality is maintained if (1) the same number is subtracted from each member of the inequality and/or (2) each member of the inequality is divided by the same *positive* number.

Example 6.6
The following are equivalent statements about x:

1. $$70 < x < 95$$

2. $$(70 - 15) < (x - 15) < (95 - 15)$$

3. $$\frac{70 - 15}{5} < \frac{x - 15}{5} < \frac{95 - 15}{5}$$

4. $$11 < \frac{x - 15}{5} < 16$$

Example 6.7
Let x be a normal random variable with mean $\mu = 100$ and standard deviation $\sigma = 4$. Find $P(92 < x < 104)$.

Solution
Recalling that $z = (x - \mu)/\sigma$, we can apply rules 1 and 2 to convert the probability statement about x to one about the standard normal random variable z.

1. $$P(92 < x < 104) = P(92 - 100 < x - 100 < 104 - 100)$$
$$= P\left(\frac{92 - 100}{4} < \frac{x - 100}{4} < \frac{104 - 100}{4}\right)$$
$$= P(-2 < z < 1)$$

2. The problem now stated in terms of z is readily solved by using the methods of Section 6.2.

$$P(92 < x < 104) = P(-2 < z < 1)$$
$$= A(-2) + A(1)$$

.4772; .3413 $$= \underline{\qquad\qquad} + \underline{\qquad\qquad}$$

.8185 $$= \underline{\qquad\qquad}$$

Example 6.8

Let x be a normal random variable with mean 100 and standard deviation 4. Find $P(93.5 < x < 105.2)$.

Solution

$$P(93.5 < x < 105.2) = P\left(\frac{93.5 - 100}{4} < z < \frac{105.2 - 100}{4}\right)$$

$$= P(-1.63 < z < \_\_\_\_\_\_)$$ 1.30

$$= \_\_\_\_\_\_ + \_\_\_\_\_\_$$ .4484; .4032

$$= \_\_\_\_\_\_$$ .8516

Self-Correcting Exercises 6B

1. If x is normally distributed with mean 10 and variance 2.25, evaluate the following probabilities:

a.	$P(x > 8.5)$	d.	$P(7.5 < x < 9.2)$
b.	$P(x < 12)$	e.	$P(12.25 < x < 13.25)$
c.	$P(9.25 < x < 11.25)$		

2. An industrial engineer has found that the standard household light bulbs produced by a certain manufacturer have a useful life which is normally distributed with a mean of 250 hours and a variance of 2500. What is the probability that a randomly selected bulb from this production process will have a useful life
   a. in excess of 300 hours?
   b. between 190 and 270 hours?
   c. not exceeding 260 hours?
   d. Ninety percent of the bulbs have a useful life in excess of how many hours?
   e. The probability is .95 that a bulb does not have a useful life in excess of how many hours?
3. Scores on a personnel evaluation form exhibit the characteristics of a normal distribution with mean and standard deviation of 50 and 5 respectively. What proportion of the scores on this evaluation form would be

a. greater than 60,
b. less than 45,
c. between 35 and 65?
d. If to be considered eligible for a given position, an applicant must score beyond the 95th percentile on this form, what score must an applicant have to be eligible?

6.4 The Normal Approximation to the Binomial Distribution

The binomial random variable x was defined in Chapter 5 as the number of successes in n independent and identical trials comprising the binomial experiment. The probabilities associated with this random variable were calculated as

$$p(x) = C_x^n p^x q^{(n-x)} \qquad \text{for } x = 0, 1, 2, \ldots, n$$

For large values of n (in fact, if n gets much larger than 10), the binomial probabilities are very tedious to compute. Fortunately, several options are available to us in an effort to avoid lengthy calculations.

1. Table 1 of the Appendix contains the tabulated values $P(x \leqslant a)$ for $n = 5, 10, 15, 20, 25$ and for $p = .01, .05, .10, .20, \ldots, .90, .95, .99$. However, if the user requires values of n and p for which the tables have not been given, Table 1 will not be useful.
2. In Section 5.5, we considered two examples in which the Poisson distribution could be used to approximate the binomial probabilities. This approximation was appropriate when n was large and p (or q) was small, so that $np < 7$. However, there are a great number of situations in which n is large, but $np \geqslant 7$. In this case, the Poisson approximation (will, will not) be accurate.

will not

3. When n is large and p (or q) is not too small, the binomial probability histogram is fairly symmetric and mound-shaped. This symmetry increases as p gets closer to $p = .5$. Hence, it would seem reasonable to approximate the distribution of a binomial random variable with the distribution of a normal random variable whose mean and variance are identical to those for the binomial random variable.

When n is *sufficiently large* and p is not too close to zero or one, the random variable x, the number of successes in n trials is approximately normal with mean np and variance npq.

When can we reasonably apply the normal approximation? For small values of n and values of p close to 0 or 1, the binomial distribution will exhibit a "pile-up" around $x =$ ________ or $x =$ ________. The data will not be ____________-shaped and the normal approximation will be poor. For a normal random variable, ________% of the measurements will be within the interval $\mu \pm 2\sigma$. For $\mu = np$ and $\sigma = \sqrt{npq}$, the interval $np \pm 2\sqrt{npq}$ should be within the bounds of the binomial random variable x, or within the interval $(0, n)$, to obtain reasonably good approximations to the binomial probabilities.

0; n
bell
95

To show how the normal approximation is used, let us consider a binomial random variable x with $n = 8$ and $p = 1/2$ and attempt to approximate some binomial probabilities with a normal random variable having the same mean, $\mu = np$, and variance, $\sigma^2 = npq$, as the binomial x. In this case

$$\mu = np = 8(1/2) = \_\_\_\_\_\_$$

4

$$\sigma^2 = npq = 8(1/2)(1/2) = \_\_\_\_\_\_$$

2

Note that the interval

$$\mu \pm 2\sigma = 4 \pm 2\sqrt{2} = (1.2, 6.8)$$

is contained within the interval (0, 8); therefore our approximations should be adquate. Consider the following diagrammatic representation of the approximation, where $p(x)$ is the frequency distribution for the binomial random variable and $f(x)$ is the frequency distribution for the corresponding normal random variable x.

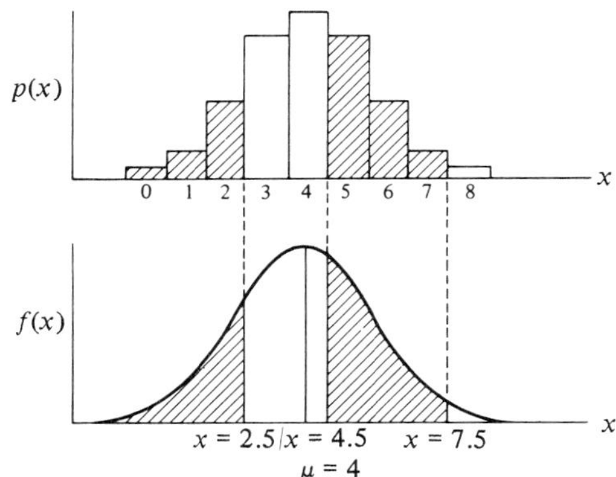

Example 6.9
Find $P(x < 3)$ using the normal approximation.

Solution
$P(x < 3)$ for the binomial random variable with mean $\mu = 4$ and $\sigma = \sqrt{2}$ corresponds to the shaded bars in the histogram over $x = 0$, 1, and 2. The approximating probability corresponds to the shaded area to the left of $x = 2.5$ in the normal distribution with mean 4 and standard deviation $\sqrt{2}$.

We proceed as follows:

$$P(x < 3) \approx P(x < 2.5)$$

$$= P\left(\frac{x - 4}{\sqrt{2}} < \frac{2.5 - 4}{\sqrt{2}}\right)$$

$$= P(z < -1.06)$$

$$= .5000 - A(-1.06)$$

.3554 $= .5000 -$ ________

.1446 $=$ ________

Example 6.10
Find $P(5 \leqslant x \leqslant 7)$.

Solution
For the binomial random variable with mean 4 and standard deviation $\sqrt{2}$,
5 — $P(5 \leqslant x \leqslant 7)$ corresponds to the shaded bars over $x =$ ________,
6; 7 — ________, and ________. This corresponds in turn to the shaded area for the approximating normal distribution with mean 4 and standard deviation
4.5; 7.5 — $\sqrt{2}$ between $x =$ ________ and $x =$ ________. Therefore,

$$P(5 \leqslant x \leqslant 7) \approx P(4.5 < x < 7.5)$$

$$= P\left(\frac{4.5 - 4}{\sqrt{2}} < \frac{x - 4}{\sqrt{2}} < \frac{7.5 - 4}{\sqrt{2}}\right)$$

$$= P(.35 < z < 2.47)$$

$$= A(2.47) - A(.35)$$

.4932; .1368 $=$ ________ $-$ ________

.3564 $=$ ________

Notice that we used $P(x < 2.5)$ to approximate the binomial probability $P(x < 3)$. In like manner we used $P(4.5 < x < 7.5)$ to approximate the binomial probability $P(5 \leqslant x \leqslant 7)$. The addition or subtraction of .5 is called the *correction for continuity* since we are approximating a discrete probability distribution with a probability distribution that is continuous. You may become confused as to whether .5 should be added or subtracted in the process of approximating binomial probabilities. A commonsense rule that always works is to examine the binomial probability statement carefully and determine which values of the binomial random variable are included in the statement. (Draw a picture if necessary.) The probabilities associated with these values correspond to the bars in the histogram centered over them. Locating the end points of the bars to be included determines the values needed for the approximating normal random variable.

Example 6.11

Suppose x is a binomial random variable with $n = 400$ and $p = .1$. Use the normal approximation to binomial probabilities to find the following:

1. $P(x > 45)$
2. $P(x \leqslant 32)$
3. $P(34 \leqslant x \leqslant 46)$

Solution

If x is binomial, then its mean and variance are

$\mu = np = 400(.1) =$ ________ 40

$\sigma^2 = npq = 400(.1)(.9) =$ ________ 36

1. To find $P(x > 45)$, we need the probabilities associated with the values 46, 47, 48, . . . , 400. This corresponds to the bars in the binomial histogram beginning at ________ . Hence 45.5

$$P(x > 45) \approx P(x > 45.5)$$

$$= P\left(z > \frac{45.5 - 40}{6}\right)$$

$$= P(z > .92)$$

$=$ ________ .1788

2. To find $P(x \leqslant 32)$, we need the probabilities associated with the values 0, 1, 2, . . . , up to and including $x = 32$. This corresponds to finding the
32.5 area in the binomial histogram to the left of ______. Hence

$$P(x \leqslant 32) \approx P(x < 32.5)$$

$$= P\left(z < \frac{32.5 - 40}{6}\right)$$

-1.25 $= P(z <$ ______$)$

.1056 $=$ ______

3. To find $P(34 \leqslant x \leqslant 46)$, we need the probabilities associated with the values beginning at 34 up to and including 46. This corresponds to finding
33.5; 46.5 the area under the histogram between ______ and ______. Hence

$$P(34 \leqslant x \leqslant 46) \approx P(33.5 < x < 46.5)$$

$$= P\left(\frac{33.5 - 40}{6} < z < \frac{46.5 - 40}{6}\right)$$

-1.08; 1.08 $= P($______ $< z$ ______$)$

.7198 $=$ ______

Notice that the interval $\mu \pm 2\sigma$, or 40 ± 12, is well within the binomial range of 0 to 400, so that these approximate probabilities should be reasonably accurate.

Example 6.12

In the population, a specific birth defect accounts for 10% of all birth defects. An investigator would like to know if this percentage is in fact higher if the mother is taking a particular medication. If a sample of 100 births to mothers taking the medication that gave birth to babies with birth defects revealed 18 with this specific birth defect, could the investigator conclude that the percentage is higher for mothers taking the medication.

Solution

1. This problem can be formulated as a test of an hypothesis concerning the value of a binomial parameter ______. The experimenter would like to show that the value of p is higher for the population of mothers taking

the medication and giving birth to birth-defective children than for the population in general.

2. Hence we wish to test

$$H_0: p = .10 \quad \text{versus} \quad H_a: \underline{\qquad\qquad}$$

p > .10

3. Using x, the number with the specific birth defect in the sample of 100, as the test statistic, we would reject H_0 for (large, small) values of x.

large

4. We can use the normal approximation to evaluate the probability of our sample results if H_0 is in fact true, since then $\mu = 100(.1) =$ ________ and $\sigma = \sqrt{100(.1)(.9)} = \sqrt{\underline{\qquad\qquad}} =$ ________, and

10

9; 3

$$P(x \geqslant 18) \approx P(x > \underline{\qquad\qquad})$$

17.5

$$= P\left(\frac{x - 10}{3} > \frac{17.5 - 10}{3}\right)$$

$$= P(z > \underline{\qquad\qquad})$$

$$= \underline{\qquad\qquad}$$

2.5

.0062

5. Since the probability of observing our sample value or a value more extreme has a probability equal to .0062, we __________ the null hypothesis and conclude that $p > .10$ for the medicated group. In fact, based on the sample data, it appears that this percentage is closer to ________% for the medicated group.

reject

20

6. Note that we could have used

$$z = \frac{x - \mu}{\sigma}$$

directly as a test statistic, rejecting H_0 if the value of z is too large, i.e., if the observation lies too many standard deviations to the right of the mean.

7. The student should note that we (have, have not) used the correction for continuity in this test of an hypothesis about p, even though the exact distribution of the test statistic x is not normal, but __________. When n is large, the student will find that the use of the correction changes the values of $z = (x - \mu)/\sigma$ only slightly. Therefore, *when testing an hypothesis about binomial p with n large, we choose to calculate z without the correction.*

have not

binomial

Example 6.13

In testing an hypothesis, the rejection region is usually specified in advance, so that the probability of a type I error is less than or equal to $\alpha = .05$. For the preceding problem, find the rejection region in the following cases:

1. If z is used as the test statistic.
2. If x is used as the test statistic.

Solution

1. If z is to be used as a test statistic, we need to find a value of z, say z_α, satisfying

$$P(z > z_\alpha) \leqslant \alpha$$

In pictorial form, for $\alpha = .05$, we have

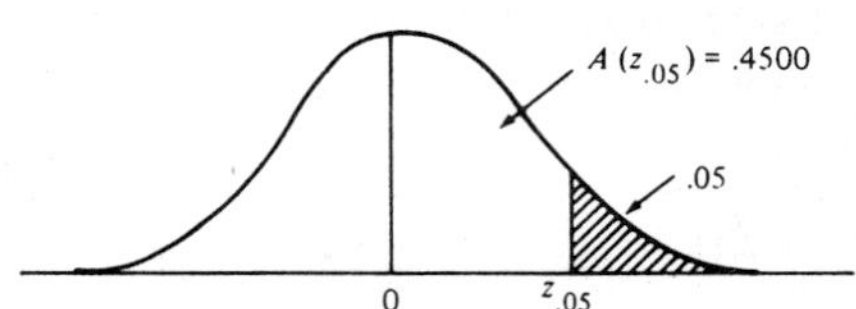

Hence $A(z_{.05}) = .45$. Searching the table of normal probabilities, we find that $A(1.64) = .4495$ and $A(1.65) = .4505$. Since our area of .4500 lies exactly halfway between the entries $z = 1.64$ and $z = 1.65$, the required value of $z_{.05}$ = __________. Hence we would reject H_0 if the observed value of $z = (x - \mu)/\sigma$ were greater than or equal to 1.645.

2. To find the rejection region if x is used as a test statistic requires the solution of the equation

$$\frac{x_\alpha - 10}{3} = 1.645$$

1.645

Solving for x_α, we find

$$x_\alpha = 10 + 3(1.645)$$

$$= 10 + \_\_\_\_\_\_\_\_\_\_$$

$$= \_\_\_\_\_\_\_\_\_\_$$

Since x takes on only integer values, we would reject H_0 if the observed x were greater than or equal to __________. For the preceding problem, the observed value of x was 18. Hence we would reject H_0 and conclude that

4.935 the percentage of birth defects is higher for mothers taking medication.

Much time is saved by using $z = (x - np)/(\sqrt{npq})$ as a test statistic when

14.935 n is large, since as n becomes large, the normal approximation becomes better and better. The calculated value of z in this case is

15

$$z = \frac{18 - 10}{3}$$

2.67

$$= \_\_\_\_\_\_\_\_\_\_$$

which is greater than $z_{.05} = 1.645$. Again H_0 is rejected in favor of H_a.

Self-Correcting Exercises 6C

1. A company claims that at most 15% of the items it produces contain defects. Assuming the maximal value of .15 for p, the probability that an item is defective, what is the probability of observing 23 or more defectives in a random sample of 100 items chosen at random from this company's production? If the sample did contain 23 defectives, would you still be willing to accept the 15% figure as claimed?
2. If the median income in a certain area is claimed to be \$22,000, what is the probability that 37 or fewer of 100 randomly chosen wage-earners from this area have incomes less than \$22,000? Would the \$22,000 figure seem reasonable if your sample actually contained 37 wage-earners whose income was less than \$22,000?
3. If the failure rate of a given component is 10%, within what limits would the number of failures in a sample of 100 be expected to lie with probability .95?
4. If it is known that 25% of newly formed small business enterprises fail within a year, what is the probability that 30 or more such enterprises in a random sample of 100 are recorded as having failed within a year?

6.5 The Uniform Distribution

The uniform probability distribution is used to model the behavior of a random variable whose values are evenly or uniformly distributed over a given interval. For example, the errors introduced by rounding observations to the nearest inch would probably have a uniform distribution over the interval from −.5 to .5 inch. The time required by lumbering trucks to travel 30 miles from a harvesting area to a lumber mill can be taken to be uniformly distributed over the interval from 30 to 40 minutes.

If x is a uniform random variable over the interval from a to b, then the probability density function for x is

$$f(x) = 1/(b - a) \quad \text{for} \quad a < x < b$$

The mean and standard deviation of x are $\mu = (a + b)/2$ and $\sigma = (b - a)/\sqrt{12}$. Notice that the mean is the midpoint of the interval and the standard deviation is directly proportional to the length of the interval.

Probabilities associated with a uniform random variable correspond to the rectangular areas under the density function and are found as

$$(\text{length of desired interval}) \times (\text{height given as } 1/(b - a))$$

The uniform distribution is a continuous distribution; hence, $P(c \leqslant x \leqslant d)$, $P(c \leqslant x < d)$, $P(c < x \leqslant d)$, and $P(c < x < d)$ are all equal, since $P(x = c) = P(x = d) = 0$.

Example 6.14
If rounding errors have a uniform distribution over the interval -.5 to .5,
a. Find the probability that the rounding error is less than .2. Find the probability that the rounding error is less than .2 in magnitude.
b. Find the mean and standard deviation of the rounding error.
c. Within what limits would you expect at least 75% of the possible rounding errors to lie?
d. What is the actual proportion of rounding errors within the limits found in part e?

Solution
Let x represent the rounding error over the interval from -.5 to .5, with probability density function

$$f(x) = 1 \quad \text{for} \quad -.5 < x < .5$$

Note that $a = -.5$, $b = .5$, $b - a = 1$ and therefore, $1/(b - a) = 1$.

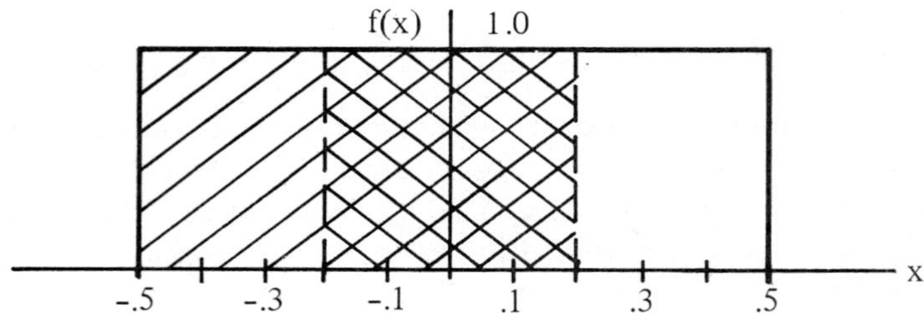

a. The probability that the rounding error is less than .2 corresponds to the area under the interval between $x = -.5$ and $x = .2$. Since the height of $f(x)$ is one,

$$P[x < .2] = [.2 - (-.5)] \times 1 = .7$$

while

$$P[-.2 < x < .2] = [.2 - (-.2)] \times 1 = .4$$

b. With $a = -.5$ and $b = .5$,

$$\mu = (a + b)/2 = [.5 + (-.5)]/2 = 0$$

and

$$\sigma = (a - b)/\sqrt{12} = [.5 - (-.5)]/\sqrt{12}$$
$$= 1/\sqrt{12} = .2887$$

c. From Tchebysheff's Theorem, we know that the interval $\mu \pm 2\sigma$ contains at least 75% of the observations. Therefore the interval

$$0 \pm 2(.2887)$$
$$0 \pm .5774, \text{ or}$$

from -.5774 to .5774 contains *at least* 75% of the rounding errors.

d. The actual proportion of rounding errors between -.5774 and .5774 is equal to the area under the curve between these endpoints. Since these endpoints extend beyond the interval -.5 to .5, all or 100% of the distribution lies within two standard deviations of the mean.

6.6 The Exponential Distribution

The exponential probability distribution is a continuous probability distribution used to model random variables that are waiting times, or random variables that are lifetimes associated with electronic components. The exponential density function is given by

$$f(x) = \lambda e^{-\lambda x} \quad \text{for} \quad x > 0;\ \lambda > 0$$

The mean and standard deviation depend only on the parameter λ with

$$\mu = 1/\lambda \quad \text{and} \quad \sigma = 1/\lambda$$

so that for the exponential distribution, $\mu = \sigma$. If the number of events occurring in a given unit of time follows a Poisson distribution with an average of μ events per unit time, then the waiting time for the next event follows an exponential distribution with mean waiting time of $\mu = 1/\lambda$.

Evaluating probabilities associated with an exponential random variable can be simplified by using the following result for *right-tailed* probabilities: $P[x > a] = e^{-\lambda a}$ for $a > 0$. Once the values of λ and a are known, $e^{-\lambda a}$ can be found from Table 2 in the Appendix or by using a calculator that has an exponential function key.

Example 6.15

Suppose that the waiting time at a grocery chain checkout counter follows an exponential distribution with an average waiting time of 10 minutes.

a. What is the probability that you wait longer than 12 minutes at a checkout counter?
b. What is the probability that you wait longer than 15 minutes?
c. With probability .05 you will wait longer than how many minutes at a checkout counter?

Solution

If x, the waiting time at a grocery chain checkout counter follows an exponential distribution with mean 10 minutes, then $\lambda = 1/10$ and

$$P[x > a] = e^{-(a/10)}$$

a. To evaluate

$$P[x > 12] = e^{-(12/10)} = e^{-1.2}$$

from Table 2, we see that $e^{-1.2} = .301194$. Therefore,

$$P[x > 12] = .3012$$

b. Similarly,

$$P[x > 15] = e^{-(15/10)} = e^{-1.5} = .223130$$

c. Since we wish to find a value of x, say x_0, with the property that

$$P[x > x_0] = .05,$$

we see that x_0 is the 95th percentile of the distribution. Hence, we need to solve

$$e^{-x_0/10} = .05$$

by using Table 2 or by solving the equation algebraically. From Table 2, we see that for $a = 2.95$, $e^{-2.95} = .052340$ while for $a = 3.00$, $e^{-3.00} = .049787$. Using linear interpolation, we have

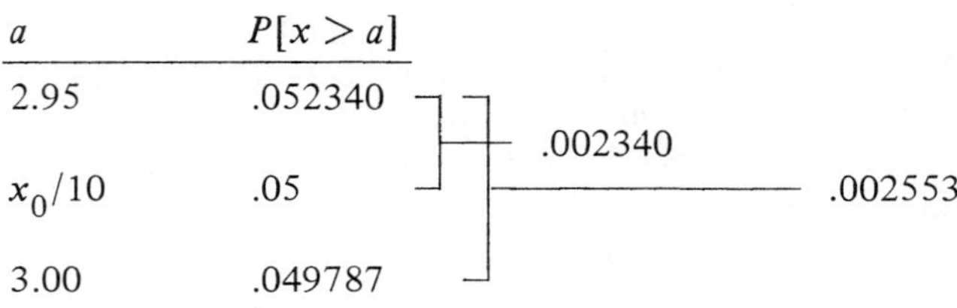

a	$P[x > a]$
2.95	.052340
$x_0/10$	.05
3.00	.049787

so that

$$x_0/10 = 2.95 + (.002340/.002553)(.05)$$
$$= 2.9958$$

and $\quad x_0 = 29.96$

Solving the equation directly, we have

$$e^{-x_0/10} = .05$$
$$\ln (e^{-x_0/10}) = \ln(.05)$$
$$-x_0/10 = -2.995732$$

or $\quad x_0 = 29.96$

which agrees with our earlier answer found using Table 2.

Self-Correcting Exercises 6D

1. When we round numbers to the nearest tenth, the rounding error is taken to be uniformly distributed between -.05 and .05.
   a. Find the probability that the rounding error will be greater than .025.
   b. Find the probability that the rounding error will be greater than .025 in magnitude.
   c. What is the mean of these rounding errors?
   d. Find the probability that the rounding error lies in the interval $\mu \pm \sigma$.
2. The length of useful life of an electronic component has an exponential distribution with a mean of 8 years.
   a. What is the probability that the component fails before 8 years?
   b. If five percent of these components last longer than x_0, what is the value of x_0?
   c. What is the median lifetime of these electronic components?
3. If calls arriving at a switchboard have a Poisson distribution with an average of 6 calls per minute, then the waiting time between calls has an exponential distribution with a mean waiting time of 10 seconds.
   a. Find the probability that the wating time between calls exceeds fifteen seconds.
   b. Find the probability that the waiting time is less than 5 seconds or greater than 15 seconds.
   c. Ninety percent of the time, the waiting time between calls is less than x_0. Find the value of x_0.
4. A library book is put on reserve in the library with a loan period of two hours. The time that the book used by a borrower is uniformly distributed over the interval from 0 to 2 hours.
   a. What is the mean and standard deviation of the time the book is used by a borrower?

b. What is the probability that a borrower keeps the book at most 1.5 hours?
c. What proportion of borrowers keep the book longer than 15 minutes, but not longer than the two hour limit?
d. Ninety-five percent of all borrowers keep the book at least how long?

EXERCISES

1. Find the following probabilites for the standard normal variable z.

a. $P[z < 1.9]$

b. $P[1.21 < z < 2.25]$

c. $P[z > -0.6]$

d. $P[-2.8 < z < 1.93]$

e. $P[-1.3 < z < 2.3]$

f. $P[-1.62 < z < 0.37]$

2. Find the value of z, say z_0, such that the following probability statements are true:

a. $P[z > z_0] = .2420$

b. $P[z < z_0] = .0668$

c. $P[z < z_0] = .9394$

d. $P[z > z_0] = .8643$

3. Find a value of z, say z_0, such that the following probability statements are true:

a. $P[-z_0 < z < z_0] = .9668$

b. $P[-z_0 < z < z_0] = .90$

4. If x is distributed normally with mean 25 and standard deviation 4, find

a. $P[x > 21]$

b. $P[x < 30]$

c. $P[15 < x < 35]$

d. $P[x < 18]$

5. The length of life of brand A television picture tubes is normally distributed with mean and standard deviation equal to 3.7 and 0.5 years, respectively. What is the probability that a tube
a. lasts at least 4 years?
b. lasts no longer than 4.5 years?

6. The test scores on a standardized examination are normally distributed with mean and standard deviation 75 and 9, respectively. What percentage of the scores
a. will be greater than 90?
b. will be less than 60?
c. will fall between 70 and 85?

7. For a given type of cannon and a fixed range setting, the distance that a shell fired from this cannon will travel is normally distributed with a mean and standard deviation of 1.5 and 0.1 miles, respectively. What is the probability that a shell will travel
a. farther than 1.72 miles?
b. less than 1.35 miles?
c. at least 1.45 miles but at most 1.62 miles?

8. For binomial experiment with $n = 20$ and $p = .7$, calculate $P[10 \leqslant x \leqslant 16]$
a. using the binomial tables.
b. using the normal approximation.

9. Using the information given in Exercise 8, repeat parts a and b for $P[x \geqslant 14]$.

10. A pre-election poll taken in a given city indicated that 40% of the voting public favored candidate A, 40% favored candidate B and 20% were as yet undecided. If these percentages are true, in a random sample of 100 voters what is the probability that

a. at most 50 voters in the sample prefer candidate A?
b. at least 65 voters in the sample prefer candidate B?
c. at least 25 but at most 45 voters in the sample prefer candidate B?

11. In introducing a new breakfast sausage to the marketing public, an advertising campaign claimed that 7 out of 10 shoppers would prefer these new sausages over other brands. If 100 people were randomly chosen, and the advertiser's claim is true, what is the probability that
    a. at most 65 people preferred the new sausages?
    b. at least 80 people preferred the new sausages?
    c. If only 60 people stated a preference for the new sausages, would this be sufficient evidence to indicate that the advertising claim is false and that in fact, less than 7 out of 10 people would prefer the new sausages?
12. Assuming that x is normally distributed with $\mu = 5$ and $\sigma^2 = 9$, find
    a. $P[2 \leqslant x \leqslant 8]$
    b. $P[-4 \leqslant x \leqslant 2]$
13. A manufacturer's process for producing steel rods can be regulated so as to produce rods with an average length of μ. If these lengths are normally distributed with a standard deviation of 0.2 inches, what should be the setting for μ if one wants at most 5% of the steel rods to have a length greater than 10.4 inches?
14. A manufacturing plant produces flashlight batteries that have a length of life which is normally distributed with mean and standard deviation equal to 300 and 25 hours, respectively. What percentage of the batteries produced will last at least 340 hours?
15. On a college campus, the student automobile registration revealed that the ratio of small to large cars (as measured by engine displacement) is 2 to 1 If 72 car owners are chosen at random from the student body, find the probability that this group includes at most 46 owners of small cars. (Use the normal approximation with the correction for continuity to find this probability.)
16. A psychological "introvert-extrovert" test produced scores which had a normal distribution with mean and standard deviation 75 and 12, respectively. If we wish to designate the *highest* 15% as extrovert, what would be the proper score to choose as the cut off point?

17. A large supermarket is located so as to service both in-town and out-of-town customers. If 60% of its customers are townspeople, use the normal approximation to find the probability that 380 or more of the 600 customers on a given day are townspeople.
18. An auto insurance company has found from past experience that it must pay approximately 20% of its customer claims. Recent indications suggest a drop in this percentage. To obtain statistical support that the percentage of customer claims requiring payment is now less than 20%, the company will examine the next 100 claims. Let p be the fraction of customer claims that must be paid. Let x be the number of claims in the sample of 100 claims that require payment.
    a. State H_0 and H_a in terms of p.
    b. If the null hypothesis is rejected when x is 15 or less, use the normal approximation (with the correction for continuity) to find α, the probability of rejecting H_0 when it is, in fact, true.
    c. Use the normal approximation to find β, the probability of falsely accepting H_0 if p is actually .10.
19. The ages of employees in a certain industry are normally distributed with mean and standard deviation 30 and 2.5 years, respectively.
    a. What is the probability that a worker chosen at random from this industry will be 34 years of age or older?
    b. If three employees are randomly selected from this industry, what is the probability that all three will be 34 years of age or older?
20. The time required for a garbage truck to make a round-trip to a disposal site and back is uniformly distributed between 0 and 1.5 hours.
    a. What is the probability that a garbage truck makes its round-trip to the disposal site in less than 75 minutes?
    b. What is the probability that the truck requires more than an hour to complete the round-trip?
21. The daily demand for gasoline at a local gas station has an exponential distribution with a mean of 2000 gallons.
    a. What proportion of the time would the demand exceed 4000 gallons?
    b. What proportion of the time would the demand exceed 1000 gallons, but be less than 4000 gallons?
    c. Ninety-five percent of the time, the demand would be less than what amount?

22. The time required to repair an electronic appliance has an exponential distribution with a mean repair time of one hour.
    a. What is the mean and standard deviation of repair times?
    b. Find the probability that the repair time exceeds $\mu + \sigma$?
    c. Fifty percent of all repair times will be shorter than x_0. What is the value of x_0?

Chapter 7

SAMPLING AND SAMPLING DISTRIBUTIONS

7.1 Introduction

Recall from earlier discussions that a population of measurements results when an experiment is repeated an infinite number of times. This population can be described using numerical descriptive measures called ______________ . A sample is some subset of the population, and can be described using numerical descriptive measures called ______________ . One of our objectives will be to use statistics (calculated from the sample) to make inferences about (or to estimate) a population parameter.

parameters

statistics

Since a statistic is computed from sample measurements, to observe the statistic over and over again, we must sample repeatedly. This repeated sampling will generate a population of possible values of the statistic. The frequency distribution associated with the population of values of the statistic is called its ______________ ______________ . Specifically, since it is generated through repeated sampling, this probability distribution is called a *sampling distribution*.

probability distribution

In this chapter, we will try to clarify the concept of a sampling distribution by deriving the sampling distributions for several statistics when sampling randomly from a finite population. We will then generalize our discussion to include random sampling from an infinite population and consider the sampling distributions of some important sample statistics.

7.2 Sampling Distributions

In making inferences about a population based on information contained in a sample, we will use sample statistics to estimate and/or make decisions about population ______________ .

parameters

Notice that each sample drawn from a population of interest to the experimenter will contain different elements. Hence, the value of a statistic (such as change — $\bar{x}$ or s^2) will (change, remain the same) from sample to sample. If one were to draw repeated samples of a constant sample size, many different values of the sample statistic would be obtained. These values could be used to create a relative frequency distribution to describe the behavior of the statistic in repeated sampling.

random variable — Since a sample statistic takes on many different numerical values depending upon the outcome of a random sample, it is classified as a ______________ ______________, and, as such, has a probability distribution associated with it. This probability distribution can be approximated by the relative frequency distribution described above.

The probability distribution for a sample statistic is called its *sampling distribution.* The sampling distribution results when random samples of size n are repeatedly drawn from the population of interest.

Example 7.1

Consider a population of $N = 6$ elements whose values are $x = 3, 3.5, 3.5, 4, 4$, and 6. If each of the population values are equally likely to be selected in a single random selection, construct the probability distribution for x. Find the mean and the variance of x.

Solution

1/6 — 1. Since each of the $N = 6$ elements has an equal chance of being selected, each has probability $1/N =$ __________ . However, some of the elements are identical. Thus,

1/6 — $p(3) =$ __________

1/6; 1/3 — but $p(3.5) = 1/6 +$ __________ $=$ __________ .

The probability distribution for x is shown below. Fill in the missing entries.

x	$p(x)$
3	1/6
3.5	________
4	1/3
6	________

1/3 (for 3.5); 1/6 (for 6)

2. Graph the probability distribution for x. The distribution (is, is not) symmetrical. — is not

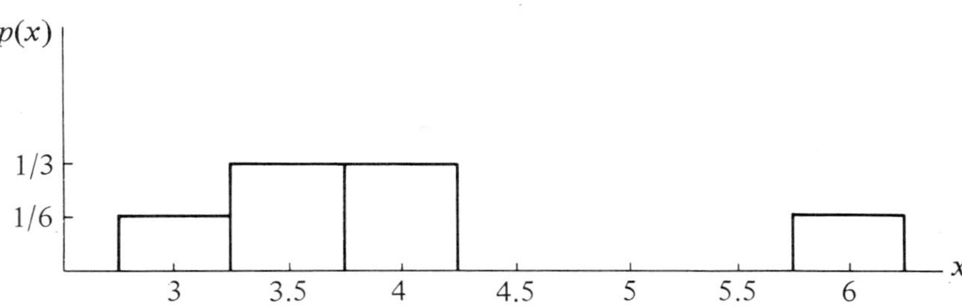

3. The mean value of x is calculated as in Chapter 4.

$$\mu = E(x) = \sum_x xp(x) = 3(1/6) + 3.5(1/3) + 4(1/3) + 6(1/6)$$

$$= 4.0$$

The variance of x is

$$\sigma^2 = \Sigma(x - \mu)^2 p(x) = \Sigma x^2 p(x) - \mu^2$$

$$= 3^2(1/6) + 3.5^2(1/3) + 4^2(1/3) + 6^2(1/6) - (\_\_\_\_\_\_)^2$$ — 4.0

$$= \_\_\_\_\_\_ - 16 = \_\_\_\_\_\_$$ — 16.9166667; .9166667

Example 7.2
Find the sampling distribution for the sample mean $\bar{x}$ when a random sample of size $n = 2$ has been drawn from the population given in Example 7.1.

Solution
When $n = 2$ observations are drawn from $N = 6$, there are $C_2^6 =$ ______ possible samples which can be drawn with equal probability. Since some of the elements in this sample are identical, let us identify the repeated measurements as 3.5 and 3.5*, 4 and 4*, respectively. The 15 possible samples are listed below. Fill in the missing entries in Column 2. — 15

	Sample	Sample Values	$\bar{x}$
	1	3, 3.5	3.25
	2	3, 3.5*	3.25
3.50	3	3, 4	______
	4	3, 4*	3.50
	5	3, 6	4.50
	6	3.5, 3.5*	3.50
3.75	7	3.5, 4	______
3.5, 4*	8	______	3.75
	9	3.5, 6	4.75
	10	3.5*, 4	3.75
3.5*, 4*	11	______	3.75
4.75	12	3.5*, 6	______
	13	4, 4*	4.00
5.00	14	4, 6	______
4*, 6	15	______	5.00

For each possible sample, the sample mean can be different. For example, sample 1 has mean

$$\bar{x} = \frac{3 + 3.5}{2} = 3.25$$

while for sample 9,

4.75 $$\bar{x} = \frac{3.5 + 6}{2} = \_\_\_\_\_\_$$

Fill in the missing entries in Column 3 of the sample table above. The value of $\bar{x}$ associated with each sample occurs with probability 1/15. The sampling distribution for $\bar{x}$ is shown and graphed below.

	$\bar{x}$	$p(\bar{x})$
	3.25	2/15
	3.50	3/15
	3.75	4/15
1/15	4.00	______
	4.50	1/15
4.75	______	2/15
	5.00	2/15

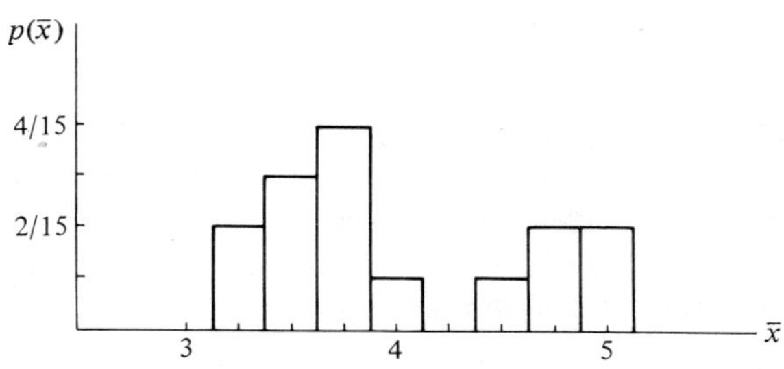

Notice several things in comparing the original population distribution to the sampling distribution of $\bar{x}$.

1. The distribution of $\bar{x}$ is (more, less) variable than the original distribution. less
2. The distribution of $\bar{x}$ appears (more, less) skewed than the original distribution. less
3. The mean of $\bar{x}$ is

$$\mu_{\bar{x}} = 3.25(2/15) + 3.5(3/15) + \ldots + 5(2/15)$$

$$= 4.0$$

which is identical to the mean of the original population.

4. The variance of $\bar{x}$ is

$$\sigma_{\bar{x}}^2 = 3.25^2(2/15) + 3.5^2(\_\_\_\_\_\_\_\_) + 3.75^2(4/15) + \ldots$$ 3/15

$$+ 5^2(2/15) - (\_\_\_\_\_\_\_\_)^2$$ 4.0

$$= \_\_\_\_\_\_\_\_ - 16 = \_\_\_\_\_\_\_\_$$ 16.366667; .36667

The variance of $\bar{x}$ is (smaller, larger) than the variance of x, confirming our earlier observation. smaller

Sampling distributions can be constructed for any finite population using this same method. For example, the experimenter might be interested in the sampling distribution of the sample median, the sample variance, s^2, or the sample standard deviation, s. For each possible sample, he calculates the value of the sample statistic and then uses the results to tabulate the appropriate sampling distribution and to describe the behavior of that statistic in repeated sampling. However, as N increases, it becomes extremely difficult to actually enumerate each sample, unless it can be done empirically on a computer. For this reason, we turn to results proven using algebra or higher mathematics to derive the sampling distributions for several commonly used statistics. It can be shown that some of these statistics have desirable properties which will be useful in inference making.

Self-Correcting Exercises 7A

1. Refer to Example 7.1. For the population given as $x = 3, 3.5, 3.5, 4, 4, 6$,
   a. Find the sampling distribution for the sample median, m, when $n = 2$.
   b. Is the sampling distribution more or less variable than the original population?
   c. Is the expected value of the sample median equal to the population median?

2. For the population described in Exercise 1,
   a. Find the sampling distribution for $\bar{x}$ when $n = 3$ elements are chosen in the sample.
   b. Find the expected value of $\bar{x}$. Does it equal the population mean?
   c. Find the variance of $\bar{x}$. Compare the variance of $\bar{x}$ when $n = 2$ and $n = 3$ to the variance of the original population. What is the effect of increasing the sample size on the value of $\sigma_{\bar{x}}^2$?
3. Consider the finite population given as $x = 3, 4, 5, 6$. A sample of size $n = 3$ is drawn from this population.
   a. Find the sampling distribution of the sample variance, s^2.
   b. Find the expected value of s^2, using the sampling distribution from part a.
   c. Find σ^2, the variance of the original population. Compare to the results of part b.

7.3 The Central Limit Theorem and the Sampling Distribution of $\bar{x}$

Consider a meat processing center which as part of its output prepares one-pound packages of bacon. If the weights of the packaged bacon were carefully checked, some weights would be slightly heavier than 16 oz. while others would be slightly lighter than 16 oz. A frequency histogram of these weights would probably exhibit the mound-shaped distribution characteristic of a normally distributed random variable. Why should this be the case? One can think of the weight of each package as differing from 16 oz. due to an error in the weighing process, to a scale that needs adjustment, to the thickness of the slices of bacon so that the package contains either one more or less slice than it should, or perhaps some of the fat has melted, and so on. Hence any one weight would consist of an average weight (hopefully 16 oz.) modified by the addition of random errors that might be either positive or negative.

The Central Limit Theorem loosely stated says that sums or averages are approximately normally distributed with a mean and standard deviation that depend upon the sampled population. If one considers the error in the weight of a one-pound package of bacon as a *sum* of various effects in which small errors are highly likely and large errors are highly improbable, then the Central Limit Theorem helps explain the apparent normality of the package weights.

Equally as important, the Central Limit Theorem assures us that sample means will be approximately normally distributed with a mean and variance that depend upon the population from which the sample has been drawn. This aspect of the Central Limit Theorem will be the focal point for making inferences about populations based upon random samples when the sample size is large.

The Central Limit Theorem (1): If random samples of n observations are drawn from a population with finite mean μ and standard deviation σ, then when n is large, the sample mean $\bar{x}$ will be approximately normally distributed with mean μ and standard deviation $\sigma/\sqrt{n}$.

The quantity $\sigma/\sqrt{n}$ is sometimes called the *standard error* of $\bar{x}$. The Central Limit Theorem could also be stated in terms of the sum of the measurements, Σx_i.

The Central Limit Theorem (2): If random samples of n observations are drawn from a population with finite mean μ and standard deviation σ, then when n is large, Σx_i will be approximately normally distributed with mean $n\mu$ and standard deviation $\sigma\sqrt{n}$.

In both cases the approximation to normality becomes more and more accurate as n becomes large.

The Central Limit Theorem is important for two reasons.

1. It partially explains *why* certain measurements possess approximately a ____________ distribution. normal
2. Many of the ____________ used in making inferences are sums or means of sample measurements and thus possess approximately ____________ distributions for large samples. Notice that the Central Limit Theorem (does, does not) specify that the sample measurements come from a normal population. The population (could, could not) have a frequency distribution that is flat or skewed or is nonnormal in some other way. It is the *sample mean* that behaves as a random variable having an approximately normal distribution. estimators normal does not could

To clarify a point we note that the sample mean $\bar{x}$ computed from a random sample of n observations drawn from any infinite population with mean μ and standard deviation σ always has a mean equal to μ and a standard deviation equal to $\sigma/\sqrt{n}$. This result is not due to the Central Limit Theorem. The important contribution of the theorem lies in the fact that when n, the sample size, is *large*, we may approximate the distribution of $\bar{x}$ with a *normal* probability distribution.

The Central Limit Theorem relies heavily on the assumption that the sample size n is large. The question of how large n must be is a difficult one to answer and depends upon the characteristics of the underlying population from which we are sampling. Many texts use the rule of thumb that allows application of the Central Limit Theorem if $n > 30$. However, this rule will not always work. If the underlying distribution is (symmetric, skewed), the symmetric

heavily skewed

Central Limit Theorem may be appropriate for $n < 30$. However, if the underlying population is (symmetric, heavily skewed), the distribution of $\bar{x}$ may still be skewed even if $n > 30$. The student will need to use judgment to determine the approximate shape of the underlying population from which he or she is sampling in order to determine whether the Central Limit Theorem will be appropriate. For specific types of applications given in the text, we will provide the sample sizes necessary to insure the applicability of the Central Limit Theorem.

Example 7.3

A production line produces items whose mean weight is 50 grams with a standard deviation of 2 grams. If 25 items are randomly selected from this production line, what is the probability that the same mean $\bar{x}$ exceeds 51 grams?

Solution

approximately symmetric; will

The underlying population from which we are sampling is the population of weights of items on the production line. Since weights tend to have a mound-shaped distribution, the sampled population is (approximately symmetric, heavily skewed). Thus, the Central Limit Theorem (will, will not) be appropriate.

According to the Central Limit Theorem, the sample mean $\bar{x}$ is approximately normally distributed with mean μ and standard deviation $\sigma/\sqrt{n}$. For our problem $\mu = 50$, $\sigma = 2$, and $n = 25$; hence

.4

$$\sigma_{\bar{x}} = \frac{\sigma}{\sqrt{n}} = \frac{2}{\sqrt{25}} = \underline{\qquad\qquad}$$

Therefore

$$P(\bar{x} > 51) = P\left(\frac{\bar{x} - 50}{.4} > \frac{51 - 50}{.4}\right)$$

$$= P(z > 2.5)$$

$$= .5000 - A(2.5)$$

.4938

$$= .5000 - \underline{\qquad\qquad}$$

.0062

$$= \underline{\qquad\qquad}$$

Example 7.4

A bottler of soft drinks packages cans of soft drink in six-packs.

1. If the fill per can has a mean of 12 fluid ounces and a standard deviation of .2 fluid ounce, what is the distribution of the total fill for a case of 24 cans?

2. What is the probability that the total fill for a case is less than 286 fluid ounces?

Solution

The population from which we are sampling is the population of fills per can, which (should, should not) be an approximately symmetric distribution. Therefore, for $n = 24$, the Central Limit Theorem (will, will not) be applicable.

should
will

1. Using the Central Limit Theorem in its second form, the total fill per case has a mean of $n\mu = 24(12) =$ ________ fluid ounces and a standard deviation (or standard error) of $\sigma\sqrt{24} = .2\sqrt{24} =$ ________ fluid ounce. The total fill is approximately ________ distributed with mean 288 and standard deviation .98.

288
.98
normally

2. Let T represent the total fill per case. We wish to evaluate $P(T < 286)$. Since T is approximately normally distributed with $\mu_T =$ ________ and $\sigma_T =$ ________ ,

288
.98

$$P(T < 286) = P\left(\frac{T - 288}{.98} < \frac{286 - 288}{.98}\right) = P(z < -2.04)$$

$$= .5000 - A(-2.04) = .5000 - \_\_\_\_\_ = \_\_\_\_\_$$

.4793; .0207

The Central Limit Theorem applies when a sufficiently (large, small) sample is randomly drawn from a very large or infinite population, regardless of its shape. However, if the population from which we are sampling is itself normal, the sampling distribution of $\bar{x}$ will be ________, regardless of the size of the sample.

large

normal

If a random sample is drawn from a *normal population* with mean μ and variance σ^2, the sampling distribution of $\bar{x}$ will be normal with mean μ and variance σ^2/n, *regardless of the sample size.*

Example 7.5

Suppose that the bottler of soft drinks in Example 7.4 packages cans of soft drinks in cans whose fill per can is normally distributed with mean 12 fluid ounces and standard deviation .2 fluid ounces. If a six-pack of soda can be considered a random sample of size $n = 6$ from the population, what is the probability that the average fill per can is less than 11.5 fluid ounces?

Solution

1. Since we are sampling from a ________ population, the sampling distribution of $\bar{x}$ will be (approximately, exactly) normal with mean $\mu =$ 12 fluid ounces and variance $\sigma^2/n = .2/6 =$ ________ .

normal
exactly
.033333

$\bar{x} < 11.5$

2. We wish to evaluate $P($__________$)$, or

$$P(\bar{x} < 11.5) = P\left(\frac{\bar{x} - \mu}{\sigma/\sqrt{n}} < \frac{11.5 - 12}{\sqrt{.03333}}\right)$$

-2.74

$$= P(z < \_\_\_\_\_\_\_\_\_\_)$$

.4969; .0031

$$= .5 - \_\_\_\_\_\_\_\_\_\_ = \_\_\_\_\_\_\_\_\_\_$$

may not

Suppose now that we are not sampling from a normal population; further, suppose that the population is not infinite. If we are sampling randomly from a *finite* population, the Central Limit Theorem (may, may not) apply. However, the following statements can be made about the sampling distribution of $\bar{x}$.

When a random sample of size n is drawn from a finite population of size N with mean μ and variance σ^2, the sampling distribution of $\bar{x}$ will have a mean or expected value equal to the population mean μ and a variance equal to

$$\sigma_{\bar{x}}^2 = \frac{\sigma^2}{n}\left(\frac{N - n}{N - 1}\right)$$

Notice the following:

1. If the population size N is large relative to the sample size, the *population correction factor,*

$$\frac{N - n}{N - 1} = \frac{N - 1}{N - 1} - \frac{n - 1}{N - 1}$$

is very close to one. For example, if $N = 10{,}000$ and $n = 100$,

.99

$$\frac{N - n}{N - 1} = \frac{9900}{9999} = \_\_\_\_\_\_\_\_\_\_$$

Therefore, as N increases, $\sigma_{\bar{x}}^2$ is approximately equal to σ^2/n, the variance of $\bar{x}$ in the case of an infinite population.

increase

decreases

2. As the original population variance increases, the variance of $\bar{x}$ will (increase, decrease). As the sample size increases (providing more information about the population), the variance of $\bar{x}$ (increases, decreases).

Example 7.6

Refer to Examples 7.1 and 7.2. Use the sampling distribution of $\bar{x}$ obtained in those examples to confirm that

$$\mu_{\bar{x}} = \mu$$

$$\sigma_{\bar{x}}^2 = \frac{\sigma^2}{n}\left(\frac{N-n}{N-1}\right)$$

Solution

1. From Example 7.2, we have $\mu_{\bar{x}} = 4$ while from Example 7.1 we have $\mu =$ __________. — 4
2. The variance of $\bar{x}$, calculated directly from the sampling distribution in Example 7.2 is $\sigma_{\bar{x}}^2 =$ __________. Using the derived result for finite populations, calculate — .36667

$$\frac{\sigma^2}{n}\left(\frac{N-n}{N-1}\right) = \frac{.916667}{2}\left(\frac{\_\_\_\_}{6-1}\right)$$ — $6 - 2$

$$= .916667\left(\_\_\_\_\right) = \_\_\_\_\_\_\_\_$$ — $\frac{4}{10}$; .36667

which (is, is not) identical to the result obtained by direct calculation. Hence, it is not necessary to derive the entire sampling distribution in order to calculate the appropriate mean and variance. — is

Self-Correcting Exercises 7B

1. A pharmaceutical company is experimenting with rats to determine if there is a difference in weights for rats fed with and without a vitamin supplement. A frequency distribution of these weights (either with or without the supplement) would probably exhibit the mound-shaped distribution characteristics of a normally distributed random variable. Why should this be the case?
2. An agricultural economist is interested in determining the average diameter of peaches produced by a particular tree. A random sample of $n = 30$ peaches is taken and the sample mean $\bar{x}$ is calculated. Suppose that the average diameter of peaches on this tree is known from previous years' production to be $\mu = 60$ millimeters with $\sigma = 10$ mm. What is the probability that the sample mean, $\bar{x}$, exceeds 65 millimeters?
3. Refer to Exercise 2, Self-Correcting Exercises 7A.
   a. When sampling $n = 3$ elements from the finite population consisting of $N = 6$ elements, $x = 3, 3.5, 3.5, 4, 4, 6$ what is the mean or expected value of $\bar{x}$?
   b. What is the variance of $\bar{x}$?
   c. Compare the derived results of parts a and b with those calculated directly from the sampling distribution of $\bar{x}$ in Exercise 2, Self-Correcting Exercises 7A.

7.4 The Sampling Distribution of the Sample Proportion

A statistic that is often used to describe a binomial population is $\hat{p}$, the *proportion* of trials in which a success is observed. In terms of previous notation,

$$\hat{p} = \frac{x}{n} = \frac{\text{number of successes in } n \text{ trials}}{n}$$

Recall that, for a binomial population, the proportion of successes in the population is defined as p. The sample proportion, $\hat{p}$, will be used to estimate or make inferences about p.

For a binomial experiment consisting of n trials, let

$x_1 = 1$ if trial one is a success
$x_1 = 0$ if trial one is a failure

$x_2 = 1$ if trial two is a success
$x_2 = 0$ if trial two is a failure

.
.
.

$x_n = 1$ if trial n is a success
$x_n = 0$ if trial n is a failure

average; Central Limit Theorem

Then x, the number of successes in n trials, can be thought of as a sum of n independent random variables. Using this fact, the statistic $\hat{p} = x/n$ is equivalent to an ______________ of these n random variables. The ______________ ______________ ______________ assures us that $\hat{p}$ will be approximately normally distributed when n is large. The mean and standard deviation of $\hat{p}$ can be shown to be

$$\mu_{\hat{p}} = p \quad \text{and} \quad \sigma_{\hat{p}} = \sqrt{\frac{p(1-p)}{n}} = \sqrt{\frac{pq}{n}}$$

Example 7.7

Past records show that at a given college 20% of the students that began as economics majors either changed their major or dropped out of school. An incoming class has 110 beginning economics majors. What is the probability that at most 30% of these students leave the economics program?

Solution

1. If p represents the proportion of students leaving the economics program, with the probability of losing a student given as $p = .2$, then the required probability for $n = 110$ is $P(\hat{p} \leqslant .30)$.

2. To use the normal approximation, we need

$$\mu_{\hat{p}} = p = \_\_\_\_\_\_\_\_$$ .2

$$\sigma_{\hat{p}} = \sqrt{\frac{p(1-p)}{n}} = \sqrt{\frac{.2(\_\_\_\_\_\_\_\_)}{110}} = \sqrt{\_\_\_\_\_\_\_\_}$$ .8; .0014545

$$= \_\_\_\_\_\_\_\_$$ .0381

We now proceed to approximate the probability required in part 1 by using a normal probability distribution with a mean of ________ and a standard deviation of ________ . .2 .0381

3. Using the normal approximation, the value $\hat{p} = .30$ corresponds to a z value of

$$z = \frac{\hat{p} - p}{\sigma_{\hat{p}}} = \frac{.30 - .20}{.0381} = \_\_\_\_\_\_\_\_$$ 2.62

and

$$P(\hat{p} \leqslant .30) \approx P(z \leqslant \_\_\_\_\_\_\_\_) = .5000 + \_\_\_\_\_\_\_\_ = \_\_\_\_\_\_\_\_$$ 2.62; .4956; .9956

In Chapter 6, we used the normal approximation to the binomial distribution to calculate probabilities associated with x, the number of successes in n trials. In that situation, it was necessary to have the interval $\mu \pm 2\sigma$ or $np \pm 2\sqrt{npq}$ fall within the binomial limits, 0 to n, in order to insure the accuracy of the approximation. Further, a "correction for continuity" was used to make the approximation more accurate. Hence, the standard normal random variable used in this earlier approximation was

$$z = \frac{x \pm \frac{1}{2} - np}{\sqrt{npq}} \approx \frac{x - np}{\sqrt{npq}}$$

If we divide both numerator and denominator of this fraction by n, we see the relationship between the sampling distributions of x and $\hat{p} = x/n$.

$$z = \frac{\frac{x}{n} \pm \frac{1}{2n} - p}{\sqrt{\frac{pq}{n}}} = \frac{\hat{p} \pm \frac{1}{2n} - p}{\sqrt{\frac{pq}{n}}} \approx \frac{\hat{p} - p}{\sqrt{\frac{pq}{n}}}$$

Hence, the sampling distributions of x and $\hat{p}$ (are, are not) equivalent. *The quantity $\pm\, 1/2n$ will be ignored for large values of n, since the value of z* are *changes very little.* The normal approximation will be appropriate if the interval $p \pm 2\sqrt{pq/n}$ falls within the limits 0 to 1.

Self-Correcting Exercises 7C

1. For a binomial experiment with $n = 20$ and $p = .5$, calculate $P(.8 \leqslant \hat{p} \leqslant .9)$ by
   a. Using the binomial tables, Table 1.
   b. Using the normal approximation to the sampling distribution of $\hat{p}$.
2. A controversial issue during the 1981 election in the state of California was a proposition to secure money to build the peripheral water canal, a canal designed to bring water from northern to southern regions of the state. Suppose that 30% of the population favor the canal, while 70% oppose it. If a random sample of $n = 50$ voters is taken, what is the probability that 50% or more favor the canal? That is, what is the probability that the sample will show a majority in favor of the canal when in fact only 30% of the population favor it?

7.5 The Sampling Distribution of the Difference Between Two Sample Means or Proportions

Chapters 2 through 7 have been concerned with statistics, the science of making inferences about a population based on information contained in a sample, as it relates to a single population of measurements of interest to the experimenter. In particular, Sections 7.3 and 7.4 involved a discussion of the sampling distributions of two important statistics:

1. The sample proportion, $\hat{p}$, based on a sample drawn from a binomial population.
2. The sample mean, $\bar{x}$, based on a sample drawn from a population of continuous measurements.

In practice, an experimenter is often concerned with two populations of measurements; and in general, is interested in knowing whether or not these populations have the same location parameters. In the case of two populations of continuous measurements, this involves a comparison of the two parameters μ_1 and μ_2, which will be made by studying the difference, $\mu_1 - \mu_2$. In the case of two binomial populations, it involves a comparison of the two parameters p_1 and p_2, which will be made by studying the difference, $p_1 - p_2$.

Example 7.8

A pharmaceutical company is interested in the effect of vitamin C on the average cholesterol level in the human body. They design an experiment in which two groups of people will be placed on a specified diet for a given length of time. One group's diet will be supplemented with a particular dose of vitamin C, while the other group's diet will not. The researchers are interested in measuring the difference in the average cholesterol levels for the two groups.

Example 7.9
An agricultural economist is interested in determining the effect of two types of fertilizer on the yield of an apple orchard. He selects 40 trees to be fertilized with one type of fertilizer, while another 40 in a different location within the orchard are fertilized with the second type of fertilizer. The economist is interested in measuring the difference in yield for two fertilizers.

Example 7.10
The political preferences of executives at two large corporations were compared, based on 50 executives from each corporation. The percentage of Democrats were recorded for each, and the difference in the two percentages was recorded.

In all of the above situations, the experimenter is considering two populations, which will be denoted as Population 1 and Population 2. In the first two examples, the populations consist of continuous measurements, although the populations are in fact hypothetical in nature. They involve the conceptual populations of measurements taken on all experimental units (people or trees) that could possibly be treated with the experimental treatment (vitamin C or fertilizer). We are concerned with making inferences about the difference in the two population means, $\mu_1 - \mu_2$. In Example 7.10, the populations are approximately binomial, since the corporations and the number of executives in each corporation are very large. The parameter of interest is $p_1 - p_2$, the difference in the proportion of Democrats in the two corporations.

Consider two populations, 1 and 2, from which we select two independent random samples of size n_1 and n_2, respectively. Sample statistics will be calculated for each of the two samples. In general, denote these sample statistics by y_1 and y_2. We will use the following theorem, which gives the sample distribution for the difference $(y_1 - y_2)$ in two specific situations. It will be used to obtain the sampling distribution for $\bar{x}_1 - \bar{x}_2$ and to obtain the sampling distribution for $\hat{p}_1 - \hat{p}_2$.

Theorem 7.1: If two independent random variables y_1 and y_2 are normally distributed with means μ_1 and μ_2 and variances σ_1^2 and σ_2^2, respectively, then the difference $(y_1 - y_2)$ will be normally distributed with mean $(\mu_1 - \mu_2)$ and variance $(\sigma_1^2 + \sigma_2^2)$.

---

1. If samples of size n_1 and n_2 are randomly and independently selected from two continuous populations with means μ_1 and μ_2, respectively, a statistic

that can be formed in order to make inferences about the difference $(\mu_1 - \mu_2)$ is __________ . If n_1 and n_2 are both larger than __________ , the __________ __________ Theorem allows us to make the following two statements:

$(\bar{x}_1 - \bar{x}_2)$; 30
Central Limit

a. $\bar{x}_1$ is approximately __________ distributed with mean $\mu_{\bar{x}_1}$ = __________ and variance

$$\sigma^2_{\bar{x}_1} = \_\_\_\_\_\_$$

normally
μ_1
$\dfrac{\sigma_1^2}{n_1}$

b. $\bar{x}_2$ is approximately __________ distributed with mean $\mu_{\bar{x}_2}$ = __________ and variance

$$\sigma^2_{\bar{x}_2} = \_\_\_\_\_\_$$

normally
μ_2
$\dfrac{\sigma_2^2}{n_2}$

Finally, using Theorem 7.1, $(\bar{x}_1 - \bar{x}_2)$ will be approximately normally distributed with mean

$$\mu_{\bar{x}_1 - \bar{x}_2} = \mu_1 - \mu_2$$

and variance

$$\sigma^2_{\bar{x}_1 - \bar{x}_2} = \frac{\sigma_1^2}{n_1} + \frac{\sigma_2^2}{n_2}$$

The standard deviation of $\bar{x}_1 - \bar{x}_2$, sometimes called the *standard error*, is

$$\sigma^2_{\bar{x}_1 - \bar{x}_2} = \sqrt{\_\_\_\_\_\_}$$

$\dfrac{\sigma_1^2}{n_1} + \dfrac{\sigma_2^2}{n_2}$

2. If samples of size n_1 and n_2 are independently drawn from two binomial populations with parameters p_1 and p_2, respectively, a statistic that can be formed in order to make inferences about the difference $(p_1 - p_2)$ is __________ , where

$(\hat{p}_1 - \hat{p}_2)$

$$\hat{p}_1 = \frac{x_1}{n_1} = \frac{\text{number of successes in sample 1}}{\text{number of trials in sample 1}}$$

and

$$\hat{p}_2 = \frac{x_2}{n_2} = \frac{\text{number of successes in sample 2}}{\text{number of trials in sample 2}}$$

As long as $p \pm 2\sqrt{pq/n}$ lies within the range 0 to 1 for both populations, the ______________ ______________ Theorem allows us to make the following two statements:

Central Limit

a. $\hat{p}_1$ is approximately ______________ distributed with mean

normally

$$\mu_{p_1} = \_\_\_\_\_\_\_\_$$

p_1

and variance

$$\sigma^2_{\hat{p}_1} = \_\_\_\_\_\_\_\_$$

$\dfrac{p_1 q_1}{n_1}$

3. $\hat{p}_2$ is approximately ______________ distributed with mean

normally

$$\mu_{\hat{p}_2} = \_\_\_\_\_\_\_\_$$

p_2

and variance

$$\sigma^2_{\hat{p}_2} = \_\_\_\_\_\_\_\_$$

$\dfrac{p_2 q_2}{n_2}$

Using Theorem 7.1, the sampling distribution of $(\hat{p}_1 - \hat{p}_2)$ is approximately normal with mean

$$\mu_{\hat{p}_1 - \hat{p}_2} = \_\_\_\_\_\_\_\_$$

$p_1 - p_2$

and variance

$$\sigma^2_{\hat{p}_1 - \hat{p}_2} = \_\_\_\_\_\_\_\_$$

$\dfrac{p_1 q_1}{n_1} + \dfrac{p_2 q_2}{n_2}$

The standard deviation of $(\hat{p}_1 - \hat{p}_2)$ is

$$\sigma_{\hat{p}_1 - \hat{p}_2} = \sqrt{\frac{p_1 q_1}{n_1} + \frac{p_2 q_2}{n_2}}$$

The sampling distributions for $\bar{x}_1 - \bar{x}_2$ and $\hat{p}_1 - \hat{p}_2$ can be used to make probability statements about the behavior of $\bar{x}_1 - \bar{x}_2$ or $\hat{p}_1 - \hat{p}_2$ in repeated sampling.

Example 7.11

Random samples of size $n_1 = 50$ and $n_2 = 40$ are drawn from two continuous populations with equal means and equal variances, $\sigma_1^2 = \sigma_2^2 = 10$. What is the probability that the sample means will differ by more than 1?

Solution

1. The sampling distribution of $\bar{x}_1 - \bar{x}_2$ is approximately normal with mean

$$\mu_{\bar{x}_1 - \bar{x}_2} = \mu_1 - \mu_2 = \_\_\_\_\_\_\_\_$$

0

since $\mu_1 = \mu_2$. The standard deviation of $\bar{x}_1 - \bar{x}_2$ is

10; .45; .6708

$$\sqrt{\frac{\sigma_1^2}{n_1} + \frac{\sigma_2^2}{n_2}} = \sqrt{\frac{\_\_\_\_\_\_}{50} + \frac{10}{40}} = \sqrt{\_\_\_\_\_\_} = \_\_\_\_\_\_$$

2. If $\bar{x}_1$ and $\bar{x}_2$ differ by more than 1, we could have either

$\bar{x}_2 - \bar{x}_1$

$$\bar{x}_1 - \bar{x}_2 > 1 \quad \text{or} \quad \_\_\_\_\_\_ > 1$$

< -1

The second inequality is equivalent to $\bar{x}_1 - \bar{x}_2$ ______, so that the probability of interest is

$$P(\bar{x}_1 - \bar{x}_2 > 1) + P(\bar{x}_1 - \bar{x}_2 < -1)$$

$$= P\left(\frac{(\bar{x}_1 - \bar{x}_2) - 0}{.6708} > \frac{1 - 0}{.6708}\right) + P\left(\frac{(\bar{x}_1 - \bar{x}_2) - 0}{.6708} < \frac{-1 - 0}{.6708}\right)$$

-1.49

$$= P(z > 1.49) + P(z < \_\_\_\_\_\_)$$

.4319; .1362

$$= 2(.5 - \_\_\_\_\_\_) = \_\_\_\_\_\_$$

14%

That is, $\bar{x}_1$ and $\bar{x}_2$ will differ by as much as 1 or more approximately ______ of the time, even when the population means are equal.

Example 7.12

A manufacturer of automobiles is conducting research to estimate the difference in the proportion of accidents on the California interstate system and on the New York interstate system that result in fatal injuries to at least one person. He randomly checks the files on 50 automobile accidents on the California interstate system and finds that 8 resulted in fatal injuries. He then randomly checks the files on 50 automobile accidents on the New York interstate system and finds that 9 resulted in fatal injuries. Suppose that the true proportion of fatal injuries is the same for both systems, and that in fact $p_1 = p_2 = .15$. What is the probability of observing a New York percentage at least 2 points higher than the California percentage, as was observed in this experiment?

Solution

1. The probability of interest is

$$P(\hat{p}_1 - \hat{p}_2 > .02)$$

New York
California

where $\hat{p}_1$ is the (New York, California) sample percentage and $\hat{p}_2$ is the (New York, California) sample percentage.

2. The sampling distribution of $\hat{p}_1 - \hat{p}_2$ is approximately normal with mean

$$\mu_{\hat{p}_1 - \hat{p}_2} = p_1 - p_2 = .15 - .15 = 0$$

and standard deviation

$$\sigma_{\hat{p}_1 - \hat{p}_2} = \sqrt{\frac{p_1 q_1}{n_1} + \frac{p_2 q_2}{n_2}} = \sqrt{\frac{.15(.85)}{\_\_\_\_\_\_} + \frac{.15(\_\_\_\_\_\_)}{50}}$$ .85 50

$$= \sqrt{2(\_\_\_\_\_\_)} = \sqrt{\_\_\_\_\_\_} = \_\_\_\_\_\_$$ .00255; .0051; .0714

3. The desired probability is

$$P(\hat{p}_1 - \hat{p}_2 > .02) = P\left(\frac{(\hat{p}_1 - \hat{p}_2) - 0}{.0714} > \frac{.02 - 0}{.0714}\right)$$

$$= P(z > \_\_\_\_\_\_)$$ .28

$$= .5 - \_\_\_\_\_\_ = \_\_\_\_\_\_$$ .1103; .3897

4. The sample result (is, is not) unlikely, even when the population proportions are identical. is not

Self-Correcting Exercises 7D

1. Random samples of size $n_1 = n_2 = 35$ are drawn from continuous populations with $\mu_1 = 20$, $\sigma_1^2 = 150$, $\mu_2 = 25$, $\sigma_2^2 = 100$. Find the following probabilities:
   a. $P(\bar{x}_1 - \bar{x}_2 > 1)$
   b. $P(0 \leqslant \bar{x}_1 - \bar{x}_2 \leqslant 6)$
   c. $P(|\bar{x}_1 - \bar{x}_2| \geqslant 2)$
2. Random samples of size $n_1 = n_2 = 100$ are drawn from binomial populations with $p_1 = .3$ and $p_2 = .4$. Find the following probabilities, describing the behavior of $\hat{p}_1 - \hat{p}_2$ in repeated sampling:
   a. $P(|\hat{p}_1 - \hat{p}_2| > .25)$
   b. $P(\hat{p}_1 > \hat{p}_2)$

7.6 Summary

The sampling distribution for a sample statistic is its probability distribution, which results when the behavior of the statistic is examined in repeated sampling. The sampling distribution can be constructed directly for small finite populations. For large or infinite populations, the sampling distribution of a statistic must be found mathematically or approximated empirically.

Central Limit Theorem

An important result called the ______________ ______________ ______________ allows us to approximate the sampling distribution for statistics which are sums or averages of random variables. Using this theorem, we examined the sampling distributions of four important sample statistics, $\bar{x}, \bar{x}_1 - \bar{x}_2, \hat{p}, \hat{p}_1 - \hat{p}_2$. All could be approximated by a normal distribution (with the appropriate mean and standard deviation) for large sample sizes. The sampling distributions of these four statistics will serve as the basis for making inferences about their corresponding population parameters. This will be the subject of Chapter 8.

EXERCISES

1. Suppose that an elevator is designed with a permissible load limit of 3000 pounds with a maximum of 20 passengers. If the weights of people using the elevator are normally distributed with a mean of $\mu = 160$ pounds and a standard deviation of 25 pounds, what is the probability that the weight of a group of 20 persons exceeds the permissible load limit?
2. In a past municipal election, a city bond issue passed with 52% of the vote. If a poll involving $n = 100$ people had been taken just prior to the election, what is the probability that the sample proportion favoring the issue would have been 49% or less?
3. Based of 1965–1974 birth records, the probability of a male livebirth in the United States is .513. Of the first $n = 100$ births in January, what is the probability that the proportion of male livebirths exceeds 60%?
4. Suppose that the average assessed values of single family dwellings in a municipality with 5000 such dwellings is $65,000 with a standard deviation of $20,000.
   a. If a random sample of $n = 100$ dwellings is selected and $\bar{x}$, the average assessed value of these dwellings calculated, what is the mean of $\bar{x}$ in repeated sampling?
   b. What is the standard deviation of $\bar{x}$?
   c. What is the standard deviation of $\bar{x}$ if the finite population correction factor is ignored?
5. Suppose that two television networks each allow an average of 5 minutes per half-hour program for advertising with a standard deviation of 2 minutes. What is the probability that the average time devoted to commercials for these two networks differs by less than one minute based on samples of 50 one-half hour programs from each network?
6. Packages of food whose average weight is 16 ounces with a standard deviation of .6 oz are shipped in boxes of 24 packages. What is the probability that a box of 24 packages will weigh more than 392 ounces (24.5 pounds)?
7. The average number of sick days per year in an electronics industry is 7 days with a standard deviation of 3 days. If a sample of $n_1 = 30$ men and $n_2 = 30$ women were selected from among the employees in this industry, what is the probability that the sample mean number of sick days for men exceed that for the women by 2 or more days?

8. Graduate students applying for entrance to many universities must take a Miller Analogies Test. It is known that the test scores have a mean of 75 and a variance of 16. If, during the past year, 100 students applied for graduate admission to a school requiring the Miller Analogies Test, what is the probability that the average score on these 100 tests exceeds 76?
9. The blood pressures for a population of individuals are normally distributed with a mean of 110 and a standard deviation of 7.
   a. If a sample of $n = 10$ individuals is chosen randomly from this population, within what limits would you expect the sample mean to lie with probability .95?
   b. What is the probability that the sample mean will exceed 115?
10. Suppose that the proportion of males and females who favor legalized abortion is the same, and equal to .6. If $n_1 = 50$ males and $n_2 = 100$ females are randomly selected from this population, what is the probability that the proportion of females in the sample favoring abortion exceeds that of the males by at least .2?

Chapter 8

LARGE-SAMPLE STATISTICAL INFERENCE

8.1 Introduction

inferences; population
sample
parameters

The objective of statistics is to make ____________ about a ____________ based on information contained in a ____________. Since populations are described by numerical descriptive measures, called ____________ of the population, we can make inferences about the population by making inferences about its parameters. For example, the test of the effectiveness of a new vaccine and lot acceptance sampling were inferences that resulted in decisions concerning the binomial parameter p. In this chapter we consider two methods for making inferences concerning population parameters: estimation and hypothesis testing.

Example 8.1

Consider the agricultural economist interested in the average diameter in millimeters of peaches in a particular orchard. Let μ be this average diameter. If an inference is to be made about μ, two questions could be asked.

1. What is the most likely value of μ for the population from which we are sampling?
2. Is the mean equal to some specified value, say μ_0, or is it not? For example, the economist may know that the average diameter of peaches in an adjacent field, or in a field sprayed with an experimental insecticide is equal to 60 millimeters. He might then be interested in finding out whether the field in question has a larger average diameter.

The first question is one of predicting or estimating the population parameter μ. The second is a question of testing an hypothesis about μ. If there is no difference between the field in question and the experimental field, then the average diameter will be $\mu = 60$. If the field in question has a larger average diameter, then $\mu > 60$. The objective is to determine which of these two hypotheses about μ is correct.

This chapter will be concerned with making inferences about four parameters:

1. μ, the mean of a population of continuous measurements.
2. $\mu_1 - \mu_2$, the difference between the means for two populations of continuous measurements.
3. p, the parameter of a dichotomous or binomial population.

4. $p_1 - p_2$, the difference in the parameters for two binomial populations.
The quantities to be used in making inferences will be sums or averages of the measurements in a random sample and consequently will possess frequency distributions in repeated sampling that are approximately ____________ due to the ____________ ____________ Theorem.

normal
Central Limit

One of the most important concepts to grasp is that estimation as well as hypothesis testing is a two-step procedure. These steps are
1. making the inference, and
2. measuring its goodness.

A measure of the goodness of an inference is essential to enable the person using the inference to measure its reliability. For example, we would wonder how close to the population parameter our estimate is expected to lie.

We will make inferences about each of the four parameters just mentioned in one of three ways:
1. By estimating the value of the parameter with a point estimate and giving a bound on the error of estimation.
2. By estimating the value of the parameter with a confidence interval.
3. By testing an hypothesis about the value of the parameter.

The techniques developed in the process of making inferences about these four parameters will also be used to determine how large the sample must be to achieve the accuracy required by the experimenter.

Rather than follow the section numbers exactly as they appear in your text, we have grouped certain topics together and will consider the following more general sections:
1. Point estimation.
2. Interval estimation.
3. Choosing the sample size.
4. A large-sample test of an hypothesis.

Part I: Large Sample Estimation

8.2 Estimation

Using the measurements in a sample to predict the value of one or more parameters of a population is called ____________. An ____________ is a rule that tells us how to calculate an estimate of a parameter based on the information contained in a sample. We can give many different estimators for a particular population parameter. An estimator is often expressed in terms of a mathematical formula in which the estimate is a function of the sample measurements. For example, $\bar{x}$ is an *estimator* of the population parameter μ. If a sample of $n = 20$ pieces of aluminum cable is tested for strength and the mean of the sample is $\bar{x} = 100.7$, then 100.7 is an *estimate* of the population mean strength μ. The estimator of a parameter is usually designated by placing a "hat" over the parameter to be estimated. Thus an estimator of μ would be $\hat{\mu} = \bar{x}$.

estimation; estimator

Estimates of a population parameter can be made in two ways:
1. The measurements in the sample can be employed to calculate a single number that is the estimate of the population parameter.
2. The measurements in the sample can also be used to calculate two points from which we acquire an estimate in the form of upper and lower limits

within which the true value of the parameter is expected to lie. This type
interval — of estimate is called an ______________ estimate since it defines an interval on the real line.

The goodness of an estimator is evaluated by observing its behavior in repeated sampling. Let us talk in general about some population parameter which we will denote as θ. An estimator $\hat{\theta}$ for the parameter θ will generate estimates in repeated sampling from the population and will produce a distribution of estimates (numerical values computed from these samples). This estimator would be considered good if the estimates cluster closely about θ.
unbiased — If the mean of the estimates is θ, then $\hat{\theta}$ is said to be an ______________ estimator for θ and $E(\hat{\theta}) = \theta$. If the spread (variance) of $\hat{\theta}$ is smaller than that
minimum — of any other estimator, then $\hat{\theta}$ is said to have ______________ variance.
Therefore, a *good estimator* should have the following properties:

unbiasedness — 1. ______________,

minimum variance — 2. ______________ ______________.

The distributions obtained in repeated sampling are shown below for four different estimators of θ. Which estimator appears to possess the most desir-
(d) $\hat{\theta}_4$ — able properties? ______________

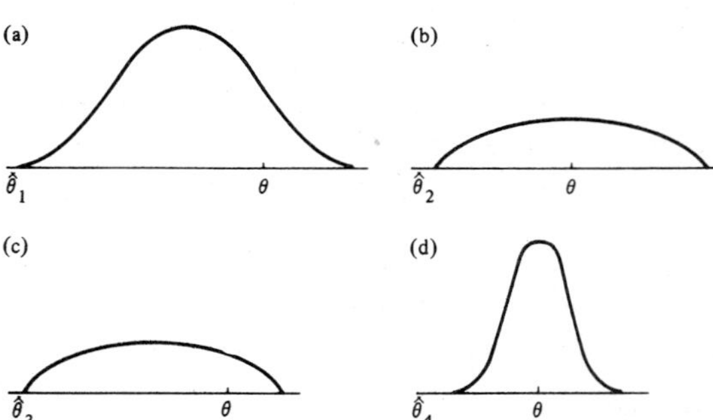

The properties of interval estimators are also determined by repeated sampling. Repeated use of an interval estimator generates a large number of
interval estimates — ______________ ______________ for estimating θ. If an interval estimator were satisfactory, a large fraction of the interval estimates would enclose the true value of θ. The fraction of such intervals enclosing θ is known as the
confidence — ______________ coefficient. This is not to be confused with the interval
interval — estimate, called the confidence ______________. The confidence coefficient actually gives the probability that a confidence interval will enclose θ.

8.3 Point Estimation

In this section we will consider point estimation for the following parameters:

1. μ, the mean of a population of continuous measurements.
2. $(\mu_1 - \mu_2)$, the difference between the means for two populations of continuous measurements.

3. p, a binomial parameter.
4. $(p_1 - p_2)$, the difference in the parameters for two binomial populations.

We assume, in all four cases, that the samples are relatively large so that the estimators possess distributions in repeated sampling that are approximately normal due to the ______________ ______________ Theorem. The basic estimation problem is the same for all four cases, and therefore we can discuss the problems in general by referring to the estimation of a parameter θ. Thus θ might be any one of the four parameters just mentioned.

Central Limit

To estimate the population parameter θ, a sample of size n $(x_1, x_2, \ldots, x_n)$ is randomly drawn from the population and an estimate of θ is calculated using $\hat{\theta}$. In repeated sampling, a distribution for $\hat{\theta}$ will be generated and will possess the following properties:

1. $E(\hat{\theta}) =$ __________.
2. $\hat{\theta}$ is approximately ______________ distributed. Therefore, approximately 95% of the values of $\hat{\theta}$ will lie within 1.96 standard deviations of their mean θ.

θ

normally

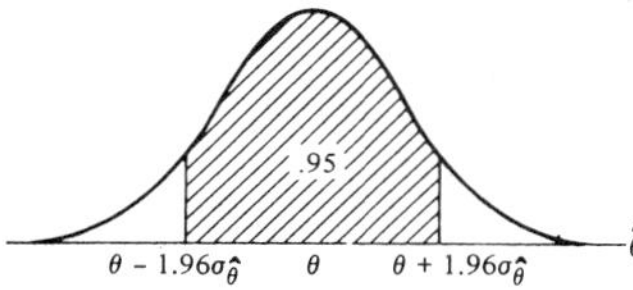

3. The symbol $\sigma_{\hat{\theta}}$ denotes the standard deviation of $\hat{\theta}$. Thus $\sigma_{\hat{\theta}}$ will be the standard deviation of the estimates generated by $\hat{\theta}$ in repeated sampling.

The measure of goodness of a particular estimate is the distance that it lies from the target θ. We call this distance ______________ ______________ ______________ ______________. Then when $\hat{\theta}$ possesses the properties stated above, the probability is approximately .95 that the error of estimation will be less than __________. We often refer to $1.96\sigma_{\hat{\theta}}$ as the *bound* on the error of estimation. By this we mean that the error will be less than $1.96\sigma_{\hat{\theta}}$ with high probability (say, near .95).

the error
of estimation

$1.96\sigma_{\hat{\theta}}$

Complete the following table, filling in the estimator and its standard error where required:

Parameter	*Estimator*	*Standard Error*
μ	$\bar{x} = \sum_{i=1}^{n} x_i/n$	$\sigma/\sqrt{n}$
p	$\hat{p} = x/n$	__________
$\mu_1 - \mu_2$	__________	__________
$p_1 - p_2$	$\hat{p}_1 - \hat{p}_2$	$\sqrt{\dfrac{p_1 q_1}{n_1} + \dfrac{p_2 q_2}{n_2}}$

$\sqrt{pq/n}$

$\bar{x}_1 - \bar{x}_2$; $\sqrt{\dfrac{\sigma_1^2}{n_1} + \dfrac{\sigma_2^2}{n_2}}$

Notice that evaluation of the standard errors given in the table may require values of parameters that are unknown. When the sample sizes are large, the sample estimates can be used to calculate an approximate standard errors. As a rule of thumb, we will consider samples of size 30 or greater to be large samples.

Example 8.2
The mean length of stay for patients in a hospital must be known in order to estimate the number of beds required. The length of stay, recorded for a sample of 400 patients at a given hospital, produced a mean and a standard deviation equal to 5.7 and 8.1 days, respectively. Give a point estimate for μ, the mean length of stay for patients entering the hospital, and place a bound of error on this estimate.

Solution

5.7 1. The point estimate for μ is $\bar{x} =$ ________.
2. Since σ is unknown, the *approximate* bound on error is

.79 $$1.96\left(\frac{s}{\sqrt{n}}\right) = 1.96\left(\frac{8.1}{\sqrt{400}}\right) = \underline{\hspace{2cm}}$$

Example 8.3
An advertising executive is interested in investigating family sizes in an attempt to determine the percentage of families having more than two children under the age of 18. She will use this information to determine the amount of advertising that should be directed toward children in this age group. She randomly samples $n = 100$ families and finds 12 families with more than two children under the age of 18. Estimate the true proportion of families with more than two children under 18 and place a bound on the error of estimation.

Solution
1. The point estimate of p is

12; .12 $$\hat{p} = \frac{x}{n} = \frac{\underline{\hspace{2cm}}}{100} = \underline{\hspace{2cm}}$$

12 That is, ________% of families have more than two children under 18.
2. The bound on the error of estimation is $1.96\sigma_{\hat{p}} = 1.96\sqrt{pq/n}$. The quantities p and q are unknown. However, since n is large, $\hat{p}$ and $\hat{q}$ may be substituted for p and q. The *approximate* bound on the error of estimation is

$\frac{(.12)(.88)}{100}$; .001056 $$1.96\sqrt{\frac{\hat{p}\hat{q}}{n}} = 1.96\sqrt{\underline{\hspace{2cm}}} = 1.96\sqrt{\underline{\hspace{2cm}}}$$

.0325; .064 $$= 1.96(\underline{\hspace{2cm}}) = \underline{\hspace{2cm}}$$

Self-Correcting Exercises 8A

1. In investigating the potential market for a new product within a given area, a market researcher asked 100 randomly chosen people to rank the new product together with four standard brands. Twenty-five people ranked the new product either first or second in a possible ranking from one to five. If p is the proportion of the population which would rank the new product either first or second, use the sample data to estimate p and place a bound on the error of estimation.
2. A random check of 50 savings accounts at the local city bank showed an average savings of \$89.50 with a standard deviation of \$25.10. Estimate the average savings in the accounts at this bank. Place a bound on the error of estimation.
3. In measuring the tensile strength of two alloys, strips of the alloys were subjected to tensile stress and the force (measured in pounds) at which the strip broke recorded for each strip. The data is summarized below.

	Alloy 1	*Alloy 2*
$\bar{x}$	150.5	160.2
s^2	23.72	36.37
n	35	35

Use these data to estimate the true mean difference in tensile strength by finding a point estimate for $\mu_1 - \mu_2$ and placing a bound on the error of estimation.

4. Using the following data, give a point estimate with bounds on error for the difference in mortality rates in breast cancers where radical or simple mastectomy was used as a treatment.

	Radical	*Simple*
Number died	31	41
Number treated	204	191

8.4 Interval Estimation

An interval estimator is a rule that tells one how to calculate two points based on information contained in a sample. The objective is to form a narrow interval that will enclose the parameter. As in the case of point estimation, one can form many interval estimators (rules) for estimating the parameter of interest. Not all intervals generated by an interval estimator will actually enclose the parameter. The probability that an interval estimate will enclose the parameter is called the ______________ ______________.

confidence coefficient

Let $\hat{\theta}$ be an *unbiased* point estimator of θ and suppose that $\hat{\theta}$ generates a normal distribution of estimates in repeated sampling. The mean of this distribution of estimates is __________ and the standard deviation is $\sigma_{\hat{\theta}}$.

θ

95 Then __________ % of the point estimates will lie within $1.96\sigma_{\hat{\theta}}$ of the
90 parameter θ. Similarly, __________ % will lie in the interval $\theta \pm 1.645\sigma_{\hat{\theta}}$ (see below).

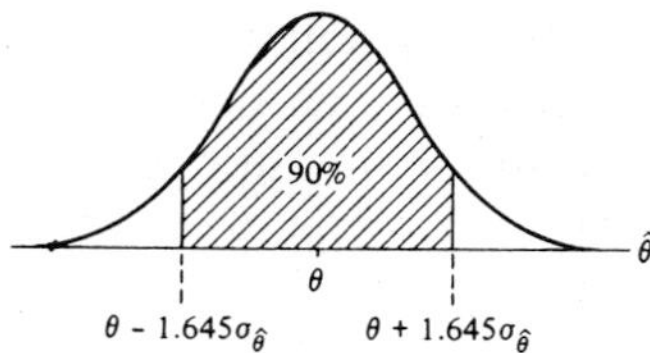

Suppose we were to construct an interval estimate by measuring the distance $1.645\sigma_{\hat{\theta}}$ on either side of $\hat{\theta}$. *Intervals constructed in this manner will*
90 *enclose* θ __________ *% of the time* (see below).

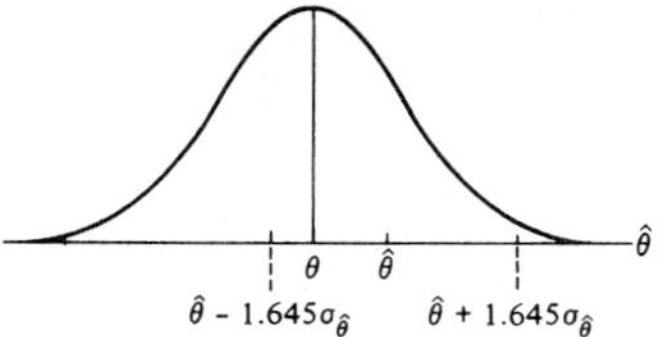

Thus for a confidence interval with confidence coefficient $(1 - \alpha)$, we use

$$\hat{\theta} \pm z_{\alpha/2}\sigma_{\hat{\theta}}$$

to construct the interval estimate. The quantity $z_{\alpha/2}$ satisfies the relation $P(z > z_{\alpha/2}) = \alpha/2$, as indicated below:

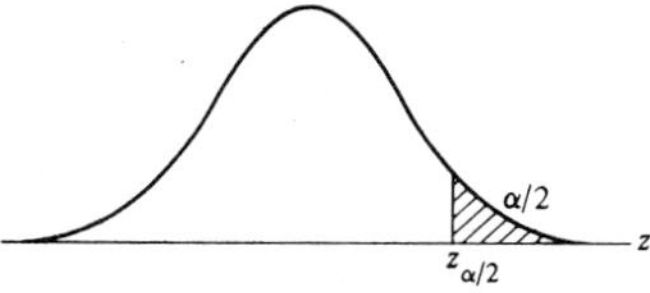

Sometimes it is convenient in reporting experimental results to refer separately to the upper and lower limits of the confidence interval. For that reason, the larger number (which locates the upper end of the interval) is called the upper confidence limit and is denoted by UCL. The smaller number (which locates the lower end of the interval) is called the lower confidence limit and is denoted by LCL. For the large sample confidence intervals discussed in this section,

$$\text{LCL} = \hat{\theta} - z_{\alpha/2}\sigma_{\hat{\theta}}$$

$$\text{UCL} = \hat{\theta} + z_{\alpha/2}\sigma_{\hat{\theta}}$$

Not all good interval estimators are constructed by measuring $z_{\alpha/2}\sigma_{\hat{\theta}}$ on either side of the best point estimator, but this is true for the parameters μ, p, $(\mu_1 - \mu_2)$, and $(p_1 - p_2)$. These confidence intervals are good for samples that are large enough to achieve approximate normality for the distribution of $\hat{\theta}$ and good approximations for unknown parameters appearing in $\sigma_{\hat{\theta}}$.

A 95% confidence interval for μ is $\bar{x} \pm$ ________ $\sigma/\sqrt{n}$. As a rule of thumb, the sample size, n, must be greater than or equal to ________ in order that s be a good approximation to σ.

1.96
30

Give the z values corresponding to the following confidence coefficients:

Confidence Coefficients	$z_{\alpha/2}$
.95	1.96
.90	________
.99	________

1.645
2.58

Example 8.4

To construct a 95% confidence interval for the mean length of hospital stay, μ, based on the sample of $n = 400$ patients ($\bar{x} = 5.7$ and $s = 8.1$) we calculate

$$\bar{x} \pm z_{\alpha/2}\,\sigma/\sqrt{n}$$

Using $z_{.025} = 1.96$ and an estimate for σ given by $s = 8.1$, we obtain the interval estimate for the mean length of hospital stay

$$5.7 \pm \text{\_\_\_\_\_\_\_\_}$$

.79

More properly, we estimate that ________ $< \mu <$ ________ with 95% confidence.

4.91; 6.49

The formula for a 95% confidence interval for a binomial parameter, p, is

____

$$\hat{p} \pm 1.96\sqrt{\frac{pq}{n}}$$

where $\hat{p}$ is used to approximate p in the formula for $\sigma_{\hat{p}}$ since its value is unknown.

Example 8.5

An experimental rehabilitation technique employed on released convicts showed that 79 of a total of 121 men subjected to the technique pursued useful and crime-free lives for a three-year period following prison release. Find a 95% confidence interval for p, the probability that a convict subjected to the rehabilitation technique will follow a crime-free existence for at least three years after prison release.

Solution

The sampling described above satisfies the requirements of a binomial experiment consisting of $n = 121$ trials. In estimating the parameter p with a 95% confidence interval we use the estimator

$$\hat{p} \pm 1.96\sqrt{\frac{pq}{n}}.$$

Since p is unknown, the sample value, $\hat{p}$, will be used in the approximation of $\sqrt{pq/n}$. Collecting pertinent information, we have

1. $$\hat{p} = \frac{x}{n} = \frac{79}{121} = .65$$

2. $$\sqrt{\frac{\hat{p}\hat{q}}{n}} = \sqrt{\frac{(.65)(.35)}{121}} = .04$$

3. The interval estimate is given as

$$.65 \pm 1.96(.04)$$

.08 or $.65 \pm$ ________

.57; .73 4. We estimate that ________ $< p <$ ________ with 95% confidence.

The exact values for standard errors of estimators cannot usually be found because they are functions of unknown population parameters. For the following estimators, give the standard error and the best approximation of the standard error for use in confidence intervals.

	Estimator ($\hat{\theta}$)	*Standard Error* ($\sigma_{\hat{\theta}}$)	*Best Approximation of Standard Error* ($\hat{\sigma}_{\hat{\theta}}$)
$s/\sqrt{n}$	$\bar{x}$	$\sigma/\sqrt{n}$	________
$\sqrt{\hat{p}\hat{q}/n}$	$\hat{p}$	$\sqrt{pq/n}$	________
	$\bar{x}_1 - \bar{x}_2$	$\sqrt{\frac{\sigma_1^2}{n_1} + \frac{\sigma_2^2}{n_2}}$	$\sqrt{\frac{s_1^2}{n_1} + \frac{s_2^2}{n_2}}$
	$\hat{p}_1 - \hat{p}_2$	$\sqrt{\frac{p_1 q_1}{n_1} + \frac{p_2 q_2}{n_2}}$	$\sqrt{\frac{\hat{p}_1\hat{q}_1}{n_1} + \frac{\hat{p}_2\hat{q}_2}{n_2}}$

The large-sample confidence intervals for μ, p, $\mu_1 - \mu_2$, and $p_1 - p_2$ will be

$$\hat{\theta} \pm z_{\alpha/2}\, \hat{\sigma}_{\hat{\theta}}$$

where $\hat{\theta}$ is given by $\bar{x}$, $\hat{p}$, $\bar{x}_1 - \bar{x}_2$, and $\hat{p}_1 - \hat{p}_2$, respectively. The table above will determine the appropriate formula for $\sigma_{\hat{\theta}}$ or $\hat{\sigma}_{\hat{\theta}}$.

Example 8.6

A company was interested in comparing the average daily sales made by two different salesmen. The daily sales of each salesman were recorded for 72 consecutive days. The mean and variance of the daily sales in hundreds of dollars for the two salesmen were found to be

$$\bar{x}_1 = 7.8,\ s_1^2 = .10,\ \bar{x}_2 = 8.4, \text{ and } s_2^2 = .06$$

respectively. Find a 95% confidence interval for the difference in average daily sales for the two salesmen.

Solution

We are interested in placing a confidence interval about the parameter __________. The confidence interval is

$\mu_1 - \mu_2$

$$(\bar{x}_1 - \bar{x}_2) \pm z_{\alpha/2}\,(\_\_\_\_\_\_\_\_\_\_\_\_)$$

$\sqrt{\dfrac{\sigma_1^2}{n_1} + \dfrac{\sigma_2^2}{n_2}}$

Using the sample approximations for σ_1^2 and σ_2^2 the interval estimate is

__________ ± __________

-.6; .092

or

__________ to __________

-.692; -.508

Example 8.7

To estimate the difference between the proportion of printed pages with misprints for two printing firms, a prospective printing contractor randomly chooses pages of works printed by each firm and has the number of pages containing errors tabulated. The results of the tabulation follow.

	Firm 1	*Firm 2*
Number of pages	200	200
Pages with errors	94	60

Construct an interval that should contain the difference in proportion of misprinted pages, $p_1 - p_2$, with 98% confidence.

Solution

From the data we calculate

.47; .30 $\hat{p}_1 = 94/200 =$ ______ and $\hat{p}_2 = 60/200 =$ ______

Using

2.58 $(\hat{p}_1 - \hat{p}_2) \pm$ ______ $\sqrt{\dfrac{\hat{p}_1\hat{q}_1}{n_1} + \dfrac{\hat{p}_2\hat{q}_2}{n_2}}$

to calculate the required confidence interval we have

$$(.47 - .30) \pm 2.58\sqrt{\frac{(.47)(.53)}{200} + \frac{(.30)(.70)}{200}}$$

.17; .048 ______ $\pm$ 2.58 (______)

.17; .12 ______ $\pm$ ______

.05; .29 Hence the required confidence interval is ______ to ______.

Example 8.8

Suppose it is desired to estimate the average purchase volume for an individual credit customer of a downtown department store for the month of December. A sample of 40 credit customers' files were examined and the latest December purchase volume available was recorded for each customer in the sample. The mean volume was found to be $\bar{x} = \$42.40$ with a standard deviation, $s = \$0.95$. Give a 90% confidence interval for the mean purchase volume for December for all the credit customers of the department store.

Solution

.90; .05 The confidence coefficient, $1 - \alpha =$ ______. Therefore, $\alpha/2 =$ ______

1.645 and $z_{\alpha/2} =$ ______. To find the interval estimate, use

1.645 $\bar{x} \pm$ ______ $s/\sqrt{n}$

Substituting,

1.645 \$42.40 $\pm$ ______ $.95/\sqrt{40}$

\$.25 \$42.40 $\pm$ ______

Hence, the 90% confidence interval for μ is

\$42.15; \$42.65 ______ to ______

To provide a brief summary of the preceding sections, complete the following tables.

1. Give the best estimator for each of the following parameters:

Parameter	*Estimator*
μ	________
p	________
$(\mu_1 - \mu_2)$	________
$(p_1 - p_2)$	________

$\bar{x}$
$\hat{p}$
$\bar{x}_1 - \bar{x}_2$
$\hat{p}_1 - \hat{p}_2$

2. Give the standard errors for the following estimators:

Estimator	*Standard Error*
$\bar{x}$	________
$\hat{p}$	________
$\bar{x}_1 - \bar{x}_2$	________
$\hat{p}_1 - \hat{p}_2$	________

$\sigma/\sqrt{n}$

$$\sqrt{\frac{pq}{n}}$$

$$\sqrt{\frac{\sigma_1^2}{n_1} + \frac{\sigma_2^2}{n_2}}$$

$$\sqrt{\frac{p_1 q_1}{n_1} + \frac{p_2 q_2}{n_2}}$$

3. Indicate the best approximations of the standard errors for use in confidence intervals:

Estimator	*Best Approximation of Standard Error*
$\bar{x}$	________
$\hat{p}$	________
$\bar{x}_1 - \bar{x}_2$	________
$\hat{p}_1 - \hat{p}_2$	________

$s/\sqrt{n}$

$$\sqrt{\frac{\hat{p}\hat{q}}{n}}$$

$$\sqrt{\frac{s_1^2}{n_1} + \frac{s_2^2}{n_2}}$$

$$\sqrt{\frac{\hat{p}_1 \hat{q}_1}{n_1} + \frac{\hat{p}_2 \hat{q}_2}{n_2}}$$

Self-Correcting Exercises 8B

1. In an attempt to update rates in a specific area, a fire insurance company randomly selects 50 fire insurance claims involving damage to one-family wooden frame dwellings with approximately 1500 square feet of living area. The average claim was found to be \$18,750 with a standard deviation of \$3050. Estimate the true mean claim for structures of this type with a 95% confidence interval estimate.
2. In studying the feasibility of expanding public television programming, an investigator found that 86 out of 200 randomly chosen families with television sets watch at least two hours of public television programming per week.
   a. Use this data to find a point estimate of the proportion of viewers that watch at least two hours of public T.V. programming per week and place a bound on the error of estimation.
   b. Find a 90% confidence interval for the proportion of viewers watching at least two hours of public T.V. programming.
3. Last year's records of auto accidents occurring on a given section of highway were classified according to whether the resulting damage was \$400 or more and to whether or not a physical injury resulted from the accident. The tabulation follows:

	Under \$400	*\$400 or more*
Number of accidents	32	41
Number involving injuries	10	23

   a. Estimate the true proportion of accidents involving injuries and damage of \$400 or more for similar sections of highway with a 95% confidence interval.
   b. Estimate the true difference in proportion of accidents involving injuries for accidents involving less than \$400 in damage and those involving \$400 or more with a 95% confidence interval.
4. The yearly incomes of employees of two manufacturing plants producing equivalent items yielded the following tabulation.

	Plant 1	*Plant 2*
Number of employees	90	60
Average income	\$20,520	\$19,210
Standard deviation	\$ 1,510	\$ 950

   a. If the employees of each plant are thought of as samples from two populations of employees in this industry, use these data to construct a 99% confidence interval for the difference in mean annual incomes.
   b. Using the results of part a, would you be willing to conclude that these plants belong to populations having the same mean annual income?

8.5 Choosing the Sample Size

The amount of information contained in a sample depends on two factors:

1. The quantity of information per observation, which depends on the sampling procedure or _______________ _______________. experimental design
2. The number of measurements or observations taken, which depends on the _______________ _______________. sample size

In this chapter, we will concentrate on choosing the sample size to obtain the desired amount of information.

One of the first steps in planning an experiment is deciding on the quantity of information that we wish to buy. At first glance it would seem difficult to specify a measure of the quantity of information in a sample relevant to a parameter of interest. However, such a practical measure is available in the bound on the error of estimation; or, alternatively, we could use the half-width of the confidence interval for the parameter.

The larger the sample size, the greater will be the amount of information contained in the sample. This intuitively appealing fact is evident upon examination of the large sample confidence intervals. The width of each of the four confidence intervals described in the preceding section is inversely proportional to the square root of the _______________ _______________. sample size

Suppose that $\hat{\theta}$ is an estimator of θ and satisfies the conditions for the large-sample estimators previously discussed. Then the bound B on the error of estimation will be $1.96\sigma_{\hat{\theta}}$. This means that the error (in repeated sampling) will be less than $1.96\sigma_{\hat{\theta}}$ with probability __________. If B represents the desired bound on the error, then .95

a. for a *point* estimator $\hat{\theta}$, the restriction is $1.96\sigma_{\hat{\theta}} = B$;
b. in an interval estimation problem with $(1 - \alpha)$ confidence coefficient, the restriction is $z_{\alpha/2}\sigma_{\hat{\theta}} = B$.

Parts a and b will be equivalent when the confidence coefficient is .95.

Rather than resolve the basic equation determining the required sample size every time the problem is encountered, we can solve the equation

$$z_{\alpha/2}\sigma_{\hat{\theta}} = B$$

in general when estimating μ, $\mu_1 - \mu_2$, p or $p_1 - p_2$. A summary of these solutions with and without some simplifying assumptions (for example, $n_1 = n_2 = n$) is given in the following display.

SAMPLE SIZE FORMULAS

Let B represent the bound on the error of estimation and $(1 - \alpha)$ the confidence coefficient.

1. Estimation of μ:

$$n = \frac{z_{\alpha/2}^2 \sigma^2}{B^2}$$

2. Estimation of $\mu_1 - \mu_2$ when $n_1 = n_2 = n$:

$$n = \frac{z_{\alpha/2}^2 (\sigma_1^2 + \sigma_2^2)}{B^2}$$

3. Estimation of p:

a. $$n = \frac{z_{\alpha/2}^2 \hat{p}\hat{q}}{B^2}$$ if a prior estimate $\hat{p}$ of p is available

b. $$n = \frac{z_{\alpha/2}^2 (.25)}{B^2}$$ if no prior estimate of p is available

4. Estimation of $p_1 - p_2$ if no prior estimates are available and assuming maximum variation with $n_1 = n_2 = n$:

$$n = \frac{z_{\alpha/2}^2 (2)(.25)}{B^2}$$

Example 8.9

Suppose it is known that $\sigma = 2.25$ and it is desired to estimate μ with a bound on the error of estimation less than or equal to .5 unit with probability .95. How large a sample should be taken?

Solution

The estimator for μ is $\bar{x}$ with standard deviation $\sigma/\sqrt{n}$; $1 - \alpha = .95$, $\alpha/2 = .025$, $z_{.025} = 1.96$. Hence we solve

$$1.96\,(\sigma/\sqrt{n}) = B$$

or

$$1.96\,(2.25/\sqrt{n}) = .5$$

$1.96\,(2.25/.5) = \sqrt{n}$

__________ $= \sqrt{n}$ 8.82

__________ $= n$ 77.79

Alternately, we could use the formula

$$n = \frac{z^2_{\alpha/2}\sigma^2}{B^2} \approx \frac{(1.96)^2(\_\_\_\_\_\_\_\_\_\_)^2}{(.5)^2} = \_\_\_\_\_\_\_\_\_\_$$ 2.25 77.79

The solution is to take a sample of size __________ or greater to insure that the bound is less than or equal to .5 unit. Had we wished to have the same bound with probability .99, the value $z_{.005}$ = __________ would have been used, resulting in the following solution: 78 2.58

$$n = \frac{(\_\_\_\_\_\_\_\_\_\_)^2(2.25)^2}{(.5)^2}$$ 2.58

$n =$ __________ 134.79

Hence a sample of size __________ or greater would be taken to insure estimation with $B = .5$ unit. 135

Example 8.10

If an experimenter wished to estimate the fraction of university students that read daily the college newspaper, correct to within .02 with probability .90, how large a sample of students should she take?

Solution

To estimate the binomial parameter with a 90% confidence interval, we would use

$\hat{p} \pm$ __________ $\sqrt{pq/n}$ 1.645

We wish to find a sample size n so that

$$1.645\sqrt{pq/n} = .02$$

Since neither p nor $\hat{p}$ is known, we can solve for n by assuming the worst possible variation, which occurs when $p = q =$ __________. Hence we solve .5

$$n = \frac{z^2_{\alpha/2}(.25)}{B^2}$$

1691.27 $$n = \frac{(1.645)^2(.25)}{(.02)^2} = \_\_\_\_\_\_\_\_$$

1,692 Therefore, we should take a sample of size ________ or greater to achieve the required bounds, even if faced with the maximum variation possible.

Example 8.11
An experiment is to be conducted to compare two different sales techniques at a number of sales centers. Suppose that the range of sales for the sales centers is expected to be \$4,000. How many centers should be included for each of the sales techniques in order to estimate the difference in mean sales correct to within \$500?

Solution
We will assume that the two sample sizes are equal, that is, $n_1 = n_2 = n$, and that the desired confidence coefficient is .95. Then

$$n = \frac{z_{\alpha/2}^2(\sigma_1^2 + \sigma_2^2)}{B^2}$$

The quantities σ_1^2 and σ_2^2 are unknown but we know that the range is ex-
1,000 pected to be \$4,000. Then we would take $\sigma_1 = \sigma_2 =$ ________ as the best available approximation. Then, substituting into the equation above,

$$n = \frac{(1.96)^2(1000^2 + 1000^2)}{(500)^2}$$

30.73 or $n =$ ________

31 Thus $n =$ ________ sales centers would be required for each of the two sales techniques.

Self-Correcting Exercises 8C

1. A device is known to produce measurements whose errors in measurement are normally distributed with a standard deviation $\sigma = 8$ mm. If the average measurement is to be reported, how many repeated measurements should be used so that the error in measurement is no larger than 3 mm. with probability .95?
2. How many items from a production line should be sampled to estimate the true proportion of defectives for the line to within .01 with probability .95? The value of p is expected to be at most 0.1.

3. In investigating what appears to be an unusually large difference in overtime pay between the accounting records for two subsidiaries, the general manager has asked that all records be checked in each subsidiary to find the average number of overtime hours per week. If a sampling plan rather than a complete audit were to be used, how many weekly records should be checked to insure that the estimate is no further than 10 hours from the true mean difference with probability .95? You may assume that the overtime hours per week will range from 10 to 160 hours for each subsidiary.
4. How many individuals from each of two politically oriented groups should be included in a poll designed to estimate the true difference in proportions favoring a tuition increase at the state university correct to within .01 with probability .95? (In the absence of any prior information regarding the values of p_1 and p_2, solve the problem assuming maximum variation.)

Part II: Large Sample Hypothesis Testing

8.6 A Statistical Test of an Hypothesis

We now leave estimation and turn our attention to a decision making form of inference, hypothesis testing. In hypothesis testing, we formulate an hypothesis about a population in terms of its ______________, and then, after observing a ______________ drawn from this population, we decide whether our sample value could have come from the hypothesized population. We then accept or reject the hypothesized value.

parameters
sample

A statistical test of an hypothesis consists of four parts:

1. ______________ ______________, (H_0): This is the hypothesis to be tested and gives hypothesized values for one or more population parameters.

Null hypothesis

2. ______________ ______________, (H_a): This is the hypothesis against which H_0 is tested. We look for evidence in the sample that will cause us to reject H_0 in favor of H_a.

Alternative hypothesis

3. Test statistic: This function of the sample values extracts the information about the parameter contained in the sample. The observed value of the test statistic leads us to reject one hypothesis and accept the other.
4. Rejection region: Once the test statistic to be used is selected, the entire set of values that the statistic may assume is divided into two regions. The acceptance region consists of those values most likely to have arisen if H_0 were true. The rejection region consists of those values most likely to have arisen if H_a were true. If the observed value of the test statistic falls in the

rejection region, H_0 is rejected; if it falls in the acceptance region, H_0 is accepted.

Our approach will be to draw a random sample from the population of interest and decide whether we will accept or reject an hypothesized value of the specified parameter. The decision will be made on the basis of whether the sample results are highly ____________ and support the hypothesized value or are ____________ and fail to support the hypothesized value. Our procedure is very similar to a court trial in which the accused is assumed innocent until proven guilty. In fact, our sample acts as the ____________ for or against the accused. What we do is to compare the hypothesized value with reality. Let us illustrate how a test of an hypothesis is conducted.

probable
improbable

evidence

Example 8.12

A large orchard has averaged 140 pounds of apples per tree per year. The manufacturer of a new fertilizer would like to use it to try to increase yield. Forty trees are randomly selected and the mean and standard deviation of yield are $\bar{x} = 143.2$ and $s = 9.4$. Do the data indicate a significant increase in yield?

Discussion

If there is no increase in the average yield for fertilized trees, then the average value μ of the hypothetical population of fertilized trees from which we have obtained a random sample is $\mu = 140$. If, on the other hand, this is not true, and the fertilizer tends to increase yield, then μ, the mean yield for fertilized trees, would be greater than 140. Since the researcher is interested in detecting an increase in yield, the statement $\mu > 140$ is the ____________ or ____________ hypothesis, while the statement $\mu = 140$ is the ____________ ____________.

research; alternative
null hypothesis

Assuming that there is no increase in the average yield for fertilized trees, it would be extremely unlikely in a sample of $n = 40$ trees to observe certain values of $\bar{x}$. Since $\bar{x}$ has an approximate normal distribution with $\mu_{\bar{x}} = 140$ and

$$\sigma_{\bar{x}} \approx \frac{s}{\sqrt{n}} = \frac{9.4}{\sqrt{40}} = \_\_\_\_\_\_\_\_$$

1.486

we can calculate the probability of observing a particular value of $\bar{x}$ or something even more extreme. For example, suppose that $\bar{x} = 150$. This is a highly unlikely event since

$$P(\bar{x} > 150) = P\left(z > \frac{150 - 140}{1.486}\right)$$

$$= P(z > \_\_\_\_\_\_\_\_) \approx \_\_\_\_\_\_\_\_$$

6.73; 0

The occurrence of $\bar{x} = 141$, however, is not so unlikely, since

$$P(\bar{x} > 141) = P\left(z > \underline{\qquad\qquad}\right)$$ $\dfrac{141 - 140}{1.486}$

$$= P(z > \underline{\qquad\qquad})$$ .67

$$= .5 - \underline{\qquad\qquad} = \underline{\qquad\qquad}$$ .2486; .2514

In conducting a test of hypothesis, the possible outcomes for $\bar{x}$ are divided into those for which we agree to reject the null hypothesis [those values of $\bar{x}$ that are much (greater, less) than $\mu = 140$] and those for which we accept the null hypothesis [those values of $\bar{x}$ that are (close to, far away from) $\mu = 140$].

greater
close to

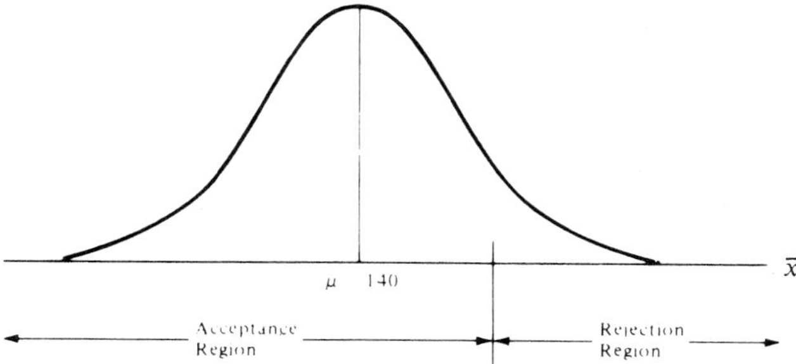

There are many possible rejection regions available to the experimenter. A sound choice among various reasonable rejection regions can be made after considering the possible errors that can be made in a test of an hypothesis.

The following table is called a *decision table* (refer to Section 5.8) and looks at the two possible states of nature (H_0 and H_a) and the two possible decisions in a test of an hypothesis. Fill in the missing entries as either "correct" or "error":

	Decision	
Null Hypothesis	*Reject H_0*	*Accept H_0*
True	________	correct
False	correct	________

error
error

An error of type I is made when we reject H_0 when H_0 is (true, false). An error of type II is made when we fail to reject H_0 when H_a is (true, false). In considering a statistical test of any hypothesis, it is essential to know the probabilities of committing errors of type I and type II when the test is used in order to assess the goodness of the test. We define

true
true

$$\alpha = P(\text{type I error}) = P(\text{reject } H_0 \text{ when } H_0 \text{ true})$$

$$\beta = P(\text{type II error}) = P(\text{accept } H_0 \text{ when } H_a \text{ true})$$

For this example, suppose we set the region $\bar{x} > 142.5$ as the rejection region.
1. If H_0 is true and $\mu = 140$,

$$\alpha = P(\text{reject } H_0 \text{ when } H_0 \text{ true})$$

$$= P(\bar{x} > 142.5) = P\left(z > \frac{142.5 - 140}{1.486}\right)$$

1.68; .4535 $= P(z >$ _________) $= .5 -$ _________

.0465 $=$ _________

2. If H_0 is false and $\mu = 145$,

$$\beta = P(\text{accept } H_0 \text{ when } H_a \text{ true})$$

$$= P(\bar{x} < 142.5 \text{ when } \mu = 145)$$

$$= P\left(z < \frac{142.5 - 145}{1.486}\right)$$

-1.68; .4535 $= P(z <$ _________) $= .5 -$ _________

.0465 $=$ _________

Notice that β is a function of H_a, since by definition,

$$\beta = P(\text{accepting } H_0 \text{ when } H_a \text{ true})$$

Using $\bar{x} > 142.5$ as rejection region, we would reject H_0, since our observed value of $\bar{x} = 143.2$ is greater than 142.5.

smaller Consider a second rejection region, $\bar{x} > 144$. This rejection region is (larger, smaller) than the first region.

1. If H_0 is true, and $\mu = 140$,

$$\alpha = P(\text{reject } H_0 \text{ when } H_0 \text{ true})$$

$$= P(\bar{x} > 144 \text{ when } \mu = 140)$$

$\dfrac{144 - 140}{1.486}$ $= P(z >$ _________)

$$= P(z > 2.69)$$

$$= .5 - .4964 = .0036$$

2. If H_0 is false and $\mu = 145$,

$$\beta = P(\text{accept } H_0 \text{ when } H_a \text{ true})$$

$$= P(\bar{x} < 144 \text{ when } \mu = 145)$$

$$= P\left(z < \frac{\quad}{\quad}\right)$$ $\dfrac{144 - 145}{1.486}$

$$= P(z < -.67)$$

$$= .5 - \underline{\qquad\qquad} = \underline{\qquad\qquad}$$ .2486; .2514

We can measure the ability of the test to perform as required by calculating

$$1 - \beta = P(\text{reject } H_0 \text{ when } H_0 \text{ is false})$$

$$= P(\text{reject } H_0 \text{ when } H_a \text{ is true})$$

which is called the *power of the test.* For this example, the power of the test when $\mu = 145$ is

$$1 - \beta = 1 - .2514 = \underline{\qquad\qquad}$$ .7486

3. If H_0 is false and $\mu = 148$, the power of the test is

$$1 - \beta = P(x \geqslant 144 \text{ when } \mu = 148)$$

$$= P(z \geqslant \underline{\qquad\qquad})$$ -2.69

$$= .5 + \underline{\qquad\qquad} = \underline{\qquad\qquad}$$ .4964; .9964

A graph of $(1 - \beta)$ as a function of μ is often constructed to chart the performance of the test. Such a graph is called a *power curve*. Notice that the power of the test increases as the distance between the true and hypothesized values of μ increases, which is a desirable property. Also notice that both α and β depend on the rejection region employed and that when the sample size n is fixed, α and β are inversely related: as one increases, the other ______________ . decreases
Increasing the sample size provides more information on which to make the decision and will reduce the probability of a type II error. Since these two quantities measure the risk of making an incorrect decision, the experimenter chooses reasonable values for α and β and then chooses the rejection region and sample size accordingly. Since experimenters have found that a 1-in-20 chance of a type I error is usually tolerable, common practice is to choose $\alpha \leqslant$ __________ and a sample size n large enough to provide the desired control of the type II error. .05

8.7 A Large-Sample Statistical Test

As in previous sections, the parameter of interest ($\mu, \mu_1 - \mu_2, p,$ or $p_1 - p_2$) will be referred to as θ. If an *unbiased* point estimator $\hat{\theta}$ exists for θ and if $\hat{\theta}$ is normally distributed, we can employ $\hat{\theta}$ as a test statistic to test the hypothesis $H_0: \theta = \theta_0$.

larger

If H_a states that $\theta > \theta_0$, that is, the value of the parameter is greater than that given by H_0, then the sample value for $\hat{\theta}$ should reflect this fact and be (larger, smaller) than a value of $\hat{\theta}$ when sampling from a population whose mean is θ_0. Hence we would reject H_0 for large values of $\hat{\theta}$. "Large" can be interpreted as too many standard deviations to the right of the mean θ_0. The value of $\hat{\theta}$ selected to separate the acceptance and rejection regions is called

critical value

the ______________ ______________ of the test statistic.

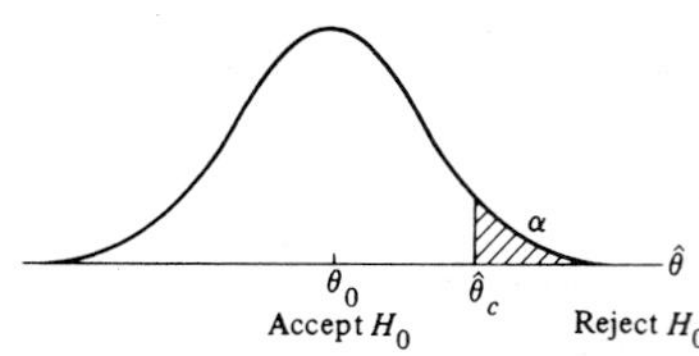

α

$\hat{\theta}_c$ in the diagram represents the critical value of $\hat{\theta}$ and the shaded area to the right of $\hat{\theta}_c$ is equal to __________. This is a one-tailed statistical test.

<

A similar picture could have been used with the critical value of $\hat{\theta}$ to the left of the mean for testing $H_0: \theta = \theta_0$ against $H_a: \theta$ __________ θ_0. Then we would reject for values of $\hat{\theta}$ lying too many standard deviations to the left of

one-tailed

θ_0 (resulting in a ______________ ______________ test in the left tail) and would reject H_0 for small values of $\hat{\theta}$.

two

A third type of alternative hypothesis would be $H_a: \theta \neq \theta_0$, where we seek departures either greater or less than θ_0. This results in a ______________ -tailed statistical test.

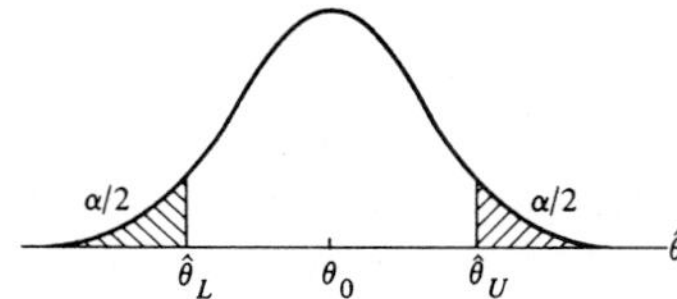

In order that the probability of a type I error be equal to α, two critical values of $\hat{\theta}$ must be found, one having area $\alpha/2$ to its right ($\hat{\theta}_U$) and one having area $\alpha/2$ to its left ($\hat{\theta}_L$). H_0 will be rejected if $\hat{\theta} \geqslant \hat{\theta}_U$ or $\hat{\theta} \leqslant \hat{\theta}_L$.

Since the estimator $\hat{\theta}$ is normally distributed, we can standardize the normal variable $\hat{\theta}$ by converting the distance that $\hat{\theta}$ departs from θ_0 to z (the number of standard deviations to the left or right of the mean). Thus we will use z as the test statistic. The four elements of the test are as follows:

1. $H_0: \theta = \theta_0$

2. One of the three alternatives:
   a. $H_a: \theta > \theta_0$ (right-tailed)
   b. $H_a: \theta < \theta_0$ (left-tailed)
   c. $H_a: \theta \neq \theta_0$ (two-tailed)
3. Test statistic z, where

$$z = (\hat{\theta} - \theta_0)/\sigma_{\hat{\theta}}$$

4. Rejection region:
   a. For $H_a: \theta > \theta_0$

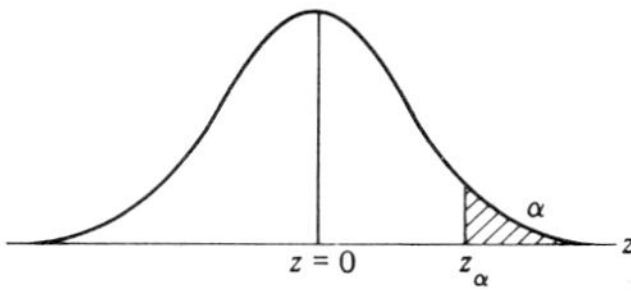

Reject H_0 if $z > z_\alpha$

   b. For $H_a: \theta < \theta_0$

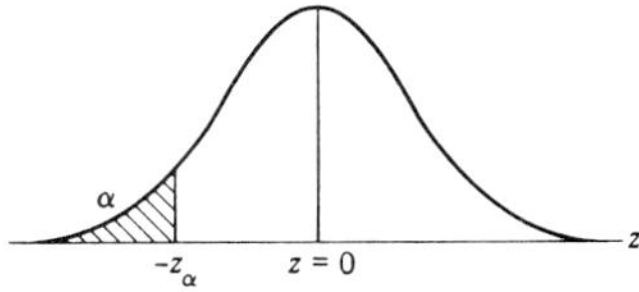

Reject H_0 if $z < -z_\alpha$

   c. For $H_a: \theta \neq \theta_0$

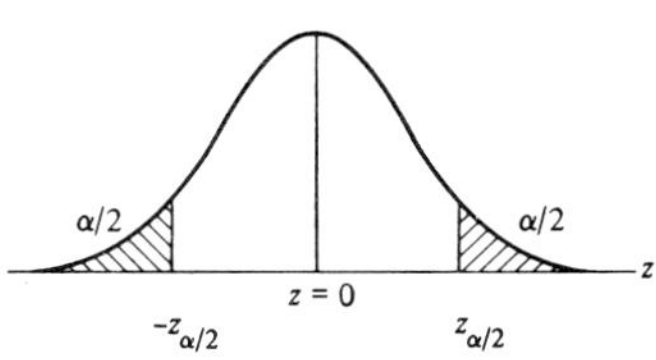

Reject H_0 if $z > z_{\alpha/2}$
or $z < -z_{\alpha/2}$
($|z| > z_{\alpha/2}$)

We now apply this test of an hypothesis.

Example 8.13
Test of a population mean μ. Test the hypothesis at the $\alpha = .05$ level, that a population mean $\mu = 10$ against the hypothesis that $\mu > 10$ if, for a sample of 81 observations, $\bar{x} = 12$ and $s = 3.2$. Note the following:

a. $\theta = \mu$

b. $\theta_0 = \mu_0 = 10$

c. $\hat{\theta} = \bar{x}$

d. $\sigma_{\hat{\theta}} = \sigma/\sqrt{n}$

e. $\alpha = .05$

Solution

Since σ is unknown, use s, the sample standard deviation, as its approximation. Then the elements of the test are as follows:

1. $H_0: \mu = 10$
2. $H_a: \mu > 10$
3. Test statistic:

$$z = \frac{\bar{x} - \mu_0}{\sigma/\sqrt{n}} \quad \text{(using } s \text{ if } \sigma \text{ is unknown)}$$

4. Rejection region:

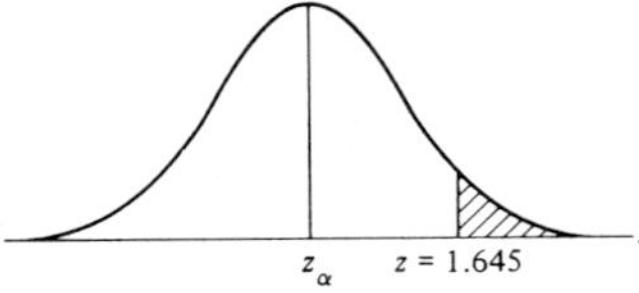

1.645 Reject H_0 if $z >$ _________

Having defined the test, calculate z.

12 $$z = \frac{\bar{x} - \mu_0}{s/\sqrt{n}} = \frac{\_\_\_\_\_\_ - 10}{\_\_\_\_\_\_/\sqrt{81}}$$

3.2

$$= 2/.356 = 5.62$$

reject Since $z = 5.62 > 1.645$, the decision is (reject, do not reject) H_0 with $\alpha = .05$.

Example 8.14

A machine shop is interested in determining a measure of the current year's sales revenue in order to compare it with known results from last year. From the 9682 sales invoices to date for the current year, the management randomly selected $n = 400$ invoices and from each recorded x, the sales revenue per invoice. Using the following data summary, test the hypothesis that the mean revenue per invoice is \$6.35, the same as last year, versus the alternative hypothesis that the mean revenue per invoice is different than \$6.35 with $\alpha = .05$.

Data Summary
$n = 400$
$\sum_{i=1}^{400} x_i = \$2464.40$
$\sum_{i=1}^{400} x_i^2 = 16156.728$

Solution

Using the values given in the data summary calculate $\bar{x}$, s^2 and s.

$$\bar{x} = \frac{\sum_{i=1}^{400} x_i}{400} = \frac{\$2464.40}{400} = \_\_\_\_\_\_\_\_$$ $6.16

$$s^2 = \frac{\sum_{i=1}^{400} x_i^2 - \frac{\left(\sum_{i=1}^{400} x_i\right)^2}{400}}{399} = \frac{\_\_\_\_\_\_\_\_ - \frac{(2464.40)^2}{400}}{399}$$ 16156.728

$$= \_\_\_\_\_\_\_\_$$ 2.4400

$$s = \sqrt{\_\_\_\_\_\_\_\_} = \_\_\_\_\_\_\_\_$$ 2.4400; 1.562

The test proceeds as follows.

1. $H_0: \mu =$ ________ 6.35

2. $H_a: \mu$ ________ $\neq 6.35$

3. Test statistic:

$$z = \frac{\bar{x} - \mu_0}{\sigma/\sqrt{n}}$$

4. Rejection region: reject H_0 if $|z| >$ ________ 1.96

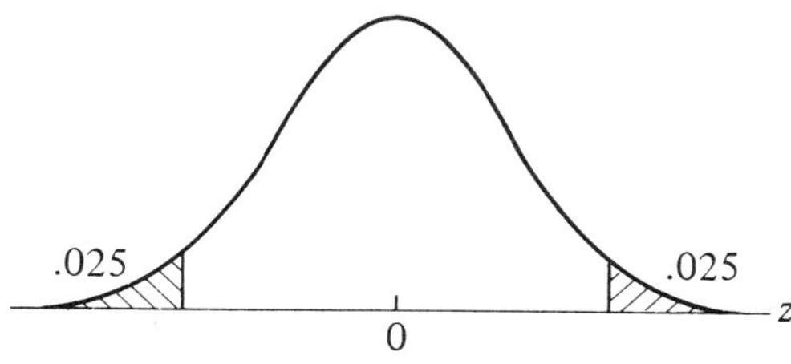

________ ________ -1.96; 1.96

Calculate the observed value of z using $\mu_0 = \$6.35$ and σ approximated by the sample standard deviation s.

$$z = \frac{6.16 - 6.35}{1.562/\sqrt{\_\_\_\_\_\_}} = \frac{-.19}{\_\_\_\_\_\_} = \_\_\_\_\_\_\_\_$$ 400; .0781; -2.43

Based upon the sample evidence we (reject, do not reject) H_0 and conclude that the mean income per invoice (is, is not) different from $6.35 with probability of error equal to .05.

reject
is

At this point the management would want to estimate the current year's mean income per invoice. A 95% confidence interval estimate would be

1.96 $$\bar{x} \pm \_\_\_\_\_\_\_\_\_ s/\sqrt{n}$$

or

1.96 $$\$6.16 \pm \_\_\_\_\_\_\_\_\_ (.0781)$$

.15 $$\$6.16 \pm \_\_\_\_\_\_\_\_\_$$

$6.01 so that the mean income per invoice is estimated to lie between _________

$6.31 and _________ with 95% confidence.

Example 8.15

A test of a binomial p. Suppose it is hypothesized that $p = 0.1$. Test this hypothesis at the $\alpha = .01$ level against the alternative that $p < 0.1$ if the number of successes is $x = 8$ in a sample of $n = 100$. In this problem

1. $\theta = p$
2. $\theta_0 = p_0 = 0.1$
3. $\hat{\theta} = \hat{p} = x/n$
4. $\sigma_{\hat{\theta}} = \sqrt{p_0 q_0/n}$
5. $\alpha = .01$

Solution

Note that p_0 and q_0 are used in $\sigma_{\hat{p}}$ to conform with $H_0: p = p_0$. The elements of the test are:

0.1 1. $H_0: p =$ _________

0.1 2. $H_a: p <$ _________

3. Test statistic:

$$z = \frac{\hat{p} - p_0}{\sqrt{p_0 q_0/n}}$$

4. Rejection region:

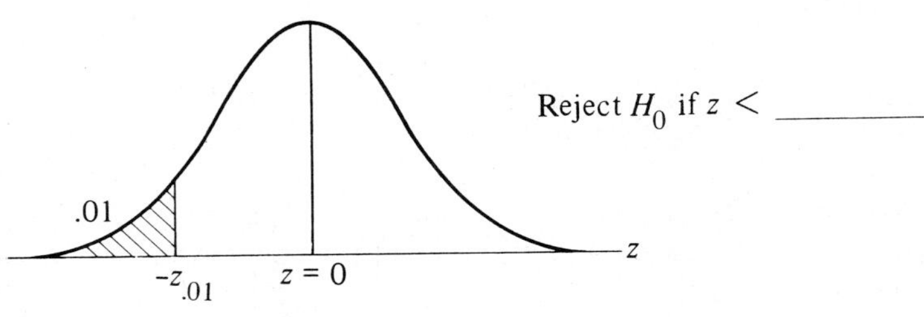

To calculate z, we need $\hat{p} = x/n$.

$$\hat{p} = (\_\_\_\_\_\_\_\_)/(\_\_\_\_\_\_\_\_) = \_\_\_\_\_\_\_\_$$

8; 100; .08

and

$$z = \frac{\hat{p} - 0.1}{\sqrt{\frac{(0.1)(0.9)}{100}}} = \frac{(\_\_\_\_\_\_\_\_) - 0.1}{\sqrt{\frac{(\_\_\_\_\_\_\_\_)}{100}}}$$

.08

.09

$$z = \frac{(\_\_\_\_\_\_\_\_)}{(\_\_\_\_\_\_\_\_)} = \_\_\_\_\_\_\_\_$$

$\frac{-.02}{.03}$; $-.667$

Since the value of z (does, does not) fall in the rejection region, we (will, will not) reject H_0.

does not
will not

Before deciding to accept H_0 as true, we may wish to evaluate the probability of a Type II error for meaningful values of p described by H_a. Until this is done, we shall state our decision as "Do not reject H_0."

Example 8.16

Test of an hypothesis concerning $(\mu_1 - \mu_2)$. Before launching a full-scale training program, a company must decide which of two manager training programs it will use. Seventy participants were randomly divided into two groups of thirty-five. During a six-week trial period one group was trained according to program A while the other was trained according to program B. At the end of the trial period the programs were evaluated by means of a test given to each participant. Assuming the test to be a valid criterion in comparing the programs, test the hypothesis that there is no difference in mean scores for the two programs at the $\alpha = .05$ level of significance. Which program should the company decide to use? The data follow.

Program A	*Program B*
$\bar{x}_1 = 80.2$	$\bar{x}_2 = 72.8$
$s_1^2 = 49.3$	$s_2^2 = 64.5$
$n_1 = 31$	$n_2 = 34$

(Not all participants completed the six-week program.)

Solution

This problem involves a test of $\mu_1 - \mu_2$. The unbiased estimator used in this test is ________ with standard deviation __________.

$\bar{x}_1 - \bar{x}_2$; $\sqrt{\frac{\sigma_1^2}{n_1} + \frac{\sigma_2^2}{n_2}}$

1. $H_0: \mu_1 - \mu_2 =$ ________

0

2. $H_a: \mu_1 - \mu_2 \neq$ ________

0

3. Test statistic:

$$z = \frac{(\bar{x}_1 - \bar{x}_2) - 0}{\sqrt{\dfrac{s_1^2}{n_1} + \dfrac{s_2^2}{n_2}}} \quad (\sigma_1 \text{ and } \sigma_2 \text{ are unknown})$$

4. Rejection region:
This is a two-tailed test with $\alpha = .05$.

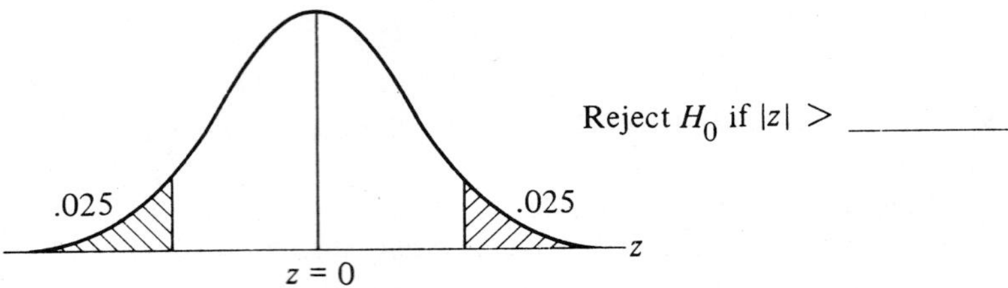

1.96 Reject H_0 if $|z| >$ ________

Computing the value of the test statistic,

80.2; 72.8

$$z = \frac{(\underline{\qquad\qquad} - \underline{\qquad\qquad}) - 0}{\sqrt{\dfrac{49.3}{31} + \dfrac{64.5}{34}}}$$

7.4

$$= \frac{\underline{\qquad\qquad}}{1.87}$$

3.96

$$= \underline{\qquad\qquad}$$

1.96 Since the calculated value of $z = 3.96$ is greater than $z_{.025} =$ __________,
reject we __________ H_0 and conclude that there is a difference in the effectiveness of the programs. The data indicate that program __________ should
A be the one adopted for full-scale use.

Example 8.17
Test of an hypothesis concerning $(p_1 - p_2)$. To investigate possible differences in attitude about a current economic problem, 100 randomly selected citizens between the ages of 18 and 25 were polled and 100 randomly selected citizens over age 25 were polled. Each was asked if he or she agreed with the government's position on the problem. Forty-five of the first group agreed, while 63% of the second group agreed. Do these data represent a significant difference in attitude for these two groups?

Solution

This problem involves a test of the difference between two binomial proportions, $p_1 - p_2$. The relevant data are given in the table.

	Group 1	Group 2
n	100	100
$\hat{p}$	.45	.63

1. $H_0: p_1 - p_2$ ________ $= 0$

2. $H_a: p_1 - p_2$ ________ $\neq 0$

3. For testing the hypothesis of *no difference* between proportions, the test statistic is

$$z = \frac{(\hat{p}_1 - \hat{p}_2) - 0}{\sqrt{\hat{p}\hat{q}\left(\frac{1}{n_1} + \frac{1}{n_2}\right)}}$$

with

$$\hat{p} = \frac{x_1 + x_2}{n_1 + n_2}$$

4. Rejection region:

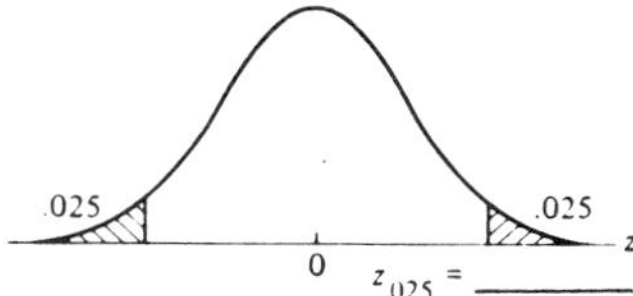

1.96

For a two-tailed test with $\alpha = .05$, we will reject H_0 if $|z| >$ ________. 1.96

To calculate the test statistic, we need

$$\hat{p} = \frac{x_1 + x_2}{n_1 + n_2} = \frac{45 + 63}{200} = \_\_\_\_\_\_$$ .54

Then

$$z = \frac{(.45 - .63) - 0}{\sqrt{(.54)(.46)(2/100)}}$$

$= \_\_\_\_\_\_ /.0705$ $-.18$

$= \_\_\_\_\_\_$ -2.55

reject Since $|-2.55| = 2.55 > 1.96$, we (reject, do not reject) H_0 and conclude that
is there (is, is not) a significant difference in opinion between these two age groups with respect to this issue.

Example 8.18
Refer to Example 8.12. Using $\alpha = .05$, set up a formal test of hypothesis to test the researcher's claim.

Solution

1. $H_0: \mu = 140$

2. $H_a: \mu > 140$

3. Test statistic:

$$z = \frac{\bar{x} - \mu_0}{\sigma/\sqrt{n}} \quad \text{(using } s \text{ if } \sigma \text{ is unknown)}$$

4. Rejection region:

1.645

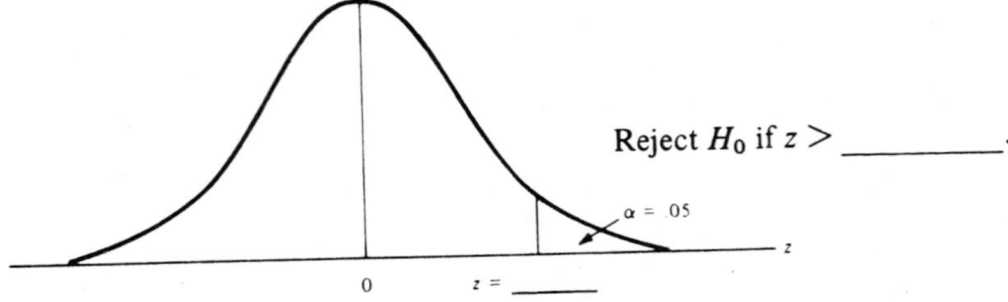

1.645

Having defined the test, calculate z.

143.2

$$z = \frac{\bar{x} - \mu_0}{\sigma/\sqrt{n}} \approx \frac{\_\_\_\_\_\_ - 140}{9.4/\sqrt{40}}$$

3.2/1.486; 2.15

$$= \frac{\_\_\_\_\_\_}{\_\_\_\_\_\_} = \_\_\_\_\_\_$$

2.15; reject Since $z =$ ________ > 1.645, the decision is to (reject, not reject) H_0 with
does $\alpha = .05$. The new fertilizer (does, does not) increase yield.

Self-Correcting Exercises 8D

1. The board of directors of an investment company is considering the possible merger of their company with another. If 34 shareholders in a random sample

of 65 shareholders stated that they were in favor of the merger, test the hypothesis that a majority of the stockholders favor merger (the proportion favoring merger is greater than .5) at the $\alpha = .05$ level of significance.

2. To compare the assembly times for two assembly techniques, 30 workers were randomly chosen to use Method 1 and 40 workers were randomly chosen to use Method 2. Using the data summary below, could you conclude that there is a significant difference in the mean assembly times for these two methods at the $\alpha = .01$ level of significance?

Method 1	*Method 2*
$n_1 = 30$	$n_2 = 40$
$\bar{x}_1 = 21.1$ min.	$\bar{x}_2 = 18.0$ min.
$s_1 = 3.5$ min.	$s_2 = 4.2$ min.

3. A market research organization found that 160 in a random sample of 400 households in City 1 had at least one color television set, while a random sample of 250 households in City 2 showed 90 with at least one color television set. Is there reason to believe that the proportion of households with color televisions differs between City 1 and City 2? Answer the question by testing the appropriate hypothesis at the $\alpha = .05$ level of significance.
4. In a manufacturing plant employing a double inspection procedure, the first inspector is expected to miss an average of 25 defective items per day with a standard deviation of 3 items. If the first inspector has missed an average of 29 defectives per day based upon the last 30 working days, is he working up to company standards? Answer the question using a test of an hypothesis at the $\alpha = .01$ level of significance.

8.8 The Level of Significance of a Statistical Test

The structure of a statistical test of hypothesis can be summarized as follows:

1. State the null and ______________ (or ______________) hypotheses. — research; alternative
2. Choose a test statistic.
3. Choose a value of α and, depending on the nature of the alternative hypothesis, establish a one- or two-tailed rejection region for which the α level is approximately the level chosen.
4. Perform the experiment, calculate the test statistic and come to a conclusion based on the observed value of the test statistic. If the value of the test statistic falls in the rejection region we ______________ the null hypothesis in favor of the alternative hypothesis. If the value of the test statistic is not in the rejection region we (can, cannot) reject the null hypothesis in favor of the alternative hypothesis. — reject; cannot

One difficulty in utilizing the approach outlined above is that the choice of the α level is to some extent subjective. Another researcher may disagree with your conclusions regarding the research hypothesis because he or she does not agree level of significance — with your choice of the α level. The __________ __________ __________ or p-value for an observed value of the test statistic is the smallest α value for which the null hypothesis could be rejected. In using the rare-event philosophy, we reject the null hypothesis in favor of the alternative whenever the total probability of the observed value of the test statistic or

small — any rarer event is __________ .

Consider the problem discussed in Example 8.15. In that problem we tested $H_0: p = 0.1$ versus $H_a: p < 0.1$ based on an observed value of $\hat{p} = .08$. Since this is a one-tailed test and "small" values of $\hat{p}$ belong in the rejection region, the smallest rejection region that contains $\hat{p}$ is the region $\hat{p} \leqslant .08$. The p-value associated with this observation is therefore

.08 — $$p\text{-value} = P(\hat{p} \leqslant \_\_\_\_\_\_)$$

$$= P\left(z \leqslant \frac{.08 - 0.1}{\sqrt{\frac{(0.1)(0.9)}{100}}}\right)$$

−.67 — $$= P(z \leqslant \_\_\_\_\_\_)$$

$$= .5 - .2486$$

.2514 — $$= \_\_\_\_\_\_$$

Thus any researcher who would specify an α value greater than or equal to

.2514; is — __________ would conclude that there (is, is not) sufficient evidence to accept the alternative hypothesis. Since this is a relatively high α value, it would prob-

not reject — ably be unacceptable, and the researcher would (reject, not reject) H_0.

The significance-level approach to hypothesis testing does not require specifying an α level before the analysis is undertaken. Rather, the degree of disagreement with the null hypothesis is quantified by the calculation of the

p value — __________ __________, which is used to make decisions regarding the alternative hypothesis.

Example 8.19

Calculate the level of significance for the data in Example 8.13.

Solution

The hypothesis to be tested is

$$H_0: \ \mu = 10$$

$$H_a: \ \mu \neq 10$$

This is a (one, two)-tailed test and the observed value of $\bar{x}$ was $\bar{x}$ = __________, or equivalently, | two; 12

$$z = \frac{\bar{x} - \mu_0}{\sigma/\sqrt{n}} \approx \_\_\_\_\_\_\_\_\_\_$$ | 5.62

This value of the test statistic is in the (upper, lower) tail of the distribution if the null hypothesis is true. The collection of all values of z as rare or rarer than $z = 5.62$ has probability $P(z \geqslant 5.62)$. Since the value $z = 5.62$ is not given in Table 3 of the Appendix, we can say only that the probability of interest is (less than, greater than) that given for the last tabled entry. That is, | upper | less than

$$P(z \geqslant 5.62) \text{ is less than } P(z \geqslant 3.09)$$

$$= .5 - \_\_\_\_\_\_\_\_\_\_ = \_\_\_\_\_\_\_\_\_\_$$ | .4990; .001

This probability accounts for only the values of $\bar{x}$ in the upper tail of the distribution. There would be values of $\bar{x}$ which are equally as rare in the lower tail of the distribution. In order to account for these realizations, the significance level is calculated by ______________ the value found above, so that | doubling

$$p\text{-value} < 2(\_\_\_\_\_\_\_\_\_\_) = \_\_\_\_\_\_\_\_\_\_$$ | .001; .002

Thus, for any researcher specifying an α value ($\geqslant, \leqslant$) .002, the conclusion would be to accept the alternative hypothesis, $\mu \neq 10$. | $\geqslant$

In summary, the procedure used to determine levels of significance is as follows:

1. Look at the alternative hypothesis. If it is an upper-tail alternative, list all values of the test statistic greater than or equal to the value observed. If it is a lower-tail alternative, list all values of the test statistic ______________ than or equal to the value observed. If it is a two-tailed alternative, determine which tail of the distribution contains the observed value and list all values as rare or rarer than the observed value that are in that tail. | less
2. Calculate the probability of getting a value of the test statistic in the collection of values given in part (1) assuming the ______________ hypothesis is true. If the test is ______________-tailed, this is the p-value. | null | one
3. If the test is two-tailed, the p-value is ______________ the probability calculated in (2). | twice

Self-Correcting Exercises 8E

1. Refer to Exercise 1, Self-Correcting Exercises 8D. Give the significance level of the test and interpret your results.
2. Refer to Exercise 2, Self-Correcting Exercises 8D. Give the significance level of the test and interpret your results.

3. A grocery store operator claims that the average waiting time at a checkout counter is 3.75 minutes. To test this claim, a random sample of 30 observations was taken.

Waiting Time in Minutes				
3	4	3	4	1
1	0	5	3	2
4	3	1	2	0
3	2	0	3	4
1	3	2	1	3
2	4	2	5	2

Give the significance level for the test of the operator's claim, and make a decision as to the validity of his claim using the p-value.

EXERCISES

1. List the two essential elements for any inference-making procedure.
2. What are two desirable properties of a point estimator, $\hat{\theta}$?
3. A bank was interested in estimating the average size of its savings accounts for a particular class of customer. If a random sample of 400 such accounts showed an average amount of \$61.23 and a standard deviation of \$18.20, place 90% confidence limits on the actual average account size.
4. A company wished to estimate the percentage of defective items produced by its local plant. In a random sample of 50 items selected from the production of this factory, three defectives were observed. Estimate the true percentage of defectives with a 95% confidence interval.
5. An appliance dealer sells toasters of two different brands, brand A and brand B. Let p_1 denote the fraction of brand A toasters which are returned to him by customers as defective, and let p_2 represent the fraction of brand B toasters which are rejected by customers as defective. Suppose that of 200 brand A toasters sold, 14 were returned as defective, while of 450 brand B toasters sold, 18 were returned as defective. Provide a 90% confidence interval for $p_1 - p_2$.
6. If 36 measurements of the specific gravity of aluminum had a mean of 2.705 and a standard deviation of 0.028, construct a 98% confidence interval for the actual specific gravity of aluminum.
7. To compare the tensile strengths of two synthetic fibers, samples of 31 of each kind were selected and tested for breaking strength. The results are summarized below. Find a 98% confidence interval for the difference between the true mean breaking strengths.

Fiber I	*Fiber II*
$\bar{x}_1 = 370$	$\bar{x}_2 = 332$
$s_1^2 = 1930$	$s_2^2 = 1670$

8. A sample of 39 cigarettes of a certain brand, tested for nicotine content, gave a mean of 22 and a standard deviation of 4 milligrams. Find a 90% confidence interval for μ.
9. A doctor wishes to estimate the average nicotine content in a certain brand of cigarettes correct to within 0.5 milligram. From previous experiments it is known that σ is in the neighborhood of 4 milligrams. How large a sample should the doctor take to be 95% confident of his estimate?
10. A manufacturer of dresses believes that approximately 20% of his product contains flaws. If he wishes to estimate the true percentage to within 8%, how large a sample should he take?
11. It is desired to estimate $\mu_1 - \mu_2$ from information contained in independent random samples from populations with variances $\sigma_1^2 = 9$ and $\sigma_2^2 = 16$. If the two sample sizes are to be equal ($n_1 = n_2 = n$), how large should n be in order to estimate $\mu_1 - \mu_2$ with an error less than 1.0 (with probability equal to .95)?
12. In order to bid competitively for the lumbering rights on a certain tract of land, a company needs to know the mean diameter of the trees on the tract to within 2.5 inches. If the company can assume $\sigma = 8$ inches, how large a sample of trees on this tract should be taken?
13. A marketing representative was assigned to observe the frequency of sales of his company's brand of canned ham at a supermarket. During a given day 25 canned hams were purchased from the supermarket. What is the probability that the percentage of those purchasing the company's brand exceeds 60%, if the true probability that any customer buying a canned ham buys the company's brand is .5?
14. What are the four essential elements of a statistical test of an hypothesis?
15. Assume that a certain set of "early returns" in an election is actually a random sample of size 400 from the voters in that election. If 225 of the voters in the sample voted for candidate A, could we assert with $\alpha = .01$ that candidate A has won?
16. Random samples of 100 shoes manufactured by machine A and 50 shoes manufactured by machine B showed 16 and 6 defective shoes, respectively. Do these data present sufficient evidence to suggest a difference in the performance of the machines? Use $\alpha = .05$.
17. In order to test the effectiveness of a vaccine, 150 experimental animals were given the vaccine; 150 were not. All 300 were then infected with the disease. Among those vaccinated, ten died as a result of the disease. Among the control group (i.e., those not vaccinated), there were 30 deaths.

Can we conclude that the vaccine is effective in reducing the mortality rate? Use a significance level of .025.

18. Refer to Exercise 17. Calculate the p-value for this test and interpret the results.
19. Two diets to be compared. Seventy-five individuals were selected at random from a population of overweight people. Forty of this group were assigned diet A and the other thirty-five were placed on diet B. The weight losses in pounds over a period of one week were found and the following quantities recorded:

	Sample Size	*Sample Mean (lbs)*	*Sample Variance*
Diet A	40	10.3	7.00
Diet B	35	7.3	3.25

   a. Do these data allow the conclusion that the expected weight loss under diet A (μ_A) is greater than the expected weight loss under diet B (μ_B)? Test at the .01 level. Draw the appropriate conclusion.
   b. Construct a 90% confidence interval for $\mu_A - \mu_B$.
20. A random sample of 400 radio tubes is drawn from a certain population of radio tubes. Let p be the fraction defective in the population. Suppose we wish to test $H_0: p = .2$ at the .01 level of significance.
   a. What statistic can be formed which has approximately the standard normal distribution when H_0 is true?
   b. State the rejection region for z if the alternative hypothesis is H_a: $p > .2$.
   c. State the rejection region for z if the alternative hypothesis is H_a: $p \neq .2$.
   d. If indeed the number of defective tubes in the sample of 400 is 80, find a 90% confidence interval for p, the true fraction defective in the population of radio tubes.
21. A manufacturer of refrigerators suspects that about 10% of his product is defective. How large a random sample should he select in order to estimate the true fraction defective to within 1% with probability .95?
22. Random samples of 200 bolts manufactured by machine A and 200 bolts manufactured by machine B showed 45 and 35 defective bolts, respectively. Do these data present sufficient evidence to suggest a difference in performances of the machines? Use $\alpha = .05$.
23. The following data pertain to breaking strengths of two types of rope, A and B.

	Type A	*Type B*
Number in sample	400	400
Mean breaking strength	168.2	149.1
Standard deviation	8.0	6.0

Determine 80% confidence limits for the difference in population mean breaking strengths.

24. A manufacturer had reason to believe that the percentage of younger people was greater than the percentage of older people who preferred his product. A sample of 800 persons under 40 years of age revealed that 200 preferred his product, while 120 of 800 persons over 40 years of age preferred his product. Does this provide sufficient evidence to support the manufacturer's claim?
25. To estimate the percentage of defective tubes produced by a certain machine, a sample of 100 tubes was taken and six were found to be defective. Find a 90% confidence interval for the true fraction defective produced by this machine.
26. In a sample of 400 seeds, 240 germinated. At the 2.5% level of significance is this reason enough to reject the claim that 64% or more will germinate?
27. Two different methods of manufacturing, die forging and casting, were used to make parts for an appliance. In service tests of 100 of each type, it was found that ten castings failed during the test, but only three forged parts failed. Place a 98% confidence interval on the true difference in the fractions of defectives produced by the two methods.
28. A manufacturer of cereal states that the average weight of cereal in his boxes is at least 20 ounces. A sample of 64 boxes of this cereal was examined and revealed a mean of 19 ounces and a standard deviation of three ounces. Does the sample provide enough evidence to reject the manufacturer's claim at the 5% significance level?
29. It is desired to test the hypothesis that the mean of a population is 145 against the alternative that the mean is less than 145. A sample of 100 measurements drawn from the population yields $\bar{x} = 140$ and $s = 20$. If α is chosen to be .05, calculate the power of the test, $1 - \beta$, if the mean actually equals 137.
30. A market research organization has decided to introduce a special group of color television advertisements for a client in cities in which more than 40% of the households have color television. If a random sample of 125 households in a specific city showed that 55 of those households had at least one color television set, would this city be one in which the advertising campaign should be introduced? Test at the $\alpha = .05$ level of significance.
31. It is thought that about one-tenth of the individuals in a given population have a certain genetic defect. In order to determine the true fraction with a maximum error of .003 with probability .95, the sample size should be at least how large?
32. It is known from long experience that the variability in a certain method of determining the concentration of a chemical in solution is indicated by a standard deviation of .005 grams per cubic centimeter. Determine the number of measurements so that the error of the estimated concentration will be less than .0005 with probability .95.

Chapter 9

INFERENCES FROM SMALL SAMPLES

9.1 Introduction

Central Limit

normal

Large-sample methods for making inferences about a population were considered in the preceding chapter. When the sample size was large, the _________ ______________ Theorem assured the approximate normality of the distribution of the estimators $\bar{x}$ or $\hat{p}$. However, time, cost, or other limitations may prevent an investigator from collecting enough data to feel confident in using large-sample techniques. When the sample size is small, $n < 30$, the Central Limit Theorem may no longer apply. This difficulty can be overcome if the investigator is reasonably sure that his or her measurements constitute a sample from a _______________ population.

randomly

The results presented in this chapter are based on the assumption that the observations being analyzed have been ______________ drawn from a normal population. This assumption is not as restrictive as it sounds, since the normal distribution can be used as a model in cases where the underlying distribution is mound-shaped and fairly symmetrical.

9.2 Student's *t* Distribution

When the sample size is large, the statistic

$$\frac{\bar{x} - \mu}{\sigma/\sqrt{n}}$$

is approximately distributed as the standard normal random variable z. What can be said about this statistic when n, the sample size, is small and the sample variance s^2 is used to estimate σ^2?

If the parent population is not normal (nor approximately normal), the behavior of the statistic given above is not known in general when n is small. Its distribution could be empirically generated by repeated sampling from the population of interest. If the parent population *is* normal, we can rely upon the results of W. S. Gosset, who published under the pen name Student. He drew repeated samples from a normal population and tabulated the distribution of a statistic which he called t, where

$$t = \frac{\bar{x} - \mu}{s/\sqrt{n}}$$

The resulting distribution for t has the following properties:

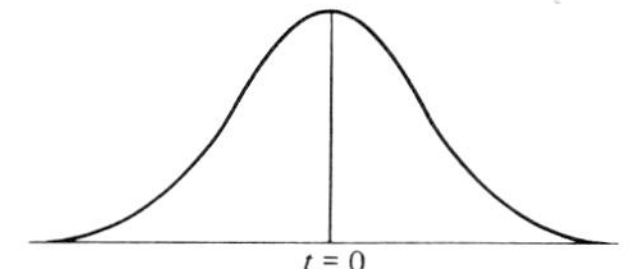

1. The distribution is ________-shaped. — mound
2. The distribution is ________ about the value $t = 0$. — symmetrical
3. The distribution has more flaring tails than z; hence t is (more, less) variable than the z statistic. — more
4. The shape of the distribution changes as the value of ________, the sample size, changes. — n
5. As the sample size n becomes large, the t distribution becomes identical to the ________ ________ distribution. — standard normal

These results are based on the following two assumptions:

1. The parent population has a ________ distribution. The t statistic is, however, relatively stable for nonnormal ________-shaped distributions. — normal; mound
2. The sample is a ________ sample. When the population is normal, this assures us that $\bar{x}$ and s^2 are independent. — random

For a fixed sample size, n, the statistic

$$z = \frac{\bar{x} - \mu}{\sigma/\sqrt{n}}$$

contains exactly ________ random quantity, the sample mean ________. — one; $\bar{x}$

However, the statistic

$$t = \frac{\bar{x} - \mu}{s/\sqrt{n}}$$

contains ________ random quantities, ________ and ________. — two; $\bar{x}$; s

more — This accounts for the fact that t is (more, less) variable than z. In fact, $\bar{x}$ may be large while s is small or $\bar{x}$ may be small while s is large. Hence it is said
independent — that $\bar{x}$ and s are ______________, which means that the value assumed by $\bar{x}$ in no way determines the value of s.

As the sample size changes, the corresponding t distribution changes so that each value of n determines a different probability distribution. This is due to the variability of s^2, which appears in the denominator of t. Large sample
more — sizes produce (more, less) stable estimates of σ^2 than do small sample sizes. These different probability curves are identified by the degrees of freedom associated with the estimator of σ^2.

The term "degrees of freedom" can be explained in the following way. The sample estimate s^2 uses the sum of squared deviations in its calculation.

0 — Recall that $\sum_{i=1}^{n} (x_i - \bar{x}) =$ __________. This means that if we know the values of $n - 1$ deviations, we can determine the last value uniquely since their sum must be zero. Therefore, the sum of squared deviations,

$n - 1$ — $\sum_{i=1}^{n} (x_i - \bar{x})^2$, contains only __________ independent deviations and not n independent deviations, as one might expect. Degrees of freedom refer to the number of independent deviations that are available for estimating σ^2. When n observations are drawn from one population, we use the estimator

$$\hat{\sigma}^2 = s^2 = \sum_{i=1}^{n} (x_i - \bar{x})^2 \Big/ (n - 1)$$

$n - 1$ — In this case, the degrees of freedom for estimating σ^2 are __________ and the
$n - 1$ — resulting t distribution is indexed as having __________ degrees of freedom.

The Use of Tables for the t Distribution

right — We define t_α as that value of t having an area equal to α to its ____________,
left — and $-t_\alpha$ is that value of t having an area equal to α to its ______________.
Consider the following diagram:

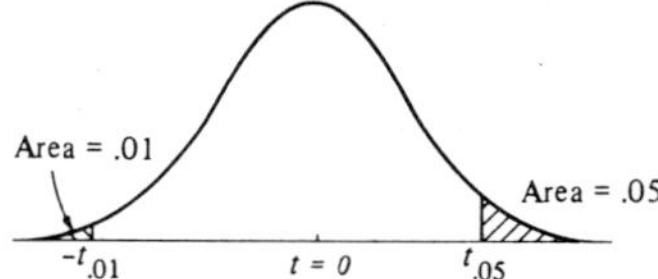

symmetrical — The distribution of t is ______________ about the value $t = 0$; hence, only the positive values of t need be tabulated. Problems involving left-tailed values of t can be solved in terms of right-tailed values, as was done with the z statistic.

A negative value of t simply indicates that you are working in the (left, right) tail of the distribution. | left

Table 4 of the text tabulates *commonly used* critical values, t_α, based on 1, 2, . . . , 29, ∞ degrees of freedom for α = .100, .050, .025, .010, .005. This table has been reproduced as Table 4 in the Appendix to this study guide. Along the top margin of the table you will find columns labeled t_α for the various values of α, while along the right margin you will find a column marked degrees of freedom, d.f. By cross-indexing you can find the value t having an area equal to α to its right and having the proper degrees of freedom.

Example 9.1

To find the critical value of t for $\alpha = .05$ with 5 degrees of freedom, find 5 in the right margin. Now by reading across, you will find $t = 2.015$ in the $t_{.05}$ column. In the same manner, we find that for 12 degrees of freedom, $t_{.025}$ = __________. In using Table 4, a student should think of his problem in terms of α, the area to the right of the value of t, and the degrees of freedom used to estimate σ^2. Compare the different values of t based on an infinite number of degrees of freedom with those for a corresponding z. You can perhaps see the reason for choosing a sample size greater than __________ as the dividing point for using the z distribution when the standard deviation s is used as an estimate for __________.

2.179

30

σ

Example 9.2

Find the critical values for t when t_α is that value of t with an area of α to its right, based on the following degrees of freedom.

	α	*d.f.*	t	
a.	.05	2	______	2.920
b.	.005	10	______	3.169
c.	.10	28	______	1.313
d.	.01	16	______	2.583
e.	.025	20	______	2.086
f.	.005	3	______	5.841
g.	.05	13	______	1.771
h.	.10	8	______	1.397
i.	.025	15	______	2.131
j.	.005	22	______	2.819

Students taking their first course in statistics usually ask the following questions at this point: "How will I know whether I should use z or t? Is sample size the only criterion I should apply?" No, sample size is not the only criterion to be used.

When the sample size is *large*, both

$$T_1 = \frac{\bar{x} - \mu}{\sigma/\sqrt{n}} \quad \text{and} \quad T_2 = \frac{\bar{x} - \mu}{s/\sqrt{n}}$$

behave as a standard normal random variable z regardless of the distribution of the parent population. When the sample size is *small* and the sampled population is *not normal*, then in general neither T_1 nor T_2 behaves as z or t. In the special case when the parent population is *normal*, then T_1 behaves as z and T_2 behaves as t.

Use this information to complete the following table when the sample is drawn from a *normal* distribution.

	Statistic	*Sample size* $n < 30$	*Sample size* $n \geqslant 30$
t	$\dfrac{\bar{x} - \mu}{s/\sqrt{n}}$	________	t or app. z
$z; z$	$\dfrac{\bar{x} - \mu}{\sigma/\sqrt{n}}$	________	________

9.3 Small-Sample Inferences About a Population Mean

Small-Sample Test Concerning a Population Mean, μ

A test of an hypothesis concerning the mean, μ, of a *normal* population when $n < 30$ and σ is unknown proceeds as follows.

1. $H_0: \mu = \mu_0$
2. H_a: Appropriate one- or two-tailed alternative.
3. Test statistic:
$$t = \frac{\bar{x} - \mu}{s/\sqrt{n}}$$
4. Rejection region with $\alpha = P$ [falsely rejecting H_0]:
   a. For $H_a: \mu > \mu_0$, reject H_0 if $t > t_\alpha$ based upon $n - 1$ degrees of freedom.
   b. For $H_a: \mu < \mu_0$, reject H_0 if $t < -t_\alpha$ based upon $n - 1$ degrees of freedom.
   c. For $H_a: \mu \neq \mu_0$, reject H_0 if $|t| > t_{\alpha/2}$ based upon $n - 1$ degrees of freedom.

Example 9.3

A new electronic device that requires two hours per item to produce on a production line has been developed by Company A. While the new product is being run, profitable production time is used. Hence the manufacturer decides to produce only six new items for testing purposes. For each of the six items, the time to failure is measured, yielding the measurements 59.2, 68.3, 57.8, 56.5, 63.7, and 57.3 hours. Is there sufficient evidence to indicate that the new device has a mean life greater than 55 hours at the $\alpha = .05$ level?

Solution

To calculate the sample mean and standard deviation we need

$$\Sigma x_i = 362.8 \text{ and } \Sigma x_i^2 = 22{,}043.60$$

Then

$$\bar{x} = \frac{1}{n}\Sigma x_i = \frac{(\_\_\_\_\_\_)}{(\_\_\_\_\_\_)} = \_\_\_\_\_\_$$ 362.8/6; 60.4667

and

$$s^2 = \frac{1}{n-1}\left[\Sigma x_i^2 - \frac{(\Sigma x_i)^2}{n}\right]$$

$$= \frac{1}{5}\left[22{,}043.60 - \frac{(362.8)^2}{6}\right]$$

$$= 21.2587$$

with $s = \sqrt{21.2587} = 4.61073$

The test proceeds as follows:

1. $H_0 : \mu$ ______ = 55

2. $H_a : \mu$ ______ > 55

3. Test statistic:

$$t = \frac{\bar{x} - 55}{s/\sqrt{n}}$$

4. Rejection region:

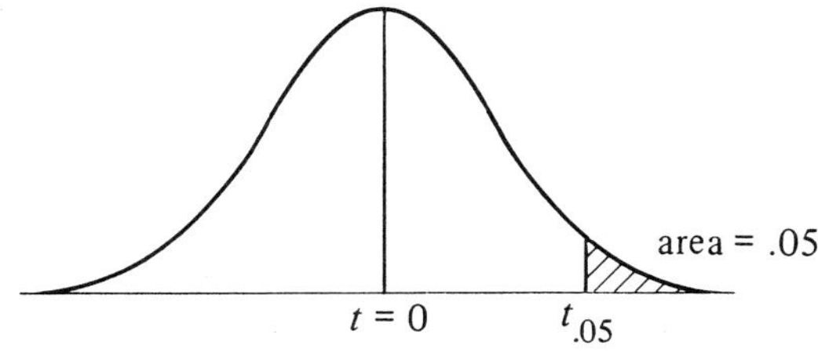

2.015

Based on 5 degrees of freedom, reject H_0 if $t >$ __________.

Now calculate the value of the test statistic:

$$t = \frac{\bar{x} - 55}{s/\sqrt{n}}$$

60.4667

$$= \frac{\_\_\_\_\_\_\_\_\_\_ - 55}{4.61073/\sqrt{6}}$$

5.4667

$$= \frac{\_\_\_\_\_\_\_\_\_\_}{1.8823}$$

2.90

$$= \_\_\_\_\_\_\_\_\_\_$$

is

reject; is

Since the observed value (is, is not) larger than 2.015, we (reject, do not reject) H_0. There (is, is not) sufficient evidence to indicate that the new device has a mean life greater than 55 hours at the 5% level of significance.

Confidence Interval for a Population Mean μ

In estimating a population mean, one can use either a point estimator with bounds on error or an interval estimator having the required level of confidence.

Small-sample estimation of the mean of a *normal* population with σ *unknown* involves the statistic

$$\frac{\bar{x} - \mu}{s/\sqrt{n}}$$

t; $n - 1$

which has a __________ distribution with (__________) degrees of freedom. The resulting $100\%(1 - \alpha)$ confidence interval estimator is given as

$$\bar{x} \pm t_{\alpha/2}\, s/\sqrt{n}$$

where $t_{\alpha/2}$ is that value of t based upon $n - 1$ degrees of freedom having an area of $\alpha/2$ to its right.

$\bar{x} - t_{\alpha/2}\, s/\sqrt{n}$

$\bar{x} + t_{\alpha/2}\, s/\sqrt{n}$; $\bar{x}$

The lower confidence limit is ______________ and the upper confidence limit is ______________. The point estimator of μ is __________ and the bound on the error of estimation can be taken to be $t_{\alpha/2}\, s/\sqrt{n}$.

$1 - \alpha$

confidence intervals

A proper interpretation of a $(1 - \alpha)$ 100% confidence interval for μ would be stated as follows: In repeated sampling, (__________) 100% of the ______________ ______________ so constructed would enclose the true value of the mean, μ.

Example 9.4

Using the data from Example 9.3, find a 95% confidence interval estimate for μ, the mean life in hours for the new device.

Solution

The pertinent information from Example 9.3 is:

$\bar{x} = 60.4667$ d.f. = ________ 5

$s/\sqrt{n} = 1.8823$ $\alpha/2 = .025$

$t_{.025}$ = ________ 2.571

The confidence interval will be found by using

$$\bar{x} \pm t_{.025}\, s/\sqrt{n}$$

Substituting $\bar{x}$, $s/\sqrt{n}$, $t_{.025}$ we have

60.4667 ± ________ (1.8823) 2.571

60.4667 ± ________ 4.84

or (________, ________) 55.63; 65.31

Thus, we can estimate with 95% confidence that the true mean life for the new device lies between 55.63 and 65.31 hours.

The MINITAB system provides two commands which are useful in making inferences about the population mean μ (MU) when σ is unknown. The command TTEST followed by a value for μ_0 and a column number will allow the user to perform a t-test on the data in the specified column. This command requires that the user provide the appropriate value of μ_0 as specified by the null hypothesis, as well as the column number. For the test of hypothesis given in Example 9.3, the appropriate command is

TTEST 55 C1

and the MINITAB printout is shown below.

```
MTB > SET C1
DATA > 59.2  68.3  57.8  56.5  63.7  57.3
DATA > END
MTB > PRINT C1
C1
59.2    68.3    57.8    56.5    63.7    57.3

MTB > TTEST 55 C1

TEST OF MU = 55.0 VS MU N.E. 55.0

        N    MEAN     STDEV    SE MEAN    T       P VALUE
C1      6    60.47    4.61     1.9        2.90    0.034
```

The quantity labeled SE MEAN is defined as $s/\sqrt{n}$, as explained earlier in the text. The value of the test statistic is found in the column labeled T, and agrees with the results of Example 9.3. The column labeled P VALUE gives the level of significance of the test, or

$$p\text{-value} = P(t \geqslant 2.90) = .034$$

The null hypothesis can be rejected for any preselected value of α greater than or equal to .034.

The program command TINTERVAL followed by the desired confidence coefficient and a column number allows the user to compute the specified confidence interval for the population mean μ. For the data of Example 9.3, the command is

TINTERVAL 95 C1

and the resulting printout is shown below.

```
MTB > TINTERVAL 95 C1

        N     MEAN     STDEV     SE MEAN     95.0 PERCENT C. I.
C1      6     60.47    4.61      1.9         (55.6,        65.3)
```

The 95% confidence interval given here agrees with the calculations obtained in Example 9.4.

Example 9.5

In a random sample of ten cans of corn from supplier B, the average weight per can of corn was $\bar{x} = 9.4$ oz. with standard deviation, $s = 1.8$ oz. Does this sample contain sufficient evidence to indicate the mean weight is less than 10 oz. at the $\alpha = .01$ level? What p-value would you report?

Solution

1. The following information is needed:

10 $n =$ ________

9.4 $\bar{x} =$ ________

1.8 $s =$ ________

.01 $\alpha =$ ________

2. Set up the test as follows:

$H_0: \mu =$ ________ 10

$H_a: \mu <$ ________ 10

3. Test statistic:

$$t = \frac{\bar{x} - \mu}{s/\sqrt{n}}$$

4. Rejection region:

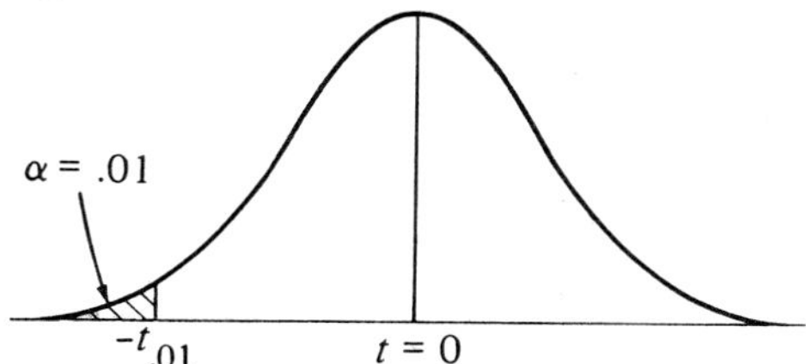

Based on 9 degrees of freedom, reject H_0 if $t <$ ________ -2.821

Calculate:

$$t = \frac{\bar{x} - \mu}{s/\sqrt{n}}$$

$$= \frac{9.4 - (\_\_\_\_\_\_)}{1.8/\sqrt{10}}$$ 10

$$= \frac{(\_\_\_\_\_\_)}{.57}$$ -.6

$= $ ________ -1.05

Since the calculated value of t (does, does not) fall in the rejection region we conclude that the data (do, do not) present sufficient evidence to indicate that the mean weight per can is less than 10 oz. does not / do not

The level of significance for this one-tailed test is defined to be

p-value $= P(t \leqslant$ ________ $) = P(t \geqslant 1.05)$ -1.05

where t has a Student's t distribution with $n - 1 =$ ________ degrees of freedom. From Table 4, with $d.f. = 9$, the critical value of $t = 1.05$ falls to the left 9

.10 of the smallest value given. That value is $t = 1.383$ with area __________ to its right.

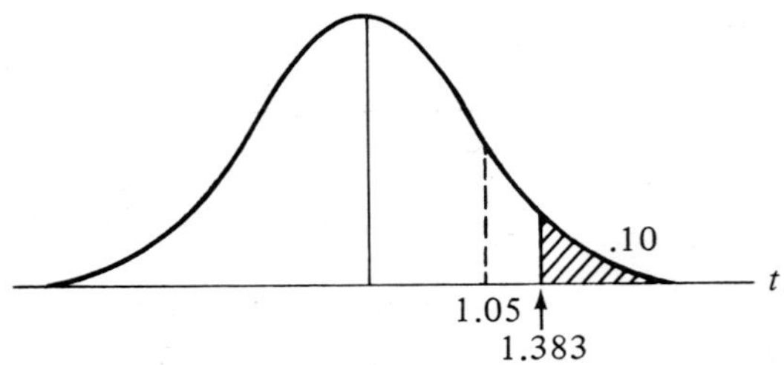

greater Hence, the area to the right of $t = 1.05$ is (greater, less) than .10, and the p-value
greater is ______________ than .10.

Example 9.6
Refer to Example 9.5. Find a 98% confidence interval for μ.

Solution

.02 $\alpha =$ __________

9 d.f. = __________

2.821 $t_{\alpha/2} =$ __________

Calculate:

$$\bar{x} \pm t_{\alpha/2}\, s/\sqrt{n}$$

9.4; .57 (__________) ± 2.821 (__________)

9.4; 1.6 (__________) ± (__________)

7.8 Therefore the 98% confidence interval required is (__________,
11.0 __________).

Self-Correcting Exercises 9A

1. In attempting to increase the number of miles traveled per gallon of gas, a designer has modified the fuel injection system on his company's six-cylinder engine. Seven modified engines were produced and installed into identical passenger cars. In road testing, the recorded miles per gallon for these seven vehicles were: 18.1, 19.7, 17.2, 18.9, 20.3, 18.5, 19.1.

a. Find a 95% confidence interval for μ, the mean number of miles per gallon achieved with the modified engine.
b. Has the modification significantly increased the average number of miles per gallon above the previous average of 17.5 mpg without the modification? What p-value would you report?

2. A pharmaceutical company must keep the amount of impurities in a certain product below .050 gram. The amount of impurities is monitored by analyzing 25 samples randomly drawn from the daily production and reporting the amount of impurities present per sample. Wednesday's sampling produced an average of .057 gram impurities with a standard deviation of .008 grams.
   a. Use the framework of a test of a statistical hypothesis with $\alpha = .01$ in making a decision as to whether Wednesday's production has an excess amount of impurities present.
   b. Find a 95% confidence interval for the mean amount of impurities present in Wednesday's production.

9.4 Small-Sample Inferences About the Difference Between Two Means

Inferences concerning $\mu_1 - \mu_2$ based on small samples are founded upon the following assumptions:

1. Each population sampled has a ______________ distribution. — normal
2. The population ______________ are equal; that is, $\sigma_1^2 = \sigma_2^2$. — variances
3. The samples are independently drawn.

An unbiased estimator for $\mu_1 - \mu_2$, regardless of sample size, is __________. — $\bar{x}_1 - \bar{x}_2$

The standard deviation of this estimator is

$$\sqrt{\frac{\sigma_1^2}{n_1} + \frac{\sigma_2^2}{n_2}}$$

When $\sigma_1^2 = \sigma_2^2$, we can replace σ_1^2 and σ_2^2 by a common variance σ^2. Then the standard deviation of $\bar{x}_1 - \bar{x}_2$ becomes

$$\sqrt{\frac{\sigma^2}{n_1} + \frac{\sigma^2}{n_2}} = (\_\_\_\_\_\_\_\_)\sqrt{\frac{1}{n_1} + \frac{1}{n_2}}$$

σ

If σ were known, then in testing an hypothesis concerning $\mu_1 - \mu_2$, we would use the statistic

$$z = \frac{(\bar{x}_1 - \bar{x}_2) - D_0}{\sigma\sqrt{\frac{1}{n_1} + \frac{1}{n_2}}}$$

where $D_0 = \mu_1 - \mu_2$. For small samples with σ unknown, we would use

$$t = \frac{(\bar{x}_1 - \bar{x}_2) - D_0}{s\sqrt{\frac{1}{n_1} + \frac{1}{n_2}}}$$

where s is the estimate of σ, calculated from the sample values. When the data are normally distributed, this statistic has a ______________ __________ distribution with degrees of freedom the same as those available for estimating __________.

Student's t

σ^2

In selecting the best estimate (s^2) for σ^2, we have three immediate choices:

a. s_1^2, the sample ______________ from population I.

b. s_2^2, the sample ______________ from population II.

c. A combination of __________ and __________.

The best choice is (a, b, c), since it uses the information from both samples. A logical method of combining this information into one estimate, s^2, is

variance

variance

s_1^2; s_2^2

c

d. $$s^2 = \frac{(n_1 - 1)s_1^2 + (n_2 - 1)s_2^2}{(n_1 - 1) + (n_2 - 1)}$$

a weighted average of the sample variances using the degrees of freedom as weights.

The expression in d can be written in another form by replacing s_1^2 and s_2^2 by their defining formulas. Then, if x_{1i} and x_{2i} represent the ith observation in samples 1 or 2, respectively,

$$s^2 = \frac{\sum_{i=1}^{n_1}(x_{1i} - \bar{x}_1)^2 + \sum_{i=1}^{n_2}(x_{2i} - \bar{x}_2)^2}{(n_1 - 1) + (n_2 - 1)}$$

In this form we see that we have pooled or added the sums of squared deviations from each sample and divided by the pooled degrees of freedom, $n_1 + n_2 - 2$. Hence s^2 is a *pooled estimate* of the common variance σ^2 and is based on ______________ degrees of freedom. Since our samples were drawn from normal populations, the statistic

$n_1 + n_2 - 2$

$$t = \frac{(\bar{x}_1 - \bar{x}_2) - (\mu_1 - \mu_2)}{s\sqrt{\frac{1}{n_1} + \frac{1}{n_2}}}$$

has a ______________ __________ distribution with __________ degrees of freedom.

Student's t; $n_1 + n_2 - 2$

Example 9.7

A restaurant owner claims that the eight-ounce steaks served at his restaurant contain, on the average, less waste than the eight-ounce steaks sold by his competitor. Twelve eight-ounce steaks were randomly selected from the claimant's restaurant, twelve from his competitor's, and their waste-free weights were recorded. The measurements yielded the following information.

Restaurant I (Claimant)	*Restaurant II (Competitor)*
$\bar{x}_1 = 6.8$ oz.	$\bar{x}_2 = 5.3$ oz.
$s_1 = 1.5$ oz.	$s_2 = 0.9$ oz.
$n_1 = 12$	$n_2 = 12$

Do these data present sufficient evidence to indicate at the $\alpha = .05$ level that the mean waste-free content of steaks from Restaurant I is greater than the waste-free content of steaks from Restaurant II? Find a 90% confidence interval for $\mu_1 - \mu_2$, the mean difference in waste-free content between the two restaurants.

Solution

We shall take the waste-free contents to be normally distributed with equal variances and calculate a pooled estimate for σ^2.

$$s^2 = \frac{(n_1 - 1)s_1^2 + (n_2 - 1)s_2^2}{n_1 + n_2 - 2}$$

$$= \frac{11(1.5)^2 + 11(0.9)^2}{12 + 12 - 2}$$

$$= \frac{(\_\_\_\_\_\_)}{22}$$ 33.66

$= \_\_\_\_\_\_$ 1.530

Then

$s = \sqrt{\_\_\_\_\_\_} = 1.237$ 1.530

The test is as follows:

1. $H_0 : \mu_1 - \mu_2 = \_\_\_\_\_\_$ 0

2. $H_a : \mu_1 - \mu_2 > \_\_\_\_\_\_$ 0

3. Test statistic:

$$t = \frac{(\bar{x}_1 - \bar{x}_2) - D_0}{s\sqrt{\frac{1}{n_1} + \frac{1}{n_2}}}$$

4. Rejection region:

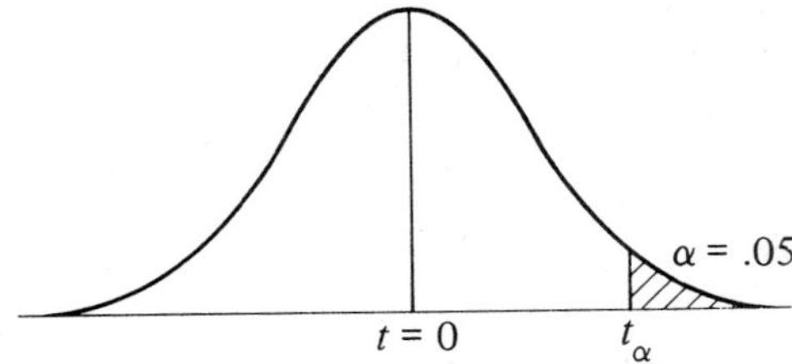

22 With $n_1 + n_2 - 2 =$ __________ degrees of freedom, we would reject H_0
1.717 if $t >$ __________. Calculate the test statistic.

$$t = \frac{(\bar{x}_1 - \bar{x}_2) - D_0}{s\sqrt{\frac{1}{n_1} + \frac{1}{n_2}}}$$

1.5; 0

$$= \frac{(\_\_\_\_\_\_) - (\_\_\_\_\_\_)}{1.237\sqrt{.1667}}$$

1.5

$$= \frac{(\_\_\_\_\_\_)}{.505}$$

2.97

$$= \_\_\_\_\_\_$$

reject H_0 Decision: __________ __________

5. To find a 90% confidence interval for $\mu_1 - \mu_2$, we need $t_{.05}$ based upon 22 degrees of freedom. $t_{.05} =$ __________.

1.717

Hence we would use

$$(\bar{x}_1 - \bar{x}_2) \pm 1.717\, s\sqrt{\frac{1}{n_1} + \frac{1}{n_2}}$$

1.5; .505 __________ ± 1.717 (__________) from part b

1.5; .867 (__________) ± (__________)

Therefore a 90% confidence interval for $\mu_1 - \mu_2$ would be

(__________, __________) .63; 2.37

The testing procedure used to make decisions about the difference between two means requires the assumptions that each underlying population possesses a __________ probability distribution, and that the population __________ are __________. Departures from the normally assumption (are, are not) serious. However, the population variances must be __________ equal for the test to be valid.

normal
variances; equal
are not
nearly

Example 9.8
A consumer-oriented magazine designed a study to compare the speed and energy efficiency of two brands of microwave ovens. In the experiment, five identical microwaves made by Company A were to be tested against five microwaves from Company B. The experimenter placed identical one-cup containers of room temperature water in each oven and measured the time in seconds until the water reached a boiling point. Unfortunately, when the experiment began, one of Company A's microwaves proved to have a defective fan mechanism and had to be eliminated from the experiment. The results from the remaining nine microwaves are given below:

Company A	*Company B*
152	171
161	170
155	174
157	180
	176

Do these data provide sufficient evidence to indicate a difference in the average boiling times for the two types of microwave ovens? Find the approximate level of significance for the test and interpret the results.

Solution
We will assume that the times for the two types of ovens are normally distributed with equal variances.
1. The hypothesis to be tested is

$$H_0: \mu_1 - \mu_2 = 0$$

$$H_a: \mu_1 - \mu_2 \text{ \_\_\_\_\_\_\_\_\_\_}$$

$\neq 0$

The following calculations are necessary:

Company A	Company B
$\Sigma x_{1i} = 625$	$\Sigma x_{2i} = 871$
$\Sigma x_{1i}^2 = 97{,}699$	$\Sigma x_{2i}^2 = 151{,}793$
$\bar{x}_1 = 156.25$	$\bar{x}_2 = 174.2$
$n_1 = 4$	$n_2 = 5$

2. Calculate the pooled estimate for σ^2 using the alternate form of s^2 as

$$s^2 = \frac{\sum_{i=1}^{n_1} (x_{1i} - \bar{x}_1)^2 + \sum_{i=1}^{n_2} (x_{2i} - \bar{x}_2)^2}{(n_1 - 1) + (n_2 - 1)}$$

$$= \frac{\Sigma x_{1i}^2 - \frac{(\Sigma x_{1i})^2}{n_1} + \Sigma x_{2i}^2 - \frac{(\Sigma x_{2i})^2}{n_2}}{n_1 + n_2 - 2}$$

151,793; 871

$$= \frac{97{,}699 - \frac{(625)^2}{4} + \underline{\qquad} - \frac{(\underline{\qquad})^2}{5}}{\underline{\qquad}}$$

7

107.55; 15.3643

$$= \frac{\underline{\qquad}}{7} = \underline{\qquad}$$

3. The test statistic is

$$t = \frac{\bar{x}_1 - \bar{x}_2 - D_0}{\sqrt{s^2\left(\frac{1}{n_1} + \frac{1}{n_2}\right)}} = \frac{(156.25 - 174.2)}{\sqrt{15.3643(1/4 + 1/5)}}$$

− 17.95

− 6.827

$$= \frac{\underline{\qquad}}{2.6294} = \underline{\qquad}$$

two-tailed

6.827

right

right

less

4. Level of Significance: The level of significance for this (one-tailed, two-tailed) test is p-value $= 2P(t >$ __________). Notice in Table 4 that this value is not tabulated. Rather, for each different value of the degrees of freedom, the table gives t_α such that $P[t > t_\alpha] = \alpha$. This is the value of t that cuts off an area equal to α to its (right, left). However, since the observed value, $t =$ 6.827 falls to the (left, right) of the largest tabulated value, $t_{.005} = 3.499$, the area to the right of $t = 6.827$ must be (greater, less) than .005. Hence, the

level of significance is p-value $< 2(.005) = .01$. This value is small enough to allow rejection of H_0. Hence, we conclude that there (is, is not) sufficient evidence to detect a difference in the two averages.

is

In order to use either MINITAB or SAS to compute a confidence interval or test an hypothesis about the parameter $\mu_1 - \mu_2$, the raw data must be stored in the computer. For the MINITAB system, the n_1 measurements constituting the first sample are stored in one column (say C1), while the n_2 measurements constituting the second sample are stored in second column (say C2). The command TWOSAMPLE C1 C2; followed by the subcommand POOLED. will perform the t-test described in this section. This command will also produce a 95% confidence interval for $\mu_1 - \mu_2$ unless a different degree of confidence is specified in the command. The computer printout for the data given in Example 9.8 is shown below. The results agree with those calculated in Example 9.8.

```
MTB > TWOSAMPLE C1 C2;
SUBC > POOLED.
TWOSAMPLE T FOR C1 VS C2

        N        MEAN        STDEV       SE MEAN
C1      4        156.25      3.77        1.9
C2      5        174.20      4.02        1.8

95 PCT CI FOR MU C1 - MU C2: (-24.2, -11.7)
TTEST MU C1 = MU C2 (VS NE): T=-6.83 P=0.0000 DF=7.0
```

If the subcommand POOLED. is omitted, the command TWOSAMPLE followed by two column numbers (to indicate the two samples upon which the test is to be performed) calculates the statistic

$$t = \frac{\bar{x}_1 - \bar{x}_2}{\sqrt{\dfrac{s_1^2}{n_1} + \dfrac{s_2^2}{n_2}}}$$

which is not the same as the pooled statistic (using s^2) found in this section. The degrees of freedom given in the printout are calculated using an approximation procedure as

$$\text{d.f.} \approx \frac{\left(\dfrac{s_1^2}{n_1} + \dfrac{s_2^2}{n_2}\right)^2}{\dfrac{\left(\dfrac{s_1^2}{n_1}\right)^2}{n_1 - 1} + \dfrac{\left(\dfrac{s_2^2}{n_2}\right)^2}{n_2 - 1}}$$

The computer printout for the data given in Example 9.8 is given below for the analysis using the TWOSAMPLE command. Note the small difference in the confidence interval and the degrees of freedom. These differences will increase if the sample sizes are unequal.

```
MTB > TWOSAMPLE C1 C2

TWOSAMPLE T FOR C1 VS C2

        N      MEAN      STDEV     SE MEAN
C1      4    156.25       3.77        1.9
C2      5    174.20       4.20        1.8

95 PCT CI FOR MU C1 − MU C2: (−24.3, −11.6)
TTEST MU C1 = MU C2 (VS NE): T=−6.88 P=0.0005 DF=6.8
```

If the sample sizes are large (n_1 and n_2 greater than 30) and the raw data are still available to you, the command TWOSAMPLE may be used to calculate the z-statistic discussed in this section, and the result may be compared to a critical value of z. The TWOSAMPLE command is often used by experimenters who are not willing to make the assumption of equal variances for the two populations. If this is the case, the TWOSAMPLE procedure is used, and the approximate degrees of freedom are used to determine the approximate rejection region from Table 4.

Self-Correcting Exercises 9B

1. What are the assumptions required for the proper use of the statistic

$$t = \frac{(\bar{x}_1 - \bar{x}_2) - (\mu_1 - \mu_2)}{s\sqrt{\dfrac{1}{n_1} + \dfrac{1}{n_2}}}$$

2. In evaluating the efficiency of each of two teams of workers, a contractor records the length of time required for these teams to complete comparable assignments with the following results.

	Team 1	*Team 2*
Number of jobs	10	8
Mean completion time	6.3 hrs.	7.2 hrs.
Standard deviation	1.1 hrs.	2.2 hrs.

Test whether there is a significant difference in mean completion times for these two teams at the .05 level of significance.

3. In the evaluation of two possible advertising campaigns, a group of 30 volunteers were randomly divided into two groups of 15 people. Group number one was presented with advertising campaign one and the second presented with advertising campaign two. After the presentations, each person filled out an evaluation form prepared by the advertising agency. The information on each form was translated into a numerical score, resulting in the following summary.

	Campaigns	
	1	*2*
n	15	15
$\bar{x}$	80.3	68.7
s	6.2	9.3

a. Is there a significant difference in mean scores for the two presentations?
b. If the mean scores differ by 10 points or more, the campaign which scored 10 points higher than the other will proceed to the next stage of development. Estimate $\mu_1 - \mu_2$ with a 95% confidence interval. Based upon your estimate, would campaign number one be given approval to proceed to the next stage?
c. If you were reporting test results, what p-value would you report?

9.5 A Paired-Difference Test

In many situations an experiment is designed so that a comparison of the effects of two *treatments* is made on the same person, on twin offspring, two animals from the same litter, two pieces of fabric from the same loom, or two plants of the same species grown on adjacent plots. Such experiments are designed so that the pairs of experimental units (people, animals, fabrics, plants) are as much alike as possible. By taking measurements on the two treatments within the relatively homogeneous pairs of experimental units, we find the difference in the measurements for the two treatments in a pair will primarily reflect the difference between ________ means rather than the difference between experimental units. This experimental design reduces the error of comparison and increases the quantity of information in the experiment.

treatment

To analyze such an experiment using the techniques of the last section would be incorrect. In planning this type of experiment, we *intentionally violate* the assumption that the measurements are *independent* and we hope that this violation will work to our advantage by (increasing, reducing) the variability of the differences of the paired observations. Consider the situation in which two products are to be compared by analyzing the sales in dollars over a one-week period for each of the products in each of three stores. Store number 1 is a department store, store number 2 is a specialty shop and store number 3 is a general merchandise store. At the end of the specified time the sales data are collected and presented for analysis.

reducing

Store	Product A	Product B	Difference
1	A_1	B_1	$A_1 - B_1$
2	A_2	B_2	$A_2 - B_2$
3	A_3	B_3	$A_3 - B_3$

small

Now A_1 and B_1 are not independent since both sales records were made during the same week in a department store. Although A_1 could be larger or smaller than B_1, if A_1 were a large amount, we would also expect B_1 to be a large amount. Since store 2 is a specialty store, it probably has less in total sales than a department store. Hence if A_2 were a small amount, then we would expect B_2 to be a (small, large) amount. Store 3 would probably produce sales for each product lying somewhere between that of store 1 and that of store 2. However, by looking at the differences $(A_1 - B_1)$, $(A_2 - B_2)$, $(A_3 - B_3)$, the volume of sales at the various stores will no longer cloud the issue, since these differences should represent the difference due to consumer choice between the two products.

In using a paired-difference design, we analyze the differences of the paired measurements and, in so doing, attempt to *reduce* the *variability* that would be present in two *randomly* selected groups without pairing.

A test of the hypothesis that the difference in two population means, $\mu_1 - \mu_2$, is equal to a constant, D_0, is equivalent to a test of the hypothesis that the mean of the differences, μ_d, is equal to a constant, D_0. That is, $H_0: \mu_1 - \mu_2 = D_0$ is equivalent to $H_0: \mu_d = D_0$. Usually, we will be interested in the hypothesis that $D_0 = 0$.

Example 9.9

In order to evaluate a new training program for sales personnel, twelve new salesmen were selected and matched as closely as possible with respect to factors that could affect their potential sales ability, such as age, personality and past sales records. One member of each pair was randomly assigned to receive training under the standard program; the other member was trained according to the new program. At the end of their training periods, their progress was measured by their observed success in the market during a one-week period. Do the following data indicate that the new training program is better than the standard program? Use $\alpha = .05$.

Pair	Sales Record: Standard	Sales Record: New	$d_i = N - S$
1	68	73	5
2	75	79	4
3	98	97	-1
4	81	83	2
5	72	78	6
6	109	109	0

Find a 95% confidence interval for the mean difference in sales records.

Solution

We analyze the set of six differences as we would a single set of six measurements. The change in notation required is straightforward.

$$\sum_{i=1}^{6} d_i = 16 \qquad \sum_{i=1}^{6} d_i^2 = 82$$

The sample mean is

$$\bar{d} = \frac{1}{6}\sum_{i=1}^{6} d_i = \underline{\hspace{2cm}}$$ 2.6667

The sample variance of the differences is

$$s_d^2 = \frac{\sum_{i=1}^{6} d_i^2 - \frac{\left(\sum_{i=1}^{6} d_i\right)^2}{6}}{5}$$

$$= \frac{\underline{\hspace{2cm}} - (\underline{\hspace{2cm}})^2/6}{5}$$ 82; 16

$$= 7.8667$$

$$s_d = \sqrt{\underline{\hspace{2cm}}} = \underline{\hspace{2cm}}$$ 7.8667; 2.8048

The test is conducted as follows. Remember that $\mu_d = \mu_N - \mu_S$.

1. $H_0 : \mu_d =$ __________ 0

2. $H_a : \mu_d$ __________ > 0

3. Test statistic:

$$t = \frac{\bar{d} - 0}{s_d/\sqrt{n}}$$

4. Rejection region: Based upon 5 degrees of freedom we will reject H_0 if the observed value of t is greater than $t_{.05} =$ __________ . Note that this is a one-tailed test. 2.015

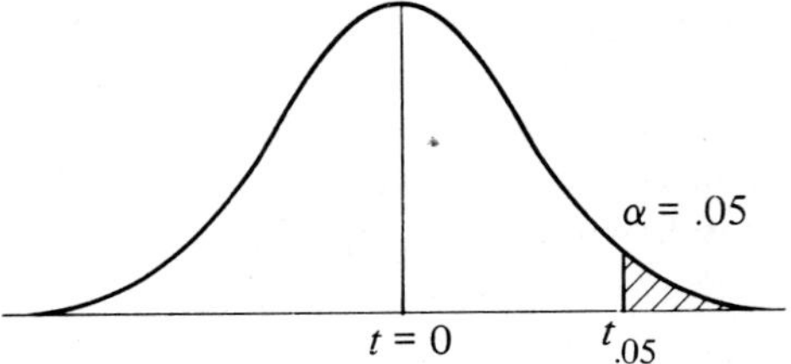

The sample value of t is

$$t = \frac{\bar{d} - 0}{s_d/\sqrt{n}}$$

$$= \frac{2.667 - 0}{2.80/\sqrt{6}}$$

$$= \frac{2.6667}{1.145}$$

$$= 2.33$$

reject

Since the value of the test statistic is greater than 2.015, we (reject, do not reject) H_0. This sample indicates that the new program appears to be superior to the standard program at the $\alpha = .05$ level, if we assume that the recorded sales are a valid criterion upon which to base our judgment.

A 95% confidence interval for μ_d is estimated by

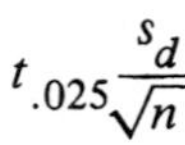

$t_{.025}\frac{s_d}{\sqrt{n}}$

$\bar{d} \pm$ ________

2.571

Using our sample values and $t_{.025} =$ ________, we have

2.571

2.6667 ± ________ (1.145)

2.9439

2.6667 ± ________

5.61

With 95% confidence, we estimate that μ_d lies within the interval −0.28 to ________ .

$n - 1$

larger

Notice that in using a paired-difference analysis, the degrees of freedom for the critical value of t drop from $2n - 2$ for an unpaired design to $n - 1$ for the paired, a loss of $(2n - 2) - (n - 1) =$ ________ degrees of freedom. This results in a (larger, smaller) critical value of t. Therefore a larger value of the test statistic is needed to reject H_0. Fortunately, *proper* pairing will reduce $\sigma_{\bar{d}}$. Hence the paired-difference experiment results in both a loss and a gain of information. However, the *loss* of $(n - 1)$ degrees of freedom is usually far overshadowed by the gain in information when $\sigma_{\bar{d}}$ is substantially reduced.

Both the MINITAB and SAS systems can be used to analyze a paired-difference experiment. The data are entered into two columns as in the unpaired experiment. The command SUBTRACT (followed by the two column numbers to be differenced and a column number into which the differences are stored) or the command LET C3 = C2 - C1 will calculate the differences, d. A one sample t-test or a confidence interval for the parameter $\mu_d = \mu_2 - \mu_1$ can be obtained by using the command TTEST or TINTERVAL followed by a column number which specifies the column of differences. The MINITAB output for the data in Example 9.9 is shown below. The SAS printout would be quite similar.

```
MTB > SET C1
DATA > 68 75 98 81 72 109
DATA > END
MTB > SET C2
DATA > 73 79 97 83 78 109
DATA > END
MTB > SUBTRACT C1 C2 C3
MTB > TTEST 0 C3

TEST OF MU = 0 VS MU N.E. 0

        N    MEAN    STDEV    SE MEAN    T       P VALUE
C3      6    2.67    2.80     1.1        2.33    0.067

MTB > TINTERVAL 95 C3

        N    MEAN    STDEV    SE MEAN    95.0 PERCENT C.I.
C3      6    2.67    2.80     1.1        (-0.3,        5.6)
```

The statistical design of the paired-difference test is a simple example of a randomized block design. In such a design, the pairing must occur when the experiment is planned and not after the data are collected. Once the experimenter has used a paired design for an experiment, he no longer has the choice of using the unpaired design for testing the difference between means. This is because we have violated the assumptions needed for the unpaired design, namely, that the samples are ______________ and ______________ .

random; independent

Self-Correcting Exercises 9C

1. The owner of a small manufacturing plant is considering a change in salary base by replacing an hourly wage structure with a per-unit rate. He hopes that such a change will increase the output per worker, but he has reservations about a possible decrease in quality under the per-unit plan. Before arriving at any decision, he formed 10 pairs of workers so that within each pair, the two workers had produced about the same number of items per day, and their work was of comparable quality. From each pair, one worker was randomly selected to be paid as usual and the other to be paid on a per-unit basis. In addition to the number of items produced, a cumulative quality score for the items produced was kept for each worker. The quality scores follow. (A high score is indicative of high quality.)

	Rate	
Pair	*Per unit*	*Hourly*
1	86	91
2	75	77
3	87	83
4	81	84
5	65	68
6	77	76
7	88	89
8	91	91
9	68	73
10	79	78

Do these data indicate that the average quality for the per-unit production is significantly lower than that based upon an hourly wage?

2. Refer to Exercise 1. The following data represent the average number of items produced per worker, based upon one week's production records.

	Rate	
Pair	*Per unit*	*Hourly*
1	35.8	31.2
2	29.4	27.6
3	31.2	32.2
4	28.6	26.4
5	30.0	29.0
6	32.6	31.4
7	36.8	34.2
8	34.4	31.6
9	29.6	27.6
10	32.8	29.8

a. Estimate the mean difference in average daily output for the two pay scales with a 95% confidence interval.

b. Test the hypothesis that a per-unit pay scale increases production at the .05 level of significance.

9.6 Inferences About a Population Variance

In many cases, the measure of variability is more important than that of central tendency. For example, an educational test consisting of 100 items has a mean score of 75 with standard deviation of 2.5. Although $\mu = 75$ may sound impressive, $\sigma = 2.5$ would imply that this test has very poor discriminating ability since approximately 95% of the scores would be between 70 and 80. In like manner a production line producing bearings with $\mu = .25$ inches and $\sigma = .5$ inches would produce many defective items; the fact that the bearings have a mean diameter of .25 inches would be of little value when the bearings are fitted together. *The precision of an instrument, whether it be an educational test or a machine, is measured by the standard deviation of the error of measurement.* Hence we proceed to a test of a population variance, σ^2.

The sample variance, s^2, is an ______________ estimator for σ^2. To use s^2 for inference making, we find that in repeated sampling, the distribution of s^2 has the following properties. unbiased

1. $E(s^2) =$ __________ σ^2
2. The distribution of s^2 is (symmetric, nonsymmetric). nonsymmetric
3. s^2 can assume any value greater than or equal to __________ . zero (0)
4. The shape of the distribution changes for different values of __________ and __________ . n; σ^2
5. In sampling from a *normal* population, s^2 is independent of the population mean, __________, and the sample mean, __________. As with the z-statistic, the distribution for s^2 when sampling from a normal population can be standardized by using μ; $\bar{x}$

$$\chi^2 = \frac{(n-1)s^2}{\sigma^2}$$

which is the chi-square random variable having the following properties in repeated sampling.

1. $E(\chi^2) =$ d.f. = __________ . $n - 1$
2. The distribution of χ^2 is (symmetric, nonsymmetric). nonsymmetric
3. $\chi^2 \geqslant$ __________. 0
4. The distribution of χ^2 depends upon the degrees of freedom, $n - 1$.

Since χ^2 does not have a symmetric distribution, critical values of χ^2 have been tabulated for both the upper and lower tails of the distribution in Table 5 of your text. This table is reproduced for your convenience as Table 5 in the Appendix to this study guide. The degrees of freedom are listed along both the right and left margins of the table. Across the top margin are values, χ^2_α, indicating a value of χ^2 having an area equal to α to its right, that is

$$P[\chi^2 > \chi^2_\alpha] = \alpha$$

Example 9.10

Use Table 5 to find the following critical values of χ^2:

		α	d.f.	χ^2_α
5.99147	a.	.05	2	______
2.55821	b.	.99	10	______
37.5662	c.	.01	20	______
18.4926	d.	.95	30	______
1.734926	e.	.995	9	______
27.4884	f.	.025	15	______
45.5585	g.	.005	24	______
10.0852	h.	.90	17	______

The statistical test of an hypothesis concerning a population variance, σ^2, at the α level of significance is given as follows:

1. H_0: $\sigma^2 = \sigma_0^2$
2. H_a: Appropriate one- or two-tailed test
3. Test statistic:

$$\chi^2 = \frac{(n - 1)\, s^2}{\sigma_0^2}$$

4. Rejection region:
   a. For H_a: $\sigma^2 > \sigma_0^2$, reject H_0 if $\chi^2 > \chi^2_\alpha$ based on $n - 1$ degrees of freedom.
   b. For H_a: $\sigma^2 < \sigma_0^2$, reject H_0 if $\chi^2 < \chi^2_{(1-\alpha)}$ based on $n - 1$ degrees of freedom.
   c. For H_a: $\sigma^2 \neq \sigma_0^2$, reject H_0 if $\chi^2 > \chi^2_{\alpha/2}$ or $\chi^2 < \chi^2_{(1-\alpha/2)}$ based on $n - 1$ degrees of freedom.

Example 9.11

A producer of machine parts claimed that the diameters of the connector rods produced by his plant had a variance of at most .03 in.^{2} A random sample of 15 connector rods from his plant produced a sample mean and variance of 0.55 in. and 0.53 in.^{2}, respectively. Is there sufficient evidence to reject his claim at the $\alpha = .05$ level of significance?

Solution

1. Collecting pertinent information:

$$s^2 = .053 \text{ in.}^2$$

$$\text{d.f.} = n - 1 = 14$$

$$\sigma_0^2 = .03 \text{ in.}^2$$

2. The test of the hypothesis is given as:

H_0: $\sigma^2 = .03$

H_a: σ^2 ________ | $> .03$

Test statistic:

$$\chi^2 = \frac{(n-1)s^2}{\sigma_0^2}$$

Rejection region:

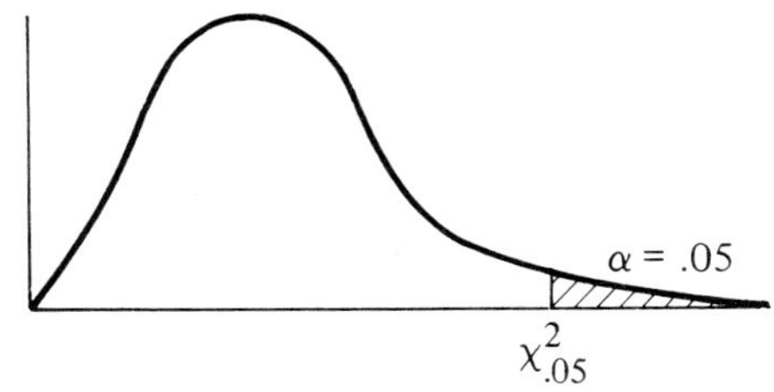

For 14 degrees of freedom, we shall reject H_0 if $\chi^2 \geqslant$ ________ | 23.6848

Calculate:

$$\chi^2 = \frac{(n-1)s^2}{\sigma_0^2}$$

$$= \frac{14\,(\_\_\_\_\_\_\_\_)}{(\_\_\_\_\_\_\_\_)}$$ | .053 | .03

$= 24.733$

Decision: (Reject, Do not reject) H_0 since | Reject

$$24.733 > \chi^2_{.05} = 23.6848$$

The data produced sufficient evidence to reject H_0. Therefore we can conclude that the variance of the rod diameters (is, is not) greater than .03 inch^2. | is

Example 9.12
Refer to Example 9.11. Find the approximate level of significance and interpret your results.

Solution
The level of significance for this test is

$$p\text{-value} = P[\chi^2 > 24.733]$$

where χ^2 has a chi-square distribution with $n - 1 = 14$ degrees of freedom. From Table 5, the observed value falls between $\chi^2_{.05}$ = ________ and $\chi^2_{.025}$ = ________ . Hence,

23.6848
26.1190

________ < p-value < ________

.025; .05

The null hypothesis can be rejected for any value of α (greater than, less than) or equal to α = ________ . Since α was .05 in Example 9.11, H_0 was rejected.

greater than
.05

The sample variance s^2 is an unbiased point estimator for the population variance σ^2. Utilizing the fact that $(n-1)s^2/\sigma^2$ has a chi-square distribution with $(n-1)$ degrees of freedom, we can show that a $(1-\alpha)100\%$ confidence interval for σ^2 is

$$\frac{(n-1)s^2}{\chi^2_U} < \sigma^2 < \frac{(n-1)s^2}{\chi^2_L}$$

where χ^2_U is the tabulated value of the chi-square random variable based on ________ degrees of freedom having an area equal to $\alpha/2$ to its right, while χ^2_L is the tabulated value from the same distribution having an area of $\alpha/2$ to its left or, equivalently, an area of $1 - \alpha/2$ to its right.

$n - 1$

Example 9.13
Find a 95% confidence interval estimate for the variance of the rod diameters from Example 9.11.

Solution
From Example 9.11 the estimate of σ^2 was $s^2 = .053$ with 14 degrees of freedom. For a confidence coefficient of .95, we need

$$\chi^2_L = \chi^2_{.975} = \_\_\_\_\_\_\_\_$$

and

$$\chi^2_U = \chi^2_{.025} = \_\_\_\_\_\_\_\_$$

5.62872

26.1190

1. Using the confidence interval estimator

$$\frac{(n-1)s^2}{\chi^2_U} < \sigma^2 < \frac{(n-1)s^2}{\chi^2_L}$$

we have

$$\frac{14(.053)}{(\_\_\_\_\_\_\_\_)} < \sigma^2 < \frac{14(.053)}{(\_\_\_\_\_\_\_\_)}$$

26.1190; 5.62872

________ < σ^2 < ________

.028; .132

2. By taking square roots of the upper and lower confidence limits, we have an equivalent confidence interval for the standard deviation σ. For this problem,

$$\_\_\_\_\_\_\_\_ < \sigma < \_\_\_\_\_\_\_\_$$ .167; .363

Comment. Although the sample variance is an unbiased point estimator for σ^2, notice that the confidence interval estimator for σ^2 *is not symmetrically located about* $\hat{\sigma}^2$ as was the case with confidence intervals that were based on the z or t distributions. This follows from the fact that a chi-square distribution is not symmetric, while the z and t distributions are symmetric.

Self-Correcting Exercises 9D

1. In an attempt to assess the variability in the time until a pain reliever became effective, a pharmaceutical research scientist on five different occasions administered a controlled dosage of the drug to a subject. The five measurements recorded for the time until effective relief were 20.2, 15.7, 19.8, 19.2, and 22.7 minutes. Would these measurements indicate that the standard deviation of the time until effective relief was less than 3 minutes for this subject?
2. An educational testing service, in developing a standardized test, would like the test to have a standard deviation of at least 10. The present form of the test has produced a standard deviation of $s = 8.9$ based on $n = 30$ test scores. Should the present form of the test be revised based on these sample data? What p-value would you report?
3. A quick technique for determining the concentration of a chemical solution has been proposed to replace the standard technique, which takes much longer. In testing a standardized solution, 30 determinations using the new technique produced a standard deviation of $s = 7.3$ parts per million.
   a. Does it appear that the new technique is less sensitive (has larger variability) than the standard technique whose standard deviation is $\sigma = 5$ parts per million?
   b. Estimate the true standard deviation for the new technique with a 95% confidence interval.

9.7 Comparing Two Population Variances

An experimenter may wish to compare the variability of two testing procedures or compare the precision of one manufacturing process with another. One may also wish to compare two population variances prior to using a t test.

To test the hypothesis of equality of two population variances,

$$H_0: \sigma_1^2 = \sigma_2^2$$

we need to make the following assumptions:

normal
independent

1. Each population sampled has a ____________ distribution.
2. The samples are ____________.

The statistic s_1^2/s_2^2 is used to test

$$H_0: \sigma_1^2 = \sigma_2^2$$

large; small

A ____________ value of this statistic implies that $\sigma_1^2 > \sigma_2^2$; a ____________ value of this statistic implies that $\sigma_1^2 < \sigma_2^2$; while a value of the statistic close to one (1) implies that $\sigma_1^2 = \sigma_2^2$. In repeated sampling this statistic has an F distribution when $\sigma_1^2 = \sigma_2^2$ with the following properties:

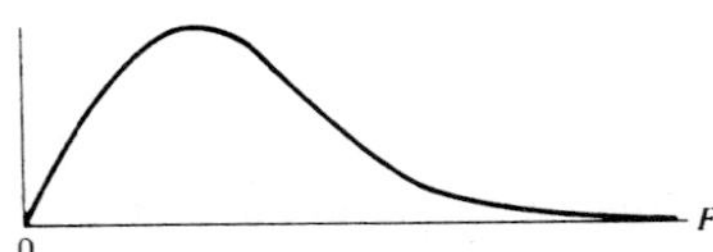

nonsymmetric

$s_1^2; s_2^2$

zero

1. The distribution of F is (symmetric, nonsymmetric).
2. The shape of the distribution depends on the degrees of freedom associated with __________ and __________.
3. F is always greater than or equal to ____________.

The tabulation of critical values of F is complicated by the fact that the distribution is nonsymmetric and must be indexed according to the values of ν_1 and ν_2, the degrees of freedom associated with the numerator and denominator of the F statistic. As we will see, however, it will be sufficient to have only right-tailed critical values of F for the various combinations of ν_1 and ν_2. Table 6 in the text has tabulated right-tailed critical values for the F statistic, where F_α is that value of F having an area of α to its right, based on ν_1 and ν_2, the degrees of freedom associated with the *numerator* and *denominator* of F, respectively. F_α satisfies the relationship $P(F > F_\alpha) = \alpha$. Table 6 has been reproduced for your convenience in the Appendix to this study guide.

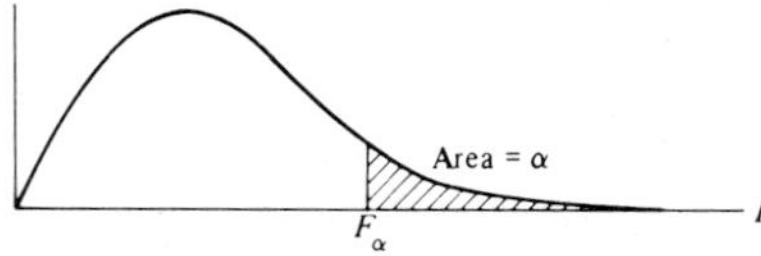

Example 9.14

Find the value of F based on $\nu_1 = 5$ and $\nu_2 = 7$ degrees of freedom such that that

$$P(F > F_{.05}) = .05$$

Solution

1. We wish to find a critical value of F with an area $\alpha = .05$ to its right based on $\nu_1 = 5$ and $\nu_2 = 7$ degrees of freedom. Therefore, we will use Table 6.

2. Values of ν_1 are found along the *top* margin of the table while values of ν_2 appear on both the right *and* left margins of the table. Find the value of $\nu_1 = 5$ along the top margin and cross-index this value with $\nu_2 = 7$ along the left margin to find $F_{.05} = 3.97$.

Example 9.15
Find the critical right-tailed values of F for the following:

	ν_1	ν_2	α	F_α	
a.	5	2	.05	______	19.30
b.	7	15	.10	______	2.16
c.	20	10	.025	______	3.42
d.	30	40	.005	______	2.40
e.	17	13	.01	______	3.76

We can always avoid using left-tailed critical values of the F distribution by using the following approach. In testing H_0: $\sigma_1^2 = \sigma_2^2$ against the alternative H_a: $\sigma_1^2 > \sigma_2^2$, we would reject H_0 *only if* s_1^2/s_2^2 *is too large* (larger than a right-tailed critical value of F). In testing H_0: $\sigma_1^2 = \sigma_2^2$ against H_a: $\sigma_1^2 < \sigma_2^2$, we would reject H_0 *only if* s_2^2/s_1^2 *were too large.* In testing H_0: $\sigma_1^2 = \sigma_2^2$ against the two-tailed alternative H_a: $\sigma_1^2 \neq \sigma_2^2$, we will agree to *designate the population that produced the larger sample variance as population* 1 *and the larger sample variance as* s_1^2. We then agree to reject H_0 if s_1^2/s_2^2 is *too large.*

When we agree to designate the population with the larger sample variance as population 1, the test of H_0: $\sigma_1^2 = \sigma_2^2$ versus H_a: $\sigma_1^2 \neq \sigma_2^2$ using s_1^2/s_2^2 will be right-tailed. However, in so doing we must remember that the tabulated tail area must be doubled to get the actual significance level of the test. For example, if the critical right-tailed value of F has been found in the row labeled "$\alpha = .05$," the actual significance level of the test will be $\alpha = 2(.05) =$ __________ . .10
If the critical value comes from the row labeled "$\alpha = .01$," the actual level will be $\alpha = 2(.01) =$ __________ , and so forth. .02

Example 9.16
An investor is studying the performance of two security portfolios. Performance of each portfolio is measured by its market closing price at the end of each market day. Use the following data to determine whether or not there is a significant difference in variability of closing prices for these two portfolios at the $\alpha = .02$ level of significance.

Portfolio I	*Portfolio II*
$s = 2.3$	$s = 5.8$
$n = 10$	$n = 10$

Solution

This problem involves a test of the equality of two population variances. Let population 1 be associated with portfolio II.

1. $H_0: \sigma_1^2 = \sigma_2^2$

2. $H_a: \sigma_1^2 \neq \sigma_2^2$

3. Test statistic:

$$F = s_1^2/s_2^2$$

4. Rejection region: With $\nu_1 = \nu_2 = 9$ degrees of freedom, reject H_0 if
5.35 $F > F_{.01} =$ __________.

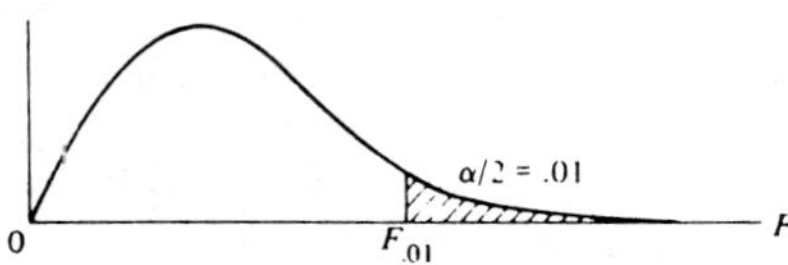

Now we calculate the test statistic.

$$F = s_1^2/s_2^2$$

$$= (5.8)^2/(2.3)^2$$

33.64; 5.29 $= ($__________$)/($__________$)$

6.36 $=$ __________

greater; is Decision: Since F is (greater, less) than $F_{.01} = 5.35$, H_0: $\sigma_1^2 = \sigma_2^2$ (is, is not) rejected.

Since the population variances were judged to be different, the investor should now also consider the mean closing price of both portfolios. The best portfolio would be the one with the smaller variance and the larger mean closing price.

Example 9.17

Refer to Example 9.16. Find the level of significance for the test and interpret your results.

Solution

two-tailed The level of significance for this (one-tailed, two-tailed) test is p-value = $2P[F >$
6.36; 9 __________$]$, where F has an F distribution with $\nu_1 =$ __________ and
9 $\nu_2 =$ __________ degrees of freedom. In order to find an approximate p-value, we must first find critical values, F_α, for various values of α with $\nu_1 = \nu_2 = 9$.

These values are found in Table 6. Fill in the missing entries in the table that follows.

α	F_α	
.10	2.44	
.05	________	3.18
.025	4.03	
.01	________	5.35
.005	________	6.54

Since the observed value, $F = 6.36$ falls between $F_{.01} =$ ________ and 5.35
$F_{.005} = 6.54$, the p-value will be between $2(.005) = .01$ and $2(.01) = .02$. That is, $.01 < p\text{-value} < .02$. Hence, H_0 can be rejected for any value of α (greater, greater
less) than or equal to ________ . .02

Example 9.18

A comparison of the precisions of two machines developed for extracting juice from oranges is to be made using the following data:

Machine A	*Machine B*
$s^2 = 3.1$ ounces^2	$s^2 = 1.4$ ounces^2
$n = 25$	$n = 25$

Is there sufficient evidence to indicate that $\sigma_A^2 > \sigma_B^2$ at the $\alpha = .05$ level?

Solution

Let population 1 be the population of measurements on machine A. The test would proceed as follows:

$$H_0: \sigma_1^2 = \sigma_2^2$$

$$H_a: \sigma_1^2 \text{ \_\_\_\_\_\_\_\_ } \sigma_2^2$$ >

Test statistic:

$$F = s_1^2/s_2^2$$

Rejection region: Based on $\nu_1 = \nu_2 =$ ________ degrees of freedom, we will 24
reject H_0 if $F > F_{.05}$ with $F_{.05} =$ ________. 1.98

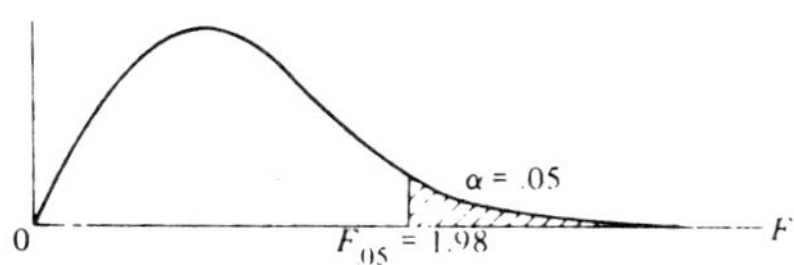

The value of the statistic is

$$F = s_1^2/s_2^2 = 3.1/1.4 = \text{ \_\_\_\_\_\_\_\_ }$$ 2.21

is

Decision: We reject H_0 and conclude that the variability of machine A (is, is not) greater than that of machine B.

Self-Correcting Exercises 9E

1. Refer to Exercise 2, Self-Correcting Exercises 9B. In using the t statistic to test an hypothesis concerning $\mu_1 - \mu_2$, one assumes that $\sigma_1^2 = \sigma_2^2$. Based on the sample information, could you conclude that this assumption had been met for this problem? Use $\alpha = .05$.
2. In following the daily fluctuations in prices for two commodities, an investor found the variability of the price for one commodity to be $s_1 = \$1.59$ while that of a second was $s_2 = \$2.49$. If 10 daily prices were involved in the calculation of each standard deviation, does it appear that both commodities are exhibiting the same basic variation?

9.8 Assumptions

The testing and estimation procedures presented in this chapter are based on the t, χ^2, and F statistics. In order that the probability statements associated with these testing and estimation procedures accurately reflect the prescribed probability values, specific assumptions concerning the sampled population(s) and the method of sampling must be satisfied.

normal

independently

equal

The valid use of the t, χ^2, and F statistics requires that all samples be randomly selected from ____________ populations. With the exception of the paired-difference experiment, when two samples are drawn, the samples must be drawn ____________. In addition, when making inferences about the difference in two population means μ_1 and μ_2 using two independent samples, the population variances σ_1^2 and σ_2^2 must be ____________.

robust

It would be unusual to have all these assumptions satisfied in practice. However, if the sampled population were not normal, or $\sigma_1^2 \neq \sigma_2^2$, we would like our procedures to produce error probabilities that are approximately equal to the specified values. A statistical procedure that is insensitive to departures from the assumptions upon which it is based is said to be ____________.

is not

Procedures based on the t statistic are fairly robust to departures from normality provided that the sampled population(s) is(are) not strongly skewed. This (is, is not) true for procedures based upon the χ^2 and F statistics. The t statistic used in comparing two means is moderately robust to departures from the assumption $\sigma_1^2 = \sigma_2^2$ when $n_1 = n_2$. However, when $\sigma_1^2 \neq \sigma_2^2$ and one sample size becomes large relative to the other, the procedure fails to be robust.

When the experimenter is aware of possible violations of assumptions, the usual procedure can be used if it is robust with respect to the assumptions violated. Otherwise, the nonparametric procedures presented in Chapter 18 can be used. Nonparametric methods require few or no assumptions concerning the sampled population(s); however, samples must nonetheless be ____________ selected, and when appropriate, the samples must also be independently drawn. When the sample sizes are relatively large, techniques such as those presented in Chapter 8 can be used in place of nonparametric procedures.

randomly

EXERCISES

1. Why can we say that the test statistics employed in Chapter 8 are approximately normally distributed?
2. What assumptions are made when Student's t statistic is used to test an hypothesis concerning a population mean μ?
3. How does one determine the degrees of freedom associated with a t statistic?
4. Let t_α be that value of t with the proper degrees of freedom, such that

$$P[t > t_\alpha] = \alpha$$

Complete the following table.

	α	*d.f.*	t_α
a.	.025	7	________
b.	.005	15	________
c.	.05	2	________
d.	.10	26	________
e.	.05	11	________

5. Ten butterfat determinations for brand G milk were carried out yielding $\bar{x} = 3.7\%$ and $s = 1.7\%$. Do these results produce sufficient evidence to indicate that brand G milk contains on the average less than 4.0% butterfat? (Use $\alpha = .05$.)
6. Refer to Exercise 5. Estimate the mean percent of butterfat for brand G milk with a 95% confidence interval.
7. A new method of producing a long-lasting headache remedy consists of varying the type of coatings used on the pill, so as to produce a continuous discharge of the drug into a person's system. If the mean time for the pill to dissolve is greater than 12 hours, the new method will be further investigated. From a sample of size $n = 16$ people, $\bar{x}$ and s were computed to be 13.2 hours and 1.5 hours, respectively. Based on this sample, would you conclude that this new pill should be further investigated?
8. Refer to Exercise 7. Estimate the mean time until dissolution with an 80% confidence interval.
9. Due to a cost factor, only ten experimental electronic devices were constructed. For each device, the time until failure was recorded. If $\bar{x} = 354.0$ hours and $s = 23.9$ hours, would you conclude that the mean time until failure was less than 370 hours?

10. During the course of one month, a truck whose capacity was given as five tons, was weighed at a weighing station five times. The tare weights on these five occasions were: 5.1, 5.2, 4.8, 5.1 and 5.2 tons. Does it appear that this truck is overloaded on the average?
11. What assumptions are made for an unpaired test of an hypothesis concerning $\mu_1 - \mu_2$ using Student's t-statistic?
12. In comparing the weights of one-pound loaves of bread from two different bakeries the following data summary was presented.

	Bakery 1	*Bakery 2*
Number of loaves	16	10
Mean weight	17.4 oz.	15.8 oz.
Standard deviation	3.0 oz.	4.0 oz.

Based on these data, could you conclude that there was a significant difference in the average weight of one-pound loaves of bread for these two bakeries?
13. Find a 90% confidence interval estimate for $\mu_1 - \mu_2$ using the data in Exercise 12.
14. In investigating which of two presentations of subject matter to use in a marketing management course, an experimenter randomly chose two groups of 18 students each, and assigned one group to receive presentation I and the second to receive presentation II. A short quiz on the presentation was given to each group and their grades recorded. Do the following data indicate that a difference in the mean quiz scores (hence, a difference in effectiveness of presentation) exists for the two methods?

	$\bar{x}$	s^2
Presentation I	81.7	23.2
Presentation II	77.2	19.8

15. To test the comparative brightness of two red dyes, nine samples of cloth were taken from a production line and each sample was divided into two pieces. One of the two pieces in each sample was randomly chosen and red dye 1 applied; red dye 2 was applied to the remaining piece. The following data represent a "brightness score" for each piece. Is there sufficient evidence to indicate a difference in mean brightness scores for the two dyes?

Sample	*Dye 1*	*Dye 2*
1	10	8
2	12	11
3	9	10
4	8	6
5	15	12
6	12	13
7	9	9
8	10	8
9	15	13

16. Before contracting to have stereo music piped into each of his suites of offices, an executive had his office manager randomly select seven offices to have the system installed. The average time spent outside these offices per excursion among the employees involved was recorded before and after the music system was installed with the following results.

Office number	*Time in minutes*	
	No music	*Music*
1	8	5
2	9	6
3	5	7
4	6	5
5	5	6
6	10	7
7	7	8

Would you suggest that the executive proceed with the installation?

17. Find the following critical values of χ^2:

	α	*d.f.*	χ^2_α
a.	.10	17	________
b.	.90	18	________
c.	.005	7	________
d.	.975	29	________
e.	.025	29	________

18. A manufacturer of odometers claimed that mileage measurements indicated on his instruments had a variance of at most .53 miles per ten miles traveled. An experiment, consisting of eight runs over a measured ten-mile stretch, was performed in order to check the manufacturer's claim. The variance obtained for the eight runs was 0.62. Does this provide sufficient evidence to indicate that $\sigma^2 > .53$? (Use $\alpha = .05$.)
19. Construct a 99% confidence interval estimate for σ^2 in Exercise 18.
20. In an attempt to assess the variability in the time until a pain reliever became effective for one of his patients, a doctor, on five different occasions, prescribed a controlled dosage of the drug for this patient. The five measurements recorded for the time until effective relief were: 20.2, 15.7, 19.8, 19.2, 22.7 minutes. Would these measurements indicate that the standard deviation of the time until effective relief was less than three minutes (i.e., $\sigma^2 < 9$)?
21. Construct a 95% confidence interval estimate for σ^2 in Exercise 20.
22. If F_α is that value of F based on ν_1 and ν_2 degrees of freedom, respectively, such that $P[F > F_\alpha] = \alpha$, find the following critical values of F_α.

	α	ν_1	ν_2	F_α
a.	.05	15	19	________
b.	.05	9	22	________
c.	.01	24	14	________
d.	.01	5	8	________

23. In a test of heat resistance involving two types of metal paint, two groups of ten metal strips were randomly selected. Group one was painted with type I paint, while group two was painted with type II paint. The metal strips were placed in an oven in random order, heated, and the temperature at which the paint began to crack and peel recorded for each strip. Do the following data indicate that the variability in the critical temperatures differs for the two types of paint?

	$\bar{x}$	s^2	n
Type I	280.1°F	93.2	10
Type II	269.9°F	51.9	10

24. Refer to Exercise 23. Can you comfortably apply Student's t-statistic in a test of $\mu_1 - \mu_2$ in this situation? Why? If you decide that you can, test the hypothesis that the mean difference in critical temperatures is zero at the $\alpha = .01$ level.
25. In an attempt to reduce the variability of machine parts produced by process A, a manufacturer has introduced process B (a modification of A). Do the following data based on two samples of 25 items indicate that the manufacturer has achieved his goal?

	n	s^2
Process A	25	6.57
Process B	25	3.19

Chapter 10

THE ANALYSIS OF VARIANCE

10.1 Introduction

Many investigations are directed toward establishing the effect of one or more variables upon a response of interest. The measurements that we record can be considered dependent variables, while their modifiers, be they treatments, classifications, or other factors, can be considered independent variables. A dependent variable, or response, is assumed to be a function of one or more independent variables that are varied and controlled by the experimenter during the investigation. These independent variables may be either qualitative or ______________. quantitative

In an investigation to determine how the amount of money invested in advertising affects the total sales, the ______________ variable would be total sales and the ______________ variable would be advertising expenditures. In this case the independent variable is (quantitative, qualitative). dependent independent quantitative

In the investigation of the relative merits of three sales training programs aimed at increasing the actual value of sales made, the dependent or response variable would be value of sales and the independent variable would be training programs. In this study, the independent variable is (quantitative, qualitative). qualitative

In this chapter we will use an analysis of variance as a statistical technique for evaluating the relationship between one or more independent variables and a response, x.

10.2 The Analysis of Variance

To perform an analysis of variance is to partition the total variation in a set of measurements, given by

$$\sum_{i=1}^{n} (x_i - \bar{x})^2$$

into portions associated with each independent variable in the experiment as well as a remainder attributable to random error. Let us investigate the partitioning of the total variation into two components with the following example.

Example 10.1
The impurities in parts per million were recorded for five batches of chemicals supplied by two different suppliers.

	Supplier 1		*Supplier 2*
	25		32
	33		43
	42		38
	27		47
	36		30
Sum	163	Sum	190
$\bar{x}_1$ =	________	$\bar{x}_2$ =	________

32.6; 38

It will save confusion if we use two subscripts to identify each observation rather than just one. Let x_{ij} designate the jth observation recorded in the ith sample. When i is either 1 or 2, j can take the values 1, 2, 3, 4, or 5. We could then write

Supplier 1	*Supplier 2*
$x_{11} = 25$	$x_{21} = 32$
$x_{12} = 33$	$x_{22} = 43$
$x_{13} = 42$	$x_{23} = 38$
$x_{14} = 27$	$x_{24} = 47$
$x_{15} = 36$	$x_{25} = 30$

1. Total variation: Let us consider all measurements as one large sample of size 10. Then the total of the 10 measurements is

$$\sum_{i=1}^{2} \sum_{j=1}^{5} x_{ij} = 353$$

and the grand mean is

35.3

$$\bar{x} = 353/10 = \_\_\_\_\_\_\_\_$$

The total variation then is given by

$$\text{Total SS} = \sum_i \sum_j (x_{ij} - \bar{x})^2$$

$$= \sum_i \sum_j x_{ij}^2 - (\sum_i \sum_j x_{ij})^2/10$$

$$= 12{,}929 - (353)^2/10$$

$$= 12{,}929 - 12{,}460.9$$

$$= \underline{\hspace{3em}}$$

468.1

This total sum of squares will be partitioned into two sources of variation: treatments and error.

2. Treatment variation: Recall that the variance of a sample mean is given to be σ^2/n, where n is the number of observations used to calculate the mean and σ^2 is the variance of the population of measurements sampled. Suppose we had two samples of size n from the same population. Then if $\bar{x}$ is the grand mean, the sample variance of the means, calculated as

$$s_{\bar{x}}^2 = \sum_{i=1}^{2} (\bar{x}_i - \bar{x})^2/(2 - 1)$$

estimates σ^2/n with one degree of freedom. If we multiply the sum of squares,

$$\sum_{i=1}^{2} (\bar{x}_i - \bar{x})^2$$

by n, we return this sum of squares to a "per measurement" basis. Then, the sum of squares due to variation of the treatment means will be

$$n \sum_{i=1}^{2} (\bar{x}_i - \bar{x})^2$$

If the sample sizes are not equal, then the sum of squares for treatments is modified to be

$$\text{SST} = \sum_{i=1}^{2} n_i(\bar{x}_i - \bar{x})^2 = \frac{n_1 n_2}{n_1 + n_2} (\bar{x}_1 - \bar{x}_2)^2$$

As the difference between the sample means increases, this sum of squares also ______________. For the problem at hand, $t = 2$ and

increases

$$\bar{x}_1 = 32.6, \quad \bar{x}_2 = 38, \quad \bar{x} = 35.3$$

$$n_1 = n_2 = 5$$

Therefore the treatment sum of squares is

$$\begin{aligned} \text{SST} &= n_1(\bar{x}_1 - \bar{x})^2 + n_2(\bar{x}_2 - \bar{x})^2 \\ &= 5(32.6 - 35.3)^2 + 5(38 - 35.3)^2 \\ &= 5(-2.7)^2 + 5(2.7)^2 \\ &= 5(7.29) + 5(7.29) \\ &= 2(36.45) \\ &= \_\_\_\_\_\_\_\_ \end{aligned}$$

72.9

3. Error variation: If the two samples have come from the same population, we can use a pooled estimate of error given by

$$\text{SSE} = \sum_{j=1}^{5} (x_{1j} - \bar{x}_1)^2 + \sum_{j=1}^{5} (x_{2j} - \bar{x}_2)^2$$

For sample 1,

$$\begin{aligned} \Sigma (x_{1j} - \bar{x}_1)^2 &= \Sigma x_{1j}^2 - (\Sigma x_{1j})^2/5 \\ &= 5{,}503 - (163)^2/5 \\ &= 5{,}503 - 5{,}313.8 \\ &= \_\_\_\_\_\_\_\_ \end{aligned}$$

189.2

For sample 2,

$$\begin{aligned} \Sigma (x_{2j} - \bar{x}_2)^2 &= \Sigma x_{2j}^2 - (\Sigma x_{2j})^2/5 \\ &= 7{,}426 - (190)^2/5 \end{aligned}$$

$= 7{,}426 - 7{,}220$

$=$ __________ 206

It follows that

$\text{SSE} = 189.2 + 206 =$ __________ 395.2

4. Therefore we see directly that

$\text{SST} = 72.9$

$\text{SSE} = 395.2$

$\text{Total SS} = 468.1$

and that

$\text{Total SS} = \text{SST} + \text{SSE}$

Since simpler calculational forms will be given presently, we defer further calculations until then.

The F Test and the Analysis of Variance

For the two-sample problem discussed in Example 10.1 the t statistic is readily available for testing the hypothesis

$$H_0: \mu_1 = \mu_2$$

versus

$$H_a: \mu_1 \neq \mu_2$$

The two-sample unpaired t test requires that both samples can be drawn randomly and independently from two normal populations with equal variances. Using these same assumptions, we can construct an F statistic, which is the ratio of two variances, to test these same hypotheses. The advantage to using the F statistic is that the procedure can be easily extended for testing the equality of several population means.

If $H_0: \mu_1 = \mu_2$ is true, then the partitioning of the total sum of squares provides us with two estimators of the common variance σ^2.

1. $\text{MSE} = \text{SSE}/(n_1 + n_2 - 2)$

where

$$\text{SSE} = \sum_{j=1}^{n_1} (x_{1j} - \bar{x}_1)^2 + \sum_{j=1}^{n_2} (x_{2j} - \bar{x}_2)^2$$

with $n_1 + n_2 - 2$ degrees of freedom.

2. $\text{MST} = \text{SST}/(2 - 1)$

where

$$\text{SST} = n_1(\bar{x}_1 - \bar{x})^2 + n_2(\bar{x}_2 - \bar{x})^2 = \frac{n_1 n_2}{n_1 + n_2} (\bar{x}_1 - \bar{x}_2)^2$$

with 2 - 1 degrees of freedom. Therefore, when H_0 is true,

$$F = \text{MST/MSE}$$

$1; n_1 + n_2 - 2$

has an F distribution with ν_1 = __________ and ν_2 = __________ degrees of freedom.

MSE

If H_0 is false and $H_a: \mu_1 \neq \mu_2$ is true, this fact should be reflected in MST, and MST should in probability be larger than __________. This implies that if H_0 is false, the F ratio,

$$F = \text{MST/MSE},$$

will be too large. Hence the rejection region for this test will consist of all values of F satisfying

$$F > F_\alpha$$

where F_α is the right-tailed critical value of F based on $\nu_1 = 1$ and $\nu_2 = n_1 + n_2 - 2$ degrees of freedom having an area of α to its right.

Example 10.2

For the data in Example 10.1, test the null hypothesis $H_0: \mu_1 = \mu_2$ versus $H_a: \mu_1 \neq \mu_2$ at the $\alpha = .05$ level of significance.

Solution

Let us first gather the information that we have compiled so far.

72.9; 72.9

SST = __________ MST = 72.9/1 = __________

395.2; 49.4

SSE = __________ MSE = 395.2/8 = __________

1. $H_0: \mu_1 = \mu_2$ versus $H_a: \mu_1 \neq \mu_2$.
2. The test statistic will be

$$F = \text{MST}/\text{MSE}$$

with ν_1 = __________ and ν_2 = __________ degrees of freedom. | 1; 8

3. Rejection region: For $\alpha = .05$, a right-tailed value of F with $\nu_1 = 1$ and $\nu_2 = 8$ degrees of freedom is $F_{.05}$ = __________. Therefore we will reject H_0 if $F >$ __________. | 5.32; 5.32
4. Using the sample values,

$$F = 72.9/49.4 = \_\_\_\_\_\_\_\_\_\_.$$ | 1.48

Since this value is (less, greater) than 5.32, we (reject, do not reject) the null hypothesis. There is not sufficient evidence to indicate that $\mu_1 \neq \mu_2$. | less; do not reject

Had we tested using the t statistic,

$$t = \frac{(\bar{x}_1 - \bar{x}_2) - 0}{\sqrt{s^2\left(\frac{1}{n_1} + \frac{1}{n_2}\right)}}$$

with $n_1 + n_2 - 2 = 8$ degrees of freedom, the calculated value would have been

$$t = \frac{32.6 - 38.0}{\sqrt{49.4\left(\frac{1}{5} + \frac{1}{5}\right)}}$$

$$= -5.4/\sqrt{19.76}$$

$$= -5.4/4.445 = \_\_\_\_\_\_\_\_\_\_$$ | -1.215

The rejection region would have consisted of values of t such that $|t| > t_{.025}$ = __________. Hence we would not have rejected H_0: $\mu_1 = \mu_2$ even had we used the t statistic. Noting that | 2.306

$$t^2 = (-1.215)^2 = 1.48 = \_\_\_\_\_\_\_\_\_\_$$ | F

and

$$(t_{.025})^2 = (2.306)^2 = 5.32 = \_\_\_\_\_\_\_\_\_\_$$ | $F_{.05}$

the results should be identical. This verifies the fact that an F with $\nu_1 = 1$ and ν_2 degrees of freedom is the same as t^2 with ν_2 degrees of freedom; further, $F_\alpha = t^2_{\alpha/2}$ *only if* ν_1 = __________. | 1

10.3 The Analysis of Variance for Comparing More than Two Populations

In extending the problem of testing for a significant difference between two population means to one of testing for significant differences among several population means, let us consider an experiment run in a completely randomized design. A completely randomized design involves the selection of randomly drawn independent samples from each of t populations.

Consider an experiment designed to compare the quality of the resulting color when identical pieces of material are dyed in one of three chemical formulations for red dye. Fifteen pieces of identical material have been randomly divided into three groups of five pieces of cloth, and each group randomly assigned to be dyed using one of the three dye formulations. Since each piece of cloth is dyed or 'treated' by using one of the formulations, the dyes in statistical terminology are called ______________.

treatments

This type of randomization procedure is called a ______________ ______________ design.

completely randomized

The completely randomized design involves one independent variable, treatments. In this design the total sum of squares of deviations of the measurements about their overall mean can be partitioned into two parts.

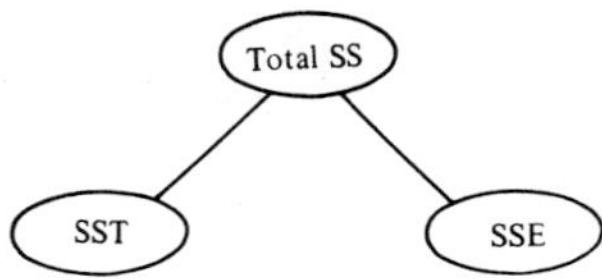

In generalizing the two-sample problem, we will now assume that *the t samples have been randomly and independently drawn from t normal populations with means $\mu_1, \mu_2, \ldots, \mu_t$, respectively, and with common variance σ^2.*

Let T_i and $\overline{T}_i$ be the sum and the mean of the n_i observations in the sample from the ith population, with $n = n_1 + n_2 + \ldots + n_t$ being the total number of observations. Then we have the following:

1.
$$\text{Total SS} = \sum_{i=1}^{t} \sum_{j=1}^{n_i} (x_{ij} - \bar{x})^2$$

with __________ degrees of freedom.

$n - 1$

2.
$$\text{SST} = \sum_{i=1}^{t} n_i(\overline{T}_i - \bar{x})^2$$

with __________ degrees of freedom. $t - 1$

3. $$\text{SSE} = \sum_{i=1}^{t} \sum_{j=1}^{n_i} (x_{ij} - \bar{T}_i)^2$$

with $\sum_{i=1}^{t} (n_i - 1) = n_1 + n_2 + \ldots + n_t - t =$ __________ degrees of freedom. Not only does $n - t$

$$\text{Total SS} = \text{SST} + \text{SSE}$$

but the same relationship holds for the degrees of freedom associated with each sum of squares.

$$\text{d.f.}_{\text{Total}} = \text{d.f.}_{\text{treatments}} + \text{d.f.}_{\text{error}}$$

since

$$n - 1 = (t - 1) + (n - t)$$

The formulas actually used for computing these sums of squares are given below. Let

$$\text{CM} = \left(\sum_{i=1}^{t} \sum_{j=1}^{n_i} x_{ij} \right)^2 \Big/ n = (\text{grand total})^2/n$$

Then

1. $$\text{Total SS} = \sum_{i=1}^{t} \sum_{j=1}^{n_i} x_{ij}^2 - \text{CM}$$

2. $$\text{SST} = \sum_{i=1}^{t} \frac{T_i^2}{n_i} - \text{CM}$$

3. $$\text{SSE} = \text{Total SS} - \text{SST}$$

Notice that in SST the square of each treatment total is divided by the number of ________________ in that total. Although SSE can be computed directly as a pooled sum of squared deviations within each sample, it is computationally easier to use the additivity property, SST + SSE = __________. observations Total SS

The mean squares for treatments and error are calculated by dividing each sum of squares by its degrees of freedom. Therefore

$$s^2 = \text{MSE} = \text{SSE}/(\_\_\_\_\_\_)$$ $n - t$

and

$t - 1$

$$\text{MST} = \text{SST}/(\_\_\_\_\_\_\_\_)$$

If all samples are from the same normal population, then MST and MSE are each estimators of the population variance σ^2. In this case the statistic

$$F = \text{MST}/\text{MSE}$$

F

has an ________ distribution with $\nu_1 = t - 1$ and $\nu_2 = n - t$ degrees of freedom.

Consider testing the hypothesis $H_0{:}\mu_1 = \mu_2 = \ldots = \mu_t$ against the alternative that at least one mean is different from at least one other. *If H_0 is true, then all samples have come from the same normal population* and the statistic

$$F = \text{MST}/\text{MSE}$$

has the F distribution specified above. However, if H_a is true (at least one of the equalities does not hold), then

$$\text{MST} = \frac{1}{t-1}[n_1(\overline{T}_1 - \bar{x})^2 + n_2(\overline{T}_2 - \bar{x})^2 + \ldots + n_t(\overline{T}_t - \bar{x})^2]$$

larger
larger; large

will in probability be ____________ than MSE and F will tend to be ____________ than expected. Hence H_0 will be rejected for ____________ values of F; that is, we will reject H_0 if

$$F > F_\alpha$$

with $\nu_1 = t - 1$ and $\nu_2 = n - t$ degrees of freedom.

Example 10.3

Do the following data provide sufficient evidence to indicate a difference in the means of the three underlying treatment populations?

9; 31; 14

	Treatment			
	1	*2*	*3*	
	3	7	5	
	4	9	4	
	2	8	5	
		7		
T_i	______	______	______	Total = 54
n_i	3	4	3	$n = 10$
$\overline{T}_i$	3	7.75	4.67	

Solution

1. We must first partition the total variation into SST and SSE.

$$CM = (54)^2/10 = 2{,}916/10 = \_\_\_\_\_\_\_\_$$ 291.6

a. $$\text{Total SS} = 3^2 + 4^2 + 2^2 + \ldots + 5^2 + 4^2 + 5^2 - 291.6$$

$$= 338 - 291.6$$

$$= \_\_\_\_\_\_\_\_$$ 46.4

b. $$\text{SST} = \frac{9^2}{3} + \frac{31^2}{4} + \frac{14^2}{3} - 291.6$$

$$= \frac{81}{3} + \frac{961}{4} + \frac{196}{3} - 291.6$$

$$= 27 + 240.25 + 65.33 - 291.6$$

$$= \_\_\_\_\_\_\_\_ - 291.6$$ 332.58

$$= \_\_\_\_\_\_\_\_$$ 40.98

c. $$\text{SSE} = 46.4 - 40.98$$

$$= \_\_\_\_\_\_\_\_$$ 5.42

d. To compute the degrees of freedom, we need the values $n = 10$ and $t = 3$. Hence SST has $t - 1 =$ ________ degrees of freedom while SSE has $n - t =$ ________ degrees of freedom. The resulting mean squares are 2 7

$$\text{MST} = 40.98/2 = \_\_\_\_\_\_\_\_$$ 20.49

$$\text{MSE} = 5.42/7 = \_\_\_\_\_\_\_\_$$ 0.77

2. We are now in a position to test $H_0\colon \mu_1 = \mu_2 = \mu_3$ versus H_a: at least one equality does not hold.

a. The test statistic is

$$F = \text{MST}/\text{MSE}$$

with $\nu_1 =$ ________ and $\nu_2 =$ ________ degrees of freedom. 2; 7

b. Rejection region: Using $\alpha = .05$, we will reject H_0 if $F > F_{.05}$ = ________. 4.74

c. Calculate

26.61 $F = 20.49/.77 =$ __________

greater; reject which is (greater, less) than $F_{.05} = 4.74$. Hence we __________ H_0 and conclude that there is evidence to indicate a difference in means for the three treatment populations at the $\alpha = .05$ level of significance.

Example 10.4

In the investigation of a citizens committee's complaint about the availability of fire protection within the county, the distance in miles to the nearest fire station was measured for each of 5 randomly selected residences in each of four areas.

		Areas				
		1	*2*	*3*	*4*	
		7 5 5 6 8	1 4 3 4 5	7 9 8 7 8	4 6 3 7 5	
31; 17; 39; 25	T_i	____	____	____	____	Total = 112
	n_i	5	5	5	5	$n = 20$
	$\bar{T}_i$	6.2	3.4	7.8	5.0	

Do these data provide sufficient evidence to indicate a difference in mean distance for the four areas at the $\alpha = .01$ level of significance?

Solution

1. We first partition the total sum of squares into SST and SSE to find MST and MSE.

112; 627.2 $$CM = \frac{(\_\_\_\_\_\_)^2}{20} = \frac{12544}{20} = \_\_\_\_\_\_$$

a. Total $SS = 7^2 + 5^2 + \ldots + 7^2 + 5^2 - CM$

708 $= \_\_\_\_\_\_ - 627.2$

80.80 $= \_\_\_\_\_\_$

b. $$SST = \frac{31^2 + 17^2 + 39^2 + 25^2}{\_\_\_\_\_\_} - CM$$

5

$$= \frac{\_\_\_\_\_\_}{5} - CM$$ | 3396

$= \_\_\_\_\_\_ - 627.2$ | 679.2

$= \_\_\_\_\_\_$ | 52.00

c. $SSE = \_\_\_\_\_\_ - \_\_\_\_\_\_$ | 80.80; 52.00

$= \_\_\_\_\_\_$ | 28.80

d. With $n = 20$ and $t = 4$,

$$MST = \frac{SST}{t-1} = \frac{52.00}{3} = \_\_\_\_\_\_$$ | 17.33

$$MSE = \frac{SSE}{n-t} = \frac{28.80}{16} = \_\_\_\_\_\_$$ | 1.80

2. Test of the null hypothesis:

a. H_0: ______ | $\mu_1 = \mu_2 = \mu_3 = \mu_4$

H_a: At least one equality does not hold.

b. Test statistic:

$F = \_\_\_\_\_\_$ | MST/MSE

with $\nu_1 = \_\_\_\_\_\_$ and $\nu_2 = \_\_\_\_\_\_$ degrees of freedom. | 3; 16

c. Rejection region: Reject H_0 if $F > F_{.01} = \_\_\_\_\_\_$. | 5.29

d. For these data,

$$F = \frac{17.33}{1.80} = \_\_\_\_\_\_$$ | 9.63

Hence, we ______ H_0 and conclude that there is sufficient evidence to indicate a difference in mean distance for the four areas. | reject

10.4 An Analysis of Variance Table for a Completely Randomized Design

The results of an analysis of variance are usually displayed in an analysis of variance (*ANOVA* or *AOV*) summary table. The table displays the sources of variation together with the degrees of freedom, sums of squares, and mean squares for each source listed in the table. The results of the F-test appear as a final entry in the table.

For a completely randomized design, the *ANOVA* table is as follows:

ANOVA

	Source	*d.f.*	*SS*	*MS*	*F*
MST/MSE	Treatments	$t - 1$	*SST*	*MST*	________
	Error	$n - t$	*SSE*	*MSE*	
n - 1; Total *SS*	Total	________	________		

This display gives all the pertinent information leading to the F-test and further emphasizes the fact that the degrees of freedom and the sums of squares are both additive.

Example 10.5
Display the results of the analysis of the data in Example 10.3.

Solution
We need but collect the results that we have for this example.

ANOVA

	Source	*d.f.*	*SS*	*MS*	*F*
2; 26.61	Treatments	________	40.98	20.49	________
7; 0.77	Error	________	5.42	________	
9; 46.40	Total	________	________		

Example 10.6
Display the results of the analysis of the data in Example 10.4.

Solution
Since the term "treatments" is a general way of describing the differences in the sampled populations, we can replace the term "treatments" in this problem by the more descriptive word "areas."

ANOVA

	Source	*d.f.*	*SS*	*MS*	*F*
17.33; 9.63	Areas	3	52.00	________	________
1.80	Error	16	28.80	________	
19; 80.80	Total	________	________		

10.5 Estimation for the Completely Randomized Design

In using the analysis of variance F test to test for significant differences among a group of population means, an experimenter can conclude that either (a) there is no difference among the means or (b) at least one mean is different from at least one other. In the second case, (b), an experimenter may wish to proceed with estimating the value of a treatment mean or with estimating the difference between two treatment means.

Since the analysis of variance requires that all samples be drawn from ____________ populations with a common variance, confidence intervals can be constructed using the t statistic with error degrees of freedom. Hence for estimating the ith treatment mean with a $(1 - \alpha)$ 100% confidence interval, use

normal

$$\bar{T}_i \pm t_{\alpha/2} \sqrt{\text{MSE}/n_i}$$

where $\bar{T}_i$ is the ith sample mean, n_i is the number of observations in the ith sample, and MSE is the pooled estimate of σ^2 from the analysis of variance with _________ degrees of freedom.

$n - t$

To estimate the difference between two population means with a $(1 - \alpha)$ 100% confidence interval, use

$$(\bar{T}_i - \bar{T}_j) \pm t_{\alpha/2} \sqrt{MSE\left(\frac{1}{n_i} + \frac{1}{n_j}\right)}$$

Example 10.7

Refer to Example 10.4. Estimate the mean distance to the nearest fire station for those residents in Area 1 with a 95% confidence interval.

Solution

1. The required information can be obtained from Examples 10.4 and 10.6.

$\bar{T}_1 = 6.2$ d.f. = _________ 16

$n_1 = 5$

$MSE =$ _________ $t_{.025} =$ _________ 1.80; 2.120

2. Therefore the estimate is given by

_________ $\pm$ _________ $\sqrt{\frac{1.80}{5}}$ 6.2; 2.120

.6 6.2 ± 2.120 (________)

1.27 $6.2 \pm$ ________ miles

or

4.93; 7.47 ________ $< \mu_1 <$ ________

Example 10.8
Refer to Examples 10.4 and 10.6. Construct a 95% confidence interval for $\mu_1 - \mu_3$.

Solution

1. Collecting pertinent information,

6.2; 7.8 $\bar{T}_1 =$ ________ $\bar{T}_3 =$ ________ $MSE = 1.80$

$n_1 = 5$ $n_3 = 5$ d.f. = 16

With 16 degrees of freedom, $t_{.025} = 2.120$.

2. The confidence interval estimate is found using

$$(\bar{T}_1 - \bar{T}_3) \pm t_{.025}\sqrt{MSE\left(\frac{1}{n_1} + \frac{1}{n_3}\right)}$$

which when evaluated becomes

$$(6.2 - 7.8) \pm 2.120\sqrt{1.80\left(\frac{1}{5} + \frac{1}{5}\right)}$$

.849 -1.6 ± 2.120 (________)

1.8 $-1.6 \pm$ ________

3. Hence with 95% confidence, we estimate that $\mu_1 - \mu_3$ lies between

-3.4; 0.2 ________ and ________ miles. Notice that even though we found that at least one area differed from at least one other area in average distance to the nearest firehouse using the analysis of variance F-test, we would conclude that there appears to be no difference between areas 1 and 3.

10.6 A Computer Printout for a Completely Randomized Design

Packaged computer programs for performing an analysis of variance are available at most computer facilities. In addition to the SAS package, the SPSS and MINITAB packages are commonly used for standard data analyses such as analysis of variance. In general, these and other packaged programs have been developed or can be modified to accommodate individual preferences with regard to available options within the programs as well as the format of the printed output. However, all produce the same basic information for an analysis of variance. The SAS and MINITAB printouts for an analysis of variance for the data in Example 10.4 are given in Example 10.9. Since these printouts are similar, we will box and explain the meanings of the various quantities that appear in the SAS printout and we will box the corresponding quantities on the MINITAB output when they are available.

Notice that the format (placement of items on the page) differs slightly from that given in your text, but the same information is given in both formats.

Example 10.9

The SAS computer printout for an analysis of variance for the data in Example 10.4 concerning the distance to the nearest fire station for four areas follows.

DISTANCES

ANALYSIS OF VARIANCE PROCEDURE

DEPENDENT VARIABLE: DISTANCE

#1

SOURCE	DF	SUM OF SQUARES	MEAN SQUARE	F VALUE
MODEL	3	52.00000000	17.33333333	9.63
ERROR	16	28.80000000	1.80000000	PR > F
CORRECTED TOTAL	19	80.80000000		.0007

#2

R-SQUARE	CV	ROOT MSE	DISTANCE MEAN
.643564	23.96	1.3416408	5.60000000

#4 #5

SOURCE	DF	ANOVA SS	F VALUE	PR > F
AREAS	3	52.00000000	9.63	.0007

#3

The corresponding MINITAB computer printout for these same data is generated using the command ONEWAY (one-way analysis of variance), with the response variable x stored in one column (C1) and the corresponding treatment numbers stored in another (C2).

```
MTB > ONEWAY C1 C2
ANALYSIS OF VARIANCE ON C1
                                                              #1
 SOURCE         DF        SS          MS          F
 C2              3        52.00       17.33       9.63
 ERROR          16        28.80        1.80
 TOTAL          19        80.80

                                      INDIVIDUAL 95 PCT CI'S FOR MEAN
                                      BASED ON POOLED STDEV
 LEVEL    N     MEAN      STDEV    ----------+---------+---------+------
 1        5     6.200     1.3038                     (-----*------)
 2        5     3.400     1.5166   (-----*------)
 3        5     7.800     0.8367                               (-----*------)
 4        5     5.000     1.5811             (------*-----)
                                   ----------+---------+---------+------
                    #4
 POOLED STDEV = 1.342                       4.0       6.0       8.0
```

Explanation of Printouts

1. The table enclosed in Box #1 is called an analysis of variance or ANOVA table. The three sources of variation given in the column labeled SOURCE are:
   a. MODEL: This source of variation is that due to variation among the sample means.
   b. ERROR: This is the variation within samples.
   c. CORRECTED TOTAL: This is the variation of all observations about the overall mean.
2. The sums of squares of deviations corresponding to the three sources of variation are found in column 3, labeled SUM OF SQUARES. The sum of squares corresponding to the source MODEL is what we have called the sum of squares for treatments; therefore

52.00 SST = ________

The sum of squares corresponding to ERROR is SSE, where

28.80 SSE = ________

The degrees of freedom (DF), mean squares (MS), and the F statistic for testing the equality of the four population means are also shown in the table. Box 2 in the SAS printout displays the level of significance for this test, given as

.0007 p-value = ________

Consistent with our earlier results, we (can, cannot) reject H_0 for any α greater than or equal to ______. can .0007

3. For some designs, the Total SS can be partitioned into sums of squares corresponding to two or more sources of variation in addition to SS. The SAS analysis of variance program always combines these sources into one source designated as MODEL in Box #1. In Box #3, the source due to MODEL is partitioned into component sources of variation. In this example, there is only one source of variation in addition to SSE. Hence, the sum of squares for MODEL in Box #1 is identical to the sum of squares for AREAS in Box #3.
4. The standard deviation s is found in Box #4. It can easily be verified that the value $s = 1.3416408$ can be calculated as

$$s = \sqrt{\text{MSE}} = \sqrt{\qquad} = 1.3416408$$ 1.8

If the standard deviation cannot easily be found on the printout from a specific computer package, it is advisable to calculate $s = \sqrt{\text{MSE}}$ directly.
5. The sample means given in Example 10.4, together with the standard deviation given in Box #4, can be used to construct confidence intervals for population means or their differences. In using the standard deviation s in the construction of a confidence interval based on the t-statistic, always index the degrees of freedom associated with ______. ERROR

Although the printed output from different packages varies in format and decimal accuracy, all analysis of variance programs will have an analysis of variance table in fairly standard form. Other items will differ, depending upon the package and the options within the package that have been requested by the user.

Self-Correcting Exercises 10A

1. In the evaluation of three rations fed to chickens grown for market, the dressed weights of five chickens fed from birth on one of the three rations were recorded.

	Rations		
	1	*2*	*3*
	7.1	4.9	6.7
	6.2	6.6	6.0
	7.0	6.8	7.3
	5.6	4.6	6.2
	6.4	5.3	7.1
Total	32.3	28.2	33.3
Averages	6.46	5.64	6.66

a. Do the data present sufficient evidence to indicate a difference in the mean growth for the three rations as measured by the dressed weights?

b. Estimate the difference in mean weight for rations 2 and 3 with a 95% confidence interval.

2. The length of time required for new employees to assemble a device was compared for four training periods of different lengths. Four employees were randomly assigned to each training group, but two were eliminated during the experiment due to sickness. The length of time to assemble the device was recorded for each employee in the experiment.

	Training Periods (in hours)			
	0.5	*1.0*	*1.5*	*2.0*
	8	9	4	4
	14	7	6	7
	9	5	7	5
	12		8	
Total	43	21	25	16
Mean	10.75	7.00	6.25	5.33

An SAS computer printout of the analysis of the variance for these data is given in the following display.

ASSEMBLY TIMES

ANALYSIS OF VARIANCE PROCEDURE

DEPENDENT VARIABLE: TIME

SOURCE	DF	SUM OF SQUARES	MEAN SQUARE	F VALUE
MODEL	3	63.33333333	21.11111111	4.78
ERROR	10	44.16666667	4.41666667	PR > F
CORRECTED TOTAL	13	107.50000000		.0257

R-SQUARE	C.V.	ROOT MSE	TIME MEAN
.0589147	28.0212	2.10158670	7.50000000

SOURCE	DF	ANOVA SS	F VALUE	PR > F
PERIOD	3	63.33333333	4.78	.0257

Use the information in the printout to answer the following questions.

a. Do the data present sufficient evidence to indicate a difference in mean time to assemble the device for the four different lengths of instructional time?

b. Estimate the difference in mean time to assemble the device for training periods of 1 hour and 2 hours with 95% confidence.

c. Estimate the difference in mean time to assemble the device for training periods of 1 and 1.5 hours, with 95% confidence.

10.7 A Randomized Block Design

The randomized block design is a natural extension of the ________ ________ experiment. Its purpose is to increase the ________ in the design by making comparisons between treatments within relatively homogeneous blocks of experimental material. The randomized block design for t treatments and b blocks assumes blocks of relatively homogeneous material with each block containing ________ experimental units. Each treatment is applied to one experimental unit in each block. Consequently, the number of observations for a given treatment for the entire experiment will equal ________. Thus, for the randomized block design, $n_1 = n_2 = \ldots = n_t = b$. A randomized block design for $t = 3$ treatments and $b = 4$ blocks is shown below. Denote the treatments as T_1, T_2, and T_3.

paired
difference; information

t

b

Blocks

1	2	3	4
T_3	T_2	T_1	T_3
T_1	T_1	T_3	T_2
T_2	T_3	T_2	T_1

The total number of observations for a randomized block design with b blocks and t treatments is $n =$ ________.

The word "randomized" means that the ________ are randomly distributed over the experimental units within each block. The randomized block design involves two independent variables: ________ and ________. For an experiment run in a randomized block design, the total variation can now be partitioned into three sources of variation, blocks (B), treatments (T), and error (E).

bt
treatments

blocks
treatments

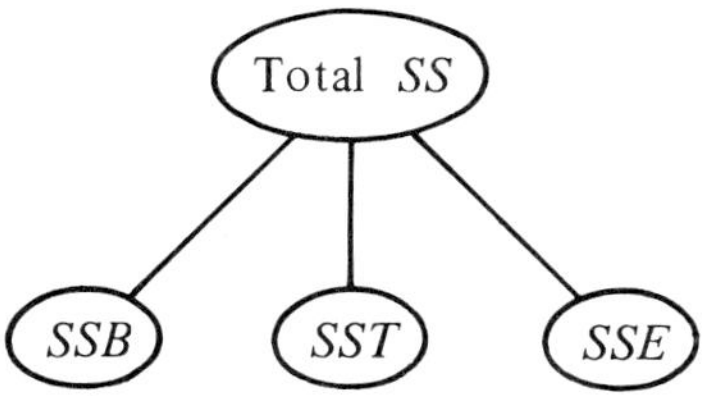

Randomized block designs prove to be very useful in business and economics. Many investigations involve human subjects which exhibit a large subject-to-subject variability.

1. By using a subject as a "________" and having each subject receive all the treatments in a random order, treatment comparisons

block

made within subjects would exhibit less variation than treatment comparisons made between subjects.

smaller

2. Since every subject receives each treatment in some random order, a ____________ number of subjects would be required in a randomized block design than in a completely randomized design.

10.8 The Analysis of Variance for a Randomized Block Design

In partitioning the sums of squares for an experiment run in a randomized block design with b blocks and t treatments, the calculational formulas for Total SS and SST remain the same except that now every treatment total will contain exactly b measurements and the total number of observations will be $n = bt$. Hence,

$$CM = \frac{\left(\sum_{i=1}^{t} \sum_{j=1}^{b} x_{ij}\right)^2}{bt} = \frac{(\text{Grand Total})^2}{bt}$$

$$\text{Total } SS = \sum_{i=1}^{t} \sum_{j=1}^{b} x_{ij}^2 - CM$$

and

$$SST = \frac{\sum_{i=1}^{t} T_i^2}{b} - CM$$

The calculation of SSB follows the same pattern as the calculation of SST, namely, square each block total; sum the squares of each total; divide by t, the number of observations per total; and subtract the correction for the mean. If $B_1, B_2, \ldots, B_b$ represent the block totals, then

$$SSB = \frac{(B_1^2 + B_2^2 + \ldots + B_b^2)}{t} - CM$$

Using the additivity of the sums of squares, we can find SSE by subtraction.

SSB; *SST*

$$SSE = \text{Total } SS - \_\_\_\_\_\_ - \_\_\_\_\_\_$$

The analysis of variance table for a completely randomized block design with b blocks and t treatments follows.

ANOVA

Source	*d.f.*	*SS*	*MS*
Blocks	________	*SSB*	$SSB/(b-1)$
Treatments	________	*SST*	$SST/(t-1)$
Error	________	*SSE*	$SSE/(b-1)(t-1)$
Total	$bt - 1$	Total *SS*	

$(b - 1)$
$(t - 1)$
$(b - 1)(t - 1)$

To test the null hypothesis: "there is no difference in treatment means," we use

$$F = MST/MSE$$

which has an F distribution with $\nu_1 = t - 1$ and $\nu_2 = (t - 1)(b - 1)$ degrees of freedom when H_0 is true. If H_0 is false, the statistic will tend to be larger than expected; hence we would reject H_0 if

$$F > F_\alpha$$

Although a test of H_0: "there is no difference in block means" is not always required, we can test this hypothesis using

$$F = MSB/MSE$$

When H_0 is true, this statistic has an F distribution with $\nu_1 = b - 1$ and $\nu_2 = (t - 1)(b - 1)$ degrees of freedom. H_0 is rejected if $F > F_\alpha$, where F_α is an α-level critical value of F with $(b - 1)$ and $(b - 1)(t - 1)$ degrees of freedom.

A significant test of block means provides a method of assessing the efficiency of the experimenter's blocking procedure, since if

$$F = \frac{MSB}{MSE}$$

is significant, the experimenter has ______________ the available information in the experiment by blocking, and would certainly use this same technique in subsequent experiments. In business and economics where subjects are often used as blocks, a nonsignificant test of block means should not be taken as a license to discontinue blocking in subsequent experiments involving different subjects, since the next group of subjects selected for participation could exhibit strong subject-to-subject variability and provide a highly significant test of blocks.

increased

Example 10.10

The readability of four different styles of textbook types was compared using a speed-reading test. The amount of reading material was identical for all four type styles. The sample material for each of the four type styles was read in random order by each of five readers in order to eliminate the natural variation in reading speed between readers. The length of time to completion of reading was needed. Thus, each reader corresponds to a

block

_____________ and comparisons of the four styles were made within readers. Do the data present evidence of a difference in mean reading times for the four type styles?

Type Style	*Readers* 1	2	3	4	5	*Totals*	*Means*
1	15	18	13	21	15	82	16.40
2	19	19	16	22	15	91	18.20
3	13	20	14	21	16	84	16.80
4	11	18	12	17	12	70	14.00
Totals	58	75	55	81	58	327	
Means	14.50	18.75	13.75	20.25	14.50		

Solution

Before analyzing these data, it should be pointed out that the order in which the type style was presented was randomized for each reader. The data layout presented *does not* represent the order of presentation for each reader.

1. *Partitioning the Sums of Squares*

327

$$CM = \frac{(\text{Total})^2}{bt} = \frac{(\_\_\_\_\_\_)^2}{20} = 5346.45$$

$$\text{Total } SS = \sum_{i=1}^{t} \sum_{j=1}^{b} x_{ij}^2 - CM$$

5346.45

$$= 5555 - \_\_\_\_\_\_$$

208.55

$$= \_\_\_\_\_\_$$

For SST and SSB remember that the respective totals are each squared and divided by the number of measurements per total. Block totals contain $t = 4$ measurements and treatment totals contain $b = 5$ measurements.

$$SSB = \sum_{j=1}^{b} \frac{B_j^2}{t} - CM$$

5346.45

$$= \frac{58^2 + 75^2 + \ldots + 58^2}{4} - \_\_\_\_\_\_$$

$= 5484.75 - 5346.45$

$= \_\_\_\_\_\_\_\_$ 138.30

$$SST = \sum_{i=1}^{t} \frac{T_i^2}{b} - CM$$

$= \frac{82^2 + 91^2 + 84^2 + 70^2}{5} - \_\_\_\_\_\_\_\_$ 5346.45

$= \_\_\_\_\_\_\_\_ - 5346.45$ 5392.20

$= \_\_\_\_\_\_\_\_$ 45.75

$SSE = \text{Total } SS - \_\_\_\_\_\_\_\_ - \_\_\_\_\_\_\_\_$ SSB; SST

$= 208.55 - 138.30 - 45.75$

$= \_\_\_\_\_\_\_\_$ 24.50

2. *The Analysis of Variance Table*

Complete the following *ANOVA* table.

ANOVA

Source	*d.f.*	*SS*	*MS*	*F*	
Blocks	4	138.30	______	______	34.58; 16.95
Treatments	3	45.75	______	______	15.25; 7.48
Error	12	24.50	______		2.04
Total	19	208.55			

In testing H_0: "no difference in treatment means," we use

$$F = \frac{MST}{MSE} = \frac{15.25}{2.04} = \_\_\_\_\_\_\_\_$$ 7.48

With $\nu_1 = 3$ and $\nu_2 = 12$ degrees of freedom, $F_{.05} = \_\_\_\_\_\_\_\_$. Hence we reject H_0 and conclude that there is a significant difference among the mean reading times for the four type styles. 3.49

Because we expected significant differences in mean reading times for the five readers, we used a randomized block design with the readers as blocks.

Let us test whether these five readers have significantly different mean reading times. To test H_0: "no difference in block means," we use

16.95

$$F = \frac{MSB}{MSE} = \frac{34.58}{2.04} = \_\_\_\_\_\_\_\_$$

3.26; reject

more

The 5% critical value of F with $\nu_1 = 4$ and $\nu_2 = 12$ degrees of freedom is ________; hence we __________ H_0 and conclude that the mean reading times for the five readers are significantly different. A significant test of blocks indicates that our experiment has been made (more, less) precise by using the randomized block design with readers as blocks.

10.9 Estimation for the Randomized Block Design

Since a randomized block design involves two classifications, not only can we estimate differences in treatment means, but we can also estimate the differences in block means. In either situation we can construct a confidence interval estimate based upon Student's t distribution with

$(b - 1)(t - 1)$

__________ degrees of freedom. Hence $(1 - \alpha)$ 100% confidence intervals would be found using

$$(\bar{T}_i - \bar{T}_j) \pm t_{\alpha/2} \sqrt{\frac{2\,MSE}{b}}$$

$(\bar{T}_i - \bar{T}_j) \pm t_{\alpha/2} s \sqrt{\frac{2}{b}}$

which is equivalent to __________, and

$$(\bar{B}_i - \bar{B}_j) \pm t_{\alpha/2} \sqrt{\frac{2\,MSE}{t}}$$

$(\bar{B}_i - \bar{B}_j) \pm t_{\alpha/2} s \sqrt{\frac{2}{t}}$

which is equivalent to __________.

Example 10.11

Refer to Example 10.10. Estimate the difference in mean reading time for type styles 1 and 2 with a 95% confidence interval.

Solution

1. Pertinent information:

Answer		
2.04	$\bar{T}_1 = 16.40$	$MSE =$ ________
12	$\bar{T}_2 = 18.20$	d.f. $=$ ________
2.179	$b = 5$	$t_{.025} =$ ________

2. Using

$$(\bar{T}_1 - \bar{T}_2) \pm t_{.025} \sqrt{\frac{2\,MSE}{b}}$$

we have

$$(16.40 - 18.20) \pm 2.179 \sqrt{\frac{2(2.04)}{5}}$$

or __________ ± __________ minutes -1.80; 1.97

Example 10.12
For the same problem, find a 95% confidence interval for the difference in mean reading time for readers 2 and 3.

Solution
To use the estimator

$$(\bar{B}_2 - \bar{B}_3) \pm t_{.025} \sqrt{\frac{2\,MSE}{t}}$$

we need the following additional information: $\bar{B}_2$ = __________, 18.75
$\bar{B}_3$ = __________, $t = 4$. Then 13.75

$$(18.75 - 13.75) \pm 2.179 \sqrt{\frac{2(2.04)}{4}}$$

simplifies to

__________ ± __________ minutes 5.00; 2.20

Confidence interval estimates for block means or the difference between two block means are not always required nor are they always useful. Oftentimes, however, blocks constitute an important factor in many experiments. For example, if a marketing research survey investigating potential sales for four products is carried out in six areas, the areas would constitute blocks for this experiment, and the differences in mean sales between areas would be of strong interest to the experimenter.

10.10 Computer Printout for a Randomized Block Design

Most computer software packages provide programs useful in analyzing data run in a randomized block design. Some of these programs include options for further techniques that can be used in the analysis. Since these techniques are not discussed in the text, these options will not be included in our discussion.

Example 10.13

Refer to Example 10.10. The following printout resulted when these data were analyzed by using a packaged analysis of variance program appropriate for an experiment run in a randomized block design.

```
GRAND MEAN = 16.35

READER MEANS ARE:
   14.5        18.75       13.75       20.25       14.5

TYPE MEANS ARE:
   16.4        18.2        16.8        14
```

ANALYSIS OF VARIANCE

SOURCE	DF	SS	MS	F
READER	4	138.3	34.575	16.934694
TYPE	3	45.75	15.25	7.4693878
ERROR	12	24.5	2.041667	
TOTAL	19	208.55		

Discussion

Except for decimal alignment and the printed accuracy, the ANALYSIS OF VARIANCE portion of this printout is the same as the ANOVA table of Example 10.10. When compared with the appropriate critical values of the *F* distribution, the values of the *F* statistics printed in the last column indicate
are that there (are, are not) significant differences among the readers and among
the type styles. Notice that this program allows the user to identify a block as a READER and a treatment as a TYPE style.

The first portion of the printout lists the GRAND MEAN, the READER MEANS, and the TYPE (style) MEANS. Estimation of the difference between two READER means or two TYPE style means is easily accomplished by using the formulas in Section 10.9 with appropriate tabulated values of the
12 *t* statistic based on __________ ERROR degrees of freedom.

The MINITAB command TWOWAY (two-way analysis of variance) can be used to analyze data run in a randomized block design in the following way. The data are entered into Column 1 of the computer while the corresponding block and treatment numbers (designated as 1, 2, 3, . . .) are entered into Columns 2 and 3 respectively. The MINITAB command

```
TWOWAY C1 C2 C3
```

will produce the ANOVA table, with blocks labeled 'C2' and treatments labeled 'C3'. For clarity of presentation, it is convenient to rename the C2 and C3 with the more descriptive labels BLOCKS and TRTS. This can be done by using the command

NAME C2 = 'BLOCKS' C3 = "TRTS'

before executing the TWOWAY C1 C2 C3 command.

Example 10.14
Give the appropriate commands necessary to generate the MINITAB output for the analysis of variance in Example 10.10. Compare the results with the ANOVA table given in Example 10.13.

Solution
In order to use the descriptive labels "Blocks" and Treatments" for the printout, use the MINITAB command

NAME C2 = '______________' __________ = 'TRTS' BL

The data are now entered into the computer in Columns 1, 2, and 3 as shown below. Fill in the missing entries.

ROW	C1	BLOCKS	TRTS	
1	15	1	1	
2	19	1	2	
3	13	1	3	
4	11	___	___	1; 4
5	18	2	1	
6	19	2	2	
7	___	___	___	20; 2; 3
8	18	2	4	
9	13	3	___	1
10	16	3	2	
11	14	3	3	
12	12	3	4	
13	21	4	1	
14	22	4	2	
15	21	___	3	4
16	17	4	___	4
17	15	5	1	
18	15	5	2	
19	16	5	3	
20	12	5	4	

C2; C3

The MINITAB output is generated using the command

TWOWAY C1 ________ ________

and is shown below. The output is identical, except for rounding, to the output given in Example 10.13.

```
MTB > TWOWAY C1 C2 C3

ANALYSIS OF VARIANCE ON C1

SOURCE      DF        SS        MS
BLOCKS       4    138.30     34.58
TRTS         3     45.75     15.25
ERROR       12     24.50      2.04
TOTAL       19    208.55
```

Self-Correcting Exercises 10B

1. In a study where the objective was to investigate methods of reducing fatigue among employees whose job involved a monotonous assembly procedure, twelve randomly selected employees were asked to perform their usual job under each of three trial conditions. As a measure of fatigue, the experimenter used the total length of time in minutes of assembly line stoppages during a four-hour period for each trial condition. The data follow.

	Conditions		
Employee	*1*	*2*	*3*
1	31	22	26
2	20	15	23
3	26	21	18
4	21	12	22
5	12	16	18
6	13	19	23
7	18	7	16
8	15	9	12
9	21	11	26
10	15	15	19
11	11	14	21
12	18	11	21

An SAS computer printout of the analysis of variance for these data is given in the following display.

CONDITIONS

ANALYSIS OF VARIANCE PROCEDURE

DEPENDENT VARIABLE: DWNTM

SOURCE	DF	SUM OF SQUARES	MEAN SQUARE	F VALUE
MODEL	13	708.61111111	54.50854701	3.69
ERROR	22	324.61111111	14.75505051	PR > F
CORRECTED TOTAL	35	1033.22222222		.0034

R-SQUARE	C.V.	ROOT MSE	DWNTM MEAN
.685826	21.6747	3.84123034	17.72222222

SOURCE	DF	ANOVA SS	F VALUE	PR > F
WRKRS	11	477.88888889	2.94	.0149
CONDS	2	230.72222222	7.82	.0027

Use the information in the printout to answer the following questions.

a. Is there a significant difference among the mean stoppage times for the three conditions?
b. Is there a significant difference in mean stoppage times for the twelve employees? Was the "blocking" effective?
c. Estimate the difference in mean stoppage time for conditions 2 and 3 with 95% confidence.

2. In a brand identification experiment involving four brands, 10 subjects in each of 5 geographic areas were asked to listen to an advertising jingle associated with each of the four brands and identify the brand through its jingle. The length of time in seconds until correct identification was averaged for the 10 people with the following results.

	Brands			
Areas	*1*	*2*	*3*	*4*
1	3.7	3.9	4.2	4.0
2	4.2	4.8	4.6	4.7
3	2.9	3.5	3.0	3.4
4	5.0	5.4	5.0	5.5
5	3.3	4.3	4.1	3.9

a. Present an analysis of variance for these data, testing for significant differences among mean recognition times for the four brands. Test for a significant difference among mean recognition times for the 5 areas.
b. Estimate the difference in mean recognition times for brands 2 and 4 with a 95% confidence interval.

c. Find a 95% confidence interval estimate for the difference in mean recognition times for areas 1 and 4.

10.11 Two-Way Classifications: The Factorial Experiment

The randomized block design is an example of an experiment that involves
a two-way classification, since an observation is classified as receiving the
i^{th} treatment in the jth block. The block classification, however, was not a
treatment classification and was introduced into the experiment to help
reduce ________ the error variation. However, in many situations, an experimenter may wish to investigate two or more independent treatment
factors variables, called ________ , with each factor held at several settings,
levels called ________. An experiment which utilizes every combination of
factorial factor levels is called a ________ experiment. When two factors are
investigated in a factorial experiment, the experiment produces a two-way
classification of the data in which each classification corresponds to a "treatment" factor.

Consider a factorial experiment involving factors A and B. By including all
factor combinations in the experiment, the investigator can assess the effect
of factor A alone, the effect of factor B alone, or their effect in concert. When
interact factors A and B do not behave independently, they are said to ________.
interaction The nonindependent behavior of factors A and B is called ________.

Example 10.15

A researcher at a pharmaceutical company wishes to investigate the effect of
hormone H and vitamin V upon the activity of laboratory animals. Two levels
of hormone H and two levels of vitamin V are to be investigated. This experi-
4 ment will involve (2)(2) = ________ factor combinations.

If hormone H tends to increase activity, we might observe the following response.

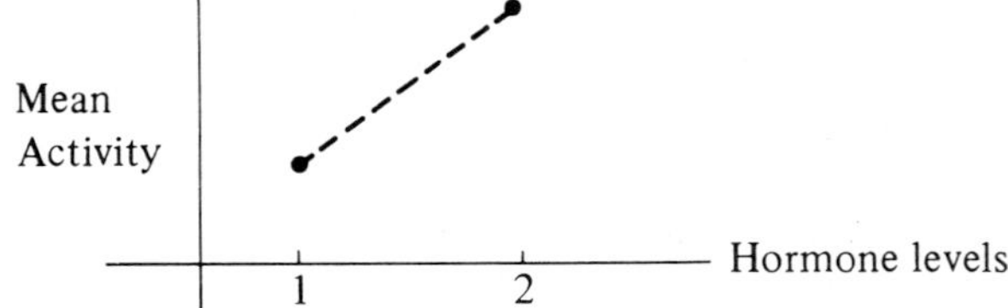

If vitamin V also increases activity, we might observe this response.

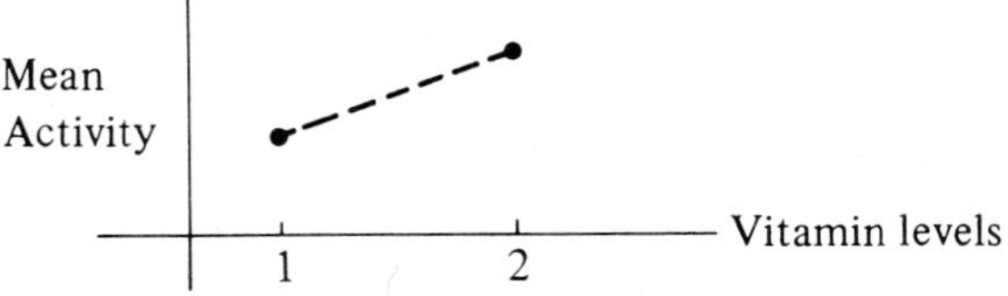

If the factors H and V do not interact, we should observe a similar effect of hormone for each vitamin dose (or vice versa).

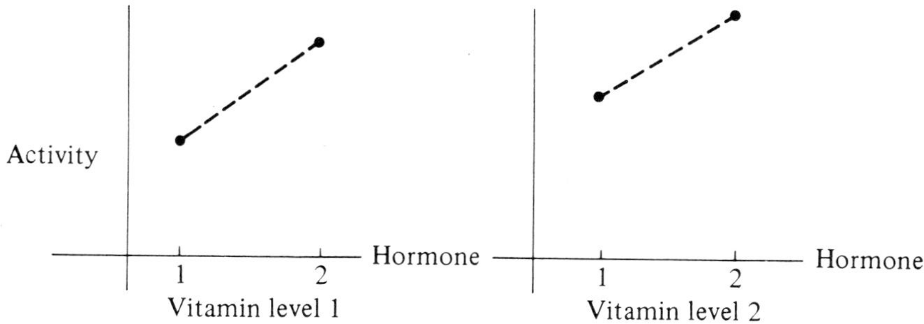

If V and H do interact, we might observe the following situation.

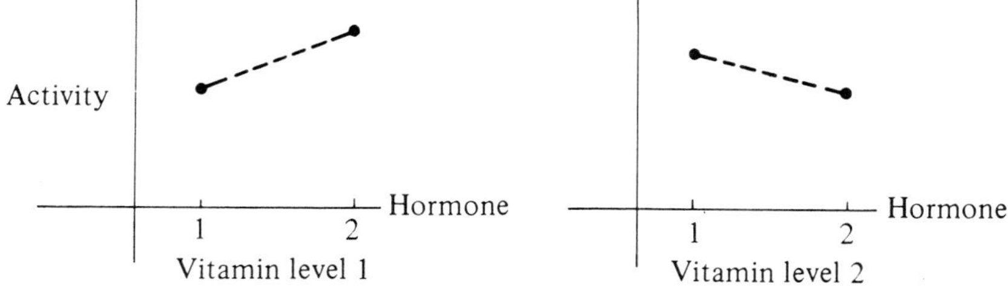

The last two diagrams indicate that at vitamin dosage (level) 1, the effect of increasing the amount of hormone is to ______________ activity, while at vitamin dosage (level) 2, the effect of increasing the amount of hormone is to ______________ activity. Hence the factors V and H do not behave independently in this situation, and would be said to ______________.

increase

decrease

interact

In the analysis of variance for a factorial experiment involving factor A at a levels and factor B at b levels with r observations of each factor combination,

$$\text{Total } SS = SSA + SSB + SS(AB) + SSE$$

To compute these sums of squares, define

A_i = the sum of all observations at the ith level of factor A, $i = 1, \ldots, a$

B_j = the sum of all observations at the jth level of factor B, $j = 1, \ldots, b$

$(AB)_{ij}$ = the sum of all observations at the ith level of factor A and the jth level of factor B, $i = 1, \ldots, a$; $b = 1, \ldots, b$

Each $(AB)_{ij}$ total will contain r observations, each A_i will contain rb observations and each B_j total will contain ra observations.

The computational formulas for the sums of squares are:

$$\text{Total } SS = \Sigma\,(\text{each observation})^2 - CM$$

$$SSA = \sum_{i=1}^{a} \frac{A_i^2}{rb} - CM$$

$$SSB = \sum_{j=1}^{b} \frac{B_j^2}{ra} - CM$$

$$SS(AB) = \sum_{i=1}^{a} \sum_{j=1}^{b} \frac{(AB)_{ij}^2}{r} - CM - SSA - SSB$$

$$SSE = \text{Total } SS - SSA - SSB - SS(AB)$$

with

$$CM = \frac{(\text{Grand total})^2}{n}$$

The corresponding mean squares are

$a - 1$ $$MSA = \text{mean square for factor } A = \frac{SSA}{(\_\_\_\_\_\_\_\_)}$$

SSB $$MSB = \text{mean square for factor } B = \frac{\_\_\_\_\_\_\_\_}{b - 1}$$

interaction $$MS(AB) = \text{mean square for } \_\_\_\_\_\_\_\_\_\_ = \frac{SS(AB)}{(a - 1)(b - 1)}$$

$$MSE = \text{mean square for error} = \frac{SSE}{n - ab}$$

Example 10.16

An experiment was conducted to investigate the effect of management training on the decision-making abilities of supervisors in a large corporation. Two factors were considered in the experiment: A, the presence or absence of managerial training, and B, the type of decision-making situation with which the supervisor was confronted. Sixteen supervisors were selected, and eight were randomly chosen to receive managerial training. Four trained and four untrained supervisors were then randomly selected to function in a situation in which a standard problem arose. The other eight supervisors were presented with an emergency situation in which standard procedures could not be used. The response was a management behavior rating for each supervisor as assessed by a rating scheme devised by the experimenter. The basic elements of the experiment are as follows.

Experimental units: ______________ supervisors

Factors: The type of training (qualitative) and the type of decision-making situation (qualitative, quantitative) qualitative

Levels of factors: Two levels for type of training, ______________ (give number) levels for type of decision-making situation. two

Treatments: The __________ (give number) training-situation combinations. 4

The data for this factorial experiment are shown below.

	A		
Situation (B)	*Trained*	*Not Trained*	*Totals*
	85	53	
	91	49	
Standard	80	38	
	78	45	
	334	185	519
	76	40	
	67	52	
Emergency	82	46	
	71	39	
	296	177	473
Totals	630	362	992

Partition the total sum of squares into SSA, SSB, SS(AB) and SSE.

Solution

Notice that in the data table, the right margin entries are the totals for the two levels of factor B, the bottom margin entries are the totals for factor A, while the entries inside the table are the subtotals for the four factorial combinations.

1. Since there are $n = 16$ observations in the experiment,

992 $$CM = \frac{(\_\_\_\_\_\_\_\_)^2}{16} = 61{,}504$$

and

$$\text{Total } SS = (85^2 + 91^2 + \ldots + 46^2 + 39^2) - CM$$

61,504 $$= 66{,}640 - \_\_\_\_\_\_\_\_$$

5136 $$= \_\_\_\_\_\_\_\_$$

2. Each A total contains eight measurements. Hence,

8 $$SSA = \frac{(630)^2 + (362)^2}{(\_\_\_\_\_\_\_\_)} - CM$$

61,504 $$= 65{,}993 - \_\_\_\_\_\_\_\_$$

4489 $$= \_\_\_\_\_\_\_\_$$

3. Each B total also contains eight measurements. Therefore

8 $$SSB = \frac{(519)^2 + (473)^2}{(\_\_\_\_\_\_\_\_)} - CM$$

61,504 $$= 61{,}636.25 - \_\_\_\_\_\_\_\_$$

132.25 $$= \_\_\_\_\_\_\_\_$$

4. Each AB total contains four measurements, and SSA and SSB have been computed, so that

$$SS(AB) = \frac{334^2 + 185^2 + 296^2 + 177^2}{4} - CM - SSA - SSB$$

$$= [66{,}181.5 - 61{,}504] - SSA - SSB$$

4677.5 $$= \_\_\_\_\_\_\_\_ - 4489 - 132.25$$

56.25 $$= \_\_\_\_\_\_\_\_$$

5. We can find SSE by using the additivity of the sums of squares.

$SSE = \text{Total } SS - SSA - SSB - SS(AB)$

$= \_\_\_\_\_\_\_\_$ | 458.5

The analysis-of-variance summary table for a $a \times b$ factorial experiment is given below. Fill in any missing entries.

ANOVA

Source	*d.f.*	*SS*	*MS*
Factor A	________	SSA	MSA
Factor B	________	SSB	MSB
$A \times B$	$(a-1)(b-1)$	$SS(AB)$	$MS(AB)$
Error	$n - ab$	________	MSE
Total	$n - 1$	Total SS	

$a - 1$

$b - 1$

SSE

The entries in the mean-square column are found by dividing each sum of squares by its appropriate degrees of freedom.

There are three tests available for a $a \times b$ factorial experiment.

1. A test of H_0: no interaction among the factors, utilizes

$$F = \frac{MS(AB)}{MSE}$$

with $\nu_1 = \_\_\_\_\_\_\_\_$ and $\nu_2 = \_\_\_\_\_\_\_\_$ degrees of freedom. H_0 is rejected if $F > F_\alpha$ with the appropriate degrees of freedom. | $(a-1)(b-1); n - ab$

2. To test H_0: no difference in the effect of levels of B, we use

$$F = \frac{MSB}{MSE}$$

with $\nu_1 = \_\_\_\_\_\_\_\_$ and $\nu_2 = \_\_\_\_\_\_\_\_$ degrees of freedom. We reject H_0 if $F > F_\alpha$ with $(b-1)$ and $(n - ab)$ degrees, respectively. | $b - 1; n - ab$

3. In testing H_0: no difference in the effect of levels of A, use

$$F = \frac{MSA}{MSE}$$

with ________ numerator and ________ denominator degrees of freedom, respectively, rejecting H_0 if $F > F_\alpha$ with the specified degrees of freedom. | $(a-1); (n - ab)$

Example 10.17

a. Present the results of Example 10.16 in an analysis-of-variance table.
b. Is there a significant interaction between A and B at the 5% level of significance?
c. Do the data indicate a significant difference in behavior ratings for the two types of situations at the 5% level of significance?
d. Do behavior ratings differ significantly for the two types of training categories at the 5% level of significance?

Solution

16
2

Recall that the experiment involved a total of $n =$ __________ observations with $a = b =$ __________ levels for each factor.

a. Collecting the results of Example 10.16, we have the following table. Fill in any missing entries.

4489.00
132.25
56.25
38.21

ANOVA

Source	*d.f.*	*SS*	*MS*
Training (A)	1	4489.00	________
Situation (B)	1	132.25	________
$A \times B$	1	56.25	________
Error	12	458.50	________
Total	15	5136.00	

b. Test H_0: no interaction between A and B using

56.25; 1.47

$$F = \frac{MS(AB)}{MSE} = \frac{\_\_\_\_\_\_\_\_}{38.21} = \_\_\_\_\_\_\_\_$$

4.75
cannot

with $\nu_1 = 1$ and $\nu_2 = 12$ degrees of freedom. $F_{.05} =$ __________; hence, we __________ reject H_0. The data indicate that there is no significant interaction between these two factors.

c. In testing H_0: no difference in behavior ratings for the two situation types, use

132.25; 3.46

$$F = \frac{MSB}{MSE} = \frac{\_\_\_\_\_\_\_\_}{38.21} = \_\_\_\_\_\_\_\_$$

4.75; cannot

Since $3.46 < F_{.05} =$ __________, we (can, cannot) conclude that there is a significant difference in behavior ratings for the two types of situations.

d. To test H_0: no difference in behavior ratings for the two training categories, use

$$F = \frac{MSA}{MSE} = \frac{\rule{2cm}{0.4pt}}{38.21} = \rule{2cm}{0.4pt}$$ 4489; 117.48

In comparing 117.48 to $F_{.05}$ = __________, we find that there is a highly significant difference in behavior ratings for the two training classifications. 4.75

e. In summary, there is no significant interaction between the factors and no significant difference in behavior ratings for standard and emergency situations. However, there is a highly significant difference in behavior ratings for the two conditions "Trained" and "Not Trained." Notice that the average behavior rating for trained supervisors was 630/8 = __________ compared to an average of 362/8 = __________ for untrained supervisors. 78.75; 45.25

The MINITAB TWOWAY analysis of variance program (as well as SAS and SPSS programs) can be used to analyze an $a \times b$ factorial experiment, as long as each factorial combination is replicated an equal number of times. The data are entered into Column 1 of the computer, while the corresponding levels of A and B are entered into C2 and C3 respectively. The MINITAB command TWOWAY (two-way analysis of variance) C1 C2 C3 will produce the necessary analysis of variance, with factor A labeled "C2" factor B labeled "C3" and the interaction AB labeled ______________. As in the MINITAB output for the randomized block design, we may choose to use more descriptive labels for C2 and C3. In this case, we use the commands INTERACTION

NAME C2 = 'A' C3 = 'B'

or some more descriptive label, and the sum of squares within the ANOVA table will be more clearly identified.

Example 10.18

Give the appropriate commands necessary to generate the MINITAB output for the analysis of variance in Example 10.16. Compare the results with the ANOVA table calculated by hand in Example 10.17.

Solution

In order to use the descriptive labels 'Training' and 'Situation' for factors A and B, use the MINITAB command

NAME C2 = '______________' __________ = 'SITUATN' TRAINING C3

The data are now entered into the computer in Columns C1, C2, and C3 as shown below. Fill in the missing entries.

```
MTB > PRINT C1-C3
```

	ROW	C1	TRAINING	SITUATN
1; 1	1	85	___	___
	2	91	1	1
	3	80	1	1
	4	78	1	1
2	5	76	1	___
67	6	___	1	2
	7	82	1	2
1	8	71	___	2
	9	53	2	1
49	10	___	2	1
	11	38	2	1
2; 1	12	45	___	___
	13	40	2	2
	14	52	2	2
	15	46	2	2
39	16	___	2	2

The MINITAB output is generated using the command

C3 TWOWAY C1 C2 ________

and is shown below.

```
MTB > TWOWAY C1 C2 C3
ANALYSIS OF VARIANCE ON C1
```

SOURCE	DF	SS	MS
TRAINING	1	4489.0	4489.0
SITUATN	1	132.3	132.3
INTERACTION	1	56.3	56.3
ERROR	12	458.5	38.2
TOTAL	15	5136.0	

The results are identical to those given in Example 10.17.

Self-Correcting Exercises 10C

1. The effect of three fungicide treatments on the germination rate of three varieties of beans was measured as the percentage of germinating beans out of 100 planted. The data follow.

	Fungicide Treatment		
Variety	*1*	*2*	*3*
A	78	82	92
	62	78	85
	72	70	87
	68	75	90
B	65	72	85
	70	68	79
	75	73	84
	69	76	80
C	81	87	94
	78	83	90
	75	82	89
	85	85	95

a. What type of experimental design has been used?
b. Perform an analysis of variance on the data.
c. Is there a significant interaction between treatments and varieties? Use $\alpha = .05$.
d. Are there significant differences among varieties? Among fungicides? Use $\alpha = .05$.

2. One aspect of a study to compare the quality of medical care delivered by two health maintenance organizations (HMO) was to get a satisfaction rating for patients using the various departments of the HMO's. Five patients were randomly selected from three departments of each HMO. The data which follow consist of a satisfaction rating on a scale from 0 (least satisfaction) to 10 (most satisfied).

	Health Maintenance Organization	
Department	*1*	*2*
Pediatrics	7	8
	6	9
	5	7
	7	9
	4	8
OB/GYN	8	6
	7	5
	5	6
	5	7
	6	5
Family Practice	4	7
	3	6
	5	5
	6	5
	5	7

a. What type of experimental design has been used?
b. Perform an analysis of variance on the data.
c. Is there evidence of a significant interaction between the type of department and HMO's ? Use $\alpha = .05$.
d. Is it appropriate to consider main effects in the presence of significant interaction?
e. Estimate the difference in ratings for the two HMO's for each of the three departments using 95% confidence intervals.

10.12 Comments on Blocking and on the Analysis of Variance Assumptions

There are two major steps in designing an experiment that must be kept conceptually separate:

1. The first step encompasses the decision about what treatments to include in the experiment and the number of observations per treatment. Each setting of the independent variable, or each combination of settings of the independent variables if there are more than one, corresponds to a single ______________.
2. The second step involves the decision of how to apply the treatments to the experimental ______________. Here is where the choice between a completely randomized and a randomized block design should be made.

treatment

units

Blocking produces a gain in information if and only if the between-block variation is (larger, smaller) than the within-block variation. But blocking also costs information because it (increases, reduces) the number of degrees of freedom associated with the sum of squares for error denoted by *SSE*. Hence, blocking is beneficial only if the gain in information due to blocking outweighs the loss due to reduced degrees of freedom associated with *SSE*.

larger
reduces

In order to validly apply the testing and estimation procedures in an analysis of variance, the following assumptions concerning the probability distribution of the response x must be met:

1. For any treatment or block combination, the response x is ______________ distributed with variance σ^2.
2. The observations are selected randomly and independently so that x_i and x_j are ______________ for all pairs i and j, $i \neq j$.

normally

independent

Although it is never known in practice whether these assumptions are satisfied, we should be reasonably sure that violations of these assumptions are moderate. If the random variable under investigation is discrete, it is possible that the distribution for x is mound-shaped and hence approximately normal. This would not be the case if the discrete random variable only assumed three or four values.

Although binomial and Poisson random variables have probability distributions that may be approximately normal, these random variables will usually violate the assumption of equal variances. Recall that for a binomial random variable, $\mu =$ ________ and $\sigma^2 =$ ________ $= \mu(1 - p)$, while for a Poisson random variable, $\sigma^2 =$ ________. In either case, if the treatments are effective in changing the means, they will also cause the variances to change. Hence the homogeneity assumption will be violated.

np; *npq*

μ

Even when the response is normally distributed, the variances for the treatment groups may still be unequal. In economic studies the variability of income within economic groupings is known to increase as the average income increases. Relationships of this sort can be detected by plotting the treatment or group means against the group variances or standard deviations. The coefficient of variation, defined as the ratio of the standard deviation to the ________ expressed as a percentage, can also be used to identify situations in which the standard deviations, and hence the variances, are unequal through their dependence on the mean.

mean

When the data fail to meet the assumptions of normality and equal variances, an appropriate transformation of the data, such as their square roots, logarithms, or some other function of the data values, may be used in order that the transformed values approximately satisfy these assumptions.

When the data consist only of rankings or ordered preferences, appropriate nonparametric testing and estimation procedures can be used. These procedures can also be used when the data fail to satisfy the assumptions of normality and equal variances, since the only requirement needed to use nonparametric techniques is that the observations be ________ within the constraints of the design used.

independent

EXERCISES

1. A large piece of cotton fabric was cut into 12 pieces and randomly partitioned into three groups of four. Three different chemicals designed to produce resistance to stain were applied to the units, one chemical for each group. A stain was applied (as uniformly as possible) over all $n = 12$ units and the intensity of the stain measured in terms of light reflection.
   a. What type of experimental design was employed?
   b. Perform an analysis of variance and construct the *ANOVA* table for the following data:

Chemical		
1	*2*	*3*
12	14	9
8	9	7
9	11	9
6	10	5

c. Do the data present sufficient evidence to indicate a difference in mean resistance to stain for the three chemicals?
d. Give a 95% confidence interval for the difference in means for chemicals 1 and 2.
e. Approximately how many observations per treatment would be required to estimate the difference in mean response for two chemicals correct to within 1.0?
f. Obtain *SSE* directly for the data of Exercise 1 by calculating the sums of squares of deviations within each of the three treatments and pooling. Compare with the value found using *SSE* = Total *SS* - *SST*.
g. Give a 90% confidence interval for the mean stain intensity for chemical 2.

2. A substantial amount of variation was expected in the amount of stain applied to the experimental units of Exercise 1. It was decided that greater uniformity could be obtained by applying the stain three units at a time. A repetition of the experiment produced the following results:

	Chemical		
Application	*1*	*2*	*3*
1	12	15	9
2	9	13	9
3	7	12	7
4	10	15	9

a. Give the type of design.
b. Conduct an analysis of variance for the data.
c. Do the data provide sufficient evidence to indicate a difference among chemicals?
d. Give the formula for a $(1 - \alpha)$ 100% confidence interval for the difference in a pair of chemical means. Calculate a 95% confidence interval for $(\mu_2 - \mu_3)$.
e. Approximately how many blocks (applications) would be required to estimate $(\mu_1 - \mu_2)$ correct to within .5?
f. We noted that the chemist suspected an uneven distribution of stain when simultaneously distributed over the 12 pieces of cloth. Do the data support this view? (That is, do the data present sufficient evidence to indicate a difference in mean résponse for applications?)

3. Refer to Exercise 1. The experimenter felt that if the chemical were applied to the fabric several times, with the fabric allowed to dry between applications, the resistance to stain might be increased. He decided to use three different levels of chemical application (once, twice, and three times) and to replicate the treatment twice for each of the three types of chemicals. A piece of fabric was therefore divided into 18 pieces, the stain was applied to two pieces for each of the nine treatment combinations, and the intensity of the stain was again measured. The results are shown below.

		Chemical Type		
		1	*2*	*3*
Number of Applications	1	11	12	9
		13	10	7
	2	14	13	13
		16	14	10
	3	22	12	10
		18	12	11

a. What type of experimental design was employed?
b. Perform an analysis of variance and construct the ANOVA table.
c. Do the data present sufficient evidence to indicate that there is an interaction between the types of chemicals and the number of applications? Use $\alpha = .05$.
d. Graph the average stain resistance as the number of chemical applications increases for each of the three chemicals. Based on the results of part c, what conclusions would you draw about stain resistance for the three chemicals?

4. Daily lost production from three production lines in a manufacturing operation were recorded for a ten-day period.

Day	Line *1*	*2*	*3*
1	15	11	8
2	9	9	6
3	6	8	4
4	7	6	5
5	16	13	9
6	23	25	14
7	12	9	7
8	10	12	9
9	12	10	11
10	16	10	9

a. Give the type of experiment.
b. Give the analysis of variance for the data.
c. Do the data present sufficient evidence to indicate a difference in mean lost daily production for the three production lines?
d. Do the data provide sufficient evidence to indicate a difference in mean daily lost production between days?
e. Find a 95% confidence interval for the difference in mean loss of production for lines 1 and 3.

5. Twenty college graduates selected by a large corporation were randomly separated into four equal groups and subjected to three months of executive training. A slightly different training program was administered to each

group. At the end of the three-month period, progress of the participants was measured by a specially designed examination. The exam scores are shown below (one participant in group three dropped out of the training program).

Group			
1	*2*	*3*	*4*
112	111	140	101
92	129	121	116
124	102	130	105
89	136	106	126
97	99		119

a. Give the type of design which appears appropriate.
b. Conduct an analysis of variance for the data.
c. Do the data present sufficient evidence to indicate a difference in mean response on the examination for the four training programs?
d. Find a 95% confidence interval for the difference in mean response on the exam for groups 1 and 2.
e. How could one employ blocking to increase the information in this problem? Under what circumstances might a blocking design applied to this problem fail to achieve the objective of the experiment?

6. The Graduate Record Examination scores were recorded for students admitted to three different graduate programs in a university.

Graduate Programs		
1	*2*	*3*
532	670	502
601	590	607
548	640	549
619	710	524
509		542
627		
690		

a. Do these data provide sufficient evidence to indicate a difference in mean level of achievement on the GRE for applicants admitted to the three programs?
b. Find a 90% confidence interval for the difference in mean GRE scores for programs 1 and 2.

7. An experiment was conducted to compare the gasoline mileage using four different gasoline additives. To eliminate the effect of the type of automobile used, the experiment was blocked on automobiles. Five different automobiles were employed with each automobile using four different tankfuls of gasoline, each with a different additive. Each set of four measured runs by one type of automobile tended to represent a rather homogeneous set of measurements and was considered a block. The data,

in miles per gallon, is shown below for each type of automobile and each gasoline additive.

	Additive			
Automobile	*1*	*2*	*3*	*4*
A	28	19	28	35
B	16	14	20	20
C	31	28	22	33
D	26	16	27	24
E	11	16	19	20

a. Give the analysis of variance for the data.
b. Do the data present sufficient evidence to indicate a difference in average gasoline mileage capability for the four gasoline additives?
c. Do the data present sufficient evidence to indicate a difference in average gasoline mileage capability among the automobiles? Was blocking desirable?

Chapter 11

LINEAR REGRESSION AND CORRELATION

11.1 Introduction

We have investigated the problem of making inferences about population parameters in the case of large and small sample sizes. We will now consider another aspect of this problem. Suppose that $E(y)$, the expected value of a random variable y, depends on the values assigned to other variables, $x_1, x_2, \ldots, x_k$. Then we say that a functional relationship exists between $E(y)$ and $x_1, x_2, \ldots, x_k$. Since the values of $E(y)$ depend on the values assumed by $x_1, x_2, \ldots, x_k$, $E(y)$ is called the *dependent variable* and $x_1, x_2, \ldots, x_k$ are called the *independent variables.* We restrict our investigation to the case where $E(y)$ is a *linear* function of one variable x. By linear, we mean that the relationship between $E(y)$ and x can be described by a straight line.

Review: The Algebraic Representation of a Straight Line

To understand the development of the following linear models, you must be familiar with the algebraic representation of a straight line and its properties.

The mathematical equation for a straight line is

$$y = \beta_0 + \beta_1 x,$$

where x is the independent variable, y is the dependent variable, and β_0 and β_1 are fixed constants. When values of x are substituted into this equation, pairs of numbers, (x_i, y_i), are generated which, when plotted or graphed on a rectangular coordinate system, form a straight line.

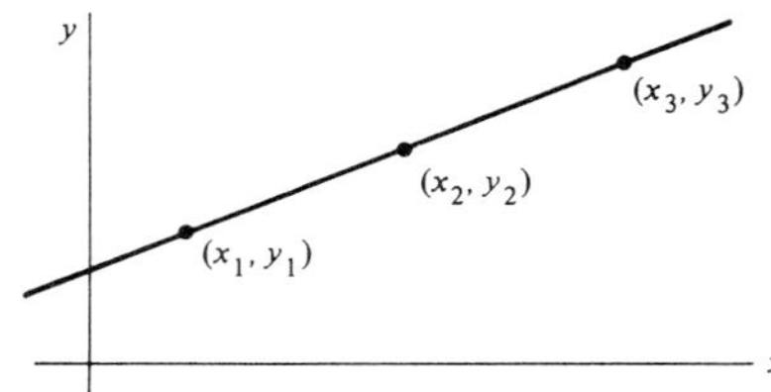

Consider the graph of a linear equation $y = \beta_0 + \beta_1 x$, shown below.

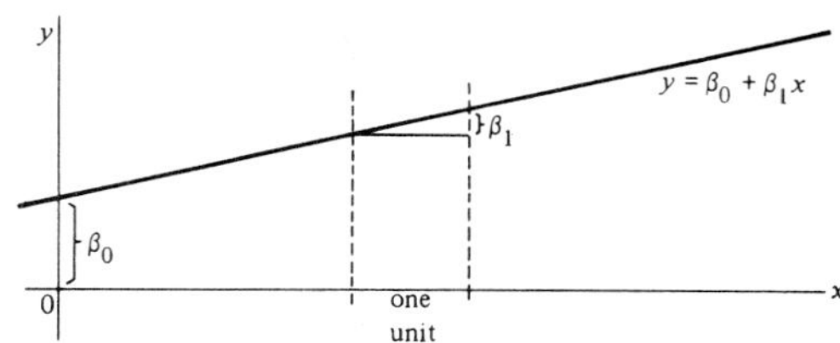

1. By setting $x = 0$, we have $y = \beta_0 + \beta_1(0) = \beta_0$. Because the line intercepts or cuts the y-axis at the value $y = \beta_0$, β_0 is called the y ________________. intercept
2. The constant β_1 represents the increase in y for a one-unit increase in x and is called the ________________ of the line. slope

Example 11.1
Plot the equation $y = 1 + .5x$ on a rectangular coordinate system.

Solution
Two points are needed to uniquely determine a straight line and therefore a minimum of two points must be found. A third point is usually found as a check on calculations.

1. Using 0, 2, and 4 as values of x, find the corresponding values of y.

When $x = 0, y = 1 + .5(0) =$ __________ 1

When $x = 2, y = 1 + .5(2) =$ __________ 2

When $x = 4, y = 1 + .5(4) =$ __________ 3

2. Plot these points on a rectangular coordinate system and join them by using a straightedge.

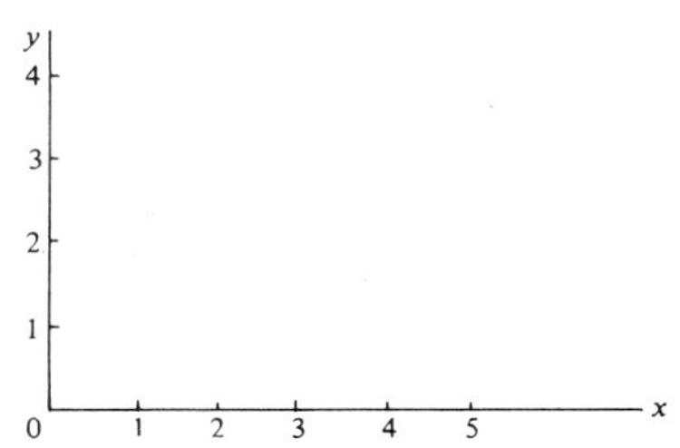

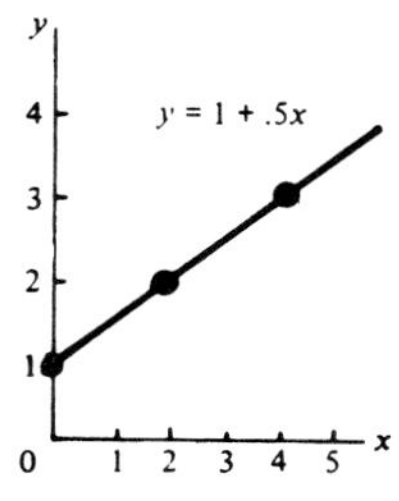

Practice plotting the following linear equations on a rectangular coordinate system:

a. $y = -1 + 3x$

b. $y = 2 - x$

c. $y = -.5 - .5x$

d. $y = x$

e. $y = .5 + 2x$

11.2 A Simple Linear Probabilistic Model

Suppose we are given a set consisting of n pairs of values for x and y, each pair representing the value of a response y for a given value of x. Plotting these points might result in the following scatter diagram:

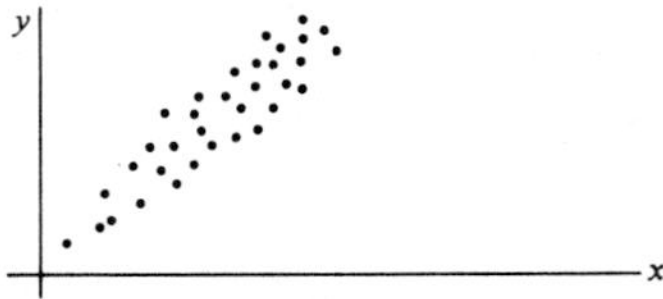

Someone might say that these points appear to lie on a straight line. This person would be hypothesizing that a *model* for the relationship between x and y is of the form

$$y_i = \beta_0 + \beta_1 x_i \qquad i = 1, 2, \ldots, n$$

deterministic

According to this model, for a given value of x, the value of y is *uniquely determined.* Therefore this is called a ______________ model.

Another person might say that these points appear to be *deviations* about a straight line, hypothesizing the model

$$y_i = \beta_0 + \beta_1 x_i + \epsilon_i \qquad i = 1, 2, \ldots, n$$

where ϵ_i represents the deviation of the ith point (x_i, y_i) from the straight line $y = \beta_0 + \beta_1 x$.

Suppose that we were able to make 4 observations on y at each of the values x_1, x_2, and x_3. We might observe the following 12 pairs of values:

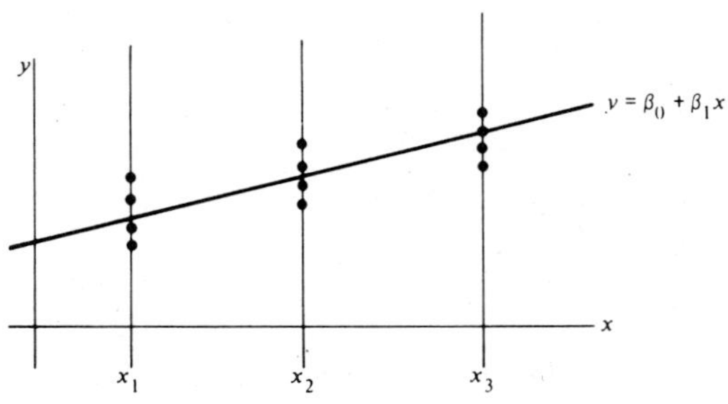

To account for what appear to be random deviations about the deterministic line $y = \beta_0 + \beta_1 x$, we will consider the deviations to be *random errors* with the following properties:

1. For any fixed value of x, in repeated sampling, the random errors have a mean of zero and a variance equal to σ^2.
2. Any two random errors are independent in the probabilistic sense.
3. Regardless of the value of x, the random errors have the same *normal* distribution with mean zero and variance σ^2.

Since this model uses a random error component having a probability distribution, it is referred to as a ______________ model. probabilistic

The probabilistic model assumes that the average value of y is linearly related to x and the observed values of y will deviate above and below the line

$$E(y) = \beta_0 + \beta_1 x$$

by a random amount. The random components all have the same normal distribution and are independent of each other. According to the properties given above, repeated observations on y at the values x_1, x_2, and x_3 would result in the following visual representation of the random errors:

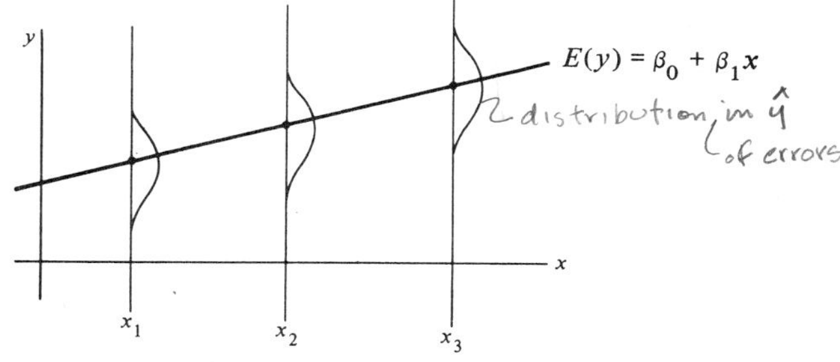

The probabilistic model appears to be the model that best describes the data and we now proceed to find an estimate for this prediction equation, the regression line

$$\hat{y} = \hat{\beta}_0 + \hat{\beta}_1 x$$

11.3 The Method of Least Squares

The criterion used for estimating β_0 and β_1 in the model

$$y_i = \beta_0 + \beta_1 x_i + \epsilon_i$$

is to find an estimated line

$$\hat{y}_i = \hat{\beta}_0 + \hat{\beta}_1 x_i$$

that in some sense minimizes the deviations of the observed values of y from the fitted line. If the deviation of the ith observed value from the fitted value is $(y_i - \hat{y}_i)$, we define the best estimated line as one that minimizes the sum of squares of the deviations of the observed values of y from the fitted values of y. The quantity

$$\sum_{i=1}^{n} (y_i - \hat{y}_i)^2$$

represents the sum of squares of deviations of the observed values of y from the fitted values and is called the sum of squares for error (SSE):

$$\text{SSE} = \sum_{i=1}^{n} (y_i - \hat{y}_i)^2 = \sum_{i=1}^{n} [y_i - (\hat{\beta}_0 + \hat{\beta}_1 x_i)]^2$$

The values of $\hat{\beta}_0$ and $\hat{\beta}_1$ are determined mathematically so that SSE will be minimum.

This process of minimization is called the *method of least squares* and produces estimates of β_0 and β_1. If we agree that all summations will be with respect to i as the variable of summation, $i = 1, 2, \ldots, n$, then the least-squares estimates of β_1 and β_0 are

$$\hat{\beta}_1 = \text{S}_{xy}/\text{S}_{xx} \quad \text{and} \quad \hat{\beta}_0 = \bar{y} - \hat{\beta}_1 \bar{x}$$

where

$$\text{S}_{xy} = \Sigma (x_i - \bar{x})(y_i - \bar{y}) = \Sigma x_i y_i - [(\Sigma x_i)(\Sigma y_i)/n]$$

and

$$\text{S}_{xx} = \Sigma (x_i - \bar{x})^2 = \Sigma x_i^2 - [(\Sigma x_i)^2/n]$$

When $\hat{\beta}_0$ and $\hat{\beta}_1$ have been calculated, their values are substituted into the equation of a straight line to obtain the least squares prediction equation

$\hat{y} = \hat{\beta}_0 + \hat{\beta}_1 x$ ____________.

Example 11.2
In this chapter we will use the following example to illustrate each type of problem encountered. Be ready to refer to the information tabulated on this page. For the following data, find the best fitting line, $\hat{y} = \hat{\beta}_0 + \hat{\beta}_1 x$:

	x_i	y_i	x_i^2	y_i^2	$x_i y_i$
	2	1	4	1	2
	3	3	9	9	9
	5	4	25	16	20
	7	7	49	49	49
	9	10	81	100	90
26; 25	Sum ____	____	168	175	170

5.2; 5 $\bar{x}$ = ____________ $\bar{y}$ = ____________

Solution

1. First find all the sums needed in the computations.

$$S_{xy} = \Sigma x_i y_i - [(\Sigma x_i)(\Sigma y_i)/n]$$

$= 170 - [(\_\_\_\_\_\_)(\_\_\_\_\_\_)/5]$ — 26; 25

$= 170 - \_\_\_\_\_\_$ — 130

$= \_\_\_\_\_\_$ — 40

$$S_{xx} = \Sigma x_i^2 - [(\Sigma x_i)^2/n]$$

$= \_\_\_\_\_\_ - [(26)^2/5]$ — 168

$= \_\_\_\_\_\_ - 135.2$ — 168

$= \_\_\_\_\_\_$ — 32.8

2. $\hat{\beta}_1 = S_{xy}/S_{xx} = 4.0/32.8 = \_\_\_\_\_\_$ — 1.2195 or 1.22

3. $\hat{\beta}_0 = \bar{y} - \hat{\beta}_1 \bar{x}$

$= (\_\_\_\_\_\_) - 1.22(\_\_\_\_\_\_)$ — 5; 5.2

$= (\_\_\_\_\_\_) - (\_\_\_\_\_\_)$ — 5; 6.34

$= -1.3415$ or -1.34

4. The best fitting line is

$\hat{y} = \_\_\_\_\_\_$ — $-1.34 + 1.22x$

We can now use the equation $\hat{y} = -1.34 + 1.22x$ to predict values of ______ for values of x in the interval $2 \leqslant x \leqslant 9$. However, we also need to place ______ of ______ on this prediction. To do this we need σ^2, or its estimator, s^2. — y; bounds; error

Self-Correcting Exercises 11A

1. The registrar at a small university noted that the pre-enrollment figures and the actual enrollment figures for the past 6 years (in hundreds of students) were

x: pre-enrollment	30	35	42	48	50	51
y: actual enrollment	33	41	46	52	59	55

a. Plot these data. Does it appear that a linear relationship exists between x and y?
b. Find the least-squares line, $\hat{y} = \hat{\beta}_0 + \hat{\beta}_1 x$.
c. Using the least-squares line, predict the actual number of students enrolled if the pre-enrollment figure is 5000 students.

2. An agricultural economist, interested in predicting cotton harvest using the number of cotton bolls per quadrate counted during the middle of the growing season, collected the following data, where y is the yield in bales of cotton per field quadrate and x is hundreds of cotton bolls per quadrate counted during mid-season.

y	21	17	20	19	15	23	20
x	5.5	2.8	4.7	4.3	3.7	6.1	4.5

a. Fit the least-squares line $\hat{y} = \hat{\beta}_0 + \hat{\beta}_1 x$ using these data.
b. Plot the least-squares line and the actual data on the same graph. Comment on the adequacy of the least-squares predictor to describe these data.

3. Refer to Exercise 2. The same economist also had available a measure of the number of damaging insects present per quadrate during a critical time in the development of the cotton plants. The data follow.

y: yield	21	17	20	19	15	23	20
x: insects	11	20	13	12	18	10	12

a. Fit the least-squares line to these data.
b. Plot the least-squares line and the actual data points on the same graph. Does it appear that the predictor line adequately describes the relationship between yield (y) and the number of insects present (x)?

11.4 Calculating s^2, an Estimator of σ^2

Before we can proceed with evaluations of the estimates $\hat{\beta}_0$ and $\hat{\beta}_1$, or assess the reliability of any forecast of y based on the estimated regression
σ^2 line, we must first estimate __________, the variance of y for a given value of x.

To estimate σ^2, we use *SSE*, the sum of squares of deviations about the line, $\hat{y} = \hat{\beta}_0 + \hat{\beta}_1 x$. The n pairs of data points provide n degrees of freedom
$n - 2$ for estimation. Having estimated β_0 and β_1, we now have __________ remaining degrees of freedom to estimate σ^2.

Therefore the estimate of σ^2 is

$$s^2 = \text{SSE}/(n - 2) = \Sigma(y_i - \hat{y}_i)^2/(n - 2)$$

The computational form for the quantity SSE is

$$\text{SSE} = \text{S}_{yy} - \hat{\beta}_1 \text{S}_{xy}$$

where

$$\text{S}_{yy} = \Sigma\,(y_i - \bar{y})^2 = \Sigma\, y_i^2 - (\Sigma\, y_i)^2/n$$

S_{xy} is the numerator used in computing $\hat{\beta}_1$ and *has already been found.*

Example 11.3
Calculate s^2 for our data.

Solution
1. Calculate S_{yy}.

$$S_{yy} = \Sigma y_i^2 - \frac{(\Sigma y_i)^2}{n} = \_\_\_\_\_\_\_\_ - \frac{(\_\_\_\_\_\_\_\_)^2}{5}$$ 175; 25

$$= \_\_\_\_\_\_\_\_$$ 50

2. Using S_{xy} from the calculations for $\hat{\beta}_1$, use the computational formula for SSE.

$$SSE = S_{yy} - \hat{\beta}_1 S_{xy}$$

$$= \_\_\_\_\_\_\_\_ - (\_\_\_\_\_\_\_\_)(\_\_\_\_\_\_\_\_)$$ 50; 1.2195; 40

$$= \_\_\_\_\_\_\_\_$$ 1.2195

3. Calculate s^2, using the formula

$$s^2 = \frac{SSE}{n-2} = \frac{1.2195}{(\_\_\_\_\_\_\_\_)} = \_\_\_\_\_\_\_\_$$ 3; 0.4065

11.5 Inferences Concerning the Slope of the Line, β_1

The slope β_1 is the average increase in ________ for a one-unit increase in ________. The question of the existence of a linear relationship between x and y must be phrased in terms of the slope β_1. If no linear relationship exists between x and y, then $\beta_1 = 0$. Hence a test of the existence of a *linear* relationship between x and y is given as $H_0: \beta_1 =$ ________ versus H_a: $\beta_1 \neq$ ________.

y
x
0
0

When the random error ϵ is *normally* distributed, the estimator $\hat{\beta}_1$ has the following properties:

normal 1. $\hat{\beta}_1$ has a ______________ distribution.

$\beta_1; \beta_1$ 2. $\hat{\beta}_1$ is an unbiased estimator for __________ so that $E(\hat{\beta}_1) =$ __________.

3. The variance of $\hat{\beta}_1$ is

$$\sigma_{\hat{\beta}_1} = \sigma^2/S_{xx}$$

The following test statistics can be constructed using the fact that $\hat{\beta}_1$ is a *normally* distributed, *unbiased* estimator of β_1:

1. $$z = \frac{\hat{\beta}_1 - \beta_1}{\sigma/\sqrt{S_{xx}}} \quad \text{if } \sigma^2 \text{ is known}$$

2. $$t = \frac{\hat{\beta}_1 - \beta_1}{s/\sqrt{S_{xx}}} \quad \text{if } s^2 \text{ is used to estimate } \sigma^2 \text{ and hence to estimate } \sigma^2_{\hat{\beta}_1}$$

Since σ^2 is rarely known, we can test for a significant linear relationship using the statistic given in 2, which has a Student's t distribution with

$n - 2$ __________ degrees of freedom. A test of the hypothesis $H_0: \beta_1 = 0$ versus $H_a: \beta_1 \neq 0$ is given as follows:

1. $H_0: \beta_1 = 0$

2. $H_a: \beta_1 \neq 0$

3. Test statistic:

$$t = \frac{\hat{\beta}_1 - (0)}{s/\sqrt{S_{xx}}}$$

4. Rejection region: Reject H_0 if $|t| > t_{\alpha/2}$ based on $n - 2$ degrees freedom.

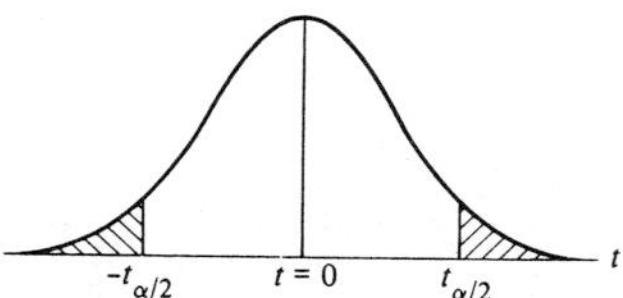

Example 11.4

For our data, test the hypothesis that there is no linear relationship between x and y at the $\alpha = .05$ level.

Solution

1. $H_0: \beta_1 =$ __________ 0

2. $H_a: \beta_1 \neq$ __________ 0

3. Test statistic:

$$t = \frac{\hat{\beta}_1 - (0)}{s/\sqrt{S_{xx}}}$$

4. Rejection region: With 3 degrees of freedom, we will reject H_0 if $|t| > t_{.025} =$ __________. 3.182

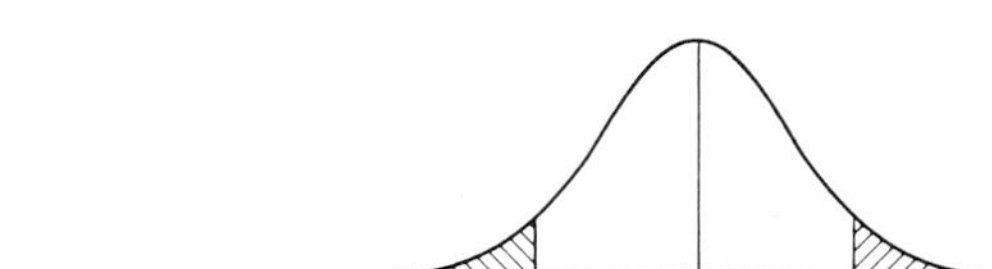

5. To calculate the test statistic, we draw upon earlier calculations for the value of s and S_{xx}.

$$s = \sqrt{s^2} = \sqrt{\_\_\_\_\_\_\_\_\_\_} = \_\_\_\_\_\_\_\_\_\_$$ 0.4065; .63758

and

$$S_{xx} = \_\_\_\_\_\_\_\_\_\_$$ 32.8

The test statistic is then

$$t = \frac{\hat{\beta}_1}{s} \cdot \sqrt{S_{xx}}$$

$$= \frac{(\_\_\_\_\_\_\_\_\_\_)}{.63758} \cdot \sqrt{\_\_\_\_\_\_\_\_\_\_}$$ 1.2195; 32.8

$$= \_\_\_\_\_\_\_\_\_\_$$ 10.95

6. Since 10.95 is larger than the critical value of $t =$ __________, we (reject, do not reject) H_0 and conclude that there (is, is not) a linear relationship between x and y. 3.182 reject; is

Confidence Interval for β_1

If x increases one unit, what is the predicted change in y? Since $\hat{\beta}_1$ is an unbiased estimator for β_1 and has a normal distribution, the t statistic, based on $n - 2$ degrees of freedom, can be used to derive the confidence interval estimator for the slope β_1:

$$\hat{\beta}_1 \pm t_{\alpha/2}\, s/\sqrt{S_{xx}}$$

Example 11.5

Find a 95% confidence interval for the average change in y for an increase of one unit in x.

Solution

.05; .025; 3
3.182

1. $1 - \alpha = .95$; $\alpha =$ __________; $\alpha/2 =$ __________; $n - 2 =$ __________; $t_{.025} =$ __________

2. $$\hat{\beta}_1 \pm t_{.025}\, s/\sqrt{S_{xx}}$$

3.182

$1.22 \pm (\_\_\_\_\_\_\_\_\_\_)(.63758)/\sqrt{32.8}$

.35

$1.22 \pm (\_\_\_\_\_\_\_\_\_\_)$

.87; 1.57

3. A 95% confidence interval for β_1 is (__________, __________).

Points Concerning Interpretation of Results

does not

If the test $H_0\colon \beta_1 = 0$ is performed and H_0 is *not rejected,* this (does, does not) mean that x and y are *not related,* since

II
linearly

1. a type __________ error may have been committed, or
2. x and y may be related, but not __________. For example, the true relationship may be of the form $y = \beta_0 + \beta_1 x + \beta_2 x^2$.

If the test $H_0\colon \beta_1 = 0$ is performed and H_0 *is rejected,*

cannot

1. we (can, cannot) say that x and y are solely linearly related, since there may be other terms (x^2 or x^3) that have not been included in our model;
2. we should not conclude that a *causal* relationship exists between x and y, since the related changes we observe in x and y may actually be *caused* by an unmeasured third variable, say z.

Consider the problem where the true relationship between x and y is a "curve" rather than a straight line. Suppose we fitted a straight line to the data for values of x between a and b.

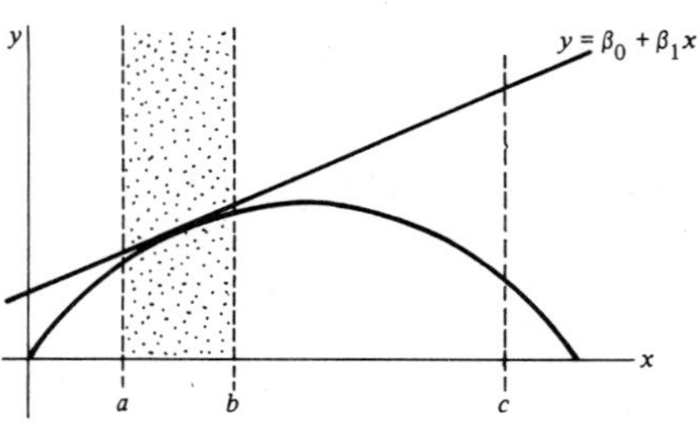

Using $\hat{y} = \hat{\beta}_0 + \hat{\beta}_1 x$ to predict values of y for $a \leqslant x \leqslant b$ would result in quite an accurate prediction. However, if the prediction line were used to predict y for the value $x = c$, the prediction would be highly ______________. Although the line adequately describes the indicated trend in the region $a \leqslant x \leqslant b$, there is no justification for assuming that the line would fit equally well for values of x outside the region $a \leqslant x \leqslant b$. The process of predicting outside the region of experimentation is called ______________. As our example shows, an experimenter should *not* extrapolate unless he or she is willing to assume the consequences of *gross errors.*

inaccurate

extrapolation

Self-Correcting Exercises 11B

1. Refer to Self-Correcting Exercises 11A, Exercise 1. Calculate SSE, s^2 and s for these data.
   a. Test the hypothesis that there is no linear relationship between actual and pre-enrollment figures at the $\alpha = .05$ level of significance.
   b. Estimate the average increase in actual enrollment for an increase of 100 in pre-enrolled students with a 95% confidence interval.
2. Refer to Self-Correcting Exercises 11A, Exercise 2. Calculate SSE, s^2 and s for these data and test for a significant linear relationship between yield and number of bolls at the $\alpha = .05$ level of significance.
3. Refer to Self-Correcting Exercises 11A, Exercise 3. Test for a significant linear relationship between yield and the number of insects present at the $\alpha = .05$ level of significance.

11.6 Estimating the Expected Value of y for a Given Value of x

Assume that x and y are related according to the model

$$y = \beta_0 + \beta_1 x + \epsilon$$

We have found an estimator for this line which is

$$\hat{y} = \_\_\_\_\_\_\_\_\_\_\_\_\_\_$$

$\hat{\beta}_0 + \hat{\beta}_1 x$

Suppose we are interested in estimating $E(y|x)$ for a given value of x, say x_p.

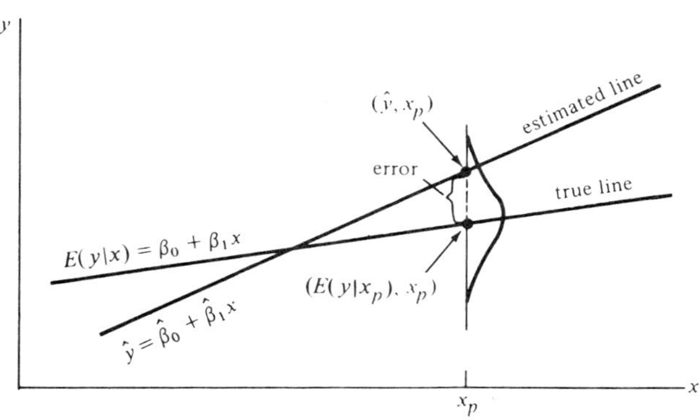

In repeated sampling, the predicted values of y will generate a distribution of estimates, $\hat{y}$, for the value of $x = x_p$, as shown in the diagram. The mean of these estimates is the true value

$$E(y|x = x_p) = \beta_0 + \beta_1 x_p$$

Therefore, we will use $\hat{y}$ to estimate the expected or average value of y for $x = x_p$, using as our estimator

$\hat{\beta}_0 + \hat{\beta}_1 x_p$

$\hat{y} =$ ____________

The estimator $\hat{y} = \hat{\beta}_0 + \hat{\beta}_1 x_p$ has the following properties:

1. $E(\hat{y}|x_p) = E(y|x_p)$
   That is, for a fixed value of x, $\hat{y}$ is an unbiased estimator for the average value of y,

$\beta_0 + \beta_1 x_p$

$E(y|x_p) =$ ____________

2. The variance, $\sigma_{\hat{y}}^2$, of the estimator $\hat{y}|x_p$ is given by
$$\sigma_{\hat{y}}^2 = \sigma^2 \left[\frac{1}{n} + \frac{(x_p - \bar{x})^2}{S_{xx}}\right]$$
3. When the random component ϵ is normally and independently distributed, estimator $\hat{y}|x$ is ____________ distributed.

normally

By using these results we can construct a z or t statistic to test an hypothesis concerning the expected value of y when $x = x_0$. Since σ^2 is rarely known, its sample estimate s^2 is used, resulting in a ________ statistic with ________ degrees of freedom.

t; $n - 2$

Test of an Hypothesis Concerning $E(y|x_p)$

1. H_0: $E(y|x_p) = E_0$
2. H_a: Appropriate one- or two-tailed test.
3. Test statistic:

$$t = \frac{\hat{y} - E_0}{s_{\hat{y}}} = \frac{\hat{y} - E_0}{s\sqrt{\dfrac{1}{n} + \dfrac{(x_p - \bar{x})^2}{S_{xx}}}}$$

4. Rejection region: Appropriate one- or two-tailed rejection region based on H_a.

Example 11.6

For our data, test the hypothesis that $\beta_0 = -1$ against the alternative that $\beta_0 < -1$ at the $\alpha = .05$ level.

Remark: By setting $x_0 = 0, E(y|x_0 = 0) = \beta_0 + \beta_1(0) = \beta_0$. Therefore, the test described above can be used to test an hypothesis about the intercept β_0.

Solution

1. $H_0: E(y|x = 0) = \beta_0 = -1$

2. $H_a: \beta_0 < -1$

3. Test statistic:

$$t = \frac{\hat{\beta}_0 - (-1)}{s\sqrt{\frac{1}{n} + \frac{(0 - \bar{x})^2}{S_{xx}}}}$$

$$= \frac{-1.3415 - (-1)}{.638\sqrt{\frac{1}{5} + \frac{(0 - 5.2)^2}{32.8}}} = \frac{-.3415}{\_\_\_\_\_\_} = \_\_\_\_\_\_$$

.64; -.53

4. Rejection region: With ______ degrees of freedom, we will reject H_0 if $t <$ ______.

3
-2.353

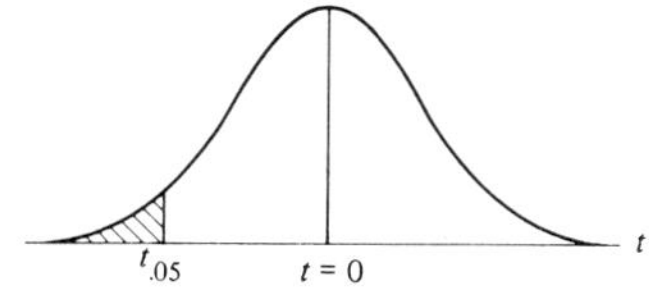

5. Decision: (Reject, Do not reject) H_0. The data (do, do not) present sufficient evidence to indicate that $\beta_0 < -1$.

Do not reject; do not

A $100(1 - \alpha)\%$ confidence interval for $E(y|x_p)$ is given as

$$(\hat{y}|x_p) \pm t_{\alpha/2}\, s\sqrt{\frac{1}{n} + \frac{(x_p - \bar{x})^2}{S_{xx}}}$$

where $(\hat{y}|x_p)$ is the value of the estimate for $x = x_p$, found by using

$$\hat{y} = \hat{\beta}_0 + \hat{\beta}_1 x_p$$

Example 11.7
Find a 95% confidence interval for $E(y|x = 6)$.

Solution

5.98 | 1. $(\hat{y}|x = 6) = -1.3415 + 1.2195(6) =$ ________

3.182 | 2. $t_{.025} =$ ________

.2987 | 3. $\hat{\sigma}_{\hat{y}} = .638\sqrt{\frac{1}{5} + \frac{(6 - 5.2)^2}{32.8}} =$ ________

4. A 95% confidence interval is constructed as follows:

$(\hat{y}|x = 6) \pm 3.182\hat{\sigma}_{\hat{y}}$

5.98; .2987 | (________) ± 3.182 (________)

5.98; .95 | (________) ± (________)

range; observed | In order to obtain reasonably accurate results when predicting $E(y)$ at a particular x_p, it is desirable that x_p lie within the ____________ of the ____________ values of x.

11.7 Predicting a Particular Value of y for a Given Value of x

true | In the last section, we were interested in estimating $E(y|x)$ when $x = x_p$. That is, we estimated a point on the ____________ regression line at the value of $x = x_p$. Now we consider the problem of predicting the actual single value of y that occurs (or will occur) when $x = x_p$, rather than the

expected *or* average; repeated | ____________ value of all the y_i that would occur at $x = x_p$ in ____________ sampling. We have as a predictor for this actual value of y, the quantity

$\hat{\beta}_0 + \hat{\beta}_1 x_p$ | $\hat{y} =$ ____________

By looking at the following graph, we can see that our error in predicting the actual value of y when $x = x_p$ will come from two sources:

II | 1. The difference between the predicted value of y, $\hat{y}$, and the expected value of y, $E(y|x_p)$. This difference is labeled ____________ in the diagram and is the source of the variance of $\hat{y}$ as a predictor of $E(y|x_p)$ that was discussed in the last section.

I | 2. The difference between the actual value of y and the expected value of y, $E(y|x_p)$. This difference is labeled ____________ in the diagram, and is identical to __________, the __________ __________ term in the probabilistic model.

ϵ; random error

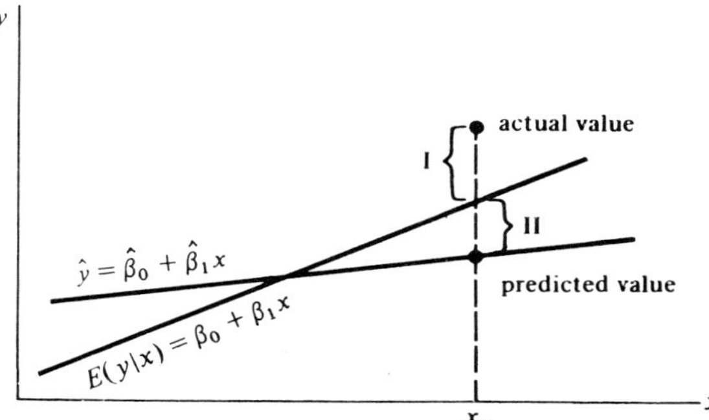

Thus the error associated with using $\hat{y} = \hat{\beta}_0 + \hat{\beta}_1 x_p$ as our prediction for the actual value of y which will occur when $x = x_p$, consists of the two components, I and II.

1. The variance associated with component I (the difference between the actual and expected values of y) is, by assumption, __________.
2. The variance associated with component II (the difference between the true and estimated regression lines) is, as shown in the last section,

____

σ^2

$\sigma^2\left[\frac{1}{n} + \frac{(x_p - \bar{x})^2}{S_{xx}}\right]$

Not surprisingly, the variance of the error $(y - \hat{y})$ in predicting a particular value of y with $\hat{y}$ can be shown to be the sum of the variances of the components of that error

$$\sigma^2_{y-\hat{y}} = \sigma^2 + \sigma^2\left[\frac{1}{n} + \frac{(x_p - \bar{x})^2}{S_{xx}}\right]$$

or more simply,

$$\sigma^2_{y-\hat{y}} = \sigma^2\left[\rule{3cm}{0.4pt}\right]$$

$1 + \frac{1}{n} + \frac{(x_p - \bar{x})^2}{S_{xx}}$

Notice that this variance is (smaller, larger) than the variance of the error associated with using $\hat{y}$ to predict the expected or average value of y, $E(y|x_p)$, for a given value of $x = x_p$. This is a consequence of the fact the mean of a population of measurements on a random variable has a (smaller, larger) variance than does any individual measurement on the random variable.

larger

smaller

When s^2 is used to estimate σ^2, a prediction interval for the actual value of y when $x = x_p$ can be constructed based on the __________ - statistic, which has an associated confidence coefficient of $(1 - \alpha)$:

t

$$(\hat{y}|x_p) \pm \rule{3cm}{0.4pt}$$

$t_{\alpha/2}s\sqrt{1 + \frac{1}{n} + \frac{(x_p - \bar{x})^2}{S_{xx}}}$

Because the variance of the error in predicting the actual value of y when $x = x_p$ is larger than the variance of the error in estimating $E(y|x_p)$, the resulting confidence or prediction interval will be (wider, narrower) when predicting the actual value of y, for a given level of α.

wider

Example 11.8
Continuing the example from previous sections, predict the particular value of y when $x = 6$, with 95% confidence.

Solution

1. $\hat{y} = -1.3415 + 1.2195(6)$

$= $ ________

5.98

2. With 3 degrees of freedom, $t_{.025} =$ ________.

3.182

3. The 95% prediction interval would be

$$5.98 \pm (\_\_\_\_\_\_)(\_\_\_\_\_\_)\sqrt{1 + \frac{1}{5} + \frac{(6 - 5.2)^2}{32.8}}$$

3.182; .638

$$5.98 \pm (\_\_\_\_\_\_)$$

2.24

Recall that the 95% confidence interval for our estimate of $E(y|x = 6)$ was $5.98 \pm .95$. Consequently, the prediction interval is ____________ for the actual value of y at $x = 6$.

wider

Self-Correcting Exercises 11C

1. Refer to Self-Correcting Exercises 11A, problem 1. Test the hypothesis that the expected enrollment is zero if there are no students pre-enrolled at the $\alpha = .05$ level. Does the line of means pass through the origin? Would you expect it to pass through the origin?
2. For Self-Correcting Exercises 11A, problem 2, predict the expected yield in cotton when the mid-season boll count is 450 with a 90% confidence interval. Could you use the prediction line to predict the cotton yield if the mid-season boll count was 250?
3. Refer to Self-Correcting Exercises 11A, problem 3. Using the least-squares prediction line for these data, predict the expected cotton yield if the insect count is 12 with a 90% confidence interval. Compare this interval with that found in problem 2 and comment on these two predictors of cotton yield.
4. Use the least-squares line from problem 1, Self-Correcting Exercises 11A to predict the enrollment with 95% confidence if the pre-enrollment figure is 4000 students.

11.8 A Coefficient of Correlation

A common measure of the strength of the ______________ relationship between two variables is the Pearson product-moment ______________ __________ ______________, symbolized by __________. This correlation coefficient is (dependent on, independent of) the scales of measurement of the two variables. The Pearson product-moment coefficient of correlation is calculated as

linear
coefficient
of correlation; r
independent of

$$r = \underline{\qquad\qquad}$$

$$\frac{S_{xy}}{\sqrt{S_{xx}S_{yy}}}$$

where S_{xx}, S_{yy} and S_{xy} are as defined earlier in this chapter, and where

$$\underline{\qquad} \leqslant r \leqslant \underline{\qquad}$$

-1; 1

Examine the formula for r above, and notice the following:

1. The denominator of r is the square root of the product of two positive quantities and will always be ______________.
2. The numerator of r is identical to the numerator used to calculate __________, whose denominator is also always positive.
3. Hence __________ and r will always have the same algebraic sign. When

positive

$\hat{\beta}_1$

$\hat{\beta}_1$

   a. $\hat{\beta}_1 > 0$, then r __________

   b. $\hat{\beta}_1 = 0$, then r __________

   c. $\hat{\beta}_1 < 0$, then r __________

> 0

$= 0$

< 0

When $r > 0$, there is a ______________ linear correlation; when $r < 0$, there is a ______________ linear correlation; when $r = 0$, there is ______________ linear correlation. See the following examples:

positive
negative
no

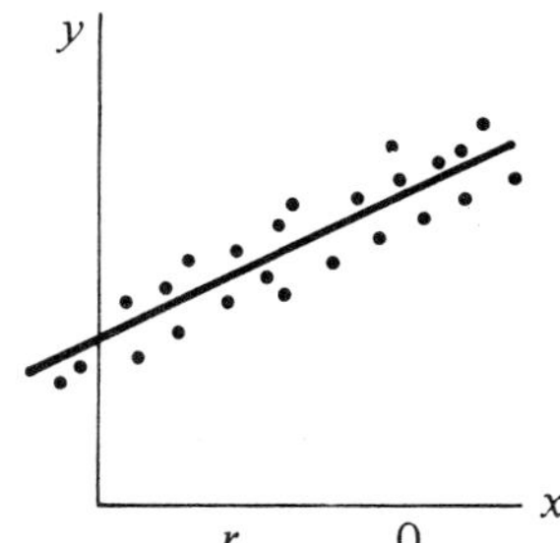

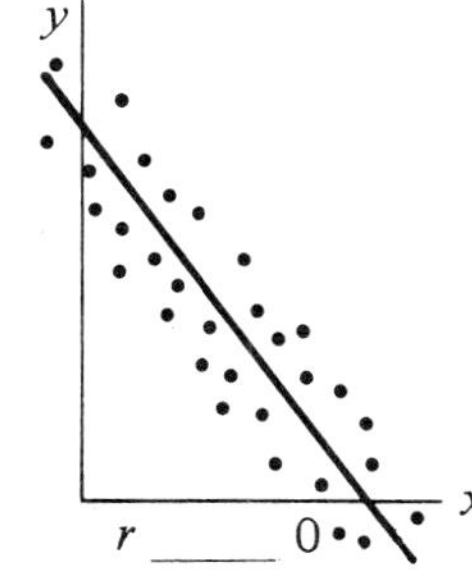

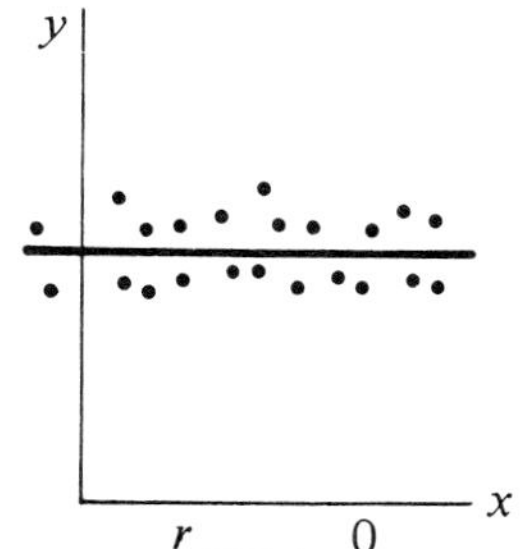

$>$; $<$;

Example 11.9

Find the coefficient of correlation for our data.

Solution

Drawing upon our earlier calculations of S_{xx}, S_{yy} and S_{xy}, we have

32.8; 50

$$r = \frac{S_{xy}}{\sqrt{S_{xx}S_{yy}}} = \frac{40}{\sqrt{(\_\_\_\_\_\_)(\_\_\_\_\_\_)}}$$

.9877

$$= \_\_\_\_\_\_$$

population
ρ; -1; 1; β_1

The coefficient r, which is calculated from sample data, is actually an estimator of the ______________ coefficient of correlation, symbolized by __________, where __________ $\leqslant \rho \leqslant$ __________. Since ρ and __________ both measure the linear relationship between x and y, the test of $H_0 : \beta_1 = 0$ is equivalent to testing $H_0 : \rho = 0$. Therefore, no separate test of the hypothesis concerning the coefficient of correlation, ρ, will be presented. (See Section 11.8 in the text.)

several

linear

nonlinear

It should be noted that a dependent random variable, y, usually depends on ______________ predictor variables, rather than just one. Consequently, the correlation between y and a single predictor variable is of doubtful value. It is even more important to bear in mind that r measures only the ______________ relationship between two variables, say x and y. So even when $r = 0$, x and y could be *perfectly* related by a ______________ function.

Suppose that we want to predict the value of y for a given value of x. Consider these two estimators for y:

a. $\hat{y} = \bar{y}$

b. $\hat{y} = \hat{\beta}_0 + \hat{\beta}_1 x$

$= \bar{y} + \hat{\beta}_1(x - \bar{x})$

a

Estimator (a, b) uses no information about the value of x in arriving at a prediction for y. These estimators are shown in the following diagram:

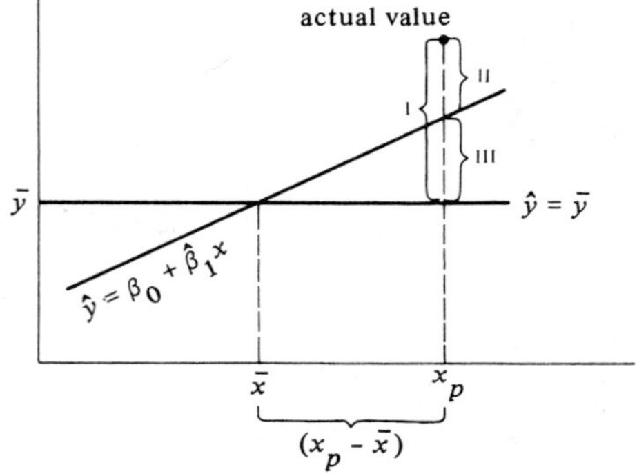

1. Distance I is equal to $y - \bar{y}$ and represents the error associated with

using __________ as a predictor of y. When this error is squared and then summed over all observations, we have | $\bar{y}$

$$\Sigma(y_i - \bar{y})^2 = \_\_\_\_\_\_\_\_\_\_$$

S_{yy}

which is the total variation in y.

2. Distance II is equal to $y_i - \hat{y}$ and represents the error associated with using __________ as a predictor of y. When this error is squared and summed over all observations, we have | $\hat{y}$

$$\Sigma(y_i - \hat{y}_i)^2 = \_\_\_\_\_\_\_\_\_\_$$

SSE

which is the variation remaining after information about x is used to help predict y.

3. Distance III is equal to $\hat{y}_i - \bar{y}$, the reduction in prediction error realized by using $\hat{y}_i$ rather than __________ as a predictor of y_i. From estimator b above, it is seen that $\hat{y}_i - \bar{y} = \hat{\beta}_1(x_i - \bar{x})$. When this quantity is squared and summed over all observations, we have | $\bar{y}$

$$\Sigma(\hat{y}_i - \bar{y})^2 = \hat{\beta}_1^2 \Sigma(x_i - \bar{x})^2$$

$$= \hat{\beta}_1^2 \, S_{xx}$$

$$= \frac{S_{xy}^2}{S_{xx}}$$

which is the portion of the total variation in y that is explained by the estimator $\hat{y}$ which utilizes information about x. $\Sigma(\hat{y}_i - \bar{y})^2$ is called the sum of squares due to regression, SSR.

Hence, we have the relationship

$$S_{yy} = SSE + \_\_\_\_\_\_\_\_\_\_$$

SSR

where $SSR = S_{xy}^2/S_{xx}$. This can be written as

$$SSR = S_{yy} - \_\_\_\_\_\_\_\_\_\_$$

SSE

which upon division by S_{yy} becomes

$$\frac{S_{xy}^2}{S_{xx}S_{yy}} = \frac{S_{yy} - SSE}{S_{yy}}$$

However, $S_{xy}^2/S_{xx}S_{yy} =$ __________, the square of Pearson product-moment coefficient of correlation. Therefore, | r^2

$$r^2 = \frac{S_{yy} - SSE}{S_{yy}}$$

determination
reduction

The quantity r^2 is called the coefficient of ______________ and is equal to the ratio of the ______________ in the sum of squares of deviations obtained by using $\hat{y}$ as a predictor, to the sum of squares of deviations which would result if $\bar{y}$ were used as a predictor, ignoring x. r^2 lies in the interval __________ $\leqslant r^2 \leqslant$ __________ and equals __________ only when all the values of y fall exactly on the fitted line. Since r^2 gives the percentage reduction in the sum of squares for error achieved by using the ______________ model as a predictor for y in preference to __________ as a predictor, r^2 gives a (more, less) meaningful interpretation of the strength of the relationship between x and y than does __________ itself.

0; 1; 1

linear

$\bar{y}$

more

r

Example 11.10

For our problem, the value of r was found to be $r = .9877$; therefore, $r^2 =$ __________. This means that we have reduced the sum of squares for error approximately ________% by using the predictor $\hat{y} = -1.34 + 1.22x$ rather than $\bar{y} = 5$.

.976
97.6

Self-Correcting Exercises 11D

1. Refer to Self-Correcting Exercises 11A, problem 2.
   a. Use the additivity of the sums of squares to find the sum of squares due to regression.
   b. From part a find r^2 and explain its significance in using the number of cotton bolls to predict yield of cotton.
   c. Find the correlation between the number of bolls and the yield of cotton. (Remember that $\hat{\beta}_1$ and r *always* have the same algebraic sign.)
2. Refer to Self-Correcting Exercises 11A, problem 3.
   a. Find the value of r^2 and r for these data and explain the value of using the number of damaging insects present to predict cotton yield.
   b. Compare the values of r^2 using these two predictors of cotton yield. Which predictor would you prefer?
3. The data in problems 2 and 3, Self-Correcting Exercises 11A are related in that for each field quadrate, the yield, the number of bolls and the number of damaging insects were simultaneously recorded. Using this fact, calculate the correlation between the number of cotton bolls and the number of insects present for the 7 field quadrates. Does this value of r explain in any way the similarity of results using the predictors found for problems 2 and 3, Self-Correcting Exercises 11A?

11.9 The Additivity of Sums of Squares: An Analysis of Variance

In a regression analysis the values of x are recorded in an effort to help explain the variation observed in y, the response of interest. The variation in y is measured by the sum of squared deviations given as

$$\sum_{i=1}^{n} (y_i - \bar{y})^2$$

and is referred to as the total variation or the total sum of squares. The difference between the total sum of squares and SSE measures the effectiveness of the regression of y on __________ and is called the sum of squares due to ______________, SSR. Therefore the total sum of squares can be partitioned into two parts:

x
regression

$$\text{Total } SS = SSR + \text{\_\_\_\_\_\_\_\_\_\_}$$

SSE

where

$$SSR = \sum_{i=1}^{n} (\hat{y}_i - \bar{y})^2$$

and

$$SSE = \sum_{i=1}^{n} \text{\_\_\_\_\_\_\_\_\_\_\_\_}$$

$(y_i - \hat{y}_i)^2$

Since Total SS = ______________, neither SSR nor SSE can be larger than Total SS.

$SSR + SSE$

Notice that SSR measures the difference between the simple predictor $\bar{y}$ and the linear predictor $\hat{y}_i = \bar{y} + \hat{\beta}_1 (x_i - \bar{x})$. Therefore a large value of SSR indicates that the values of x are contributing (little, much) to the estimation of the values of y. SSR is said to be the amount of the total variation ______________ by the auxiliary variable x.

much

explained

SSE measures the difference between the observed values y_i and the values predicted using $\hat{y}_i = \bar{y} + \hat{\beta}_1 (x_i - \bar{x})$. A (small, large) value of SSE indicates that the linear predictor is effectively reproducing the observed values $y_1, y_2, \ldots, y_n$. SSE is said to be the amount of the total variation that is ______________ by the auxiliary variable x.

small

unexplained

The additivity of the sums of squares is important for several reasons.

1. SSR can be used to measure the contribution of the auxiliary variable x, since

$$r^2 = \frac{\text{Total } SS - SSE}{\text{Total } SS}$$

SSR

$$= \frac{\rule{2cm}{0.4pt}}{\text{Total } SS}$$

x

In this form it is easily seen that r^2 represents the proportion of the total variation explained by the auxiliary variable __________.

2. When more than one auxiliary variable is included in the linear model, the additivity property still holds, and the ratio

$$R^2 = \frac{SSR}{\text{Total } SS}$$

now measures the joint contribution of the auxiliary variables in explaining the variation in y. R, the positive square root of R^2 is called the multiple correlation coefficient and is the multivariate counterpart of r.

3. The additivity of the sums of squares, Total $SS = SSR + SSE$, makes it possible to use the analysis of variance technique presented in Chapter 10 to present the results of the analysis. Only two of the quantities,

$$\text{Total } SS = \Sigma y_i^2 - \frac{(\Sigma y_i)^2}{n}$$

and

$$SSR = \frac{(S_{xy})^2}{S_{xx}}$$

need to be calculated, since the third can be obtained by subtraction. The analysis of variance table is presented below.

Source	*d.f.*	*SS*	*MS*
Regression	1	*SSR*	$MSR = SSR/1$
Error	$n - 2$	*SSE*	$MSE = SSE/(n-2) = s^2$
Total	$n - 1$	Total *SS*	

Consider the quantity

$$\frac{MSR}{MSE} = \frac{(S_{xy})^2/S_{xx}}{MSE} = \frac{(S_{xy}/S_{xx})^2}{s^2/S_{xx}} = \frac{\rule{2cm}{0.4pt}}{s^2/S_{xx}}$$

This is exactly t^2 where

$$t = \underline{\qquad\qquad}$$

$$\frac{\hat{\beta}_1}{s/\sqrt{S_{xx}}}$$

was used in testing H_0: $\beta_1 = 0$ in Section 11.5. Hence, the quantity

$$F = \frac{MSR}{MSE} = t^2$$

which has an F distribution with $\nu_1 = 1$ and $\nu_2 = (n - 2)$ degrees of freedom can be used to test for a significant linear relationship as an alternative to the t test used in Section 11.5.

Example 11.11
Present the data used in this chapter as an analysis of variance. Test for a significant linear relationship using the analysis of variance F test.

Solution
From Example 11.3, we have

$$\text{Total } SS = S_{yy} = 50$$

$$SSE = 1.2195$$

The analysis of variance table is shown below. Fill in the missing entries.

Source	*d.f.*	*SS*	*MS*	*F*
Regression	1	______	______	120.00
Error	______	1.2195	0.4065	
Total	4	50.0000		

48.7805; 48.7805
3

The test statistic for testing for a significant linear relationship is

$$F = \frac{MSR}{MSE} = 120.0$$

and the rejection region, with $\alpha = .05$ and 1 and 3 degrees of freedom, is $F >$ 10.13. The null hypothesis of no linear relationship is rejected. Notice that

$$\sqrt{F} = \sqrt{120.0} = 10.95$$

which is the value of the test statistic calculated in Example 11.4.

11.10 Computer Printout for a Regression Analysis

The calculations required for a regression analysis can be cumbersome when working with a large set of data points. Since the MINITAB and/or SAS systems as well as several other excellent packaged regression programs are available at most computer facilities, many researchers prefer to rely on these programs for the analysis of a regression problem. We will discuss the salient points of the output resulting from the MINITAB and SAS programs using the data given in Example 11.2, which is reproduced below.

y	1	3	4	7	10
x	2	3	5	7	9

The analysis of these data using the MINITAB command REGRESSION requires that the dependent variable y is stored in one column, say C1, the independent variable x is stored in another column, say C2. The linear regression analysis is performed using the command REGRESS followed by the column number to specify y, the number of independent variables (in linear regression this integer is 1) and another column number to specify x. The MINITAB command for the linear regression of y on x,

REGRESS C1 1 C2

resulted in the following output:

```
MTB > REGRESS C1 1 C2

THE REGRESSION EQUATION IS
C1 = - 1.34 + 1.22 C2

                                 ST. DEV.     T-RATIO =
COLUMN       COEFFICIENT         OF COEF.     COEF/S.D.
               -1.3415           0.6453       -2.08
C2              1.2195           0.1113       10.95
S = 0.6376                                    #1

R-SQUARED = 97.6 PERCENT
R-SQUARED = 96.7 PERCENT, ADJUSTED FOR D.F.

ANALYSIS OF VARIANCE              #2

DUE TO         DF                   SS        MS=SS/DF
REGRESSION      1               48.780          48.780
RESIDUAL        3                1.220           0.407
TOTAL           4               50.000

DURBIN-WATSON STATISTIC = 2.71
```

We can identify the regression equation,

$$\hat{y} = \_\_\_\_\_\_\_\_$$

-1.34 + 1.22x

and the value of the coefficient of determination, $r^2 =$ ________, both of which are clearly labeled on the printout. The portion of the printout contained in Box #1 contains four columns. The second column, labeled COEFFICIENT, contains the estimates of β_0 and β_1 in the first and second positions, respectively. The first column lists the programmer's identification of the parameters. Hence, the row labeled C2 contains the coefficient of x, $\hat{\beta}_1$, since the values of x were stored in C2. The unlabeled row contains the y-intercept.

.976

The estimated standard deviations, $s_{\hat{\beta}_0}$ and $s_{\hat{\beta}_1}$, of the regression coefficients $\hat{\beta}_0$ and $\hat{\beta}_1$ are given in the column labeled ST. DEV. OF COEF. In particular, we can use $s_{\hat{\beta}_1}$ to test an hypothesis about β_1 or to construct a confidence interval for β_1.

The entries in the fourth column, headed T-RATIO = COEF/S.D., are the computed values of the t statistic used in testing hypotheses about the regression parameters. In testing $H_0: \beta_1 = 0$ versus $H_a: \beta_1 \neq 0$, the computed value of

$$t = \frac{\hat{\beta}_1}{s_{\hat{\beta}_1}}$$

is the second entry in this column and is equal to ________. This value of t is large enough to conclude that $\beta_1 \neq 0$. However, in order to find critical values of t, we note that the degrees of freedom with t are $n - 2$, or ________. (The degrees of freedom for testing and estimation appear in the RESIDUAL line and DF column of the ANALYSIS OF VARIANCE portion of the printout.)

10.95

3

A confidence interval estimate for β_1 is easily calculated using the information provided in the printout. A general confidence interval estimator of β_1 is given as

$$\hat{\beta}_1 \pm t s_{\hat{\beta}_1}$$

where t is a tabulated value of t from Table 4 of the text with $n - 2$ degrees of freedom. With 3 degrees of freedom, $t_{.025} =$ ________. Therefore, a 95% confidence interval estimate of the slope is

3.182

$$\hat{\beta}_1 \pm t_{.025}\, s_{\hat{\beta}_1}$$

$$1.22 \pm 3.182\,(.1113)$$

$$1.22 \pm .35$$

This agrees with the result obtained by direct calculation in Example 11.5.

Box #2: Analysis of Variance

As explained in Section 11.9, an analysis of variance is a technique that partitions the total variation in the response y into one portion associated with random error and another portion associated with the variability accounted for by regression. The RESIDUAL line in this portion of the printout provides the degrees of freedom for error in the DF column, the value of SSE in the SS (sum of squares) column, and the value of s^2 in the MS (mean square) column. The value of the standard deviation s found elsewhere on the printout, is the square root of s^2. For this problem the degrees of freedom for error is __________, SSE = __________, s^2 = __________, and

3
1.220; .407

$$s = \sqrt{\_\_\_\_\_\_\_\_} = \_\_\_\_\_\_\_\_$$

.407; .6376

These results agree with those obtained earlier in this chapter.

The SAS printout for the regression analysis of these same data is shown below. Notice that the boxes labeled #1 and #2 contain results which are very similar to the MINITAB results, except that they are reported to a greater degree of accuracy. In Box #1, the computed values of the t statistic for testing the regression coefficients are followed by the appropriate level of significance for the particular test, in the column labeled PR > |T|.

The value that appears in the F-VALUE column of the MODEL line in Box #2 is the calculated value of an F statistic used in testing $H_0:\beta_1 = 0$ versus H_a: $\beta_1 \neq 0$. This value is the square of the t-value for testing this same hypothesis found in Box #1. Note that

$$(t\text{-value})^2 = (10.95)^2 = 120.00 = \text{F-VALUE}$$

will not

within rounding errors. This relationship (will, will not) hold when two or more independent variables are included in the regression equation and subsequently in the regression analysis.

GENERAL LINEAR MODELS PROCEDURE

#2

DEPENDENT VARIABLE: Y

SOURCE	DF	SUM OF SQUARES	MEAN SQUARE
MODEL	1	48.78048780	48.78048780
ERROR	3	1.21951220	0.40650407
CORRECTED TOTAL	4	50.00000000	
MODEL F =	120.00		PR > F 0.0016

R-SQUARE	C.V.	ROOT MSE	Y MEAN
0.975610	12.7515	0.63757671	5.00000000

#1

PARAMETER	ESTIMATE	T FOR H0: PARAMETER=0	PR > |T|	STD ERROR OF ESTIMATE
INTERCEPT	-1.34146341	-2.08	0.1292	0.64530520
X	1.21951220	10.95	0.0016	0.11132572

11.11 Assumptions

For the techniques in this chapter to be valid, the pairs of data points must satisfy the following assumptions:

1. The response y can be modeled as

$$y = \beta_0 + \beta_1 x + \epsilon$$

2. The independent variable x is measured without error.
3. The quantity ϵ is a random variable such that for any fixed value of x,

$$E(\epsilon) = 0, \quad \sigma_\epsilon^2 = \sigma^2$$

and all pairs ϵ_i, ϵ_j are independent.

4. The random variable ϵ has a ________________ distribution. normal

The first assumption requires that the response y be ________________ linearly related to the independent variable x. If the response is not just a simple linear function of x, but the fit to the data as evidenced by a high value of r^2 is good, the least-squares equation will produce adequate predictions within the range of the experimental values of x. Extrapolation, however, can cause problems in prediction, since the fitted linear relationship may fail to adequately describe the data outside the range of values used in the analysis. This is especially true when the independent variable is ___________. time

The assumption of constant variance for the ϵ's may not be valid in all situations. For example, the variability in the amount of impurities in a chemical mixture as well as the amount of impurities itself may increase with increasing temperature of the mixture. However, if repeated values of the independent variable x are included within the experiment, a plot of the data points will usually reveal whether the variance of the ϵ's depends on x. When this is the case, weights are assigned to each value of x and a regression analysis is performed on y and the weighted values of x.

It is not unusual to have the error terms correlated when the data are collected over time. For example, a high inflation rate during the first 3 months of the year is likely to be followed by a high inflation rate during the next quarter as well. Ordinary regression techniques applied to such data produce underestimates of the true variance and hence cause distortion in significance levels and confidence coefficients. Time series analysis should be used in the analysis of such data.

Departure from the normality assumption will not distort results too strongly provided the distributions of the ϵ's are not strongly skewed.

EXERCISES

1. For the following equations (i) give the y intercept, (ii) give the slope, and (iii) graph the line corresponding to the equation:

a. $y = 3x - 2$

b. $2y = 4x$

c. $-y = .5 + x$

d. $3x + 2y = 5$

e. $y = 2$

2. a. Find the least-squares line for the following data:

x	-3	-2	-1	0	1	2	3
y	-1	-1	0	1	2	2	3

b. As a check on your calculations, plot the data points and graph the least-squares line.
c. Calculate SSE and s^2. Under what conditions could $SSE = 0$?
d. Do the data present sufficient evidence to indicate that x and y are linearly related at the $\alpha = .05$ level of significance?
e. Estimate the average change in y for a one-unit change in x with a 95% confidence interval.
f. Calculate the coefficient of linear correlation for the data and interpret your results.
g. Calculate r^2 and state in words the significance of its magnitude.
h. Construct a 90% confidence interval estimate for a particular value of y when $x = 1$.
i. Test the hypothesis that $E(y|x = 0) = 0$ at the $\alpha = .05$ level of significance. (This is actually a test of H_0: $\beta_0 = 0$.)

3. For the following data,

x	0	2	4	6	8	10
y	9	7	3	1	-2	-3

a. Fit the least-squares line, $\hat{y} = \hat{\beta}_0 + \hat{\beta}_1 x$.
b. Plot the points, and graph the line to check your calculations.
c. Calculate SSE, s^2, and s.
d. Is there a linear relationship between x and y at the $\alpha = .05$ level of significance?
e. Calculate r^2, and explain its significance in predicting the response, y.
f. Predict the particular value of y when $x = 5$ with 80% confidence.
g. Predict the expected value of y when $x = 5$ with 80% confidence.

4. What happens if the coefficient of linear correlation, r, assumes the value one? The value -1?

5. The following data were obtained in an experiment relating the dependent variable, y (texture of strawberries), with x (coded storage temperature).

x	-2	-2	0	2	2
y	4.0	3.5	2.0	0.5	0.0

a. Find the least-squares line for the data.

b. Plot the data points and graph the least-squares line as a check on your calculations.
c. Calculate SSE, s^2, and s.
d. Do the data indicate that texture and storage temperature are linearly related? ($\alpha = .05$)
e. Predict the expected strawberry texture for a coded storage temperature of $x = -1$ with a 90% confidence interval.
f. Of what value is the *linear* model in increasing the accuracy of prediction as compared to the predictor, $\bar{y}$?
g. Estimate the particular value of y when $x = 1$ with a 98% confidence interval.
h. At what value of x will the width of the confidence interval for a particular value of y be a minimum, assuming n remains fixed?

6. In addition to increasingly large bounds on error, why should an experimenter refrain from predicting y for values of x outside the experimental region?
7. If the experimenter stays within the experimental region, when will the error in predicting a particular value of y be maximum?
8. An agricultural experimenter, investigating the effect of the amount of nitrogen (x) applied in 100 pounds per acre on the yield of oats (y) measured in bushels per acre, collected the following data:

x	1	2	3	4
y	22	38	57	68
	19	41	54	65

a. Fit a least-squares line to the data.
b. Calculate SSE and s^2.
c. Is there sufficient evidence to indicate that the yield of oats is linearly related to the amount of nitrogen applied? ($\alpha = .05$)
d. Predict the expected yield of oats with 95% confidence if 250 pounds of nitrogen per acre are applied.
e. Predict the average increase in yield for an increase of 100 pounds of nitrogen with 90% confidence.
f. Calculate r^2 and explain its significance in terms of predicting y, the yield of oats.

9. In an industrial process, the yield, y, is thought to be linearly related to temperature, x. The following coded data is available:

Temperature	0	0.5	1.5	2.0	2.5
Yield	7.2	8.1	9.8	11.3	12.9
	6.9	8.4	10.1	11.7	13.2

a. Find the least-squares line for this data.
b. Plot the points and graph the line. Is your calculated line reasonable?
c. Calculate SSE and s^2.

d. Do the data indicate a linear relationship between yield and temperature at the $\alpha = .01$ level of significance?
e. Calculate r, the coefficient of linear correlation and interpret your results.
f. Calculate r^2, and interpret its significance in predicting the yield, y.
g. Test the hypothesis that $E(y|x = 1.75) = 10.8$ at the $\alpha = .05$ level of significance.
h. Predict the particular value of y for a coded temperature $x = 1$ with 90% confidence.

10. A food technologist employed by a large supermarket chain devised a scale to measure the freshness of packaged meats that were frozen and displayed for varying periods of time before sale. In the following table, y represents the freshness measurement and x represents the length of time in days the meat is frozen and on display.

x	5	10	15	20	25
y	15.3	13.6	9.8	5.5	1.8
	16.8	13.8	8.7	4.7	1.0

Use the MINITAB output shown below to answer the following questions:

```
MTB > REGRESS C1 1 C2

THE REGRESSION EQUATION IS
C1 = 20.5 - 0.758 C2

                               ST. DEV.      T-RATIO =
COLUMN       COEFFICIENT       OF COEF.      COEF/S.D.
                 20.4700         0.5659          36.17
C2              -0.75800        0.03412         -22.21

S = 0.7631

R-SQUARED = 98.4 PERCENT
R-SQUARED = 98.2 PERCENT, ADJUSTED FOR D.F.

ANALYSIS OF VARIANCE

DUE TO                DF            SS       MS=SS/DF
REGRESSION             1        287.28         287.28
RESIDUAL               8          4.66           0.58
TOTAL                  9        291.94
```

a. Fit a least-square line to the data.
b. Calculate SSE and s^2 for the data.
c. Is there sufficient evidence to indicate that a linear relationship exists between freshness and storage time? (Use $\alpha = .05$.)

d. Estimate the mean rate of change in freshness for a 1-day increase in storage time using a 95% confidence interval.
e. Predict the expected freshness measurement for a storage time of 14 days with a 95% prediction interval.
f. Of what value is the linear model in preference to $\bar{y}$ in predicting freshness?

Chapter 12

MULTIPLE LINEAR REGRESSION

12.1 Introduction

We have examined estimation, testing, and prediction techniques for the situation in which y, the response of interest, was linearly related to an independent variable x in the following way.

$$y = \beta_0 + \beta_1 x + \epsilon$$

In this chapter, we extend these techniques to the more general situation in which the response y is linearly related to one or more independent variables. These extended techniques can be used when the response is linearly related to several different independent variables, or when the response is a polynomial function of just one variable. Modeling, testing, and prediction in these cases belong to an area of statistics called multiple regression analysis.

12.2 The Multiple Linear Regression Model and Associated Assumptions

The general results given in the remainder of this chapter are applicable and produce standard solutions for a multiple regression problem when the response

linear — y is a ____________ function of the unknown regression coefficients. That is, we write

$$y = \beta_0 + \beta_1 x_1 + \beta_2 x_2 + \cdots + \beta_k x_k + \epsilon$$

where

1. y is the response variable we wish to predict,

unknown — 2. $\beta_0, \beta_1, \ldots, \beta_k$ are (known, unknown) constants,

3. $x_1, x_2, \ldots, x_k$ are independent variables that (are, are not) measured without error, — are
4. ϵ is a random error having a normal distribution with mean zero and variance σ^2, independent of $x_1, x_2, \ldots, x_k$. Further, the error terms for any two values of y are taken to be __________. — independent
5. Since $E(\epsilon) = 0$, we can write the mean value of y for a given set $x_1, x_2, \ldots, x_k$ as

$$E(y) = \beta_0 + \beta_1 x_1 + \beta_2 x_2 + \cdots + \beta_k x_k$$

   Although the actual observed values of y will not exactly equal the values generated by the model, they will deviate from $E(y)$ by a random amount ϵ if the model is in fact true.

The methodology that we use requires only that the β_i's occur in a linear fashion. That is, β_i must be the coefficient of a term that does not involve any *unknown* parameters.

Formulation of the linear model to be used in the data analysis is perhaps the most difficult aspect of regression analysis since the results we achieve depend strictly on the model we have chosen to fit. For example, if y is related to x in a quadratic fashion and we include only a linear term in x in our model, our analysis would produce a poor estimator of y in general. In like manner, if we include the independent predictor variables x_1 and x_2 in our model, but fail to include x_3, which has high predictive potential, we may indeed end up with a poor estimator of y. Model formulation will be addressed in Section 12.7, but we present an illustrative example at this point.

Example 12.1

An agricultural economist interested in predicting cotton harvest using the number of cotton bolls per quadrate counted during the middle of the growing season and the number of damaging insects per quadrate present during a critical time in the development of the plant, collected data on the response y, the yield in bales of cotton, x_1, hundreds of cotton bolls per quadrate counted during mid-season, and x_2, the insect count per quadrate. If we can expect a straight line relationship between the cotton yield, y, and each of the two predictor variables, x_1 and x_2, write a linear model relating y and the predictor variables x_1 and x_2.

Solution

We might expect the yield y to (increase, decrease) linearly as x_1, the number of cotton bolls increases and x_2, the number of damaging insects decreases. The simplest model relating y and the predictors x_1 and x_2 is — increase

$$E(y) = \beta_0 + \beta_1 x_1 + \beta_2 x_2$$

When x_2 is held constant we can write

$$E(y) = (\beta_0 + \beta_2 x_2) + \beta_1 x_1$$

with β_1 the rate of increase in $E(y)$ for a one unit increase in the boll count, while the intercept, which depends on x_2, is given as $\beta_0(x_2) = \beta_0 + \beta_2 x_2$. For different values of x_2, $E(y)$ would plot as a series of parallel lines, each with slope β_1 as shown in the following graph.

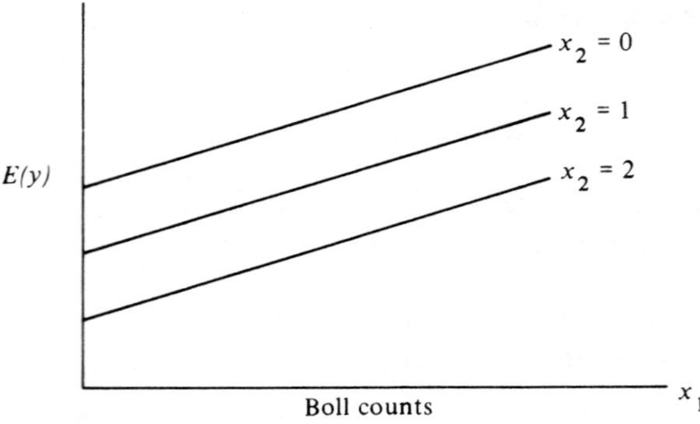

Since yield is expected to decrease as the number of damaging insects increases, the lines in the preceding graph are drawn assuming β_2 is negative.

When x_1 is held constant, we can write the model as

$$E(y) = (\beta_0 + \beta_1 x_1) + \beta_2 x_2$$

β_2
$\beta_0 + \beta_1 x_1$

which plots as a series of parallel lines with negative slope __________ and varying intercepts that depend upon x_1 and are given by $\beta_0(x_1) =$ __________. Assuming β_2 is negative, a plot of $E(y)$ for three values of x_1 is given in the next graph.

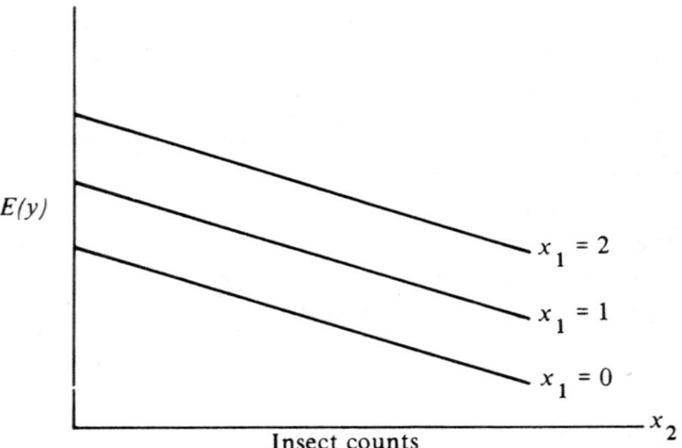

An alternative model that is a linear function of x_1 and x_2, but allows for differing slopes as well as differing intercepts, is given by

$$E(y) = \beta_0 + \beta_1 x_1 + \beta_2 x_2 + \beta_3 x_1 x_2$$

In this case, if x_2 is held constant, we can write

$$E(y) = (\beta_0 + \beta_2 x_2) + (\beta_1 + \beta_3 x_2) x_1$$

where (__________) is the intercept and (__________) is the slope. $E(y)$ would plot as a series of lines with changing slopes and intercepts. If β_3 is negative, the plots would appear as in the following graph.

$\beta_0 + \beta_2 x_2; \beta_1 + \beta_3 x_2$

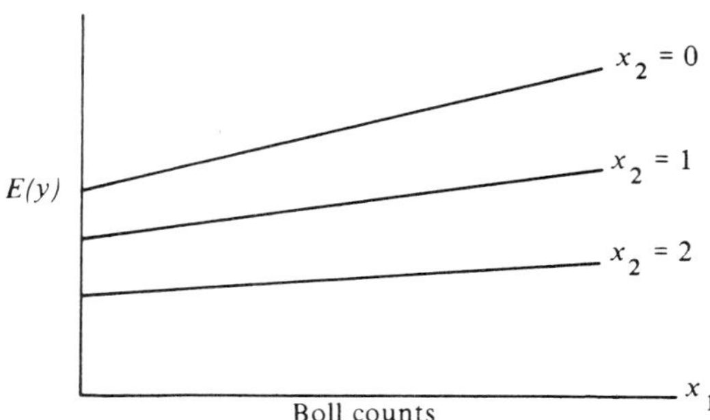

If x_2 is held constant, a similar plot would result with varying negative slopes. Hence both models allow for a straight line relationship between y and each of the predictor variables x_1 and x_2, but the model given by

$$E(y) = \beta_0 + \beta_1 x_1 + \beta_2 x_2 + \beta_3 x_1 x_2$$

is more flexible since it allows for differing slopes and intercepts as either x_1 or x_2 is held constant.

Self-Correcting Exercises 12A

1. Graph the following equations:
   a. $E(y) = 1 + 2x$
   b. $E(y) = 1 + .5x$
   c. $E(y) = 2 - 2x$
2. Graph the following equations, which graph as parabolas:
   a. $E(y) = x^2$
   b. $E(y) = 1 + x^2$
   c. $E(y) = -x^2$
   d. How does the sign of the coefficient of x^2 affect the graph of the parabola?
3. Graph the following equation:
   a. $E(y) = 1 - 2x + x^2$
   b. Compare the graph in part a with the graph in Exercise 2, part b. What effect does the term $-2x$ have on the graph?
   c. How would the graph change if $-2x$ were replaced by $+2x$?
4. Suppose $E(y)$ is related to two predictor variables x_1 and x_2 by the equation

$$E(y) = 2 + 3x_1 - x_2$$

   a. Graph the relationship between $E(y)$ and x_1 when $x_2 = 0$. Repeat for $x_2 = 1$ and $x_2 = 2$.
   b. How are the graphs of the three lines in part a related?

c. Graph the relationship between $E(y)$ and x_2 when $x_1 = 0$. Repeat for $x_1 = 1$ and $x_1 = 2$.
d. How are the graphs of the three lines in part c related?

12.3 A Multiple Regression Analysis

In generalizing the results of the simple linear regression to multiple linear regression, we have considered the model

$$y = \beta_0 + \beta_1 x_1 + \beta_2 x_2 + \cdots + \beta_k x_k + \epsilon$$

independent

minimize

where ϵ is a normally distributed random error component with a mean of zero and a variance σ^2. In addition, the error terms for any two values of y are taken to be ____________. The parameters $\beta_1, \beta_2, \ldots, \beta_k$ are the partial slopes associated with the nonrandom quantities $x_1, x_2, \ldots, x_k$. The slope, β_i, represents the expected increase in the response y corresponding to a one-unit increase in x_i when the values of all other x's are held constant. Estimates of the unknown parameters in the model are found by using the method of least squares. Using this method, the estimates $\hat{\beta}_0, \hat{\beta}_1, \ldots, \hat{\beta}_k$ are chosen so as to ____________ the quantity

$$\text{SSE} = \sum_{i=1}^{n} (y_i - \hat{y}_i)^2$$

This minimization technique leads to a set of $(k + 1)$ simultaneous equations in the unknowns $\hat{\beta}_0, \hat{\beta}_1, \ldots,$ and $\hat{\beta}_k$, which are easily solved using any multiple regression analysis computer program. Such programs are usually available at any computing facility, and provide not only the estimates of the regression parameters, but also additional information required for prediction, estimation and hypothesis testing. These programs require only that the user provide the proper commands to activate the program, and then submit the data in the proper format.

In this section we will analyze two data sets using a multiple regression program and interpret the results of the analyses.

Example 12.2
An agricultural economist interested in California cotton production gathered the following data concerning the mean number of cotton bolls per plant during the growing season in the San Joaquin Valley of California. Here y is the mean number of bolls per plant and x is the time measured in weeks.

y	110	470	1040	1100	1000	820
x	1	4	7	9	12	15

Use a multiple regression program to fit a second degree polynomial to these data.

Solution

1. A second degree polynomial model is given by

$$E(y) = \beta_0 + \beta_1 x + \beta_2 x^2$$

In this case $E(y)$ is a general linear model with $x_1 = x$ and $x_2 = x^2$. If a multiple regression program requires that the data be entered as (y, x_1, x_2) for each of the n data points, the user would enter the triples (y, x, x^2) for each of the n observations. For example, the first data point would be (110, 1, 1) and the last would be (820, 15, 225). A standard multiple regression program produced the following computer output in fitting a second degree polynomial to these data.

MULTIPLE R .97733784
R-SQUARE .95518926
STD ERROR OF EST 106.66744

INDIVIDUAL ANALYSIS OF VARIABLES

VARIABLE	COEFFICIENT	STD ERROR	T	PR > |T|
INTERCEPT	−175.54726	125.43558	−1.40	.2560
X	244.21642	35.96951	6.79	.0065
X-SQ	−11.87811	2.17192	−5.47	.0120

ANALYSIS OF VARIANCE

SOURCE	DF	SUM OF SQUARES	MEAN SQUARE	F	PR > F
MODEL	2	727599.50	363799.75	31.97	.0095
ERROR	3	34133.83	11377.94		
TOTAL	5	761733.33			

---

2. Using the estimated coefficients $\hat{\beta}_0$, $\hat{\beta}_1$, and $\hat{\beta}_2$ found in the column labeled COEFFICIENTS, the prediction equation is

$$\hat{y} = -175.55 + 244.22x - 11.88x^2$$

A plot of the prediction curve and the observed data values are given in the following graph. Notice that the curve appears to fit the observed data points very well.

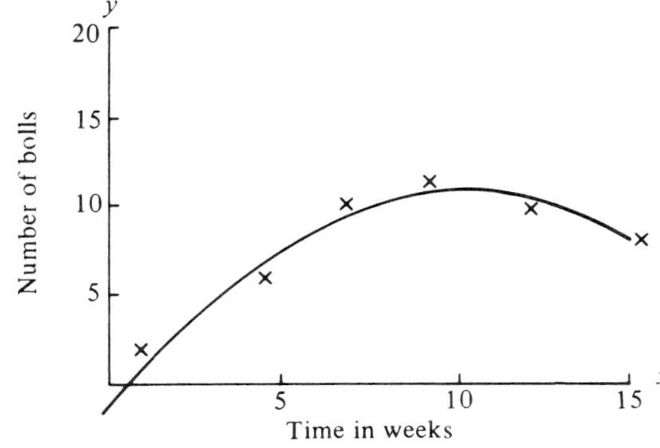

Some computer facilities may have a program written specifically to perform polynomial regression analysis. For such programs it is sufficient to enter the pairs (y, x) since the values of x^2, x^3 and other power terms are generated within the program itself. However, any multiple regression program can be used to fit a polynomial model.

Example 12.3

In order to study the relationship of advertising and capital investment on corporate profits, the following data, recorded in units of $100,000, was collected for ten medium-sized firms within the same year. The variable y represents profit for the year, x_1 represents capital investment, and x_2 represents advertising expenditures.

y	x_1	x_2
15	25	4
16	1	5
2	6	3
3	30	1
12	29	2
1	20	0
16	12	4
18	15	5
13	6	4
2	16	2

Using the model

$$y = \beta_0 + \beta_1 x_1 + \beta_2 x_2 + \epsilon$$

find the least-squares prediction equation for these data.

Solution

1. A standard multiple regression analysis program produced the following computer output for these data.

```
MULTIPLE R              .907204123
R-SQUARE                .82301932
STD ERROR OF EST       3.3033503

INDIVIDUAL ANALYSIS OF VARIABLES

VARIABLE        COEFFICIENT       STD ERROR        T          PR > |T|

INTERCEPT       - 8.17702         4.20599         - 1.94      .1913
X1                 .29213          .13571           2.15      .0684
X2               4.43430           .80024           5.54      .0009

ANALYSIS OF VARIANCE

                             SUM OF        MEAN
SOURCE          DF           SQUARES       SQUARE         F        PR > F

MODEL           2            355.21514     177.60757      16.28    .0002
ERROR           7             76.38486      10.91212
TOTAL           9            431.60000
```

At this point we are interested in that portion of the printout labeled INDIVIDUAL ANALYSIS OF VARIABLES. The first column identifies the estimated coefficients and the second column their values. Thus, the INTERCEPT is estimated to be $\hat{\beta}_0 = -8.17702$, the partial regression coefficient corresponding to the variable X1((capital) is $\hat{\beta}_1 = .29213$ and the partial regression coefficient corresponding to X2 (Advertising) is $\hat{\beta}_2 =$ 4.43430.

2. The least-squares prediction equation is

$$\hat{y} = \underline{\hspace{3em}} + .29213x_1 + 4.43430x_2$$ -8.17702

The fitted prediction equation can be used to __________ the mean value of y for given values of $x_1, x_2, \ldots, x_k$ or to __________ specific values of y for given values of $x_1, x_2, \ldots, x_k$. Estimates and predictions are obtained by substituting the required values of $x_1, x_2, \ldots, x_k$ into the prediction equation.

estimate
predict

Example 12.4

Use the prediction equation derived in Example 12.3 to estimate yearly corporate profits for a medium sized firm whose capital investment was \$2,200,000 and whose advertising expenditure was \$400,000.

Solution

The prediction equation is given as

$$\hat{y} = -8.17702 + .29213x_1 + 4.43430x_2$$

Since x_1, capital investment, and x_2, advertising expenditure, were given in units of \$100,000, the values to be entered into the prediction equation are $x_1 =$ ________ and $x_2 =$ ________. Therefore 22; 4

$$\hat{y} = -8.17702 + .29213(\underline{\hspace{3em}}) + 4.43430(\underline{\hspace{3em}})$$ 22; 4

$$= -8.17702 + \underline{\hspace{3em}} + \underline{\hspace{3em}}$$ 6.42686; 17.7372

$$= \underline{\hspace{3em}}$$ 15.98704

To find the actual profit, multiply 15.98704 by ________ to find that when capital investment is \$2,200,000 and advertising expenditure is \$400,000, profit is estimated to be ________.

\$100,000

\$1,598,704

The point estimate found in Example 12.4 is the best estimate of either $E(y)$, the average value of y, or a particular value of y. We can construct confidence interval estimates for $E(y)$ or y using a procedure similar to that for the simple linear regression model presented in Chapter 11. However, the computational aspects of this problem are best handled by a computer. Some, but not all, regression analysis programs have options that allow the user to include confidence interval estimates for $E(y)$ and y in the computer output. In both cases, the point estimate for $E(y)$ and y remain the same;

it is the width of the confidence interval that differs. The confidence interval
narrower — for $E(y)$ is (narrower, wider) than the confidence interval for a particular value of y.

In addition to the least-squares estimates of the regression coefficients, the INDIVIDUAL ANALYSIS OF VARIABLES portion of the computer printout provides the estimated standard deviation of the regression coefficients as well as the value of an F- or t-statistic used in testing.

Refer to the INDIVIDUAL ANALYSIS OF VARIABLES portion of the computer printout in Example 12.3. The estimated standard deviations of $\hat{\beta}_1$ and $\hat{\beta}_2$
standard errors — are often referred to as ______ ______. These standard errors, $s_{\hat{\beta}_1}$ and $s_{\hat{\beta}_2}$, are found in the column labeled STD. ERROR. These quantities can be used for producing confidence intervals for the parameters β_1 and β_2, or in testing hypotheses concerning their values. A $100(1 - \alpha)\%$ confidence interval for β_i is given as

$$\hat{\beta}_i \pm t_{\alpha/2} s_{\hat{\beta}_i}$$

The tabled value of $t_{\alpha/2}$ is based upon $n - (k + 1)$ degrees of freedom when the model contains k regression coefficients in addition to the intercept, or
$(k + 1)$ — ______ β's in all.

Example 12.5

Find a 95% confidence interval for the average increase in profit, β_2, for an increase of $100,000 in advertising expenditure.

Solution

.80024 — 1. From the computer printout we find $\hat{\beta}_2 = 4.43430$ with $s_{\hat{\beta}_2} =$ ______.
The number of data points is $n = 10$, and the number of estimated
3 — parameters in the model is ______. Therefore the tabulated value
3; 7 — of t based upon 10 – ______ = ______ degrees of freedom is
2.365 — $t_{.025} =$ ______.

2. The resulting 95% confidence interval for β_2 is

$$\hat{\beta}_2 \pm t_{.025} s_{\hat{\beta}_2}$$

.80024 — $$4.43430 \pm 2.365\ (\underline{\qquad\qquad})$$

or

1.89257 — $$4.43430 \pm \underline{\qquad\qquad}$$

With 95% confidence we estimate that on the average, profit will in-
$254,173; $632,687 — crease $443,430 ± $189,257 or between ______ and ______ for an increase of $100,000 in advertising expenditure.

This same information can be utilized in testing an hypothesis concerning β_1 or β_2. For example, the test of the hypothesis $H_0: \beta_1 = 0$ versus $H_a: \beta_1 \neq 0$, is based upon the statistic

$$t = \frac{\hat{\beta}_1 - 0}{s_{\hat{\beta}_1}}$$

with $n - (k + 1)$ degrees of freedom. It can be shown that the square of a t-statistic with ν degrees of freedom has an F distribution with one numerator degree of freedom and ν denominator degrees of freedom. Therefore a two-tailed t-test is equivalent to a one-tailed F-test and the user may choose to use one test or the other.

Example 12.6

Refer to Example 12.3. Test the hypothesis $H_0{:}\beta_1 = 0$ against the alternative $H_a{:}\beta_1 \neq 0$ at the 5% level of significance.

Solution

Collecting pertinent information we have

$$\hat{\beta}_1 = \_\_\_\_\_\_\_\_ \qquad s_{\hat{\beta}_1} = \_\_\_\_\_\_\_\_$$

.29213; .13571

Using a t-statistic with 7 degrees of freedom, we would reject H_0 if $|t| > t_{.025} =$ ________. For our problem,

2.365

$$t = \frac{\hat{\beta}_1 - 0}{s_{\hat{\beta}_1}} = \frac{(\_\_\_\_\_\_)}{(\_\_\_\_\_\_)} = \_\_\_\_\_\_$$

.29213; 2.15
.13571

Hence there (is, is not) sufficient evidence to reject H_0.

is not

Some computer packages use the F-statistic to test the hypothesis given in Example 12.6. Had we used the F-statistic for testing in Example 12.6, the value of the test statistic would be

$$F = t^2 = (2.1526)^2 = 4.63.$$

This value is compared with a critical value of F with one numerator and 7 denominator degrees of freedom, given as $F_{.05} = 5.59$. Again, we (would, would not) reject H_0. Notice that

would not

$$t^2_{.025} = (2.365)^2 = 5.5932 = F_{.05}$$

within rounding errors. Hence when testing the hypothesis $H_0{:}\ \beta_i = 0$ against the two-tailed alternative $H_a{:}\ \beta_i \neq 0$, the F-test rejects H_0 whenever the t-test rejects H_0.

In testing $H_0{:}\ \beta_i = 0$ against the one-tailed alternative $H_a{:}\ \beta_i > 0$ (or $H_a{:}\ \beta_i < 0$), the t-statistic is easier to use than the F-statistic. In testing $H_0{:}\ \beta_i = 0$ against $H_a{:}\ \beta_i > 0$ at the α-level of significance, H_0 is rejected if $t > t_\alpha$. For the alternative $H_a{:}\beta_i < 0$, we reject H_0 if $t < -t_\alpha$.

Self-Correcting Exercises 12B

1. A chemical company interested in maximizing the output of a chemical process by selection of the reaction temperature recorded the following data where y is the yield in kilograms and x is the coded temperature:

y	7.5	8.1	8.8	10.9	12.5	11.8	11.1	10.4	9.5
x	−4	−3	−2	−1	0	1	2	3	4

In chemical reactions, the amount of the substance produced may increase until a critical temperature is reached, at which point the amount of substance produced begins to decrease due to its decomposition by the increasing temperature. Anticipating that this would be the case, the model

$$E(y) = \beta_0 + \beta_1 x + \beta_2 x^2$$

was fitted using a multiple regression program. The computer output follows.

MULTIPLE R	.926652421
R-SQUARE	.85868471
STD ERROR OF EST	.73888298

INDIVIDUAL ANALYSIS OF VARIABLES

VARIABLE	COEFFICIENT	STD ERROR	T	PR > |T|
INTERCEPT	11.43463	.37342	30.62	.0000
X	.34000	.09539	3.56	.0119
X-SQ	−.20519	.04210	−4.87	.0028

ANALYSIS OF VARIANCE

SOURCE	DF	SUM OF SQUARES	MEAN SQUARE	F	PR > F
MODEL	2	19.90431	9.95216	18.23	.0028
ERROR	6	3.27569	.54595		
TOTAL	8	23.18000			

a. Use the printout to find the least squares estimates of β_0, β_1 and β_2. Write the least squares prediction equation.
b. Find a 90% confidence interval for β_1.
c. Test for significant curvature in the fitted response by testing $H_0: \beta_2 = 0$ against $H_a: \beta_2 \neq 0$ with $\alpha = .05$.
d. Use the fitted prediction equation to predict the yield when the coded temperature is $x = 1$.

2. Data on cotton yield, the number of cotton bolls, and the number of damaging insects as described in Example 12.1 are shown as follows:

y	x_1	x_2
21	5.5	11
17	2.8	20
20	4.7	13
19	4.3	12
15	3.7	18
23	6.1	10
20	4.5	12

These data were analyzed by a multiple regression program using the model

$$E(y) = \beta_0 + \beta_1 x_1 + \beta_2 x_2 + \beta_3 x_1 x_2$$

MULTIPLE R	.96788336
R-SQUARE	.93649819
STD ERROR OF EST	.93644526

INDIVIDUAL ANALYSIS OF VARIABLES

VARIABLE	COEFFICIENT	STD ERROR	T	PR > |T|
INTERCEPT	10.98293	7.78372	1.41	0.2532
X1	4.43713	1.61861	2.74	0.0713
X2	0.64905	0.47073	1.38	0.2619
X1*X2	−0.35151	0.14466	−3.43	0.0934

ANALYSIS OF VARIANCE

SOURCE	DF	SUM OF SQUARES	MEAN SQUARE	F	PR > F
MODEL	3	38.79778	12.93259	14.75	0.0311
ERROR	3	2.63079	0.87693		
TOTAL	6	41.42857			

a. Using the output given above, find the least squares prediction equation.
b. Using the least-squares prediction equation, predict the cotton yield when 16 damaging insects are found and the number of cotton bolls is 4.4.
c. Test for a significant partial regression of y on x_1. That is, test H_0: $\beta_1 = 0$, in the presence of the second variable, x_2.
d. Test for a significant partial regression of y on x_2.
e. Find a 95% confidence interval for β_1.

12.4 Measuring the Goodness of Fit of the Model

In the case of simple linear regression, we showed that the total sum of squares given by

$$\text{Total } SS = \sum_{i=1}^{n} (y_i - \bar{y})^2$$

could be partitioned into two parts, referred to as *SSR* and *SSE*. The sum of squares due to regression is given by

$$SSR = \sum_{i=1}^{n} (\hat{y}_i - \bar{y})^2$$

while the sum of squares for error is given by

$$SSE = \sum_{i=1}^{n} (y_i - \hat{y}_i)^2$$

Therefore

SSR; SSE

Total *SS* = ______________ + ______________

Notice that *SSR* measures the difference between the regression predictor $\hat{y}_i$ which uses the information contained in the independent variables $x_1, x_2, \ldots, x_k$ and the simple predictor $\bar{y}$ which uses none of the information from the independent variables. Large values of *SSR* indicate that the independent variables (are, are not) contributing strongly to the estimation of y. *SSR* is said to be that part of the total variation explained by the auxiliary variables $x_1, x_2, \ldots, x_k$. The quantity *SSE* measures the discrepancy between observed and ______________ values of y using the linear predictor $\hat{y}_i$. A (small, large) value of *SSE* indicates that the predictor is accurately reproducing the observed values of y.

are

predicted

small

The additivity property of the sums of squares is important for two reasons.

1. Only two of the quantities need to be calculated since the third can be obtained by ______________.
2. *SSR* can be used to measure the joint contribution of the independent variables $x_1, x_2, \ldots, x_k$ in the prediction of y.

subtraction

The quantity R^2 defined as

$$R^2 = \frac{SSR}{\text{Total } SS}$$

is called the coefficient of ______________. R^2, which measures the proportion of the variation in y explained by the independent variables, takes values in the interval

determination

_________ $\leq R^2 \leq$ _________ 0; 1

R, the positive square root of R^2, called the multiple correlation coefficient, is the multivariate counterpart of the simple correlation coefficient, _________. R measures the correlation between the response y and that portion of the model involving the predictor variables $x_1, x_2, \ldots, x_k$. r

Refer to Example 12.3 concerning corporate profits, capital investments, and advertising expenditures. The first three lines of the computer printout of the multiple regression program using profit as the response of interest are produced below.

MULTIPLE R	.907204123
R-SQUARE	.82301932
STD ERROR OF EST	3.3033503

1. The first line of output gives the value of the multiple correlation coefficient, R. For this example, the multiple correlation between corporate profits and the variables capital investments and advertising expenditures is _________, indicating the existence of a fairly (weak, strong) correlation (since the maximum value of R is one). .9072; strong
2. The second line in the printout gives the value of the coefficient of determination, R^2. In this example, $R^2 = .8230$, indicating that (_________)% of the total variation in y can be explained by the model. The remaining 19.7% of the variation is due to _________ _________ as well as the omission of other possible predictor variables that could have been included in the model. 82.3; random variation
3. The third line gives the value of s, the estimate of σ. The value of s is the positive square root of s^2 where

$$s^2 = \frac{SSE}{n - (k + 1)}$$

and $(k + 1)$ is the number of parameters in the model. For this example, $s =$ _________. The value of s is utilized in two important ways. 3.3033
   a. The quantity s (or s^2) may be required for use in calculating a test statistic or confidence interval other than those given in the printout.
   b. The quantity s can be used to detect errors in computation or unusual observations called outliers. When the deviations between the observed and predicted values of y have been calculated, approximately 95% of these deviations should be within the interval $(-2s, 2s)$ and almost all should lie within the interval (_________, _________). Values lying outside these limits are suspect, and indicate that all corresponding input values could be checked, or minimally, that the suspect observations should be checked for validity. $-3s$; $3s$

always

Some problems can arise when we use R^2 as a measure of the goodness of fit of the regression model. If additional variables are added to the model, the coefficient of determination will (always, never) increase regardless of whether the additional variables are good predictors of y. Hence, we could force R^2 to become very close to 1 by adding a sufficiently large number of additional variables. A measure of fit which does not always increase with the addition of more independent variables is an *adjusted value of* R^2 calculated as

$$R_a^2 = 1 - \left(\frac{n-1}{n-k-1}\right)\left(\frac{SSE}{\text{Total } SS}\right)$$

$$= 1 - \frac{s^2}{\text{Total } SS/n-1}$$

decrease
increase

If additional variables are good predictors, then s^2 will (increase, decrease) and R_a^2 will (increase, decrease). However, if the variables are not valuable to the regression analysis, SSE will not change significantly, the degrees of freedom for s^2, $(n - k - 1)$, will decrease, so that

$$s^2 = SSE/(n-k-1)$$

increase

will (increase, decrease) and the value of R_a^2 will decrease. That is, R_a^2 will decrease if a poor predictor variable is added to the model. If R^2 and R_a^2 are quite different in value, we would suspect that at least one independent variable, x_1, is contributing very little to the prediction of y, in the presence of the other independent variables.

.823
431.60

In Example 12.3, we found from the computer printout that $R^2 =$ __________, Total $SS =$ __________, and $s^2 = 10.9121$. Then

10.91212
.2275; .7725

$$R_a^2 = 1 - \frac{\_\_\_\_\_\_}{431.6/9} = 1 - \_\_\_\_\_\_ = \_\_\_\_\_\_$$

x_1

Hence, we would suspect that at least one of the variables is not increasing our prediction ability. In this case, the suspect variable is (x_1, x_2), which is not significant, based on its individual t-value of $t = 2.15$ (p-value = .0684).

12.5 Testing the Utility of the Regression Model

analysis of variance

The partitioning of the total sum of squares into component parts is called an __________ __________ __________. In regression analysis,

SSR; SSE

$$\text{Total } SS = \_\_\_\_\_\_ + \_\_\_\_\_\_$$

where SSR represents the variation of the linear predictor $\hat{y}_i$ from the simple predictor $\bar{y}$, while SSE represents the variation between the observed and the predicted values of y. These sums of squares divided by their appropriate degrees of freedom can be used to test the effectiveness of the regression model in predicting y.

In testing the hypothesis $H_0: \beta_1 = \beta_2 = \ldots = \beta_k = 0$, that the predictor variables contribute no information in the prediction of y, the quantities

$$MSR = \frac{SSR}{k}$$

and

$$MSE = \frac{SSE}{n - (k + 1)}$$

are independent estimates of σ^2 when H_0 is true. When H_0 is false, and one or more of the predictor variables do contribute information in predicting y, MSR will in general be significantly (smaller, larger) than MSE. Therefore, the hypothesis $H_0: \beta_1 = \beta_2 = \ldots = \beta_k = 0$ is tested using the statistic

larger

$$F = \frac{MSR}{MSE}$$

which has an F distribution with $\nu_1 =$ __________ and $\nu_2 =$ __________ degrees of freedom, respectively, when H_0 is true. The null hypothesis is rejected at the α-level of significance only if the observed value of F exceeds F_α, a right-tailed critical value of F with $\nu_1 = k$ and $\nu_2 = n - (k + 1)$ degrees of freedom.

$k; n - (k + 1)$

The results of the test for a significant regression appear in the section of the computer printout labeled ANALYSIS OF VARIANCE. For the data in Example 12.3 relating profits to capital investment and advertising expenditures, this portion of the printout appears as follows.

ANALYSIS OF VARIANCE

	DF	SUM OF SQUARES	MEAN SQUARE	F
MODEL	2	355.21514	177.60757	16.28
ERROR	7	76.38486	10.91212	

The entries in the third column give the quantities SSR and SSE where SSE corresponds to the entry in the line labeled ERROR. The entries in the MEAN SQUARE column are found by dividing the SUM OF SQUARES entry by its respective degrees of freedom in the DF column. For this example, SSR = 355.21514, SSE = 76.38486, and

$$MSR = 355.21514/\_\_\_\_\_\_\_\_ = \_\_\_\_\_\_\_\_$$

2; 177.60757

7; 10.91212	$MSE = 76.38486/$________ = ________
	In testing for significant regression,
177.60757	$$F = \frac{MSR}{MSE} = \frac{(\_\_\_\_\_\_)}{10.91212} = 16.28$$
2; 7	with $\nu_1 =$ ________ and $\nu_2 =$ ________ degrees of freedom. This calculated value appears in the column labeled F. The .05 critical value
4.74	of F based upon $\nu_1 = 2$ and $\nu_2 = 7$ degrees of freedom is $F_{.05} =$ ________.
reject	Since the observed value of F exceeds 4.74, we (reject, do not reject) the null hypothesis

$$H_0: \beta_1 = \beta_2 = 0$$

and conclude that at least one predictor variable contributes significant information for the prediction of y.

Self-Correcting Exercises 12C

1. Refer to Exercise 1, Self-Correcting Exercises 12B.
   a. Test the hypothesis $H_0: \beta_1 = \beta_2 = 0$ at the $\alpha = .05$ level of significance. Is there a significant regression of y on x and x^2?
   b. What percentage of the variation in y is accounted for by the auxiliary variables x and x^2?
   c. Calculate R_a^2. Does it appear that any of the independent variables are contributing little information for the prediction of y?
2. Refer to Exercise 2, Self-Correcting Exercises 12B.
   a. What percentage of the variation in y is accounted for by the auxiliary variables x_1, x_2, and x_1x_2? Calculate R_a^2, and compare to R^2.
   b. Test the hypothesis $H_0: \beta_1 = \beta_2 = \beta_3 = 0$ at the $\alpha = .05$ level of significance Is there a significant regression of y on x_1, x_2, and x_1x_2?
   c. Refer to Exercise 1, Self-Correcting Exercises 11D. What additional percentage of the variation in y is accounted for by adding x_2, the number of damaging insects present, to the model using x_1, the average number of bolls per quadrate?
   d. Can you explain the results of part b, as well as parts c and d, Exercise 2, Self-Correcting Exercises 12B, in the light of the results of part c?

12.6 Comparison of Computer Printouts

Multiple regression programs can be found in most statistical program packages. Three commonly used packages that contain multiple regression programs are

SAS, MINITAB, and SPSS. The computer printouts for each of these multiple regression programs are given in your text. Although the format (which refers to the use of headings and the placement of the results on the printed page) vary from package to package, essentially the same information appears on all outputs. Rather than reexplain all the entries on these three programs, we will note only the differences as they relate to the information we have presented.

The estimates of the regression coefficients given in our INDIVIDUAL ANALYSIS OF VARIABLES section appear in the column labeled ESTIMATE in the SAS package, in the column labeled COEF in the MINITAB package, and in the column labeled B in the SPSS package.

The estimated standard deviations of the estimated regression coefficients are labeled STD ERROR OF ESTIMATE in the SAS package, ST DEV in the MINITAB package, and STD ERROR OF B in the SPSS package.

The ANALYSIS OF VARIANCE sections are similar for all three, except that MINITAB does not calculate the F-statistic for testing the fit of the model. This is easily found by calculating

$$F = \text{MSR}/\text{MSE}$$

with the appropriate degrees of freedom.

The SPSS printout differs from SAS and MINITAB in that individual model parameters are tested using an F-statistic rather than the t-statistic that we have used, given by

$$t = \hat{\beta}_i / s_{\hat{\beta}_i}$$

with error degrees of freedom equal to n minus the number of model parameters. The SPSS package uses the fact that the square of a t-statistic with ν degrees of freedom is the same as an F-statistic with one numerator and ν denominator degrees of freedom. That is

$$(t_\nu)^2 = F_\nu^1$$

or equivalently,

$$t_\nu = \sqrt{F_\nu^1}$$

with the sign of t the same as the sign of the coefficient tested.

Both MINITAB and SPSS printouts give the adjusted value of R^2, which is adjusted for degrees of freedom. The adjusted value of R^2 is calculated as

$$R^2(\text{adjusted}) = 1 - \frac{s^2}{\text{Total SS}/(n-1)}$$

where n is the number of observations. Without adjustment,

$$R^2 = 1 - \frac{\text{SSE}}{\text{Total SS}}$$

less

Notice that the adjusted value of R^2 will always be (less, greater) than or equal to the unadjusted value.

12.7 Some Comments on Model Formulation (Optional)

qualitative

quantitative

Variables are classified as being either quantitative or qualitative. A quantitative variable takes values corresponding to the points on the real line. If a variable is not quantitative, then it is said to be qualitative. Variables such as advertising expenditure, number or age of employees, per unit production cost, and number of delivery trucks are examples of quantitative variables while geographic region, plant size, and kind of stock are examples of ____________ variables. Although predictor variables can be quantitative or qualitative, a dependent variable must be ____________ in order to satisfy the assumptions given in Section 12.2.

level

three

four

three

The intensity setting of an independent variable is called a ____________. The levels of a quantitative independent variable correspond to the number of distinct values that the variable assumes in an investigation. For example, if an experimenter interested in maximizing the output of a chemical process observed the process when the temperature was set at 100°F, 200°F and 300°F, the independent variable "temperature" was observed at ____________ levels. The levels of a qualitative independent variable are defined by describing them. For example, the independent variable "occupational groups" might be described as white-collar workers, blue-collar workers, service workers, and farm workers. If all four groups were included in an investigation, the qualitative variable "occupational groups" would be taken to have ____________ levels. Similarly, if an investigation were to be conducted in three regions, the qualitative variable "regions" would have ____________ levels.

It is necessary to differentiate between quantitative and qualitative variables to be included in a regression analysis because these variables are entered into a regression model in different ways. Quantitative variables, in general, are entered directly into a regression equation, while qualitative variables are entered through the use of dummy variables, which in effect produce different response curves at each setting of the qualitative independent variable.

one

k

When two or more quantitative independent variables appear in a regression model, the resulting response function produces a graph called a response surface in three or more dimensions. These graphs become difficult to produce when three or more independent variables are included in the model. A model involving quantitative variables is said to be a first-order model if each independent variable appears in the model with power ____________. The model

$$E(y) = \beta_0 + \beta_1 x_1 + \beta_2 x_2 + \cdots + \beta_k x_k$$

is a first-order model involving __________ independent variables, since the model is linear in each x. The graph of a first-order model is a response plane, which means that the surface is "flat" but has some directional tilt with respect to its axes. Second-order linear models in k quantitative predictor variables include all the terms in a first-order model, all crossproduct terms such as $x_1x_2, x_1x_3, x_2x_3, \ldots, x_{k-1}x_k$, and all pure quadratic terms $x_1^2, x_2^2, \ldots, x_k^2$. A second order model with two predictor variables is given as

$$E(y) = \beta_0 + \beta_1 x_1 + \beta_2 x_2 + \beta_3 x_1^2 + \beta_4 x_1 x_2 + \beta_5 x_2^2$$

The quadratic terms x_1^2 and x_2^2 allow for curvature while the crossproduct or interaction term x_1x_2 allows for warping or twisting of the response surface.

Two predictor variables are said to *interact* if the change in $E(y)$ corresponding to a change in one predictor variable depends upon the value of the other variable.

In Example 12.1, the model included the interaction term x_1x_2. The resulting graphs in Example 12.1 show how the change in $E(y)$ as x_1 changes depends upon the value of x_2 and vice versa.

Qualitative variables are entered into a regression model using dummy variables. For each independent qualitative variable in the model, the number of dummy variables required is one less than the number of ____________ associated with that qualitative variable. The following example will demonstrate how this technique is implemented. — levels

Example 12.7

An investigator is interested in predicting the strength of particle board (y) as a function of the size of the particles (x_1) and two types of bonding compounds. If the basic response is expected to be a quadratic function of particle size, write a linear model that incorporates the qualitative variable "bonding compound" into the predictor equation.

Solution

The basic response equation for a specific type of bonding compound would be

$$E(y) = \beta_0 + \beta_1 x_1 + \beta_2 x_1^2$$

Since the qualitative variable "bonding compound" is at two levels, one dummy variable is needed to incorporate this variable into the model. Define the dummy variable x_2 as follows:

x_2 = 1 if bonding compound 2

x_2 = __________ if not — 0

The expanded model would now be written as

$$E(y) = \beta_0 + \beta_1 x_1 + \beta_2 x_1^2 + \beta_3 x_2 + \beta_4 x_1 x_2 + \beta_5 x_1^2 x_2$$

1. When $x_2 = 0$, the response has been measured using bonding compound 1 and the resulting equation is

$x_1; x_1^2$ $E(y) = \beta_0 + \beta_1$ ________ $+ \beta_2$ ________

2. When $x_2 = 1$, the response has been measured using bonding compound 2 and the resulting equation is

$\beta_1 + \beta_4$ $E(y) = (\beta_0 + \beta_3) + ($________$)x_1 + (\beta_2 + \beta_5)x_1^2$

3. The use of the dummy variable x_2 has allowed us to simultaneously describe two quadratic response curves for each of the two bonding compounds. Notice that β_3, β_4, and β_5 measure the differences between the intercepts, the linear components, and the quadratic components, respectively, for the two bonding compounds.
4. Had another bonding compound been included in the investigation, x_3, a second dummy variable, would be defined as

1 $x_3 =$ ________ if bonding compound 3

0 $x_3 =$ ________ if not

and the model would be expanded to include the terms x_3, $x_1 x_3$, and

$x_1^2 x_3$ ________ to produce in effect a third quadratic response curve for compound 3.

The formulation of the model is perhaps the most important aspect of a regression analysis since the fit of the model will depend not only upon the independent variables included in the model, but also upon the way in which the variables are introduced into the model. If, for example, the response increases with some variable x, achieves a maximum, and then begins to decrease, both linear and quadratic terms in x should be included in the model. Failure to include a term in x^2 may cause the model to fit poorly and/or fail in predicting the response y for all values of x. Accurate formulation of a model requires experience and a knowledge of the mechanism underlying the response of interest. The latter is sometimes achieved by running several exploratory investigations, and combining this information within a more elaborate model.

Self-Correcting Exercises 12D (Optional)

1. Graph the following polynomials in x:

   a. $E(y) = 1 + x + x^2$

   b. $E(y) = 1 - x + x^2$

   c. $E(y) = 2 + 3x^2$

   d. $E(y) = 2 - 3x^2$

2. Consider a situation in which the output (y) of an industrial plant is related to the number of individuals employed (x_1) and the area in which the plant is located. Define the following dummy variable:

   $x_2 = 1$ if area 2

   $x_2 = 0$ if not

   Write a linear model relating output to x_1 and x_2 if we assume that the relationship between y and x_1 is linear for both areas.
3. Refer to Exercise 2. Suppose that three areas were involved in the experiment. Define the second dummy variable:

   $x_3 = 1$ if area 3

   $x_3 = 0$ if not

   Write a linear model relating output to x_1, x_2, and x_3 if we assume again that the relationship between y and x_1 is linear for all areas.
4. Suppose, in Exercise 3, that an experiment is conducted and the following least-squares predictor equation is obtained (data are ficticious):

   $$\hat{y} = 2 + x_1 + x_2 + 3x_1x_2 + 2x_3 + x_1x_3$$

   Graph the three least-squares lines for the three areas, 1, 2, and 3.

12.8 Testing Portions of a Model

In previous sections we have presented procedures for testing the contribution of individual independent variables in predicting a response y, and the joint contribution of ______________ the independent variables in the model in predicting y. Interpretation of the results of tests concerning individual parameters in the model was difficult because of the possible

all

presence in the model of other independent variables contributing similar or perhaps identical information in the prediction of the response y. In this section a more general version of the procedure for testing the joint contribution of a set of independent variables in predicting y is given.

The rationale in implementing this procedure is quite simple. A regression model utilizing all the independent variables of interest is fitted. To test the contribution of any group of these independent variables, a second

difference | model with these variables deleted is fitted and the ____________ in the two sums of squares for error is found. This difference is used to assess the additional contribution of the deleted variables above and beyond

were not | the information contained in the variables that (were, were not) deleted from the model.

This procedure is formalized in the following way. Suppose we have k predictor variables, $x_1, x_2, \ldots, x_g, x_{g+1}, \ldots, x_k$ available for predicting the response y. For the *complete* or full model,

$$E(y) = \beta_0 + \beta_1 x_1 + \ldots + \beta_g x_g + \beta_{g+1} x_{g+1} + \ldots + \beta_k x_k$$

Testing whether the variables $x_{g+1}, x_{g+2}, \ldots, x_k$ contribute additional significant information in predicting y is equivalent to testing the hypothesis

0 |

$$H_0\colon \beta_{g+1} = \beta_{g+2} = \ldots = \beta_k = \text{\_\_\_\_\_\_\_\_}$$

When H_0 is true, the reduced model is

$$E(y) = \beta_0 + \beta_1 x_1 + \ldots + \beta_g x_g$$

reduced | Whenever terms are added to the model, SSE is ____________. Hence, if SSE_1 is the sum of squares for error with the *reduced* model involving g predictor variables and SSE_2 is the sum of squares for error with the

larger | *complete* model, then SSE_1 will be (smaller, larger) than SSE_2. If the difference $(SSE_1 - SSE_2)$ is significantly large, we conclude that at least one of the variables $x_{g+1}, x_{g+2}, \ldots, x_k$ contributes significant information beyond that contained in the variables $x_1, x_2, \ldots, x_g$.

In testing the hypothesis $H_0\colon \beta_{g+1} = \beta_{g+2} = \ldots = \beta_k = 0$ we use the test statistic given as

$$F = \frac{MS(\text{Drop})}{MSE_2}$$

$n - k - 1$ | where MS (Drop) $= (SSE_1 - SSE_2)/(k - g)$ and $MSE_2 = SSE_2/($________$)$. When the random errors are normally and independently distributed with mean zero and variance σ^2, this statistic has an F distribution with ν_1

$k - g; n - k - 1$ | $= ($________$)$ and $\nu_2 = ($________$)$ degrees of freedom. If H_0 is false and one or more of the variables tested contribute significant additional information in predicting y, then MS(Drop) would tend to be significantly larger than MSE_2. Therefore the test is one-tailed, and H_0 is rejected if the observed value of F exceeds a (left, right)-tailed critical value of F. — right

Example 12.8
Refer to Example 12.3 in which the complete model was given as

$$y = \beta_0 + \beta_1 x_1 + \beta_2 x_2 + \epsilon$$

Test the hypothesis $H_0: \beta_2 = 0$ versus $H_a: \beta_2 \neq 0$ using the testing procedure presented in this section.

Solution

1. If H_0 is true, the reduced model is

$$y = \beta_0 + \beta_1 x_1 + \epsilon$$

the simple linear regression model discussed in Chapter 11. The computer printout of the regression analysis using this model appears below.

MULTIPLE R	.2161
R SQUARE	.0467
STD. ERROR OF EST.	7.1715

	DF	SUM OF SQUARES	MEAN SQUARE	F RATIO
REGRESSION	1	20.1604	20.1604	.3920
RESIDUAL	8	411.4396	51.4300	

INDIVIDUAL ANALYSIS OF VARIABLES

VARIABLE	COEFFICIENT	STD. ERROR	F VALUE
(CONSTANT	12.1894)		
CAPITAL	-.1493	.2385	.3920

In the ANALYSIS OF VARIANCE portion of the printout, we find that the sum of squares for error in the reduced model is SSE_1 = __________ with __________ degrees of freedom. — 411.4396; 8

2. From the regression analysis printout using the complete model, we find SSE_2 = __________ and MSE_2 = __________ with 7 degrees of freedom. Then — 76.3849; 10.9121

$$SS(\text{Drop}) = SSE_1 - SSE_2$$

$$= 411.4396 - 76.3849$$

$$= \_\_\_\_\_\_\_\_\_\_$$

335.0547

with 8 - 7 = 1 degree of freedom. In this case MS(Drop) is the same as SS(Drop).

3. To test $H_0: \beta_2 = 0$ versus $H_a: \beta_2 \neq 0$, calculate

$$F = \frac{MS(\text{Drop})}{MSE_2}$$

$$= \frac{335.0547}{10.9121}$$

30.7048 $= \_\_\_\_\_\_\_\_$

With $\alpha = .05$, the critical value of F based with $\nu_1 = 1$ and $\nu_2 = 7$ degrees
5.59 of freedom is $F_{.05} = \_\_\_\_\_\_\_\_$. Hence, we reject H_0 and conclude
does that the variable advertising expenditure (does, does not) contribute
significant information in predicting y.

4. In comparing this result with the F VALUE for this same test in the INDIVIDUAL ANALYSIS OF VARIABLES portion of the computer print-
30.7081 out for the complete model, we find the value $F = \_\_\_\_\_\_\_\_$ which, within rounding errors, is the same as the value we have just computed.

The general testing procedure just described is more appropriately applied when we are interested in assessing the joint contribution of several variables in predicting a response y. It is worth pointing out, however, that in applying this procedure to one predictor variable as we have done, we produced results identical to those obtained directly from the computer printout for the complete model. This should help clarify and unify the test procedure which produces the F VALUE in the INDIVIDUAL ANALYSIS OF VARIABLES portion of the computer printout.

Self-Correcting Exercises 12E

1. A particular savings and loan corporation is interested in determining how well the amount of money in family savings accounts can be predicted using the three independent variables, annual income, number in the family unit, and area in which the family lives. Suppose that there are two specific areas of interest to the corporation. The following data were collected, where

y = amount in all savings accounts

x_1 = annual income

x_2 = number in family unit

x_3 = 0 if area 1; 1 if not

Both y and x_1 were recorded in units of \$1000.

y	x_1	x_2	x_3
0.5	19.2	3	0
0.3	23.8	6	0
1.3	28.6	5	0
0.2	15.4	4	0
5.4	30.5	3	1
1.3	20.3	2	1
12.8	34.7	2	1
1.5	25.2	4	1
0.5	18.6	3	1
15.2	45.8	2	1

The following computer printout resulted when the data was processed using a multiple regression computer program.

MULTIPLE R	.96043325
R SQUARE	.92243203
STD. ERROR OF EST.	1.89645250

	DF	SUM OF SQUARES	MEAN SQUARE	F RATIO
REGRESSION	3	256.62059	85.54020	23.78
RESIDUAL	6	21.57941	3.59657	

INDIVIDUAL ANALYSIS OF VARIABLES

VARIABLE	COEFFICIENT	STD. ERROR	F VALUE
(CONSTANT	– 3.11171)		
X1	0.50314	0.07670	43.03
X2	– 1.61259	0.65785	6.01
X3	– 1.15479	1.79064	0.42

a. Test the hypothesis H_0: $\beta_1 = \beta_2 = \beta_3 = 0$ at the $\alpha = .05$ level of significance. Is there a significant regression of y on x_1, x_2 and x_3?

b. Suppose that we are interested in testing the hypothesis that the variables x_2 and x_3 contribute no information for the prediction of y. To do so, we fit the reduced model, $y = \beta_0 + \beta_1 x_1 + \epsilon$ and obtain $SSE = 49.08683$. Test the above hypothesis in terms of the regression coefficients at the $\alpha = .05$ level of significance.

c. Refer to part b. Suppose instead that we hypothesize that the variable x_1 contributes no information. The reduced model is $y = \beta_0 + \beta_2 x_2 + \beta_3 x_3 + \epsilon$ and $SSE = 176.3438$. Test the hypothesis H_0: $\beta_1 = 0$ at the $\alpha = .05$ level. Does the value of the test statistic appear in the computer printout?

d. Interpret the results of part b and part c in terms of their practical significance.

12.9 Problems in Using Multiple Linear Regression Analysis

would not

In a multiple regression problem, the regression coefficients are called *partial* regression coefficients, since they are determined in conjunction with other variables in the model and only partially determine the value of y. Further, the values of these partial regression coefficients (would, would not) in general be the same as those found by using several simple linear regression models, each with one independent variable. Estimates of the partial regression coefficients are correlated with each other to the extent that the underlying independent variables share the same predictive information.

When the independent variables included in a regression analysis are correlated among themselves, the values of the estimated β's in the model take into account the amount of shared and independent information available in the x's for estimating the response y. In this situation, individual tests of the regression coefficients are of little value. More information concerning the utility of the independent variables $x_1, x_2, \ldots, x_k$ in predicting y can be obtained by testing the hypothesis

$$H_0: \beta_1 = \beta_2 = \ldots = \beta_k = 0$$

A test of this hypothesis is given in Section 12.5.

Multicollinearity

straight line

When two or more of the independent variables are highly correlated with each other, we are confronted with the problem of multicollinearity. Multicollinearity is the technical way of saying, for example, that if one is given pairs of values for two independent variables that are highly correlated with each other, the pairs of values will exhibit a strong linear relationship when plotted on graph paper. When the correlation is very high, the points will almost plot as a ______________ ______________. Hence we say that these variables are collinear, and, for all practical purposes, one is working with one independent variable. When this situation is repeated for several pairs of independent variables, we refer to the problem as one of multicollinearity.

Stepwise Regression

Many investigators prefer to use a *stepwise regression program* which at each step adds an independent variable to the regression model only if its inclusion significantly reduces *SSE* below the value achieved without the variable included. In this way, the investigator can look at the stepwise decrease in *SSE* and assess the additional contribution of the independent variable just added, above and beyond the contribution of those variables already in the model.

Residual Analysis and Serial Correlation

Another problem sometimes results when a multiple regression problem involves time series data. When one or more important variables have been omitted from the model, the residuals $(y_i - \hat{y}_i)$ will not be independent.

In fact, if these residuals are plotted over time, the plot will exhibit some systematic pattern. When this happens, the residuals are said to be autocorrelated or serially correlated. Serial correlation may cause serious underestimation of the true error variation, which in turn causes observed values of t- or F-statistics to be (smaller, larger) than they should be. larger

The potential problems of multicollinearity and serial correlation require that we exercise caution when interpreting the results of tests involving individual parameters appearing in the model.

12.10 Summary

Multiple regression analysis is an extension of ______________ linear regression analysis to accommodate situations in which the response y is a function of a number of independent variables $x_1, x_2, \ldots, x_k$. The procedures given in Chapter 11 for the simple linear model have analogies in the multiple regression model. Hence, any simple linear regression problem (can, cannot) be analyzed using multiple regression techniques. simple can

Although identical in concept, simple and multiple regression analysis differ in two important aspects. Simple linear regression analysis can be done (with, without) the use of a computer; for multiple regression analysis, this is generally not the case. However, multiple regression analysis programs are available at most computing facilities. These programs, though very similar in their approach to the multiple regression problem, are all slightly different in format, available options, and in the procedure used for finding the best model of the form without

$$y = \beta_0 + \beta_1 x_1 + \ldots + \beta_k x_k + \epsilon$$

The interested reader may consult a programmer at his local computing facility to determine which of the multiple regression programs are available. Secondly, very few real life situations (can, cannot) be adequately described by a simple linear regression model. Multiple regression analysis provides greater utility and latitude in data analysis by allowing the inclusion of k independent variables, $x_1, x_2, \ldots, x_k$ in the regression model. can

EXERCISES

1. A manufacturer, concerned about the number of defective items being produced within his plant, recorded the number of defective items produced on a given day (y) by each of 10 machine operators, recording also the average output per hour (x_1) for each operator and the time from the last machine servicing (x_2) in weeks. The data were

y	x_1	x_2
13	20	3
1	15	2
11	23	1.5
2	10	4
20	30	1
15	21	3.5
27	38	0
5	18	2
26	24	5
1	16	1.5

The following computer output resulted when these data were analyzed using a multiple regression analysis program based on the model

$$E(y) = \beta_0 + \beta_1 x_1 + \beta_2 x_2$$

MULTIPLE R	.99881232
R-SQUARE	.99762606
STD ERROR OF EST	.54843279

INDIVIDUAL ANALYSIS OF VARIABLES

VARIABLE	COEFFICIENT	STD ERROR	T	PR > |T|
INTERCEPT	−28.39063	.82733	−34.32	.0000
X1	1.46306	.02699	54.20	.0000
X2	3.84459	.14256	26.97	.0000

ANALYSIS OF VARIANCE

SOURCE	DF	SUM OF SQUARES	MEAN SQUARE	F	PR > F
MODEL	2	884.79455	442.39728	1470.84	.0000
ERROR	7	2.10545	.30078		
TOTAL	9	886.90000			

a. Interpret R^2 and comment on the fit of the model.
b. Is there sufficient evidence to indicate that the model contributes significant information in predicting y at the .01 level of significance?
c. What is the prediction equation relating $\hat{y}$ and x_1 when $x_2 = 4$?
d. Use the fitted prediction equation to predict the number of defective items produced for an operator whose average output per hour is 25 and whose machine was serviced three weeks ago.

2. An experiment was conducted to investigate the relationship between the degree of metal corrosion and the length of time the metal is exposed to the action of soil acids. In the data which follow, y is the percentage corrosion and x is the exposure time measured in weeks.

y	.1	.3	.5	.8	1.2	1.8	2.5	3.4
x	1	2	3	4	5	6	7	8

The following computer output resulted in fitting the model:

$$E(y) = \beta_0 + \beta_1 x + \beta_2 x^2$$

MULTIPLE R	.99925528
R-SQUARE	.99851112
STD ERROR OF EST	.05300494

INDIVIDUAL ANALYSIS OF VARIABLES

VARIABLE	COEFFICIENT	STD ERROR	T	PR > |T|
INTERCEPT	.19643	.07396	2.66	.0450
X	−.10000	.03770	−2.65	.0453
X-SQ	.06190	.00409	15.14	.0000

ANALYSIS OF VARIANCE

SOURCE	DF	SUM OF SQUARES	MEAN SQUARE	F	PR > F
MODEL	2	9.42095	4.71047	1676.61	.0000
ERROR	5	.01405	.00281		
TOTAL	7	9.43500			

a. What percent of the total variation is explained by the quadratic regression of y on x?
b. Is the regression of y on x and x^2 significant at the $\alpha = .05$ level of significance?
c. Is the linear regression coefficient significant at the .05 level of significance?
d. Is the quadratic regression coefficient significant at the .05 level of significance?
e. When the model with the linear term omitted given by $E(y) = \beta_0 + \beta_2 x^2$ was fitted to the data, $R^2 = .99641629$ and SSR = 9.40119. What could you say about the contribution of the linear term in x in explaining the total variation in y? Should the linear term be deleted from the prediction model?

3. In a study to examine the relationship between the time required to complete a construction project and several pertinent independent variables, an analyst compiled a list of four variables that might be useful in predicting the time to completion. These four variables were size of the contract (in \$1,000 units) (x_1), number of workdays adversely affected by the weather (x_2), number of subcontractors involved in the project (x_4), and a variable (x_3) that measured the presence or absence of a workers' strike during the construction. In particular,

$$x_3 = 0 \text{ if no strike}$$

$$x_3 = 1 \text{ if strike}$$

Fifteen construction projects were randomly chosen, and each of the four variables as well as the time to completion were measured. The data are given in the following table:

y	x_1	x_2	x_3	x_4
29	60	7	0	7
15	80	10	0	8
60	100	8	1	10
10	50	14	0	5
70	200	12	1	11
15	50	4	0	3
75	500	15	1	12
30	75	5	0	6
45	750	10	0	10
90	1200	20	1	12
7	70	5	0	3
21	80	3	0	6
28	300	8	0	8
50	2600	14	1	13
30	110	7	0	4

An analysis of these data using a first-order model in x_1, x_2, x_3, and x_4 produced the following computer printout. Notice that the t-statistic has been replaced by its equivalent F-statistic, which appears in the column labeled F VALUE and the intercept is referred to as CONSTANT.

MULTIPLE R .9204
R-SQUARE .8471
STD ERROR OF EST 11.8450

ANALYSIS OF VARIANCE

	DF	SUM OF SQUARES	MEAN SQUARE	F RATIO	PR > F
REGRESSION	4	7770.2972	1942.5743	13.8455	.0004
RESIDUAL	10	1403.0362	140.3036		

INDIVIDUAL ANALYSIS OF VARIABLES

VARIABLE	COEFFICIENT	STD ERROR	F VALUE	PR > F
(CONSTANT	− 1.5887)			
X1	−.00784	.00623	1.5846	.2367
X2	.67533	.99978	.4563	.5147
X3	28.01342	11.37143	6.0688	.0335
X4	3.4889	1.93516	3.2504	.1016

Give a complete analysis of the printout and interpret your results.

4. Refer to Exercise 3. For the fifteen construction projects used in the analysis, calculate the predicted values, $\hat{y}_i$, and the residuals, $(y_i - \hat{y}_i)$. Use the information given in the computer printout to verify that each of these residuals lies within the interval $(-2s, 2s)$.
5. Refer to Exercise 3. The analyst suspects that the variables x_1 and x_2 are not contributing significantly to the prediction. Test the null hypothesis $H_0{:}\beta_1 = \beta_2 = 0$, at the $\alpha = .05$ level. Note that when the reduced model is fitted, $SSE = 1656.6729$.
6. Refer to Exercise 3. Test the null hypothesis $H_0{:}\beta_3 = \beta_4 = 0$ at the $\alpha = .05$ level. When the reduced model is fitted $SSE = 4697.117$. Interpret the results of problems 5 and 6 in terms of the variables necessary to predict time to completion.

Chapter 13

ELEMENTS OF TIME SERIES ANALYSIS

13.1 Introduction

The businessperson and the economist are constantly faced with variables whose values are measured at different points in time. Quite often these points in time are equidistant. For example, the total sales of a particular salesperson may be recorded *daily*, profits may be recorded *monthly* and/or *yearly*, and the Dow Jones Industrial Average may be recorded at the close of each business day. In many decision-making situations, time may be one of the most important variables affecting the response variable. In other situations, it may be a "nuisance" variable, which tends only to obscure the behavior of the response variable.

A *time series variable* is one that is observed at specific (usually equidistant) points in time. A *time series* is a set of sequential measurements on a time series variable.

---

time series

time

Any sequence of measurements taken on a process variable over time is called a ____________ ____________. The time series is usually represented by a mathematical equation listing the process values as a function of time, or by a curve on a graph whose vertical axis represents the value of the random response plotted against ____________ on the horizontal axis. It is the *pattern* generated by a time series that is of special interest to a business planner or forecaster attempting to forecast the behavior of the time series at some future point in time.

decreases

The analysis of time series is a difficult task. Response measurements appearing in a time series are often correlated, with the correlation increasing as the time interval between a pair of measurements (increases, decreases). As a result, time series data will often defy the basic assumption of *independence* required for the methods we have learned thus far. Since the methodology of time series analysis has not yet been developed to an advanced state, analytical methods used are often quite subjective. Newer techniques of time series analysis are often very complex. In this chapter, we will discuss some of the more elementary procedures used in analyzing time series. We will also discuss several types of index numbers, descriptive statistics sometimes used in time series analysis.

13.2 Components of Time Series

Time series are often conceptually divided into four components. These are:

1. secular or long-term trends
2. cyclical fluctuation
3. seasonal variation
4. random variation

Long-term trends are often present in time series because of such things as a steady increase in population. Such factors do not cause sudden changes in the response, but produce steady change over time. *Cyclic* effects in a time series are apparent when the response rises and falls in a gentle, wavelike manner on a ______ ______ trend curve. Cyclic effects could be caused by many factors, for example, pulsations in the demand for a product or business cycles. *Seasonal effects* in time series are rises and falls that always occur at a particular time of year. The essential difference between seasonal and cyclic effects is that seasonal effects are (predictable, unpredictable), occurring at a given interval of time from the last occurrence, while cyclic effects are completely ______. *Random variation* represents the random *upward* and *downward* movement of the series after adjustment for the other components. It is the unexplained shifting and bobbing of the series in the short-term period. These variations are caused by factors such as weather and political events. Any time series may contain any number of the above components: cyclic effect, ______ ______, long-term ______, or ______ ______; however, all time series will contain ______ ______. With most time series processes, the *non-random* components are not easily separable.

long-term

predictable

unpredictable

seasonal variation; trend;
random variation
random variation

The communications engineer refers to the long-term, cyclic, and seasonal effects as the *signal* of the time series. The random variations are called *noise*. The amplitude, or strength, of the noise is an important consideration. It is possible for the noise to be so great that it completely hides the signal.

The objective of time series analysis is to identify the components which do exist in order to identify their causes and to forecast future values of the time series. Accurate estimation of future values of time series is possible only when the magnitude of the ______ ______ is small. Otherwise, its fluctuations may overwhelm or even cancel the signal components.

random variation

13.3 Smoothing Methods

Traditional methods of time series analysis have rested heavily upon *smoothing techniques*. These techniques attempt to cancel out the effect of random variation and reveal the underlying components. In the terms of the communication engineer, we filter out the small high frequency variations (noise) present in the signal, making the signal more easily detectable.

Smoothing can be accomplished by utilizing a centered *moving average* of the response measurements over a set number of time periods.

The centered moving average $\bar{y}_t$ at time t of the response measurements over M time periods is given by

$$\bar{y}_t = \frac{y_{t-(M-1)/2} + y_{t+1-(M-1)/2} + y_{t+2-(M-1)/2} + \cdots + y_{t+(M-1)/2}}{M}$$

where M is a positive integer, y_t is the process response at time t, y_{t-1} is the process response at time $t - 1$, and so forth.

For example, with a five-period centered moving average, $\bar{y}_{10}$ is given by

$$\frac{y_8 + y_9 + y_{10} + y_{11} + y_{12}}{5}$$

$\bar{y}_{10} =$ ________

between

odd

When M is an even number, the centered moving averages will occur ________ the time points. Therefore, it is more useful to select (odd, even) values for M. If an even number is selected, the series can be smoothed again, using a small even value such as $M = 2$.

1

small

The primary disadvantage of using a centered moving average for smoothing is that the technique will not produce a smoothed value corresponding to each response value (observation), unless $M =$ ________ . This can be a serious problem when the number of response measurements is ________ .

Example 13.1

The weekly sales of a foreign-based electronics company are given in the table below. Compute the centered moving average of sales for the period shown when $M = 3$. The ten centered moving averages are computed in a manner similar to the computation shown for $\bar{y}_2$.

109.3
120.3
131.7
120.3
119.7
95.7
97.7

t	y_t	$\bar{y}_t$
1	132	
2	100	116.3
3	117	102.3
4	90	105.0
5	108	______
6	130	______
7	123	______
8	142	______
9	96	______
10	121	______
11	70	______
12	102	

$$\bar{y}_2 = \frac{y_1 + y_2 + y_3}{3} = \frac{(132) + (100) + (117)}{3} = \frac{(349)}{3} = 116.3$$

Another method of smoothing which is more efficient than the moving-average method is the process of ______________ smoothing. | exponential

This technique is more efficient because it produces a ______________ value corresponding to each response measurement—one does not "lose" observations. The smoothed value, under exponential smoothing, at time period t is denoted by __________. | smoothed; S_t

---

The basic equation of exponential smoothing is

$$S_t = y_t + (1 - \alpha)S_{t-1}$$

where $S_1 = y_1$, y_t is the value of the time series at time t, and $0 \leqslant \alpha \leqslant 1$ is the smoothing constant.

Hence, for $t = 1$, $S_1 = y_1$. For the second time period, t = __________, we have $S_2 = \alpha y_2 + (1 - \alpha)S_1$. | 2

It is interesting to note that whereas the moving average considers process values only over the M time periods, the exponential smoothing method considers ______________ past process values at each stage in the computations. Even though remote responses are not dropped in the exponential smoothing scheme as they are in a moving average, their contribution to the smoothed value S_t becomes (greater, less) at each successive time point. The speed at which remote responses are dampened out is determined by the ______________ constant, __________. For values of __________ near __________, remote values are dampened out slowly. For values of α near one, they are dampened out more ______________. For a volatile series, we would select a (large, small) smoothing constant. For a stable process, we would select a (large, small) constant. | all; less; smoothing; α; α; 0; quickly; small; large

Example 13.2

The sales manager of the foreign-based electronics company is dissatisfied with the results of the moving-average technique employed in Example 13.1. He has suggested that you try exponential smoothing with $\alpha = .5$ and $\alpha = .1$. On the graph following, plot the original data, the moving average for $M = 3$ from Example 13.1, and the exponentially smoothed curves for both α levels.

Solution

1.

t	y_t	$S_t(\alpha = .1)$	$S_t(\alpha = .5)$
1	132	132	132
2	100	128.8	116.0
3	117	127.6	116.5
4	90	123.8	103.3
5	108	122.2	________

$$S_t(\alpha = .1) = (\alpha)y_t + (1 - \alpha)S_{t-1}$$

$$= .1y_t + .9S_{t-1}$$

105.7

117.9	6	130	123.0	______
123.0; 120.5	7	123	______	______
124.9; 131.3	8	142	______	______
122.0; 113.7	9	96	______	______
121.9; 117.4	10	121	______	______
116.7; 93.7	11	70	______	______
115.2; 97.9	12	102	______	______

$$S_2(\alpha = .1) = (.1)(y_2) + .9(S_1)$$
$$= 10 + 118.8$$
$$= 128.8$$

The 24 exponentially smoothed values are computed in a manner similar to the computation shown for $S_2(\alpha = .1)$.

2. Plot the smoothed series for $\alpha = .1$ and $\alpha = .5$.

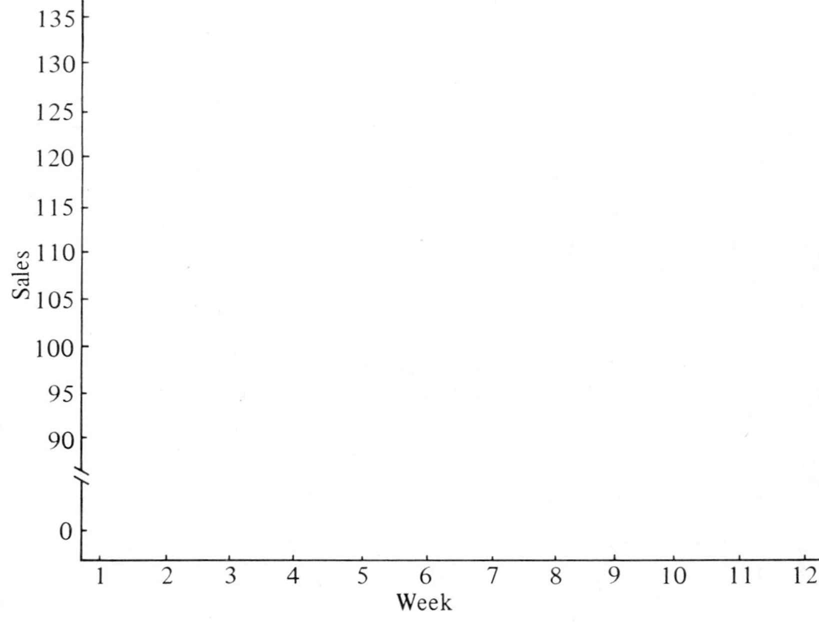

13.4 Adjustment of Seasonal Data

When a time series exhibits a seasonal component, the centered moving-average smoothing technique can be used to remove the seasonal component by using a moving average of order M, where M is the number of time points in one complete seasonal cycle. In most seasonal economic time series, the seasonal period usually consists of either 4 or 12 time periods, corresponding, respectively, to quarterly and yearly cycles. Once the series has been *deseasonalized*, the deseasonalized series can be examined to detect other important components, such as a long-term trend or a cyclic effect. The technique used here for deseasonalizing a time series is called the *ratio-to-moving-average method*.

In using the ratio-to-moving average technique to remove a seasonal component whose cycle consists of M time periods,

1. Compute the M-period centered moving averages for the series.
2. If M is an even number, adjust the centered moving average values by averaging adjacent centered moving averages.

3. Using the series in step 2, calculate a series of **specific seasonal indexes**, by dividing the original value of the series at time t, y_t, by the adjusted centered moving average at time t.
4. Calculate the **seasonal indexes,** $\bar{s}_i$, for season i by averaging all of the specific seasonal indexes for season i, found in step 3.
5. Normalize the seasonal indexes, forcing them to sum to M, the number of periods in one season. For quarterly data, $M = 4$, while for yearly date, $M = 12$.
6. Deseasonalize the series, dividing the original series value y_t by the appropriate **normalized seasonal index**.

The loss of several observations at each end of the time series is not a serious problem if the number of observations is (small, large). In any case, we should have observations over at least three complete seasons in order to apply the ratio-to-moving average technique for deseasonalizing the data. large

Example 13.3

A newly founded community college operates on the basis of three academic terms each year. Enrollment at the college during the years 1982 through 1988 was as follows:

Academic year	*Enrollment*		
	Fall	*Winter*	*Spring*
1982–1983	910	1180	1580
1983–1984	1060	1210	2080
1984–1985	1720	2640	3320
1985–1986	3090	3250	3570
1986–1987	3730	3680	4690
1987–1988	3560	3760	4450

Use a centered moving average of order 3 to deseasonalize these data.

Solution

1. The sequential time listing for these data together with the centered moving-average series are given as follows:

Time	*Enrollment*	*Centered Moving Average*	*Time*	*Enrollment*	*Centered Moving Average*	
1	910	–	10	3090	______	3220.00
2	1180	1223.33	11	3250	______	3303.33
3	1580	1273.33	12	3570	______	3516.67
4	1060	1283.33	13	3730	______	3660.00
5	1210	1450.00	14	3680	______	4033.33
6	2080	1670.00	15	4690	______	3976.67
7	1720	2146.67	16	3560	______	4003.33
8	2640	2560.00	17	3760	______	3923.33
9	3320	3016.67	18	4450	–	

Since $M = 3$ is odd, there is no reason to perform a second moving average for the purpose of centering the moving-average time series.

2. Specific seasonal indexes are calculated as y_t divided by the corresponding centered moving average. Fill in the blanks in the table below, calculating the three seasonal indexes (Fall, Winter, Spring) as the average of the specific seasonal indexes.

		Fall	*Winter*	*Spring*
1.241		*	.965	______
		.826	.834	1.246
1.031		.801	______	1.101
.960		______	.984	1.015
1.179		1.019	.912	______
.889		______	.958	*
.899; .947	*Seasonal Index*	______	______	1.156

3. Since the sum of the three seasonal indexes is 3.002, the normalized indexes are

.899; .898

$s_1 = 3(\_\_\_\_\_\_)/(3.002) = \_\_\_\_\_\_$

.947; .946

$s_2 = 3(\_\_\_\_\_\_)/(3.002) = \_\_\_\_\_\_$

$s_3 = 3(1.156)/(3.002) = 1.155$

4. The deseasonalized series is obtained by dividing each original observation by the appropriate seasonal index. Fill in the table below.

	Time	y_t	Deseasonalized Series	Time	y_t	Deseasonalized Series
3440.98	1	910	1013.36	10	3090	______
	2	1180	1247.36	11	3250	3435.52
1367.97	3	1580	______	12	3570	3090.91
	4	1060	1180.40	13	3730	4153.67
	5	1210	1279.07	14	3680	3890.06
1800.87	6	2080	______	15	4690	4060.61
	7	1720	1915.37	16	3560	3964.37
2790.70; 3974.63	8	2640	______	17	3760	______
	9	3320	2874.46	18	4450	3852.81

5. A plot of the original enrollment data is given below. Plot the ratio-to-moving-average deseasonalized series superimposed on this graph.

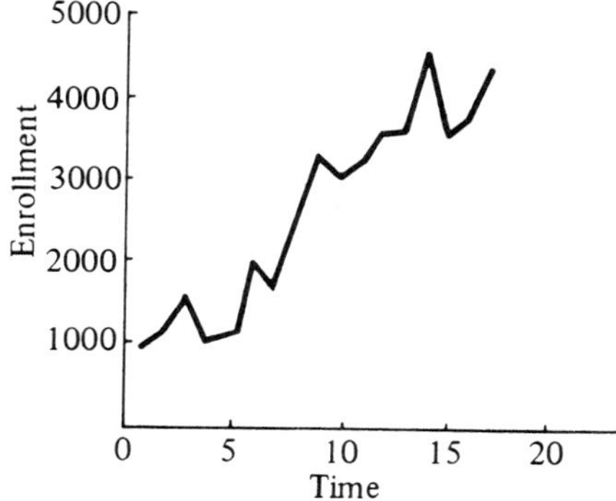

6. The ratio-to-moving-average series shows (more, less) variation than do the original data. less
7. With the seasonal component removed, it appears that the rate of increase of enrollment is (increasing, leveling off). leveling off

Self-Correcting Exercises 13A

1. The owner of a suburban liquor store has indicated that the following represents his gross monthly sales (in thousands of dollars) for the years 1987 and 1988:

1987		*1988*	
Month	*Sales*	*Month*	*Sales*
Jan.	9.5	Jan.	11.3
Feb.	11.6	Feb.	12.7
Mar.	16.4	Mar.	15.9
Apr.	13.5	Apr.	14.3
May	17.6	May	18.0
June	21.3	June	23.1
July	19.7	July	20.3
Aug.	17.5	Aug.	18.6
Sept.	22.1	Sept.	23.4
Oct.	23.0	Oct.	24.1
Nov.	25.8	Nov.	27.6
Dec.	33.2	Dec.	35.0

a. Plot the sales values against time and construct the time series.
b. Which time series components appear to exist within the sales pattern?
c. Smooth the monthly sales values by computing a three-month centered moving average. Plot the smoothed series and the original series on the same set of graph paper. Has smoothing helped to identify the components of the series?

d. Smooth the sales data by computing an exponentially smoothed series using the smoothing constant $\alpha = .1$.
e. Smooth the sales data by computing an exponentially smoothed series using the smoothing constant $\alpha = .5$.
f. On a sheet of graph paper, superimpose the two smoothed series on the original series. Are any hidden time series components suggested?
g. Was the larger or the smaller smoothing constant most appropriate, or is there no detectable difference? Explain.

2. The data in the accompanying table represent the quarterly earnings per share for the shareholders of a soft drink company for a period of five years. Remove the seasonal component from the earnings data by applying the ratio-to-moving-average technique with $M = 4$. Plot the original series and the deseasonalized series together on the same piece of graph paper and describe the results.

Year	*Quarter 1*	*Quarter 2*	*Quarter 3*	*Quarter 4*
1	.13	.21	.26	.12
2	.15	.21	.27	.14
3	.16	.24	.30	.16
4	.18	.26	.33	.18
5	.22	.31	.39	.22

13.5 Index Numbers

index numbers

Because of the variability in the buying power of the dollar over time, it is necessary to deflate some values and inflate others in order to make meaningful comparisons. This is done through the use of ____________ ____________. The application of index numbers is not limited strictly to monetary comparisons, but in business problems, this is a very common application.

An index number is a ratio or an average of ratios. Two or more time periods are involved, one of which is called the *base time period*. The value at the base time period serves as the standard point of comparison, while values at other time periods are used to show the percentage change in value from the standard value of the base period. If we let

$$I_k = \frac{(\text{average dollar value of concern in year } k)\,(100)}{\text{average dollar value in year one}}$$

then we are using one as our ______________ ______________. Each year's ______________ is a percentage of the base year's combined dollar values.

base period
index

Example 13.4

You are employed as an hourly worker by an electronics firm, and have worked for the company for 10 years. Over this time period your average yearly wages have risen, but you suspect you have little more buying power than you had when you were hired. To find out, use year 1 as the base year and calculate the simple index number, I_k, for years 2 through 10. The average hourly wages for each year are given below.

Year	*Average hourly wages*	*Simple wage index,* I_k	
1	6.25	________	100.00
2	6.37	________	101.92
3	6.44	________	103.04
4	6.57	________	105.12
5	6.62	________	105.92
6	6.75	________	108.00
7	6.89	________	110.24
8	6.96	________	111.36
9	7.02	________	112.32
10	7.17	________	114.72

Solution

Let y_k be the average hourly wages in year k, and let y_0 be the average hourly wages in the base year. With $y_0 = 6.25$, use the formula

$$I_k = \frac{y_k}{y_0}(100) \qquad \text{for } k = 2, 3, \ldots, 10$$

For example,

$$I_2 = \frac{y_2}{y_0}(100) = \frac{\_\_\_\_\_\_}{6.25}(100) = \_\_\_\_\_\_$$

6.37; 101.92

$$I_3 = \frac{y_3}{y_0}(100) = \frac{\_\_\_\_\_\_}{6.25}(100) = \_\_\_\_\_\_$$

6.44; 103.04

The other simple wage indices are computed similarly.

Example 13.5

Continuing Example 13.4, suppose you have obtained the Consumer Price Index for the ten years in question. Compare the simple index calculated in Example 13.4 with the CPI. Do you have more or less buying power than you had when you were hired?

Solution

The CPI for years 1 through 10 are shown below. Fill in the appropriate simple wage indices from Example 13.4.

	Year	*CPI*	I_k
100.00	1	100.0	________
101.92	2	104.3	________
103.04	3	107.5	________
105.12	4	112.2	________
105.92	5	116.6	________
108.00	6	121.4	________
110.24	7	124.7	________
111.36	8	128.3	________
112.32	9	132.0	________
114.72	10	137.4	________

greater than For each year (2 through 10) the Consumer Price Index is (greater than, less than) your personal wage index. Hence, your buying power is consistently
less (less, greater) than when you were hired.

A list of index numbers for two or more periods of time, where each index number employs the same base year, is called an *index time series*.

Example 13.6

Plot the index time series in Example 13.4.

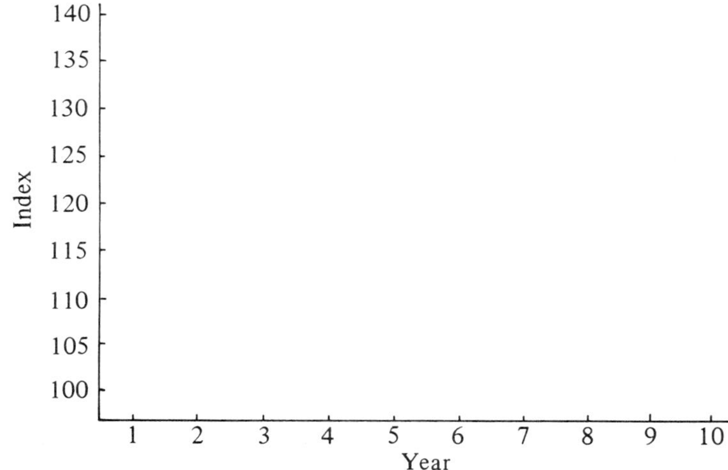

A commonly used index to compare two sets of prices from a wide variety of items is called a *simple aggregate index.* An aggregate index is the ratio of an aggregate (sum) of commodity prices for a given year k to an aggregate of the prices of the same commodities in some base year.

The *simple aggregate index* for year k is calculated as

$$I_k = \frac{\sum_{i=1}^{n} p_{ki}}{\sum_{i=1}^{n} p_{0i}} (100)$$

p_{ki} = price in year k of item i where i ranges from 1 to n

p_{0i} = base year price of the same item i.

An index number I_k measures the ______________ changes in a set of monetary values at period k compared with a base period index of __________. When computing an index number, one must multiply the monetary value ratios or averages by __________ so that the resultant index number is comparable to the base period index of __________. The percentage change from the base period to period k is __________. Thus, if I_t is equal to 100, no change is implied; if I_k is less than 100, (increase, decrease) of the time series values is implied; and if I_k is

percentage

100
100
100
I_k - 100

decrease

increase

greater than 100, (increase, decrease) of the time series value is assumed. If the time series values are in fact monetary, the increase or decrease in the index I_k will be a measure of inflation. That is, if I_k is equal to 100, no change is implied; if I_k is less than 100, (inflation, deflation) of the monetary values is implied; and if I_k is greater than 100, (inflation, deflation) of the monetary values is assumed.

deflation
inflation

Most formulas for the computation of an index number contain the constant multiple __________ to insure that the index number for period k is a ______________ which is comparable to the base period time series value index, 100.

100
percentage

Example 13.7

You have decided to quit your job at the electronics firm (as a result of the previous example), and are accepting a job offer in Tokyo. A friend who lived in Tokyo during 1968 says the prices there are very low, and has produced an old account book to prove his point. The prices of some commodities listed in his book are given below. Another friend just returned from a vacation in Tokyo, says the prices are high, and quotes some prices he remembers. You are curious and wish to compute the price change over the 1968-to-1988 period, using 1968 as the base period. Using the data below, compute the aggregate price index for 1988. Prices are per pound.

Commodity	*1968 Price*	*1988 Price*
Gohan	10	35
Tofu	15	24
Miso	8	57
Nori	12	42
Sakana	17	63
Mochi	5	15

24; 57; 42; 63
15; 8; 12; 17

$$I_{1988} = \frac{(35) + (\_\_\_\_) + (\_\_\_\_) + (\_\_\_\_) + (\_\_\_\_) + (15)}{(10) + (\_\_\_\_) + (\_\_\_\_) + (\_\_\_\_) + (\_\_\_\_) + (5)}(100)$$

236; 67; 352

$$= \frac{(\_\_\_\_)}{(\_\_\_\_)}(100) = \_\_\_\_\_\_\_\_$$

The simple aggregate index has its greatest weakness in that changes in the measuring units may drastically affect the value of the index. An index that gives a better indication of relative changes is called a *weighted aggregate index*. A weighted aggregate index is the ratio of a sum of weighted commodity prices for a given year k to a sum of the weighted prices of the same commodities in some base time period. In this case, the prices (do, do not) contribute equally to the value of the index. Each price is weighted by a value that measures its relative importance in the index. The weights can be chosen in different ways, but in the case of commonly used price indices, the weights

do not

are usually the quantities of items produced or the numbers of units purchased or consumed. In using these weights, each item contributes to the index according to its importance in the sum of prices of the items being described by the index.

The weighted aggregate index is given as

$$I_k = \frac{\sum_{i=1}^{n} p_{ki}q_{ki}}{\sum_{i=1}^{n} p_{0i}q_{0i}}(100)$$

p_{ki} = price of item i in period k

p_{0i} = price of item i in base period

q_{ki} = relative quantity of item consumed in time period k

q_{0i} = relative quantity of item consumed in base time period.

Example 13.8

After computing the simple aggregate index of the previous example, you realize that your average diet has changed over the time period, as your tastes changed. In order to make a more meaningful comparison, you assign the following average q_{ki}'s, average quantities you might have bought per month during the time the prices were in effect. Compute the aggregate weighted index for the period, using 1968 as the base period.

Commodity	*1968 Price*	*1988 Price*	q_{1968}	q_{1988}
Gohan	10	35	5	3
Tofu	15	24	4	9
Miso	8	57	1	2
Nori	12	42	3	4
Sakana	17	63	15	12
Mochi	5	15	2	1

$$I_{1988} = \frac{(35)(3) + (24)(9) + (57)(2) + (42)(4) + (63)(12) + (15)(1)}{(10)(5) + (15)(4) + (8)(1) + (12)(3) + (17)(15) + (5)(2)}(100)$$

$$= \frac{(105) + (216) + (114) + (168) + (756) + (15)}{(50) + (60) + (8) + (36) + (255) + (10)}(100)$$

1374; 419; 327.9

$$= \frac{(\_\_\_\_\_\_)}{(\_\_\_\_\_\_)}(100) = \_\_\_\_\_\_$$

weighted aggregate

The U.S. Department of Labor uses a special index, called the *Laspeyres Index*. It is a special form of the ______ ______ index.

The *Laspeyres Index* is calculated as

$$L = \frac{\sum_{i=1}^{n} p_{ki}\, q_{0i}}{\sum_{i=1}^{n} p_{0i}\, q_{0i}} (100)$$

where p_{ki}, q_{0i}, and p_{0i} are defined as before.

---

less
more

In using the Laspeyres Index, base period weights are used for all other time periods. In the specific case of price indices, this allows us to make more meaningful comparisons of changes in price and buying power over time, since we are only considering the change in price per given number of units and not changing the number of units. One disadvantage of this method is that it tends to overstate the effect of price increases. This is because the demand for most goods shows some sensitivity to price changes. This means that as the prices of certain goods increase, consumers tend to buy (more, less) of these goods and to buy (more, less) of substitute goods whose prices have remained unchanged. This problem can usually be ignored in the case of necessities, which have no close substitutes. The Paasche Index, I_t, uses time period t rather than base period quantities as weights for the index. The Paasche Index tends to underweight rather than overweight commodities whose prices have increased, and should be used and interpreted with caution.

Example 13.9

Refer to Example 13.8. Compute the Laspeyres and Paasche Indices for 1988, using 1968 as the base year.

Commodity	*1968 Price*	*1988 Price*	q_{1968}	q_{1988}
Gohan	10	35	5	3
Tofu	15	24	4	9
Miso	8	57	1	2
Nori	12	42	3	4
Sakana	17	63	15	12
Mochi	5	15	2	1

Solution

1. For the Laspeyres Index, q_1 = __________, q_2 = __________, . . . , $q_6 = 2$. Then

5; 4

$$L = \frac{(35)(5) + (24)(4) + (57)(1) + (42)(3) + (63)(15) + (15)(2)}{(10)(5) + (15)(4) + (8)(1) + (12)(3) + (17)(15) + (5)(2)}(100)$$

$$= \frac{(175) + (96) + (57) + (126) + (945) + (30)}{(50) + (60) + (8) + (36) + (255) + (10)}(100)$$

$$= \frac{(\_\_\_\_\_\_\_\_\_\_)}{(\_\_\_\_\_\_\_\_\_\_)}(100) = \_\_\_\_\_\_\_\_\_\_$$

1429; 419; 341.05

2. For the Paasche Index, $q_1 = 3, q_2 = 9, \ldots q_6 = 1$. Then

$$P = \frac{35(3) + 24(9) + 57(2) + 42(4) + 63(12) + 15(1)}{10(3) + 15(9) + 8(2) + 12(4) + 12(17) + 5(1)}(100)$$

$$= \frac{\_\_\_\_\_\_\_\_\_\_}{438}(100) = \_\_\_\_\_\_\_\_\_\_$$

1374; 313.70

Both indices show a large amount of (inflation, deflation) during this period. The Paasche Index appears to be smaller than either the simple aggregate index (Example 13.7) or the Laspeyres Index.

inflation

The __________ __________ index is the __________ mean of the Laspeyres and the Paasche indices. It is found by computing

Fisher's ideal; geometric

$$I_F = \sqrt{I_L I_P}$$

where I_F = Fisher's ideal index

I_L = Laspeyres index

I_P = Paasche index

Although this method probably yields a more accurate value than either the Paasche or Laspeyres methods, it is seldom used in practice.

Two important indices computed regularly by the Bureau of Labor Statistics are the __________ __________ index and the __________ __________ index. Both of these can be somewhat misleading. The consumer price index (CPI) is published monthly. It is a(n) __________ __________ index. The year 1967 is currently used as the base period; however, beginning in January 1988, most CPI's have shifted to 1982–84 as their base year. The following factors should be considered in examining the CPI.

consumer price; wholesale price
weighted
aggregate

1. The CPI (is, is not) representative of all American families.
2. The CPI says (little, much) about the cost of living for a professional man.

is not
little

ignores

3. The CPI (ignores, considers) taxation and product quality changes over time.

Any computed price index, including the CPI, should always mention the relevant base period and the class of items or people for which the index has meaning.

is not
producers'

Another index computed by the Bureau of Labor Statistics is the wholesale price index (WPI). One difficulty in the use of this index is that it (is, is not) really an indicator of wholesale prices, but actually represents the change in ______________ selling prices.

differently from

Security market indices, such as the Dow-Jones industrial average, are computed (similarly to, differently from) the wage and price indices we have discussed. Dow-Jones averages might be described as averages of a group of time series rather than as indicators of changes in value or price.

30
mergers
stock splits
less

The Dow-Jones industrial average tries to compute the average of the daily closing prices of the securities of __________ predetermined industrial firms. The computations become involved when events such as __________ and ______________ ______________ occur. Each time these more involved computations are necessary, the index becomes (less, more) meaningful.

Self-Correcting Exercises 13B

1. Using 1983 as the base year, compute the simple price index for the manufacturer's suggested retail price for a small portable color television set. The prices over the years 1983 through 1988 are listed below.

Year	1983	1984	1985	1986	1987	1988
Price	\$340	\$325	\$350	\$380	\$400	\$410

2. An accountant employed in the state auditor's office of a western state has earned the following annual salaries in his three years' employment.

Year	1986	1987	1988
Salary	\$17,880	\$18,400	\$18,850

During these three years, the state's wage indices were 121.4, 125.2, and 129.0, respectively, computed from 1975 as the base year. Have the accountant's real wages increased during his time of employment in his current position? Explain.

3. The cost of operating an automobile was compared for the years 1970 and 1980. It was decided that operating costs were to exclude the cost of insurance because of the many different types of insurance policies available to the automobile owner. The items, and their costs, included in the analysis were:

Item	*1970 Price* (p_0)	*1980 Price* (p_k)
Gasoline (gallon)	$ .35	$1.10
Oil (quart)	.75	1.35
Mechanic's time (per hour)	4.25	7.25

These figures were computed as averages over the entire United States for the period of time under consideration. Using the prices for 1970 as the base year prices, compute the simple aggregate index for the cost of car care for 1980.

4. After further studying the problem of comparing the cost of operating an automobile in 1970 versus 1980, it was thought necessary to consider not only the cost per unit of gasoline, oil, and mechanic time but also the quantity of each of these items used in a year's time. The average use of gasoline and oil and the average hours required of an automobile mechanic per car owner were computed for 1970 and 1980. They are:

Item	*1970 Quantity* (q_0)	*1980 Quantity* (q_k)
Gasoline (gallons)	500	700
Oil (quarts)	50	40
Mechanic's time (hours)	8	11

Using the price information given in Exercise 3 and the quantities of each item used given here, compute the weighted aggregate index of car cost for 1980 using 1970 as the base year. Comment on the difference between the index computed here and the index computed in Exercise 3. (That is, how do you account for their difference and what is the meaning of this difference?)

5. Refer to Exercises 3 and 4. Use these data to compute the Laspeyres index for 1980 with 1970 data considered as base year data. Account for any difference between the Laspeyres index computed here and the weighted aggregate index computed in Exercise 4.
6. Refer to Exercises 3 and 4. Use these data to compute the Paasche index for 1980 with 1970 data considered as base year data. Account for any differences between the Paasche index computed here, the Laspeyres index computed in Exercise 5, and the weighted aggregate index computed in Exercise 4.
7. Refer to Exercises 5 and 6. Use the results obtained in these two exercises to compute Fisher's ideal index for the automobile cost data. Let the base year be 1970.

13.6 Summary

A time series is a sequence of measurements taken on a response that varies over ______________. A time series may consist of several

time

components, such as long-term trend, a cyclic effect, or a seasonal effect. All time series may contain any number of these components, but, in addition, all time series contain random variation. Smoothing techniques are used to smooth the time series whereby the random variation is damped and the underlying components of the series are more clearly revealed.

Index numbers are used to show the relative changes of a response with respect to some chosen point in time. Index numbers can be used to measure the change in price or value of a single commodity or a group or commodities when compared to some base time period. A weighted index incorporates the values of the time series variables together with weights that reflect the relative importance of the variables in the index. The Consumer Price Index (CPI), which is published monthly by the Bureau of Labor Statistics, is a measure of the level of consumer prices as compared to the base year of 1967. Although the CPI (is, is not) representative of all American families, it (does, does not) provide a legal basis on which to base adjustments in salaries, social security, and other benefits.

is not
does

EXERCISES

1. The total national health expenditures in billions of dollars are given below for the years 1982–1986.

Year	*Amount*
1982	73.5
1983	69.4
1984	82.0
1985	92.8
1986	99.1

Find the simple indices for the years 1983–1986 using 1982 as the base year.

2. The total production amounts (in millions of bushels) and the price per bushel for five different grain commodities in two different years are given in the following table.

	Year 1		*Year 2*	
Commodity	*Production*	*Price/bushel*	*Production*	*Price/bushel*
Flaxseed	30.900	1.420	30.400	2.650
Soybeans	78.000	.900	555.100	2.130
Sorghum grain	86.000	.478	620.000	.836
Rye for grain	39.725	.420	33.108	.882
Buckwheat	6.476	.538	.847	1.160

a. Construct a simple aggregate price index for year 2 using year 1 as a base year.

b. Compute the Paasche Index using year 1 as the base year, and using production units as the weights.
c. Compute the Laspreyres Index using year 1 as the base year, and using production units as the weights.
d. Comment on the differences among the indices calculated in parts a, b, and c.

3. The stumpage prices (the value of the standing timber) in dollars per thousand board feet for four species of lumber in three different years are given below.

Species	*Year 1*	*Year 2*	*Year 3*
Douglas fir	32.00	42.60	41.90
Southern pine	34.50	31.70	44.10
Sugar pine	29.00	23.30	38.50
Ponderosa pine	19.10	19.80	32.10

a. Calculate the simple aggregate index for year 2 using year 1 as the base year.
b. Calculate the simple aggregate index for year 3 using year 1 as the base year.

4. The table that follows gives the annual sales data for the sales of Crest toothpaste in millions of dollars for the years 1971 through 1980. (*Business Economics*, May 1982, Vol. 17, No. 3, p. 44).

Year	*Sales* (y_t)
1971	113.750
1972	124.150
1973	133.000
1974	126.000
1975	162.000
1976	191.625
1977	189.000
1978	210.000
1979	224.250
1980	245.000

a. Plot the sales data against time and construct the time series.
b. Which time series components appear to exist within the sales pattern?
c. Smooth the series by computing a three-month centered moving average. Plot the smoothed series and the original series on the same set of axes. Has the smoothing helped to identify the components of the series?
d. Smooth the sales data by computing exponentially smoothed series using $\alpha = .2$ and $\alpha = .6$. Superimpose the two smoothed series on the original series. Was the larger or the smaller smoothing constant most helpful, or is there no detectable difference?

Chapter 14

FORECASTING MODELS

14.1 Introduction

In Chapter 13, we considered variables often encountered in business and economics whose values are measured at different points in time. When a sequence of measurements is taken on this type of random variable over time, the resulting sequence is called a ______________ ______________.

time series

It is natural for businessmen and economists to try to forecast the future behavior of such time series, and to take actions appropriate to the forecast suggestions. Depending on how far into the future we are attempting to forecast, we distinguish between short-term and long-term forecasts. (Short-, Long-) term forecasts generally make predictions no more than one year in advance, while (short-, long-) term forecasts usually look from two to ten years ahead.

Short-

long-

Because the future is always (certain, uncertain), we can never expect complete forecast accuracy. Forecasting the future behavior of a time series using the smoothing methods of Chapter 13 can be very inaccurate, because such attempts require the very strong assumption that past trends and cycles will continue unchanged into the future. Due to uncertain economic, political and business developments, such an assumption is often unjustified. If the smoothed forecasts are used unilaterally, without any adjustment based on the researcher's subjective judgment, the forecast accuracy will be questionable. For this reason, forecasting remains as much an art as a science.

uncertain

14.2 Choosing an Appropriate Forecasting Model

Forecasting models can be classified as one of four types:

1. Naive models
2. Econometric models
3. Time series models
4. Qualitative forecasting models

The primary focus in this chapter will be on forecasting using the first three types of models. For naive, econometric and time series models, we assume that a *sample data base* (a set of sample observations from the time series process) is available, and that it can be used to create a model to reliably predict the future activity of the series. The *econometric model* uses auxiliary independent variables and a regression approach to construct an equation for predicting future values of the time series process. The *time series model* (does, does not) use auxiliary variables; it uses only the sample data base and extends the patterns inherent in these observations to develop a prediction equation. *Qualitative forecasting models* differ from the other two types because they use no sample data in developing a forecast. This type of model can be used in a situation where it is too costly (either in time or money) to obtain a data base, or in which a data base is not available.

does not

14.3 Four Common Measures of Forecast Accuracy

When presented with several possible forecasting models, all of which could be used to predict the future outcome of a time series y_t, it is difficult for an experimenter to make a decision as to which model is the most appropriate. In Chapters 8, 9 and 11, an estimate or prediction was accompanied by a measure of its ______________ in the form of a bound on error or a confidence interval. However, most time series violate the basic assumptions necessary for the use of these methods; namely, a time series, $y_1, y_2, \ldots, y_t$, does not generally represent a set of ______________ measurements on the random variable y. For this reason, it is necessary to find a more general measure to judge the forecast accuracy of a model.

goodness

independent

There are four commonly used measures of forecast accuracy. Each is appropriate in different situations. Let y_t be the observed response measurement and $\hat{y}_t$ be the predicted response measurement.

1. *Mean Absolute Deviation* (MAD): This is the average of the absolute deviations of the observed values from the ______________ values. It is calculated as

predicted

$$\text{MAD} = \frac{\sum_{t=1}^{n} |y_t - \hat{y}_t|}{n}$$

for $y_1, y_2, \ldots, y_n$.

2. *Mean Square Error* (MSE): This is the average of the squares of the deviations $(y_t - \hat{y}_t)$. It is calculated as

$$\text{MSE} = \frac{\sum_{t=1}^{n} (y_t - \hat{y}_t)^2}{n}$$

3. *Root Mean Square Error* (RMSE) is the square root of the MSE, calculated as

$$\text{RMSE} = \sqrt{\frac{1}{n} \sum_{t=1}^{n} (y_t - \hat{y}_t)^2}$$

4. *Mean Absolute Percentage Error* (MAPE) is the average of the absolute error measured as a percentage of the observed value for each observation $y_1, y_2, \ldots, y_n$. MAPE is calculated as

$$\text{MAPE} = \frac{1}{n} \sum_{t=1}^{n} \frac{|y_t - \hat{y}_t|}{y_t} \times 100\%$$

more

MSE
smallest

small

future

The basic difference between the MAD and MSE (or RMSE) is that extreme errors in forecasting are given (less, more) weight in the calculation of MSE than in the calculation of MAD, since the error in prediction, $(y_t - \hat{y}_t)$, is squared. Hence, an experimenter wishing to avoid large (and perhaps costly) errors of prediction should use (MSE, MAD). In either case, the model yielding the (smallest, largest) value of MSE or MAD is the more accurate model.

Because MAPE is a unitless measure of accuracy, it can be used to compare model accuracy for different time series. However, MAPE will be seriously inflated if the fitted series contains extremely (small, large) values.

It is very important to remember that the test of a model is how well it predicts the ______________. The fit of the model to the past response measurements, though important, is secondary. Hence, in developing a model for a time series, it is often valuable to divide the available data into two parts. The first part of the series is used to develop an appropriate forecast model. Once this model is established, the remaining unused data can be considered "future" data. The utility of the fitted model is then assessed using MAD, MSE, RMSE or MAPE, calculated using the forecast errors for the second part of the time series.

14.4 Naive Models

Models that have a very simplistic structure are usually examined prior to fitting more sophisticated or complex models.

A **no-change forecasting model** assumes that the current value of a series is a good estimate of the next value in the series. Hence, the present value y_t is used as an estimate of y_{t+1}, so that

$$\hat{y}_{t+1} = y_t.$$

The **percent-change model** assumes that the forecast for the next value in the series will reflect a percentage increase (or decrease) over the present value. In this case,

$$\hat{y}_{t+1} = (1 + k)y_t$$

where k is the percentage change expressed in decimal form.

When a company assumes that next year's sales will be about the same as this year's sales, that company is using a (no-change, percent-change) forecasting model. On the other hand, if a company feels that next year's sales should reflect a 5% increase over this year's sales, the company is using a (no-change, percent-change) model. The no-change model would be appropriate if the series exhibited no trends of any kind. The percent-change model can be used to model an exponential growth or decline in the series.

no-change

percent-change

14.5 Econometric Forecasting Models

Econometric models consist of one or more equations which describe the probabilistic relationship between a dependent time series and one or more auxiliary independent variables. The linear model of earlier chapters is an example of an econometric model. Econometric forecasting models are distinguished from time series models in that the latter ignore any relationship between a given time series and other economic variables. Rather, time series models predict the future behavior of a time series solely on the basis of its own past behavior.

A simple long-term linear trend might be represented by

$$y = \beta_0 + \beta_1 x + \epsilon \qquad \text{where } x = \underline{\hspace{3cm}}$$

time

We can estimate the values of β_0 and β_1 by the procedures of Chapter 11. A curvilinear long-term trend might be represented by

$$y = \beta_0 + \beta_1 x + \underline{\hspace{2cm}} + \epsilon \qquad (x = \text{time})$$

$\beta_2 x^2$

We could estimate the parameters of this equation also by the method of least squares, as explained in Chapter 12.

On the graph below, plot a time series (real or imaginary) to which the linear model might appropriately be fitted.

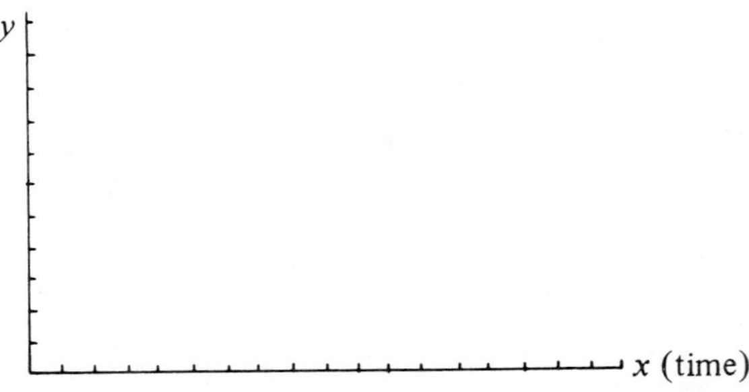

On the graph below, plot an imaginary or real time series to which the curvilinear model might appropriately be fitted.

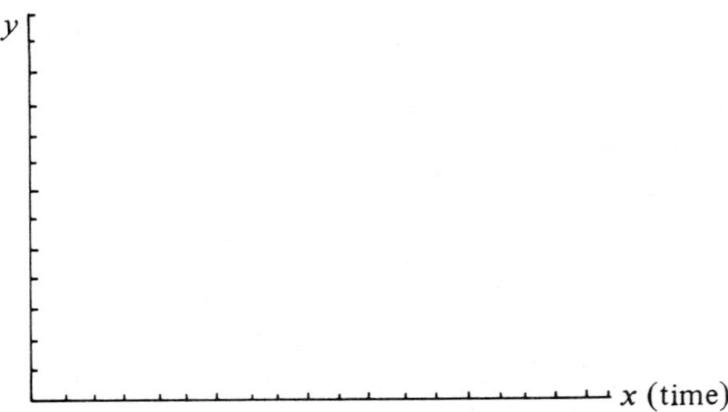

independent

narrow; correlation

average

independence

One problem generally encountered in practice is that the random error terms (denoted by ϵ_i) associated with the y_i's are often not ______________ between successive measurements. As a result, any probabilistic intervals which might be constructed around the expected process value will be too ______________. It is possible that an examination of the ______________ patterns present in the series will enable one to improve the accuracy of prediction and estimation. If the response is an ______________ over a period of time, serial correlation of the ϵ_i's will be reduced, and may enable us to assume the ______________ required by the method of least squares.

A great deal of ingenuity can be shown in the choice of predictors in a multivariate regression prediction model. For instance, if

x_1 = price of tea

x_2 = price of coffee

$x_3 = t$, the index of time

x_4 = price of cream

x_5 = price of cream substitutes

$$x_6 = x_1 x_2$$

$$x_7 = \sin\left(\frac{2\pi t}{12}\right)$$

we might predict the monthly demand for cream by the additive prediction model

$$y = \beta_0 + \beta_1 x_1 + \beta_2 x_2 + \ldots + \beta_7 x_7 + \epsilon$$

where x_6 takes into account an _______________ effect between tea and coffee prices, and x_7 allows for a cyclic effect in sales, with a period of one year (12 months). The term $\beta_3 x_3$ allows for a long-term growth trend which is (linear, curvilinear) over time.

interaction

linear

Another type of econometric forecasting model results from using transfer function analysis. In addition to having the features of regression analysis, this technique also allows for the inclusion of lagged variables such as y_{t-1} or x_{t-1}. Correlated errors cause no problems since the residuals in these equations can be modeled as moving average processes. Transfer function analysis is a powerful single equation forecasting technique that requires trained experienced analysts for implementation.

When the dependent variable influences the values of explanatory variables, known as *feedback*, the validity of single equation forecasting models becomes questionable. Multiple equation forecasting models must be used when feedback is present in the system to be modeled.

The general procedure most commonly employed in the development of a time series forecasting model is as follows:

1. Select a number of variables which are believed to be closely related to the process variable of interest.
2. Construct transformations of these variables in an attempt to model observed patterns of the response variable over time or interactions between predictors.
3. Estimate the parameters of the model by the method of _______________ _______________.
4. Test the model to see how well it fits the response measurements and how well it forecasts the future, using the methods of Section 14.2.
5. Revise the model by adding new variables as predictors and removing certain predictors currently in the model whenever it appears appropriate.

least squares

The method of least squares, as used in the estimation of the parameters in a regression model, requires, in a practical sense, the use of an electronic computer. The computations involved make hand calculations or the use of a desk calculator almost prohibitive.

Self-Correcting Exercises 14A

1. The Public Welfare Administrator for the state of Nevada claims that the number of people who will request funds each month in the next calendar

year under the state's Aid to Families of Dependent Children can be predicted by the equation

$$\hat{y}_t = 33.0 + 0.5t + 11.5 \cos\left(\frac{2\pi t}{12}\right)$$

where the $\hat{y}_t$ is computed in thousands of claimants and t is the monthly index; $t = 1$ (January), $t = 2$ (February), . . . , $t = 12$ (December). Use the administrator's forecast equation to forecast the number of claims under the Nevada AFDC program for each month of the next calendar year.

2. Based on the following sales data, the manager of a small grocery store claims that his gross monthly sales volume (in \$1000) can be forecast using the prediction equation

$$y_t = 10.29 + .13t$$

Month	*Sales*
Jan.	10.0
Feb.	10.6
Mar.	10.9
Apr.	10.8
May	11.1
June	11.3
July	11.0
Aug.	11.5
Sept.	11.6
Oct.	11.2
Nov.	11.7
Dec.	11.8

With $t = 1$ for January, . . . , $t = 12$ for December, use the suggested forecasting model to forecast the gross monthly sales volume. Compare the actual sales volumes with those predicted. Find MSE as a measure of forecast accuracy.

3. Refer to Exercise 2.
   a. Plot the sales volume data and notice the apparent quarterly fluctuation in the data.
   b. As an alternative to the forecasting model in Exercise 2, use least squares to fit the model

$$y_t = \beta_0 + \beta_1 x_1 + \beta_2 x_2 + \beta_3 x_3 + \beta_4 x_4 + \epsilon$$

where

$$x_1 = t$$

$x_2 = 1$ if Quarter 2
0 otherwise

x_3 = 1 if Quarter 3
0 otherwise

x_4 = 1 if Quarter 4
0 otherwise

c. Find the forecasts for January through December using the forecasting model in part b.
d. Using MSE as a measure of forecasting accuracy, how does this model compare with the model given in Exercise 2?

14.6 Moving Average Forecasting Models

In Chapter 13, the moving average was used to smooth a time series by averaging out the random fluctuations present in the series. When neither a marked trend nor a seasonal fluctuation is present in a time series, a moving average can be used to generate reliable short-term forecasts.

In using a moving average forecast of order M, the average of the last M available observations is used to forecast the next observation. A one-period ahead forecast with a moving average of order $M = 4$ is given by

$$\hat{y}_{t+1} = \frac{y_t + y_{t-1} + y_{t-2} + y_{t-3}}{4}$$

Moving average forecasts are appropriate only when the series exhibits no trends. Therefore, as in the naive no-change model, the moving average forecast for any number of periods ahead of available data is the one-period ahead forecast.

Moving Average Forecast of Order M

One-period ahead forecast:

$$\hat{y}_{t+1} = \frac{y_t + y_{t-1} + \ldots + y_{t-M+1}}{M}$$

Example 14.1

The data which follows represents the monthly sales revenues (in thousands of dollars) over two years for a local convenience market.

Month	*Year 1*	*Year 2*
January	21.2	23.1
February	19.1	20.9
March	21.0	19.6
April	18.9	22.3
May	17.0	20.1
June	22.8	23.5

July	24.3	25.2
August	23.7	24.1
September	20.9	23.0
October	23.3	26.2
November	25.7	25.6
December	26.2	27.5

a. Calculate the one month ahead forecasts for year 2 using a moving average of order 4.
b. Calculate the two-month ahead forecasts for year 2 using a moving average of order 4.
c. Compare the reliability of the forecasts generated in parts a and b, using MSE.

Solution

a. The one-month ahead forecasts are generated using

$$\hat{y}_{t+1} = \frac{y_t + y_{t-1} + y_{t-2} + y_{t-3}}{4}$$

For January of year 2, $t = 13$; therefore

$y_{10}; y_9$

$$\hat{y}_{13} = \frac{y_{12} + y_{11} + \underline{\qquad} + \underline{\qquad}}{4}$$

26.2; 25.7

$$= \frac{\underline{\qquad} + \underline{\qquad} + 23.3 + 20.9}{4}$$

96.1; 24.025

$$= \frac{\underline{\qquad}}{4} = \underline{\qquad}$$

The one-month ahead forecast for February ($t = 14$) is found to be

$$\hat{y}_{14} = \frac{y_{13} + y_{12} + y_{11} + y_{10}}{4}$$

26.2; 25.7

$$= \frac{23.1 + \underline{\qquad} + \underline{\qquad} + 23.3}{4}$$

98.3; 24.575

$$= \frac{\underline{\qquad}}{4} = \underline{\qquad}$$

Notice that

$$\hat{y}_{14} = \hat{y}_{13} + \left(\frac{23.1 - 20.9}{4}\right)$$

0.55; 24.575

$$= 24.025 + \underline{\qquad} = \underline{\qquad}$$

The remaining one-month ahead forecasts are given in the following table.

	Year 2		
t	*Month*	*Sales*	*One-month ahead forecast*
13	January	23.1	24.025
14	February	20.9	24.575
15	March	19.6	________
16	April	22.3	________
17	May	20.1	21.475
18	June	23.5	20.725
19	July	25.2	21.375
20	August	24.1	22.775
21	September	23.0	23.225
22	October	26.2	23.950
23	November	25.6	24.625
24	December	27.5	24.725

23.975

22.450

Since the two-month ahead forecasts using a moving average are the same as the one-month ahead forecasts, the calculated forecasts found in part a will also be used as the two-month ahead forecasts. Therefore, the two-month ahead forecast for January is the same as the one-month ahead forecast for December, or

$$\hat{y}_{13} = 23.4$$

These and the remaining two-month ahead forecasts for year 2 are given in the following table.

		Year 2		
t	*Month*	*Actual Sales*	*One-month*	*Two-month*
13	January	23.1	24.025	23.4
14	February	20.9	24.575	24.025
15	March	19.6	23.975	24.575
16	April	22.3	22.450	23.975
17	May	20.1	21.475	22.450
18	June	23.5	20.725	21.475
19	July	25.2	________	________
20	August	24.1	________	________
21	September	23.0	________	________
22	October	26.2	________	________
23	November	25.6	________	________
24	December	27.5	________	________

21.375; 20.725
22.775; 21.375
23.225; 22.775
23.950; 23.225
24.625; 23.950
24.725; 24.625

c. For the one-month ahead forecasts for year 2, $MAD = 24.65/12 =$ ________ while $MSE = SSE/12 =$ ________ $/12 =$ ________ ($\sqrt{MSE} = 2.47$). For the two-month ahead forecasts, $MAD = 29.3750/12 =$ ________ while $MSE = 94.3756/12 =$ ________ ($\sqrt{MSE} = 2.80$). Using either the *MAD* or *MSE* criterion, we see that the two-month ahead forecasts have a larger forecasting error than does the one-month ahead forecasts.

2.05
73.26625; 6.10
2.05
7.86

If a time series exhibits a pronounced positive or negative linear trend, applying a moving average forecast directly will produce misleading forecasts that underestimate the series values when linear growth is present and overestimate the series values when a linear decline is present. To see how this happens, consider a time series which can be modeled by the linear relationship

$$y_t = \alpha + \beta t + \epsilon_t$$

Using a moving average forecast of order $M = 5$ would predict the next value to be

$$\hat{y}_{t+1} = \frac{y_t + y_{t-1} + y_{t-2} + y_{t-3} + y_{t-4}}{5}$$

$$= \alpha + \beta (t - 2) + \bar{\epsilon}$$

which is the value of the series at the earlier period $t - 2$ plus an average residual $\bar{\epsilon}$.

A *first-order difference transformation* is a technique to filter out or remove a linear trend component in a time series. The first-order difference transformation produces a new series found by computing the differences between successive terms in a time series.

The First-Order Difference Transformation

The first-order differences are given by

$$\nabla y_t = y_t - y_{t-1}$$

for $t = 2, 3, 4, \ldots, n$. The time series formed by taking first differences is called the **series of first differences.** Notice that there is no difference corresponding to time period $t = 1$.

If $y_t = \alpha + \beta t + \epsilon_t$, then a first-difference would be given by

$$\nabla y_t = [\alpha + \beta t + \epsilon_t] - [\alpha + \beta(t - 1) + \epsilon_{t-1}] = \beta + (\epsilon_t - \epsilon_{t-1})$$

The new series of differences would behave as the constant β plus a random difference between two error terms. The first-order difference transformation has filtered out the linear trend which was present in the original series, and a moving average forecast can now be computed for the series of differences. If $\hat{\nabla} y_{t+1}$ is the moving average forecast for the difference at time $t + 1$, then $\hat{\nabla} y_{t+1}$ estimates $\nabla y_{t+1} = y_{t+1} - y_t$. Therefore we have

$$\hat{\nabla} y_{t+1} = \hat{y}_{t+1} - y_t$$

or equivalently,

$$\hat{y}_{t+1} = y_t + \hat{\nabla} y_{t+1}$$

where $\hat{y}_{t+1}$ is the forecast for the original series at time $t + 1$. We will clarify this procedure with the next example.

Example 14.2
The data which follows gives the sales revenues (in $10,000) for a new product during the first 12 months that the product was on the market.

Month t	*Sales*	∇y_t	*MA (5) Forecast of* ∇y_t	*Forecast of* y_t
1	25	–	–	–
2	31	6	–	–
3	34	3	–	–
4	42	8	–	–
5	46	4	–	–
6	50	4	–	–
7	53	3	5.0	55.0
8	59	6	4.4	57.4
9	66	7	5.0	64.0
10	71	5	4.8	70.8
11	77	6	5.0	76.0
12	81	4	5.4	82.4
13			5.6	86.6

a. Find a 5-period moving average forecast for the series of first differences from $t = 7$ to $t = 13$.
b. Using the results in part a, find the forecast for the original series, beginning with month $t = 7$.

Solution
a. The original series exhibits a marked linear growth trend during the first twelve months. Hence a moving average forecast using first-differences would be an appropriate forecasting technique. The differences between consecutive values of y_t are given in the preceding table. Therefore

$$\hat{\nabla} y_7 = \frac{\nabla y_6 + \nabla y_5 + \nabla y_4 + \nabla y_3 + \nabla y_2}{5}$$

$$= \frac{\_\_\_\_ + \_\_\_\_ + 8 + 3 + 6}{5} = \frac{\_\_\_\_}{5} = \_\_\_\_$$ 4; 4; 25; 5

Similarly,

5; 4.4 $$\hat{\nabla} y_8 = \frac{3+4+4+8+3}{\_\_\_\_\_\_} = \_\_\_\_\_\_$$

$$\vdots \qquad\qquad\qquad \vdots$$

3; 5.4 $$\hat{\nabla} y_{12} = \frac{6+5+7+6+\_\_\_}{5} = \_\_\_\_\_\_$$

$$\hat{\nabla} y_{13} = \frac{4+6+5+7+6}{5} = 5.6$$

b. To generate forecasts for the original series, we use the relationship

$$\hat{y}_{t+1} = y_t + \hat{\nabla} y_{t+1}$$

For month $t = 7$

$$\hat{y}_7 = y_6 + \hat{\nabla} y_7 = 50 + 5.0 = 55.0$$

In generating succeeding forecasts, we have

4.4; 57.4 $$\hat{y}_8 = 53 + \_\_\_\_\_\_ = \_\_\_\_\_\_$$

59; 64.0 $$\hat{y}_9 = \_\_\_\_\_\_ + 5.0 = \_\_\_\_\_\_$$

$$\vdots \qquad\qquad\qquad \vdots$$

77 $$\hat{y}_{12} = \_\_\_\_\_\_ + 5.4 = 82.4$$

86.6 $$\hat{y}_{13} = 81 + 5.6 = \_\_\_\_\_\_$$

The results of parts a and b are given with the original data. Notice that the forecasts are fairly accurate and reflect the linear growth trend present in the original series.

As we have seen, a first-order difference transformation will remove a linear trend in a time series. When quadratic or other nonlinear trend is present in a time series, a second-order difference transformation is useful in detrending the series. A second-order difference transformation, $\nabla^2 y_t$, produces a times series found by computing the successive differences of the first-order differences.

A Second-Order Difference Transformation

The second-order differences of a time series are given by

$$\begin{aligned}\nabla^2 y_t &= \nabla y_t - \nabla y_{t-1} \\ &= (y_t - y_{t-1}) - (y_{t-1} - y_{t-2})\end{aligned}$$

for $t = 2, 3, \ldots, n$.

In using a second-order difference transformation to detrend a time series, we proceed in three steps:

1. Compute the second differences of the values of the time series.
2. We use a moving average of order M to forecast the series of second differences, given by

$$\hat{\nabla}^2 y_t = \frac{\nabla^2 y_t + \nabla^2 y_{t-1} + \ldots + \nabla^2 y_{t-M+1}}{M}$$

3. Forecasts for the original series $\hat{y}_t$ are developed using

$$\hat{\nabla}^2 y_{t+1} = (\hat{y}_{t+1} - y_t) - (y_t - y_{t-1})$$

   which can be expressed as

$$\hat{y}_{t+1} = y_t + \nabla y_t + \hat{\nabla}^2 y_{t+1}$$

   or equivalently as

$$\hat{y}_{t+1} = 2y_t - y_{t-1} + \hat{\nabla}^2 y_{t+1}$$

We shall illustrate this procedure with the next example.

Example 14.3

Refer to Example 14.2. Sales of acceptable new products tend to exhibit a linear or exponential growth trend during the initial period of introduction, and then to stabilize somewhat as the market nears saturation. Suppose that the sales revenues for this new product over the next six months are as follows:

t	13	14	15	16	17	18
Sales	89	94	98	101	102	105

Beginning with month $t = 8$,

a. Find the second differences of the series.
b. Use a 3-month moving average to generate forecasts of the original series values based on the second-difference estimates.

Solution

a. The first and second differences are given in the table which follows.

Month t	*Sales*	∇y_t	$\nabla^2 y_t$	$\hat{\nabla}^2 y_t$	$\hat{y}_t$
8	59	–	–	–	–
9	66	7	–	–	–
10	71	5	-2	–	–
11	77	8	3	–	–
12	81	4	-4	–	–
13	89	8	4	-1	84.00
14	94	5	-3	1	98.00
15	97	3	-2	-1	98.00
16	101	4	1	-0.33	99.67
17	102	1	-2	-1.33	103.67
18	105	3	2	-1	102.00
19				.33	108.33

Notice that no second-differences are available for $t = 8$ or $t = 9$ when considering only the data for months $t = 8$ through $t = 18$.

A plot of the actual values of y_t exhibits a damped linear trend; a plot of the first differences exhibits a slight negative trend; while a plot of second differences appears as deviations about the line $\nabla^2 y_t = 0$. Therefore the second difference transformation seems appropriate for these data.

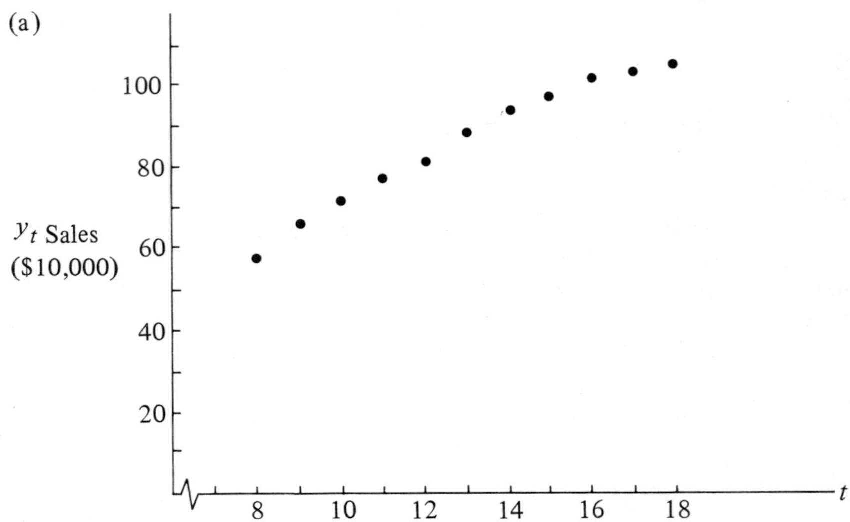

(b)

(c)

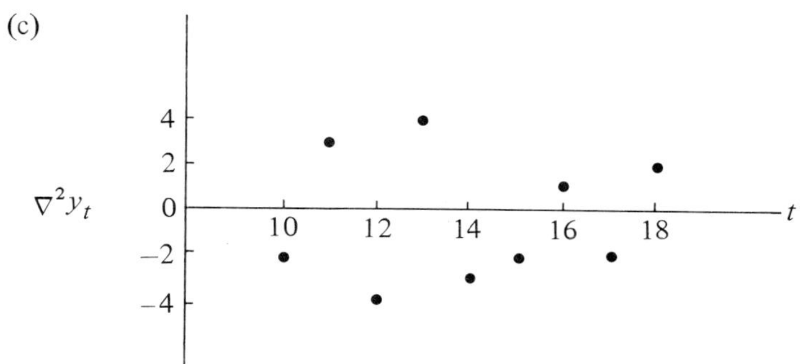

Plots of (a) the original series y_t, (b) the first-order differences ∇y_t, and (c) the second-order differences $\nabla^2 y_t$.

b. To compute forecasts for the original series, we must first calculate the 3-month moving average forecasts for the series of second differences. With $M = 3$,

$$\hat{\nabla}^2 y_{t+1} = \frac{\nabla^2 y_t + \nabla^2 y_{t-1} + \nabla^2 y_{t-2}}{3}$$

Beginning with period 13,

$$\hat{\nabla}^2 y_{13} = \frac{(-2) + 3 + (-4)}{3} = -1.0$$

$$\hat{\nabla}^2 y_{14} = \frac{3 + (\_\_) + 4}{3} = \_\_\_\_\_\_$$

-4; 1.0

$$\vdots \qquad\qquad \vdots$$

$$\hat{\nabla}^2 y_{19} = \frac{\_\_ + (\_\_) + 2}{3} = \_\_\_\_\_\_$$

1; -2; .33

The second difference forecasts appear in the fifth column of the preceding table.

Forecasts for the original series y_t are found using either

$$\hat{y}_{t+1} = y_t + \nabla y_t + \hat{\nabla}^2 y_{t+1}$$

or

$$\hat{y}_{t+1} = 2y_t - y_{t-1} + \hat{\nabla}^2 y_{t+1}$$

Using the first expression,

∇y_{12} $$\hat{y}_{13} = y_{12} + \_\_\_\_\_\_\_\_ + \hat{\nabla}^2 y_{13}$$

4; 84.00 $$= 81 + \_\_\_\_\_\_\_\_ + (-1) = \_\_\_\_\_\_\_\_$$

and

$$\hat{y}_{14} = \_\_\_\_\_\_\_\_ + \nabla y_{13} + \hat{\nabla}^2 y_{14}$$

y_{13}

89; 98.00 $$= \_\_\_\_\_\_\_\_ + 8 + 1 = \_\_\_\_\_\_\_\_$$

Continuing in this manner, we find the one-month ahead forecast for $t = 19$ to be

$\hat{\nabla}^2 y_{19}$ $$\hat{y}_{19} = y_{18} + \nabla y_{18} + \_\_\_\_\_\_\_\_$$

0.33; 108.33 $$= 105 + 3 + \_\_\_\_\_\_\_\_ = \_\_\_\_\_\_\_\_$$

The resulting forecasts are given in column six of the preceding table.

Self-Correcting Exercises 14B

1. Under what conditions is a simple moving average forecast appropriate?
2. How do simple moving average forecasts compare to the actual series values if a positive linear trend is present in the original series?
3. What is the effect of using a first-order difference transformation on a time series? When is it appropriate to use this transformation?
4. When is it appropriate to use a second-order difference transformation? How can one assess the effectiveness of a second-order difference transformation in removing a trend from a time series?
5. The sales revenues (in thousands of dollars) of a local hardware store for the first six months of the year are given as follows:

Month	Jan	Feb	Mar	Apr	May	June
Sales	15.2	14.1	13.6	14.1	15.1	14.6

a. Find the one-month ahead forecast for July revenues using a three-month moving average.
b. Find the two-month ahead forecast for August revenues using a three-month moving average.

6. The gold reserves of the United States in millions of Troy ounces for an eight year period follow.

Year	*Reserves*
1	274.7
2	277.6
3	276.4
4	264.6
5	264.3
6	264.1
7	264.0
8	263.4

a. Plot the gold reserves against time. Does there appear to be a significant trend in the data?
b. Use a 3-period moving average to find a one-period ahead forecast for the years 5 to 9.
c. Find a one-period ahead forecast for the years 5 to 9 using a 3-period moving average on the series of first-differences.
d. Using MAD as the criteria, compare the accuracy of the year 5-9 forecasts in parts b and c.

7. The following data are the budget receipts (in trillions of dollars) of the United States government from 1970 through 1983.

Year	*Receipts*
1970	196
1971	192
1972	210
1973	238
1974	269
1975	294
1976	303
1977	358
1978	400
1979	460
1980	520
1981	602
1982	618
1983	601

a. Plot the budget receipts against time. Is there an apparent trend in the data? Would you suggest using a first- or second-order difference transformation to detrend this series?

b. Calculate the first and second differences of the time series, and plot ∇y_t and $\nabla^2 y_t$ against time. Has either transformation effectively detrended the series?

c. Find the one-year ahead forecasts for the years 1980–1984 using a 4-period moving average of first differences.

d. Find the one-year ahead forecasts for the years 1980–1984 using a 4-period moving average of the second differences.

e. Using the MAD of the forecasts for 1980–1983 to compare the forecasts in parts c and d.

14.7 An Exponential-smoothing Forecasting Model

smoothing
random variation
time
forecasts; future
exponential-smoothing

In Chapter 13, we explored ____________ methods which are used in an attempt to average out the effect of ____________ ____________ in a ____________ series. Now we consider the direct use of smoothing methods to compute ____________ of ____________ process values.

We specifically consider Brown's ____________ ____________ forecasting model, which uses observations from a time series, $y_1, y_2, \ldots, y_t$ to compute a forecast of the time series process value y_{t+T}, that is, ________ time periods ahead of the available data. Brown's method gives a convenient way of expressing this forecast in terms of easily computable ____________ ____________ statistics.

T

exponentially smoothed
first

1. If the time series appears constant over time, we would use a ____________-order exponential-smoothing forecasting model given by

S_t; $1 - \alpha$

$$\hat{y}_{t+T} = \text{\_\_\_\_\_\_\_\_} = \alpha y_t + (\text{\_\_\_\_\_\_\_\_})\, S_{t-1}$$

That is, if the time series appears constant over time, the forecast is equal to the ____________ statistic, __________.

smoothed; S_t
linear

2. If the time series is ____________ over time, we would employ a second-order exponential-smoothing forecasting model given by

$2 + \dfrac{\alpha T}{(1-\alpha)}$; $1 + \dfrac{\alpha T}{(1-\alpha)}$

$$\hat{y}_{t+T} = (\text{\_\_\_\_\_\_\_\_})\, S_t - (\text{\_\_\_\_\_\_\_\_})\, S_t(2)$$

double

where $S_t(2)$ is called the ____________-smoothed statistic and is found by computing

S_t; $S_{t-1}(2)$

$$S_t(2) = \alpha\ \text{\_\_\_\_\_\_\_\_} + (1 - \alpha)\ \text{\_\_\_\_\_\_\_\_}$$

S_t
trend
constant; linear

This statistic is a smoothing of the smoothed values, __________, and gives an indication of the ____________ changes over time.

3. If the time series is neither ____________ nor ____________ with time, we would use a third-order exponential-smoothing forecasting model given by

$$\hat{y}_{t+T} = [6(1-\alpha)^2 + (6-5\alpha)\alpha T + \alpha^2 T^2] \frac{(\_\_\_\_\_\_)}{2(1-\alpha)^2}$$

$$- [6(1-\alpha)^2 + 2(5-4\alpha)\alpha T + 2\alpha^2 T^2] \frac{(\_\_\_\_\_\_)}{2(1-\alpha)^2}$$

$$+ [2(1-\alpha)^2 + (4-3\alpha)\alpha T + \alpha^2 T^2] \frac{(\_\_\_\_\_\_)}{2(1-\alpha)^2}$$

S_t

$S_t(2)$

$S_t(3)$

The statistic $S_t(3)$ is called the ______________-smoothed statistic and measures the average rate of change of the trend over time. $S_t(3)$ is found by computing

triple

$$S_t(3) = \alpha \_\_\_\_\_\_\_\_\_\_ + (1-\alpha) \_\_\_\_\_\_\_\_\_\_$$

$S_t(2)$; $S_{t-1}(3)$

Thus, Brown's method provides a means by which forecasts can be computed based upon the three ______________ ______________ S_t, $S_t(2)$, and $S_t(3)$. The advantage of Brown's method is that it is a ______________ scheme developing a new, updated forecast model each time new ________ ________ become available. Updating of least-squares models each time new data become available is often too costly and, hence, becomes prohibitive.

smoothed statistics
recursive
process
data

The primary disadvantage of Brown's method is that it may tend to ______________ ______________ certain cycles or seasonal patterns within the process. Since the model is computed as a function of the smoothed statistics, these statistics tend to consider any departure of the process values from a constant or linear trend as ______________ ______________ in the time series. Thus, Brown's method should not be used to generate forecasts for a process in which a distinct ______________ or ____________ pattern exists.

smooth out

random variation

cyclic; seasonal

The forecast model is initiated by setting the smoothed statistics S_t, $S_t(2)$ and $S_t(3)$ all equal to __________, the ______________ observation. The ______________ ______________, α, is then selected as a function of the apparent volatility of random variation within the process. If the process appears quite volatile, α is given a (large, small) value; if the process is rather stable, a (larger, smaller) value for α is selected. But in any case, the selection of the smoothing constant is ______________, and the statistician must use his judgment in choosing α. One chooses the ______________ of the model according to whether or not the time series is ____________ or ______________ over time. One chooses __________, the forecast lead time, according to the number of time points ahead one is attempting to ______________. Care should be taken when attempting to forecast more than __________ time period(s) ahead. The values of T and α are substituted into the model of the appropriate order and the forecasting equation is computed as a function of the smoothed statistics S_t, $S_t(2)$ and $S_t(3)$.

y_1; first
smoothing constant

small
larger
arbitrary
order
constant
linear; T

forecast
one

updated

The smoothed statistics are ______________ with each subsequent observation, and then entered into the forecasting equation to obtain the forecast for the next time period.

Example 14.4

The following data represent the daily high temperature in Fahrenheit degrees recorded at O'Hare Field in Chicago for 15 consecutive days during the month of February. Use Brown's method to forecast the daily high temperatures one day ahead of available data over this period ($T = 1$) and then compare the forecasts with the actual, observed temperatures. Temperature, y_t: 19.0, 24.5, 20.5, 25.0, 24.8, 30.1, 38.5, 33.0, 29.8, 27.0, 32.7, 42.5, 44.0, 48.2, 46.0.

Solution

A plot of the temperature values against time would show that the relationship is nearly linear over small segments of time. Thus, an appropriate forecasting model for this process

$$\hat{y}_{t+T} = \left(2 + \frac{\alpha T}{(1-\alpha)}\right) S_t - \left(1 + \frac{\alpha T}{(1-\alpha)}\right) S_t(2)$$

Suppose, for the sake of discussion, that we let $\alpha = .1$. Then, since $T = 1$, the forecast equation becomes

2.11; 1.11

$$\hat{y}_{t+1} = \_\_\_\_\_\_\_\_ S_t - \_\_\_\_\_\_\_\_ S_t(2)$$

For the time period $t = 1$, the smoothing statistics S_t and $S_t(2)$ are

19.0

set equal to the first process value, __________. Thereafter, they are computed from the recursive equations

$$S_t = \alpha y_t + (1-\alpha) S_{t-1}$$

and

$$S_t(2) = \alpha S_t + (1-\alpha) S_{t-1}(2)$$

At the second time period ($t = 2$),

$$S_2 = (.1)(24.5) + (1 - .1)(19.0)$$

$$= 19.55$$

and

19.55; 19.0

$$S_2(2) = (.1)(\_\_\_\_\_\_\_\_) + (1 - .1)(\_\_\_\_\_\_\_\_)$$

19.06

$$= \_\_\_\_\_\_\_\_$$

Compute the smoothed statistics S_t and $S_t(2)$ for the remaining 13 time periods and place them in the table below.

Day	*Temperature*			
t	y_t	S_t	$S_t(2)$	
1	19.0	19.0	19.0	
2	24.5	19.55	19.06	
3	20.5	_____	_____	19.65; 19.12
4	25.0	_____	_____	20.19; 19.23
5	24.8	_____	_____	20.65; 19.37
6	30.1	_____	_____	21.60; 19.59
7	38.5	_____	_____	23.29; 19.96
8	33.0	_____	_____	24.26; 20.39
9	29.8	_____	_____	24.81; 20.83
10	27.0	_____	_____	25.03; 21.25
11	32.7	_____	_____	25.80; 21.70
12	42.5	_____	_____	27.47; 22.28
13	44.0	_____	_____	29.12; 22.96
14	48.2	_____	_____	31.03; 23.77
15	46.0	_____	_____	32.53; 24.65

Forecasts may now be computed directly by substituting into the forecasting equation. Computing the forecast for time $t = 2$ using the data available from time $t = 1$, we have

$$\hat{y}_2 = \_\_\_\_\_(19.0) - \_\_\_\_\_(19.0)$$ 2.11; 1.11

$$= \_\_\_\_\_$$ 19.0

Using data through $t = 2$ to forecast the temperature at $t = 3$,

$$\hat{y}_3 = 2.11\ (19.55) - 1.11\ (\_\_\_\_\_)$$ 19.06

$$= \_\_\_\_\_$$ 20.09

Use the forecast equation and the smoothed statistics to compute the remaining forecasts for periods $t = 4$ through $t = 15$.

Day t	*Actual Temperature* y_t	*Forecast Temperature* $\hat{y}_t$	
1	19.0		
2	24.5	19.00	
3	20.5	20.09	
4	25.0	_____	20.24
5	24.8	_____	21.26
6	30.1	_____	22.07
7	38.5	_____	23.83
8	33.0	_____	26.99

28.56
29.23
29.23
30.35
33.23
35.96
39.09

Day t	Actual Temperature y_t	Forecast Temperature $\hat{y}_t$
9	29.8	________
10	27.0	________
11	32.7	________
12	42.5	________
13	44.0	________
14	48.2	________
15	46.0	________

Example 14.5

The forecasts which were computed in Example 14.4 do not appear to be very accurate. Thus, if Brown's method is an appropriate device to use to generate forecasts for this process, either—

larger
third

1. we should have used a ______________ smoothing constant, or
2. we should have used the ______________-order exponential-smoothing forecasting model. Use such a model with a smoothing constant of 0.2 to forecast the temperature data from Example 14.4 one period ahead of available data.

Solution

The model we have chosen to use is

$$\hat{y}_{t+T} = [6(1-\alpha)^2 + (6-5\alpha)\alpha T + \alpha^2 T^2]\,\frac{S_t}{2(1-\alpha)^2}$$

$$-\,[6(1-\alpha)^2 + 2(5-4\alpha)\alpha T + 2\alpha^2 T^2]\,\frac{S_t(2)}{2(1-\alpha)^2}$$

$$+\,[2(1-\alpha)^2 + (4-3\alpha)\alpha T + \alpha^2 T^2]\,\frac{S_t(3)}{2(1-\alpha)^2}$$

Since $\alpha = .2$ and $T = 1$, the coefficients of the model give us the forecasting equation

3.813; 4.375: 1.563

$$\hat{y}_{t+1} = \_\_\_\_\_\_\_\_ S_t - \_\_\_\_\_\_\_\_ S_t(2) + \_\_\_\_\_\_\_\_ S_t(3)$$

smoothed statistics
recursively
19.0

In order to forecast the process values, we must first compute the values for the ______________ ______________ $S_t, S_t(2)$, and $S_t(3)$. These statistics are computed ______________ by first setting S_1, $S_1(2)$, and $S_1(3)$ equal to __________ and then employing the smoothing equations

$$S_t = \alpha y_t + (1-\alpha)S_{t-1}$$

$$S_t(2) = \alpha S_t + (1-\alpha)S_{t-1}(2)$$

and

$$S_t(3) = \alpha S_t(2) + (1 - \alpha)S_{t-1}(3)$$

Since $\alpha = .2$, at the second time period ($t = 2$), the smoothed statistics are

$S_2 \quad = (.2)$ (________) + (1 - .2) (________) — 24.5; 19.0

= ________ — 20.10

$S_2(2) = (.2)$ (________) + (1 - .2) (________) — 20.10; 19.0

= ________ — 19.22

and

$S_2(3) = (.2)$ (________) + (1 - .2) (________) — 19.22; 19.0

= ________ — 19.04

Compute the remaining 13 values for each of the smoothed statistics and enter them in the table below.

t	S_t	$S_t(2)$	$S_t(3)$	
1	19.0	19.0	19.0	
2	20.10	19.22	19.04	
3	________	________	________	20.18; 19.41; 19.11
4	________	________	________	21.14; 19.76; 19.24
5	________	________	________	21.87; 20.18; 19.43
6	________	________	________	23.52; 20.85; 19.71
7	________	________	________	26.52; 21.98; 20.16
8	________	________	________	27.82; 23.15; 20.76
9	________	________	________	28.22; 24.16; 21.44
10	________	________	________	27.98; 24.92; 22.14
11	________	________	________	28.92; 25.72; 22.86
12	________	________	________	31.64; 26.90; 23.67
13	________	________	________	34.11; 28.34; 24.60
14	________	________	________	36.93; 30.06; 25.69
15	________	________	________	38.74; 31.80; 26.91

Forecasts one period ahead of available data can now be generated by substituting the smoothed statistics computed above into the forecasting equation

$$\hat{y}_{t+1} = 3.813S_t - 4.375S_t(2) + 1.563S_t(3)$$

Thus, at $t = 1$, our forecast for the second period is

$$\hat{y}_2 = 3.813(19) - 4.375(19) + 1.563(19)$$

$$= 19.0$$

At time $t = 2$, our forecast for the third period is

20.10; 19.22; 19.04

$$\hat{y}_3 = 3.813\ (\_\_\_\_\_\_) - 4.375\ (\_\_\_\_\_\_) + 1.563\ (\_\_\_\_\_\_)$$

22.31

$$= \_\_\_\_\_\_$$

Compute the one period ahead of available data forecasts for time periods 4 through 15 and list them below.

21.90
24.23
25.47
29.27
36.47
37.24
35.41
32.27
33.48
39.95
44.52
49.46

t	y_t	$\hat{y}_t$
1	19.0	
2	24.5	19.0
3	20.5	22.31
4	25.0	______
5	24.8	______
6	30.1	______
7	38.5	______
8	33.0	______
9	29.8	______
10	27.0	______
11	32.7	______
12	42.5	______
13	44.0	______
14	48.2	______
15	46.0	______

Plot the actual values against the forecast values for the process on the graph below. Note the improved accuracy over the method of Example 14.4.

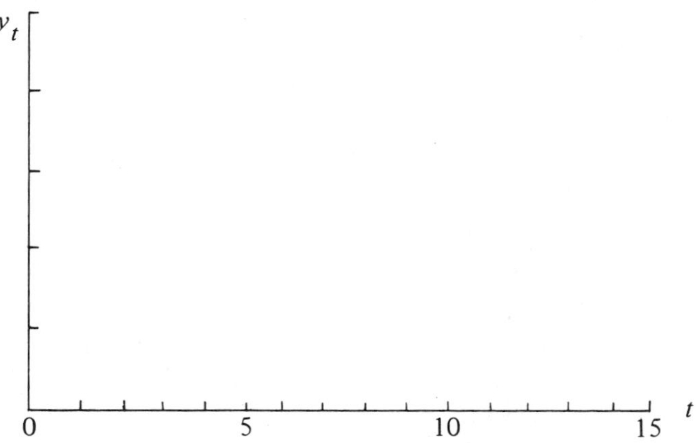

turning

over

true; forecast

The multiple exponential-smoothing model can be used as a tracking model to discover ________ points in a time series. According to this interpretation, a time series has bottomed out when the true values cut (under, over) the smoothing forecasts. A process has peaked out when the ________ values cut under the ________ values.

From the plot in Example 14.5, the temperature time series peaked out on the ______, ______ and ______ days. Similarly, the time series bottomed out on the __________ and __________ days.

2nd; 7th; 14th
3rd; 10th

If the reader has access to a computer or a computer facility, he may wish to use a program to forecast using the multiple exponential-smoothing model. One such program is given in the Appendix to this study guide.

14.8 The Exponentially Weighted Moving-Average Forecasting Model

An exponential-smoothing forecasting model is inappropriate to use when the process values follow a ______________ or ______________ pattern over time. The exponentially weighted moving average (EWMA) model is quite often very effective for generating forecasts for a process with a definite ______________ effect.

cyclic; seasonal

seasonal

The difference between a cyclic effect and a seasonal effect is that the seasonal effect is recurrent and ______________ and, hence, predictable. The EWMA attempts to take advantage of this predictability by separately estimating at each point in time (1) a smoothed process ______________, (2) the trend ______________, and (3) the ______________ ______________. The model then combines these three statistics in a unique fashion to compute a forecast of a future process value. Like the exponential-smoothing forecasting model, the EWMA is a recursive scheme and is therefore efficient in that each forecast is based upon ______________ available past process information. The three components of the EWMA model are:

periodic

average
gain; seasonal factors

all

1. The smoothed process ______________ at time t:

average

$$S_t = (\alpha)y_t/F_{t-L} + (\_\_\_\_\_\_\_\_\_\_)(S_{t-1} + R_{t-1})$$

$1 - \alpha$

2. The ______________ gain at time t:

trend

$$R_t = (\beta)(S_t - S_{t-1}) + (\_\_\_\_\_\_\_\_\_\_)R_{t-1}$$

$1 - \beta$

3. The updated ______________ factor at time t:

seasonal

$$F_t = (\gamma)y_t/S_t + (\_\_\_\_\_\_\_\_\_\_)F_{t-L}$$

$1 - \gamma$

The constants α, β, and γ are arbitrarily selected ______________ constants having values between __________ and __________. Usually, the process generates accurate forecasts when α and β are near __________ and γ is near __________. The index L in the seasonal factor F_{t-L} is the __________ of the seasonal effect (the number of time periods required for the process to complete one seasonal pattern). If the process under study represented the monthly sales pattern of a department store, L would equal __________, the number of months before the seasonal pattern would again repeat itself.

smoothing
zero; one
.1
.4; period

12

The EWMA develops a model by asking the following questions:

1. What is the average value of the process at time t?
2. What is the best estimate of the gain in the average trend over the forecast period?
3. What is the multiplicative relationship between the process average and the actual process value during the forecast period?

All these questions can be answered by the above described components.

S_t

R_t

1. ________ is the average value of the process at time t.
2. ________ is the best estimate of the gain in average trend per unit of time based on all available process information. Thus, if we are forecasting T time periods ahead, the best estimate of the gain in average trend over these T time periods is ________.

$(T)R_t$

F_{t-L+T}

3. The multiplicative relationship between the process average and the process value at time $t + T$ is ________, the multiplicative relationship computed during the last seasonal period.

Thus, consistent with a rather logical development, the EWMA forecast model to forecast the value of a process T time periods ahead of available data is

$$\hat{y}_{t+T} = [S_t + (T)R_t]\,F_{t-L+T}$$

L

Initial values are needed for S and R so that S_t and R_t can be computed at time $t = 1$. Also, a total of ________ initial values are needed for the seasonal factors, F_t; one is computed for each partition (day, week, month, etc.) of the complete seasonal period.

two

It is usually best to derive these initial estimates from part of the process data available from past information. Hopefully, one has at least ________ complete periods of seasonal data from which to compute these estimates. A method for determining the original estimates was discussed in detail in Example 14.4 in the text. In this case, two complete periods of sample data from the past were used. Then,

slope

trend

L

trend

1. S_0, the original estimate for S was the first process value from the sample;
2. R_0, the original value for R was selected as the ________ of the linear ________ line fitted to the sample data;
3. the ________ seasonal factors were computed by taking the ratio, at each point in the first seasonal period, of the process value to the corresponding value at that point in time on the ________ line fitted to the data.

Reference to Example 14.4 should make these points more clear.

initial

After the original estimates are developed, these values are then smoothed over the available sample data by use of the above smoothing equations for S_t, R_t, and F_t. The last values computed from the sample data for S, R, and the L-values of F are then used as the ________ estimates for the forecast period.

The EWMA model is useful only when the time series is seasonal and has a predictable period. Furthermore, the peaks and valleys of each seasonal pattern must always occur at the same partitions through the seasonal pattern.

Example 14.6
The data which appear below represent the monthly sales (in thousands of dollars) of a state liquor store in Eugene, Oregon. Use the EWMA forecasting method to forecast these sales figures one period ahead of available data. Let $\alpha = .1$, $\beta = .1$, and $\gamma = .4$.

Month	*Year 1*	*Year 2*
Jan.	15.07	16.91
Feb.	15.86	17.08
Mar.	20.24	20.63
Apr.	18.33	18.64
May	19.87	21.15
June	20.93	20.43
July	17.16	18.67
Aug.	18.93	20.42
Sept.	18.80	19.40
Oct.	22.58	23.83
Nov.	25.35	26.71
Dec.	28.32	29.83

Solution
Suppose that based upon preliminary sales data, initial estimates have been obtained for S_0, R_0, and the 12 initial values of the seasonal factor, F. These values are as follows:

$$S_0 = 17.53, \qquad R_0 = 0.05$$

and

$$F_{\text{Jan.}} = 0.89 \qquad F_{\text{Feb.}} = 0.93 \qquad F_{\text{Mar.}} = 1.10 \qquad F_{\text{Apr.}} = 1.03$$

$$F_{\text{May}} = 1.10 \qquad F_{\text{June}} = 1.09 \qquad F_{\text{July}} = 0.98 \qquad F_{\text{Aug.}} = 1.04$$

$$F_{\text{Sept.}} = 1.04 \qquad F_{\text{Oct.}} = 1.25 \qquad F_{\text{Nov.}} = 1.35 \qquad F_{\text{Dec.}} = 1.56$$

Suppose we arbitrarily label the months beginning with January of Year 1 and ending with December of Year 2, $t = 1, 2, 3, \ldots, 24$. Our forecast for $t = 1$ based on the initial estimates is then

$$\hat{y}_1 = (S_0 + R_0)F_{\text{Jan.}}$$

$= \_\_\_\_\_\_\_\_$ (17.53 + 0.05)(0.89)

$= \_\_\_\_\_\_\_\_$ 15.65

15.07 which compares to the actual January sales figure of ________. To find further forecasts, we must first find the smoothed estimates for the values of S_t, R_t, and F_{t-L}. Let us compute the forecast of sales for February of Year 1 ($t = 2$), based on available sales data through January of Year 1 ($t = 1$).

The smoothed process average at time $t = 1$ is

$$S_1 = (.1)\frac{y_1}{F_{\text{Jan.}}} + (1 - .1)(S_0 + R_0)$$

$$= (.1)\frac{15.07}{0.89} + (.9)(17.53 + 0.05)$$

$$= 17.52$$

The trend gain at time $t = 1$ is

$$R_1 = (.1)(S_1 - S_0) + (1 - .1)R_0$$

$$= (.1)(17.52 - 17.53) + (.9)(0.05)$$

$$= 0.044$$

The updated seasonal factor to use during the next January is

$$F_1 = (.4)\frac{y_1}{S_1} + (1 - .4)F_{\text{Jan.}}$$

$$= (.4)\frac{(15.07)}{17.52} + (.6)(0.89)$$

$$= 0.88$$

The forecast of sales for February of the first year ($t = 2$) is then

$$\hat{y}_2 = (S_1 + R_1)F_{\text{Feb.}}$$

$$= (17.52 + 0.044)(0.93)$$

$$= 16.33$$

which compares to the actual value of $y_2 = 15.86$.

To find $\hat{y}_3$ based upon sales data through $t = 2$, we need values for S_2 and R_2. They are obtained as follows:

$$S_2 = (.1)\frac{y_2}{F_{\text{Feb.}}} + (.9)(S_1 + R_1)$$

$= (.1)\dfrac{(\_\_\_\_\_\_\_\_)}{(0.93)} + (.9)(\_\_\_\_\_\_\_\_ + \_\_\_\_\_\_\_\_)$ 15.86; 17.52; 0.044

$= \_\_\_\_\_\_\_\_$ 17.51

and

$R_2 = (.1)(S_2 - S_1) + (.9)R_1$

$= (.1)(\_\_\_\_\_\_\_\_ - \_\_\_\_\_\_\_\_) + (.9)(\_\_\_\_\_\_\_\_)$ 17.51; 17.52; 0.044

$= \_\_\_\_\_\_\_\_$ 0.039

The forecast of sales for time period $t = 3$ is then

$\hat{y}_3 = (S_2 + R_2)F_{\text{Mar.}}$

$= (\_\_\_\_\_\_\_\_ + \_\_\_\_\_\_\_\_)(\_\_\_\_\_\_\_\_)$ 17.51; 0.039; 1.10

$= \_\_\_\_\_\_\_\_$ 19.30

which compares to the true sales at $t = 3$ of $y_3 = 20.24$. For each of the remaining time periods, $t = 4$ through $t = 24$, compute the smoothed process average S_t, the trend gain R_t, and the seasonal factor, F_t. Then use the EWMA forecasting method to find the estimate of sales in period $t + 1$ based on sales data through period t. List the values in the table below.

t	S_t	R_t	F_t	$\hat{y}_t$	y_t
1	17.52	0.044	0.88	15.65	15.07
2	17.51	0.039	0.92	16.33	15.86
3				19.30	20.24
4					18.33
5					19.87
6					20.93
7					17.16
8					18.93
9					18.80
10					22.58
11					25.35
12					28.32
13					16.91
14					17.08
15					20.63
16					18.64
17					21.15
18					20.43
19					18.67
20					20.42
21					19.40
22					23.83
23					26.71
24					29.83

If the reader has access to a computer or a computer facility, he may wish to use a program to forecast using the EWMA method. One such program, for monthly forecasting, is given in the Appendix to this study guide.

The correct values are given in the table which follows.

t	S_t	R_t	F_t	$\hat{y}_t$	y_t
1	17.52	0.044	0.88	15.65	15.07
2	17.51	0.039	0.92	16.33	15.86
3	17.63	0.047	1.12	19.30	20.24
4	17.69	0.048	1.03	18.21	18.33
5	17.77	0.051	1.11	19.51	19.87
6	17.96	0.065	1.12	19.42	20.93
7	17.97	0.060	0.97	17.66	17.16
8	18.05	0.062	1.04	18.75	18.93
9	18.11	0.062	1.04	18.84	18.80
10	18.16	0.061	1.25	22.72	22.58
11	18.28	0.067	1.36	24.60	25.35
12	18.33	0.065	1.55	28.62	28.32
13	18.48	0.074	0.89	16.19	16.91
14	18.56	0.075	0.92	17.07	17.08
15	18.61	0.073	1.12	20.87	20.63
16	18.62	0.067	1.02	19.24	18.64
17	18.72	0.070	1.12	20.74	21.15
18	18.74	0.065	1.11	21.04	20.43
19	18.85	0.070	0.98	18.24	18.67
20	18.99	0.077	1.05	19.68	20.42
21	19.03	0.073	1.03	19.83	19.40
22	19.10	0.073	1.25	23.88	23.83
23	19.22	0.078	1.37	26.08	26.71
24	19.29	0.077	1.55	29.91	29.83

Self-Correcting Exercises 14C

1. Consider the following sales data, and assume that the data for the year given are linear over time.

Month	*Sales*
January	10.0
February	10.6
March	10.9
April	10.8
May	11.1
June	11.3
July	11.0
August	11.5
September	11.6
October	11.2
November	11.7
December	11.5

Use a first-order multiple exponential smoothing (Brown's method) forecasting model to forecast the sales volume one month ahead of available information. Let $\alpha = .1$.

2. Refer to the data given in Self-Correcting Exercises 13A. Since the sales volume for the liquor store appears to be quite seasonal, use the exponentially weighted moving-average model to forecast the monthly sales volume of the liquor store one month ahead of available sales data. Based upon earlier sales data, initial values for the process average and trend gain are $S_0 = 18.0$ and $R_0 = 0.2$, respectively, while initial values for the seasonal indices are:

Jan.	.53	May	.92	Sept.	1.12
Feb.	.61	June	1.11	Oct.	1.16
Mar.	.89	July	1.02	Nov.	1.30
Apr.	.72	Aug.	.90	Dec.	1.66

Let the smoothing constants be $\alpha = .1$, $\beta = .1$, $\gamma = 0.4$.

14.9 The Box-Jenkins Forecasting Procedure

When patterns in a time series are very complex or difficult to discern, the Box-Jenkins forecasting methodology can be a useful and efficient technique. **Autoregressive integrated moving average (ARIMA) models** are a class of time series models of the form

$$y_t = \phi_1 y_{t-1} + \phi_2 y_{t-2} + \ldots + \phi_p y_{t-p} + \epsilon_t - \theta_1 \epsilon_{t-1} - \ldots - \theta_q \epsilon_{t-q}$$

where $\phi_1, \phi_2, \ldots, \phi_p$ are the autoregressive parameters in the model, while $\theta_1, \theta_2, \ldots, \theta_q$ are the moving average parameters of the model. The past q error terms in the model are given by $\epsilon_t, \epsilon_{t-1}, \ldots \epsilon_{t-q}$.

1. The autoregressive component is a linear combination of the lagged values $y_{t-1}, \ldots, y_{t-p}$.
2. The moving average component is a linear combination of current and past error terms.

Before fitting an ARIMA model to a set of time series data, we must first remove any trends in the data by using differencing. If a linear trend is present, a difference of order $d = 1$ is used. If the data exhibit a quadratic trend, then a difference of order $d = 2$ is used. When the series is detrended, the number of autoregressive terms, denoted by p, and the number of moving average terms, denoted by q, must be selected. The resulting model is referred to as an ARIMA (p, d, q) model.

One aid in the determination of which lag values to use as autoregressive predictors is a correlogram, a graphical display of the correlations existing between responses in a time series separated by a constant interval of time. These time-lag correlations are called ______________. The ______________ of process values separated by k units of time is computed by

autocorrelations; autocorrelation

$$r_k = \frac{\sum_{t=1}^{n} (y_t - \bar{y})(y_{t+k} - \bar{y})}{\sum_{t=1}^{n} (y_t - \bar{y})^2}, \quad -1 \leqslant r_k \leqslant 1$$

where $y_1, y_2, \ldots, y_n$ are the values for n consecutive time periods in a time series and $\bar{y}$ is the average of the n series values. Differencing is applied to the time series as many times as is necessary to remove any inherent ______________. (The autocorrelation analysis is actually performed on the time series which is generated by first-differencing the underlying time series.)

trend

The autocorrelation function (acf) summarizes the correlations that a series has with itself. The acf can be calculated using the MINITAB command ACF followed by the appropriate column designation. The acf which follows summarizes the autocorrelations present in the data given in Example 14.1, while the MINITAB PLOT of the time series (C1) against time (C2) exhibits a definite linear trend.

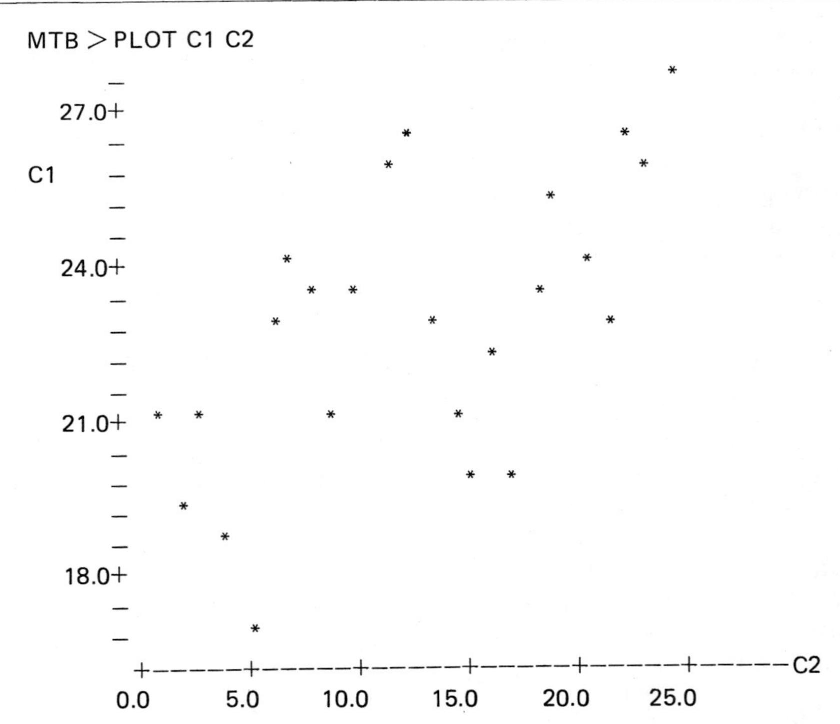

```
MTB > ACF C1
ACF of C1

       -1.0  -0.8  -0.6  -0.4  -0.2   0.0   0.2   0.4   0.6   0.8   1.0
         +----+----+----+----+----+----+----+----+----+----+----+
 1    0.529                         XXXXXXXXXXX
 2    0.187                         XXXXX
 3    0.046                         XX
 4    0.078                         XXX
 5   -0.062                       XXX
 6   -0.183                    XXXXXX
 7   -0.286                  XXXXXXXX
 8   -0.152                     XXXXX
 9   -0.156                     XXXXX
10    0.032                         XX
11    0.205                         XXXXX
12    0.362                         XXXXXXXX
13    0.196                         XXXXX
14   -0.030                        XX
MTB >
```

The acf can be used to determine which terms should be included in the model. An approximate test concerning ρ_k, the population autocorrelation of lag k, is to reject H_0: $\rho_k = 0$ in favor of H_a: $\rho_k \neq 0$ when $|r_k| \geqslant 2/\sqrt{n}$ with $\alpha \approx .05$.

Example 14.7

Determine which autocorrelations are significantly non-zero in developing an ARIMA model for the data in Example 14.1.

Solution

1. For any sample autocorrelation coefficient which exceeds $2/\sqrt{n}$ in magnitude, we shall reject the null hypothesis H_0: $\rho_k = 0$.
2. Since $n = 24$, $2/\sqrt{24} = .408$. Hence any autocorrelation whose absolute value exceeds .408 is deemed significant. From the MINITAB ACF printout, we see that only $r_1 = .529$ exceeds .408. Hence, within the class of ARIMA (p, d, q) models, we should fit a model with $p = 1$ and $d = 1$. If $q = 0$, then the model will be an autoregressive model of order $p = 1$ fitted to first differences.

The results of fitting the ARIMA (1, 1, 0) model to the data in Example 14.1 using MINITAB follows. Notice that the ARIMA (1, 1, 0) model is fitted to the data in C1 using the MINITAB command

```
ARIMA 1 1 0 C1
```

```
MTB > ARIMA 1 1 0 C1;
SUBC > FORECAST 23 1.

ESTIMATES AT EACH ITERATION
ITERATION        SSE        PARAMETERS
     0         135.592        0.100
     1         130.003       -0.050
     2         129.297       -0.118
     3         129.288       -0.125
     4         129.288       -0.126
     5         129.288       -0.126

RELATIVE CHANGE IN EACH ESTIMATE LESS THAN 0.0010

FINAL ESTIMATES OF PARAMETERS
TYPE         ESTIMATE        ST. DEV.        T-RATIO
AR  1         -0.1262         0.2145          -0.59

DIFFERENCING: 1 REGULAR DIFFERENCE
NO. OF OBS.:    ORIGINAL SERIES 24, AFTER DIFFERENCING 23
RESIDUALS:      SS = 129.219  (BACKFORECASTS EXCLUDED)
                MS =    5.874  DF = 22

MODIFIED BOX-PIERCE CHISQUARE STATISTIC
LAG                      12            24            36            48
CHISQUARE      9.4(DF = 11)    * (DF = *)    * (DF = *)    * (DF = *)

FORECASTS FROM PERIOD 23
                             95 PERCENT LIMITS
PERIOD        FORECAST        LOWER        UPPER        ACTUAL
    24         25.6757      20.9246      30.4268       27.5000
```

The subcommand FORECAST followed by the numbers 23 and 1 is an instruction to predict the value of the series one-step ahead (1) beginning with the twenty-third (23) observation. Notice that the forecast value $\hat{y}_{24} = 25.6757$ is close to the actual value of $y_{24} = 27.5$, which is contained within the prediction interval (20.9246, 30.4268).

Further information about fitting Box-Jenkins models can be found in the references given in the text.

There are limitations on the usefulness of Box-Jenkins forecasting models:

1. The necessary computer programs can be very expensive to use.
2. The EWMA model will give at least as good results when applied to a time series with a clear ______________ component.
3. Such models rely heavily on subjective judgment and forecasting experience at the model specification stage.

seasonal

14.10 Qualitative Forecasting Models

Forecasting models that do not rely on an historical data base are called *qualitative forecasting models*. These models play important roles in projecting demand and sales of new products for which there is no sales history. Four of the more commonly used qualitative forecasting models are: the panel consensus method; the Delphi method; the historical analogy; and, in situations concerning consumer behavior, market research methods.

The *panel consensus method* assumes that an organization has experts who have the knowledge and experience to evaluate future economic aspects, and arrive at a consensus about the appropriate sales forecast for the new product. An alternative method which tends to eliminate biases due to deference to rank in the organization or the reputation of one or more of the experts is the *Delphi method* in which successive questionnaires are circulated among in-house experts or possibly outside consultants, with each questionnaire revised according to the responses given on the previous questionnaire, until agreement among the group is reached. In addition to eliminating the biases mentioned earlier, the Delphi method allows for the dissemination of expert information among the group as successive questionnaires are developed.

The *historical analogy* assumes that the unknown sales history of a new product will be similar to a product whose sales history is known. This assumption implies that the economic environment for the new product will be similar to the economic environment when the analogous product was first introduced.

Rather than rely wholly on the opinion of experts, an organization may prefer to implement one or more *market research methods* in which opinions and other important information is gathered from a random sample of consumers selected from the target population of interest. Market research methods generally involve survey sampling techniques, which is the subject of Chapter 16.

14.11 Combining Forecasts

In developing a forecasting model for a time series, most analysts examine several possible models and select the model with the smallest forecasting error.

Each of the models developed as a forecasting model may be sensitive to one or more salient aspects of the series that is not detected by other possible models. Researchers now suggest that the forecasting accuracy of any single forecasting model can be improved by combining the forecasts generated by several single forecasting models. This *multiple model* approach is most easily implemented using multiple regression analysis in which the original series y_t assumes the role of the dependent variable, and the several single model forecasts assume the role of the independent variables, $x_1, x_2, \ldots, x_p$.

Even though the basic assumptions required for a valid regression analysis are not satisfied, the forecasting error using the multiple model approach as measured by *MSE* or R^2 in the regression analysis is always better than that for

increase

starting point

dormant

change
fits

forecasts

time
linear
regression; additive

cyclic

exponential-smoothing

seasonal; exponentially weighted

same
seldom

any single forecasting model, since the addition of independent variables in the regression equation will never cause *MSE* to (increase, decrease.)

14.12 Summary

At best, statistical methods provide only a ______ ______ in the computation of the forecast of a process value because of the uncertainties which exist over time. Certain variables may lie ______ for a period of time only later to exhibit a considerable influence on a time series. Other variables may simply ______ their apparent relationship with a time series. Thus, a model which ______ a set of sample data may not accurately forecast future process values. The ultimate criterion of a forecasting model is how well it ______ the future. Model selection can be aided by observing the relationship of the process variable with ______ and with other variables over time.

The most commonly used forecasting model is the ______ ______ model. Such a model uses an ______ combination of related variables to generate a forecast. Trigonometric terms can also be used in the model to track ______ patterns of the process value over time.

Recursive forecasting methods do not employ predictor variables formally in the model. The multiple ______ ______ model (Brown's method) is useful when the time series can be considered a polynomial over time. For processes which exhibit a pronounced ______ effect, the ______ ______ moving-average model often generates accurate forecasts.

Only a few of the available forecasting methods were presented in Chapter 14. It must be remembered that the development of a good forecasting model requires a great deal of ingenuity on the part of the statistician. Seldom would two statisticians select the ______ model for a particular process and ______ would one particular model be found appropriate for forecasting two different time series.

Chapter 15

QUALITY CONTROL

15.1 Introduction

The field of quality control is concerned with the ______________ of products and with techniques for attaining consistently high quality in their production. Statistical quality control techniques are not limited to manufacturing environments, but can be employed to monitor any business activity that requires reliability and consistency in its goods or its services.

design

In addition to maintaining high quality and reliability in goods or services, quality control is also used in achieving a good design for new products. A well-designed product is usually the result of "off-line" quality control consisting of statistical techniques for finding optimum conditions for use in manufacturing or providing the product or service. When the design or optimum operating conditions have been determined, then "on-line" quality control techniques can be used to monitor and hence maintain the process producing the good or the service provided.

15.2 Modern Terminology and Concepts

Every step in a manufacturing line or in a service-related business is referred to as a ______________ with its own inputs and outputs. Producing a good or a service can be viewed as a series of related processes. The use of statistical quality control techniques is called ______________ ______________ ______________.

process

Statistical Process Control (SPC)

There are two basic approaches to monitoring the output quality of a given process. One approach is to wait until products are produced, and then to isolate the good from the bad. This approach is called the (detection, prevention) approach. The information about the process when obtained in this manner may be too old to be very useful. The second approach to monitoring a process

detection

prevention
before
superior

is the ______________ approach. With this approach, important process variables are monitored while the process is in operation and (before, after) the final product is made. The prevention approach is (superior, inferior) to the detection approach and is the approach commonly used today.

control chart

variables
attribute
control charts for attributes

When using the prevention approach, measurements on important process variables are monitored using a ______________ ______________. A control chart that monitors a continuous variable is called a control chart for ______________. When the variable measured is discrete, the resulting data is called ______________ data. Control charts for monitoring attribute data are called ______________ ______________ ______________ ______________.

controllable

Variation exhibited by variables consists of variation that is caused by changes in important process variables and by random variation in the process. Variation that is caused by variables such as machine wear, machine adjustments, and machine operators is referred to as (controllable, uncontrollable) variation. Control charts are designed to separate controllable variation from uncontrollable process variation. Using control charts is an example of "on-line" quality control, while experimental design procedures are examples of "off-line" quality control techniques.

15.3 Simple Graphical Techniques

A graphical display of data serves several purposes in quality control.

1. Graphs provide a clear visual summary of what otherwise might be a complicated numerical summary.
2. Graphs are a common medium for communicating ideas.
3. Graphs are useful for making decisions about process variables.
4. Graphs can help focus attention on problem areas within a process.

Four graphical techniques are widely used in quality control: histograms, Pareto charts, fishbone diagrams and scatter plots.

upper
specification limit (USL)
lower specification limit (LSL)

Histograms are simple graphical displays that show both the central tendency and the range of a process variable measured over sequential times. In general, a process variable has a specific range within which it is required to lie. The largest allowable value of a process variable is called the ______________ ______________ ______________, and the smallest allowable value is called the ______________ ______________ ______________. A histogram of process readings makes it easy to determine whether a process is capable of staying within specification limits.

Example 15.1

The data which follow represent the diameters of $n = 50$ drill bits whose final machined size should be .500 in. Specifications dictate that these drill bits should have diameters between .490 in. and .510 in. Is the production process capable of meeting these specifications?

.497	.501	.504	.499	.509
.498	.505	.497	.492	.496
.504	.508	.490	.491	.496
.485	.506	.500	.494	.501
.500	.494	.498	.497	.497
.500	.488	.507	.497	.487
.511	.505	.489	.496	.501
.495	.493	.507	.495	.499
.501	.499	.497	.503	.496
.506	.493	.491	.510	.503

Solution
A MINITAB printout of the histogram for the $n = 50$ diameters follows.

```
HISTOGRAM OF C3   N = 50

MIDPOINT    COUNT
 0.48400        1   *
 0.48800        3   ***
 0.49200        6   ******
 0.49600       14   **************
 0.50000       12   ************
 0.50400        6   ******
 0.50800        6   ******
 0.51200        2   **
```

The midpoints of the histogram classes are .484, .488, __________, .496, .500, __________, __________ and .512. Therefore, the boundary points of the histogram are .482, .486, __________, .494, .498, __________, .506, .510 and .514. From the count we see that there are __________ observations less than or equal to .490 and __________ observations greater than .510. Hence, __________ or __________% of these bits fail to meet the required specifications. However, if the specification limits were changed to .480 and .520, it would appear that the process is capable of meeting these new specifications.

.492
.504; .508
.490; .502
4
2
6/50; 12

A Pareto chart is another graphical technique used to identify process problems. A Pareto chart is a bar graph in which each bar represents an area of concern within the process, with the bars drawn in order of decreasing height. Pareto charts help sort out the few serious process problems from the many minor ones.

Example 15.2
The manager of an electronic assembly shop recorded the number of defective items at sub-assembly during a one month period by type of defect. The data summary follows.

Type of Defect	Number of Defectives
Improper mounting of a component	21
Incorrect wiring	121
Missing component	20
Soldering	183
Wrong component	32
Miscellaneous	43

Provide a Pareto chart for these data, including a plot of the cumulative relative frequency of the numbers of defectives. Which types of defect account for approximately 80% of observed defects?

Solution

Since a Pareto chart is a bar graph in which the bars are arranged in decreasing heights, we must first rearrange the defect categories so that the observed frequencies associated with these categories are decreasing in magnitude. Fill in the missing entries in the table.

	Type of Defect	Frequency	Cumulative Frequency
	Soldering	183	183
121	Incorrect wiring	______	304
336	Wrong component	32	______
	Improper mounting	21	357
20; 377	Missing component	______	______
	Miscellaneous	43	420

The Pareto chart is shown below. Although the frequency in the miscellaneous category exceeds three of the frequencies in the other five categories, it is correctly placed last in the listing, because it is the total of defectives from infrequently occurring classes.

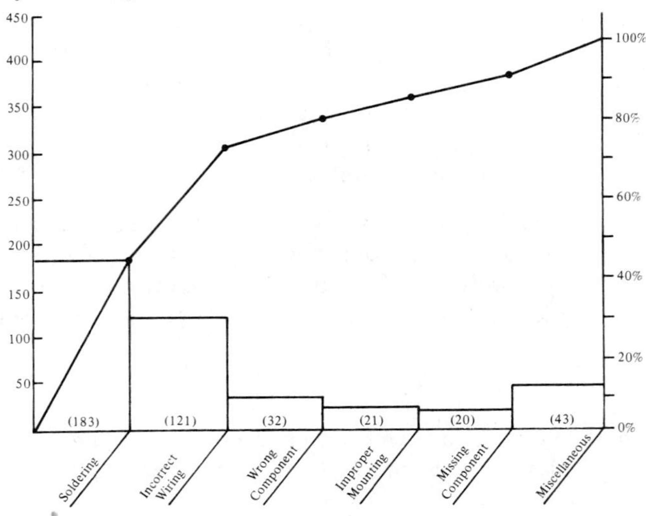

The first three types of defects, namely _______________, _______________ _______________ and _______________ _______________, account for exactly 80% of the observed defectives.

soldering; incorrect wiring; wrong component

The results of a Pareto analysis in which dollar amounts are used to replace the number of defectives could be very different from that just reported, since the categories contributing most to the dollar volume may be quite different from the categories contributing most to the number of defectives.

Once the problem areas have been pinpointed using a Pareto analysis, the next step is to remedy these problems when possible. One method of graphically displaying the reasons for, or causes of a particular problem is called the _______________ _______________ or an Ishikawa diagram, named for the person who introduced its use in quality control.

fishbone diagram

To construct a fishbone diagram, the problem area selected for investigation becomes the head of the diagram. Next, causes, including the five basic causes, are added to the diagram as "fishbones" radiating from the "spine" or problem area. The five basic causes are methods, equipment, materials, workforce and the environment. These basic causes are often referred to as the four M's (Methods, Machinery, Material and Manpower) and an E (Environment).

Example 15.3

Production operators in metal fabricating industries generally inspect machine tools before starting and after ending each job. Additionally major maintenance machine inspections take place from one to four times per year, depending upon whether the machine must maintain high precision, is costly to replace, and so on. In investigating a problem with a drilling process, the fishbone diagram which follows was put forward by a team representing maintenance, management, and machine operators.

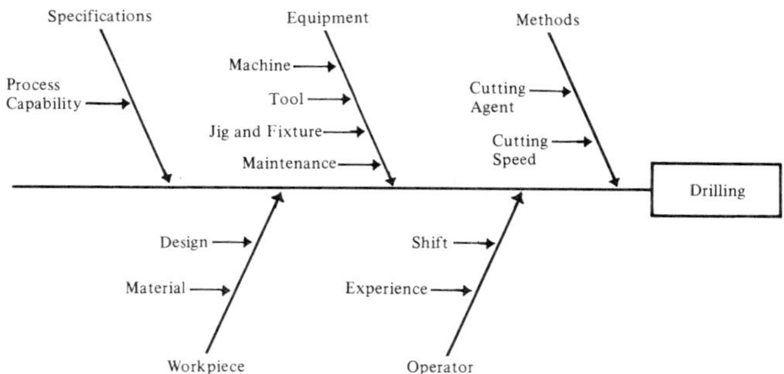

Discuss the implications of this fishbone diagram.

Solution

The five basic causes (four M's and an E) appear in this diagram under slightly different designations. In order to have a successful drilling operation, one must have the proper machinery, with appropriate fixtures, that are calibrated and well maintained. The process itself must be capable of producing items that conform to specifications. A successful drilling operation requires operators with ____________ ____________ who can work with production items made of different materials and of varying designs. The production staff should implement known standard cutting rates and ____________ ____________ that depend upon the type of metals used to produce the items being drilled.

on-the-job experience

cutting agents

The fishbone diagram is used to show possible problem areas in the process. Each of the causes must now be thoroughly examined and appropriate actions taken.

Scatter plots can be used to explore the relationship between a response variable y and a related, possibly causal variable x. A scatter plot is a precursor to a regression analysis relating y and x. If the scatter plot exhibits the form of a relationship between x and y, then a ____________ ____________ can be used to further explore this relationship.

regression analysis

15.4 Control Charts

Product quality during the manufacturing process is monitored by a ____________ ____________. A control chart plots sample measurements derived from the process at different points in time. If the items issuing from the process are measurable and must conform to measurable specifications such as length, weight, volume, potency, or cost, the quality of the process is monitored by an $\bar{x}$ chart and an ____________. These charts plot, respectively, sample ____________ and ranges computed from samples selected from the process at different points in time. Control charts designed to monitor a process with measurable characteristics are called control charts for ____________.

control chart

R chart

means

variables

If the items are merely categorized as either possessing or not possessing a given characteristic, samples drawn from the process are referred to as attribute samples. In such a case, we are usually concerned with either the acceptability or unacceptability of each item – either it works or does not work, either it is of the correct dimensions or it is not. Control charts to monitor such a process are called control charts for ____________, the most common of which is the p-chart, which plots the proportion of defectives found in successive samples selected from the production process.

attributes

The construction of a quality control chart is based on the Central Limit Theorem and the Empirical Rule. When the production process is operating satisfactorily, whether the items are measurable or not, almost all of the sample values will oscillate within ____________ standard deviations of the mean of the process values. Hence, it is very unlikely that we would observe any sample values outside this band. The mean of the process values obtained from the process which is in statistical control forms what is called the ____________ on the control chart. The bands located ____________ standard deviations on each side of the centerline are called the upper and lower ____________ ____________.

three

centerline; three

control limits

It is important to remember that the centerline and the control limits are constructed from process values obtained from the production process at times when the process is known to be in statistical control. The control chart is then used to monitor the production process and in effect continually gauge its production capabilities. When sample statistics computed from process data fall outside the control limits, the process is said to be (in control, out of control) and corrective action is required to locate and eliminate the implicit controllable variation.

out of control

Sometimes a process may be detected to be out of control before a sample value outside the control limits is observed. As in the control chart below, successive sample values may be continually decreasing (or increasing, depending on the process) over time. Thus, we could be fairly certain that a sample value will soon appear below the lower control limit. If this were an $\bar{x}$ chart, a deterioration of average product quality would be assumed; if it were a p-chart, we would assume that the fraction defective was improving and the production process was becoming more effective. Thus, impending trouble or changes in process capabilities can sometimes be detected before the process is judged to be statistically out of control.

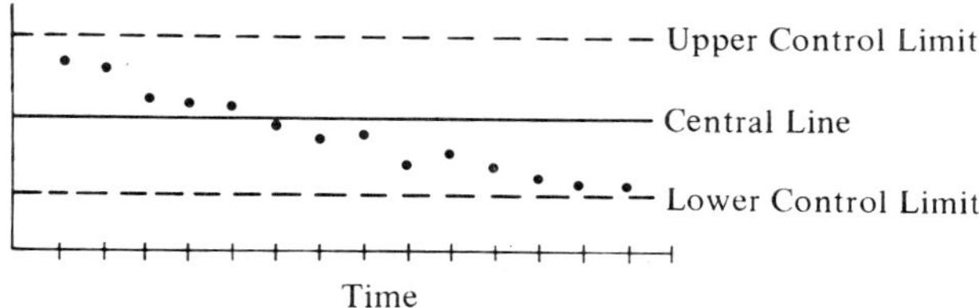

A process which is in statistical control does not necessarily meet buyer specifications. Specifications give limits within which the buyer wishes the measures to fall while control limits are determined solely by the capabilities of the process.

15.5 $\bar{x}$ Charts and R Charts

Control charts designed to monitor the measurable characteristics of a production process are the __________ chart and the __________ chart. The $\bar{x}$ chart plots means of samples drawn from the production process at equally spaced points in time. It provides an ongoing check of average product quality. However, the $\bar{x}$ chart tells us very little about the internal variability of process values. This is the task of the R chart, which plots the ____________ of successive samples drawn from the production process at equally spaced points in time.

$\bar{x}$; R

ranges

The control limits for the $\bar{x}$ chart and the R chart are constructed from sample data gathered from the production process at a time when the process is known to be (in control, out of control). At least 25 different samples of

in control

size $n = 3, 4$ or 5 observations each are recommended for use in constructing the control charts.

The $\bar{x}$ chart should not be used without first constructing an R chart, since the control limits on the $\bar{x}$ chart are calculated using $\bar{R}$, the value of the centerline on the R chart. For the R chart, we must first compute the sample

range _______________ for each of the k different samples. Remember, the range is simply the difference between the largest and smallest measurement in each sample. The centerline for the range chart is located at

$$\bar{R} = \frac{R_1 + R_2 + R_3 + \ldots + R_k}{k}$$

where the sample ranges are denoted by $R_1, R_2, \ldots, R_k$. The centerline is

mean simply the _______________ of all the sample range values.

The value of $\bar{R}$ is the estimate of μ_R. When the process is in control, the

three sample ranges should vary within _______________ standard deviations of their mean. Therefore, the upper and lower control limits are given by

$$\text{UCL} = \mu_R + 3\sigma_R \quad \text{and} \quad \text{LCL} = \mu_R - 3\sigma_R.$$

In practice the control limits are estimated as

$$\text{UCL} = D_4\bar{R} \quad \text{and} \quad \text{LCL} = D_3\bar{R}.$$

The values of D_3 and D_4, which depend on the sample size n, are found in Table 12 of the Appendix.

Example 15.4

A manufacturing process is designed to produce drill bits which are precisely one-half inch in diameter. The sample data which follows represents 25 samples selected from the production process with four measurements in each sample. The sample measurements were obtained during a time when the production process was deemed to be in statistical control. Use the data to construct an R chart to monitor the production process. Does the process appear to be in statistical control?

Diameters of Drill Bits (Inches)						
	Measurement Number				Mean	Range
Sample	1	2	3	4	$\bar{x}$	R
1	.501	.499	.496	.500	.499	.005
2	.499	.497	.494	.498	.497	.005
3	.503	.501	.502	.494	.500	.009
4	.509	.511	.516	.508	.511	.008
5	.507	.494	.505	.510	.504	.016
6	.500	.503	.506	.491	.500	.015
7	.488	.483	.501	.512	.496	.029
8	.497	.499	.495	.501	.498	.006
9	.492	.485	.480	.483	.485	.012
10	.480	.480	.490	.498	.487	.018
11	.496	.493	.493	.489	.490	.014
12	.496	.506	.504	.506	.503	.010
13	.503	.507	.504	.510	.506	.007
14	.508	.502	.509	.509	.507	.007
15	.505	.510	.515	.502	.508	.013
16	.501	.503	.505	.499	.502	.006
17	.503	.500	.497	.500	.500	.006
18	.490	.500	.498	.496	.496	.010
19	.502	.509	.523	.502	.506	.011
20	.506	.509	.510	.507	.508	.004
21	.501	.505	.498	.508	.503	.010
22	.500	.497	.497	.502	.499	.005
23	.491	.499	.498	.500	.497	.009
24	.497	.487	.488	.492	.491	.010
25	.489	.493	.503	.507	.498	.018

Solution

The centerline for the R chart is located at the mean of the 25 sample range measurements. Thus,

$$\bar{R} = \frac{.005 + .005 + \ldots + .018}{25}$$

$$= \frac{\_\_\_\_\_\_}{25}$$

$$= \_\_\_\_\_\_$$

.263

.01052

2.282 With $n = 4$ observations per sample the value of $D_3 = 0$ and $D_4 =$ __________. Therefore

.01052

$$\text{LCL} = (0)(\_\_\_\_\_\_\_\_\_\_) = 0$$

and

.02401

$$\text{UCL} = (2.282)(.01052) = \_\_\_\_\_\_\_\_\_\_.$$

The control chart for the sample ranges follows.

R-chart for the Drill Bit Manufacturing process

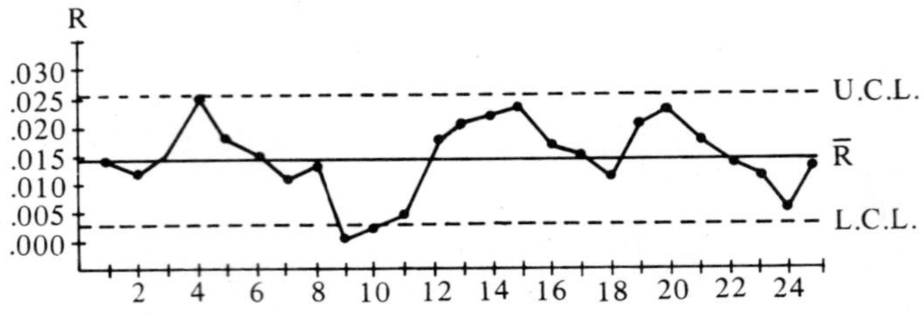

Sample Number

The sample standard deviation can also be used to monitor process variation. However, *R* charts are the choice of most practitioners because the range is an easily calculated sample statistic and for the small sample sizes used in constructing a control chart, the sample range and sample standard deviation differ but little in their efficient use of the sample information. (This last statement (is, is not) true for larger values of n.)

is not

In constructing an $\bar{x}$ chart, the centerline is located at $\bar{\bar{x}}$, the average of the sample means, given by

$$\bar{\bar{x}} = \frac{\bar{x}_1 + \bar{x}_2 + \ldots + \bar{x}_k}{k}$$

where $\bar{x}_1, \bar{x}_2, \ldots, \bar{x}_k$ are each based on n observations. Using only sample information, the upper and lower control limits would be found using

$$\text{UCL} = \bar{\bar{x}} + 3s/\sqrt{n} \quad \text{and} \quad \text{LCL} = \bar{\bar{x}} - 3s/\sqrt{n},$$

where s is the sample standard deviation of all kn observations. However, we can estimate σ from the range using

$$\hat{\sigma} = \frac{\bar{R}}{d_2}$$

The value of d_2 depends upon the sample size n, and can be found in Table 12 of the Appendix.

For the drill bit data, $\bar{R} = .01052$, $n = 4$ and $d_2 = 2.059$. Therefore

$$\hat{\sigma} = \frac{.01052}{\_\_\_\_\_\_} = \_\_\_\_\_\_$$

.005109
2.059

and

$$\frac{3\hat{\sigma}}{\sqrt{n}} = \frac{3(\_\_\_\_\_\_)}{\sqrt{4}} = \_\_\_\_\_\_$$

.005109
.007664

However, the calculation of this quantity can be accomplished by multiplying $\bar{R}$ by the number A_2, found in Table 12 because

$$\frac{3\hat{\sigma}}{\sqrt{n}} = \frac{3}{d_2\sqrt{n}}(\bar{R}) = A_2 R$$

The upper and lower control limits for an $\bar{x}$ chart are given by

$$\text{UCL} = \bar{\bar{x}} + A_2\bar{R} \quad \text{and} \quad \text{LCL} = \bar{\bar{x}} - A_2\bar{R}.$$

Example 15.5

Construct an $\bar{x}$ chart for monitoring the mean of the process producing drill bits using the data given in Example 15.4.

Solution

The centerline of the $\bar{x}$ chart is located at the average of the sample means which is given by

$$\bar{\bar{x}} = \frac{.499 + .497 + \ldots + .498}{25}$$

$$= \frac{\_\_\_\_\_\_}{25} = \_\_\_\_\_\_$$

12.491
.49964

To calculate the upper and lower control limits, we also need the value of $\bar{R} = .01052$ and the value of $A_2 =$ ______ based on a common sample size of $n = 4$. Hence .729

$$\text{UCL} = \bar{\bar{x}} + A_2\bar{R}$$

$$= \_\_\_\_\_\_ + .729(.01052)$$

.49964

$$= \_\_\_\_\_\_$$

.50731

and

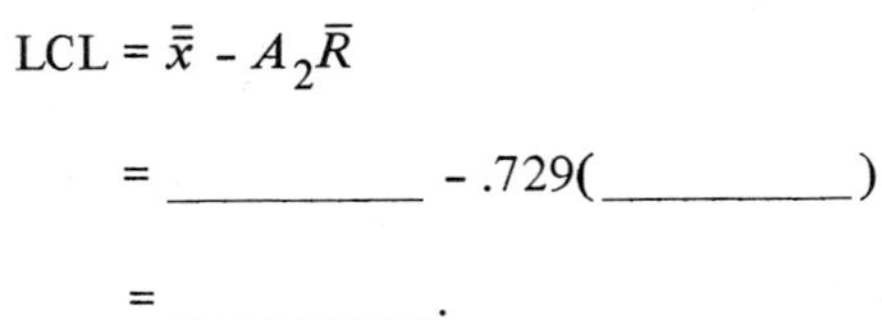

$$\text{LCL} = \bar{\bar{x}} - A_2\bar{R}$$

.49964, .01052 $= \_\_\_\_\_\_\_\_\_ - .729(\_\_\_\_\_\_\_\_\_)$

.49197 $= \_\_\_\_\_\_\_\_\_.$

The resulting $\bar{\bar{x}}$ chart follows.

$\bar{x}$-chart for the Drill Bit Manufacturing Process

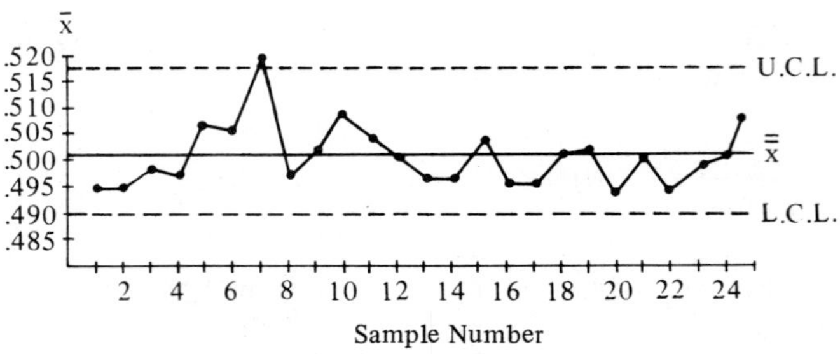

Example 15.6
At a time when the state of the production process discussed in Examples 15.4 and 15.5 was unknown, four samples of four measurements each were selected at half-hour intervals yielding the following results.

	Measurement Number					
Sample	*1*	*2*	*3*	*4*	$\bar{x}$	*R*
1	.506	.512	.508	.506	.507	.006
2	.498	.483	.505	.514	______	______
3	.509	.514	.510	.515	______	______
4	.510	.506	.499	.501	______	______

.500; .031
.512; .006
.504; .501

Use the $\bar{x}$ chart and the R chart which were constructed in Examples 15.4 and 15.5 to monitor the production process for the time during which these four samples were selected.

Solution
The simplest method of monitoring the sample measurements is by plotting the sample means and ranges on the $\bar{x}$ chart and the R chart, respectively.

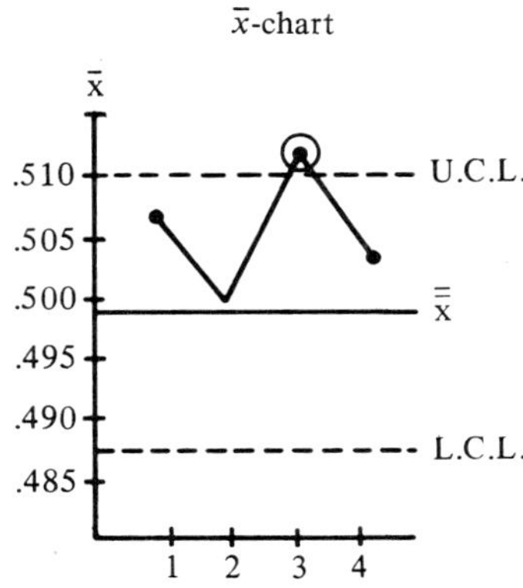

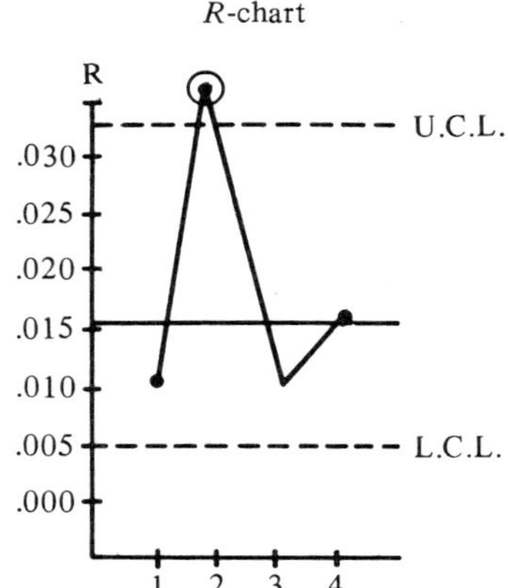

At each point in time when a sample measurement is observed (inside, outside) the control limits, it can be assumed that either the production process is out of control due to the presence of excess controllable variation or it is not out of control but, by chance, random variation or a sampling error caused the measurement to appear outside the control limits. Since the mean of the ______________ sample exceeded the UCL for the $\bar{x}$ chart and the range of the ______________ sample exceeded the UCL for the R chart, the production process should be examined to determine whether controllable variation is present in the process.

outside

third

second

Self-Correcting Exercises 15A

1. In the production of two-liter bottles of a particular brand of soft drink, the fill machine is designed to fill these bottles with 67.6 fluid ounces of soda. Quality control limitations require that all bottles contain between 67.4 and 67.8 fluid ounces. During a production period when the fill process was known to be in statistical control, a series of 30 samples of size $n = 10$ bottles were randomly selected. The average fill was $\bar{\bar{x}} = 67.54$ and the average range was $\bar{R} = .12$.
   a. Construct an $\bar{x}$ chart to monitor the fill process. Explain how this chart will be used.
   b. Construct an R chart to monitor the process. Explain how this chart will be used.
   c. What is the probability that the process is capable of meeting the specification limits?
2. Refer to Exercise 1. The manager of the plant is concerned about the performance of the fill machine, since it has not been adjusted for a long period of time. She selected a series of 5 samples of size $n = 10$ at hourly intervals and obtained the following measurements:

Hour	$\bar{x}$	R
1	67.77	.10
2	67.76	.13
3	68.01	.12
4	67.62	.10
5	67.65	.11

Use the $\bar{x}$ and R charts constructed in Exercise 1 to monitor the process. Does the process appear to be in control?

3. The side pieces for aluminum picture frames are manufactured in various lengths and packaged in pairs of equal lengths, so that the consumer can construct his own custom frame by purchasing two pairs of side pieces. The machine which cuts the side pieces can be set to cut pieces in varying lengths. During a period in which the process is in control, the cutting machine is set to cut 18 inch side pieces, and the following measurements are obtained.

Sample	Length	Sample	Length
1	18.02, 18.04, 17.95, 17.96	9	17.99, 18.00, 18.01, 17.99
2	17.96, 18.00, 17.99, 17.97	10	18.02, 18.01, 18.03, 17.99
3	18.00, 18.05, 18.01, 18.00	11	17.95, 18.00, 17.98, 18.01
4	17.97, 18.00, 17.99, 18.02	12	17.99, 17.99, 18.00, 17.95
5	18.00, 18.01, 17.98, 17.97	13	17.96, 18.01, 18.02, 17.97
6	17.99, 17.97, 18.01, 18.02	14	17.96, 17.96, 17.99, 18.00
7	17.97, 17.96, 17.99, 18.00	15	18.01, 17.95, 18.02, 18.03
8	17.97, 17.98, 17.97, 18.03	16	18.00, 18.01, 17.98, 18.03

a. Construct an $\bar{x}$ chart for the process. Explain how it will be used.
b. Construct an R chart for the process. Explain how it will be used.

15.6 Process Capability

Even though a production process is in statistical control, it may not meet product specifications. Process capability refers to the ability of a process to stay within specification limits.

Histograms can be used to determine to what extent a process stays within specification limits. However, we can also calculate one or more capability indexes to describe process capability. One simple capability index uses the ratio of the range between specification limits to the range of process values, given by

$$C_p = \frac{\text{USL - LSL}}{6\hat{\sigma}}$$

where $\hat{\sigma}$ is an estimate of the standard deviation of process values. The process is capable of meeting the specification limits if C_p is (greater than, less than) one; the process is not capable of meeting the specification limits if C_p is (greater than, less than) one. If $C_p = 1$, the process is minimally capable of meeting the specification limits. The value of $C_p = 1.33$ which occurs when $\text{USL} - \text{LSL} = 8\hat{\sigma}$ is considered good, and is often used as a target figure for C_p. Since C_p is a unitless measure, capabilities of two or more processes can be compared on the basis of their C_p values.

greater than

less than

It is apparent that the C_p index measures the ______________ process capability since it considers the spread of process values but not the location of these values. A second index which does take the process mean into consideration is given by

potential

$$C_{pk} = \text{minimum}\left(\frac{\text{USL} - \bar{\bar{x}}}{3\hat{\sigma}}, \frac{\bar{\bar{x}} - \text{LSL}}{3\hat{\sigma}}\right)$$

with $\hat{\sigma} = \bar{R}/d_2$. The factor k in the subscript of this measure of process capability is given by

$$k = \frac{|(\text{USL} + \text{LSL})/2 - \bar{\bar{x}}|}{(\text{USL} - \text{LSL})/2}$$

which measures the amount by which the mean process value $\bar{\bar{x}}$ differs from the value centered midway between the upper and lower specification limits. When $\text{LSL} < \bar{\bar{x}} < \text{USL}$, $0 < k < 1$ and these two capability indexes are related by the formula

$$C_{pk} = C_p(1 - k)$$

Therefore, when $\bar{\bar{x}}$ is located midway between USL and LSL, $k = 0$ and $C_{pk} = C_p$.

Example 15.7

Suppose that in Example 15.4 acceptable drill bits were required to have diameters within the specification limits of .500 ± .020. Calculate C_p and C_{pk} for the drill bit data and interpret the results.

Solution

1. To calculate C_p we need an estimate of the process standard deviation, found using

$$\hat{\sigma} = \bar{R}/d_2$$

With $\bar{R} =$ __________ and $d_2 =$ __________ $(n = 4)$

.01052; 2.059

$$\hat{\sigma} = .01052/2.059$$

.005109 $= \underline{\qquad\qquad}$

Therefore,

$$C_p = (\text{USL} - \text{LSL})/6\hat{\sigma}$$

.005109 $= (.5200 - .4800)/6(\underline{\qquad\qquad})$

1.304816 $= \underline{\qquad\qquad}$

2. The second index of process capability is given by

$$C_{pk} = \text{minimum}\left(\frac{\text{USL} - \bar{\bar{x}}}{3\hat{\sigma}}, \frac{\bar{\bar{x}} - \text{LSL}}{3\hat{\sigma}}\right)$$

With $\bar{\bar{x}} = .49964$,

.49964
1.3283

$$\frac{\text{USL} - \bar{\bar{x}}}{3\hat{\sigma}} = \frac{.5200 - \underline{\qquad\qquad}}{3(.005109)} = \underline{\qquad\qquad}$$

.4800
1.2813

$$\frac{\bar{\bar{x}} - \text{LSL}}{3\hat{\sigma}} = \frac{.49964 - \underline{\qquad\qquad}}{3(.005109)} = \underline{\qquad\qquad}$$

1.2813 Therefore, $C_{pk} = \text{minimum}\,(1.3283, 1.2813) = \underline{\qquad\qquad}$

The value of C_{pk} could also be found using the relationship $C_{pk} = C_p(1 - k)$ where

$$k = \frac{|(\text{USL} + \text{LSL})/2 - \bar{\bar{x}}|}{(\text{USL} - \text{LSL})/2}$$

.5200
.4800

$$= \frac{|(\underline{\qquad\qquad} + .4800)/2 - .49964|}{(.5200 - \underline{\qquad\qquad})/2}$$

.00036
.018

$$= \frac{\underline{\qquad\qquad}}{.02} = \underline{\qquad\qquad}$$

Hence,

.018; 1.2813 $C_{pk} = 1.3048(1 - \underline{\qquad\qquad}) = \underline{\qquad\qquad}$

In summary, the value of $C_p = 1.31$ indicates that the process is capable of

variability producing drill bits whose ________________ is within the specified limits.

Further, the value of $C_{pk} = 1.28$ indicates that the process is capable of producing items within the actual specification limits from .48 to .52.

Self-Correcting Exercises 15B

1. Refer to Exercise 1, Self-Correcting Exercises 15A. Calculate the process capability index, C_p. Interpret its value. Is the process capable of meeting its specifications?
2. Refer to Exercise 1, Self-Correcting Exercises 15A. Calculate the C_{pk} index. Use this value to describe the extent to which the location of the process differs from 67.6 fluid ounces.
3. Refer to Exercise 3, Self-Correcting Exercises 15A.
   a. Estimate the population standard deviation σ using two different estimators.
   b. If the specification limits are $18 \pm .02$, calculate C_p using the two different estimates from a. Is the process capable of meeting its specifications?

15.7 The *p*-chart

If the items of a continuous production process can be classified as either "good" or defective," a ______________ is used to monitor the process capabilities. Such items as flash bulbs, transistors, electron tubes, and dry cell batteries when operable can be almost guaranteed to possess uniformity in operating characteristics. However, due to the complexity of design of such items and the rapid pace of the production process, many such items cannot be guaranteed 100% operability in the production process. Data observed from a process whose characteristics need not conform to measurable characteristics is called ______________ data.

p-chart

attribute

As in the construction of any control chart, the *p*-chart should be constructed from sample data obtained during periods of time when the process is known to be in ______________ ______________. At least 100 sample items should be observed in constructing the *p*-chart, but usually many more than 100 are observed.

statistical control

Since the *p*-chart is designed to control the ______________ of defective units produced by a production process, the attribute sampling problem can be modeled by the ______________ distribution. The center line of the *p*-chart is the fraction (proportion) of defective items observed from all samples selected when the process is known to be in statistical control and is denoted by $\bar{p}$. Thus,

proportion

binomial

$$\bar{p} = \frac{\text{total number of defectives in all samples}}{\text{total number of observations in all samples}}$$

Since $\bar{p}$ estimates the true fraction defective of the process, we recall that the

$\sqrt{\dfrac{\bar{p}(1-\bar{p})}{n}}$

3-sigma

standard deviation of $\bar{p}$ is estimated by $\sigma_{\hat{p}}$ = ______________, where n is the size of the sample selected at each sampling interval. The upper and lower control limits for the p-chart are, as with the previous control charts, the ______________ limits around the mean. That is,

$$\text{U.C.L.} = \bar{p} + 3\sqrt{\frac{\bar{p}(1-\bar{p})}{n}}$$

and

$$\text{L.C.L.} = \bar{p} - 3\sqrt{\frac{\bar{p}(1-\bar{p})}{n}}$$

lower

lower

As with the R-chart, the ______________ control limit for the p-chart is rather meaningless as a monitor of the efficiency of the manufacturing process. Observing a sample fraction defective below the lower control limit of a p-chart would imply that the fraction defective is much ______________ than normal. This is what is desired, not something to be avoided. Such an observation may imply that the efficiency of the manufacturing process has increased and that new control limits should be constructed to reflect this new capability of the process.

Example 15.8

A manufacturing process is designed to produce electron tubes for use in small, portable television sets. The tubes are all of standard size and need not conform to any measurable characteristic but are sometimes inoperable when emerging from the manufacturing process. Fifteen samples were selected from the process at times when the process was known to be in statistical control. Fifty tubes were observed within each sample, tests were performed to determine their operability, and the number of defective tubes was recorded. Construct a p-chart to monitor the manufacturing process.

Sample Number	*Sample Size*	*Number of Defectives*	$\hat{p}$
1	50	6	.12
2	50	7	.14
3	50	3	.06
4	50	5	.10
5	50	6	.12
6	50	8	.16
7	50	4	.08
8	50	5	.10
9	50	7	.14
10	50	3	.06
11	50	1	.02
12	50	6	.12
13	50	5	.10
14	50	4	.08
15	50	5	.10
Totals	750	75	

Solution

The central line for the p-chart is found by computing the average proportion defective using all the sample data. Thus,

$$\bar{p} = \frac{(\underline{\qquad\quad})}{750} = \underline{\qquad\quad}$$

75; .10

Using the formula ______________ for the standard deviation, we find that

$\sqrt{\frac{\bar{p}(1-\bar{p})}{n}}$

$$\hat{\sigma}_{\hat{p}} = \sqrt{\frac{(.1)(.9)}{50}}$$

$$= \sqrt{.0018}$$

$$= \underline{\qquad\quad}$$

.0415

The control limits for the p-chart are then found as follows:

$$\text{U.C.L.} = \bar{p} + 3\sqrt{\frac{\bar{p}(1-\bar{p})}{n}}$$

$$= \underline{\qquad\quad} + 3(\underline{\qquad\quad})$$

.1; .0415

$$= \underline{\qquad\quad}$$

.2245

while the lower control limit is

$$\text{L.C.L.} = \bar{p} - 3\sqrt{\frac{\bar{p}(1-\bar{p})}{n}}$$

$$= \underline{\qquad\quad} - 3(\underline{\qquad\quad})$$

.1; .0415

$$= \underline{\qquad\quad}$$

- .0245

Since a sample fraction defective, $\hat{p}$, cannot be negative, the computed lower control limit is ignored and we use ______________ instead. The p-chart for the electron tube manufacturing process is shown below.

zero

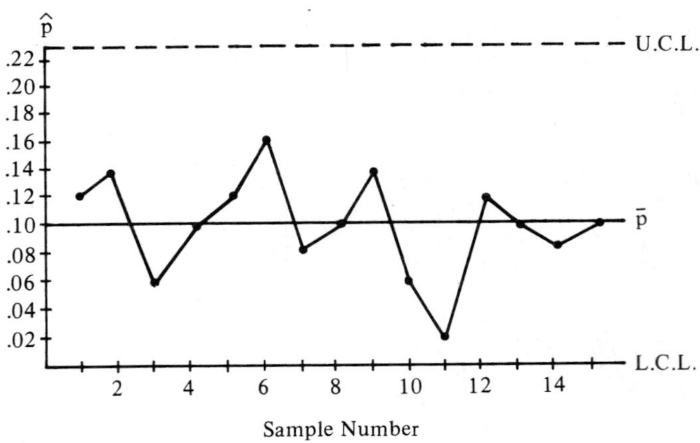

Example 15.9
Consider the electron tube manufacturing process discussed in the previous example. During a day in which the state of the manufacturing process was unknown, sample of size 50 were selected from the manufacturing process at one-hour intervals. The numbers of defectives found in eight samples of size 50 were 9, 8, 4, 7, 8, 12, 9, and 13, respectively. Comment on the state of the process during the day in question.

Solution
Using the control chart developed in the previous example, plot the eight observations given above.

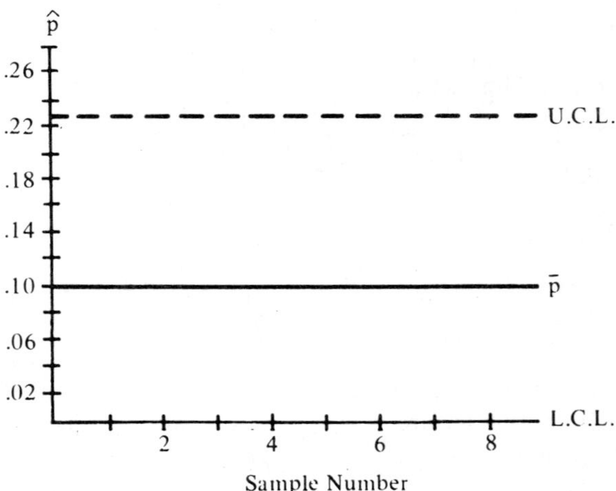

Thus, the manufacturing process appeared to be producing an excessively large fraction of defectives during the ______________ and ______________ hours. One might also comment that the overall fraction defective appeared much greater than average during the day, implying that even when the process was not technically out of control, there was evidence to suggest that the process was not performing up to its capability.

sixth; eighth

Example 15.10

Refer to the electron tube manufacturing process in Example 15.9. Suppose the true fraction defective in the production process suddenly shifts to .20. What is the probability that the shift will be detected in the first sample of size 50 selected from the process?

Solution

We want to find the probability that the next sample $\hat{p}$ exceeds the U.C.L., .2245, when the true fraction defective $p =$ __________. In other words, we want to find the probability that __________ or more defectives will be observed in the next sample of size 50 selected from the manufacturing process. Using the Central Limit Theorem as applied to binomial the distribution, we find

.20
12

$$P[x \geqslant 12] \cong P\left[z > \frac{11.5 - np}{\sqrt{np(1-p)}}\right]$$

$$= P\left[z > \frac{11.5 - 50(\_\_\_\_\_\_)}{\sqrt{50(\_\_\_\_\_\_)(\_\_\_\_\_\_)}}\right]$$

$$= P\left[z > \frac{11.5 - (\_\_\_\_\_\_)}{\sqrt{(\_\_\_\_\_\_)}}\right]$$

$$= P\left[z > \_\_\_\_\_\_\right]$$

$$= \_\_\_\_\_\_ .$$

.20
.20; .80
10
2.82
.52
.3015

When the sample sizes are not all equal, we can modify the charting procedure in one of three ways.

1. When the samples are not strongly different, use the average sample size, n, in calculating the control limits where

$$\bar{n} = \sum_{i=1}^{k} n_i/k$$

2. Construct a control chart by plotting

$$z = \frac{\hat{p}_i - \bar{p}}{\sqrt{\dfrac{\bar{p}\,\bar{q}}{n_i}}}$$

with UCL = 3 and LCL = -3.

3. Use variable control limits for each sample whereby

$$\text{UCL} = \bar{p} + 3\sqrt{\bar{p}(1 - \bar{p})/n_i}$$

and

$$\text{LCL} = \bar{p} - 3\sqrt{\bar{p}(1 - \bar{p})/n_i}$$

When the sample sizes do not differ strongly, procedures one and three produce similar results.

15.8 The *c*-chart

number
c-chart

If we are interested in monitoring the ______________ of defects per unit and not the proportion of units possessing defects, we use a ______________. The *c*-chart is used where defects are allowed in a finished unit but we want the number of defects per unit to be controlled. An automobile, a man's suit, and a finished roll of steel need not be considered worthless if they contain only a few minor imperfections.

sampling
defect

The sampling inspector must clearly define what comprises a ______________ unit and exactly what will be categorized as a ______________. Sampling units are sometimes well defined, such as each finished man's suit or each completed automobile. But occasionally sampling units have to be defined, as in the case of observing the number of typographical errors in an evening newspaper. Since the newspaper will likely have different numbers of pages from day to day, it is best to define the sampling unit as each page of the newspaper and to attempt to control the average number of errors per page.

defects

equally spaced

Poisson; Poisson
mean; variance

A *c*-chart is a control chart on which is plotted the number of ______________ per sampling unit from samples drawn from a production process at ______________ ______________ points over time. The probability distribution of c, the number of defects per sampled unit, is closely approximated by the ______________ distribution. Since the ______________ distribution possesses the characteristic that its ______________ and ______________ are equal, the center line and control limits for the *c*-chart are found as follows:

center line = $\bar{c}$ = the average number of defects per sampled unit

$$= \frac{\text{number of defects in all sampled units}}{\text{number of sampling units selected}}$$

U.C.L. = $\bar{c} + 3\sqrt{\bar{c}}$

L.C.L. = __________ | $\bar{c} - 3\sqrt{\bar{c}}$

The center line, U.C.L. and L.C.L. for the c-chart are constructed from data obtained from at least __________ sampling units during times when the production process is known to be in ______________ ______________ . | 100 statistical control

Example 15.11

A manufacturing process produces heavy-duty dinner plates for use by restaurants. During equally spaced intervals of time when the process was known to be in statistical control, 100 plates were selected from the process and the number of defects (scratches, bubbles, and small cracks) on each plate was observed. The total number of defects observed was 260. Construct a c-chart to monitor the process.

Solution

The average number of defects per plate is

$$\bar{c} = 260/100 = 2.6$$

Thus, the control limits are

U.C.L. = 2.6 + __________ | $3\sqrt{2.6}$

= __________ | 7.43

and

L.C.L. = 2.6 - __________ | $3\sqrt{2.6}$

= __________ | - 2.23

Since the computed lower control limit is negative and, thus, unrealistic, we use ______________ as the lower control limit. The c-chart is shown below. Sample points are not displayed since they were not given. The c-chart, as it appears, can be used to directly monitor the plate manufacturing process by randomly selecting a finished plate from the process and noting the number of defects it contains. If the number of defects, c, is greater than __________ , the process is assumed to be out of statistical control. | zero | 7

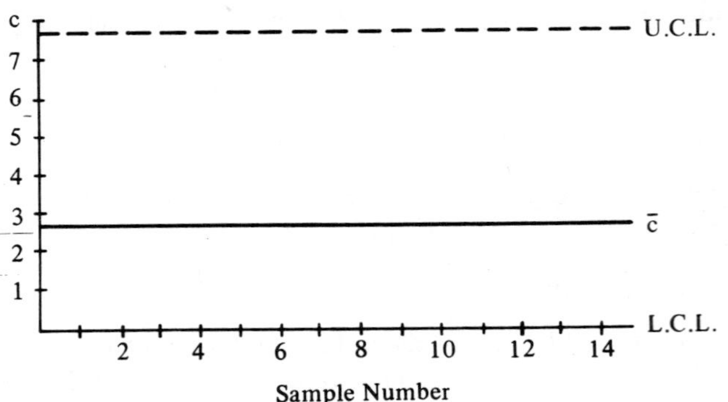

Self-Correcting Exercises 15C

1. The data which follows summarizes the results of testing permanent magnets used in electric relays. During each of ten weeks, 700 magnets were inspected per week and the number of defective magnets recorded.

Weeks	*Number Inspected*	*Number Defective*
1	700	38
2	700	60
3	700	36
4	700	39
5	700	28
6	700	37
7	700	41
8	700	47
9	700	32
10	700	30
Totals	7000	388

   Construct a p-chart using these data, under the assumption that the process was under control during this time period.

2. Refer to Exercise 1. The next five weeks produced the following data on the number of defective electromagnets per $n = 700$ weekly samples.

   25, 37, 42, 47, 55

   Use the control chart in Exercise 1 to plot the proportion defective per week. Comment on your results.
3. In order to control the number of pinholes in sheets of paper, specimen sheets of paper measuring 8.5 × 11 inches were taken from production at

specified intervals, and colored ink applied to one side of the paper. Each inkblot appearing on the opposite side of the paper within 3 minutes was counted as a defect. The data which follows gives the number of defects measured for 20 different sheets of paper tested at consecutive time intervals.

Time	*Number of Defects*	*Time*	*Number of Defects*
1	6	11	9
2	8	12	10
3	10	13	6
4	7	14	9
5	5	15	10
6	11	16	8
7	8	17	7
8	9	18	11
9	10	19	8
10	12	20	10
		TOTAL	174

a. Construct a c-chart using these data.
b. If the next 5 test samples produced 8, 10, 13, 15 and 16 defects per sheet, respectively, what would your conclusions be?

15.9 Acceptance Sampling

Most manufacturing plants can be thought of as processors that accept raw materials and turn them into finished products. Efficient operation would require that the number of defective items accepted for processing be kept to a minimum and the number of acceptable finished products be kept at a maximum.

These goals can be achieved in different ways. A manufacturer producing television sets would obviously test and adjust *each* set before it leaves the plant but would probably not test each transistor in an incoming lot before accepting the whole shipment. He would probably accept or reject the shipment depending on the number of defective transistors observed in a random sample drawn from that lot. Sometimes the act of testing an item is destructive, so that each item cannot be individually tested. Testing whether a flashbulb produces the required intensity of light obviously destroys the flashbulb.

The process of screening lots is an inferential procedure in which a decision about the proportion defective in a lot (population) is made. The sampling of items from incoming or outgoing lots or the sampling of items from a production line closely approximates the defining characteristics of a binomial experiment. Therefore, the number of defectives in a sample of size n will be distributed as a binomial random variable with parameter p, the proportion of defective items in the population sampled.

A number of sampling schemes are used in industry, the simplest of which is the following:

> From the lot select n items at random. Record the number x of defective items found in the sample. If x is less than or equal to a prescribed number a, accept the lot; otherwise reject the lot. This maximum number a of allowable defectives is called the *acceptance number* for the plan.

$n; a$

The plan above is called a *single sampling plan.* Any such plan is defined by specifying values for the numbers _________ (sample size) and _________ (acceptance number).

high

low

How does one decide whether to use plan A ($n = 10, a = 1$), or plan B ($n = 20, a = 2$), or some other plan? One acceptable criterion is that the probability of accepting a good lot should be (high, low) and that the probability of accepting a bad lot should be ___________. Thus we might select plan B (with the larger sample size) rather than plan A if good lots have a higher probability of acceptance and bad lots have a lower probability of acceptance when plan B is used. To obtain this comparison, we construct the *operating characteristic curve* for each of these plans. The operating characteristic curve is a graph that shows the probability of acceptance for an incoming lot with fraction defective p. The curve will be shown for values of p ranging from 0 (perfect lot) to 1 (totally defective). If a lot contains no good items

1; 0

0

1

($p =$ _________), then the probability that it will be accepted is _________. If a lot contains no defective items ($p =$ _________), it is certain to be accepted; that is, the probability of acceptance is _________. For intermediate values of p, the operating characteristic curves for two different plans will not, in general, coincide.

Example 15.12

Construct an operating characteristic curve for the sampling plan $n = 10$, $a = 1$.

Solution

large

binomial

Using this particular plan, we take a sample of size 10 and accept the lot if no more than 1 defective item is found. We assume that the lot is (large, small) enough to justify treating x, the number of defectives found in the sample, as a _____________ random variable.

1. Suppose that the lot contains 10% defective items ($p = .1$). The probability of accepting this lot is

$$P(x \leqslant 1) = p(0) + p(1) = C_0^{10}(.1)^0(.9)^{10} + C_1^{10}(.1)^1(.9)^9$$

It is not necessary to complete this calculation since the result, correct to the nearest thousandth, may be read directly from Table 1. Thus,

$$C_0^{10}\,(.1)^0\,(.9)^{10} + C_1^{10}\,(.1)^1\,(.9)^9 = \_\_\_\_\_\_\_\_$$ .736

2. By referring to Table 1, obtain the probabilities of acceptance that are omitted in the following table. Complete the table by filling in the missing entries when $n = 10$ and $a = 1$.

Fraction Defective, p	*Probability of Lot Acceptance*	
.01	.996	
.05	________	.914
.10	.736	
.20	________	.376
.30	________	.149
.40	________	.046
.50	.011	

3. A graph may now be constructed showing the probability of acceptance as a function of the fraction defective in the incoming lot. The curve so obtained is called the *operating characteristic curve* for the sampling plan.

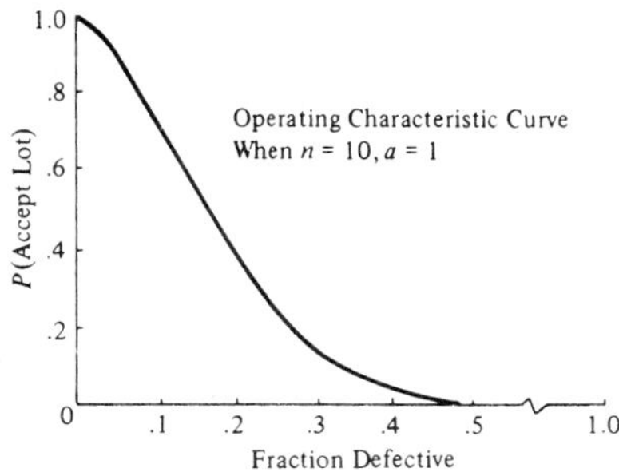

Example 5.20
Construct an operating characteristic curve for the plan $n = 20, a = 2$.

Solution
The probability of accepting a lot under this plan is the probability of obtaining no more than ________ defective items in a random sample of size 20. 2
Thus the probability of accepting an incoming lot with fraction defective p is

2

$$P(x \leqslant 2) = \sum_{x=\_\_\_}^{\_\_\_} C_x^{20} p^x (1-p)^{20-x}$$

0 (fill in the summation limits)

1. Using Table 1 complete the following table:

	Fraction Defective, *p*	*Probability of Lot Acceptance*
.925	.05	______
.677	.10	______
.206	.20	______
.035	.30	______

2. Complete the operating characteristic curve by labeling and scaling the following axes, plotting the points obtained from the table above, and joining the points with a smooth curve.

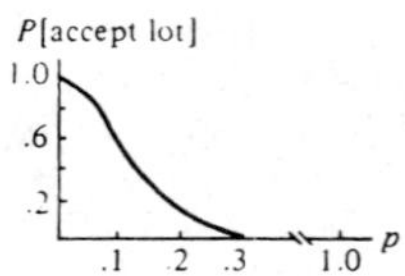

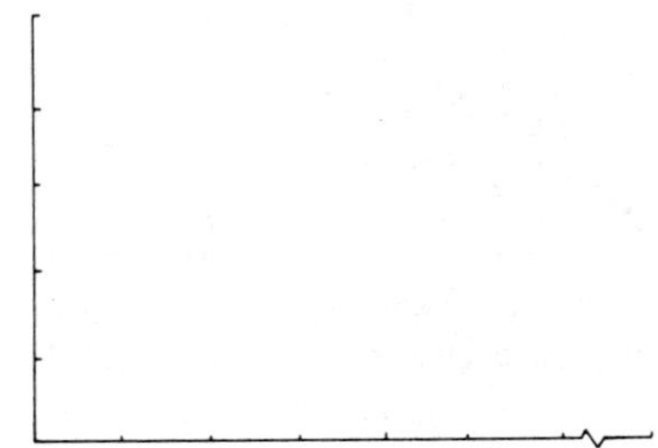

less Since an operating characteristic curve falls as one moves to the right, the probability of accepting a lot containing a high fraction defective is (more, less) than the probability of accepting a good lot.

Example 15.13

To aid in the comparison of plan A ($n = 10, a = 1$) and plan B ($n = 20, a = 2$), we will show their operating characteristic curves on the same graph, using acceptance values recorded in the following table:

Fraction Defective, *p*	*Probability of Acceptance* Plan A	*Probability of Acceptance* Plan B
.00	1.000	1.000
.05	.914	.925
.10	.736	.677
.20	.376	.206
.30	.149	.035
.40	.046	.004
.50	.011	.000

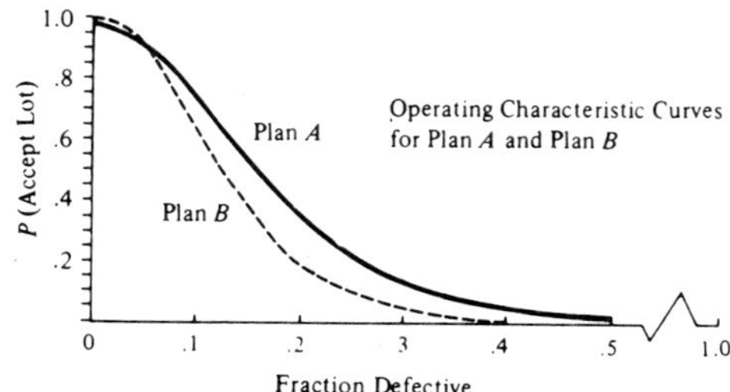

The two curves should cross at about $p = .06$. Thus the probability of accepting a lot with fraction defective less than .06 is (higher, lower) with plan B than with plan A. The probability of accepting a lot with fraction defective more than .06 is ______________ with plan B than with plan A. Thus plan B is more sensitive in discriminating between good and bad lots. The expense of inspecting a larger sample (as in plan B) may be justified by the greater sensitivity of plan B as compared with plan A.

higher

lower

Self-Correcting Exercises 15D

1. Large lots of portable radios are accepted in accordance with the sampling plan with sample size $n = 4$ and acceptance number $a = 1$.
   a. Complete the following table and construct the OC curve for this plan. The axes should be properly labeled and scaled.

Fraction Defective, p	0	.10	.30	.50	1
Probability of acceptance	______	.95	______	.31	______

   b. State two essentially different ways in which one might modify the above sampling plan to increase the probability of accepting a lot with fraction defective $p = .10$.

2. To discover the effect on acceptance probabilities of varying the sample size we study the additional sampling plans ($n = 10$, $a = 1$) and ($n = 25$, $a = 1$).
   a. Use Table 1 to complete the following table.

Fraction Defective, p		0	.10	.30	.50	1.0
Probability of acceptance	$n = 10$, $a = 1$	______	.74	______	.01	______
	$n = 25$, $a = 1$	______	______	.00	______	______

   b. Construct the OC curves for the plan in Exercise 1 and the plans considered in part a on the same set of axes.

c. If the acceptance number is kept the same and the sample size increased, what is the effect on the probability of accepting a given lot?

3. To discover the effect on acceptance probabilities of varying the acceptance number we study the additional sampling plans ($n = 25, a = 3$) and ($n = 25, a = 5$).

a. Use Table 1 to complete the following table.

Fraction Defective, p		0	.10	.30	.50	1.0
Probability of acceptance	$n = 25$, $a = 3$	______	______	.03	______	______
	$n = 25$, $a = 5$	______	.97	______	______	______

b. Construct the *OC* curves for the plans considered in part a together with the *OC* curve for the plan ($n = 25$, $a = 1$) (see Exercise 2) on the same set of axes.

c. If the sample size is kept the same and the acceptance number increased, what is the effect on the probability of accepting a given lot?

15.10 Summary

controllable
variation
control charts
$\bar{x}, R$

attribute
screen
sampling
plan
n
a

Quality control techniques are used to identify the presence of ________ ________ in the manufacturing process. The devices used to monitor the capability of the process are called ________ ________. The ________- and ________-charts are used to monitor a process whose measurements constitute a set of variable data, while the p-chart and c-chart are used to monitor a process consisting of ________ data.

A manufacturer of goods often finds it wise to ________ incoming lots of items for defectives. He does so by establishing a ________ ________, a rule which specifies two numbers, n and a. Under this rule, the manufacturer samples ________ items from the incoming lot and accepts the lot if no more than ________ defectives are observed. The numbers n and a are selected to balance the risks of an erroneous decision to the producer and the consumer of the items being screened.

EXERCISES

1. What are the distinguishing characteristics of the manufacturing situations where each of the following quality control devices are applicable:
   (a) A control chart
   (b) The $\bar{x}$-chart
   (c) The R-chart
   (d) The p-chart
   (e) The c-chart
   (f) An (n, a) sampling rule
   (g) An operating characteristic curve

2. Discuss the following statement: "The $\bar{x}$-chart and R-chart are internal control devices used by the manufacturer to monitor process capabilities, while lot acceptance sampling techniques are used externally by the buyer of the goods to see whether the process is capable of meeting his product specifications."
3. A hardwoods manufacturing plant has several different production lines to manufacture baseball bats of differing weights. One such production line is designed to produce bats weighing 32 ounces. During a period of time when the production process was known to be in statistical control, the average bat weight was found to be 31.7 ounces. The observed data was gathered from 50 samples each consisting of 5 measurements. The average range of all samples was found to be $\bar{R} = .48$ ounces. Construct an $\bar{x}$-chart and an R-chart to monitor the 32-ounce bat production process.
4. Refer to Exercise 3 and suppose that during a day when the state of the 32-ounce bat production process was unknown the following measurements were obtained at hourly intervals:

Hour	$\bar{x}$	R
1	31.6	0.90
2	32.5	2.31
3	33.4	1.95
4	33.1	2.40
5	31.6	0.40
6	31.8	1.23

Each measurement represents a statistic computed from a sample of five bat weights selected from the production process during a certain hour. Use the control charts constructed in Exercise 3 to monitor the process.
5. A sporting goods distributor buys large quantities of 32-ounce bats from the manufacturer described in Exercises 3 and 4. His specifications are that all 32-ounce bats he purchases must be between 31 ounces and 32.5 ounces. If the process is in control, find the values of the process capability indexes C_p and C_{pk}, and interpret your results.
6. A manufacturing process, designed to produce flashlight batteries, was examined at 20 different points in time when the process was known to be in control. At each sampling interval, 100 batteries were randomly selected from the process, they were tested, and the number of defective (inoperable) batteries was recorded. The numbers of defectives found in the 20 samples were as follows:

   5, 7, 6, 8, 10, 3, 2, 5, 8, 4, 9, 5, 7, 5, 2, 3, 8, 2, 1, 4

   a. Construct a p-chart to monitor the process.
   b. During a day when the state of the process was unknown, five different samples of size 100 each yielded 7, 9, 11, 12, and 6 defectives, respectively. Comment on the state of the process.

7. Suppose that the flashlight battery manufacturing process suddenly shifts in the proportion of defectives produced to 10%. What is the probability that the next sample of 100 will detect this shift by finding the process to be out of control?
8. A buyer of flashlight batteries from the manufacturer described in the previous two exercises specifies that each shipment he receives must contain no more than 7% defectives. When the manufacturing process is in control, what is the probability that the buyer's specifications are met?
9. The number of defects per electric clock was recorded for 100 clocks in a manufacturing process at times when the process was known to be in statistical control. A total of 325 defects were observed on the 100 clocks.
   (a) Construct a c-chart to monitor the clock manufacturing process.
   (b) During a period when the state of the manufacturing process was unknown, six clocks were randomly selected from the process. The numbers of defects found on the six clocks were 4, 7, 9, 6, 8, and 2, respectively. Comment on the state of the manufacturing process.
10. Large lots of portable radios are accepted in accordance with the sampling plan with sample size $n = 4$ and acceptance number $a = 1$.
   (a) Complete the following table and construct the O.C. curve for this plan. The axes should be properly labeled and scaled.

Fraction Defective, p	0	.10	.30	.50	1.0
Probability of Accepting	______	.95	______	.31	______

   (b) State two essentially different ways in which one might modify the above sampling plan to increase the probability of accepting a lot with fraction defective $p = .10$.
11. To discover the effect on acceptance probabilities of varying the sample size we study the additional sampling plans ($n = 10$, $a = 1$) and ($n = 25$, $a = 1$).
   a. Use Table 1 in your text to complete the following table.

Fraction Defective, p		0	.10	.30	.50	1.0
Probability of Accepting	$n = 10$, $a = 1$	______	.74	______	.01	______
	$n = 25$, $a = 1$	______	______	.00	______	______

b. Construct the O.C. curves for the plan in Exercise 1 and the plans considered in part a on the same set of axes.
c. If the acceptance number is kept the same and the sample size increased, what is the effect on the probability of accepting a given lot?

12. To discover the effect on acceptance probabilities of varying the acceptance number we study the additional sampling plans ($n = 25$, $a = 3$) and ($n = 25$, $a = 5$).
   a. Use Table 1 in your text to complete the following table.

Fraction Defective, p		0	.10	.30	.50	1.0
Probability of Accepting	$n = 25$, $a = 3$	______	______	.03	______	______
	$n = 25$, $a = 5$	______	.97	______	______	______

   b. Construct the O.C. curves for the plans considered in part a together with the O.C. curve for the plan ($n = 25$, $a = 1$) (see Exercise 11) on the same set of axes.
   c. If the sample size is kept the same and the acceptance number increased, what is the effect on the probability of accepting a given lot?

13. A buyer and a seller agree to use sampling plan ($n = 25$, $a = 2$) or sampling plan ($n = 10$, $a = 1$). Under each of these plans, determine the probability that the buyer would accept the lot if the fraction defective of the lot is:
   a. $p = 0$ b. $p = .05$ c. $p = .10$
   d. $p = .20$ e. $p = .50$ f. $p = 1.0$

Chapter 16

SURVEY SAMPLING

16.1 Introduction

The topics presented in previous chapters were mainly concerned with methods for describing and analyzing available sets of data, with the major emphasis on analysis and interpretation of results. In this chapter, the emphasis will be on the methods used to select the sample that gives rise to the sample observations. Methods for selecting the sample are called sampling designs.

The objective of a sampling design is to produce a sample that is representative of the ______________ from which it was drawn. The type of sampling design chosen depends mainly on the ______________ of the population with regard to the characteristic under investigation; however, other factors may also affect the sampling design ultimately chosen.

population
uniformity

A ______________ is an enumeration of every element contained in the population, whereas a sample survey involves only those elements of the population included in the ______________. Although a census certainly provides more information than would a sample survey, a sample survey has many advantages when compared to a complete census. In addition to economy and feasibility, a sample survey has the following advantages.

census

sample

1. Sampling provides the opportunity for rapid information retrieval not usually available with a complete census.
2. When the evaluation of the characteristics under study results in the destruction of the elements tested, a census is not reasonable.
3. A complete census will not necessarily provide complete information since, for example, people may refuse to answer what they feel are sensitive or very personal questions, or the sheer volume of data may cause careless recording and/or handling of results.

In order to ensure that the sample is representative of the population sampled, and that the sample is chosen so that valid inferences can be made

random — about the population, the sample must be drawn in a ____________ manner. A random sample is a sample selected in such a way that every sample of n observations has the same probability of being selected. When

sample — a sample is not random, only descriptive statements about the (sample, population) can be made.

A sampling design or a survey design specifies the method for collecting

element — the elements in the sample. An ____________ is an object on which a

does not — measurement is taken. The design itself (does, does not) specify the method in which an element in the sample will give rise to an observation. Sampling units are nonoverlapping collections of elements from the population. A

may not — sampling unit (may, may not) be an individual element. A list of all sam-

frame — pling units contained in the population is called a ____________. In conducting a sample survey, the sampling units must first be identified, and an appropriate frame constructed. The sampling units to be included are then

frame — randomly chosen from the ____________ in accordance with the desired sampling design.

16.2 Bias and Error in Sampling

The reliability of an inference concerning a population parameter θ is measured by the error in estimation, defined as $|\hat{\theta} - \theta|$, the absolute difference between the estimate and the true value of the parameter estimated. When the experimenter can specify a tolerable bound B on the error of estimation, a minimum sample size can be found that will ensure that the estimate $\hat{\theta}$ will not differ from θ by more than B with a high probability. The

larger — smaller the value of B, the (smaller, larger) will be the sample size required to achieve the specified bound on the error of estimation.

Three factors that may affect the validity of the results of a sample survey are random variation, misspecification, and nonresponse. Misspecification and nonresponse may cause estimates to be biased, while random variation introduces the possibility that the sample observations constitute one of the very unlikely samples possible under random sampling.

1. Random Variation

When sampling has been done in a random manner, so that every combination of n elements from the population has an equal chance of being selected, the distribution of sample estimates can be determined, and confidence interval estimates for the parameter under investigation can be constructed. When, for example, the estimator is unbiased and the distribution of estimates is approximately normal, a 95% confidence interval esti-

1.96 — mate means that approximately 95% of such estimates will be within ______ standard deviations of the true value of the parameter. However, it also

5% — means that approximately ____________ of such estimates will lie farther than 1.96 standard deviations from the true value of the parameter. Since random sampling always introduces random variation into the estimation scheme, there is always the possibility that any single estimate will be farther than 1.96 standard deviations from the true value of the parameter. For example, if a random sampling plan implemented to determine the average assessed value of single-family residences in a given area happened to produce a sample containing only those homes with four or more bedrooms when the area has a preponderance of residences with at most three bedrooms, the sample average would lead the sampler to conclude that the average assessed value in the area is (lower, higher) than it actually is. Hence, random variation introduces the probability of error in estimation. higher

2. Misspecification

In order to make valid inferences from sample information, the sample must be drawn from the target population of interest. If a sample drawn from a related, but essentially different, population is used to make inferences about the target population, any resulting inferences about the target population will be ______________ in some way. When the frame used to select a sample does not accurately contain the elements in the target population, we have the problem of ______________. Using a telephone directory as a frame for all family residences in a given city systematically excludes residences without phones or residences with unlisted telephone numbers. Such a systematic exclusion could produce bias in inferences made from sample data collected using this frame. It may be that the frame contains elements not in the population, or perhaps contains incorrect information concerning these elements. In either case, misspecification can produce ______________ in the survey sample results.

biased
misspecification
bias

3. Nonresponse

Another major source of error in sample surveys is due to nonresponse by some members of the sample. Nonresponse is quite common in telephone surveys, in surveys in which a questionnaire is mailed to a household, and in door-to-door surveys involving individual households. Nonresponse results in bias because researchers in general assume that respondents and nonrespondents would provide ______________ information in the survey when this is rarely the case. In preference surveys, very often nonrespondents are satisfied with the status quo, or have no strong feelings about a given matter. In door-to-door surveys, nonrespondents are usually those employed outside the home, while respondents are homemakers, retired persons, and others who can perform their work at home. Some control over nonresponse can be accomplished by revisiting nonrespondents or randomly choosing an ______________ sampling unit.

similar
alternate

Errors due to random variation can be controlled to some extent by the choice of sample ______________ and by the choice of the survey ______________ to be used. Careful definition of the target population

size
design

misspecification

nonresponse

and the associated frame can eliminate bias due to ______________. Attempts to contact nonrespondents or the random selection of an alternate will help reduce bias due to ______________. In light of these sources of error, great care should be exercised in designing a sample survey and in the interpretation of the results.

16.3 How to Select a Random Sample

The selection of a simple random sample is a basic technique that is used in all sampling designs. Therefore, it is important to know in detail how to select a simple random sample of size n from a *finite* population consisting of N elements.

> When a sample is drawn in such a way that every possible sample of size n has the same probability of being selected, the sampling is said to be random and the resulting sample is called a *simple random sample.*

---

random number

0; 9

Although random sampling is difficult to achieve in practice, the use of a ______________ ______________ table in selecting a random sample is the best way to implement a random sampling design. A random number table contains the digits __________ through __________ with equal frequency and in a random order. The digits are in random order if there is no pattern of any kind with respect to their occurrence. For example, in a random number table you would not find the digit 9 always followed by a 1 or 2. Neither, for example, would you find a two-digit combination such as 57 or 75 always followed by a combination such as 68 or 86. When a random number table is used to select a simple random sample, the choice of elements to be included in the sample reflects the properties of the random number table used in the selection. We illustrate the procedure with the next example.

Example 16.1

In order to estimate the number of visits to a doctor per household in an area containing $N = 1000$ households, an investigator has decided to select a simple random sample of size 20 households. Use the random number table in your text to select a sample of size $n = 20$ drawn in such a way as to satisfy a simple random sampling plan.

Solution

The frame to be used in this problem consists of a list of the 1000 households in the given area. Since each of the numbers 1 through 1000 corresponds to one and only one household in the area, we need to select

20 numbers between 1 and 1000 from the random number table to identify the households to be included in the sample.

1. Suppose we decide to use the first three digits of the five-digit numbers appearing in the columns of the table. We must first randomly select a line and column in the table as a starting point and then decide in which direction we will move within the table. This can be done by turning to a page containing the random numbers and setting your pencil point on the page. In pinpointing a five-digit block of numbers, we can use the first two digits to find the row and the next two digits to find the column in which to begin. Suppose that our pencil pointed to the five-digit group 21361 in line 81, column 7. The first two digits in
the group 21361 can identify the line as line __________, while the 21
second two digits in the group 21361 can identify the column. Since there are only 14 columns, divide 36 by 14 and use the *remainder* to
identify the column. Since 36/14 is 2 with a remainder of __________, 8
we begin with column __________. 8
2. Using line 21, column 8 as a starting point, we can now list the five-digit entries by moving in any direction we wish. Let us list lines 21 through 25 for columns 8, 9, 10 and 11 to produce the 20 random numbers required to identify the sample elements. We will associate households 1 through 999 with the entries 001 through 999 in the table and household 1000 with the entry 000.

04734	59193	22178	30421
26384	58151	06646	21524
28728	35806	06912	17012
15398	46557	41135	10367
61280	50001	67658	32586

By reading the first three digits in each five-digit group, we have identified the households to be included in the sample.

If a household number appeared more than once in the list of random numbers, that household would only appear *once* in the sample. Further entries in the table would be used until 20 distinct households had been identified for inclusion in the sample.

Example 16.2

How would the selection procedure in Example 16.1 be modified if the area contained $N = 500$ households?

Solution

1. By using three-digit entries to identify the $n = 20$ households when the population size is $N = 500$, we could associate households 1 through
500 with the digits __________ through __________ and discard or 001; 500
not record 000 and any random digits between 501 and 999.

2. Alternatively, to avoid excessive table listings, we could use the random
digits 001 through 500 directly, and for any number in the range 501
500 through 999, use its remainder upon division by __________. Under
this scheme, household 228 would be associated with the three-digit
728 random numbers 228 and __________. Finally, by associating house-
500 hold 500 with the random numbers 000 and __________, our sample
will be drawn so that every household has a 2 in 1000 or 1 in 500
chance of being included in the sample.

Self-Correcting Exercises 16A

1. An auditing firm has been hired by a company to examine its accounts receivable. If the company has 100 current accounts and the auditing firm proposes to examine 20 of those accounts, explain how you would randomly select 20 accounts from the 100 accounts using a random number table.
2. To investigate employee satisfaction with regard to company fringe benefits, the management of a company employing 250 workers proposes to survey 30 workers concerning their views on company fringe benefits. If these 30 workers are to be randomly chosen from the 250 workers employed by the company, provide an efficient selection scheme for choosing the 30 workers, using random number tables. Implement the sampling plan and record the 30 workers who are to be interviewed.

16.4 Estimation Based on a Simple Random Sample

The objective of any sampling design is to produce valid inferences about the population sampled. Most investigations are concerned with estimating the population mean, μ, or a population total, τ. For example, a large wholesale firm might be interested in the mean sales per account as well as the total sales. This same firm would also be interested in the proportion of delinquent accounts. In addition to a point estimator for each of these population parameters, we need the variance of these estimators in order to place bounds on the error of estimation. Recall that in Chapter 8, we used bounds on error

$$\hat{\theta} \pm 1.96\,\sigma_{\hat{\theta}}$$

in order to estimate a parameter θ. This result was due to the fact that the
Central Limit estimator $\hat{\theta}$ satisfied the requirements of the __________ __________
Theorem; normal __________, and hence $\hat{\theta}$ had an approximately __________ dis-
tribution in repeated sampling.

In general, the estimators of μ and τ in survey sampling will not always satisfy the requirements of the Central Limit Theorem. However, Tchebysheff's Theorem is applicable to any population, and the Empirical Rule is applicable if the distribution of the estimator is *approximately* mound shaped. For this reason, we can and shall consistently use 1.96 standard deviations as the approximate bound on error, implying minimally that at least ________% (and more likely ________%) of such estimates will lie within 1.96 standard deviations of the true value of the estimated parameter.

75
95

1. Estimation of the Population Mean and Total for a Simple Random Sample
The estimator of the population mean μ of a finite population of size N based on a simple random sample of size n is

$$\bar{x} = \frac{\Sigma x_i}{n}$$

with variance

$$\hat{\sigma}^2_{\bar{x}} = \frac{s^2}{n}\left(\frac{N-n}{N}\right)$$

The point estimate with approximate bounds on the error of estimation is $\bar{x} \pm 1.96\hat{\sigma}_{\bar{x}}$. The quantity s^2 is the sample variance of the n sample observations, discussed earlier in this text.

The estimator of the population total τ uses the information contained in $\bar{x}$ by inflating this average by a factor of ________, the population size. Hence,

N

$$\hat{\tau} = N\bar{x}$$

with variance

$$\hat{\sigma}^2_{\hat{\tau}} = N^2\hat{\sigma}^2_{\bar{x}}$$

The point estimate with bounds on the error of estimation is given as

$$N\bar{x} \pm 1.96\sigma_{\hat{\tau}}$$

Notice that the variance of $\bar{x}$ when sampling from a finite population of size N is

$$\frac{s^2}{n}\left(\frac{N-n}{N}\right)$$

the same as the quantity given in earlier chapters multiplied by ________.

$(N - n)/N$

correction factor

The quantity $(N - n)/N$ is called the finite population ______________ ______________ and accounts for the fact that sampling does deplete a finite population. When n is small relative to N, $(N - n)/N$ is close to

one

__________. When $N \geqslant 20n$, the correction factor is often ignored and the quantity s^2/n is used as the variance of $\bar{x}$. However, we will use the finite population correction factor where appropriate, regardless of the population and sample sizes.

Example 15.3

A wholesale firm that has 325 active accounts is interested in estimating the average sales per account as well as the total sales over the last four weeks. In a random sample of 20 accounts, the average sales per account was found to be $\bar{x}$ = \$849 with a sample standard deviation of s = \$89. Estimate the average sales per account and the total sales for the last four weeks. Place bounds of error on these estimates.

Solution

A summary of the pertinent information follows.

$$\bar{x} = 849 \qquad n = 20$$

$$s = 89 \qquad N = 325$$

849

a. The estimate of the mean sales per account is $\bar{x}$ = __________. To place bounds of error on this estimate, we need to evaluate $\hat{\sigma}_{\bar{x}}$.

$$\hat{\sigma}^2_{\bar{x}} = \frac{s^2}{n}\left(\frac{N - n}{N}\right)$$

$$= \frac{(89)^2}{20}\left(\frac{325 - 20}{325}\right)$$

.9385

$$= \frac{(89)^2}{20}(\_\_\_\_\_\_\_\_\_\_)$$

371.6777

$$= \_\_\_\_\_\_\_\_\_\_$$

Hence,

$$\hat{\sigma}_{\bar{x}} = \sqrt{371.6777}$$

19.28

$$= \_\_\_\_\_\_\_\_\_\_$$

The estimate of the mean sales per account with a bound on the error of estimation is

$$849 \pm 1.96(19.28)$$

$$\_\_\_\_\_\_\_\_ \pm \_\_\_\_\_\_\_\_$$ \$849; \$37.79

b. The estimate of the total sales is given by

$$\hat{\tau} = N\bar{x}$$

$$= \_\_\_\_\_\_\_\_(849)$$ 325

$$= \_\_\_\_\_\_\_\_$$ 275,928

Evaluating $\hat{\sigma}_{\hat{\tau}}$, we have

$$\hat{\sigma}^2_{\hat{\tau}} = N^2\hat{\sigma}^2_{\bar{x}}$$

$$= (\_\_\_\_\_\_\_\_)^2(371.6777)$$ 325

$$= 39{,}258{,}456$$

with

$$\hat{\sigma}_{\hat{\tau}} = \sqrt{39{,}258{,}456}$$

$$= \_\_\_\_\_\_\_\_$$ 6265.66

The estimate of total sales with bounds on the error of estimation is given as

$$275{,}928 \pm 1.96(6265.66)$$

or

$$\_\_\_\_\_\_\_\_ \pm \_\_\_\_\_\_\_\_$$ \$275,928; \$12,281

2. Estimation of the Population Prcportion for a Simple Random Sample

In estimating the proportion p of the population that possesses a given characteristic, we use the computational procedures of Chapter 8 with a modification to account for sampling from a finite population of size N.

If x is the number of elements in the sample of size n possessing the specified characteristic, the estimate of p is

$$\hat{p} = \_\_\_\_\_\_\_\_$$ $\frac{x}{n}$

with variance

$$\hat{\sigma}^2_{\hat{p}} = \frac{\hat{p}\hat{q}}{(n-1)}\left(\frac{N-n}{N}\right)$$

$1 - \hat{p}$ where $\hat{q}$ = __________. The point estimate for p with bounds on the error of estimation is

$$\hat{p} \pm 1.96\hat{\sigma}_{\hat{p}}$$

Example 16.4

Refer to Example 16.3. Suppose that 2 of the 20 sampled accounts were found to be delinquent. Estimate the proportion of the firm's accounts that are delinquent.

Solution

a. The estimate of the proportion of delinquent accounts is

.1 $$\hat{p} = \frac{x}{n} = \frac{2}{20} = \_\_\_\_\_\_\_\_\_\_$$

and

.9 $$\hat{q} = 1 - \hat{p} = \_\_\_\_\_\_\_\_\_\_$$

b. The estimated variance of $\hat{p}$ is

$$\hat{\sigma}^2_{\hat{p}} = \frac{\hat{p}\hat{q}}{(n-1)}\left(\frac{N-n}{N}\right)$$

$$= \frac{(.1)(.9)}{19}\left(\frac{325-20}{325}\right)$$

$$= \frac{.09}{19}(.9385)$$

.004445 $$= \_\_\_\_\_\_\_\_\_\_$$

and

$$\hat{\sigma}_{\hat{p}} = \sqrt{.004445}$$

.0667 $$= \_\_\_\_\_\_\_\_\_\_$$

c. The point estimate of the proportion of delinquent accounts with bounds on the error of estimation is

$$.1 \pm 1.96(.0667)$$

$$\_\_\_\_\_\_\_\_ \pm \_\_\_\_\_\_\_\_$$

.1; .1307

Self-Correcting Exercises 16B

1. To estimate the average assessed value of $N = 1000$ single-family residences within a given area of a city, a simple random sample of $n = 25$ residences provided the following information.

$\bar{x} = \$86{,}500$ $\qquad$ $s = \$8{,}600$

   a. Estimate the average assessed value of the 1000 homes in this area, and place a bound on the error of estimation.
   b. Estimate the total assessed value of the homes in this area, and place a bound on the error of estimation.
2. A quality control scheme required that a random sample of $n = 50$ items be selected from each incoming lot of $N = 1000$ items. If 8 defective items were found in a sample of 50 items from lot number 18, estimate the percentage of defective items in lot 18, and place a bound on the error of estimation.

16.5 Stratified Random Sampling

In many situations the population of interest consists of one or more subpopulations. Workers within a given industry may be grouped into several natural job categories; business firms or cities may be grouped according to size; areas may be classified as urban, suburban or rural. In such cases, it is desirable to have each subpopulation represented in the sample.

A *stratified random sample* is a sample obtained by dividing a population into nonoverlapping subpopulations called strata and then selecting a simple random sample within each stratum.

Stratified random sampling, when appropriate, has three major advantages over simple random sampling.

1. The cost of collecting and analyzing data is often reduced by stratifying a population into homogeneous subgroups, which are different from one another.

2. The variance of the estimator is also reduced by stratification, since the
smaller — variation within subgroups is usually (smaller, larger) than the overall population variance.
3. Stratified sampling provides separate estimates for parameters in each
stratum — ______________, without selecting a separate sample.

The cost of sampling and the bound on the error of estimation are two factors that determine the sample allocation across the strata. In general, one takes a larger sample if

large — 1. the stratum is (small, large)
large — 2. the variance within that stratum is (small, large), or
less — 3. sampling costs (less, more) in that stratum.

One method of allocation, called the proportional allocation procedure,
size — partitions the sample size across the strata proportional to the __________ of the strata. We will use this procedure throughout this chapter because of its simplicity and because of inherent problems usually encountered in optimum allocation procedures.

In allocating a sample of size n across L strata using the proportional allocation procedure, n_i elements are selected from the ith stratum, where

$$n_i = n\left(\frac{N_i}{N}\right)$$

when the ith stratum contains N_i elements and the total population size is

$$N = \sum_{i=1}^{L} N_i$$

Example 16.5

An investigator has sufficient funds to include 50 wholesale dealers of farm implements in a products liability insurance survey. Of the 1000 dealers, 600 have annual sales under \$5 million, 300 have annual sales between \$5 and \$25 million, and the remaining 100 have annual sales in excess of \$25 million. Produce the proportional sample allocation appropriate for this situation.

Solution

600 — The population size is $N = 1000$, with stratum sizes $N_1 =$ __________,
300; 100 — $N_2 =$ __________, $N_3 =$ __________.

1. The sample size for stratum 1 is

$$n_1 = n\left(\frac{N_1}{N}\right)$$

$$= 50\left(\frac{600}{1000}\right)$$

$$= \_\_\_\_\_\_\_\_$$ 30

2. For stratum 2,

$$n_2 = 50\left(\frac{300}{1000}\right)$$

$$= \_\_\_\_\_\_\_\_$$ 15

3. For stratum 3,

$$n_3 = 50\left(\frac{100}{1000}\right)$$

$$= \_\_\_\_\_\_\_\_$$ 5

Proportional allocation would allot n_1 = ________, n_2 = ________, and n_3 = ________. 30; 15 5

Estimation of the Mean and Variance of Each Stratum

If x_{ij} is the jth observation in the ith stratum, $j = 1, 2, \ldots, n_i$, the mean and variance for the ith stratum are estimated by

$$\bar{x}_i = \frac{\sum_{j=1}^{n_i} x_{ij}}{n_i}$$

and

$$s_i^2 = \frac{\sum_{j=1}^{n_i} (x_{ij} - \bar{x}_i)^2}{n_i - 1}$$

respectively, where $i = 1, 2, \ldots, L$. The sum of squared deviations is calculated as usual:

$$\sum_{j=1}^{n_i} (x_{ij} - \bar{x}_i)^2 = \sum_{j=1}^{n_i} x_{ij}^2 - \frac{\left(\sum_{j=1}^{n_i} x_{ij}\right)^2}{n_i}$$

Estimation of the Population Mean for a Stratified Random Sample

The estimator of the population mean is the weighted average of the strata means, using the strata sizes as weights. This estimator is

$$\bar{x}_{st} = \frac{1}{N} \sum_{i=1}^{L} N_i \bar{x}_i$$

with variance

$$\hat{\sigma}^2_{\bar{y}_{st}} = \frac{1}{N^2} \sum_{i=1}^{L} N_i^2 \left(\frac{N_i - n_i}{N_i}\right) \left(\frac{s_i^2}{n_i}\right)$$

1.96 standard deviations are used as bounds on the error of estimation.

Example 16.6

The following tabulation provides a partial summary of the results of the products liability insurance survey of Example 16.5. The amount of products liability insurance carried by each dealer was recorded in units of one million dollars. Stratum 1 included all dealers with annual sales under $5 million, stratum 2 included those dealers with annual sales between $5 and $25 million, and stratum 3 included those dealers whose annual sales exceeded $25 million.

	Stratum 1	*Stratum 2*	*Stratum 3*
N_i	600	300	100
n_i	30	15	5
$\bar{x}_i$	6.2	47.3	150.2
s_i^2	2.5	25.4	100.8

Estimate the average amount of products liability insurance carried, and place bounds on the error of estimation.

Solution

1. Using the tabled information, the estimate of the average amount of products liability insurance carried is found using

$$\bar{x}_{st} = \frac{1}{N} \sum_{i=1}^{L} N_i \bar{x}_i$$

There are $L = 3$ strata with $N = 1000$. Hence,

$$\bar{x}_{st} = \frac{1}{1000} [600(6.2) + 300(47.3) + 100(150.2)]$$

$$= \frac{1}{1000} [3720 + 14{,}190 + \_\_\_\_\_\_\_\_]$$ 15,020

$$= \frac{1}{1000} (\_\_\_\_\_\_\_\_)$$ 32,930

$$= \_\_\_\_\_\_\_\_$$ 32.93

2. To calculate bounds on error, we need to evaluate the variance of $\bar{x}_{st}$. Using proportional allocation, the finite population correction factors should be equal within each stratum. For stratum 1,

$$\frac{N_1 - n_1}{N_1} = \frac{600 - 30}{600} = \_\_\_\_\_\_\_\_$$ .95

For stratum 2,

$$\frac{N_2 - n_2}{N_2} = \frac{300 - 15}{300} = \_\_\_\_\_\_\_\_$$ .95

For stratum 3,

$$\frac{N_3 - n_3}{N_3} = \frac{100 - 5}{100} = \_\_\_\_\_\_\_\_$$ .95

Hence,

$$\hat{\sigma}^2_{\bar{x}_{st}} = \frac{1}{N^2} \sum_{i=1}^{L} N_i^2 \left(\frac{N_i - n_i}{N_i}\right)\left(\frac{s_i^2}{n_i}\right)$$

$$= \frac{.95}{(1000)^2}\left[(600)^2\left(\frac{2.5}{30}\right) + (300)^2\left(\frac{25.4}{15}\right) + (100)^2\left(\frac{100.8}{5}\right)\right]$$

$$= \frac{.95}{(1000)^2}[30{,}000 + 151{,}800 + 201{,}600]$$

383,400 $= \frac{.95}{(1000)^2}$ [________]

.36423 = ________

and

.6035147 $\hat{\sigma}_{\bar{x}_{st}} = \sqrt{.36423} =$ ________

3. The estimate of the average amount of liability insurance carried is

$$\$32{,}930{,}000 \pm 1.96(603{,}514.7)$$

or

\$32,930,000; \$1,182,888.8 ________ ± ________

Example 16.7
Using the information in Example 16.6 estimate the total amount of products liability insurance carried by these dealers and place a bound on the error of estimation.

Solution
32.93 From Example 16.6, we have $\bar{x}_{st} =$ ________ with estimated variance
.6035 ________. Therefore,

$$\hat{\tau} = N\bar{x}_{st}$$

$$= 1000(32.93)$$

32,930 = ________

and

$$\hat{\sigma}_{\hat{\tau}} = \sqrt{N^2 \hat{\sigma}^2_{\bar{x}_{st}}}$$

$$= \sqrt{(1000)^2(.6035147)}$$

$$= \sqrt{\underline{\qquad\qquad}}$$ 603,514.7

$$= \underline{\qquad\qquad}$$ 776.86

The estimate of the total amount of products liability insurance carried is

$32,930MM ± 1.96($776.86MM)

$32,930MM ± $1,522.65MM

where MM represents 1 million.

Estimation of the Population Proportion for a Stratified Random Sample

The estimator of the population proportion p for a stratified random sample is the weighted average of the sample proportions in each stratum using the strata sizes as weights.

$$\hat{p}_{st} = \frac{1}{N} \sum_{i=1}^{L} N_i \hat{p}_i$$

with

$$\hat{\sigma}^2_{\hat{p}_{st}} = \frac{1}{N^2} \sum_{i=1}^{L} N_i^2 \left(\frac{N_i - n_i}{N_i}\right) \left(\frac{\hat{p}_i \hat{q}_i}{n_i - 1}\right)$$

Again, 1.96 standard deviations are used as bounds on the error of estimation.

Example 16.8

In addition to the amount of products liability insurance carried, each dealer in the survey was asked whether or not he carried excess or "umbrella" coverage, which covers claims in excess of the usual products liability insurance. The number in each stratum carrying umbrella coverage is given in the following table.

Strata	*Sample Size*	*Number Having Umbrella Coverage*	$\hat{p}_i$	
1	30	21	______	.70
2	15	9	______	.60
3	5	4	______	.80

Estimate p, the proportion of dealers who carry excess coverage, and place bounds on the error estimation.

Solution

1. In the table, fill in the values for $\hat{p}_1, \hat{p}_2$ and $\hat{p}_3$. The estimate for p is

$$\hat{p}_{st} = \frac{1}{N} \sum_{i=1}^{3} N_i \hat{p}_i$$

.70; .60; .80 $$= \frac{1}{1000} [600(\_\_\_\_\_\_) + 300(\_\_\_\_\_\_) + 100(\_\_\_\_\_\_)]$$

$$= \frac{1}{1000} (420 + 180 + 80)$$

.68 $$= \_\_\_\_\_\_$$

2. In evaluating the variance of $\hat{p}_{st}$, we can use the fact that the finite population correction factor $(N_i - n_i)/N_i = .95$ for $i = 1, 2, 3$. Hence,

$$\hat{\sigma}^2_{\hat{p}_{st}} = \frac{1}{N^2} \sum_{i=1}^{3} N_i^2 \left(\frac{N_i - n_i}{N_i}\right) \left(\frac{p_i q_i}{n_i - 1}\right)$$

600; 300 $$= \frac{.95}{(1000)^2} \left[(\_\_\_\_\_\_)^2 \frac{(.7)(.3)}{29} + (\_\_\_\_\_\_)^2 \frac{(.6)(.4)}{14}\right.$$

100 $$\left. + (\_\_\_\_\_\_)^2 \frac{(.8)(.2)}{4}\right]$$

$$= \frac{.95}{(1000)^2} (2606.8966 + 1542.8571 + 400)$$

.004322 $$= \_\_\_\_\_\_$$

and

.066 $$\hat{\sigma}_{\hat{p}_{st}} = \_\_\_\_\_\_$$

3. The estimate of the proportion of dealers who carry excess coverage with bounds on the error of estimation is

$.68 \pm 1.96(.066)$

which, correct to 2 decimal accuracy, is ________ ± ________. .68; .13

Using a stratified random sampling procedure allows an investigator to estimate parameters within a stratum, as well as parameters of the total population. If, for example, we wished to estimate the percentage of dealers in the first stratum (less than \$5 million annual sales) carrying umbrella coverage, we would use

$$\hat{p}_1 \pm 1.96 \sqrt{\left(\frac{N_1 - n_1}{N_1}\right)\left(\frac{\hat{p}_1\hat{q}_1}{n_1 - 1}\right)}$$

or

$$\_\_\_\_\_\_ \pm 1.96 \sqrt{(.95)\frac{(.7)(.3)}{29}}$$ .70

________ ± ________ .70; .16

Self-Correcting Exercises 16C

1. The home office would like to estimate the value of the items on the machine inventory lists at its four branch offices. If $n = 60$ items are to be sampled, use proportional allocation to determine the number of inventory items to be sampled at each branch office if the inventory lists at the four branch offices contain $N_1 = 1100, N_2 = 600, N_3 = 800$ and $N_4 = 500$ items, respectively.
2. When the stratified sampling plan in Exercise 1 was implemented, the following information was obtained.

	Branch Office			
	1	*2*	*3*	*4*
Number of items, N_i	1,100	600	800	500
Sample size, n_i	22	12	16	10
Sample mean, $\bar{x}_i$	1,050	820	990	1,280
Sample variance, s_i^2	1,210	930	1,080	1,510

a. Estimate the average value of the inventoried items on all four branch office inventory lists, and place a bound on the error of estimation.
b. Estimate the total value of the inventoried items on all four branch office inventory lists, and place a bound on the error of estimation.

c. Estimate the average value of the inventoried items at branch office 1 and place a bound on the error of estimation.

3. In addition to the value of the inventoried items, the number of items five years old or older at each branch office was also recorded.

	Branch Office			
	1	*2*	*3*	*4*
Sample size	22	12	16	10
Number of items 5 years old or older	12	5	6	3

Estimate the proportion of inventoried items five years old or older on all branch office inventory lists, and place a bound on the error of estimation.

16.6 Cluster Sampling

In order to select a simple random sample or a stratified random sample, an investigator must have available a frame listing all of the elements in the population to be sampled. When an appropriate frame is not available or is very costly to obtain, a ______________ sampling design can be used.

cluster

A *cluster sample* is a simple random sample in which the sampling units are collections or clusters of elements in the population. A cluster sample is obtained by randomly selecting m clusters from the population and then conducting a complete census within each cluster.

In sampling households in a given city, an appropriate cluster of households might be a city block or a political ward. In sampling airline passengers, an appropriate cluster would be an arriving or departing plane load. In sampling students within a large school, an appropriate cluster would be a classroom.

Although a current frame listing all the households in a given city may not exist, a frame listing arriving or departing passengers should be fairly complete, and a frame listing the students in a given school certainly exists. However, the selection of a simple or stratified random sample would not be practically feasible in any large airport because of the large number of flights and the distance between gates. The administrators of a large school would probably allow some classrooms to be disrupted for a short time, but would be adverse to disrupting all classrooms in order to obtain a simple or stratified random sample.

Cluster sampling provides an effective design when

1. a frame listing all the elements in the population (is, is not) available or (is, is not) costly to obtain, or — is not; is
2. the population is (small, large) and spread over a wide area and/or the cost of obtaining an observation (increases, decreases) as the distance between elements increases. — large; increases

In preparing a cluster sampling design, an experimenter is often faced with choosing between a design involving a small number of large clusters and a design involving a large number of small clusters. When costs are not prohibitive, the (former, latter) design should be chosen since it is more likely to include a more representative cross-section of the sampled population. — latter

Estimation of a Population Mean for a Cluster Sample

In cluster sampling, m clusters are randomly selected from a frame listing the ________ and a complete ________ of the n_i elements in the ith cluster is conducted. The value of n_i (is always, may not be) known in advance. (The number of airline passengers may vary from flight to flight.) Let t_i represent the total of the measurements in the ith cluster. The estimator of the population mean μ is — clusters; census — may not be

$$\bar{x}_{cl} = \frac{\sum_{i=1}^{m} t_i}{\sum_{i=1}^{m} n_i}$$

an aggregate mean based on the grand total of all observations divided by the total number of elements in the sample. Let M denote the number of clusters in the population, and let the average cluster size be denoted by

$$\bar{n} = \frac{1}{m} \sum_{i=1}^{m} n_i$$

The variance of the estimator $\bar{x}_{cl}$ is

$$\hat{\sigma}^2_{\bar{x}_{cl}} = \left(\frac{M - m}{Mm\bar{n}^2}\right)\left(\frac{\sum_{i=1}^{m} (t_i - \bar{x}_{cl} n_i)^2}{m - 1}\right)$$

1.96 standard deviations are used as bounds on the error of estimation.

Estimation of the Population Total for a Cluster Sample

Let $\bar{t}$ be the average cluster total defined as

$$\bar{t} = \frac{1}{m} \sum_{i=1}^{m} t_i$$

The estimator of the population total τ is given as

$$\hat{\tau} = M\bar{t}$$

with variance

$$\hat{\sigma}_{\hat{\tau}}^2 = M^2 \left(\frac{M - m}{Mm}\right)\left(\frac{\sum_{i=1}^{m} (t_i - \bar{t})^2}{m - 1}\right)$$

1.96 standard deviations are used as a bound on the error of estimation.

Example 16.9

A dealer in electronic equipment offers his customers a twelve-month service contract at a fixed annual cost. In order to update cost estimates for the 200 installations under service contracts, the dealer randomly selected 20 installations and recorded the number of service calls, including regular maintenance, and the actual cost incurred for each call during the last six months. For sampling purposes, each installation represents a cluster, and each repair call at a given installation constitutes an element in the population of interest. The data follow.

Installation	*Service Calls*	*Cost*	*Installation*	*Service Calls*	*Cost*
1	6	$1,250	11	6	$1,050
2	4	600	12	9	1,700
3	5	1,150	13	7	1,250
4	6	1,550	14	9	2,150
5	8	2,000	15	5	850
6	6	1,150	16	6	1,000
7	4	750	17	4	850
8	10	2,250	18	6	1,100
9	4	900	19	7	1,650
10	5	950	20	10	1,950

127; $26,100

$\sum_{i=1}^{20} n_i =$ ________ $\sum_{i=1}^{20} t_i =$ ________

Estimate the average cost per repair call, and place bounds on the error of estimation.

Solution

1. The estimate of the average cost per repair call is

$$\bar{x}_{cl} = \frac{\sum_{i=1}^{m} t_i}{\sum_{i=1}^{m} n_i}$$

$$= \frac{26{,}100}{127}$$

$$= \_\_\_\_\_\_\_\_\_\_$$

$205.51

2. To calculate the variance of the estimator $\bar{x}_{cl}$, we need the following sum of squares.

$$\sum_{i=1}^{m} (t_i - \bar{x}_{cl} n_i)^2 = \sum_{i=1}^{m} t_i^2 - 2\bar{x}_{cl} \sum_{i=1}^{m} t_i n_i + \bar{x}_{cl}^2 \sum_{i=1}^{m} n_i^2$$

Now

$$\sum_{i=1}^{20} t_i^2 = 1250^2 + 600^2 + \ldots + 1950^2 = 38{,}665{,}000$$

$$\sum_{i=1}^{20} t_i n_i = (1250)(6) + (600)(4) + \ldots + (1950)(10)$$

$$= 182{,}700$$

$$\sum_{i=1}^{20} n_i^2 = 6^2 + 4^2 + \ldots + 10^2 = 879$$

Therefore,

182,700 $$\sum_{i=1}^{20} (t_i - \bar{x}_{cl} n_i)^2 = 38{,}665{,}000 - 2(205.51)(\_\_\_\_\_\_\_\_)$$

879 $$+ (205.51)^2(\_\_\_\_\_\_\_\_)$$

695,648.5279 $$= \_\_\_\_\_\_\_\_$$

The average cluster size is

6.35 $$\bar{n} = \frac{1}{m} \sum_{i=1}^{m} n_i = \frac{1}{20}(127) = \_\_\_\_\_\_\_\_$$

With $M = 200$ clusters in the population,

$$\hat{\sigma}^2_{\bar{x}_{cl}} = \left(\frac{M - m}{Mm\bar{n}^2}\right)\left(\frac{\sum_{i=1}^{m} (t_i - \bar{x}_{cl} n_i)^2}{m - 1}\right)$$

$$= \frac{(200 - 20)}{(200)(20)(6.35)^2} \; \frac{(695{,}648.5279)}{19}$$

40.8603 $$= \_\_\_\_\_\_\_\_$$

Hence,

40.8603 $$\hat{\sigma}_{\bar{x}_{cl}} = \sqrt{\_\_\_\_\_\_\_\_}$$

\$6.39 $$= \_\_\_\_\_\_\_\_$$

3. The estimate of the average cost per repair call with a bound on the error of estimation is

6.39 $$\$205.51 \pm 1.96(\_\_\_\_\_\_\_\_)$$

or

\$12.53 $$\$205.51 \pm \_\_\_\_\_\_\_\_$$

Example 16.10
Estimate the total cost of repair calls for all 200 installations in Example 16.9 and place a bound on the error of estimation.

Solution
1. The estimate of the population total is

$$\hat{\tau} = \frac{M}{m} \sum_{i=1}^{m} t_i$$

$$= \frac{200}{20}(26{,}100)$$

$$= \underline{\hspace{3cm}}$$ $261,000

Equivalently, the average repair cost per cluster is

$$\bar{t} = \frac{1}{m} \sum_{i=1}^{m} t_i$$

$$= \frac{1}{20}(26{,}100)$$

$$= \underline{\hspace{3cm}}$$ $1305

and the estimate of the population total based on $M = 200$ clusters is

$$\hat{\tau} = M\bar{t}$$

$$= (200)(1305)$$

$$= \underline{\hspace{3cm}}$$ $261,000

2. To evaluate the variance of $\hat{\tau}$, we need to calculate

$$\sum_{i=1}^{m} (t_i - \bar{t})^2 = \sum_{i=1}^{m} t_i^2 - \frac{\left(\sum_{i=1}^{m} t_i\right)^2}{m}$$

26,100

$$= 38{,}665{,}000 - \frac{(\_\_\_\_\_\_\_\_)^2}{20}$$

34,060,500

$$= 38{,}665{,}000 - \_\_\_\_\_\_\_\_$$

4,604,500

$$= \_\_\_\_\_\_\_\_$$

Therefore,

$$\hat{\sigma}^2_{\hat{\tau}} = \left(\frac{M - m}{Mm}\right)\left(\frac{\sum_{i=1}^{m} (t_i - \bar{t})^2}{m - 1}\right)$$

$$= \frac{(200 - 20)}{(200)(20)}\left(\frac{4{,}604{,}500}{19}\right)$$

10,905.3947

$$= \_\_\_\_\_\_\_\_$$

and

$$\hat{\sigma}_{\hat{\tau}} = \sqrt{10{,}905.3947}$$

\$104.43

$$= \_\_\_\_\_\_\_\_$$

3. The estimate of the total cost with a bound on the error of estimation is

\$104.43

\$261,000 ± 1.96(________)

or

\$204.68

\$261,000 ± ________

Estimation of the Population Proportion for a Cluster Sample

In estimating the proportion p of those elements in the population possessing a specified characteristic from a cluster sample, a_i, the number of elements in the ith cluster possessing that characteristic is tabulated for each cluster. The estimate of p is

$$\hat{p}_{cl} = \frac{\sum_{i=1}^{m} a_i}{\sum_{i=1}^{m} n_i}$$

with variance

$$\hat{\sigma}^2_{\hat{p}_{cl}} = \left(\frac{M - m}{Mm\bar{n}^2}\right)\left(\frac{\sum_{i=1}^{m} (a_i - \hat{p}_{cl}n_i)^2}{m - 1}\right)$$

Notice that the formula for the variance of $\hat{p}_{cl}$ is the same as that for $\bar{x}_{cl}$ with t_i replaced by __________. Further, an equivalent form for the sum of squares in this formula can be calculated as a_i

$$\sum_{i=1}^{m} (a_i - \hat{p}_{cl}n_i)^2 = \sum_{i=1}^{m} a_i^2 - 2\hat{p}_{cl} \sum_{i=1}^{m} a_i n_i + \hat{p}_{cl}^2 \sum_{i=1}^{m} \text{\_\_\_\_\_\_\_\_}$$ n_i^2

The variance formula above is an unbiased estimator when the cluster sizes are all _______________. When the cluster sizes are unequal, the estimator of the variance is a good estimator only when the number of clusters is greater than or equal to __________. equal; 20

Example 16.11
In conducting the survey reported in Example 16.9 the number of service calls requiring only adjustments with no replacement parts was also recorded.

Installation	*Service Calls*	*Adjustments Only*	Installation	*Service Calls*	*Adjustments Only*
1	6	4	11	6	0
2	4	2	12	9	5
3	5	2	13	7	5
4	6	5	14	9	4
5	8	3	15	5	3
6	6	4	16	6	3
7	4	0	17	4	2
8	10	7	18	6	1
9	4	2	19	7	4
10	5	3	20	10	4
	$\Sigma n_i =$ ________			$\Sigma a_i =$ ________	

127; 63

Estimate the proportion of service calls involving adjustments only, and place a bound on the error of estimation.

Solution
The problem is similar to Example 16.9 except that the quantities $t_1, t_2, \ldots, t_{20}$ are replaced with the quantities $a_1, a_2, \ldots, a_{20}$. A summary of relevant information follows.

Answer	
200; 63	$M =$ ______ $\qquad \Sigma a_i =$ ______ $\qquad \Sigma a_i^2 = 257$
20; 127	$m =$ ______ $\qquad \Sigma n_i =$ ______ $\qquad \Sigma n_i^2 = 879$
6.35	$\bar{n} =$ ______ $\qquad \Sigma a_i n_i = 444$

1. The estimate of the proportion of service calls requiring only adjustments is

.4961

$$\hat{p}_{cl} = \frac{\Sigma a_i}{\Sigma n_i} = \frac{63}{127} = \underline{\qquad}$$

2. Evaluate

$$\Sigma(a_i - \hat{p}_{cl} n_i)^2 = \Sigma a_i^2 - 2\hat{p}_{cl}\, \Sigma a_i n_i + \hat{p}_{cl}^2\, \Sigma n_i^2$$

.4961; .4961

$$= 257 - 2(\underline{\qquad})(444) + (\underline{\qquad})^2(879)$$

32.7985

$$= \underline{\qquad}$$

The variance of $\hat{p}_{cl}$ is

$$\hat{\sigma}^2_{\hat{p}_{cl}} = \left(\frac{M - m}{Mm\bar{n}^2}\right)\left(\frac{\sum_{i=1}^{m} (a_i - \hat{p}_{cl} n_i)^2}{m - 1}\right)$$

32.7985

6.35

$$= \frac{(200 - 20)}{200(20)(\underline{\qquad})^2} \; \frac{(\underline{\qquad})}{19}$$

.001926

$$= \underline{\qquad}$$

with

$$\hat{\sigma}_{\hat{p}_{cl}} = \sqrt{.001926}$$

.0439

$$= \underline{\qquad}$$

3. The estimate of the number of service calls requiring only adjustments is

.4961; .0439

$$\underline{\qquad} \pm 1.96(\underline{\qquad})$$

or

.50; .09

$$\underline{\qquad} \pm \underline{\qquad}$$

Self-Correcting Exercises 16D

1. A survey was designed to estimate the amount spent on utilities during the year for households in a city. Because a list of households was not available, a cluster sampling design was used with blocks as the clusters. From the $M = 200$ city blocks within the city limits, a random sample of $m = 10$ blocks produced the following information.

City Block	*Number of Households*	*Amount for Utilities*
1	16	$19,210
2	10	9,130
3	14	12,340
4	20	16,480
5	15	9,570
6	8	10,420
7	15	12,290
8	30	20,920
9	10	9,980
10	18	16,750

   a. Estimate the average yearly amount spent on utilities per household, and place a bound on the error of estimation.
   b. Estimate the total amount spent on utilities in this city, and place a bound on the error of estimation.

2. A cancer research organization wishes to determine whether recent advances made in the treatment of cancer are being implemented in hospitals having radiation therapy units. In designing the survey, it was decided to randomly sample $m = 10$ of the possible $M = 75$ geographic areas designated as clusters. In the following tabulation, a_i is the number of hospitals having radiation units that have implemented at least one recent recommendation in the treatment of cancer. (Data are fictitious.)

Cluster	n_i	a_i
1	20	8
2	10	5
3	30	16
4	8	2
5	15	7
6	28	17
7	48	19
8	64	38
9	22	10
10	13	4

Estimate the proportion of hospitals utilizing new treatment recommendations, and place a bound on the error of estimation.

16.7 Finding the Sample Size

cost

variability

large
small

known; estimate

An effective sampling plan is one in which a specified amount of information is obtained at a minimum ________. The number of elements to be included in a sample will depend upon the specified bound on the error of estimation as well as the ________ of the elements in the population to be sampled. In general, small bounds on error require (small, large) sample sizes, while small sample sizes are required when the population is fairly uniform and exhibits (small, large) variability. Formulas for determining the sample size required to achieve a given precision in estimation vary from one sampling design to another. In every case, however, B, the maximum tolerable bound on the error of estimation must be specified, and the variability of the elements in the population must be ________, or a reasonable ________ must be available.

When using a *simple random sampling design,* the sample size required to estimate the population mean μ with a bound B on the error of estimation is

$$n = \frac{N\sigma^2}{(N-1)D + \sigma^2}$$

where $D = B^2/z^2$, z^2 is the value of the standard normal random variable corresponding to $(1 - \alpha)$, the desired level of confidence, N is the size of the population, and σ^2 is the population variance. When N is very large (so that the finite population correction factor can be ignored), this formula reduces to

$$n = \frac{z^2\sigma^2}{B^2}$$

When σ is unknown and a prior estimate is not available, a rough estimate of σ based upon the Empirical Rule is $\hat{\sigma} = (\text{range})/4$. When estimating the population total τ, earlier formulas apply with $D = B^2/zN^2$.

Example 16.12

A department store would like to estimate the average monthly sales for its 10,000 credit-card customers. How many credit-card accounts should be included in the sample in order to estimate μ, the average monthly credit-card sales with 95% confidence and a bound on the error of estimation of B = \$20? It is known that monthly credit-card sales in general range from \$20 to \$500.

Solution

1. Since the standard deviation is unknown, we will use the range to estimate σ. The range is \$500–\$20 = \$480. Therefore, σ = \$480/4 = \$120 and $\hat{\sigma}^2 = 120^2 = 14{,}400$.

10,000; \$20
104.123

2. N = ________ and B = ________. The quantity D used in finding the sample size is $D = B^2/(1.96)^2 = (20)^2/(1.96)^2$ = ________. Then,

$$n = \frac{N\sigma^2}{(N-1)D + \sigma^2}$$

$$= \frac{(10{,}000)(\_\_\_\_\_\_\_\_)}{(9999)D + \_\_\_\_\_\_\_\_}$$ 14,400 14,400

$$= \frac{144{,}000{,}000}{1{,}055{,}528.70}$$

$$= \_\_\_\_\_\_\_\_$$ 136.42

A random sample of __________ accounts should be selected in order to estimate the average monthly credit-card sales to within \$20. 137

3. Since $N = 10{,}000$ is large, we can use the approximate solution

$$n = \frac{(1.96)^2\sigma^2}{B^2}$$

$$= \frac{(1.96)^2(14{,}400)}{400}$$

$$= \_\_\_\_\_\_\_\_$$ 138.3

This result differs only slightly from the sample size found using the exact formula.

In estimating the population proportion p, the sample size formulas for the population mean μ can be used with σ^2 replaced by __________. However, since p is unknown, some estimate for p must be available. This estimate could be in the form of an educated guess, or one can assume maximum variation, attained when $p = q = 1/2$, and take $\sigma^2 =$ __________. pq .25

In determining the total sample size n to be allocated among the L strata in a *stratified random sampling design,* in addition to B, the bound on the error of estimation, we must also know the strata sizes, $N_1, N_2, \ldots, N_L$ as well as the variances within the strata, $\sigma_1^2, \sigma_2^2, \ldots, \sigma_L^2$. Previous samples or the range approximation can be used to estimate the variances if they are unknown. The sample size required to estimate the population mean μ with a bound B on the error of estimation is

$$n = \frac{\sum_{i=1}^{L} N_i\sigma_i^2}{ND + \frac{1}{N}\sum_{i=1}^{L} N_i\sigma_i^2}$$

where $D = B^2/z^2$. By substituting $D = B^2/z^2N^2$ into this formula, the sample size required to estimate the population total τ with a bound B on the error of estimation can be found.

Example 16.13
In order to update the current group life insurance plan, the personnel department of a company was asked to estimate the average amount of group life insurance held by the company's $N = 2000$ employees. The company employs $N_1 = 1500$ machine operators, $N_2 = 350$ support personnel, and $N_3 = 150$ persons in managerial positions. The latest available information indicates that $\sigma_1 = \$3000$, $\sigma_2 = \$1500$ and $\sigma_3 = \$5000$. How large a sample should be taken to ensure that the bound on the error of estimation be no larger than $B = \$1000$? Using proportional allocation, how many persons from each stratum would be included in the sample if $1 - \alpha = .95$?

Solution

1. Large intermediate values in the calculation of n can be avoided by recording B, σ_1, σ_2, and σ_3 in units of \$1000. Complete the following summary.

3 $\sigma_1 =$ ________ $N_1 = 1500$

350 $\sigma_2 = 1.5$ $N_2 =$ ________

5; 150 $\sigma_3 =$ ________ $N_3 =$ ________

$B = 1$ $N = 2000$

$z = 1.96$

We also need to evaluate the quantity D and $\sum_{i=1}^{3} N_i\sigma_i^2$.

.26 $D = B^2/z^2 = (1)^2/(1.96)^2 =$ ________

$$\sum_{i=1}^{3} N_i\sigma_i^2 = 1500(3)^2 + 350(1.5)^2 + 150(5)^2$$

$$= 13{,}500 + 787.5 + 3750$$

18,037.5 $=$ ________

Then

$$n = \frac{\sum_{i=1}^{3} N_i \sigma_i^2}{ND + \frac{1}{N} \sum_{i=1}^{3} N_i \sigma_i^2}$$

$$= \frac{18{,}037.5}{2000(.26) + \frac{18{,}037.5}{2000}}$$

$$= \frac{18{,}037.5}{(\_\_\_\_\_\_\_\_)}$$ 529.635

$$= \_\_\_\_\_\_\_\_$$ 34.06

The sample size required to estimate the average amount of group life insurance per employee with bound on the error of estimation equal to \$1000 is $n =$ ________. 35

2. Using proportional allocation,

$$n_1 = 35\left(\frac{1500}{2000}\right) = \_\_\_\_\_\_\_\_$$ 26.25

$$n_2 = 35\left(\frac{350}{2000}\right) = \_\_\_\_\_\_\_\_$$ 6.125

$$n_3 = 35\left(\frac{150}{2000}\right) = \_\_\_\_\_\_\_\_$$ 2.625

We would randomly select $n_1 =$ ________, $n_2 =$ ________, and $n_3 =$ ________ people from strata 1, 2, and 3, respectively. 26; 6 3

To find the sample size required to estimate a population proportion using stratified random sampling, we substitute $\sigma_i^2 = p_i q_i$, the variance of the ith stratum, and $D = B^2/z^2$. A prior estimate or guess can be substituted for p_i or the maximum variation of $p_i q_i =$ ________ can be used. Using maximum variation and proportional allocation, the sample size required to estimate the population proportion p with a bound on error equal to B is approximately .25

$$n = \frac{N}{NB^2 + 1}$$

For example, the sample size required to estimate p in a population of $N = 2000$ elements with a bound on error equal to $B = 0.1$ is

$$n = \frac{2000}{2000(.01) + 1}$$

21 $$= \frac{2000}{(\underline{\qquad\qquad})}$$

95.24 $$= \underline{\qquad\qquad}$$

96 or $n =$ __________ elements.

frame Simple random sampling and stratified random sampling both require the existence of a ______________ listing the elements in the population. In contrast, *cluster sampling* utilizes a frame in which the sampling units are

clusters ______________ of elements. The size of the clusters in many situations are actually random quantities. However, the information in a cluster sample depends not only on m, the number of clusters, but also on the size of the clusters. If we assume that the relative cluster size has been selected in advance, the number m of clusters required to estimate the population mean μ with a bound B on the error of estimation is given as

$$m = \frac{M\,\sigma_{cl}^2}{MD + \sigma_{cl}^2}$$

with

$$D = \frac{B^2 \bar{N}^2}{z^2}$$

where σ_{cl}^2 and $\bar{N}^2$ are estimated by $\bar{n}^2$ and

$$s_{cl}^2 = \frac{\Sigma(t_i - \bar{x}_{cl} n_i)^2}{m - 1}.$$

In general, more information can be obtained in a cluster sample by selecting

larger a (smaller, larger) number of smaller-sized clusters.

Self-Correcting Exercises 16E

1. A professional organization listing approximately 12,000 members on its national roster would like to conduct a mail survey of its members in order to estimate the proportion of its members favoring the establishment of a second journal to be made available to its members. Assuming

maximum variation within a simple random sampling design, how large a sample should be taken in order that the estimate of p be no farther than $B = .05$ from the true value?

2. Suppose that the professional organization in Exercise 1 can actually classify its members into the following three strata.

Stratum	*Classification*	N_i
1	Employed by academic institution	6,000
2	Employed by industrial organization	4,000
3	Self-employed	2,000

a. Using a stratified random design with proportional allocation, how large a sample should be taken to estimate the proportion of members favoring a second journal to within $B = .05$ if it is assumed that the proportions for the three strata would be approximately $p_1 = .7, p_2 = .6$, and $p_3 = .5$?
b. What is the resulting proportional allocation among the three strata?
c. How would your results differ if you were to assume that $p_1 = p_2 = p_3 = .5$?

3. A bank offering two kinds of checking accounts would like to estimate the average monthly balance in the checking accounts of its customers. In the $N_1 = 10{,}000$ "no minimum balance" accounts, the average monthly balance is between \$25 and \$500, while in the $N_2 = 5000$ "\$300 minimum balance" accounts, the average monthly balance ranges between \$300 and \$1500. How large a sample should be taken in order to estimate the average monthly balance to within \$30? What is the proportional allocation across the two strata?

16.8 Other Sampling Designs and Procedures

We have described the three most commonly used sampling designs. In this section, we will briefly review some other sampling designs and some procedures that can be used within any design.

Systematic Sampling

A *systematic sample* is obtained by randomly selecting one of the first k elements in the frame and then selecting every __________ element thereafter. Systematic sampling is especially useful when the elements (or information) in the population are recorded in some systematic way. Computer-stored data, for example, is easily sampled using systematic samples. Systematic sampling (should, should not) be used when periodicities exist in the population. Periodicities or cyclical behavior may be present in financial records or in production records kept over __________.

kth

should not

time

By systematically sampling either the peaks or the troughs in such records, we may obtain a biased sample that is not representative of the total population.

Two-Stage Cluster Sampling

A *two-stage cluster sample* is obtained by selecting a simple random sample of clusters and then selecting a random sample of elements within each

cluster

______________. For example, in a study of overtime expenditures, a large company might randomly select m of its subsidiaries and then randomly select several departments within each subsidiary to be included in the sampling. When clusters constitute

geographic

______________ areas, cluster sampling of the areas is referred to as *area sampling.* The chief advantage of two-stage or multistage sampling designs over other designs is cost savings, since a frame listing only

clusters

______________ is required and the elements sampled within a cluster would be physically nearer each other than would be elements selected at random from the population. However, any type of cluster sampling may result in biased estimates because of the intentional exclusion of part of the population from our sample.

Ratio Estimation

Ratio estimation is a procedure that can be used within any appropriate sampling design. This procedure uses an observed relationship between two variables, x and y, measured on the same set of sample elements, to predict μ_y or τ_y. For example, one might wish to estimate the selling price of a home using the square footage of the home, or one might wish to predict the juice content of fruit, using its observed weight. Ratio estimation assumes that the relationship between two variables is of the form

$$R = \frac{\tau_y}{\tau_x}$$

so that $\tau_y = R\tau_x$. Two variables, x and y, are measured for each element in the sample, and the quantity R is estimated as

$$\hat{R} = \frac{\sum_{i=1}^{n} y_i}{\sum_{i=1}^{n} x_i}$$

The population total τ_y can be estimated using

$\hat{R}\tau_x$

$$\hat{\tau}_y = \_\_\_\_\_\_\_\_\_\_$$

provided τ_x is known. When there is a strong positive correlation between x and y (greater than 1/2), the variance of the ratio estimator $\hat{R}\tau_x$ is (smaller, larger) than the variance of the estimator $N\bar{y}$. We would expect the ratio estimator to be more precise in this case, since we are using the additional information provided by the variable _________ in estimating τ_y.

smaller

x

Randomized Response Sampling

Two nonsampling errors that frequently bias the results of sample surveys are the refusal of a respondent to answer all, or part of, a questionnaire or the deliberate falsification of information. These errors often result when the questionnaire, or certain parts of the questionnaire, deal with sensitive or potentially embarrassing topics. _____________ _____________ sampling is an attempt to alleviate this problem by pairing a sensitive question with another question that the respondent should feel comfortable in answering. The respondent then answers one of the questions, which he or she selects at random using some randomization device. For example, the question "Have you ever smoked marijuana?" could be paired with the question "Have you ever drunk coffee?" The interviewer receives an answer but is unaware of which question is being answered by the respondent. The analysis of randomized response data utilizes the fact that the randomization device selects the sensitive question with a known _____________. Randomized response sampling is a procedure that can be utilized within any of the sampling designs.

Randomized response

probability

16.9 Summary and Comments

In addition to random sampling designs, there are some nonrandom sampling designs that are commonly used. However, with nonrandom sampling designs, only _____________ statements can be made. Convenience sampling, judgment sampling, and quota sampling are three forms of nonrandom sampling.

1. A *convenience sample* consists of elements that can easily be obtained. A group of volunteer subjects (would, would not) comprise a convenience sample.
2. *Judgment sampling* involves the selection of the elements in the sample by "experts" so that the sample is "representative" of the _____________ of interest. For example, one city in the United States might be picked as a typical city to represent all the cities in the United States.
3. *Quota sampling* involves the selection of a predetermined number of elements from specific portions of the population so as to construct a sample _____________ to the population with respect to certain variables. National opinion polls might rely on quota sampling to insure that given ethnic, socioeconomic, religious, political, and other groups are represented in the sample in roughly the same proportions that they appear in the _____________. The selection of the elements within the quotas often depends upon the sampler and usually results in a _____________ sample.

Samples arising from the use of random, stratified, cluster, and systematic sampling designs (can, cannot) be used to make inferential statements about

descriptive

would

population

proportional

population

nonrandom

can

random

ratio estimation
randomized
response

the population from which they were drawn because these designs produce ______________ samples with a known probability of including or excluding elements of the population in the sample. Within these sampling designs, the ______________ ______________ procedure can be used when observations on a highly correlated auxiliary variable are available, while the ______________ ______________ technique can be used to elicit responses to embarrassing or sensitive topics within the sample survey.

EXERCISES

1. When is a sample a random sample? Why is a random sample preferred to a nonrandom sample?
2. What are the sources of error in a sample survey?
3. Differentiate between an element, a cluster, and a sampling unit.
4. In a random sample of $n = 20$ accounts, the average amount due was $\bar{x} = \$130.25$ with a standard deviation of $s = \$15.30$.
   a. Estimate μ, the average amount due for all $N = 100$ current accounts held by this company, and place a bound on the error of estimation.
   b. Estimate the total amount due for all $N = 100$ accounts, and place a bound on the error of estimation.
5. Refer to Exercise 4. If 3 of the 20 accounts sampled are delinquent, estimate the proportion of delinquent accounts, and place a bound on the error of estimation.
6. Refer to Exercise 5. Estimate the total number of delinquent accounts using the estimator $N\hat{p}$, and place a bound on the error of estimation. (The variance of $N\hat{p}$ is $N^2\sigma^2_{\hat{p}}$.)
7. Using simple random sampling, how large a sample is required to estimate the population mean with a bound $B = 15$ if the range of the observations for the $N = 9000$ elements in the population is expected to be approximately 400?
8. Refer to Exercise 2, Self-Correcting Exercises 16E. The following information resulted when a stratified random sample survey involving $n = 350$ of the 12,000 members of the professional organization was conducted.

	Strata		
	1	*2*	*3*
Stratum size, N_i	6,000	4,000	2,000
Sample size, n_i	175	117	58
Number favoring second journal	130	76	32

   Estimate the proportion of the members favoring the establishment of a second journal, and place a bound on the error of estimation.
9. A stratified random sampling design involving three strata is to be used in estimating the population mean. From the following information deter-

mine the sample size required to estimate μ with a bound on error of $B = 10$ if proportional allocation is to be used.

Strata	*1*	*2*	*3*
N_i	2300	1200	4500
σ_i^2	4250	2500	5750

Determine the allocation of the sample across the three strata.

10. In order to obtain travel information concerning its passengers, an airline randomly selected $n = 10$ departing flights from its $N = 180$ flight listings and asked all the passengers on these ten flights to complete a questionnaire. The following data was extracted from the questionnaire. The third column records the ground distance between the terminal airport and the passengers' ultimate destination. (Data are fictitious.)

Flight	*Number of Passengers*	*Total Distance*	*Number with Distance over 50 Miles*
1	131	3,275	27
2	103	3,090	21
3	189	8,505	57
4	93	2,046	10
5	205	7,175	52
6	148	7,400	26
7	172	6,880	69
8	110	3,520	23
9	165	6,270	64
10	193	9,071	87

By considering the flights included in the sample as $m = 10$ clusters randomly selected from $M = 180$ clusters,

a. Estimate the average ground distance between the terminal airport and ultimate destination per passenger, and place a bound on the error of estimation.
b. Estimate the proportion of passengers who will travel over 50 ground miles to their ultimate destination, and place a bound on the error of estimation.

11. In order to update the actual dcllar value of its inventory, a firm randomly selects $n = 10$ of the $N = 600$ types of items from its inventory list and determines the actual dollar value per type of item sampled. Computer-stored records are used to determine the actual dollar value and the inventoried dollar value of the types of items included in the sample. These data are summarized in units of \$100.

Item	Computer Value (x)	Actual Value (y)
1	6.1	5.4
2	48.6	45.0
3	3.2	2.9
4	25.4	22.4
5	43.9	37.3
6	68.6	62.4
7	187.4	172.1
8	45.2	33.9
9	5.1	4.4
10	170.9	153.6

a. Estimate the ratio of the actual inventory value to the computer inventory value.

b. If the total of the computer inventory value is $\tau_x = 34{,}920$, use the ratio estimator to estimate τ_y, the total actual value of the inventoried items.

c. Estimate τ_y using the estimator $N\bar{y}$ and compare this estimate with that found in part b.

12. A bank having 10,000 checking accounts would like to estimate the average monthly balance using a 1-in-100 systematic sample from its list of accounts.

 a. What is the size of the sample using this scheme?

 b. Describe how the sample should be drawn from the 10,000 checking accounts.

 c. Implement your plan in part b, and indicate which accounts would be included in the sample.

Chapter 17

ANALYSIS OF ENUMERATIVE DATA

17.1 A Description of the Multinomial Experiment

Examine the following experimental situations for any general similarities.

1. Two hundred people are classified according to their ages. The number of people in each of the age groups 0-20, 21-40, 41-60, and over 60 is recorded.
2. A sample of 100 items is randomly selected from a production line. Each item is classified as belonging to one of three groups: acceptables, seconds, or rejects, and the number in each group is recorded.
3. A random sample of 50 people holding valid driver's licenses is selected from state records and each person is classified as having: no previous accidents, one accident, two accidents, or three or more accidents.

Each of these situations is similar to the others in that classes or categories are defined and the number of items falling into each category is recorded. Hence, these experiments result in enumerative or ______________ data and have the following general characteristics which define the ______________ experiment.

count

multinomial

1. The experiment consists of n identical trials.
2. The outcome of each trial falls into one of k classes or cells.
3. The probability that the outcome of a single trial falls into cell i is p_i, $i = 1, 2, \ldots, k$, where p_i is ______________ from trial to trial and

constant

$$\sum_{i=1}^{k} p_i = \_\_\_\_\_\_\_\_$$

1

4. The trials are ______________.

independent

5. We are interested in $n_1, n_2, n_3, \ldots, n_k$, where n_i is the number of trials in which the outcome falls in cell i, and

n $$\sum_{i=1}^{k} n_i = \_\_\_\_\_\_\_\_$$

The binomial experiment is a special case of the multinomial experiment.
2 This can be seen by letting k = ________, and noting the following correspondences.

		Binomial	*Multinomial* (k = 2)
	a.	n	n
	b.	p	p_1
p_2	c.	q	________
	d.	x	n_1
n_2	e.	$n - x$	________
	f.	$E(x) = np$	$E(n_1) = np_1$
np_2	g.	$E(n - x) = nq$	$E(n_2)$ = ________

For the multinomial experiment, we wish to make inferences about the associated population parameters, $p_1, p_2, \ldots, p_k$. A statistic that allows us to make inferences of this sort was developed by the British statistician, Karl Pearson, around 1900.

17.2 The Chi-square Test

For a multinomial experiment consisting of n trials with known (or hypothesized) cell probabilities, p_i, $i = 1, 2, \ldots, k$, we can find the expected number of items falling into the ith cell by using

$$E(n_i) = np_i \qquad i = 1, 2, \ldots, k$$

The cell probabilities are rarely known in practical situations. Consequently, we wish to estimate, or test hypotheses concerning, their values. If the hypothesized cell probabilities are the correct values, then the *observed* number of items falling in each of the cells, n_i, should differ but slightly from the expected number, $E(n_i) = np_i$. Pearson's statistic (given below) utilizes the squares of the deviations of the observed from the expected number in each cell.

$$X^2 = \sum_{i=1}^{k} \frac{[n_i - E(n_i)]^2}{E(n_i)}$$

or

$$X^2 = \sum_{i=1}^{k} \frac{(n_i - np_i)^2}{np_i}$$

Note that the deviations are divided by the expected number so that the deviations are weighted according to whether the expected number is large or small. A deviation of 5 from an expected number of 20 contributes $(5)^2/20 =$ __________ to X^2, while a deviation of 5 from an expected number of 10 contributes $(5)^2/10 =$ __________, or *twice* as much, to X^2. 1.25 2.50

When n, the number of trials, is large, this statistic has an approximate χ^2 distribution, provided the expected numbers in each cell are not too small. We will require as a rule of thumb that $E(n_i) \geqslant$ __________. This requirement can be satisfied by combining those cells with small expected numbers until every cell has an expected number of at least __________. For small deviations from the expected cell counts, the value of the statistic would be (large, small). supporting the hypothesized cell probabilities. However, for large deviations from the expected counts, the value of the statistic would be (large, small), and the hypothesized values of the cell probabilities would be __________. Hence a one-tailed test is used, rejecting H_0 when X^2 is __________. 5 5 small large rejected large

To find the critical value of χ^2 used for testing, the degrees of freedom must be known. Since the degrees of freedom change as Pearson's statistic is applied to different situations, the degrees of freedom will be specified for each application that follows. In general, the degrees of freedom are equal to the number of cells less one degree of freedom for each independent linear restriction placed upon the cell counts. One linear restriction that will always be present is that

$$n_1 + n_2 + n_3 + \ldots + n_k = \text{\_\_\_\_\_\_\_\_\_\_}. \qquad n$$

Other restrictions may be imposed by the necessity to estimate certain unknown cell parameters or by the method of sampling employed in the collection of the data.

17.3 A Test of an Hypothesis Concerning Specified Cell Probabilities

Let us consider the following application of Pearson's statistic to a problem concerning cell probabilities:

Example 17.1

A manufacturer claims that his production line produces 85% Grade A items, 10% Grade B items, and 5% rejects. A random sample of 100 items from this production line included 80 Grade A's, 9 Grade B's, and 11 rejects. Does this sample contain sufficient evidence to refute the manufacturer's claim at the $\alpha = .05$ level?

Solution

This experiment consists of classifying 100 items by assigning them to one of three cells, cell 1 (Grade A's), cell 2 (Grade B's), and cell 3 (rejects) where $p_1 = .85$, $p_2 = .10$, and $p_3 = .05$. The expected cell numbers are found to be

$$E(n_1) = np_1 = 100(.85) = \text{\_\_\_\_\_\_\_\_\_\_} \qquad 85$$

.10; 10

$E(n_2) = np_2 = 100$ (__________) = __________

100; .05; 5

$E(n_3) = np_3 =$ (__________) (__________) = __________

Tabulating the results, we have:

	Cell		
	1	*2*	*3*
Expected cell frequency	85	10	5
Observed cell frequency	80	9	11

Using Pearson's statistic we can test the hypothesis that the cell probabilities remain as before against the alternative hypothesis that at least one cell probability is different from those claimed. The value of X^2 will be compared with a critical value of $\chi^2_{.05}$ based on the degrees of freedom found as follows. The degrees of freedom are equal to the number of cells ($k = 3$) less one degree of freedom for the linear restriction $n_1 + n_2 + n_3 = n = 100$.

5.991

Therefore, the degrees of freedom are $k - 1 = 3 - 1 = 2$ and $\chi^2_{.05} =$ __________.

Formalizing this discussion we have the following statistical test of the manufacturer's claim at the $\alpha = .05$ level.

1. $H_0: p_1 = .85, p_2 = .10, p_3 = .05$

2. H_a: at least one value of p_i is different from that specified by H_0.

3. Test statistic:

$$X^2 = \sum_{i=1}^{3} \frac{[n_i - E(n_i)]^2}{E(n_i)}$$

5.991

4. Rejection region: Reject H_0 if $X^2 \geq \chi^2_{.05} =$ __________. Now we calculate the test statistic.

$$X^2 = \frac{(80 - 85)^2}{85} + \frac{(9 - 10)^2}{10} + \frac{(11 - 5)^2}{5}$$

$$= .2941 + .1 + 7.2$$

7.5941

$$= \_\_\_\_\_\_\_\_\_\_$$

reject

5. Decision: $X^2 = 7.594 > 5.991$; hence, we (reject, do not reject) H_0.

Therefore, the data produce sufficient evidence to contradict the manufacturer's statement that $p_1 = .85, p_2 = .10$, and $p_3 = .05$.

Example 17.2

A botanist performs a secondary cross of petunias involving independent factors controlling leaf shape and flower color where the factor "A" represents red color, "a" represents white color, "B" represents round leaves, and "b" represents long leaves. According to the Mendelian Model, the plants should exhibit the characteristics AB, Ab, aB, and ab in the ratio 9:3:3:1. Of 160 experimental plants, the following numbers are observed: AB, 95; Ab, 30; aB, 28; ab, 7. Is there sufficient evidence to refute the Mendelian Model at the $\alpha = .01$ level?

Solution

Translating the ratios into proportions, we have

$P(\text{AB}) = p_1 = 9/16$

$P(\text{Ab}) = p_2 = 3/16$

$P(\text{aB}) = p_3 =$ ________ 3/16

$P(\text{ab}) = p_4 =$ ________ 1/16

The data are tabulated as follows:

	Cell			
	AB	*Ab*	*aB*	*ab*
Expected	90	30	30	10
Observed	95	30	28	7

Perform a statistical test of the Mendelian Model using Pearson's statistic.

1. $H_0\colon p_1 = 9/16, p_2 = 3/16, p_3 = 3/16, p_4 = 1/16$

2. $H_a\colon p_i \neq p_{i0}$ for at least one value of $i = 1, 2, 3, 4$

3. Test statistic:

$$X^2 = \sum_{i=1}^{4} \frac{[n_i - E(n_i)]^2}{E(n_i)}$$

4. Rejection region: With 3 degrees of freedom, we shall reject H_0 if

$X^2 > \chi^2_{.01} =$ ________ 11.3449

Now we calculate

$$X^2 = \frac{(95-90)^2}{90} + \frac{(30-30)^2}{30} + \frac{(28-30)^2}{30} + \frac{(7-10)^2}{10}$$

$$= .2778 + .0000 + .1333 + .9000$$

1.3111

$= \_\_\_\_\_\_\_\_$

do not reject
is not

5. Decision: Since $X^2 = 1.3111 < 11.3449$, (reject, do not reject) H_0. There (is, is not) sufficient evidence to refute the Mendelian model.

Self-Correcting Exercises 17A

1. A company specializing in kitchen products has produced a mixer in five different colors. A random sample of $n = 250$ sales has produced the following data:

Color	White	Almond	Avocado	Brown	Gold
Number sold	62	48	56	39	45

   Test the hypothesis that there is no preference for color at the $\alpha = .05$ level of significance. (Hint: if there is no color preference, then $p_1 = p_2 = p_3 = p_4 = p_5 = 1/5$.)
2. The number of Caucasians possessing the four blood types, A, B, AB, and O, are said to be in the proportions .41, .12, .03 and .44, respectively. Would the observed frequencies of 90, 16, 10 and 84, respectively, furnish sufficient evidence to refute the given proportions at the $\alpha = .05$ level of significance?

17.4 Contingency Tables

We now examine the problem of determining whether *independence* exists between two methods for classifying observed data. If we were to classify people first according to their incomes, and second according to their brand preference, would these methods of classification be independent of each other? We might classify salesmen first according to their age class, where age classes range from 20 to 65, and second according to their average weekly sales volume. Would these methods of classification be independent? In each problem we are asking whether one method of classification is contingent on another. We investigate this problem by displaying our data according to the two methods of classification in an array called a ________ table.

contingency

Example 17.3

A criminologist studying criminal offenders under age 25 who have a record of one or more arrests is interested in knowing whether the educational achievement level of the offenders influences the frequency of arrests. He has classified his data using four educational achievement level classifications:

A: completed 6th grade or less

B: completed 7th, 8th, or 9th grade

C: completed 10th, 11th, or 12th grade

D: education beyond 12th grade

	Educational Achievement				
Number of Arrests	*A*	*B*	*C*	*D*	*Totals*
1	55 (45.39)	40 (43.03)	43 (43.03)	30 (36.55)	168
2	15 (21.61)	25 (20.49)	18 (20.49)	22 (17.40)	80
3 or more	7 (10.00)	8 (9.48)	12 (9.48)	10 (8.05)	37
Totals	77	73	73	62	285

The contingency table shows the number of offenders in each cell together with the expected cell frequency (in parentheses). The expected frequencies are obtained as follows:

1. Define p_A as the unconditional probability that a criminal offender will have completed grade 6 or less. Define p_B, p_C, and p_D in a similar manner.
2. Define p_1, p_2, p_3 to be the unconditional probability that the offender has 1, 2, or 3 or more arrests, respectively.

If two events, A and B, are independent, then $P(AB) =$ ______________. $P(A) \cdot P(B)$

Hence, if the two classifications are independent, a cell probability will equal the product of the two respective unconditional row and column probabilities. For example, the probability that an offender who has completed grade 6 is arrested 3 or more times is

$$p_{A3} = p_A \cdot p_3$$

whereas the probability that a person with a 10th grade education is arrested twice is

$$p_{C2} = \_\_\_\_\_\_\_\_\_\_ \qquad p_C \cdot p_2$$

Since the row and column probabilities are unknown, they must be estimated from the data. The estimators for these probabilities are defined in terms of r_i, the row totals, c_j, the column totals, and n.

$$\hat{p}_A = c_1/n = 77/285$$
$$\hat{p}_B = c_2/n = 73/285$$
$$\hat{p}_C = c_3/n = 73/285$$
$$\hat{p}_D = c_4/n = 62/285$$
$$\hat{p}_1 = r_1/n = 168/285$$
$$\hat{p}_2 = r_2/n = 80/285$$
$$\hat{p}_3 = r_3/n = 37/285$$

If the observed cell frequency for the cell in row i and column j is denoted by n_{ij}, then an estimate for the expected cell number in the ijth cell under the hypothesis of independence can be calculated by using the estimated cell probabilities.

$$E(n_{ij}) = n(p_{ij}) = n(p_i)\,(p_j)$$

$$\hat{E}(n_{ij}) = n(r_i/n)\,(c_j/n) = r_i c_j/n$$

The expected cell numbers enclosed in parentheses for the contingency table in the above are found in this way. For example,

45.39 $$\hat{E}(n_{11}) = \frac{(168)\,(77)}{285} = \_\_\_\_\_\_\_\_$$

43.03 $$\hat{E}(n_{12}) = \frac{(168)\,(73)}{285} = \_\_\_\_\_\_\_\_$$

8.05 $$\hat{E}(n_{34}) = \frac{(37)\,(62)}{285} = \_\_\_\_\_\_\_\_$$

80; 62; 17.40 $$\hat{E}(n_{24}) = \frac{(\_\_\_\_\_\_)\,(\_\_\_\_\_\_)}{285} = \_\_\_\_\_\_\_\_$$

Pearson's statistic can now be calculated accordingly as

$$X^2 = \sum_{i=1}^{3} \sum_{j=1}^{4} \frac{[n_{ij} - \hat{E}(n_{ij})]^2}{\hat{E}(n_{ij})}$$

$$= \frac{(55 - 45.39)^2}{45.39} + \frac{(40 - 43.03)^2}{43.03} + \dots$$

$$+ \frac{(12 - 9.48)^2}{9.48} + \frac{(10 - 8.05)^2}{8.05}$$

$$= \underline{\qquad\qquad}$$ 10.23

Recall that the number of degrees of freedom associated with the χ^2-statistic used in testing X^2 equals the number of cells less one degree of freedom for each independent linear restriction on the cell counts. The first restriction is that $\Sigma n_i =$ __________; hence __________ degree of freedom is lost here. Then $(r - 1)$ independent linear restrictions have been placed on the cell counts due to the estimation of $(r - 1)$ row probabilities. Note that we need only estimate $(r - 1)$ independent row probabilities since their sum must equal __________. In like manner, $(c - 1)$ independent linear restrictions have been placed on the cell counts due to the estimation of the column probabilities.

n; one

one (1)

Since there are rc cells, the number of degrees of freedom for testing X^2 in an $r \times c$ contingency table is

$$rc - (1) - (r - 1) - (c - 1)$$

which can be factored algebraically as

__________ $(r - 1)(c - 1)$

In short, the number of degrees of freedom for an $r \times c$ contingency table, where all expected cell frequencies must be estimated from sample data (that is, from estimated row and column probabilities), is the number of rows minus one, times the number of columns minus one.

For the problem concerning criminal offenders, the degrees of freedom are

$$(r - 1)(c - 1) = (\underline{\qquad})(\underline{\qquad}) = \underline{\qquad}$$ 2; 3; 6

We can now formalize the test of the hypothesis of independence of the two methods of classification at the $\alpha = .05$ level.

1. H_0: the two classifications are independent
2. H_a: the two classifications are not independent
3. Test statistic:

$$X^2 = \sum_{i=1}^{3} \sum_{j=1}^{4} \frac{[n_{ij} - \hat{E}(n_{ij})]^2}{\hat{E}(n_{ij})}$$

4. Rejection region: With 6 degrees of freedom, we shall reject H_0 if $X^2 > \chi^2_{.05} =$
12.5916 ________. The calculation of X^2 results in the value of $X^2 = 10.23$.
do not 5. Decision: Since $X^2 < 12.5916$, (do, do not) reject H_0.
do not Since we were unable to reject H_0, the data (do, do not) present sufficient evidence to indicate that educational achievement and the number of arrests are dependent.

Example 17.4

A marketing research director wishes to test the hypothesis that the number of children in a family is independent of the family income. A random sample of 385 families resulted in the following contingency table.

	Income Brackets in Thousands of Dollars				
Number of Children	*0–\$8*	*\$8–16*	*\$16–24*	*Above \$24*	*Total*
0	10 (14.26)	9 (15.05)	18 (16.48)	24 (15.21)	61
1	8 (17.77)	12 (18.75)	25 (20.53)	31 (18.95)	76
2	14 (21.74)	28 (22.95)	23 (25.12)	28 (23.19)	93
3	26 (17.77)	24 (18.75)	20 (20.53)	6 (18.95)	76
4 or more	32 (18.47)	22 (19.49)	18 (21.34)	7 (19.70)	79
Totals	90	95	104	96	385

If the number in parentheses is the estimated expected cell number, do these data present sufficient evidence at the $\alpha = .01$ level to indicate an independence of family size and family income?

Solution

The estimated cell counts have been found using

$$\hat{E}(n_{ij}) = \frac{r_i c_j}{n}$$

and are given in parentheses within each cell. The degrees of freedom are
12 $(r - 1)(c - 1) =$ ________.

1. H_0: the two classifications are independent
2. H_a: the classifications are not independent
3. Test statistic:

$$X^2 = \sum_{i=1}^{5} \sum_{j=1}^{4} \frac{[n_{ij} - \hat{E}(n_{ij})]^2}{\hat{E}(n_{ij})}$$

4. Rejection region: With 12 degrees of freedom, we will reject H_0 if

$$X^2 > \chi^2_{.01} = \_\_\_\_\_\_\_\_\_\_ .$$

Calculate X^2:

$$X^2 = \frac{(10 - 14.26)^2}{14.26} + \frac{(9 - 15.05)^2}{15.05} + \ldots + \frac{(18 - 21.34)^2}{21.34} + \frac{(7 - 19.70)^2}{19.70}$$

$$= \_\_\_\_\_\_\_\_\_\_$$

5. Decision: (Reject, Do not reject) H_0. Therefore, we can conclude that family size and family income (are, are not) independent classifications.
6. From Table 5, with __________ degrees of freedom, the observed value $X^2 = 63.4783$ exceeds $X^2_{.005}$ = __________ . Hence, the approximate level of significance is

   p-value __________

   The null hypothesis could be rejected for any α (greater than, less than) or equal to __________ .

26.2170

63.4783

Reject
are not
12
28.2995

$< .005$

greater than
.005

Self-Correcting Exercises 17B

1. On the basis of the following data, is there a significant relationship between levels of income and political party affiliation at the $\alpha = .05$ level of significance?

	Income		
Party Affiliation	*Low*	*Average*	*High*
Republican	33	85	27
Democrat	19	71	56
Other	22	25	13

2. Three hundred people were interviewed to determine their opinions regarding a uniform driving code for all states.

	Opinion	
Sex	*For*	*Against*
Male	114	60
Female	87	39

Is there sufficient evidence to indicate that the opinion expressed is dependent upon the sex of the person interviewed?

17.5 $r \times c$ Tables with Fixed Row or Column Totals

To avoid having rows or columns that are absolutely empty, it is sometimes desirable to fix the row or column totals of a contingency table in the design of the experiment. In Example 17.4, the design could have been to randomly sample 100 families in each of the four income brackets, thereby insuring that each of the income brackets would be represented in the sample. On the other hand, a random sample of 80 families in each of the family size categories could have been taken so that all family size categories would appear in the overall sample.

When using fixed row or column totals the number of independent linear restrictions on the cell counts is the same as for an $r \times c$ contingency table. Therefore the data is analyzed in the same way that an $r \times c$ contingency table is analyzed, using Pearson's χ^2 based on $(r - 1)(c - 1)$ degrees of freedom.

In the following example we examine a case where the column totals are fixed in advance.

Example 17.5

A manufacturer of ladies' garments wished to determine whether the percentage of unacceptable dresses differed for three different styles produced in his factory. A lot of 300 dresses of each style was produced in his factory with the following results:

Style	1	2	3
Number Unacceptable	9	4	11

Is there sufficient evidence to indicate that the percentage of unacceptable dresses varies from style to style at the $\alpha = .05$ level?

Solution

The above table displays only half of the pertinent information. Extend the table to include the acceptable category, allowing space for the expected cell frequencies.

8; 8; 8

	Style			
	1	*2*	*3*	*Totals*
Unacceptable	9 (________)	4 (________)	11 (________)	24
Acceptable	291 (292)	296 (292)	289 (292)	876
Totals	300	300	300	900

By fixing the column totals at 300, we have assured that the unconditional probability of selecting style 1, 2, or 3 is a constant and equal to

1/3 __________ for each style.

If the percentage of unacceptable dresses does not vary from style to style, then the probability of observing an unacceptable dress for a given style is the *same* for each style and is equal to a common value, p. Therefore, the unconditional probability of observing an unacceptable dress is p, and in like manner, the unconditional probability of observing an acceptable dress is $1 - p =$ __________ . If the percentage of defective dresses *is the same for the three styles*, then the probability of observing an unacceptable dress in style j will be

q

$$p_{1j} = (1/3)(p) \qquad \text{for } j = 1, 2, 3$$

while the probability of observing an acceptable dress in style j will be

$$p_{2j} = (1/3)(q) \qquad \text{for } j = 1, 2, 3$$

However, if the probability of observing an unacceptable dress varies from style to style, then

$$p_{1j} \neq (1/3)(p) \text{ and } p_{2j} \neq (1/3)(q)$$

for at least one value of $j = 1, 2, 3$. But, this is the same as asking whether the row and column classifications are independent; hence, this test is equivalent to a test of independence of the two classifications based on $(r - 1)(c - 1)$ degrees of freedom.

The test proceeds as follows:

$H_0: p_1 = p_2 = p_3 = p$

H_a: at least one proportion differs from at least one other

Test statistic:

$$X^2 = \sum_i \sum_j \frac{[n_{ij} - \hat{E}(n_{ij})]^2}{\hat{E}(n_{ij})}$$

Rejection region: For $(2 - 1)(3 - 1) =$ __________ degrees of freedom, we will reject H_0 if $X^2 > \chi^2_{.05} =$ __________.

2

5.991

To calculate the value of the test statistic, we must first find the estimated expected cell counts.

$$\hat{E}(n_{11}) = \hat{E}(n_{12}) = \hat{E}(n_{13}) = \frac{24\,(300)}{900} = \text{\_\_\_\_\_\_\_\_\_\_}$$

8

$$\hat{E}(n_{21}) = \hat{E}(n_{22}) = \hat{E}(n_{23}) = \frac{876\,(300)}{900} = \text{\_\_\_\_\_\_\_\_\_\_}$$

292

Then

11 - 8

$$X^2 = \frac{(9-8)^2}{8} + \frac{(4-8)^2}{8} + \frac{(\_\_\_\_\_\_\_\_)^2}{8}$$

289 - 292

$$+ \frac{(291-292)^2}{292} + \frac{(296-292)^2}{292} + \frac{(\_\_\_\_\_\_\_\_)^2}{292}$$

26; 26

$$= \frac{(\_\_\_\_\_\_\_\_)}{8} + \frac{(\_\_\_\_\_\_\_\_)}{292}$$

3.3390

$$= \_\_\_\_\_\_\_\_$$

cannot

does not

Decision: Since $X^2 = 3.3390 < \chi^2_{.05} = 5.991$, we (can, cannot) reject the null hypothesis. We can conclude that the percentage of defectives (does, does not) vary from style to style.

17.6 Analysis of an $r \times c$ Contingency Table Using Computer Packages

Packaged computer programs for performing a contingency table analysis are available at most computer facilities, or can be done on a home computer with the proper statistical software. The SAS, MINITAB, and SPSS computer program packages are referenced in the text and are commonly used for contingency table analysis. All of these programs, and others which may be available at a specific computer facility, produce the same basic information. The reader need only become familiar with the different printouts in order to be able to interpret the results.

Example 17.6

Refer to Example 17.3. The following computer printout resulted when the data in this example were analyzed using the SAS program.

STATISTICAL ANALYSIS SYSTEM

TABLE OF ARRESTS BY EDUCATION

ARRESTS FREQUENCY EXPECTED	EDUCATION A	B	C	D	TOTAL
1	55 45.4	40 43.0	43 43.0	30 36.6	168
2	15 21.6	25 20.5	18 20.5	22 17.4	80
3	7 10.0	8 9.5	12 9.5	10 8.0	37
TOTAL	77	73	73	62	285

STATISTICS FOR 2-WAY TABLES

CHI-SQUARE	10.227	DF = 6	PROB = .1154
PHI	.189		
CONTINGENCY COEFFICIENT	.186		
CRAMER'S V	.109		
LIKELIHOOD RATIO CHI-SQUARE		DF =	PROB =

Discussion

The TABLE OF ARRESTS BY EDUCATION, which appears first in the printout, gives observed and estimated expected cell counts for each cell (rounded to one decimal place) as well as row and column totals. The program allows the user to enter specific names for the designations "ROW" and "COLUMN" in its printout. In particular, we have asked that the word "ROW" be replaced by "__________" and that the word "COLUMN" be replaced by "__________."

ARRESTS
EDUCATION

Directly below the table, several statistics are given. The first is CHI-SQUARE, which is the value of the test statistic calculated in Section 17.4. In this example, $X^2 =$ __________ with DF = __________ degrees of freedom. In the same row, the value PROB = .1154 is the observed significance level for the test. Using this portion of the printout, the student may test the hypothesis of independence of the two classifications. The quantities listed below the line labeled CHI-SQUARE are descriptive statistics used in measuring the degree of association or dependence between the two qualitative variables. They often appear on computer printouts, but will not be discussed in this text. The interested student may check the references at the end of Chapter 17 in the text.

10.227; 6

Example 17.7

Refer to Example 17.3. The following computer printouts resulted when the data were analyzed using the MINITAB and SPSS programs.

1. MINITAB:

EXPECTED FREQUENCIES ARE PRINTED BELOW OBSERVED FREQUENCIES

	A	B	C	D	TOTALS
1	55 45.4	40 43.0	43 43.0	30 36.6	168
2	15 21.6	25 20.5	18 20.5	22 17.4	80
3	7 10.0	8 9.5	12 9.5	10 8.0	37
TOTALS	77	73	73	62	285

TOTAL CHI SQUARE =

2.03 + .21 + .00 + 1.17 +
2.02 + .99 + .30 + 1.21 +
.90 + .23 + .67 + .47 +
= 10.23

DEGREES OF FREEDOM = (3 − 1) X (4 − 1) = 6

2. *SPSS:*

	COUNT ROW PCT COL PCT TOT PCT	EDUCATION A	B	C	D	ROW TOTAL
ARRESTS	1	55 32.7 71.4 19.3	40 23.8 54.8 14.0	43 25.6 58.9 15.1	30 17.9 48.4 10.5	168 58.9
	2	15 18.8 19.5 5.3	25 31.2 34.2 8.8	18 22.5 24.7 6.3	22 27.5 35.5 7.7	80 28.1
	3	7 18.9 9.1 2.5	8 21.6 11.0 2.8	12 32.4 16.4 4.2	10 27.0 16.1 3.5	37 13.0
	COLUMN TOTAL	77 27.0	73 25.6	73 25.6	62 21.8	285 100.0

CHI SQUARE = 10.227 WITH 6 DEGREES OF FREEDOM SIGNIFICANCE = .1154

Discussion

The MINITAB printout gives the observed and estimated expected cell counts in the body of the table, as did the SAS printout. The chi-square statistic is calculated below the table, with the individual elements in the sum listed as $(n_{ij} - \hat{E}(n_{ij}))^2/\hat{E}(n_{ij})$. For example, the contribution to X^2 made by row 1, column 1, is

$$\frac{(n_{11} - \hat{E}(n_{11}))^2}{\hat{E}(n_{11})} = \frac{(\_\_\_\_\_\_\_\_)^2}{45.4} = \_\_\_\_\_\_\_\_$$

55 − 45.4; 2.03

Then $X^2 = 10.23$ is given by the label ____________. Notice that the level of significance (is, is not) given on the MINITAB printout. The experimenter must consult Table 5, the Appendix, to obtain an appropriate rejection region for the test.

TOTAL CHI SQUARE
is not

The SPSS printout (does, does not) display the estimated expected cell counts. It (does, does not) display in each cell the observed cell count, the cell count as a percentage of the row total, as a percentage of the column total, and as a percentage of the total observations, n. The value of the test statistic X^2 is labeled ____________ and is shown directly below the table along with the appropriate degrees of freedom and significance level. Other entries, such as CRAMER'S V, LAMBDA, and KENDALL'S TAU may be requested by the user and will appear below the line labeled CHI SQUARE.

does not
does

CHI SQUARE

Self-Correcting Exercises 17C

1. A survey of voter sentiment was conducted in four mid-city political wards to compare the fraction of voters favoring a "city manager" form of government. Random samples of 200 voters were polled in each of the four wards with results as follows:

	Ward			
	1	*2*	*3*	*4*
Favor	75	63	69	58
Against	125	137	131	142

   Can you conclude that the fractions favoring the city manager form of government differ in the four wards?

2. A personnel manager of a large company investigating employee satisfaction with their assigned jobs collected the following data for 200 employees in each of four job categories:

	Categories				
Satisfaction	*I*	*II*	*III*	*IV*	*Totals*
High	40	60	52	48	200
Medium	103	87	82	88	360
Low	57	53	66	64	240
Totals	200	200	200	200	800

Use the MINITAB printout given below. Do these data indicate that the satisfaction scores are dependent on the job categories? (Use α .05.)

```
MTB > CHISQUARE C1 C2 C3 C4

EXPECTED FREQUENCIES ARE PRINTED BELOW OBSERVED
FREQUENCIES
```

	C1	C2	C3	C4	TOTALS
1	40 50.0	60 50.0	52 50.0	48 50.0	200
2	103 90.0	87 90.0	82 90.0	88 90.0	360
3	57 60.0	53 60.0	66 60.0	64 60.0	240
TOTALS	200	200	200	200	800

```
TOTAL CHI SQUARE =

        2.00 + 2.00 + 0.08 + 0.08 +
        1.88 + 0.10 + 0.71 + 0.04 +
        0.15 + 0.82 + 0.60 + 0.27 +

          = 8.73

DEGREES OF FREEDOM = (3 - 1) X (4 - 1) = 6
```

17.7 Other Applications

The specific uses of the chi-square test that we have dealt with in this chapter can be divided into two categories:

1. The first category is called "goodness-of-fit tests," whereby observed frequencies are compared with hypothesized frequencies which depend upon the hypothesized cell probabilities for a multinomial probability distribution. A decision is made as to whether the data fit the hypothesized model.
2. The second category is called "tests of independence," whereby a decision is made as to whether two methods of classifying the observations are statistically independent. If it is decided that the classifications are independent, then the probability that an observation would be classified as belonging to a specific row classification would be constant across the columns, or vice versa. If it is decided that the classifications are not independent, then the implication is that the probability that an observation would be classified as belonging to a specific row classification varies from column to column.

To illustrate the general nature of the goodness-of-fit test, we could test whether a set of data comes from any specified distribution such as the normal distribution with mean μ and variance σ^2, or a binomial distribution based on n trials with probability of success p, or perhaps a Poisson distribution (we have not studied this distribution in any detail) with mean λ. Binomial data produce their own natural grouping corresponding to the cells of a multinomial experiment if one counts the number of zeros, ones, twos, and so on occurring in the data. If the expected cell frequencies are less than the required number, cells can be combined before using Pearson's statistic. Data from a normal distribution, on the other hand, do not produce an inherent natural grouping and must be grouped as in a frequency histogram. In conjunction with a table of normal curve areas and the hypothesized normal distribution, the boundary points for the histogram should be chosen so that each "cell" has approximately the same probability and an expected frequency greater than ____________. Grouping the sample data accord- 5
ingly, one can compare the "observed" group frequencies against the theoretical ones using Pearson's chi-square statistic. If population parameters need to be estimated, the point estimates given in earlier chapters are used and
__________ degree of freedom subtracted for each independent estimate. one

Tests of independence of two methods of classification are easily extended to three or more classifications by first estimating the expected cell frequencies and applying Pearson's statistic with the proper degrees of freedom. For example, in testing the independence of three classifications with c_1, c_2, and c_3 categories in the respective classifications, the test statistic would be

$$X^2 = \sum_{i=1}^{c_1} \sum_{j=1}^{c_2} \sum_{k=1}^{c_3} \frac{[n_{ijk} - \hat{E}(n_{ijk})]^2}{\hat{E}(n_{ijk})},$$

which has an approximate χ^2 distribution with $(c_1 - 1)(c_2 - 1)(c_3 - 1)$ degrees of freedom.

Further applications involving the χ^2 test are usually specifically tailored solutions to special problems. An example would be the test of a linear trend in a binomial proportion observed over time, as discussed in the text. Modifications such as this usually require the use of calculus and are beyond the scope of this text.

Self-Correcting Exercises 17D

1. A company producing wire rope has recorded the number of "breaks" occurring for a given type of wire rope within a 4-hour period. These records were kept for fifty 4-hour periods. If y is the number of "breaks" recorded for each 4-hour period and μ is the mean number of "breaks" for a 4-hour period, does the following Poisson model adequately describe these data when $\mu = 2$?

$$p(x) = \frac{\mu^x e^{-\mu}}{x!}, \quad x = 0, 1, 2, \ldots.$$

x	0	1	2	3 or more
Number observed	4	15	16	15

Hint: Find $p(0)$, $p(1)$, and $p(2)$. Use the fact that

$$P(x \geqslant 3) = 1 - p(0) - p(1) - p(2).$$

After finding the expected cell numbers, you can test the model by applying Pearson's chi-square test.

2. In standardizing a score, the mean is subtracted and the result divided by the standard deviation. If 100 scores are so standardized and then grouped, test, at the $\alpha = .05$ level of significance, whether these scores were drawn from the standard normal distribution.

Interval	*Frequency*
less than -1.5	8
-1.5 to -.5	20
-.5 to .5	40
.5 to 1.5	29
greater than 1.5	3

17.8 Assumptions

In order that the statistic

$$X^2 = \sum_{i=1}^{k} \frac{[n_i - E(n_i)]^2}{E(n_i)}$$

have an approximate χ^2 distribution, the following assumptions are made:

1. The cell counts, $n_1, n_2, \ldots, n_k$, must satisfy the conditions of a ______________ experiment (or several multinomial experiments).

multinomial

2. All expected cell counts should be at least __________.

5

Although valid multinomial data arise under various sampling plans, in order to be confident in the use of the X^2 statistic, the sample size should be large enough to ensure that all the expected cell counts are 5 or more. This is a conservative figure; some authors have stated that some expected cell counts can be as small as one. By asking for expected cell counts of 5 or more, we automatically satisfy experimental situations in which these counts can in fact be allowed to be less than 5. In so doing, we should realize that sensitivity may be sacrificed for the sake of safety and simplicity.

EXERCISES

1. What are the characteristics of a multinomial experiment?
2. Do the following situations possess the properties of a multinomial experiment?
   a. A shipment of 40 pairs of shoes from a manufacturer contained men's shoes, women's shoes, and children's shoes. The number of men's shoes, women's shoes, and children's shoes are recorded.
   b. An investor has the option of choosing among three portfolios, one of which hedges against inflation, one which is best under a stable economy, and one which provides protection in time of recession. The payoff to the investor is dependent upon the portfolio he selects and the state of nature which results.
   c. Four production lines are checked for defectives during an eight-hour period and the number of defectives for each production line recorded.
3. The probability of receiving grades of A, B, C, D, and E are .07, .15, .63, .10, and .05, respectively, in a certain business course. In a class of 120 students,
   a. what is the expected number of A's?
   b. what is the expected number of B's?
   c. what is the expected number of C's?
4. A department store manager claims that his store has twice as many customers on Fridays and Saturdays as on any other day of the week (the store is closed on Sundays). That is, the probability that a customer visits the store Friday is 2/8, the probability that a customer visits the store Saturday is 2/8, while the probability that a customer visits the store on each of the remaining weekdays is 1/8. During an average week, the following numbers of customers visited the store:

Monday	95	Thursday	75
Tuesday	110	Friday	181
Wednesday	125	Saturday	214

   Can the manager's claim be refuted at the $\alpha = .05$ level of significance?
5. If the probability of a female birth is 1/2, according to the binomial model, in a family containing four children, the probability of 0, 1, 2, 3, or 4 female births is 1/16, 4/16, 6/16, 4/16, and 1/16, respectively. A sample of 80 families each containing four children resulted in the following data:

Female births	0	1	2	3	4
Number of families	7	18	33	16	6

   Do the data contradict the binomial model with $p = 1/2$ at the $\alpha = .05$ level of significance?
6. A sales training program thought to be effective in increasing sales activity is administered to 500 real estate salesmen. Their weekly sales immediately after the training program were compared to those of 500 salesmen of the

same sales area who did not participate in the training program. The results were as follows:

	More Than One Sale	*One Sale*	*No Sale*
Trained	252	146	102
Untrained	224	136	140

Test the hypothesis that the two classifications are independent at the $\alpha = .05$ level of significance.

7. A manufacturer wished to know whether the number of defectives produced varied for four different production lines. A random sample of 100 items was selected from each line and the number of defectives recorded.

Production lines	1	2	3	4
Defectives	8	12	7	9

Do these data produce sufficient evidence to indicate that the percentage of defects is varying from line to line?

8. In a random sample of 50 male and 50 female undergraduates, each member was asked if he was for, against, or indifferent to the practice of having unannounced in-class quizzes. Do the following data indicate that attitude toward this practice is dependent upon the sex of the student interviewed? A computer printout for the chi-square test is given below.

	Male	*Female*
For	20	10
Against	15	30
Indifferent	15	10

CHI-SQUARE TEST OF INDEPENDENCE

THE ROW TOTALS ARE:

30 45 25

THE COLUMN TOTALS ARE:

50 50

THE GRAND TOTAL IS:

100

R	C	O–F	E–F	D–F	CHSQ
1	1	20	15.00	5.00	1.67
1	2	10	15.00	–5.00	1.67
2	1	15	22.50	–7.50	2.50
2	2	30	22.50	7.50	2.50
3	1	15	12.50	2.50	.50
3	2	10	12.50	–2.50	.50

CHSQ = 9.333 ** WITH 2 DF

9. In an experiment performed in a laboratory, a ball is bounced within a container whose bottom (or floor) has holes just large enough for the ball to pass through. The ball is allowed to bounce until it passes through one of the holes. For each of 100 trials, the number of bounces until the ball falls through one of the holes is recorded. If x is the number of bounces until the ball does fall through a hole, does the model

$$p(x) = (.6)(.4)^x \qquad x = 0, 1, 2, 3, \ldots$$

adequately describe the following data?

x	0	1	2	3 or more
Number observed	65	28	4	3

Hint: First find $p(0)$, $p(1)$, $p(2)$, and $P(x \geqslant 3)$ from which the expected numbers for the cells can be calculated using np_0, np_1, np_2, etc. Then a goodness of fit test will adequately answer the question posed.

Chapter 18

NONPARAMETRIC STATISTICS

18.1 Introduction

In earlier chapters we tested various hypotheses concerning populations in terms of their parameters. These tests represent a group of tests that are called ______________ tests, since they specifically involve parameters such as means, variances, or proportions. To apply the techniques of Chapter 8, a large number of observations were required to assure the approximate ______________ of the statistics employed in testing. In Chapter 9, 10, and 11, it was assumed that the sampled populations had ______________ distributions. Further, if two or more populations were studied in the same experiment, it was necessary to assume that these populations had a common ______________. In this chapter we will be concerned with hypotheses that do not involve population parameters directly but deal rather with the form of the distribution. The hypothesis that two distributions are identical versus the hypothesis that one distribution has typically larger values than the other are nonparametric statements of H_0 and H_a.

parametric

normality

normal

variance

Nonparametric tests are appropriate in many situations where one or more of the following conditions exist:

1. Nonparametric methods can be used when the form of the distribution is unknown, so that descriptive parameters may be of little use.
2. Nonparametric techniques are particularly appropriate if the measurement scale is that of rank ordering.
3. If a response can be measured on a continuous scale, a nonparametric method may nevertheless be desirable because of its relative simplicity when compared to its parametric analogue.
4. Most parametric tests require that the sampled population satisfy certain assumptions. When an experimenter cannot reasonably expect that these assumptions are met, a nonparametric test would be a valid alternative.

The following hypotheses would be appropriate for nonparametric tests:

1. H_0: a given population is normally distributed.
2. H_0: populations I and II have the same distribution.
3. H_0: a sequence of observations exhibits the property of randomness.

Since these hypotheses are less specific than those required for parametric tests, we might expect a nonparametric test to be (more, less) efficient than a corresponding parametric test when all the conditions required for the use of the parametric test are met. less

18.2 The Sign Test for Comparing Two Population Distributions

The sign test is based on the ______________ of the observed differences. signs

Thus in a paired-difference experiment, we may observe in each pair only whether the first element is larger (or smaller) than the second. If the first element is larger (smaller), we assign a plus (minus) sign to the difference. We will define the test statistic x to be the number of ______________ signs observed. plus

It is worth emphasizing that the sign test *does not* require a numerical measure of a response but merely a statement of which of two responses within a matched pair is larger. Thus the sign test is a convenient and even necessary tool in many brand preference investigations. If within a given pair it is impossible to tell which response is larger (a tie occurs), the pair is omitted. Thus if 20 differences are analyzed and 2 of them are impossible to classify as plus or minus, we will base our inference on __________ (give number) differences. 18

Let p denote the probability that a difference selected at random from the population of differences would be given a plus sign. If the two population distributions are identical, the probability of a plus sign for a given pair would equal __________. 1/2

Then the null hypothesis, "the two populations are identical," could be stated in the form H_0: $p = 1/2$. The test statistic, x, will have a ______________ distribution whether H_0 is true or not. binomial

If H_0 is true, then the number of trials, n, will be the number of pairs in which a difference can be detected and the probability of success (i.e., a plus sign) on a given trial will be __________. $p = 1/2$

If the alternative hypothesis is H_a: $p > 1/2$, then (large, small) values of x would be placed in the rejection region. large

If the alternative hypothesis is H_a: $p < 1/2$, then ______________ values of x would be used in the rejection region. small

With H_a: $p \neq 1/2$, the rejection region would include both ______________ and ______________ values of x. large small

Example 18.1

In an experiment designed to compare the relative effectiveness of two alloys with respect to their resistance to corrosion, fifteen pairs of metal strips were subjected to corrosive elements, and at the end of a specified time, a measure of the amount of corrosion that had taken place was recorded for each strip. A preliminary investigation of the 15 pairs revealed that in 12 of the 15 pairs, alloy number one showed more corrosion. Does this constitute sufficient evidence to indicate that the alloys differ in their resistance to corrosion?

Solution

If there is no difference in ability to resist corrosion, then the probability that a strip of alloy number one shows more corrosion than a strip of alloy number two is $p = 1/2$. If alloy number one is more resistant than alloy
$< 1/2$ number two, then p __________, while if alloy number one is less resistant
$> 1/2$ than two, then p __________. Using this information, the test proceeds as follows.

1. $H_0: p = \frac{1}{2}$

$p \neq \frac{1}{2}$

2. H_a: __________

3. The test statistic is x, the number of pairs in which alloy one showed more corrosion than alloy two. The number of pairs is $n = 15$, and the
12 observed value of x is __________.
4. Rejection region: The alternative hypothesis indicates that we should reject H_0 for very large or very small values of x. Using the table of binomial probabilities in your text with $p = 1/2$ and $n = 15$, evaluate the following possible rejection regions.

	Rejection region	α
.008	$x = 0, 1, 2, 13, 14, 15$	__________
.036	$x = 0, 1, 2, 3, 12, 13, 14, 15$	__________
.118	$x = 0, 1, 2, 3, 4, 11, 12, 13, 14, 15$	__________

Choosing the rejection region so that the probability of a Type I error is less than or equal to .05, we would agree to reject $H_0: p = 1/2$ if $y = 0$,
.036 1, 2, 3, 12, 13, 14, or 15 with α = __________.

5. reject With the observed value of $x = 12$, we (accept, reject) H_0 and conclude that there is a difference in resistance to corrosion for these two alloys.
two In fact, it appears that of the two alloys, alloy number __________ is the more resistant to corrosion.

We observed in Chapter 6 that the normal approximation to binomial probabilities is reasonably accurate if $p = 1/2$ even when n is as small as
10 __________. Thus, the normal distribution can ordinarily be used to

approximate __________ for a given rejection region. Furthermore, when n is at least __________, the test can be based on the statistic | α
25

$$z = \frac{x - .5n}{.5\sqrt{n}}$$

which will have approximately the standard normal distribution when H_0 is ______________. | true

Example 18.2

The productivity of 25 employees was observed and measured both before and after the installation of new lighting in a workroom. The productivity of 18 of the 25 workers was observed to have improved while the productivity of the others appeared to show no perceptible gain as a result of the new lighting. Test whether the new lighting was effective in increasing employee productivity.

Solution

Let p denote the probability that one of the 25 employees selected at random exhibits increased productivity after the installation of new lighting. This constitutes a paired-difference test where the productivity measures are paired on the employees. Such pairing tends to block out employee variations.

1. The null hypothesis is $H_0: p$ __________. | $= 1/2$
2. The appropriate one-sided alternative hypothesis is $H_a: p$ __________. | $> 1/2$
3. If x denotes the number of employees who show improved productivity after the installation of the new lighting, then x has a binomial distribution with mean $np = 25(1/2) =$ __________ and a variance equal to $npq = 25(1/2)(1/2) =$ __________. Therefore the test statistic can be taken to be | 12.5
6.25

$$z = \frac{x - 12.5}{\sqrt{6.25}}$$

4. We would reject H_0 at the $\alpha = .05$ level of significance if the calculated value of z is greater than $z_{.05} =$ __________. | 1.645
5. Since $x = 18$,

$$z = \frac{18 - 12.5}{2.5} = \text{__________}$$ | 2.2

would; has

Hence we (would, would not) reject H_0; the new lighting (has, has not) improved employee productivity.

18.3 The Mann-Whitney U Test: Two Population Distributions and Independent Random Samples

When the actual magnitudes of the observations are known, more information than that used by the sign test can be gleaned from the data for use in hypothesis testing. However, in order to make more efficient use of this information, the simplicity of the sign test must be sacrificed and a slightly more complex testing procedure introduced.

independent

If an experimenter has two ______________ random samples in which the observations can be ranked in order of magnitude, the Mann-Whitney U statistic can be used to test whether the samples have been drawn from

identical

______________ populations. The Mann-Whitney U test is appropriate when we have two independent samples of size n_1 and n_2 from populations A and B, respectively. If the null hypothesis is true, and both samples have been drawn from the same population, we then have one sample of size $N = n_1 + n_2$ from the same population.

1. All $N = n_1 + n_2$ observations are ranked from small to large with the smallest observation assigned rank 1 and the largest assigned rank $N = n_1 + n_2$. Tied observations are assigned the average of the ranks they would have been assigned if there were no ties. For example, if the sixth and seventh smallest observations have the same magnitude, each

   6.5

   is assigned the value ______________.

   If the null hypothesis is true, we would expect to see the A and B observations randomly mixed in the ranking positions. If H_0 is false and the A observations come from a population whose values tend to be larger than the B observations, the A's will tend to occupy the

   higher

   lower

   ______________ rank positions. If the B's tend to be larger than the A's, then the A observations will tend to occupy the ______________ rank positions
2. A statistic that reflects the positions in the total ranking of the observations from population A and from population B is the sum of the rank positions occupied by the first sample or the sum of the rank positions

   T_A; T_B

   occupied by the second sample, denoted by _________ and _________, respectively.

The stronger the discrepancy between T_A and T_B, the greater is the evi-

different

dence to indicate that the samples have been drawn from two __________ populations. The Mann-Whitney U statistic uses this information in testing for a difference in the population frequency distributions giving rise to the sample observations.

The Mann-Whitney U statistic is the smaller of U_A and U_B where

$$U_A = n_1 n_2 + \frac{n_1(n_1+1)}{2} - T_A$$

$$U_B = n_1 n_2 + \frac{n_2(n_2+1)}{2} - T_B$$

with $U_A + U_B =$ __________. The quantity U_A counts the number of times that an A observation precedes a B observation in the ranking while U_B counts the number of times that a B observation precedes an A observation. Since U is the smaller of U_A and U_B, the smaller the value of U, the (more, less) likely it is that the underlying distributions are different. $n_1 n_2$ more

The Mann-Whitney U statistic is used in testing whether population A and population B have identical frequency distributions. The specification of the rejection region depends upon the alternative hypothesis. A (one, two) -tailed test is used when the alternative hypothesis is that the two populations are not identical. If the alternative hypothesis is that the frequency distribution for population A lies to the right (or left) of the frequency distribution for population B, a (one, two) -tailed test is used. two one

The selection of the rejection region depends upon the value of α, the sample sizes, n_1 and n_2, and the alternative hypothesis. Tabled values for $P(U \leqslant U_0)$ when n_1 and n_2 are less than or equal to 10 are given in Table 7 in the Appendix of your text. Notice that the entries in Table 7 are indexed with $n_1 \leqslant n_2$. When the sample sizes are not equal, always designate the population with the smaller sample size as population __________. A

1. A one-tailed rejection region consists of the values of $U \leqslant U_0$ where U_0 is chosen from Table 7 such that $P(U \leqslant U_0) =$ __________. In this case the U statistic will be chosen specifically to be U_A or U_B. α
2. The rejection region for a two-tailed test consists of the values $U \leqslant U_0$ where $P(U \leqslant U_0) =$ __________. In this case U is the smaller of U_A or U_B. $\alpha/2$

Example 18.3

Five sample observations for each of two samples are given below:

Sample A: 19 (___) 20 (___) 16 (___) 12 (___) 23 (___) 5; 6; 2; 1; 9
Sample B: 17 (___) 21 (___) 22 (___) 25 (___) 18 (___) 3; 7; 8; 10; 4

In the space provided, fill in the rank of each of the 10 observations and calculate T_A and T_B.

$T_A = 5 + 6 + 2 + 1 + 9 =$ __________ 23

$T_B = 3 + 7 + 8 +$ __________ $+$ __________ $=$ __________ 10; 4; 32

Example 18.4
Use the data in Example 18.3 to test H_0: the population frequency distributions for A and B are identical against H_a: the population frequency distributions are not identical.

Solution
1. We must first calculate U_A and U_B.

$$U_A = n_1 n_2 + \frac{n_1(n_1 + 1)}{2} - T_A$$

17 $$= 5(5) + \frac{5(6)}{2} - 23 = \_\_\_\_\_\_\_\_$$

and

$$U_B = n_1 n_2 + \frac{n_2(n_2 + 1)}{2} - T_B$$

8 $$= 5(5) + \frac{5(6)}{2} - 32 = \_\_\_\_\_\_\_\_$$

As a check on our calculations, notice that

$n_1 n_2$ $$U_A + U_B = \_\_\_\_\_\_\_\_ = 25$$

8; smaller

2. The Mann-Whitney U statistic is equal to ________, the ____________ of U_A and U_B.

5; 3
.0278

3. For a two-tailed test the rejection region consists of values of $U \leqslant U_0$ such that $P(U \leqslant U_0) \approx \alpha$ with U_0 found in Table 7 of the text when $n_1 = n_2 =$ ________. An appropriate choice is $U_0 =$ ________, since that insures that $P(U \leqslant U_0) =$ ________, which is approximately equal to $\alpha/2$ for $\alpha = .05$.

do not reject

4. Since $U = 8$ is greater than $U_0 = 3$, we (reject, do not reject) the null hypothesis of identical population frequency distributions.

Example 18.5
Before filling several new managerial positions which were created due to company expansion, the personnel director of the company formed a review board consisting of five people who were asked to interview the twelve qualified applicants and rank them in order of merit. Seven of the twelve applicants held college degrees but had limited on-the-job experi-

ence. Of the remaining five applicants, all did not necessarily have college degrees, but all did have substantial experience. The review board's rankings follow.

Limited experience	Substantial experience
4	1
6	2
7	3
9	5
10	8
11	
12	

Do these rankings indicate that the review board considers on-the-job experience to be more important than formal education?

Solution

1. In testing the null hypothesis that the underlying populations are identical versus the alternative hypothesis that the population consisting of applicants having substantial experience is better qualified (will receive low ranks), we require a ____________-tailed test. — one
2. In deciding upon the test statistic and the rejection region, we must take care to note that the tables are given with $n_1 \leqslant n_2$. Hence we take $n_1 = 5$ and $n_2 = 7$ and identify the five applicants with substantial experience as A's and the remaining seven applicants as B's. If H_a is true, the A's will occupy the ____________ ranks and U_A will be ____________ because T_A is ____________. Similarly, the B's will have generally higher ranks, making T_B ____________ and U_B ____________. Hence, if H_a is true, (U_A, U_B) will be smaller than __________, and will be used as our test statistic U. — lower *or* smaller; large; small; large; small; U_B; U_A
3. $T_B = 4 + 6 + 7 +$ ________ $+$ ________ $+$ ________ $+$ ________ $=$ ________ — 9; 10; 11; 12; 59
4. Using U_B as the test statistic, with $\alpha \approx .05$, $n_1 = 5$ and $n_2 = 7$, an appropriate rejection region would consist of the values $U \leqslant$ __________ with $\alpha =$ __________, using Table 7 in the text. — 7; .0530

$$U_B = n_1 n_2 + \frac{n_2(n_2+1)}{2} - T_B$$

$$= 5(7) + \frac{7(8)}{2} - \underline{\qquad\qquad}$$ — 59

$$= \underline{\qquad\qquad}$$ — 4

5. Since $U =$ __________ is less than $U_0 =$ __________, we (reject, do not — 4; 7; reject

reject) H_0 and conclude that the review board does consider on-the-job experience to be more important than formal education alone.

The MINITAB software package provides a program called MANN WHITNEY (Mann-Whitney U test). Data from the first and second samples are stored in two separate columns in the computer. The command MANN WHITNEY followed by two column numbers will implement the program. For the data given in Example 18.5, stored in C1 and C2, the commpand MANN WHITNEY C1 C2 produced the following output.

```
MTB > MANN WHITNEY 1  C1  C2
C1                 N =  7            MEDIAN =   9.0000
C2                 N =  5            MEDIAN =   3.0000
A POINT ESTIMATE FOR ETA1-ETA2 IS                  5.00
A 96.5 PERCENT C.I. FOR ETA1-ETA2 IS        (        1.0,     9.0)

W =          59.0
TEST OF ETA1 = ETA 2 VS. ETA1 G.T. ETA 2
THE TEST IS SIGNIFICANT AT 0.0174
```

is not

The test statistic is given in line 5 of the output as $W = 59.0$. This (is, is not) the value of U, but is instead the rank sum for the observations in column 1, T_A. Although the value for U_A could be calculated from T_A, this is unnecessary, since line 6 provides the observed significance level, p-value = .0174. Hence, we (can, cannot) reject H_0 with $\alpha = .05$. The MINITAB program allows the user to specify an upper-tailed, lower-tailed, or two-tailed alternative hypothesis, rather than choosing the minimum of U_A or U_B. This is done by specifying −1 (left-tailed), 0 (two-tailed), or 1 (right-tailed) before C1 and C2.

can

When the sample sizes both exceed ten, Table 7 can no longer be used to locate rejection regions for tests involving the Mann-Whitney U statistic. However, when the sample sizes exceed __________, the distribution of U can be approximated by a ____________ distribution with mean

10
normal

$$E(U) = \frac{n_1 n_2}{2}$$

and variance

$$\sigma_U^2 = \frac{n_1 n_2 (n_1 + n_2 + 1)}{12}$$

Therefore, we can use as a test statistic:

$$z = \frac{U - E(U)}{\sigma_U}$$

with the appropriate one- or two-tailed rejection region expressed in terms of z, the ____________ ____________ random variable.

standard normal

Example 18.6

A manufacturer uses a large amount of a certain chemical. Since there are just two suppliers of this chemical, the manufacturer wishes to test whether the percent of contaminants is the same for the two sources against the alternative that there is a difference in the percent of contaminants for the two suppliers. Data from independent random samples are given below.

Supplier			*Percent contaminants*		
	.86	.69	.72	.65	1.13
A	.65	1.18	.45	1.41	.50
	1.04	.41			
	.55	.40	.22	.58	.16
B	.07	.09	.16	.26	.36
	.20	.15			

Solution

1. We combine the obtained contaminant percentages in a single ordered arrangement, and identify each percentage by letter.

Percent	.07	.09	.15	.16	.16	.20	.22	.26
Rank	1	2	3	4.5	4.5	6	7	8
Supplier	B	B	B	B	B	B	B	B
Percent	.36	.40	.41	.45	.50	.55	.58	.65
Rank	9	10	11	12	13	14	15	16.5
Supplier	B	B	A	A	A	B	B	A
Percent	.65	.69	.72	.86	1.04	1.13	1.18	1.41
Rank	16.5	18	19	20	21	22	23	24
Supplier	A	A	A	A	A	A	A	A

2. Since the sample sizes of $n_1 = 12$ and $n_2 = 12$ are beyond those given in Table 7, we can use the normal approximation to the distribution of U. The manufacturer, in asking whether there is a difference between the two suppliers, has specified a __________-tailed test. Therefore we would reject H_0 if U were either too large or too small. (For a two-tailed test using the normal approximation, we are at liberty to use either U_A or U_B as the value of U to be tested.) two
3. Using $n_1 = n_2 = 12$, $E(U) =$ __________ and $\sigma_U^2 =$ __________. 72; 300

$$U_A = n_1 n_2 + \frac{1}{2} n_1(n_1 + 1) - T_A$$

$$= 144 + 78 - \_\_\_\_\_\_ \qquad 216$$

$$= \_\_\_\_\_\_ \qquad 6$$

while

$$U_B = n_1 n_2 + \frac{1}{2} n_2(n_2 + 1) - T_B$$

84 $= 144 + 78 -$ ________

138 $=$ ________

4. The rejection region in terms of $z = (U - E(U))/\sigma_U$ would be to reject
1.96 H_0 if $|z| >$ ________. With U_A as the value of U,

-3.81 $$z = \frac{6 - 72}{\sqrt{300}} = \frac{-66}{17.32} = \_\_\_\_\_\_\_\_$$

is Hence we would conclude that there (is, is not) a significant difference in percent contaminants for the two suppliers.

5. Had we used U_B as the value of U, our result would have been

3.81 $$z = \frac{138 - 72}{\sqrt{300}} = \frac{66}{17.32} = \_\_\_\_\_\_\_\_$$

and we would have arrived at the same conclusion.

Use of the Mann-Whitney U test eliminates the need for the restrictive assumptions of Student's t-test which requires that the samples be
normal; equal randomly drawn from __________ populations having __________ variances.

Self-Correcting Exercises 18A

1. An experiment was designed to compare the durabilities of two highway paints, Paint A and Paint B, under actual highway conditions. An A strip and a B strip were painted across a highway at each of 30 locations. At the end of the test period, the experimenter observed the following results. At 8 locations Paint A showed the least wear, at 17 locations Paint B showed the least wear, and at the other 5 locations the paint samples showed the same amount of wear. Can we conclude (use $\alpha = .05$) that Paint B is more durable?
2. Refer to Chapter 9, Exercise 15. Use the sign test to test the null hypothesis that there is no difference in brightness scores versus the alternative hypothesis that dye 1 produces higher brightness scores than does dye 2. Select the rejection region so that α is as close to .05 as possible.
3. An investigation was conducted to determine whether a state's strict charter regulations for forming a new business are effective in minimizing

the chance of the new business's failing. To investigate this question, ten small businesses who had applied for a business charter at least three years ago were randomly selected from the state, and ten were selected from a neighboring state without such restrictive regulations. Recorded below is the number of days each small business survived for the 10 businesses selected from each state. An S is recorded for each business in the sample which is solvent (has not failed) at the time of the investigation.

State with strict regulations	*State without strict regulations*
315	45
474	112
737	251
894	340
S	412
S	533
S	712
S	790
S	845
S	974

Use the Mann-Whitney U and $\alpha = .0526$ to obtain a one-tailed test of whether the state with the strict charter requirements charters businesses which are more likely to succeed than those chartered by its neighboring state.

4. The score on a certain psychological test, P, is used as an index of status frustration. The scale ranges from $P = 0$ (low frustration) to $P = 10$ (high frustration). This test was administered to independent random samples of seven corporate executives and eight Federal government administrators with the following results:

	Status frustration score							
Corporate executives	6	10	3	8	8	7	9	
Federal govt. administrators	3	5	2	0	3	1	0	4

Use the Mann-Whitney U statistic with α as close to .05 as possible to test whether the distribution of status frustration scores is the same for the two groups against the alternative that the status frustration scores are higher among corporate executives.

18.4 Comparing $t > 2$ Population Distributions: Independent Random Samples

In comparing several populations based upon independent samples from these populations, the Kruskal-Wallis H test, which uses the rank sums for each sample, is an extension of the Mann-Whitney U test. The test statistic for comparing t populations is

$$H = \frac{12}{n(n-1)} \sum_{j=1}^{t} \frac{R_j^2}{n_j} - 3(n+1)$$

for R_j, the rank sum of the n_j observations in the jth sample, based upon the total ranking of all $n = n_1 + n_2 + \ldots + n_k$ observations.

The hypothesis to be tested using the Kruskal-Wallis H test is

H_0: all k population distributions are identical

H_a: at least one of the t population distributions is different

If H_0 is true, and all the samples are being drawn from the same population,
little there should be (little, large) variation in the rank sums, $R_1, R_2, \ldots, R_t$
However, if one or more samples are from different populations, the rank sums
large will exhibit (little, large) variation and the value of H will increase. This statistic then always uses an upper-tailed rejection region. Furthermore, when the null hypothesis is true, the test statistic H has an approximate Chi-square distribution with $(t - 1)$ degrees of freedom. Hence, Table 5 can be used to determine the appropriate rejection region for the test.

Example 18.7

Three job-training programs were tested on 15 new employees by randomly assigning 5 employees to participate in each program. After completing the programs and having performed on the job for one week, the fifteen were ranked according to their ability to perform the task for which they had been trained, with a high rank indicating a low ability.

	Program		
	A	*B*	*C*
	2	6	10
	13	7	15
	1	9	8
	5	3	12
	4	11	14
Sums	______	______	______

Do these rankings indicate that one program is better than another at the $\alpha = .05$ level of significance?

Solution:

1. We are interested in testing whether these three samples of 5 measurements come from the same population, against the alternative that at least one sample comes from a population different from the others.
2. Since the data are given directly as ranks, we need but calculate the statistic H using $R_1 = 25$, $R_2 = 36$, and $R_3 = 59$ with $n_1 = n_2 = n_3 = 5$
15 and $n =$ __________.

$$H = \frac{12}{n(n+1)} \sum_{j=1}^{3} \frac{R_j^2}{n_j} - 3(n+1)$$

$$= \frac{12}{15(16)} \left(\frac{25^2}{5} + \frac{36^2}{5} + \frac{59^2}{5} \right) - 3(16)$$

$$= \frac{12}{15(16)} \left(\frac{5402}{5} \right) - \_\_\_\_\_\_\_\_$$ 48

$$= \_\_\_\_\_\_\_\_ - 48$$ 54.02

$$= \_\_\_\_\_\_\_\_$$ 6.02

3. Using Table 5 with $(t - 1) =$ ________ degrees of freedom and $\alpha = .05$, the rejection region consists of values of $H \geqslant \chi_{.05} =$ ________. Since the calculated value of H exceeds 5.99, we (reject, do not reject) H_0 and conclude that a difference (exists, does not exist) among the three job-training programs. Although this is all that can be said statistically, by looking at the rank sums for the three programs, program ________ seems to produce employees with higher job abilities.

2
5.99
reject
exists

A

Example 18.8

In Example 10.4, we considered an investigation of a citizens committee's complaint about the availability of fire protection within the county. The distance in miles to the nearest fire station was measured for each of 5 randomly selected residences in each of four areas. The data are reproduced below.

Areas			
1	*2*	*3*	*4*
7 (14.5)	1 (1)	7 (14.5)	4 (5)
5 (8.5)	4 (5)	9 (________)	6 (11.5)
5 (________)	3 (2.5)	8 (________)	3 (2.5)
6 (11.5)	4 (________)	7 (14.5)	7 (________)
8 (18)	5 (8.5)	8 (18)	5 (8.5)

20
8.5; 18
5; 14.5

Suppose that the experimenter was not willing to assume that the distribution of distances for each of the four areas was normal. Use the Kruskal-Wallis H test to determine if there is sufficient evidence to indicate a difference in the distributions of distances for the four areas. Use $\alpha = .01$.

Solution

1. The data are first ranked according to their magnitude, the ranks of the

combined sample of $n = 20$ are shown in parentheses above. Fill in the missing entries. The rank sums are

61; 85

$R_1 =$ ________ $R_3 =$ ________

22; 42

$R_2 =$ ________ $R_4 =$ ________

5

with $n_1 = n_2 = n_3 = n_4 =$ ________.

2. The test statistic is calculated as

$$H = \frac{12}{n(n+1)} \sum_{j=1}^{4} \frac{R_j^2}{n_j} - 3(n+1)$$

$$= \frac{12}{20(21)} \left[\frac{61^2 + 22^2 + 85^2 + 42^2}{5} \right] - 3(21)$$

2638.8; 63

$$= \frac{12}{420}(\_\_\_\_\_\_) - \_\_\_\_\_\_$$

12.39

$$= \_\_\_\_\_\_$$

3

11.3449; reject

is

3. Using Table 5 with $(t - 1) =$ ________ degrees of freedom and $\alpha = .01$, the rejection region is $H \geqslant \chi_{.01} =$ ________. Hence, we (reject, do not reject) H_0. There (is, is not) sufficient evidence to indicate that there is a difference in the distributions of distances for the four areas.

Self-Correcting Exercises 18B

1. In Exercise 1, Self-Correcting Exercises 10A, the dressed weights of five chickens fed from birth on one of three rations were recorded. The data are reproduced below.

Rations		
1	*2*	*3*
7.1	4.9	6.7
6.2	6.6	6.0
7.0	6.8	7.3
5.6	4.6	6.2
6.4	5.3	7.1

Use the Kruskal-Wallis H Test to determine whether the data present sufficient evidence to indicate a difference in the distribution of weights for the three rations. Use $\alpha = .05$.

2. Refer to Exercise 2, Self-Correcting Exercises 10A, in which the length of time required for new employees to assemble a device was compared for four training periods of different lengths. Four employees were randomly assigned to each training group, but two were eliminated during the experiment due to sickness. The length of time to assemble the device was recorded for each employee in the experiment.

Training Periods (in hours)			
.5	*1.0*	*1.5*	*2.0*
8	9	4	4
14	7	6	7
9	5	7	5
12		8	

Use the Kruskal-Wallis H test to determine whether the data present sufficient evidence to indicate a difference in the distribution of times for the four different lengths of instruction time. Use $\alpha = .01$.

18.5 The Wilcoxon Signed Rank Test for a Paired Experiment

We have previously discussed the sign test, a nonparametric test which can be used for a paired-difference experiment. The sign test utilizes only the ______________ of the difference within each matched pair. A more efficient test (that is, one which makes better use of the information contained in the sample data) would also consider the ______________ of the differences if they are available. Such a test is the Wilcoxon signed rank test. The Wilcoxon signed rank test employs as a test statistic, T, the (smaller, larger) sum of ranks for differences of the same sign where the differences are ranked in order of their ______________ ______________. In calculating T, zero differences are ______________ and ties in the absolute values of nonzero differences are treated in the same manner as prescribed for the ______________ test. Critical values of T are given in Table 8 of the text.

direction *or* sign

size *or* magnitude

smaller

absolute values

omitted

Mann-Whitney U

Example 18.9

Twelve office machinery salesmen were sent to a three-week training program in hopes of improving their sales efficiency. The average weekly sales volume for each salesman was computed before entering the training program and after a considerable lapse of time following the training program. The results follow. The differences in average sales volume (Before-After) have been ranked according to their absolute values and appear in the fifth column. It is these ranks which are important in a signed rank test such as the Wilcoxon test.

Salesman	Average weekly sales Before	After	Difference	Rank for the absolute value of the difference
1	$380	$520	-$140	9
2	330	400	- 70	5
3	310	290	20	1.5
4	400	440	- 40	4
5	350	370	- 20	1.5
6	410	410	*	*
7	350	450	- 100	7
8	310	430	- 120	8
9	375	375	*	*
10	290	440	- 150	10
11	345	425	- 80	6
12	370	405	- 35	3

*Zero differences (not included in ranks)

Solution

For a one-sided test with $\alpha = .05$, we should reject H_0: "training program has no effect on average weekly sales volume" when $T \leqslant$ __________. The sample value of T is __________. Hence, we ______________ the null hypothesis, H_0.

11
1.5; reject

The MINITAB program WTEST (Wilcoxon Test) implements the Wilcoxon signed rank test for a paired experiment. When the paired measurements are stored in C1 and C2, their differences can be stored in C3 using the command

```
LET C3 = C1 - C2
```

The Wilcoxon Test is then implemented using the command

```
WTEST 0 C3
```

The output for the data in Example 17.9 is shown below. The value of the test statistic is shown in the column labeled WILCOXON STATISTIC and the observed level of significance in the column labeled P-VALUE.

```
MTB > WTEST 0 C3;
SUBC> ALT -1.

TEST OF MEDIAN = 0.000000000 VERSUS MEDIAN L.T. 0.000000000

              N FOR  WILCOXON              ESTIMATED
        N     TEST   STATISTIC   P-VALUE   MEDIAN
C3      12    10     1.5         0.005     -60.00
MTB >
```

When n, the number of ____________ in the experiment, is large ($n \geqslant$ ________), T is approximately ____________ distributed with mean

pairs
25; normally

$$E(T) = \frac{n(n+1)}{4}$$

and variance

$$\sigma_T^2 = \frac{n(n+1)(2n+1)}{24}$$

In such cases, we may employ the test statistic

$$z = \frac{T - E(T)}{\sigma_T}$$

which will have approximately the standard normal distribution when H_0 is ____________.

true

Example 18.10

A drug was developed for reducing the cholesterol level in heart patients. The cholesterol levels before and after drug treatment were obtained for a random sample of 25 heart patients with the following results:

	Cholesterol level			*Cholesterol level*	
Patient	*Before*	*After*	*Patient*	*Before*	*After*
1	257	243	13	364	343
2	222	217	14	210	217
3	177	174	15	263	243
4	258	260	16	214	198
5	294	295	17	392	388
6	244	236	18	370	357
7	390	383	19	310	299
8	247	233	20	255	258
9	409	410	21	281	276
10	214	216	22	294	295
11	217	210	23	257	227
12	340	335	24	227	231
			25	385	374

Test whether this drug has an effect on the cholesterol level of heart patients.

Solution

Differences, Before-After, arranged in order of their absolute values are shown below together with the corresponding ranks. Fill in the missing ranks.

	Difference	*Rank*	*Difference*	*Rank*
	-1	2	7	14
	-1	2	-7	14
	-1	2	7	14
	-2	4.5	8	16
17.5	-2	4.5	11	____
17.5	3	6.5	11	____
	-3	6.5	13	19
20.5	-4	8.5	14	____
20.5	4	8.5	14	____
22	5	11	16	____
	5	11	20	23
	5	11	21	24
			30	25

Suppose the alternative hypothesis of interest to the experimenter is the statement, "the drug has the effect of reducing cholesterol levels in heart
-1.645 patients." Thus, the appropriate rejection region for $\alpha = .05$ is $z <$ ______ where, in calculating z, we take T to be the smaller sum of ranks (the sum
negative of ranks of the ______________ differences).

When H_0 is true,

325

$$E(T) = \frac{1}{2}n(n+1) = \_\_\_\_\_\_\_\_$$

and

1381.25

$$\sigma_T^2 = \frac{1}{24}n(n+1)(2n+1) = \_\_\_\_\_\_\_\_$$

Thus, we shall reject H_0 at the $\alpha = .05$ significance level if

$$z = \frac{T - 325}{\sqrt{1381.25}} < -1.645$$

44 Summing the ranks of the negative differences, we obtain $T =$ __________
-7.56 and hence, $z =$ __________. Comparing z with its critical value, we
reject ______________ H_0 in favor of the alternative hypothesis that the drug has the effect of reducing cholesterol levels in heart patients.

It is interesting to see what conclusion is obtained by using the sign test. Recall that x is equal to the number of positive differences and that the test statistic

$$z = \frac{x - .5n}{.5\sqrt{n}}$$

has approximately the ______________ ______________ distribution when n is greater than ten and $H_0: p = 1/2$ is true. With $\alpha = .05$ the rejection region for z is z __________. But $x = 17$, so that $z =$ __________. Thus, we obtain the same conclusion as before, though the sample value of the test statistic does not penetrate as deeply into the rejection region as when the Wilcoxon signed rank test was used. Since the Wilcoxon signed rank test makes fuller use of the information available in the experiment, we say that the Wilcoxon signed rank test is more ______________ than the sign test.

standard normal

> 1.645; 1.8

efficient

Self-Correcting Exercises 18C

1. Two real estate appraisers, call them A and B, were asked to each independently appraise ten properties. The results of the appraisals are shown below. (All appraisals are dollar values of assessed valuation.)

Property	*1*	*2*	*3*	*4*	*5*	*6*	*7*	*8*	*9*	*10*
Appr. A	4630	2680	8710	7300	4740	4320	5380	3050	1730	5920
Appr. B	2770	1300	5220	6100	4820	3400	3190	2660	2050	5400

   Can it be said (use a two-tailed sign test with $\alpha = .02$) that appraisers A and B differ in their assessed valuation of different properties?
2. The sign test is not as efficient as the Wilcoxon signed rank test for data of the type presented in Exercise 1. Analyze the data of Exercise 1 by using the two-tailed Wilcoxon signed rank test with $\alpha = .02$. Can it be said that appraisers A and B differ in their assessed valuation of different properties?
3. Analyze the data of Exercise 15, Chapter 9 by use of the two-sided Wilcoxon signed rank test with $\alpha = .05$. Is there sufficient evidence to indicate a difference in mean brightness scores for the two dyes?
4. The sign test is sometimes used as a "quick and dirty" substitute for more powerful tests which require lengthy computations. The following differences were obtained in a paired-difference experiment: −.93, .95, .52, −.26, −.75, .25, 1.08, 1.47, .60, 1.20, −.65, −.15, 2.50, 1.22, .80, 1.27, 1.46, 3.05, −.43, 1.82, −.56, 1.08, −.16, 2.64.
   Use the sign test with $\alpha = .05$ to test $H_0: \mu_D = 0$ against the one-sided alternative $H_a: \mu_D > 0$.
5. Refer to problem 4. Use the large sample Wilcoxon signed rank test with $\alpha = .05$ to test $H_0: \mu_D = 0$ against the alternative hypothesis $H_a: \mu_D > 0$. Compare (in efficiency and in computational requirements) the sign test and the Wilcoxon signed rank test as substitute tests in a paired differences experiment.

18.6 The Friedman Test for a Randomized Block Design

The randomized block design is used in situations where the individual experimental units may be quite different, but where blocks of relatively ______________ experimental units may be formed. In this situation, the

homogeneous

Friedman Test provides an extension of the Wilcoxon Signed Rank test and makes use of the individual measurements. Instead of determining the ranks of the observations with respect to the entire data set as was done in the case of the Kruskal-Wallis test, the ranks of the observations are determined within each ______________. Tied measurements in the same block are each given the ______________ of the ranks the measurements would have received if there had been slight differences in the observed values.

block
average

The hypothesis to be tested is

H_0: the distributions for the t treatment populations are identical

H_a: At least one of the distributions differs from the other $t - 1$.

The Friedman X^2 statistic is given by

$$X^2 = \frac{12}{bt(t+1)}\left(\sum_{j=1}^{t}\right) R_j^2 - 3b(t+1)$$

where t is the number of ______________, b is the number of ______________ and $R_1, R_2, \ldots, R_t$ are the ______________ ______________ for the t treatments. Wide discrepancies in the values of $R_1, R_2, \ldots, R_t$ occur if high or low ranks tend to be concentrated in certain treatments, which indicates that the population distributions are not identical. Discrepancies in the values of the rank sums cause X^2 to be large. For this reason, the rejection region consists of ______________ values of X^2. As with the Kruskal-Wallis Test, the sampling distribution of the statistic X^2 is approximately __________ with __________ degrees of freedom. Thus, for significance level α, the null hypothesis that the t treatments have the same population frequency distributions should be rejected if $X^2 >$ __________ with $t - 1$ degrees of freedom.

treatments; blocks
rank sums

large

χ^2; $t - 1$

χ^2_α

Example 18.11

In an applicant-screening interview, four applicants were ranked by six panel members with the following results:

Panel Member	Applicant			
	A_1	A_2	A_3	A_4
1	3	4	1	2
2	4	2	3	1
3	4	3	2	1
4	3	4	1	2
5	4	3	1	2
6	4	2	1	3

Do these rankings indicate agreement among the panel members with respect to their ranking of the four applicants at the $\alpha = .05$ level of significance?

Solution

1. Since the observations are in fact rank orderings, to test the hypothesis that the panel members' rankings represent a random rank assignment versus the alternative that there is "agreement," we need to find the rank sum for each applicant.

$R_1 =$ ________; $R_2 =$ ________; $R_3 =$ ________; 22; 18; 9

$R_4 =$ ________ 11

2. The value of X^2 is found as

$$X^2 = \frac{12}{bt(t+1)} \sum_{j=1}^{4} R_j^2 - 3b(t+1)$$

$$= \frac{12}{6(4)(5)}(22^2 + 18^2 + 9^2 + 11^2) - 3(6)(5)$$

$$= \frac{12}{120}(1010) - \_\_\_\_\_\_\_\_$$ 90

$$= \_\_\_\_\_\_\_\_$$ 11

3. Using Table 5 with $(t - 1) =$ ________ degrees of freedom and $\alpha = .05$, the rejection region consists of values of $X^2 \geq \chi^2_{.05} =$ ________. Since the calculated value of X^2 exceeds 7.81, we (reject, do not reject) H_0 and conclude that significant agreement does exist among the six panelists. 3 7.81 reject

Example 18.12

In a study where the objective was to investigate methods of reducing fatigue among employees whose jobs involved a monotonous assembly procedure, twelve randomly selected employees were asked to perform their usual job under each of three trial conditions. As a measure of fatigue, the experimenter used the number of assembly-line stoppages during a four-hour period for each trial condition. Do the following data indicate that employee fatigue as measured by stoppages differ for these three conditions? Use $\alpha = .05$.

Margin answer	Employees	Conditions 1	Conditions 2	Conditions 3
3; 1; 2	1	31 (______)	22 (______)	26 (______)
	2	20 (2)	15 (1)	23 (3)
	3	26 (3)	21 (2)	18 (1)
	4	31 (2)	22 (1)	32 (3)
1; 2; 3	5	12 (______)	16 (______)	18 (______)
	6	22 (1)	29 (2)	34 (3)
3; 1; 2	7	28 (______)	17 (______)	26 (______)
	8	15 (3)	9 (1)	12 (2)
	9	41 (2)	31 (1)	46 (3)
1.5; 1.5; 3	10	19 (______)	19 (______)	25 (______)
	11	31 (1)	34 (2)	41 (3)
	12	18 (2)	11 (1)	21 (3)
24.5; 16.5; 31	Rank Sums	R_1 = ______	R_2 = ______	R_3 = ______

Solution

1. In order to use the Friedman test as an alternative to the parametric analysis of variance, we need to rank the responses within employees and find the rank totals for each of the three conditions. Complete any missing rank entries and find the rank sums in the table above.
2. In testing for significant differences among the three conditions, we shall use Friedman's statistic, given as

$$X^2 = \frac{12}{bt(t+1)}\left(\sum_{j=1}^{t} R_j^2\right) - 3b(t+1)$$

For $b =$ ________, $t =$ ________, $R_1 = 24.5$, $R_2 = 16.5$, $R_3 = 31$, — 12; 3

$$X^2 = \frac{12}{(12)(3)(4)}[24.5^2 + 16.5^2 + 31^2] - 3(12)(4)$$

$= 152.79 -$ ________ — 144

$=$ ________ — 8.79

3. We shall use the chi-square distribution in finding a rejection region. With $t - 1 =$ ________ degrees of freedom, $\chi^2_{.05} =$ ________. Since the observed value of $X^2 = 8.79$ is __________ than 5.99, we (reject, do not reject) H_0 and conclude that there (are, are not) significant differences among the three conditions at the $\alpha = .05$ level of significance.

2; 5.99
greater; reject
are

Self-Correcting Exercises 18D

1. Refer to Example 10.10, in which the readability of four different styles of textbook type was compared using a speed-reading test. The experiment was run using a randomized block design, and the data are reproduced below.

Type Style	Readers 1	2	3	4	5
1	15	18	13	21	15
2	19	19	16	22	15
3	13	20	14	21	16
4	11	18	12	17	12

Use Friedman's test to determine whether there is a significant difference among the distributions of reading times for the four type styles. Use $\alpha = .01$.

2. Refer to Exercise 2, Self-Correcting Exercises 10B, in which average identification times were recorded for each of four brands of a particular product, using five different geographical areas as blocks. The data is reproduced below.

Areas	Brands 1	2	3	4
1	3.7	3.9	4.2	4.0
2	4.2	4.8	4.6	4.7
3	2.9	3.5	3.0	3.4
4	5.0	5.4	5.0	5.5
5	3.3	4.3	4.1	3.9

Use Friedman's Test to determine whether there is a significant difference in the distribution of times among the four brands. Use $\alpha = .05$.

18.7 The Runs Test: A Test for Randomness

The data for a runs test is obtained in the form of a ________ where each element in the ________ is either a "success" (S) or a "failure" (F). A run is defined as a ________ sequence of like elements. R is the number of ________ in a sequence. The number of runs in the sequence SSFSFFFSSS is ______. A very small or very large number of runs in a sequence would indicate nonrandomness. If there is at least one failure and at least one success then the minimum value for R is ______.

sequence
sequence
maximal
runs
5
2

If n_1 be the number of S elements and n_2 be the number of F elements in the sequence, the probability distribution for R when $n_1 \leqslant n_2$ and both n_1 and n_2 are less than or equal to 10 is provided by Table 9 in the text. If $n_1 \geqslant n_2$, simply interchange these symbols.

The runs test is used to test the null hypothesis: the sequence of S's and F's has been produced in a ________ manner. The alternative hypothesis will determine whether one is performing a one- or two-tailed test. When the alternative hypothesis is H_a: the sequence has been produced in a nonrandom manner, a two-tailed rejection region is used, since too many

random

runs is indicative of overmixing while too few runs is indicative of undermixing in which like elements tend to follow one another. A two-tailed rejection region consists of values of R such that $R \leqslant k_1$ and $R \geqslant k_2$ where k_1 and k_2 are appropriately chosen from Table 9 of the text so that

α

$$P(R \leqslant k_1) + P(R \geqslant k_2) = \_\_\_\_\_\_$$

I the probability of a Type ______ error. If the alternative hypothesis specifies that the sequence is nonrandom due to overmixing, the rejection
large region would consist of ______ values of R, since overmixing would lead to a larger number of runs than would be expected in a random
$\geqslant$ sequence. The appropriate rejection region consists of values of R ______
α k_2 where $P(R \geqslant k_2) =$ ______. If the alternative hypothesis specifies that the sequence is nonrandom due to undermixing, the rejection region
$\leqslant$ would consist of values of R ______ k_1 where $P(R \leqslant k_1) = \alpha$.

10 When n_1 and n_2 are both greater than ______ one may use the large-sample test statistic,

$$z = \frac{R - E(R)}{\sigma_R}$$

in which the expected value and variance of R are

$$E(R) = 1 + \frac{2n_1 n_2}{n_1 + n_2}$$

and

$$\sigma_R^2 = \frac{2n_1 n_2(2n_1 n_2 - n_1 - n_2)}{(n_1 + n_2)^2 (n_1 + n_2 - 1)}$$

1.96 The rejection region for a two-tailed test with $\alpha = .05$ is $|z| \geqslant$ ______.

Example 18.13

A salesman has contacted 12 customers on a certain day. Let S represent a sale and F a failure to make a sale. The sequential record for the day was: SSSFFFFSSSSF. Is there evidence of nonrandomness in this sequence?

Solution

5; 7 $n_1 =$ ______ and $n_2 =$ ______. If we agree to reject when $R \leqslant 3$
.06 and when $R \geqslant 10$ then $\alpha =$ ______. With this rejection region we
would not (would, would not) reject the hypothesis of randomness.

Example 18.14

Refer to the previous example. A lower tail test could be justified in the following situation. Suppose the district sales manager had reason to believe that this particular salesman was unusually sensitive to success and failure. Thus, a failure to sell seemed to reduce his confidence which in turn reduced his selling effectiveness. The opposite effect seemed to be true when a sale was consummated. If this theory were correct, the number of runs would tend to be considerably (more, less) than if H_0 were true. Hence, an appropriate test would utilize the rejection region $R \leqslant 3$ for $\alpha =$ ________ or the rejection region $R \leqslant 4$ for $\alpha =$ ________. If the latter rejection region were used, the district sales manager would ____________ H_0 and perhaps enroll his salesman in a Dale Carnegie school.

less

.015; .076

reject

Example 18.15

A control chart is widely used in industry to provide a sequential record on some measured characteristic. This chart has a central line representing the process average. A measurement shall be classified as S if above this line and F if below. Does the following sequence indicate a lack of randomness in the distribution of this measured characteristic over time?

SSSFFFSSSSSSFFFSFFFFSSSSSF

Solution

Though n_1 and n_2 are too large to allow use of Table 9, both n_1 and n_2 are greater than ten. Hence, the statistic, z, can be used in a test of randomness. Now $n_1 =$ ________, $n_2 =$ ________. Hence,

15; 11

$E(R) =$ ____________ (give formula)

See 18.6(3)

$=$ ____________ (evaluate)

13.7

and $\sigma_R^2 =$ ____________ (give formula)

See 18.6(3)

$=$ ____________ (value)

5.94

Hence, $\sigma_R =$ ____________

2.44

The test statistic is thus

$z =$ ________

$$\frac{R - 13.7}{2.44}$$

With $\alpha = .05$ a two-sided test would reject when $|z| > 1.96$. The sample value of R is ________ and hence the sample value of z is ________. The decision is to ____________ H_0.

8; -2.34

reject

Example 18.16

A runs test can be used to study Example 18.10. We shall use the label S for a positive difference and F for a negative difference. The sequence of ordered differences produces the arrangement: FFFFFSFFSSSSSFSSSSSSSSSSS. The num-
6; 17 ber of runs is R = __________. n_1 (the number of S elements) = __________. n_2
8 (the number of F elements) = __________. Though n_2 is less than ten we shall for illustrative purposes employ the large sample test statistic,

$$z = \frac{R - E(R)}{\sigma_R}$$

Now

11.9 $$E(R) = 1 + \frac{2n_1 n_2}{n_1 + n_2} = \_\_\_\_\_\_\_\_\_\_$$

4.48 $$\sigma_R^2 = \frac{2n_1 n_2 (2n_1 n_2 - n_1 - n_2)}{(n_1 + n_2)^2 (n_1 + n_2 - 1)} = \_\_\_\_\_\_\_\_\_\_$$

To compare the runs test with the one-tailed Wilcoxon test we shall reject
1.645 H_0 at the level $\alpha = .05$ when $z <$ __________. The sample value of z is
-2.79; reject __________, and hence we __________ H_0.

18.8 Rank Correlation Coefficient

The Spearman rank correlation coefficient, r_s, is a numerical measure of the association between two variables, y and x. As implied in the name of
ranks the test statistic, r_s makes use of ______________ and hence the exact value of numerical measurements on y and x need not be known. Con-
r veniently r_s is computed in exactly the same manner as __________, the
sample ______________ correlation coefficient of Chapter 11.
random To determine whether variables y and x are related, we select a __________ sample of n experimental units (or items) from the population of interest. Each of the n items is ranked first according to the variable x and then
y according to the variable __________. Thus, for each item in the experi-
ranks ment we obtain two ______________. (Tied ranks are treated as in other parts of this chapter.) Let x_i and y_i denote the respective ranks assigned to item i. Then,

$$r_s = \frac{S_{xy}}{\sqrt{S_{xx} S_{yy}}}$$

and

$$S_{xy} = \sum_{i=1}^{n} (x_i - \bar{x})(y_i - \bar{y}) = \_\_\_\_\_\_\_\_\_\_$$

$\Sigma x_i y_i - \dfrac{(\Sigma x_i)(\Sigma y_i)}{n}$

$$S_{xx} = \sum_{i=1}^{n} (x_i - \bar{x})^2 = \_\_\_\_\_\_\_\_\_\_$$

$\Sigma x_i^2 - \dfrac{(\Sigma x_i)^2}{n}$

$$S_{yy} = \sum_{i=1}^{n} (y_i - \bar{y})^2 = \_\_\_\_\_\_\_\_\_\_$$

$\Sigma y_i^2 - \dfrac{(\Sigma y_i)^2}{n}$

When there are no __________ in either the x observations or the y observations, r_s is given by the simpler expression:

ties

$$r_s = 1 - \frac{6\Sigma d_i^2}{n(n^2 - 1)}$$

where $d_i =$ ________.

$x_i - y_i$

This formula can be used as a good approximation for r_s even when ties are present, provided their number is (large, small) in comparison with the number of pairs.

small

Example 18.17

An investigator wished to determine whether "leadership ability" is related to the amount of a certain hormone present in the blood. Six individuals were selected at random from the membership of the Junior Chamber of Commerce in a large city and ranked on the characteristic "leadership ability." A determination of hormone content for each individual was made from blood samples. The leadership ranks and hormone measurements are recorded below. Fill in the missing hormone ranks. Note that no difference in leadership ability could be detected for individuals 2 and 5.

Individual	*Leadership ability rank* (y_i)	*Hormone content*	*Hormone rank* (x_i)	
1	6	131	1	
2	3.5	174	____	3
3	1	189	____	5
4	2	200	6	
5	3.5	186	____	4
6	5	156	____	2

To calculate r_s, form an auxiliary table which facilitates the calculation of S_{xy}, S_{xx} and S_{yy}.

Fill in the missing quantities:

36
10.5
25
6
3.5
10

21

Individual	y_i	y_i^2	x_i	x_i^2	$x_i y_i$
1	6	______	1	1	6
2	3.5	12.25	3	9	______
3	1	1	5	______	5
4	2	4	______	36	12
5	______	12.25	4	16	14
6	5	25	2	4	______
Total	______	90.5	21	91	57.5

-16

Thus, $S_{xy} = 57.5 - \dfrac{(21)(21)}{6} =$ ______

17.5

$S_{xx} = 91 - \dfrac{(21)^2}{6} =$ ______

17

$S_{yy} = 90.5 - \dfrac{(21)^2}{6} =$ ______

and finally,

-16
17.5; 17

$$r_s = \frac{\_\_\_\_\_\_}{\sqrt{(\_\_\_\_\_\_)(\_\_\_\_\_\_)}} = -.93$$

Thus high leadership ability (reflected in a low rank) seems to be associated with higher amounts of hormone.

no association

The Spearman rank correlation coefficient may be employed as a test statistic to test an hypothesis of ______ between two characteristics. Critical values of r_s are given in Table 10 of the text. The tabulated quantities are values of r_0 such that $P[r_s > r_0] = .05, .025, .01$ or $.005$ as indicated. For a lower tail test, reject H_0: "no association between the two characteristics" when $r_s <$ ______.

$-r_0$

0.10
0.05; 0.02; 0.01

Two-tailed tests require doubling the stated values of α, and hence critical values for two-tailed tests may be read from Table 10 if $\alpha =$ ______, ______, ______, or ______.

Example 18.18
Continuing Example 18.17, we may wish to test whether leadership ability is associated with hormone level. If the experimenter had designed the experiment with the objective of demonstrating that low leadership ranks (high leadership abilities) are associated with high hormone levels, the appropriate test would be (a lower, an upper) tail test.

a lower
.829

For $\alpha = .05$ the critical value of r_s is $r_0 =$ ______. Hence, we reject

H_0 if $r_s <$ ________. Since the sample value of r_s found in Example 18.17 (does, does not) fall in the rejection region we (do, do not) reject H_0.

-.829
does; do

Self-Correcting Exercises 18E

1. An automobile agency wished to study whether advertising has an effect on sales. The sales manager advertised only model A during the first week and only model B during the second week of the study. The sequential record of sales during the two-week period was A, A, B, B, B, A, A, A, A, B, A, A, A, A, A, B, B, B, A, B, B, B, B, B, B, A, A. If advertising increases the sales of the model advertised, the number of runs would tend to be less than the number expected in a random sequence. State the null hypothesis and test H_0 against the alternative that advertising increases sales of the model advertised. Use $\alpha = .05$.
2. Refer to Self-Correcting Exercises 18A, Exercise 4. Use a one-sided runs test, with α as close to .05 as possible, to test whether the distribution of status frustration scores is the same in the two groups. The alternative hypothesis is that status frustration scores are higher among the corporate executives.
3. An interviewer was asked to rank seven applicants as to their suitability for a given position. The same seven applicants took a written examination that was designed to rate an applicant's ability to function in the given position. The interviewer's ranking and the examination score for each applicant are given below.

Applicant	*Interview rank*	*Examination score*
1	4	49
2	7	42
3	5	58
4	3	50
5	6	33
6	2	65
7	1	67

Calculate the value of Spearman's rank correlation for these data. Test for a significant negative rank correlation at the $\alpha = .05$ level of significance.

4. Nine salespeople from a particular company were randomly selected and ranked according to their average monthly sales. These same nine people were also ranked on a personality measure that integrated friendliness, extroversion and a keen sense for details. The following rankings resulted.

Salesperson	*1*	*2*	*3*	*4*	*5*	*6*	*7*	*8*	*9*
Sales rank	6	4	2	9	7	8	5	3	1
Personality rank	4	7	6	3	2	1	5	9	8

Calculate r_s for these data. Is there a significant negative rank correlation between sales and personality measure at the .05 level of significance?

18.9 A Comparison of Statistical Tests

The conditions of an experiment are often such that two or more different tests would be valid for testing the hypotheses of interest. How could we compare the efficiencies of two such tests? Statisticians examine the power of a test and use power as a measure of efficiency. The power of a test is defined to be __________. If β is the probability that H_0 is accepted when H_a is true, then the complement of this event, $1 - \beta$, is the probability that H_0 is ______________ when H_a is true. Since the object of a statistical test is to reject H_0 when it is ______________, $1 - \beta$ represents the probability that the test will perform its designated task.

$1 - \beta$

rejected

false

One method of comparing two tests utilizing the same sample size and the same significance level (α) is to compare their powers for alternatives of concern to the experimenter. The most common method of comparing two tests is to find the relative efficiency of one test with respect to the other. Since the sample sizes represent a measure of the costs of the tests in question, we would choose the test requiring (fewer, more) sample observations to achieve the same level of significance (α) and the same power ($1 - \beta$) as the (more, less) efficient test. If n_A and n_B denote the sample sizes required for tests A and B to achieve the same specified values of α and $1 - \beta$ for a specific alternative hypothesis, then the relative efficiency of test A with respect to test B is __________. If this ratio is greater than one, test A is said to be (more, less) efficient than B.

fewer

more

n_B/n_A

more

Nonparametric tests may be used in spite of the fact that a corresponding parametric test would be valid, to avoid lengthy ______________ and thus shorten the ______________ required to come to a decision. If used in this manner, it should be kept in mind that the nonparametric test may be less ______________ than the corresponding parametric test. However, when experimental observations cannot be measured exactly, or when the assumptions required by parametric tests cannot be met, nonparametric methods are appropriate.

calculations

time

efficient

EXERCISES

1. For each of the following tests, state whether the test would be used for related samples or for independent samples: sign test, Mann-Whitney U test, Wilcoxon test, runs test.
2. About 1.2% of our combat forces in a certain area develop combat fatigue. To find identifying characteristics of men who are predisposed to this breakdown, the level of a certain adrenal chemical was measured in samples from two groups: men who had developed battle fatigue and men who

had adjusted readily to combat conditions. The following determinations were recorded:

Battle fatigue group	23.35 21.69 20.00 22.21	21.08 21.54 23.40	22.36 21.26 21.43	20.24 20.71 21.54
Well-adjusted group	21.66 20.19 20.40 21.15	21.85 19.26 19.92	21.01 21.16 20.52	20.54 19.97 19.78

Use a large-sample one-tailed Mann-Whitney U test with α approximately equal to .05 to test whether the distributions of levels of this chemical are the same in the two groups against the alternative that the mean level is higher in the combat fatigue group.

3. Refer to Self-Correcting Exercises 18A, Exercise 3. Use a one-tailed runs test with $\alpha = .051$ to test whether strict charter requirements enhance the chance of a business's success. What do you surmise about the efficiency of the runs test relative to the Mann-Whitney U test for detecting a difference in population means?
4. Refer to Self-Correcting Exercises 9C, Exercise 1. Use Wilcoxon's signed rank to test if the quality of items produced under the per unit rate is inferior to the quality of those items produced under the hourly rate.
5. Refer to Self-Correcting Exercises 9C, Exercise 2. Use the sign test to test if the per unit rate has the effect of increasing the mean number of items produced per worker.
6. The value of r (defined in Chapter 11) for the following data is .636.

x	y
.05	1.08
.14	1.15
.24	1.27
.30	1.33
.47	1.41
.52	1.46
.57	1.54
.61	2.72
.67	4.01
.72	9.63

Calculate r_s for this data. What advantage of r_s was brought out in this example?

7. A ranking of the quarterbacks in the top eight teams of the National Football League was made by polling a number of professional football coaches and sports writers. This "true ranking" is shown below with my ranking.
   a. Calculate r_s.
   b. Do the data provide evidence at the $\alpha = .05$ level of significance to

indicate a positive correlation between my ranking and that of the experts?

Quarterback	*A*	*B*	*C*	*D*	*E*	*F*	*G*	*H*
True ranking	1	2	3	4	5	6	7	8
My ranking	3	1	4	5	2	8	6	7

8. Construction firms A and B are the only firms bidding for contracts in a certain area. Any cooperative arrangement between these firms would assure that any run of bids favorable to a given firm would be kept short (and thus the number of runs would be high). Does the following sequence of winning bids indicate that the two firms are acting in collusion? Use $\alpha \leqslant .05$, A, B, B, A, B, A, B, A, A, B, A, B, A, B, B, A.
9. The data from Exercise 4, Chapter 10 is reproduced below. Daily lost production from three production lines in a manufacturing operation were recorded for a ten-day period.

		Line					
Day	*1*	*2*	*3*	*Day*	*1*	*2*	*3*
1	15	11	8	6	23	25	14
2	9	9	6	7	12	9	7
3	6	8	4	8	10	12	9
4	7	6	5	9	12	10	11
5	16	13	9	10	16	10	9

a. What type of experimental design has been used?
b. If the assumptions required for the parametric analysis of variance have been violated, use an alternative nonparametric test to determine whether there is a difference in the distributions of lost daily production for the three production lines. Use $\alpha = .01$.

10. Refer to Exercise 5, Chapter 10. Four different types of training were used to train executives, and examination scores were recorded at the end of a three-month period. The data are reproduced below.

	Group		
1	*2*	*3*	*4*
112	111	140	101
92	129	121	116
124	102	130	105
89	136	106	126
97	99		119

a. Give the type of design which has been used in this experiment.
b. Use an appropriate nonparametric test to determine whether there is a significant difference in the distribution of examination scores for the four training programs. Use $\alpha = .05$.

Chapter 19

DECISION ANALYSIS

19.1 Introduction

The objective of the ______________ or empirical approach to statistics is to make ______________ about certain characteristics of a ______________ based on information contained in a ______________ drawn from the population. With this approach, certain assumptions are made about the distribution of the population. Given these assumptions, we can determine a sampling distribution for our statistic of interest and thus construct an appropriate confidence interval or test of an hypothesis. In contrast, decision analysis enables the decision maker to formally integrate his personal preferences and perceptions regarding uncertainty and value into the decision framework. Decision analysis can be defined as the logical and quantitative analysis of all of the factors that influence a decision.

classical
inferences; population
sample

Classical statistical inference and decision analysis differ in the way they treat ______________ that may result from the use of each procedure. In classical inference, the levels of α and β, the levels of ______________ and ______________ errors, respectively, are often chosen arbitrarily, without regard to the losses associated with the errors they define, and without regard to any prior information that is not formally contained in the sample. Decision analysis uses ______________ loss or gain as the criterion for comparing testing or decision-making procedures. That is, decision analysis uses the concept of gain or loss associated with every possible ______________ available and selects the decision that (maximizes, minimizes) the expected gain.

errors
Type I
Type II
expected
decision
maximizes

Classical statistical inference and decision analysis (are, are not) in fundamental conflict. They instead differ mostly in the degree of ______________ used in the decision-making procedures.

are not
formality

19.2 The Analysis of the Decision Problem

Associated with every decision-making situation are:

1. A mutually exclusive and collectively exhaustive set of ______________

alternatives

a_i

available to the decision maker, one of which must be chosen. These actions or alternatives are generally symbolized by ________, $i = 1, 2, \ldots, n$.

states of nature
has no; s_j

2. A mutually exclusive and collectively exhaustive set of events called ________ ________ ________, over which the decision maker (has, has no) control. These are denoted by ________, $j = 1, 2, \ldots, k$.

prior probabilities

3. A set of ________ ________ assigned to the states of nature (prior to experimentation) indicating the decision maker's degree of belief regarding the likelihood of occurrence of each state of nature.

payoffs
alternative *or* action

4. A list of ________ representing the value consequences to the decision maker if he takes a specific ________, assuming that each of the states of nature occurs.

mutually exclusive

collectively exhaustive

Recall that alternatives (or states of nature) are (mutually exclusive, collectively exhaustive) if no two can be in effect at the same time. Alternatives (or states of nature) are (mutually exclusive, collectively exhaustive) if all possible alternatives (or states) are included within the analysis.

rank

optimal

Before a decision maker can evaluate alternative actions, he must clearly identify his goals and objectives. He must then define a payoff measure that can ________ the outcomes according to the amount by which they satisfy his goals and objectives. The decision which best satisfies the decision maker's objectives is called the ________ decision. In the initial discussion, we shall restrict our attention to monetary payoffs measurable by the profit or opportunity loss associated with each outcome.

Example 19.1

states
of nature
decision
alternatives
46 cents

21 cents

The operator of a newsstand buys copies of the Evening News at a cost of 23 cents and sells them for 30 cents each. The possible levels of demand for the Evening News from the newsstand constitute the ________ ________ ________. The number of copies of the Evening News purchased by the operator constitutes his ________ which is one of many possible ________ available to him. His opportunity loss for buying two more newspapers than he can sell is ________; his opportunity loss for buying 22 newspapers if he has the opportunity to sell 25 newspapers is ________.

Example 19.2

states
of nature
prior probability

An oil wildcatter holds a lease on a plot of land and must decide whether to drill for oil on that land or to abandon his lease. Should he decide to drill, the outcomes "oil" or "no oil" represent the ________ ________ ________. The likelihood of striking oil assumed by the wildcatter is referred to as a ________ ________.

Example 19.3

A production manager must decide which of two machines, machine A or machine B, to buy to manufacture a novelty item. Machine A is quite expensive to operate if few items are produced but economical for large lots; the opposite is true for machine B. The ______________ ______________ for the novelty item represent the states of nature, while the ______________ are to select machine A or select machine B.

levels of demand
alternatives

A *profit table* is a listing, in tabular form, of the profit $P_{i,j}$ for selecting action __________ given that the state of nature __________ is in effect.

a_i; s_j

An *opportunity loss table* is a tabulation of the opportunity losses, $L_{i,j}$, associated with a decision problem where $L_{i,j}$ is the opportunity loss for selecting action a_i given that state of nature s_j is in effect. More precisely, $L_{i,j}$ is the difference between the ______________ profit which could be realized if state of nature s_j occurs and the profit realized by selecting action __________.

maximum

a_i

Example 19.4

A building contractor must decide how many speculative mountain cabins to build in a resort area. He builds each cabin at a cost of $30,000 and sells each for $45,000. All cabins unsold after six months will be sold to a local investor for $25,000 so that costs can be recovered. The contractor estimates that it would be impossible to sell more than four cabins. Construct the profit table and the opportunity loss table for this decision problem.

Solution

The alternatives available to the contractor are to build from __________ to __________ cabins. The states of nature would be represented by the possible levels of demand, 0 through 4. The profit per cabin sold is __________ as the contractor's costs per cabin are $30,000 and the selling price is __________. Since unsold cabins are sold at a loss of $5000 each, the contractor's profit for building 3 cabins and selling 2 is $30,000 - $5000 = __________. Similarly, his profit for building 4 cabins and selling 1 is $15,000 - $15,000 = __________. Fill in the missing entries below.

zero
four

$15,000
$45,000

$25,000
$0

Profit Table

Number of cabins built	*Number of cabins demanded* 0	1	2	3	4
0	0	0	0	0	0
1	________	15,000	15,000	15,000	15,000
2	-10,000	________	________	30,000	30,000
3	-15,000	________	25,000	________	45,000
4	-20,000	0	20,000	________	________

-5000
10,000; 30,000
5,000; 45,000
40,000; 60,000

The opportunity loss table is computed by noting the largest payoff in each column (under each state of nature) of the profit table and then subtracting each entry in the column from this maximum value. Fill in the missing entries in the opportunity loss table which follows.

Opportunity Loss Table

	Number of cabins built	*Number of cabins demanded* 0	1	2	3	4
0	0	______	15,000	30,000	45,000	60,000
15,000; 30,000	1	5,000	0	______	______	45,000
10,000; 5,000	2	______	______	0	15,000	30,000
10,000; 15,000	3	15,000	______	5,000	0	______
15,000	4	20,000	______	10,000	5,000	0

Example 19.5

A store owner must decide whether to stock one, two, or three units of a perishable commodity each morning. It is assumed that demand will always exist for at least one unit but will never exceed three units per day. The units are purchased at a cost of $4.00 each and are sold for $6.00 each. Construct the store owner's profit table and opportunity loss table.

Solution

The store owner's available alternatives are to stock 1, 2, or 3 units per day while the states of nature are represented by the possible levels of demand, 1, 2, and 3 units. Complete the profit table below.

Profit Table

	Stock level	*Demand level* 1	2	3
	1	2	2	2
-2; 4	2	______	______	4
0; 6	3	-6	______	______

Fill in the missing entries in the opportunity loss table shown below.

Opportunity Loss Table

	Stock level	*Demand level* 1	2	3
2; 4	1	0	______	______
	2	4	0	2
8; 4	3	______	______	0

Self-Correcting Exercises 19A

1. A delivery service must decide how many new delivery vehicles it will purchase in a planned expansion of service routes. At least one, but not more than three new vehicles will be required. For each truck purchased, the delivery service will be required to pay $250 per month to cover

installment payments, insurance, and other expenses. Each truck in service for a given month will earn about $1250, cost $150 for gas and service expenses, and require $500 in salary for the driver. Let us assume that one driver will be hired for each new service vehicle purchased and that each driver hired must be paid whether or not his vehicle is in service for a given month. Using these figures as monthly averages, construct a monthly profit table and the corresponding opportunity loss table for this decision problem.

2. A contractor must decide whether to submit one, two or three bids for three independent contracts, each for $100,000. The research and preparation of a $100,000 bid amounts to $5000. The cost of labor and materials per contract is expected to be about $80,000. If more than one contract is awarded to this contractor, he can save $5000 in the cost of materials by buying the materials for two jobs in bulk, and he can save $15,000 by buying the materials for three jobs in bulk. Construct a profit table and an opportunity loss table for this decision problem.

19.3 Expected Monetary Value Decisions

An expected monetary value decision is a decision to select an available alternative based on the expected ______________ ______________ or expected profit of the alternative. The ______________ decision is a decision by the decision maker to select the alternative which best satisfies his objective. Expected opportunity loss decisions and expected profit decisions are ______________ associated with the same optimal decision. The ______________ ______________ associated with the states of nature are used as weights or multipliers on the opportunity losses or profits associated with each possible alternative in an expected monetary value decision.

opportunity loss
optimal

always
prior probabilities

The expected opportunity loss for a given alternative a_i is found by computing

$$E(L_i) = \sum_{\text{all } j} \text{\_\_\_\_\_\_\_\_\_\_} \quad \text{where}$$

$L_{i,j}P(s_j)$

$L_{i,j}$ is the opportunity loss for selecting alternative a_i when state of nature s_j is in effect and $P(s_j)$ is the prior probability assigned to state of nature s_j. The decision which ______________ the decision maker's expected opportunity loss is then to select the ______________ associated with the smallest expected opportunity loss, $E(L_i)$.

minimizes
alternative

If the decision maker's objective is to maximize his expected profits, his optimal decision is to select the alternative associated with the __________ expected gain, $E(G_i)$, where

largest

$$E(G_i) = \sum_{\text{all } j} \text{\_\_\_\_\_\_\_\_\_\_}$$

$G_{i,j}P(s_j)$

and $G_{i,j}$ is the profit associated with the selection of alternative a_i under state of nature s_j. Notice that the difference between the expected opportunity losses from any two actions is ______________ in magnitude to, but __________ in sign from, the difference between their expected ______________.

equal; opposite
profits

Example 19.6
Return to the problem of the building contractor, Example 19.4. Suppose that after a careful analysis of the demand for mountain cabins in the resort area, the contractor decides the following distribution best represents his likelihood of selling from 0 through 4 cabins.

Number	0	1	2	3	4
Probability	.1	.2	.4	.2	.1

How many cabins should the contractor build if he wishes to minimize his expected opportunity loss?

Solution
The opportunity loss table for the contractor's problem was given in Example 19.4. To find the optimal decision, we must compute the ______________ ______________ ______________ for each alternative, 0, 1, 2, 3, or 4 cabins. The expected opportunity loss for building 0 cabins and 1 cabin are, respectively

expected
opportunity loss

$$E(L\text{ “build 0”}) = \$0(.1) + 15{,}000(.2) + 30{,}000(.4) + 45{,}000(.2) + 60{,}000(.1) = \$30{,}000$$

$$E(L\text{ “build 1”}) = \$5000(.1) + 0(.2) + 15{,}000\,(.4) + 30{,}000(.2) + 45{,}000(.1) = \$17{,}000$$

Compute the expected opportunity losses for the remaining alternatives.

$E(L$ "build 2") = _________ — $8000

$E(L$ "build 3") = _________ — $7000

$E(L$ "build 4") = _________ — $10,000

His minimum expected opportunity loss is __________ which is associated with the alternative of building __________ cabins. Thus, the decision which minimizes the contractor's expected opportunity loss is the decision to build __________ cabins.

$7000
3

3

Example 19.7
The portfolio manager for a firm must choose between either portfolio A

or portfolio B. After a careful examination of the securities within each portfolio, the manager listed the following information:

		Annual Return per $100 Invested	
		Portfolio	
State of the Economy	*Probability*	*A*	*B*
Depression	.2	$ 40	$ 80
Stable	.5	105	95
Inflation	.3	190	110

Which portfolio should the manager select if he wishes to maximize his expected annual return?

Solution

The expected return for each portfolio is the weighted average return, found by weighting the ______________ under each portfolio by the ______________ ______________ of occurrence of the states of the economy associated with each return. Thus,

returns
prior probabilities

$$E(\text{Return "portfolio A"}) = \$40(.2) + \$105(.5) + \$190(.3) = \$117.50$$

$$E(\text{Return "portfolio B"}) = \_\_\_\_\_\_\_\_\_$$

$96.50

The portfolio manager's optimal decision is then to choose portfolio __________.

A

An expected monetary analysis provides a model which combines both real economic data with qualitative or subjective information available to the decision maker related to the outcome of the economic data. It makes the decision maker more than just an impartial observer by forcing him to construct meaningful ______________ ______________ to associate with the states of nature. Expected monetary value decisions, since they employ the prior probabilities in the decision analysis, assume that the priors assigned to the states of nature are the ______________ priors for that problem. The optimal expected monetary value decision is meaningful only in terms of its associated ______________.

prior probabilities

true

priors

Example 19.8

Suppose the portfolio manager from Example 19.7 is approached by an economist who states, "I have a much different impression about the state of the economy a year from now than you do. I believe the likelihoods of depression, a stable economy, and inflation are represented by the probabilities .5, .3, and .2, respectively." Find the expected monetary value decision based upon the economist's set of prior probabilities.

Solution

$$E(\text{Return "portfolio A"}) = \$40(.5) + \$105(.3) + \$190(.2) = \$89.40$$

and

$90.50

$$E(\text{Return "portfolio B"}) = \underline{\hspace{2cm}}$$

B

Hence, using the economist's prior probabilities, the decision which maximizes the expected portfolio return is to select portfolio ________. Under one set of priors, portfolio A is best, while under another, portfolio B is best. The portfolio manager, or any expected monetary value decision maker, must carefully assess all available information before selecting

prior probabilities; likelihoods fixed

____________ ____________ to represent the ____________ of occurrence associated with the various states of nature. Once a set of priors has been selected, it should be assumed as ____________ and should be used with confidence in an expected monetary value analysis.

19.4 The Economic Impact of Uncertainty

certainty
uncertainty
maximum

When decisions must be made under uncertainty, the expected gains cannot be as great as the gains one would expect if the true state of nature were known with ____________. The expected opportunity loss associated with the optimal decision under uncertainty is called the cost of ____________, and is sometimes referred to as the expected value of perfect information (EVPI). The cost of uncertainty is the (maximum, minimum) amount the decision maker would pay to know which state of nature will be in effect.

less
true *or* correct
reliability

Since perfect information is hardly ever available, a decision maker usually would be only willing to pay an amount (more, less) than the EVPI. The difference between the amount the decision maker would pay for information concerning the ____________ state of nature and the EVPI is a function of the ____________ of the information.

Example 19.9

3
$7000
$7000

Refer to Example 19.6. The cost of uncertainty is defined to be the expected opportunity loss associated with the optimal decision. In this example, the optimal decision is to build ________ cabins and hence, the cost of uncertainty is ________. That is, the building contractor would be willing to pay up to ________ to know exactly how many cabins he is able to sell on the open market.

The cost of uncertainty can also be determined when the payoff table does not list the opportunity losses associated with the decision problem. Consider the following example.

Example 19.10

Refer to Example 19.7. If the portfolio manager knows the future state of the economy with certainty, he would make the following decisions. If the state of the economy is

a. Depressed, he selects portfolio __________, B

b. Stable, he selects portfolio __________, A

c. Inflated, he selects portfolio __________. A

Under certainty, his expected return is then

$$(80)(.2) + (105)(.5) + (\_\_\_\_\_\_)(.3) = \$125.50$$ 190

Under uncertainty, the best that he can expect is a return of __________ by selecting portfolio __________. The portfolio manager's cost of uncertainty is then __________, the difference between his expected return under *certainty* and his expected return under *uncertainty*.

$117.50
A
$8.00

Perfect information is rarely, if ever, available at any price. The best that can be expected is that auxiliary information may ______________ the uncertainty associated with the decision problem. reduce

Self-Correcting Exercises 19B

1. Refer to Self-Correcting Exercises 19A, problem 1. Suppose that further study of this situation assessed the probability that 1, 2 or 3 trucks would be required in a given month to be .3, .6 and .1 respectively.
   a. How many trucks should be purchased in order to minimize the expected opportunity loss?
   b. What is the cost of uncertainty for this problem?
2. A farmer, under contract to sell his entire crop to a dealer, has the option of planting one of three crops the next season. From past experience he estimates that the yields in units per acre for the three crops under dry, average rain or excess rain weather conditions to be those given below. The contracted price per unit is also listed.

	Crop		
Weather	*1*	*2*	*3*
Dry	15	15	35
Average rain	30	25	30
Excess rain	35	15	20
Price/unit	$15	$20	$10

   a. Assuming that the cost to the farmer per acre to be $60 for each of the three crops, construct a profit table and an opportunity loss table per acre by using the prices given above.
   b. If the following represents a set of prior probabilities of the weather

conditions for the coming season, what crop should be planted to minimize the farmer's expected opportunity loss?

Weather	*Probability*
Dry	.2
Average rain	.7
Excess rain	.1

c. What is the cost of uncertainty associated with this problem?

19.5 Decision Making That Involves Sample Information

uncertainty

sample

Occasionally a decision maker has the opportunity to reduce the __________ in a decision-making problem by obtaining additional information. Ordinarily such information is in the form of __________ data and is intended and used to update the values of the prior probabilities. In some cases, the auxiliary information consists of an expert opinion, or the result of a scientific or a behavioral experiment. In any case, it is of interest to find the value of the auxiliary information measured in terms of the amount by which the auxiliary information has __________ the *uncertainty* in the decision problem.

reduced

posterior

Bayes'

Prior probabilities which have been revised to incorporate auxiliary information are called __________ probabilities. Posterior probabilities are computed by employing __________ Law, Section 3.7. The posterior probability $P(s_k|x)$ represents the chance of occurrence of the state of nature, s_k, given the experimental information, x. This probability is computed from Bayes' Law by

$$\frac{P(x|s_k)\,P(s_k)}{\sum_{\text{all } j} P(x|s_j)\,P(s_j)}$$

$$P(s_k|x) = \frac{\qquad\qquad}{\qquad\qquad}$$

The probabilities $P(x|s_j)$ are the conditional probabilities of observing the observational information x under the state of nature s_j and the probabilities $P(s_j)$ are the priors.

posterior

prior; experimental

posterior

prior

The __________ probabilities which have been computed as a function of the __________ probabilities and the __________ information are then used as the weights in an expected monetary value analysis. Expected opportunity losses or expected profits are computed for all alternatives as was done earlier except that __________ probabilities are now used where __________ probabilities were employed earlier.

Example 19.11

A labor union is considering publishing a monthly journal for its 2000 members. The union leader believes the following probabilities adequately represents the likelihood that a given percentage of union members will subscribe to the journal.

Percentage, p	.20	.30	.40	.50
Probability, $P(p)$	.1	.3	.4	.2

Fixed costs of printing (rental of a printing press) will amount to $320 per month with a variable cost (materials, labor) of $.50 per journal. If the union publishes only as many journals as demand requires, each journal is to sell for $1.00 per copy:

1. What is the decision which minimizes the union's expected opportunity loss?
2. What is the union's cost of uncertainty?

Solution

The profits which would be incurred for publishing or not publishing are as listed below.

	Decision	
p	*Publish*	*Do not publish*
.20	-$120	$0
.30	-20	0
.40	________	0
.50	________	0

$80
$180

The opportunity losses can be found by noting the difference between the ________ ________ at each level of p and the profit associated with each possible decision under level of p. For example, under $p = .20$, the maximum possible profit is $0. Thus, the opportunity loss for publishing when $p = .20$ is equal to $0 - (-$120) = $120 while the opportunity loss for not publishing is $0 - $0 = $0. Fill in the missing opportunity losses.

maximum profit

p	*Publish*	*Do not publish*
.20	$120	$0
.30	________	________
.40	________	________
.50	________	________

$20; $0
$0; $80
$0; $180

1. The expected opportunity loss associated with each possible decision is

$$E(\text{opportunity loss "publish"}) = \$120(.1) + \$20(.3) + \$0(.4) + \$0(.2)$$

$$= \_\_\_\_\_\_\_\_$$

$18

$68 E(opportunity loss "do not publish") = ________

Thus, the optimal decision is for the labor union to publish the journal.

2. The cost of uncertainty is the expected opportunity loss associated with
optimal the ________ decision. Thus, the cost of uncertainty for the
$18; maximum union is ________ which is the ________ amount the union would pay to know the exact percentage of members who will subscribe.

Example 19.12

Refer to Example 19.11. Suppose that 20 union members are randomly selected from the membership and that three indicate they would subscribe to the journal.

1. What is the decision which minimizes the union's expected opportunity loss in light of this sample information?
2. What is the value of the sample information to the union?

Solution

1. Employing Bayes' Law, we first want to find the likelihoods of occurrence of each level of p in light of the sample information that 3 of 20 respondents indicated they would subscribe to the journal. The use of Bayes' Law is most clearly illustrated by using the columnar approach. In column (1) are listed the states of nature and in column (2) their associated prior probabilities.

	(1) s_j	(2) $P(s_j)$	(3) $P(x\|s_j)$	(4) $P(s_j)\,P(x\|s_j)$	(5) $P(s_j\|x)$
.435	.20	.10	.205	.0205	________
.459	.30	.30	.072	.0216	________
.012; .102	.40	.40	________	.0048	________
.001; .004	.50	.20	________	.0002	________
				.0471	

In column (3) we find the probability of occurrence of the sample information under each state of nature. In this case, since the states of nature are proportions, the experimental probabilities are binomial probabilities, and we can use Table 1 of the Appendix to compute the respective probabilities. Let n equal the sample size, x the number within the sample who indicate they would subscribe, and p the state of nature.

When $p = .20$, the probability that y is equal to three is found to be

$$P(x = 3,\ n = 20 \text{ when } p = .20) = \sum_{x=0}^{3} p(x) - \sum_{y=0}^{2} p(x)$$

$= .411 - .206$

$= .205$

In like manner we find that

$P(x = 3, n = 20 \text{ when } p = .30) = .072$

$P(x = 3, n = 20 \text{ when } p = .40) =$ __________ .012

$P(x = 3, n = 20 \text{ when } p = .50) =$ __________ .001

These values comprise the entries within column (3). In column (4), corresponding entries within columns (2) and (3) are multiplied together. Column (5) then lists the *posterior* probabilities computed by dividing each entry from column (4) by the *total* of the column (4) entries. Using the posterior probabilities as weights, we find the expected opportunity loss associated with the union's possible decisions.

E(opportunity loss "publish") = \$120(.435) + \$20(.459) + \$0(__________) + \$0(________) .102; .004

= __________ \$61.38

E(opportunity loss "do not publish") = __________ \$8.88

Therefore, in light of the sample information, the optimal decision is for the union to (abandon, proceed with) plans to publish the journal. abandon

2. The union's optimal decision is now associated with an expected opportunity loss equal to __________. The sample information has, therefore, reduced the union's cost of uncertainty from \$18 to \$8.88, implying that the value of the sample information to the union is __________. \$8.88 \$9.12

19.6 Other Topics in Decision Analysis

A. Decisions Ignoring Priof Information

Some decision makers choose to ignore prior information regarding the likelihood of occurrence of the states of nature. The most common decision maker of this type is called a ______________ decision maker. His objective is to ______________ his ______________ opportunity loss; hence the name, minimax. The minimax decision maker is characterized by an individual with a small bankroll who is concerned that the occurrence of a large loss may cause him severe financial harm. The minimax decision minimax minimize; maximum maker uses prior information only to identify the possible outcomes and focuses his entire attention on the magnitudes of the ______________ ______________ associated with these outcomes.

opportunity losses

Example 19.13
Refer to the building contractor's decision problem Example 19.4. Find the contractor's minimax decision.

Solution
From the opportunity loss table constructed for Example 19.4, we can find the maximum opportunity loss associated with each possible alternative. List these maximum opportunity losses below.

	Number of cabins built				
Alternative	0	1	2	3	4
Maximum oppor- tunity loss	60,000	45,000	________	________	________

30,000; 15,000; 20,000

Thus, the minimax decision is for the building contractor to build __________ cabins.

three

Only by chance are the minimax decision and the expected monetary value decision the same. The minimax procedure offers a more ______________ approach toward decision making than does the expected monetary value procedure.

conservative

Example 19.14
Suppose the portfolio manager from Example 19.7 seeks to select the portfolio which will minimize his maximum opportunity loss. What is his minimax decision?

Solution
The opportunity loss table associated with the two portfolios is as follows:

	A	*B*
Depression	40	________
Stable	0	________
Inflation	________	80

0
10
0

Since the maximum possible losses associated with the two portfolios are

portfolio A: ______________ (40)

portfolio B: ______________ (80)

the minimax decision is for the manager to select portfolio ____________. (A)

Similarly, the ______ criterion selects the action that maximizes the maximum possible profit, while maximin criterion entails ______ the ______ profit.
Minimax, maximax, or maximin decision criteria ______ prior information regarding the probability distribution of the ______ of ______. They are generally used for one-shot or one-time-only decisions and, in practice, (are, are not) good criteria for repeated decision making.

maximax
maximizing
minimum
ignore
states
nature
are not

B. Decision Trees

A ______ ______ is a diagram used to illustrate a multistage decision analysis problem. Decision trees are most useful for ______ decision problems, especially decision problems sequenced over ______
In a tree diagram, decision points are represented by ______ while chance points (points over which the decision maker has no ______) are represented by ______. The available first-stage alternatives are shown at the ______ of the tree. From each alternative, the decision tree constructs the ______ path through chance points and other decision points to each assumed ______ outcome. A decision tree also shows the ______ associated with each path and the ______ of the chance events.

decision tree
multistage
time
squares
control
circles
base
chronological
terminal
payoffs; probabilities

Example 19.15

Consider the data in Example 19.7. A decision tree diagram could be constructed as follows:

Think of the decision problem as proceeding in two steps:

a. At the first stage, the portfolio manager must choose between portfolios A and B. That choice will be represented in the tree diagram as a ______ point between ______ A and B.
b. At the second stage, the portfolio manager discovers the true state of the economy: depression, stability, or inflation. This ______ point will be represented by a circle.
c. The decision tree is shown below. It consists of ______ paths, each with its own payoff (profit).

decision; alternatives

chance

six

			Profits
a_1: Buy Portfolio A	(.2)	s_1 (depression)	$40
	( )	s_2 (stable)	$105
	(.3)	s_3 (inflation)	$190
a_2: Buy Portfolio B	( )	s_1 ( )	$80
	(.5)	s_2 (stable)	$ ______
	(.3)	s_3 (inflation)	$ ______

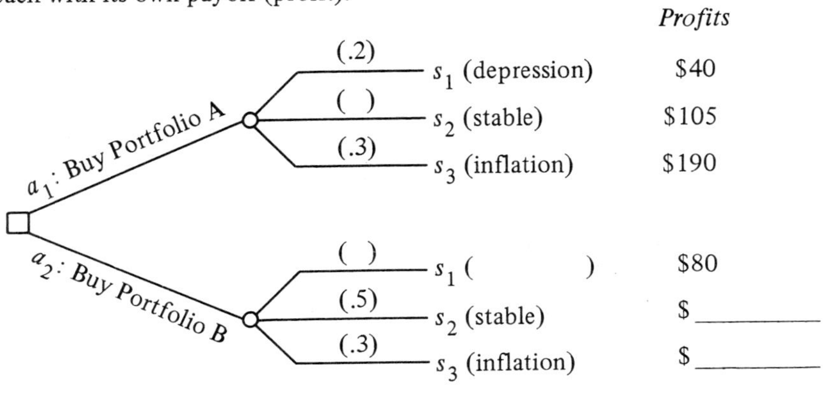

.5

.2
depression

$95

$110

C. The Utility for Money

The theory of utility allows for the outcomes of a decision problem to be scaled according to their relative ______________ to the decision maker. The scalar units are then used in place of the ______________ values associated with each outcome, such that maximization of utility insures maximization of ______________ in terms of the way the decision maker perceives value. Utility measures are necessary *unless* we can assume that:

a. The value of a dollar (does, does not) differ from one person to the next.
b. The value of D dollars is (equal, not equal) to D times the value of a single dollar.

value
monetary
value
does not
equal

Example 19.16

Reconsider the problem of the building contractor given in Example 19.4. After constructing his profit table, the contractor noticed that it is possible for him to lose as much as $20,000 on the mountain cabin venture. As the contractor was very concerned with his liquidity and was interested in avoiding alternatives likely to lose him a significant amount of money, he sought to place all the possible dollar-valued outcomes in their proper perspective. In so doing, he constructed the utility curve, which follows, over the range of possible outcomes. He believes this curve to properly scale the outcomes according to their relative value to him. How many cabins should the contractor build in order to maximize his expected utility?

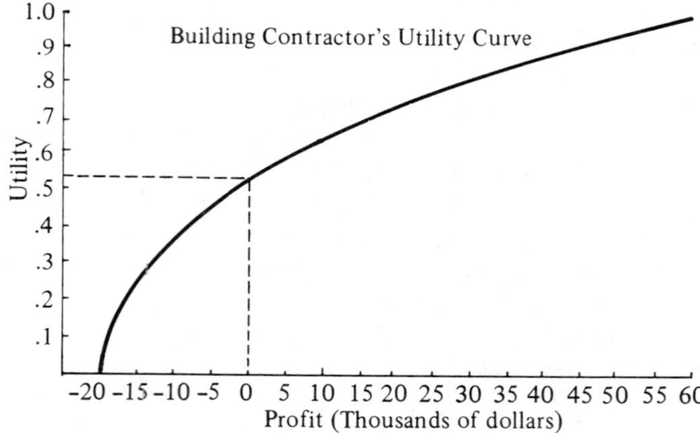

Solution

The building contractor's profit table appears below.

Profit Table

Number of cabins built	*Number of cabins demanded* 0	1	2	3	4
0	0	0	0	0	0
1	-5000	15,000	15,000	15,000	15,000
2	-10,000	10,000	30,000	30,000	30,000
3	-15,000	5000	25,000	45,000	45,000
4	-20,000	0	20,000	40,000	60,000

We now must find utility units from the utility curve associated with each profit value. For instance, the utility of \$0 is found by noting the point on the utility curve at profit equal to \$0, and reading the corresponding point on the utility axis. We can see the utility of \$0 is .55. Similarly, we find the utility of \$10,000 is .64 and the utility of –\$5000 is __________. Fill in the missing entries in the following table. .45

Utility Table

Number of cabins built	*Number of cabins demanded* 0	1	2	3	4
0	.55	.55	.55	.55	.55
1	.45	.70	.70	.70	.70
2	______	.64	______	.80	.80
3	______	______	.78	.90	.90
4	______	.55	______	.86	______

.37; .80
.25; .60
0; .73; 1.00

The decision which maximizes the contractor's expected utility can then be found by computing the expected utility for each ______________. alternative

$$E(\text{utility "build 0"}) = .55(.1) + .55(.2) + .55(.4) + .55(.2) + .55(.1) = .55$$

$$E(\text{utility "build 1"}) = .45(.1) + .70(.2) + .70(.4) + .70(.2) + .70(.1) = \_\_\_\_\_\_$$

.675

Compute the expected utility for the remaining alternatives.

$$E(\text{utility "build 2"}) = \_\_\_\_\_\_$$

.725

$$E(\text{utility "build 3"}) = \_\_\_\_\_\_$$

.727

$$E(\text{utility "build 4"}) = .674$$

Therefore, the decision which maximizes the contractor's expected utility is to build __________ cabins. 3

Utility measures are needed when the decision problem contains some possible ______________ that, should they occur, might place the decision maker in personal or financial ____________. However, unlike a minimax decision, an expected utility decision allows the use of information concerning the ______________ distribution of uncertain events.

outcomes
jeopardy
probability

Self-Correcting Exercises 19C

1. An equipment rental agency must decide whether to continue to keep one, two or three large pieces of equipment for rental purposes. These large pieces of equipment are usually leased to contractors for a period of a week or more. If the required equipment is not available, a contractor, because of time limitations and schedules, will take his business elsewhere. Let us assume that the rental fee for one of these pieces of equipment is $500 per week. Repair, fuel, storage, insurance and other overhead costs to the agency are $50 a week for each piece of equipment.
   a. Construct a weekly profit table for this problem by considering either 1, 2, or 3 available pieces of equipment, together with the possibility of either 0, 1, 2 or, 3 weekly rental requests.
   b. Find the rental agency's minimax decision.
2. Refer to Self-Correcting Exercises 19A, problem 1. Find the delivery service's minimax decision.
3. Refer to Self-Correcting Exercises 19B, problem 2. Find the farmer's minimax decision.
4. Refer to problem 1 of Self-Correcting Exercises 19A and 19B. Suppose that the company has replaced the dollar valued outcomes with the following utility values.

Profits	-1150	-400	-50	350	700	1050
Utility	0	.05	.05	.30	.60	1.00

   How many bids should the contractor submit to maximize his expected utility?
5. Refer to problem 1 of Self-Correcting Exercises 19A and 19B. Construct a decision tree diagram for this decision problem.

EXERCISES

1. Consider yourself the decision maker associated with each of the following decision-making situations. List what you would consider your available alternatives in each situation and the states of nature which might result to affect your economic payoff.
   a. Investment of a company's pension fund in either a mutual fund, corporate bonds, mortgages, government bonds, or a combination of the four.
   b. Investment of a personal windfall profit of $10,000 in either a savings account or a mutual fund.
   c. An opportunity to bid on a construction job when your competitor may submit a bid on the job.
   d. Whether or not to market a new product after observing the results of sales for the product in a trial area.

e. Whether to keep an old assembly machine or buy a new one when the new machine can be expected to produce items at a lower cost per unit than the old machine.
f. Whether the promoter of an outdoor sporting event should buy an insurance policy to cover possible losses should unfavorable weather occur on the day of the sporting event.

2. A grocer must stock a certain number of units of a perishable commodity each morning. He sells the item for \$0.50 each and pays \$0.30 each for them. His knowledge of the business as well as past sales records tell the grocer that daily demand for the product is described by the following probability distribution:

Demand (d)	27	28	29	30
Probability $P(d)$	.3	.4	.2	.1

a. Construct the grocer's profit table.
b. Construct the grocer's opportunity loss table.
c. Find the grocer's minimax inventory level.
d. Find the inventory level which minimizes the grocer's expected daily opportunity loss.

3. An investor must decide whether to finance an oil-drilling venture proposed by an oil wildcatter or to invest in a savings account. The amount of \$2000 either will be supplied to the oil wildcatter or will be invested in the savings account at an annual rate of 6% interest. If the wildcatter strikes oil, he will pay the investor \$10,000 at the end of one year, but if he finds no oil, the investor will lose his investment. If the probability of the wildcatter's striking oil is .2, what is the investor's best decision if he wishes to maximize his expected annual return?
4. Refer to Exercise 3. How great must be the probability of the oil wildcatter's striking oil before the investor rejects the savings alternative and decides to support the oil-drilling venture?
5. The promoter of an outdoor sporting event must decide whether or not to purchase an insurance policy costing \$2000 to cover possible losses should it rain on the day of the event. The promoter figures to earn \$20,000 if there is no rain but will lose \$5000 in event of rain. According to the insurance policy, the promoter will receive \$5000 to cover his losses if it rains but will receive nothing if no rain falls. Suppose the chance of rain on the day of the sporting event is .25.
   a. Construct the promoter's profit table.
   b. If the decision maker's (promoter's) objective is to maximize his expected profit, should he purchase the insurance policy?
6. Refer to Exercise 5. Find the maximum amount the promoter would have been willing to pay for the insurance policy.
7. The representative of a publishing company must decide whether or not to

publish a certain book. The following profits and losses are associated with the actions the publishing company might take.

	Unfavorable market	*Favorable market*
Publish	-$5000	$20,000
Do not publish	0	- 10,000

a. Suppose the representative calculates the expected profits for each alternative, and discovers that either decision is equally profitable. What value must he be assuming for the probability of a favorable market? Hint: Let p = probability of a favorable market, and $(1 - p)$ = probability of an unfavorable market.
b. Suppose the representative actually assumes a probability of .20 for the existence of a favorable market. What is the company's expected profit for publishing?

8. A businessman is trying to decide which of two contracts he should accept. He will accept either contract A, contract B, or neither, but he will not accept both. He has computed his profits for accepting either contract under three states of the economy as follows:

	Depressed economy	*Stable economy*	*Inflated economy*
Contract A	$ 1,000	$12,000	$30,000
Contract B	-10,000	20,000	50,000

The businessman assigns the probabilities .4, .5, and .1 to the events "Depressed economy," Stable economy," and "Inflated economy," respectively.

a. If the businessman seeks to minimize his maximum opportunity loss, what is his optimum decision?
b. What is his optimum decision if he wishes to maximize his expected profits?

9. A baker believes that the daily demand for a large specialty cake is as follows:

Demand	0	1	2	3	4
Probability of demand	.10	.20	.40	.25	.05

The cakes are baked in the morning and sold on demand for $4.00 each during the day. Each cake costs $2.00 to bake and unsold cakes at the day's end are worthless.

a. Construct the opportunity loss for the baker's problem.
b. What is the minimax decision to the baker's problem?

c. How many cakes should the baker prepare if his objective is to minimize his expected opportunity loss?
d. What is the practical meaning to the baker of the expected opportunity value associated with the optimal inventory level found in part c?

10. A toy manufacturer must decide whether or not to manufacture and market a new novelty toy for the Christmas season. An affirmative decision would require that he purchase *either* special stamping tools at a cost of \$1000 *or* a special machine at a cost of \$2000 to manufacture the toys. Each toy will be sold for \$2.00, and the variable cost of manufacturing will be \$1.00 per unit if the stamping tools are used or \$0.50 per unit if the machine is used. Neither the stamping tools nor the machine will have any value after the season. The manufacturer's probability distribution for sales volume for the toy is shown below.

Sales volume	*Probability*
1000	.4
2000	.4
5000	.2

a. Construct the manufacturer's profit table remembering that there are three possible alternatives.
b. What is the manufacturer's minimax decision?
c. What is the optimum decision if the manufacturer wishes to maximize his expected profits.

11. A heavy equipment salesman can contact either one or two customers per day with probability 1/5 and 4/5, respectively. Each contact will result in either no sale or a \$50,000 sale with probability 9/10 and 1/10, respectively.
a. What is the salesman's expected daily sales volume?
b. Knowing that the salesman transacted \$50,000 worth of business during a given day, what is the probability that he contacted only one customer? (Hint: Use Bayes' Law.)
c. What is his probability of transacting \$9000 worth of business during a given day?

12. A manufacturer wishes to accept all incoming lots of widgets with fewer than 8% defectives. Based on historical observation, he believes that a certain supplier of widgets supplies lots described by the following information:

Proportion of Lot Defective (p_D)	*Probability* $P(p_D)$	*Manufacturer's Loss*	
		Accepting	*Rejecting*
.01	.6	\$ 0	\$13
.05	.2	0	7
.10	.1	15	0
.20	.1	25	0

a. If the manufacturer wishes to minimize his expected losses, using only the above information should he accept or reject lots of widgets from this supplier?
b. Suppose the manufacturer randomly selects 25 items from a lot of widgets furnished by the supplier and observes 3 defectives. Should he accept or reject the lot? (Use Table 1, Appendix).
c. Suppose the manufacturer selects 10 and observes 2 defectives. Should he accept or reject? (Use Table 1, Appendix).
d. What is the value to the manufacturer of the sample information supplied in part b?
e. What is the value to the manufacturer of the sample information supplied in part c?

13. The owner of a camera shop must decide whether to buy a shipment of 10,000 flash bulbs from a domestic or a foreign supplier. He knows from past experience that the domestic bulbs are usually about 98% operable (2% defective per shipment). He is doubtful about the defective rate of the foreign flash bulbs and subjectively assigns the following probability distribution to the fraction defective of lots supplied by the foreign manufacturer.

Fraction defective	*Probability*
.01	.4
.05	.4
.10	.2

The cost of replacing defective flash bulbs is estimated to amount to $0.50. and the foreign flash bulbs cost the shop owner one cent per unit less than the domestic bulbs.

a. Based on only his subjective information, should the shop owner buy the foreign flash bulbs?
b. Suppose the owner randomly selects 25 flash bulbs from a shipment supplied by the foreign distributor and notes one defective bulb. Should he buy the foreign or domestic bulbs? (Use Table 1, Appendix).

14. Refer to Exercise 8. In an attempt to rescale the possible outcomes of each contract according to his risk preferences, the businessman has defined the following utility values associated with the dollar valued outcomes accompanying each contract.

Utility	0	.60	.75	.80	.90	1.0
Dollar valued outcome	-$10,000	1,000	12,000	20,000	30,000	50,000

Which contract should the businessman accept if he wishes to maximize his expected utility?

APPENDIX TABLES

TABLE 1 Binomial probability

Tabulated values are $P(y \le a) = \sum_{y=0}^{a} p(y)$. (Computations are rounded at the third decimal place.)

(a) $n = 5$

	p													
a	*0.01*	*0.05*	*0.10*	*0.20*	*0.30*	*0.40*	*0.50*	*0.60*	*0.70*	*0.80*	*0.90*	*0.95*	*0.99*	*a*
0	.951	.774	.590	.328	.168	.078	.031	.010	.002	.000	.000	.000	.000	0
1	.999	.977	.919	.737	.528	.337	.188	.087	.031	.007	.000	.000	.000	1
2	1.000	.999	.991	.942	.837	.683	.500	.317	.163	.058	.009	.001	.000	2
3	1.000	1.000	1.000	.993	.969	.913	.812	.663	.472	.263	.081	.023	.001	3
4	1.000	1.000	1.000	1.000	.998	.990	.969	.922	.832	.672	.410	.226	.049	4

TABLE 1 (*Continued*)

(b) $n = 10$

	p													
a	*0.01*	*0.05*	*0.10*	*0.20*	*0.30*	*0.40*	*0.50*	*0.60*	*0.70*	*0.80*	*0.90*	*0.95*	*0.99*	*a*
0	.904	.599	.349	.107	.028	.006	.001	.000	.000	.000	.000	.000	.000	0
1	.996	.914	.736	.376	.149	.046	.011	.002	.000	.000	.000	.000	.000	1
2	1.000	.988	.930	.678	.383	.167	.055	.012	.002	.000	.000	.000	.000	2
3	1.000	.999	.987	.879	.650	.382	.172	.055	.011	.001	.000	.000	.000	3
4	1.000	1.000	.998	.967	.850	.633	.377	.166	.047	.006	.000	.000	.000	4
5	1.000	1.000	1.000	.994	.953	.834	.623	.367	.150	.033	.002	.000	.000	5
6	1.000	1.000	1.000	.999	.989	.945	.828	.618	.350	.121	.013	.001	.000	6
7	1.000	1.000	1.000	1.000	.998	.988	.945	.833	.617	.322	.070	.012	.000	7
8	1.000	1.000	1.000	1.000	1.000	.998	.989	.954	.851	.624	.264	.086	.004	8
9	1.000	1.000	1.000	1.000	1.000	1.000	.999	.994	.972	.893	.651	.401	.096	9

(c) $n = 15$

	p													
a	*0.01*	*0.05*	*0.10*	*0.20*	*0.30*	*0.40*	*0.50*	*0.60*	*0.70*	*0.80*	*0.90*	*0.95*	*0.99*	*a*
0	.860	.463	.206	.035	.005	.000	.000	.000	.000	.000	.000	.000	.000	0
1	.990	.829	.549	.167	.035	.005	.000	.000	.000	.000	.000	.000	.000	1
2	1.000	.964	.816	.398	.127	.027	.004	.000	.000	.000	.000	.000	.000	2
3	1.000	.995	.944	.648	.297	.091	.018	.002	.000	.000	.000	.000	.000	3
4	1.000	.999	.987	.836	.515	.217	.059	.009	.001	.000	.000	.000	.000	4
5	1.000	1.000	.998	.939	.722	.403	.151	.034	.004	.000	.000	.000	.000	5
6	1.000	1.000	1.000	.982	.869	.610	.304	.095	.015	.001	.000	.000	.000	6
7	1.000	1.000	1.000	.996	.950	.787	.500	.213	.050	.004	.000	.000	.000	7
8	1.000	1.000	1.000	.999	.985	.905	.696	.390	.131	.018	.000	.000	.000	8
9	1.000	1.000	1.000	1.000	.996	.966	.849	.597	.278	.061	.002	.000	.000	9
10	1.000	1.000	1.000	1.000	.999	.991	.941	.783	.485	.164	.013	.001	.000	10
11	1.000	1.000	1.000	1.000	1.000	.998	.982	.909	.703	.352	.056	.005	.000	11
12	1.000	1.000	1.000	1.000	1.000	1.000	.996	.973	.873	.602	.184	.036	.000	12
13	1.000	1.000	1.000	1.000	1.000	1.000	1.000	.995	.965	.833	.451	.171	.010	13
14	1.000	1.000	1.000	1.000	1.000	1.000	1.000	1.000	.995	.965	.794	.537	.140	14

TABLE 1 (*Continued*)

(d) $n = 20$

	p													
a	*0.01*	*0.05*	*0.10*	*0.20*	*0.30*	*0.40*	*0.50*	*0.60*	*0.70*	*0.80*	*0.90*	*0.95*	*0.99*	*a*
0	.818	.358	.122	.012	.001	.000	.000	.000	.000	.000	.000	.000	.000	0
1	.983	.736	.392	.069	.008	.001	.000	.000	.000	.000	.000	.000	.000	1
2	.999	.925	.677	.206	.035	.004	.000	.000	.000	.000	.000	.000	.000	2
3	1.000	.984	.867	.411	.107	.016	.001	.000	.000	.000	.000	.000	.000	3
4	1.000	.997	.957	.630	.238	.051	.006	.000	.000	.000	.000	.000	.000	4
5	1.000	1.000	.989	.804	.416	.126	.021	.002	.000	.000	.000	.000	.000	5
6	1.000	1.000	.998	.913	.608	.250	.058	.006	.000	.000	.000	.000	.000	6
7	1.000	1.000	1.000	.968	.772	.416	.132	.021	.001	.000	.000	.000	.000	7
8	1.000	1.000	1.000	.990	.887	.596	.252	.057	.005	.000	.000	.000	.000	8
9	1.000	1.000	1.000	.997	.952	.755	.412	.128	.017	.001	.000	.000	.000	9
10	1.000	1.000	1.000	.999	.983	.872	.588	.245	.048	.003	.000	.000	.000	10
11	1.000	1.000	1.000	1.000	.995	.943	.748	.404	.113	.010	.000	.000	.000	11
12	1.000	1.000	1.000	1.000	.999	.979	.868	.584	.228	.032	.000	.000	.000	12
13	1.000	1.000	1.000	1.000	1.000	.994	.942	.750	.392	.087	.002	.000	.000	13
14	1.000	1.000	1.000	1.000	1.000	.998	.979	.874	.584	.196	.011	.000	.000	14
15	1.000	1.000	1.000	1.000	1.000	1.000	.994	.949	.762	.370	.043	.003	.000	15
16	1.000	1.000	1.000	1.000	1.000	1.000	.999	.984	.893	.589	.133	.016	.000	16
17	1.000	1.000	1.000	1.000	1.000	1.000	1.000	.996	.965	.794	.323	.075	.001	17
18	1.000	1.000	1.000	1.000	1.000	1.000	1.000	.999	.992	.931	.608	.264	.017	18
19	1.000	1.000	1.000	1.000	1.000	1.000	1.000	1.000	.999	.988	.878	.642	.182	19

TABLE 1 (*Concluded*)

(e) $n = 25$

							p							
a	*0.01*	*0.05*	*0.10*	*0.20*	*0.30*	*0.40*	*0.50*	*0.60*	*0.70*	*0.80*	*0.90*	*0.95*	*0.99*	a
0	.778	.277	.072	.004	.000	.000	.000	.000	.000	.000	.000	.000	.000	0
1	.974	.642	.271	.027	.002	.000	.000	.000	.000	.000	.000	.000	.000	1
2	.998	.873	.537	.098	.009	.000	.000	.000	.000	.000	.000	.000	.000	2
3	1.000	.966	.764	.234	.033	.002	.000	.000	.000	.000	.000	.000	.000	3
4	1.000	.993	.902	.421	.090	.009	.000	.000	.000	.000	.000	.000	.000	4
5	1.000	.999	.967	.617	.193	.029	.002	.000	.000	.000	.000	.000	.000	5
6	1.000	1.000	.991	.780	.341	.074	.007	.000	.000	.000	.000	.000	.000	6
7	1.000	1.000	.998	.891	.512	.154	.022	.001	.000	.000	.000	.000	.000	7
8	1.000	1.000	1.000	.953	.677	.274	.054	.004	.000	.000	.000	.000	.000	8
9	1.000	1.000	1.000	.983	.811	.425	.115	.013	.000	.000	.000	.000	.000	9
10	1.000	1.000	1.000	.994	.902	.586	.212	.034	.002	.000	.000	.000	.000	10
11	1.000	1.000	1.000	.998	.956	.732	.345	.078	.006	.000	.000	.000	.000	11
12	1.000	1.000	1.000	1.000	.983	.846	.500	.154	.017	.000	.000	.000	.000	12
13	1.000	1.000	1.000	1.000	.994	.922	.655	.268	.044	.002	.000	.000	.000	13
14	1.000	1.000	1.000	1.000	.998	.966	.788	.414	.098	.006	.000	.000	.000	14
15	1.000	1.000	1.000	1.000	1.000	.987	.885	.575	.189	.017	.000	.000	.000	15
16	1.000	1.000	1.000	1.000	1.000	.996	.946	.726	.323	.047	.000	.000	.000	16
17	1.000	1.000	1.000	1.000	1.000	.999	.978	.846	.488	.109	.002	.000	.000	17
18	1.000	1.000	1.000	1.000	1.000	1.000	.993	.926	.659	.220	.009	.000	.000	18
19	1.000	1.000	1.000	1.000	1.000	1.000	.998	.971	.807	.383	.033	.001	.000	19
20	1.000	1.000	1.000	1.000	1.000	1.000	1.000	.991	.910	.579	.098	.007	.000	20
21	1.000	1.000	1.000	1.000	1.000	1.000	1.000	.998	.967	.766	.236	.034	.000	21
22	1.000	1.000	1.000	1.000	1.000	1.000	1.000	1.000	.991	.902	.463	.127	.002	22
23	1.000	1.000	1.000	1.000	1.000	1.000	1.000	1.000	.998	.973	.729	.358	.026	23
24	1.000	1.000	1.000	1.000	1.000	1.000	1.000	1.000	1.000	.996	.928	.723	.222	24

TABLE 2 Values of e^{-x}

x	e^{-x}	x	e^{-x}
0.00	1.000000	1.90	0.149569
0.05	0.951229	1.95	0.142274
0.10	0.904837	2.00	0.135335
0.15	0.860708	2.05	0.128735
0.20	0.818731	2.10	0.122456
0.25	0.778801	2.15	0.116484
0.30	0.740818	2.20	0.110803
0.35	0.704688	2.25	0.105399
0.40	0.670320	2.30	0.100259
0.45	0.637628	2.35	0.095369
0.50	0.606531	2.40	0.090718
0.55	0.576950	2.45	0.086294
0.60	0.548812	2.50	0.082085
0.65	0.522046	2.55	0.078082
0.70	0.496585	2.60	0.074274
0.75	0.472367	2.65	0.070651
0.80	0.449329	2.70	0.067206
0.85	0.427415	2.75	0.063928
0.90	0.406570	2.80	0.060810
0.95	0.386741	2.85	0.057844
1.00	0.367879	2.90	0.055023
1.05	0.349938	2.95	0.052340
1.10	0.332871	3.00	0.049787
1.15	0.316637	3.05	0.047359
1.20	0.301194	3.10	0.045049
1.25	0.286505	3.15	0.042852
1.30	0.272532	3.20	0.040762
1.35	0.259240	3.25	0.038774
1.40	0.246597	3.30	0.036883
1.45	0.234570	3.35	0.035084
1.50	0.223130	3.40	0.033373
1.55	0.212248	3.45	0.031746
1.60	0.201897	3.50	0.030197
1.65	0.192050	3.55	0.028725
1.70	0.182684	3.60	0.027324
1.75	0.173774	3.65	0.025991
1.80	0.165299	3.70	0.024724
1.85	0.157237	3.75	0.023518

TABLE 2 (*Continued*)

x	e^{-x}	x	e^{-x}
3.80	0.022371	5.75	0.003183
3.85	0.021280	5.80	0.003028
3.90	0.020242	5.85	0.002880
3.95	0.019255	5.90	0.002739
4.00	0.018316	5.95	0.002606
4.05	0.017422	6.00	0.002479
4.10	0.016573	6.05	0.002358
4.15	0.015764	6.10	0.002243
4.20	0.014996	6.15	0.002133
4.25	0.014264	6.20	0.002029
4.30	0.013569	6.25	0.001930
4.35	0.012907	6.30	0.001836
4.40	0.012277	6.35	0.001747
4.45	0.011679	6.40	0.001662
4.50	0.011109	6.45	0.001581
4.55	0.010567	6.50	0.001503
4.60	0.010052	6.55	0.001430
4.65	0.009562	6.60	0.001360
4.70	0.009095	6.65	0.001294
4.75	0.008652	6.70	0.001231
4.80	0.008230	6.75	0.001171
4.85	0.007828	6.80	0.001114
4.90	0.007447	6.85	0.001059
4.95	0.007083	6.90	0.001008
5.00	0.006738	6.95	0.000959
5.05	0.006409	7.00	0.00912
5.10	0.006097	7.05	0.000867
5.15	0.005799	7.10	0.000825
5.20	0.005517	7.15	0.000785
5.25	0.005248	7.20	0.000747
5.30	0.004992	7.25	0.000710
5.35	0.004748	7.30	0.000676
5.40	0.004517	7.35	0.000643
5.45	0.004296	7.40	0.000611
5.50	0.004087	7.45	0.000581
5.55	0.003887	7.50	0.000553
5.60	0.003698	7.55	0.000526
5.65	0.003518	7.60	0.000500
5.70	0.003346	7.65	0.000476

TABLE 2 (*Concluded*)

x	e^{-x}	x	e^{-x}
7.70	0.000453	8.85	0.000143
7.75	0.000431	8.90	0.000136
7.80	0.000410	8.95	0.000130
7.85	0.000390	9.00	0.000123
7.90	0.000371	9.05	0.000117
7.95	0.000353	9.10	0.000112
8.00	0.000335	9.15	0.000106
8.05	0.000319	9.20	0.000101
8.10	0.000304	9.25	0.000096
8.15	0.000289	9.30	0.000091
8.20	0.000275	9.35	0.000087
8.25	0.000261	9.40	0.000083
8.30	0.000249	9.45	0.000079
8.35	0.000236	9.50	0.000075
8.40	0.000225	9.55	0.000071
8.45	0.000214	9.60	0.000068
8.50	0.000203	9.65	0.000064
8.55	0.000194	9.70	0.000061
8.60	0.000184	9.75	0.000058
8.65	0.000175	9.80	0.000055
8.70	0.000167	9.85	0.000053
8.75	0.000158	9.90	0.000050
8.80	0.000151	9.95	0.000048
		10.0	0.000045

TABLE 3 Normal curve areas

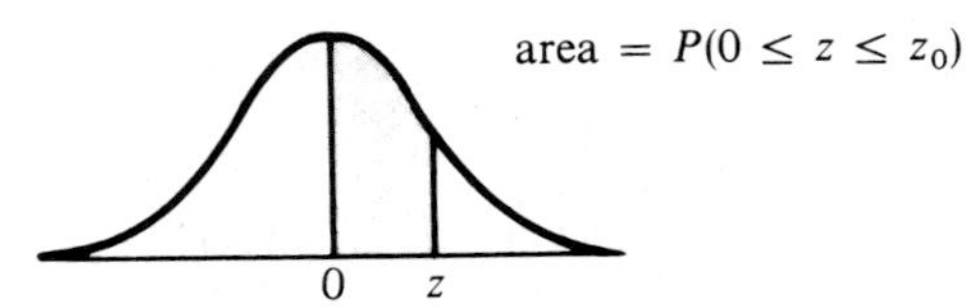

z_0	.00	.01	.02	.03	.04	.05	.06	.07	.08	.09
0.0	.0000	.0040	.0080	.0120	.0160	.0199	.0239	.0279	.0319	.0359
0.1	.0398	.0438	.0478	.0517	.0557	.0596	.0636	.0675	.0714	.0753
0.2	.0793	.0832	.0871	.0910	.0948	.0987	.1026	.1064	.1103	.1141
0.3	.1179	.1217	.1255	.1293	.1331	.1368	.1406	.1443	.1480	.1517
0.4	.1554	.1591	.1628	.1664	.1700	.1736	.1772	.1808	.1844	.1879
0.5	.1915	.1950	.1985	.2019	.2054	.2088	.2123	.2157	.2190	.2224
0.6	.2257	.2291	.2324	.2357	.2389	.2422	.2454	.2486	.2517	.2549
0.7	.2580	.2611	.2642	.2673	.2704	.2734	.2764	.2794	.2823	.2852
0.8	.2881	.2910	.2939	.2967	.2995	.3023	.3051	.3078	.3106	.3133
0.9	.3159	.3186	.3212	.3238	.3264	.3289	.3315	.3340	.3365	.3389
1.0	.3413	.3438	.3461	.3485	.3508	.3531	.3554	.3577	.3599	.3621
1.1	.3643	.3665	.3686	.3708	.3729	.3749	.3770	.3790	.3810	.3830
1.2	.3849	.3869	.3888	.3907	.3925	.3944	.3962	.3980	.3997	.4015
1.3	.4032	.4049	.4066	.4082	.4099	.4115	.4131	.4147	.4162	.4177
1.4	.4192	.4207	.4222	.4236	.4251	.4265	.4279	.4292	.4306	.4319
1.5	.4332	.4345	.4357	.4370	.4382	.4394	.4406	.4418	.4429	.4441
1.6	.4452	.4463	.4474	.4484	.4495	.4505	.4515	.4525	.4535	.4545
1.7	.4554	.4564	.4573	.4582	.4591	.4599	.4608	.4616	.4625	.4633
1.8	.4641	.4649	.4656	.4664	.4671	.4678	.4686	.4693	.4699	.4706
1.9	.4713	.4719	.4726	.4732	.4738	.4744	.4750	.4756	.4761	.4767
2.0	.4772	.4778	.4783	.4788	.4793	.4798	.4803	.4808	.4812	.4817
2.1	.4821	.4826	.4830	.4834	.4838	.4842	.4846	.4850	.4854	.4857
2.2	.4861	.4864	.4868	.4871	.4875	.4878	.4881	.4884	.4887	.4890
2.3	.4893	.4896	.4898	.4901	.4904	.4906	.4909	.4911	.4913	.4916
2.4	.4918	.4920	.4922	.4925	.4927	.4929	.4931	.4932	.4934	.4936
2.5	.4938	.4940	.4941	.4943	.4945	.4946	.4948	.4949	.4951	.4952
2.6	.4953	.4955	.4956	.4957	.4959	.4960	.4961	.4962	.4963	.4964
2.7	.4965	.4966	.4967	.4968	.4969	.4970	.4971	.4972	.4973	.4974
2.8	.4974	.4975	.4976	.4977	.4977	.4978	.4979	.4979	.4980	.4981
2.9	.4981	.4982	.4982	.4983	.4984	.4984	.4985	.4985	.4986	.4986
3.0	.4987	.4987	.4987	.4988	.4988	.4989	.4989	.4989	.4990	.4990

This table is abridged from Table 1 of *Statistical Tables and Formulas*, by A. Hald (New York: John Wiley & Sons, Inc., 1952). Reproduced by permission of A. Hald and the publishers, John Wiley & Sons, Inc.

TABLE 4 Critical values of t

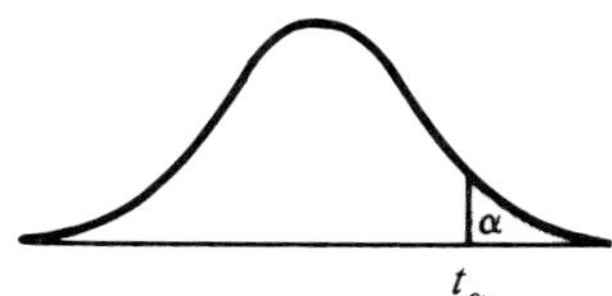

d.f.	$t_{.100}$	$t_{.050}$	$t_{.025}$	$t_{.010}$	$t_{.005}$	d.f.
1	3.078	6.314	12.706	31.821	63.657	1
2	1.886	2.920	4.303	6.965	9.925	2
3	1.638	2.353	3.182	4.541	5.841	3
4	1.533	2.132	2.776	3.747	4.604	4
5	1.476	2.015	2.571	3.365	4.032	5
6	1.440	1.943	2.447	3.143	3.707	6
7	1.415	1.895	2.365	2.998	3.499	7
8	1.397	1.860	2.306	2.896	3.355	8
9	1.383	1.833	2.262	2.821	3.250	9
10	1.372	1.812	2.228	2.764	3.169	10
11	1.363	1.796	2.201	2.718	3.106	11
12	1.356	1.782	2.179	2.681	3.055	12
13	1.350	1.771	2.160	2.650	3.012	13
14	1.345	1.761	2.145	2.624	2.977	14
15	1.341	1.753	2.131	2.602	2.947	15
16	1.337	1.746	2.120	2.583	2.921	16
17	1.333	1.740	2.110	2.567	2.898	17
18	1.330	1.734	2.101	2.552	2.878	18
19	1.328	1.729	2.093	2.539	2.861	19
20	1.325	1.725	2.086	2.528	2.845	20
21	1.323	1.721	2.080	2.518	2.831	21
22	1.321	1.717	2.074	2.508	2.819	22
23	1.319	1.714	2.069	2.500	2.807	23
24	1.318	1.711	2.064	2.492	2.797	24
25	1.316	1.708	2.060	2.485	2.787	25
26	1.315	1.706	2.056	2.479	2.779	26
27	1.314	1.703	2.052	2.473	2.771	27
28	1.313	1.701	2.048	2.467	2.763	28
29	1.311	1.699	2.045	2.462	2.756	29
inf.	1.282	1.645	1.960	2.326	2.576	inf.

From "Table of Percentage Points of the t-Distribution." *Biometrika*, Vol. 32 (1941), p. 300. Reproduced by permission of the Biometrika Trustees.

TABLE 5 Critical values of chi-square

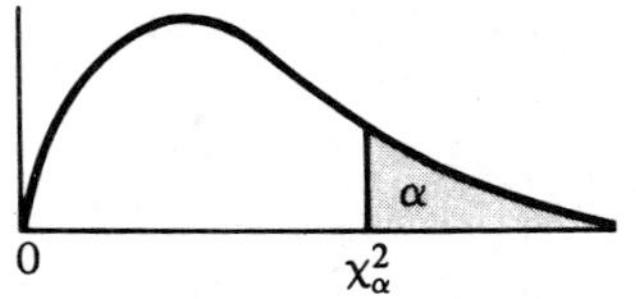

d.f.	$\chi^2_{0.995}$	$\chi^2_{0.990}$	$\chi^2_{0.975}$	$\chi^2_{0.950}$	$\chi^2_{0.900}$
1	0.0000393	0.0001571	0.0009821	0.0039321	0.0157908
2	0.0100251	0.0201007	0.0506356	0.102587	0.210720
3	0.0717212	0.114832	0.215795	0.351846	0.584375
4	0.206990	0.297110	0.484419	0.710721	1.063623
5	0.411740	0.554300	0.831211	1.145476	1.61031
6	0.675727	0.872085	1.237347	1.63539	2.20413
7	0.989265	1.239043	1.68987	2.16735	2.83311
8	1.344419	1.646482	2.17973	2.73264	3.48954
9	1.734926	2.087912	2.70039	3.32511	4.16816
10	2.15585	2.55821	3.24697	3.94030	4.86518
11	2.60321	3.05347	3.81575	4.57481	5.57779
12	3.07382	3.57056	4.40379	5.22603	6.30380
13	3.56503	4.10691	5.00874	5.89186	7.04150
14	4.07468	4.66043	5.62872	6.57063	7.78953
15	4.60094	5.22935	6.26214	7.26094	8.54675
16	5.14224	5.81221	6.90766	7.96164	9.31223
17	5.69724	6.40776	7.56418	8.67176	10.0852
18	6.26481	7.01491	8.23075	9.39046	10.8649
19	6.84398	7.63273	8.90655	10.1170	11.6509
20	7.43386	8.26040	9.59083	10.8508	12.4426
21	8.03366	8.89720	10.28293	11.5913	13.2396
22	8.64272	9.54249	10.9823	12.3380	14.0415
23	9.26042	10.19567	11.6885	13.0905	14.8479
24	9.88623	10.8564	12.4011	13.8484	15.6587
25	10.5197	11.5240	13.1197	14.6114	16.4734
26	11.1603	12.1981	13.8439	15.3791	17.2919
27	11.8076	12.8786	14.5733	16.1513	18.1138
28	12.4613	13.5648	15.3079	16.9279	18.9392
29	13.1211	14.2565	16.0471	17.7083	19.7677
30	13.7867	14.9535	16.7908	18.4926	20.5992
40	20.7065	22.1643	24.4331	26.5093	29.0505
50	27.9907	29.7067	32.3574	34.7642	37.6886
60	35.5346	37.4848	40.4817	43.1879	46.4589
70	43.2752	45.4418	48.7576	51.7393	55.3290
80	51.1720	53.5400	57.1532	60.3915	64.2778
90	59.1963	61.7541	65.6466	69.1260	73.2912
100	67.3276	70.0648	74.2219	77.9295	82.3581

TABLE 5 (*Concluded*)

$\chi^2_{0.100}$	$\chi^2_{0.050}$	$\chi^2_{0.025}$	$\chi^2_{0.010}$	$\chi^2_{0.005}$	d.f.
2.70554	3.84146	5.02389	6.63490	7.87944	1
4.60517	5.99147	7.37776	9.21034	10.5966	2
6.25139	7.81473	9.34840	11.3449	12.8381	3
7.77944	9.48773	11.1433	13.2767	14.8602	4
9.23635	11.0705	12.8325	15.0863	16.7496	5
10.6446	12.5916	14.4494	16.8119	18.5476	6
12.0170	14.0671	16.0128	18.4753	20.2777	7
13.3616	15.5073	17.5346	20.0902	21.9550	8
14.6837	16.9190	19.0228	21.6660	23.5893	9
15.9871	18.3070	20.4831	23.2093	25.1882	10
17.2750	19.6751	21.9200	24.7250	26.7569	11
18.5494	21.0261	23.3367	26.2170	28.2995	12
19.8119	22.3621	24.7356	27.6883	29.8194	13
21.0642	23.6848	26.1190	29.1413	31.3193	14
22.3072	24.9958	27.4884	30.5779	32.8013	15
23.5418	26.2962	28.8454	31.9999	34.2672	16
24.7690	27.5871	30.1910	33.4087	35.7185	17
25.9894	28.8693	31.5264	34.8053	37.1564	18
27.2036	30.1435	32.8523	36.1908	38.5822	19
28.4120	31.4104	34.1696	37.5662	39.9968	20
29.6151	32.6705	35.4789	38.9321	41.4010	21
30.8133	33.9244	36.7807	40.2894	42.7956	22
32.0069	35.1725	38.0757	41.6384	44.1813	23
33.1963	36.4151	39.3641	42.9798	45.5585	24
34.3816	37.6525	40.6465	44.3141	46.9278	25
35.5631	38.8852	41.9232	45.6417	48.2899	26
36.7412	40.1133	43.1944	46.9630	49.6449	27
37.9159	41.3372	44.4607	48.2782	50.9933	28
39.0875	42.5569	45.7222	49.5879	52.3356	29
40.2560	43.7729	46.9792	50.8922	53.6720	30
51.8050	55.7585	59.3417	63.6907	66.7659	40
63.1671	67.5048	71.4202	76.1539	79.4900	50
74.3970	79.0819	83.2976	88.3794	91.9517	60
85.5271	90.5312	95.0231	100.425	104.215	70
96.5782	101.879	106.629	112.329	116.321	80
107.565	113.145	118.136	124.116	128.299	90
118.498	124.342	129.561	135.807	140.169	100

From "Tables of the Percentage Points of the χ^2-Distribution." *Biometrika Tables for Statisticians*, Vol. 1, 3rd ed. (1966). Reproduced by permission of the Biometrika Trustees.

TABLE 6 Percentage Points of the F Distribution

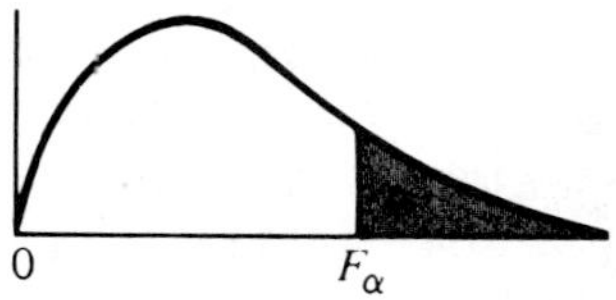

		ν_1								
ν_2	α	1	2	3	4	5	6	7	8	9
1	.100	39.86	49.50	53.59	55.83	57.24	58.20	58.91	59.44	59.86
	.050	161.4	199.5	215.7	224.6	230.2	234.0	236.8	238.9	240.5
	.025	647.8	799.5	864.2	899.6	921.8	937.1	948.2	956.7	963.3
	.010	4052	4999.5	5403	5625	5764	5859	5928	5982	6022
	.005	16211	20000	21615	22500	23056	23437	23715	23925	24091
2	.100	8.53	9.00	9.16	9.24	9.29	9.33	9.35	9.37	9.38
	.050	18.51	19.00	19.16	19.25	19.30	19.33	19.35	19.37	19.38
	.025	38.51	39.00	39.17	39.25	39.30	39.33	39.36	39.37	39.39
	.010	98.50	99.00	99.17	99.25	99.30	99.33	99.36	99.37	99.39
	.005	198.5	199.0	199.2	199.2	199.3	199.3	199.4	199.4	199.4
3	.100	5.54	5.46	5.39	5.34	5.31	5.28	5.27	5.25	5.24
	.050	10.13	9.55	9.28	9.12	9.01	8.94	8.89	8.85	8.81
	.025	17.44	16.04	15.44	15.10	14.88	14.73	14.62	14.54	14.47
	.010	34.12	30.82	29.46	28.71	28.24	27.91	27.67	27.49	27.35
	.005	55.55	49.80	47.47	46.19	45.39	44.84	44.43	44.13	43.88
4	.100	4.54	4.32	4.19	4.11	4.05	4.01	3.98	3.95	3.94
	.050	7.71	6.94	6.59	6.39	6.26	6.16	6.09	6.04	6.00
	.025	12.22	10.65	9.98	9.60	9.36	9.20	9.07	8.98	8.90
	.010	21.20	18.00	16.69	15.98	15.52	15.21	14.98	14.80	14.66
	.005	31.33	26.28	24.26	23.15	22.46	21.97	21.62	21.35	21.14
5	.100	4.06	3.78	3.62	3.52	3.45	3.40	3.37	3.34	3.32
	.050	6.61	5.79	5.41	5.19	5.05	4.95	4.88	4.82	4.77
	.025	10.01	8.43	7.76	7.39	7.15	6.98	6.85	6.76	6.68
	.010	16.26	13.27	12.06	11.39	10.97	10.67	10.46	10.29	10.16
	.005	22.78	18.31	16.53	15.56	14.94	14.51	14.20	13.96	13.77
6	.100	3.78	3.46	3.29	3.18	3.11	3.05	3.01	2.98	2.96
	.050	5.99	5.14	4.76	4.53	4.39	4.28	4.21	4.15	4.10
	.025	8.81	7.26	6.60	6.23	5.99	5.82	5.70	5.60	5.52
	.010	13.75	10.92	9.78	9.15	8.75	8.47	8.26	8.10	7.98
	.005	18.63	14.54	12.92	12.03	11.46	11.07	10.79	10.57	10.39
7	.100	3.59	3.26	3.07	2.96	2.88	2.83	2.78	2.75	2.72
	.050	5.59	4.74	4.35	4.12	3.97	3.87	3.79	3.73	3.68
	.025	8.07	6.54	5.89	5.52	5.29	5.12	4.99	4.90	4.82
	.010	12.25	9.55	8.45	7.85	7.46	7.19	6.99	6.84	6.72
	.005	16.24	12.40	10.88	10.05	9.52	9.16	8.89	8.68	8.51
8	.100	3.46	3.11	2.92	2.81	2.73	2.67	2.62	2.59	2.56
	.050	5.32	4.46	4.07	3.84	3.69	3.58	3.50	3.44	3.39
	.025	7.57	6.06	5.42	5.05	4.82	4.65	4.53	4.43	4.36
	.010	11.26	8.65	7.59	7.01	6.63	6.37	6.18	6.03	5.91
	.005	14.69	11.04	9.60	8.81	8.30	7.95	7.69	7.50	7.34
9	.100	3.36	3.01	2.81	2.69	2.61	2.55	2.51	2.47	2.44
	.050	5.12	4.26	3.86	3.63	3.48	3.37	3.29	3.23	3.18
	.025	7.21	5.71	5.08	4.72	4.48	4.32	4.20	4.10	4.03
	.010	10.56	8.02	6.99	6.42	6.06	5.80	5.61	5.47	5.35
	.005	13.61	10.11	8.72	7.96	7.47	7.13	6.88	6.69	6.54
10	.100	3.29	2.92	2.73	2.61	2.52	2.46	2.41	2.38	2.35
	.050	4.96	4.10	3.71	3.48	3.33	3.22	3.14	3.07	3.02
	.025	6.94	5.46	4.83	4.47	4.24	4.07	3.95	3.85	3.78
	.010	10.04	7.56	6.55	5.99	5.64	5.39	5.20	5.06	4.94
	.005	12.83	9.43	8.08	7.34	6.87	6.54	6.30	6.12	5.97
11	.100	3.23	2.86	2.66	2.54	2.45	2.39	2.34	2.30	2.27
	.050	4.84	3.98	3.59	3.36	3.20	3.09	3.01	2.95	2.90
	.025	6.72	5.26	4.63	4.28	4.04	3.88	3.76	3.66	3.59
	.010	9.65	7.21	6.22	5.67	5.32	5.07	4.89	4.74	4.63
	.005	12.23	8.91	7.60	6.88	6.42	6.10	5.86	5.68	5.54
12	.100	3.18	2.81	2.61	2.48	2.39	2.33	2.28	2.24	2.21
	.050	4.75	3.89	3.49	3.26	3.11	3.00	2.91	2.85	2.80
	.025	6.55	5.10	4.47	4.12	3.89	3.73	3.61	3.51	3.44
	.010	9.33	6.93	5.95	5.41	5.06	4.82	4.64	4.50	4.39
	.005	11.75	8.51	7.23	6.52	6.07	5.76	5.52	5.35	5.20

ν_1											
10	12	15	20	24	30	40	60	120	∞	α	ν_2
60.19	60.71	60.22	61.74	62.00	62.26	62.53	62.79	63.06	63.33	.100	1
241.9	243.9	245.9	248.0	249.1	250.1	251.2	252.2	253.3	254.3	.050	
968.6	976.7	984.9	993.1	997.2	1001	1006	1010	1014	1018	.025	
6056	6106	6157	6209	6235	6261	6287	6313	6339	6366	.010	
24224	24426	24630	24836	24940	25044	25148	25253	25359	25465	.005	
9.39	9.41	9.42	9.44	9.45	9.46	9.47	9.47	9.48	9.49	.100	2
19.40	19.41	19.43	19.45	19.45	19.46	19.47	19.48	19.49	19.50	.050	
39.40	39.41	39.43	39.45	39.46	39.46	39.47	39.48	39.49	39.50	.025	
99.40	99.42	99.43	99.45	99.46	99.47	99.47	99.48	99.49	99.50	.010	
199.4	199.4	199.4	199.4	199.5	199.5	199.5	199.5	199.5	199.5	.005	
5.23	5.22	5.20	5.18	5.18	5.17	5.16	5.15	5.14	5.13	.100	3
8.79	8.74	8.70	8.66	8.64	8.62	8.59	8.57	8.55	8.53	.050	
14.42	14.34	14.25	14.17	14.12	14.08	14.04	13.99	13.95	13.90	.025	
27.23	27.05	26.87	26.69	26.60	26.50	26.41	26.32	26.22	26.13	.010	
43.69	43.39	43.08	42.78	42.62	42.47	42.31	42.15	41.99	41.83	.005	
3.92	3.90	3.87	3.84	3.83	3.82	3.80	3.79	3.78	3.76	.100	4
5.96	5.91	5.86	5.80	5.77	5.75	5.72	5.69	5.66	5.63	.050	
8.84	8.75	8.66	8.56	8.51	8.46	8.41	8.36	8.31	8.26	.025	
14.55	14.37	14.20	14.02	13.93	13.84	13.75	13.65	13.56	13.46	.010	
20.97	20.70	20.44	20.17	20.03	19.89	19.75	19.61	19.47	19.32	.005	
3.30	3.27	3.24	3.21	3.19	3.17	3.16	3.14	3.12	3.10	.100	5
4.74	4.68	4.62	4.56	4.53	4.50	4.46	4.43	4.40	4.36	.050	
6.62	6.52	6.43	6.33	6.28	6.23	6.18	6.12	6.07	6.02	.025	
10.05	9.89	9.72	9.55	9.47	9.38	9.29	9.20	9.11	9.02	.010	
13.62	13.38	13.15	12.90	12.78	12.66	12.53	12.40	12.27	12.14	.005	
2.94	2.90	2.87	2.84	2.82	2.80	2.78	2.76	2.74	2.72	.100	6
4.06	4.00	3.94	3.87	3.84	3.81	3.77	3.74	3.70	3.67	.050	
5.46	5.37	5.27	5.17	5.12	5.07	5.01	4.96	4.90	4.85	.025	
7.87	7.72	7.56	7.40	7.31	7.23	7.14	7.06	6.97	6.88	.010	
10.25	10.03	9.81	9.59	9.47	9.36	9.24	9.12	9.00	8.88	.005	
2.70	2.67	2.63	2.59	2.58	2.56	2.54	2.51	2.49	2.47	.100	7
3.64	3.57	3.51	3.44	3.41	3.38	3.34	3.30	3.27	3.23	.050	
4.76	4.67	4.57	4.47	4.42	4.36	4.31	4.25	4.20	4.14	.025	
6.62	6.47	6.31	6.16	6.07	5.99	5.91	5.82	5.74	5.65	.010	
8.38	8.18	7.97	7.75	7.65	7.53	7.42	7.31	7.19	7.08	.005	
2.54	2.50	2.46	2.42	2.40	2.38	2.36	2.34	2.32	2.29	.100	8
3.35	3.28	3.22	3.15	3.12	3.08	3.04	3.01	2.97	2.93	.050	
4.30	4.20	4.10	4.00	3.95	3.89	3.84	3.78	3.73	3.67	.025	
5.81	5.67	5.52	5.36	5.28	5.20	5.12	5.03	4.95	4.86	.010	
7.21	7.01	6.81	6.61	6.50	6.40	6.29	6.18	6.06	5.95	.005	
2.42	2.38	2.34	2.30	2.28	2.25	2.23	2.21	2.18	2.16	.100	9
3.14	3.07	3.01	2.94	2.90	2.86	2.83	2.79	2.75	2.71	.050	
3.96	3.87	3.77	3.67	3.61	3.56	3.51	3.45	3.39	3.33	.025	
5.26	5.11	4.96	4.81	4.73	4.65	4.57	4.48	4.40	4.31	.010	
6.42	6.23	6.03	5.83	5.73	5.62	5.52	5.41	5.30	5.19	.005	
2.32	2.28	2.24	2.20	2.18	2.16	2.13	2.11	2.08	2.06	.100	10
2.98	2.91	2.85	2.77	2.74	2.70	2.66	2.62	2.58	2.54	.050	
3.72	3.62	3.52	3.42	3.37	3.31	3.26	3.20	3.14	3.08	.025	
4.85	4.71	4.56	4.41	4.33	4.25	4.17	4.08	4.00	3.91	.010	
5.85	5.66	5.47	5.27	5.17	5.07	4.97	4.86	4.75	4.64	.005	
2.25	2.21	2.17	2.12	2.10	2.08	2.05	2.03	2.00	1.97	.100	11
2.85	2.79	2.72	2.65	2.61	2.57	2.53	2.49	2.45	2.40	.050	
3.53	3.43	3.33	3.23	3.17	3.12	3.06	3.00	2.94	2.88	.025	
4.54	4.40	4.25	4.10	4.02	3.94	3.86	3.78	3.69	3.60	.010	
5.42	5.24	5.05	4.86	4.76	4.65	4.55	4.44	4.34	4.23	.005	
2.19	2.15	2.10	2.06	2.04	2.01	1.99	1.96	1.93	1.90	.100	12
2.75	2.69	2.62	2.54	2.51	2.47	2.43	2.38	2.34	2.30	.050	
3.37	3.28	3.18	3.07	3.02	2.96	2.91	2.85	2.79	2.72	.025	
4.30	4.16	4.01	3.86	3.78	3.70	3.62	3.54	3.45	3.36	.010	
5.09	4.91	4.72	4.53	4.43	4.33	4.23	4.12	4.01	3.90	.005	

TABLE 6 (*Continued*)

ν_2	α	ν_1 1	2	3	4	5	6	7	8	9
13	.100	3.14	2.76	2.56	2.43	2.35	2.28	2.23	2.20	2.16
	.050	4.67	3.81	3.41	3.18	3.03	2.92	2.83	2.77	2.71
	.025	6.41	4.97	4.35	4.00	3.77	3.60	3.48	3.39	3.31
	.010	9.07	6.70	5.74	5.21	4.86	4.62	4.44	4.30	4.19
	.005	11.37	8.19	6.93	6.23	5.79	5.48	5.25	5.08	4.94
14	.100	3.10	2.73	2.52	2.39	2.31	2.24	2.19	2.15	2.12
	.050	4.60	3.74	3.34	3.11	2.96	2.85	2.76	2.70	2.65
	.025	6.30	4.86	4.24	3.89	3.66	3.50	3.38	3.29	3.21
	.010	8.86	6.51	5.56	5.04	4.69	4.46	4.28	4.14	4.03
	.005	11.06	7.92	6.68	6.00	5.56	5.26	5.03	4.86	4.72
15	.100	3.07	2.70	2.49	2.36	2.27	2.21	2.16	2.12	2.09
	.050	4.54	3.68	3.29	3.06	2.90	2.79	2.71	2.64	2.59
	.025	6.20	4.77	4.15	3.80	3.58	3.41	3.29	3.20	3.12
	.010	8.68	6.36	5.42	4.89	4.56	4.32	4.14	4.00	3.89
	.005	10.80	7.70	6.48	5.80	5.37	5.07	4.85	4.67	4.54
16	.100	3.05	2.67	2.46	2.33	2.24	2.18	2.13	2.09	2.06
	.050	4.49	3.63	3.24	3.01	2.85	2.74	2.66	2.59	2.54
	.025	6.12	4.69	4.08	3.73	3.50	3.34	3.22	3.12	3.05
	.010	8.53	6.23	5.29	4.77	4.44	4.20	4.03	3.89	3.78
	.005	10.58	7.51	6.30	5.64	5.21	4.91	4.69	4.52	4.38
17	.100	3.03	2.64	2.44	2.31	2.22	2.15	2.10	2.06	2.03
	.050	4.45	3.59	3.20	2.96	2.81	2.70	2.61	2.55	2.49
	.025	6.04	4.62	4.01	3.66	3.44	3.28	3.16	3.06	2.98
	.010	8.40	6.11	5.18	4.67	4.34	4.10	3.93	3.79	3.68
	.005	10.38	7.35	6.16	5.50	5.07	4.78	4.56	4.39	4.25
18	.100	3.01	2.62	2.42	2.29	2.20	2.13	2.08	2.04	2.00
	.050	4.41	3.55	3.16	2.93	2.77	2.66	2.58	2.51	2.46
	.025	5.98	4.56	3.95	3.61	3.38	3.22	3.10	3.01	2.93
	.010	8.29	6.01	5.09	4.58	4.25	4.01	3.84	3.71	3.60
	.005	10.22	7.21	6.03	5.37	4.96	4.66	4.44	4.28	4.14
19	.100	2.99	2.61	2.40	2.27	2.18	2.11	2.06	2.02	1.98
	.050	4.38	3.52	3.13	2.90	2.74	2.63	2.54	2.48	2.42
	.025	5.92	4.51	3.90	3.56	3.33	3.17	3.05	2.96	2.88
	.010	8.18	5.93	5.01	4.50	4.17	3.94	3.77	3.63	3.52
	.005	10.07	7.09	5.92	5.27	4.85	4.56	4.34	4.18	4.04
20	.100	2.97	2.59	2.38	2.25	2.16	2.09	2.04	2.00	1.96
	.050	4.35	3.49	3.10	2.87	2.71	2.60	2.51	2.45	2.39
	.025	5.87	4.46	3.86	3.51	3.29	3.13	3.01	2.91	2.84
	.010	8.10	5.85	4.94	4.43	4.10	3.87	3.70	3.56	3.46
	.005	9.94	6.99	5.82	5.17	4.76	4.47	4.26	4.09	3.96
21	.100	2.96	2.57	2.36	2.23	2.14	2.08	2.02	1.98	1.95
	.050	4.32	3.47	3.07	2.84	2.68	2.57	2.49	2.42	2.37
	.025	5.83	4.42	3.82	3.48	3.25	3.09	2.97	2.87	2.80
	.010	8.02	5.78	4.87	4.37	4.04	3.81	3.64	3.51	3.40
	.005	9.83	6.89	5.73	5.09	4.68	4.39	4.18	4.01	3.88
22	.100	2.95	2.56	2.35	2.22	2.13	2.06	2.01	1.97	1.93
	.050	4.30	3.44	3.05	2.82	2.66	2.55	2.46	2.40	2.34
	.025	5.79	4.38	3.78	3.44	3.22	3.05	2.93	2.84	2.76
	.010	7.95	5.72	4.82	4.31	3.99	3.76	3.59	3.45	3.35
	.005	9.73	6.81	5.65	5.02	4.61	4.32	4.11	3.94	3.81
23	.100	2.94	2.55	2.34	2.21	2.11	2.05	1.99	1.95	1.92
	.050	4.28	3.42	3.03	2.80	2.64	2.53	2.44	2.37	2.32
	.025	5.75	4.35	3.75	3.41	3.18	3.02	2.90	2.81	2.73
	.010	7.88	5.66	4.76	4.26	3.94	3.71	3.54	3.41	3.30
	.005	9.63	6.73	5.58	4.95	4.54	4.26	4.05	3.88	3.75
24	.100	2.93	2.54	2.33	2.19	2.10	2.04	1.98	1.94	1.91
	.050	4.26	3.40	3.01	2.78	2.62	2.51	2.42	2.36	2.30
	.025	5.72	4.32	3.72	3.38	3.15	2.99	2.87	2.78	2.70
	.010	7.82	5.61	4.72	4.22	3.90	3.67	3.50	3.36	3.26
	.005	9.55	6.66	5.52	4.89	4.49	4.20	3.99	3.83	3.69
25	.100	2.92	2.53	2.32	2.18	2.09	2.02	1.97	1.93	1.89
	.050	4.24	3.39	2.99	2.76	2.60	2.49	2.40	2.34	2.28
	.025	5.69	4.29	3.69	3.35	3.13	2.97	2.85	2.75	2.68
	.010	7.77	5.57	4.68	4.18	3.85	3.63	3.46	3.32	3.22
	.005	9.48	6.60	5.46	4.84	4.43	4.15	3.94	3.78	3.64
26	.100	2.91	2.52	2.31	2.17	2.08	2.01	1.96	1.92	1.88
	.050	4.23	3.37	2.98	2.74	2.59	2.47	2.39	2.32	2.27
	.025	5.66	4.27	3..67	3.33	3.10	2.94	2.82	2.73	2.65
	.010	7.72	5.53	4.64	4.14	3.82	3.59	3.42	3.29	3.18
	.005	9.41	6.54	5.41	4.79	4.38	4.10	3.89	3.73	3.60

ν_1											
10	12	15	20	24	30	40	60	120	∞	α	ν_2
2.14	2.10	2.05	2.01	1.98	1.96	1.93	1.90	1.88	1.85	.100	13
2.67	2.60	2.53	2.46	2.42	2.38	2.34	2.30	2.25	2.21	.050	
3.25	3.15	3.05	2.95	2.89	2.84	2.78	2.72	2.66	2.60	.025	
4.10	3.96	3.82	3.66	3.59	3.51	3.43	3.34	3.25	3.17	.010	
4.82	4.64	4.46	4.27	4.17	4.07	3.97	3.87	3.76	3.65	.005	
2.10	2.05	2.01	1.96	1.94	1.91	1.89	1.86	1.83	1.80	.100	14
2.60	2.53	2.46	2.39	2.35	2.31	2.27	2.22	2.18	2.13	.050	
3.15	3.05	2.95	2.84	2.79	2.73	2.67	2.61	2.55	2.49	.025	
3.94	3.80	3.66	3.51	3.43	3.35	3.27	3.18	3.09	3.00	.010	
4.60	4.43	4.25	4.06	3.96	3.86	3.76	3.66	3.55	3.44	.005	
2.06	2.02	1.97	1.92	1.90	1.87	1.85	1.82	1.79	1.76	.100	15
2.54	2.48	2.40	2.33	2.29	2.25	2.20	2.16	2.11	2.07	.050	
3.06	2.96	2.86	2.76	2.70	2.64	2.59	2.52	2.46	2.40	.025	
3.80	3.67	3.52	3.37	3.29	3.21	3.13	3.05	2.96	2.87	.010	
4.42	4.25	4.07	3.88	3.79	3.69	3.58	3.48	3.37	3.26	.005	
2.03	1.99	1.94	1.89	1.87	1.84	1.81	1.78	1.75	1.72	.100	16
2.49	2.42	2.35	2.28	2.24	2.19	2.15	2.11	2.06	2.01	.050	
2.99	2.89	2.79	2.68	2.63	2.57	2.51	2.45	2.38	2.32	.025	
3.69	3.55	3.41	3.26	3.18	3.10	3.02	2.93	2.84	2.75	.010	
4.27	4.10	3.92	3.73	3.64	3.54	3.44	3.33	3.22	3.11	.005	
2.00	1.96	1.91	1.86	1.84	1.81	1.78	1.75	1.72	1.69	.100	17
2.45	2.38	2.31	2.23	2.19	2.15	2.10	2.06	2.01	1.96	.050	
2.92	2.82	2.72	2.62	2.56	2.50	2.44	2.38	2.32	2.25	.025	
3.59	3.46	3.31	3.16	3.08	3.00	2.92	2.83	2.75	2.65	.010	
4.14	3.97	3.79	3.61	3.51	3.41	3.31	3.21	3.10	2.98	.005	
1.98	1.93	1.89	1.84	1.81	1.78	1.75	1.72	1.69	1.66	.100	18
2.41	2.34	2.27	2.19	2.15	2.11	2.06	2.02	1.97	1.92	.050	
2.87	2.77	2.67	2.56	2.50	2.44	2.38	2.32	2.26	2.19	.025	
3.51	3.37	3.23	3.08	3.00	2.92	2.84	2.75	2.66	2.57	.010	
4.03	3.86	3.68	3.50	3.40	3.30	3.20	3.10	2.99	2.87	.005	
1.96	1.91	1.86	1.81	1.79	1.76	1.73	1.70	1.67	1.63	.100	19
2.38	2.31	2.23	2.16	2.11	2.07	2.03	1.98	1.93	1.88	.050	
2.82	2.72	2.62	2.51	2.45	2.39	2.33	2.27	2.20	2.13	.025	
3.43	3.30	3.15	3.00	2.92	2.84	2.76	2.67	2.58	2.49	.010	
3.93	3.76	3.59	3.40	3.31	3.21	3.11	3.00	2.89	2.78	.005	
1.94	1.89	1.84	1.79	1.77	1.74	1.71	1.68	1.64	1.61	.100	20
2.35	2.28	2.20	2.12	2.08	2.04	1.99	1.95	1.90	1.84	.050	
2.77	2.68	2.57	2.46	2.41	2.35	2.29	2.22	2.16	2.09	.025	
3.37	3.23	3.09	2.94	2.86	2.78	2.69	2.61	2.52	2.42	.010	
3.85	3.68	3.50	3.32	3.22	3.12	3.02	2.92	2.81	2.69	.005	
1.92	1.87	1.83	1.78	1.75	1.72	1.69	1.66	1.62	1.59	.100	21
2.32	2.25	2.18	2.10	2.05	2.01	1.96	1.92	1.87	1.81	.050	
2.73	2.64	2.53	2.42	2.37	2.31	2.25	2.18	2.11	2.04	.025	
3.31	3.17	3.03	2.88	2.80	2.72	2.64	2.55	2.46	2.36	.010	
3.77	3.60	3.43	3.24	3.15	3.05	2.95	2.84	2.73	2.61	.005	
1.90	1.86	1.81	1.76	1.73	1.70	1.67	1.64	1.60	1.57	.100	22
2.30	2.23	2.15	2.07	2.03	1.98	1.94	1.89	1.84	1.78	.050	
2.70	2.60	2.50	2.39	2.33	2.27	2.21	2.14	2.08	2.00	.025	
3.26	3.12	2.98	2.83	2.75	2.67	2.58	2.50	2.40	2.31	.010	
3.70	3.54	3.36	3.18	3.08	2.98	2.88	2.77	2.66	2.55	.005	
1.89	1.84	1.80	1.74	1.72	1.69	1.66	1.62	1.59	1.55	.100	23
2.27	2.20	2.13	2.05	2.01	1.96	1.91	1.86	1.81	1.76	.050	
2.67	2.57	2.47	2.36	2.30	2.24	2.18	2.11	2.04	1.97	.025	
3.21	3.07	2.93	2.78	2.70	2.62	2.54	2.45	2.35	2.26	.010	
3.64	3.47	3.30	3.12	3.02	2.92	2.82	2.71	2.60	2.48	.005	
1.88	1.83	1.78	1.73	1.70	1.67	1.64	1.61	1.57	1.53	.100	24
2.25	2.18	2.11	2.03	1.98	1.94	1.89	1.84	1.79	1.73	.050	
2.64	2.54	2.44	2.33	2.27	2.21	2.15	2.08	2.01	1.94	.025	
3.17	3.03	2.89	2.74	2.66	2.58	2.49	2.40	2.31	2.21	.010	
3.59	3.42	3.25	3.06	2.97	2.87	2.77	2.66	2.55	2.43	.005	
1.87	1.82	1.77	1.72	1.69	1.66	1.63	1.59	1.56	1.52	.100	25
2.24	2.16	2.09	2.01	1.96	1.92	1.87	1.82	1.77	1.71	.050	
2.61	2.51	2.41	2.30	2.24	2.18	2.12	2.05	1.98	1.91	.025	
3.13	2.99	2.85	2.70	2.62	2.54	2.45	2.36	2.27	2.17	.010	
3.54	3.37	3.20	3.01	2.92	2.82	2.72	2.61	2.50	2.38	.005	
1.86	1.81	1.76	1.71	1.68	1.65	1.61	1.58	1.54	1.50	.100	26
2.22	2.15	2.07	1.99	1.95	1.90	1.85	1.80	1.75	1.69	.050	
2.59	2.49	2.39	2.28	2.22	2.16	2.09	2.03	1.95	1.88	.025	
3.09	2.96	2.81	2.66	2.58	2.50	2.42	2.33	2.23	2.13	.010	
3.49	3.33	3.15	2.97	2.87	2.77	2.67	2.56	2.45	2.33	.005	

TABLE 6 *(Continued)*

		ν_1								
ν_2	α	1	2	3	4	5	6	7	8	9
27	.100	2.90	2.51	2.30	2.17	2.07	2.00	1.95	1.91	1.87
	.050	4.21	3.35	2.96	2.73	2.57	2.46	2.37	2.31	2.25
	.025	5.63	4.24	3.65	3.31	3.08	2.92	2.80	2.71	2.63
	.010	7.68	5.49	4.60	4.11	3.78	3.56	3.39	3.26	3.15
	.005	9.34	6.49	5.36	4.74	4.34	4.06	3.85	3.69	3.56
28	.100	2.89	2.50	2.29	2.16	2.06	2.00	1.94	1.90	1.87
	.050	4.20	3.34	2.95	2.71	2.56	2.45	2.36	2.29	2.24
	.025	5.61	4.22	3.63	3.29	3.06	2.90	2.78	2.69	2.61
	.010	7.64	5.45	4.57	4.07	3.75	3.53	3.36	3.23	3.12
	.005	9.28	6.44	5.32	4.70	4.30	4.02	3.81	3.65	3.52
29	.100	2.89	2.50	2.28	2.15	2.06	1.99	1.93	1.89	1.86
	.050	4.18	3.33	2.93	2.70	2.55	2.43	2.35	2.28	2.22
	.025	5.59	4.20	3.61	3.27	3.04	2.88	2.76	2.67	2.59
	.010	7.60	5.42	4.54	4.04	3.73	3.50	3.33	3.20	3.09
	.005	9.23	6.40	5.28	4.66	4.26	3.98	3.77	3.61	3.48
30	.100	2.88	2.49	2.28	2.14	2.05	1.98	1.93	1.88	1.85
	.050	4.17	3.32	2.92	2.69	2.53	2.42	2.33	2.27	2.21
	.025	5.57	4.18	3.59	3.25	3.03	2.87	2.75	2.65	2.57
	.010	7.56	5.39	4.51	4.02	3.70	3.47	3.30	3.17	3.07
	.005	9.18	6.35	5.24	4.62	4.23	3.95	3.74	3.58	3.45
40	.100	2.84	2.44	2.23	2.09	2.00	1.93	1.87	1.83	1.79
	.050	4.08	3.23	2.84	2.61	2.45	2.34	2.25	2.18	2.12
	.025	5.42	4.05	3.46	3.13	2.90	2.74	2.62	2.53	2.45
	.010	7.31	5.18	4.31	3.83	3.51	3.29	3.12	2.99	2.89
	.005	8.83	6.07	4.98	4.37	3.99	3.71	3.51	3.35	3.22
60	.100	2.79	2.39	2.18	2.04	1.95	1.87	1.82	1.77	1.74
	.050	4.00	3.15	2.76	2.53	2.37	2.25	2.17	2.10	2.04
	.025	5.29	3.93	3.34	3.01	2.79	2.63	2.51	2.41	2.33
	.010	7.08	4.98	4.13	3.65	3.34	3.12	2.95	2.82	2.72
	.005	8.49	5.79	4.73	4.14	3.76	3.49	3.29	3.13	3.01
120	.100	2.75	2.35	2.13	1.99	1.90	1.82	1.77	1.72	1.68
	.050	3.92	3.07	2.68	2.45	2.29	2.17	2.09	2.02	1.96
	.025	5.15	3.80	3.23	2.89	2.67	2.52	2.39	2.30	2.22
	.010	6.85	4.79	3.95	3.48	3.17	2.96	2.79	2.66	2.56
	.005	8.18	5.54	4.50	3.92	3.55	3.28	3.09	2.93	2.81
∞	.100	2.71	2.30	2.08	1.94	1.85	1.77	1.72	1.67	1.63
	.050	3.84	3.00	2.60	2.37	2.21	2.10	2.01	1.94	1.63
	.025	5.02	3.69	3.12	2.79	2.57	2.41	2.29	2.19	2.11
	.010	6.63	4.61	3.78	3.32	3.02	2.80	2.64	2.51	2.41
	.005	7.88	5.30	4.28	3.72	3.35	3.09	2.90	2.74	2.62

Source: A portion of "Tables of percentage points of the inverted beta (E) distribution" *Biometrika*, vol. 33 (1943) by M. Merrington and C. M. Thompson and from Table 18 of *Biometrika Tables for Statisticians*, vol. 1, Cambridge University Press, 1954, edited by E. S. Pearson and H. O. Hartley. Reproduced with permission of the authors, editors, and *Biometrika* trustees.

ν_1											
10	12	15	20	24	30	40	60	120	∞	α	ν_2
1.85	1.80	1.75	1.70	1.67	1.64	1.60	1.57	1.53	1.49	.100	27
2.20	2.13	2.06	1.97	1.93	1.88	1.84	1.79	1.73	1.67	.050	
2.57	2.47	2.36	2.25	2.19	2.13	2.07	2.00	1.93	1.85	.025	
3.06	2.93	2.78	2.63	2.55	2.47	2.38	2.29	2.20	2.10	.010	
3.45	3.28	3.11	2.93	2.83	2.73	2.63	2.52	2.41	2.29	.005	
1.84	1.79	1.74	1.69	1.66	1.63	1.59	1.56	1.52	1.48	.100	28
2.19	2.12	2.04	1.96	1.91	1.87	1.82	1.77	1.71	1.65	.050	
2.55	2.45	2.34	2.23	2.17	2.11	2.05	1.98	1.91	1.83	.025	
3.03	2.90	2.75	2.60	2.52	2.44	2.35	2.26	2.17	2.06	.010	
3.41	3.25	3.07	2.89	2.79	2.69	2.59	2.48	2.37	2.25	.005	
1.83	1.78	1.73	1.68	1.65	1.62	1.58	1.55	1.51	1.47	.100	29
2.18	2.10	2.03	1.94	1.90	1.85	1.81	1.75	1.70	1.64	.050	
2.53	2.43	2.32	2.21	2.15	2.09	2.03	1.96	1.89	1.81	.025	
3.00	2.87	2.73	2.57	2.49	2.41	2.33	2.23	2.14	2.03	.010	
3.38	3.21	3.04	2.86	2.76	2.66	2.56	2.45	2.33	2.21	.005	
1.82	1.77	1.72	1.67	1.64	1.61	1.57	1.54	1.50	1.46	.100	30
2.16	2.09	2.01	1.93	1.89	1.84	1.79	1.74	1.68	1.62	.050	
2.51	2.41	2.31	2.20	2.14	2.07	2.01	1.94	1.87	1.79	.025	
2.98	2.84	2.70	2.55	2.47	2.39	2.30	2.21	2.11	2.01	.010	
3.34	3.18	3.01	2.82	2.73	2.63	2.52	2.42	2.30	2.18	.005	
1.76	1.71	1.66	1.61	1.57	1.54	1.51	1.47	1.42	1.38	.100	40
2.08	2.00	1.92	1.84	1.79	1.74	1.69	1.64	1.58	1.51	.050	
2.39	2.29	2.18	2.07	2.01	1.94	1.88	1.80	1.72	1.64	.025	
2.80	2.66	2.52	2.37	2.29	2.20	2.11	2.02	1.92	1.80	.010	
3.12	2.95	2.78	2.60	2.50	2.40	2.30	2.18	2.06	1.93	.005	
1.71	1.66	1.60	1.54	1.51	1.48	1.44	1.40	1.35	1.29	.100	60
1.99	1.92	1.84	1.75	1.70	1.65	1.59	1.53	1.47	1.39	.050	
2.27	2.17	2.06	1.94	1.88	1.82	1.74	1.67	1.58	1.48	.025	
2.63	2.50	2.35	2.20	2.12	2.03	1.94	1.84	1.73	1.60	.010	
2.90	2.74	2.57	2.39	2.29	2.19	2.08	1.96	1.83	1.69	.005	
1.65	1.60	1.55	1.48	1.45	1.41	1.37	1.32	1.26	1.19	.100	120
1.91	1.83	1.75	1.66	1.61	1.55	1.50	1.43	1.35	1.25	.050	
2.16	2.05	1.94	1.82	1.76	1.69	1.61	1.53	1.43	1.31	.025	
2.47	2.34	2.19	2.03	1.95	1.86	1.76	1.66	1.53	1.38	.010	
2.71	2.54	2.37	2.19	2.09	1.98	1.87	1.75	1.61	1.43	.005	
1.60	1.55	1.49	1.42	1.38	1.34	1.30	1.24	1.17	1.00	.100	α
1.83	1.75	1.67	1.57	1.52	1.46	1.39	1.32	1.22	1.00	.050	
2.05	1.94	1.83	1.71	1.64	1.57	1.48	1.39	1.27	1.00	.025	
2.32	2.18	2.04	1.88	1.79	1.70	1.59	1.47	1.32	1.00	.010	
2.52	2.36	2.19	2.00	1.90	1.79	1.67	1.53	1.36	1.00	.005	

TABLE 12 Factors Used when Constructing Control Charts

Number of Observations in Sample	Chart for Averages			Chart for Standard Deviations						Chart for Ranges							
	Factors for Control Limits			Factors for Central Line		Factors for Control Limits				Factors for Central Line		Factors for Control Limits					
n	A	A_1	A_2	c_2	$1/c_2$	B_1	B_2	B_3	B_4	d_2	$1/d_2$	d_3	D_1	D_2	D_3	D_4
2	2.121	3.760	1.880	0.5642	1.7725	0	1.843	0	3.267	1.128	0.8865	0.853	0	3.686	0	3.276
3	1.732	2.394	1.023	0.7236	1.3820	0	1.858	0	2.568	1.693	0.5907	0.888	0	4.358	0	2.575
4	1.501	1.880	0.729	0.7979	1.2533	0	1.808	0	2.266	2.059	0.4857	0.880	0	4.698	0	2.282
5	1.342	1.596	0.577	0.8407	1.1894	0	1.756	0	2.089	2.326	0.4299	0.864	0	4.918	0	2.115
6	1.225	1.410	0.483	0.8686	1.1512	0.026	1.711	0.030	1.970	2.534	0.3946	0.848	0	5.078	0	2.004
7	1.134	1.277	0.419	0.8882	1.1250	0.105	1.672	0.118	1.882	2.704	0.3698	0.833	0.205	5.203	0.076	1.924
8	1.061	1.175	0.373	0.9027	1.1078	0.167	1.638	0.185	1.815	2.847	0.3512	0.820	0.387	5.307	0.136	1.864
9	1.000	1.094	0.337	0.9139	1.0942	0.219	1.609	0.239	1.761	2.970	0.3367	0.808	0.546	5.394	0.184	1.816
10	0.949	1.028	0.308	0.9227	1.0837	0.262	1.584	0.284	1.716	3.078	0.3249	0.797	0.687	5.469	0.223	1.777
11	0.905	0.973	0.285	0.9300	1.0753	0.299	1.561	0.321	1.679	3.173	0.3152	0.787	0.812	5.534	0.256	1.744
12	0.866	0.925	0.266	0.9359	1.0684	0.331	1.541	0.354	1.646	3.258	0.3069	0.778	0.924	5.592	0.284	1.719
13	0.832	0.884	0.249	0.9410	1.0627	0.359	1.523	0.382	1.618	3.336	0.2998	0.770	1.026	5.646	0.308	1.692
14	0.802	0.848	0.235	0.9453	1.0579	0.384	1.507	0.406	1.594	3.407	0.2935	0.762	1.121	5.693	0.329	1.671
15	0.775	0.816	0.223	0.9490	1.0537	0.406	1.492	0.428	1.572	3.472	0.2880	0.755	1.207	5.737	0.348	1.652
16	0.750	0.788	0.212	0.9523	1.0501	0.427	1.478	0.448	1.552	3.532	0.2831	0.749	1.285	5.779	0.364	1.636
17	0.728	0.762	0.203	0.9551	1.0470	0.445	1.465	0.466	1.534	3.588	0.2787	0.743	1.359	5.817	0.379	1.621
18	0.707	0.738	0.194	0.9576	1.0442	0.461	1.454	0.482	1.518	3.640	0.2747	0.738	1.426	5.854	0.392	1.608
19	0.688	0.717	0.187	0.9599	1.0418	0.477	1.443	0.497	1.503	3.689	0.2711	0.733	1.490	5.888	0.404	1.596
20	0.671	0.697	0.180	0.9619	1.0396	0.491	1.433	0.510	1.490	3.735	0.2677	0.729	1.548	5.922	0.414	1.586
21	0.655	0.679	0.173	0.9638	1.0376	0.504	1.424	0.523	1.477	3.778	0.2647	0.724	1.606	5.950	0.425	1.575
22	0.640	0.662	0.167	0.9655	1.0358	0.516	1.415	0.534	1.466	3.819	0.2618	0.720	1.659	5.979	0.434	1.566
23	0.626	0.647	0.162	0.9670	1.0342	0.527	1.407	0.545	1.455	3.858	0.2592	0.716	1.710	6.006	0.443	1.557
24	0.612	0.632	0.157	0.9684	1.0327	0.538	1.399	0.555	1.445	3.895	0.2567	0.712	1.759	6.031	0.452	1.548
25	0.600	0.619	0.153	0.9696	1.0313	0.548	1.392	0.565	1.435	3.931	0.2544	0.709	1.804	6.058	0.459	1.541
Over 25	$\frac{3}{\sqrt{n}}$	$\frac{3}{\sqrt{n}}$	–	–	–	a	b	a	b	–	–	–	–	–	–	–

Source: Reproduced by permission from *ASTM Manual on Quality Control of Materials*, American Society for Testing Materials, Philadelphia, Pa., 1951.

$^a 1 - \frac{3}{\sqrt{2n}}$

$^b 1 + \frac{3}{\sqrt{2n}}$

APPENDIX
COMPUTER PROGRAMS

```
C   PROGRAM:   AUTOCORRELATION
C
C   THIS PROGRAM CALCULATES THE AUTOCORRELATION COEFFICIENTS
C   WITH LAGS K= 1,2,....,N1 BASED ON OBSERVATIONS TAKEN AT
C   N CONSECUTIVE TIME PERIODS.
C
C   USER SPECIFICATIONS
C
C   THE USER MUST SPECIFY THE VALUES FOR N AND N1, AND
C   MODIFY THE DIMENSION STATEMENT AND THE FIRST READ
C   STATEMENT ACCORDINGLY.
C
       DIMENSION Y(36),Z(36),YT(36),RNUM(6),R(6)
       READ(5,10) (Y(1),I=1,36)
    10 FORMAT(8F10.0)
       N=36
       N1=6
       DO 30 I=1,N
       Z(I)=(1.0)*I
    30 CONTINUE
       ZB=0.0
       DO 34 I=1,N
       ZB=Z(I)+ZB
    34 CONTINUE
       ZB=ZB/N
       SSN=0.0
       SSD=0.0
       DO 35 I=1,N
       SSN=(Z(I)-ZB)*Y(I)+SSN
       SSD=(Z(I)-ZB)**2+SSD
    35 CONTINUE
```

```
      B1=SSN/SSD
      YB=0.0
      DO 39 I=1,N
      YB=Y(I)+YB
   39 CONTINUE
      YB=YB/N
      BO=YB-B1*ZB
      DO 40 I=1,N
      YT(I)=BO+B1*Z(I)
   40 CONTINUE
      DEN=0.0
      DO 45 I=1,N
      DEN=(Y(I)-YT(I))**2+DEN
   45 CONTINUE
      DO 50 I=1,N1
      RNUM(I)=0.0
   50 CONTINUE
      DO 55 I=1,N1
      DO 60 J=1,N-N1
      RNUM(I)=(Y(J)-YT(J))*(Y(I-J)-YT(I-J))+RNUM(I)
   60 CONTINUE
   55 CONTINUE
      DO 65 I=1,N1
      R(I)=RNUM(I)/DEN
   65 CONTINUE
      WRITE(6,70)
   70 FORMAT('1',1X,'I= ',9X,'R= ')
      DO 80 I=1,N1
      WRITE(6,75)I,R(I)
   75 FORMAT(' 'I3,8X,F9.4)
   80 CONTINUE
      STOP
      END
```

```
C   PROGRAM:   MULTIPLE EXPONENTIAL SMOOTHING
C
C   THIS PROGRAM PRODUCES THE FORECAST VALUES FOR A TIME
C   SERIES WITH A FORECAST LEAD TIME OF T UNITS USING
C   FIRST, SECOND, AND THIRD ORDER EXPONENTIAL SMOOTHING
C   FORECAST MODELS TOGETHER WITH THE ERROR SUM OF SQUARES
C   FOR EACH MODEL.
C
C   USER SPECIFICATIONS
C
C   THE USER MUST SPECIFY THE VALUES OF N, THE SIZE OF
C   THE DATA SET; A, THE SMOOTHING CONSTANT; AND LT,
```

```
C   THE FORECAST LEAD TIME.  THE TWO DIMENSION STATEMENTS
C   AND THE FIRST READ STATEMENT MUST BE MODIFIED TO
C   CONFORM TO N, THE SIZE OF THE DATA SET.
C
      DIMENSION Y(60),S(60),S2(60),S3(60),Y1(60),Y2(60)
      DIMENSION Y3(60),E1(60),E2(60),E3(60)
      READ(5,10) (Y(I),I=1,60)
   10 FORMAT(8F10.0)
      A=0.2
      LT=1
      N=60
      S(1)=Y(1)
      S2(1)=Y(1)
      S3(1)=Y(1)
      DO 20 I=2,N
      S(I)=A*Y(I)+(1.0-A)*S(I-1)
      S2(I)=A*S(I)+(1.0-A)*S2(I-1)
      S3(I)=A*S2(I)+(1.0-A)*S3(I-1)
   20 CONTINUE
      DO 25 I=1+LT,N
      Y1(I)=S(I-LT)
      E1(I)=(Y(I)-Y1(I))**2
   25 CONTINUE
      B1=(2.0+(A*LT)/(1.0-A))
      B2=(1.0+(A*LT)/(1.0-A))
      DO 30 I=1+LT,N
      Y2(I)=B1*S(I-LT)-B2*S2(I-LT)
      E2(I)=(Y(I)-Y2(I))**2
   30 CONTINUE
      C1=(6.0)*((1.0-A)**2)+(6.0-(5.0)*A)*A*LT
      C1=C1+(A**2)*(LT**2)
      C2=(6.0)*((1.0-A)**2)+(2.0)*(A**2)*(LT**2)
      C2=C2+(2.0)*(5.0-(4.0)*A)*A*LT
      C3=(2.0)*((1.0-A)**2)+(A**2)*(LT**2)
      C3=C3+(4.0-(3.0)*A)*A*LT
      C1=C1/((2.0)*((1.0-A)**2))
      C2=C2/((2.0)*((1.0-A)**2)
      C3=C3/((2.0)*((1.0-A)**2))
      DO 35 I=1+LT,N
      Y3(I)=C1*S(I-LT)-C2*S2(I-LT)+C3*S3(I-LT)
      E3(I)=(Y(I)-Y3(I))**2
   35 CONTINUE
      DO 40 I=1,LT
      Y1(I)=0.0
      Y2(I)=0.0
      Y3(I)=0.0
      E1(I)=0.0
```

```
      E2(I)=0.0
      E3(I)=0.0
   40 CONTINUE
      SSE1=0.0
      SSE2=0.0
      SSE3=0.0
      DO 45 I=1,N
      SSE1=SSE1+E1(I)
      SSE2=SSE2+E2(I)
      SSE3=SSE3+E3(I)
   45 CONTINUE
      WRITE(6,50)
   50 FORMAT('1',10X,'I= ',11X,'Y= ',10X,'Y1= ',10X,'Y2= ',10X,'Y3= ')
      DO 60 I=1,N
      WRITE(6,55)I,Y(I),Y1(I),Y2(I),Y3(I)
   55 FORMAT(' ',8X,I3,3X,4(5X,F9.4))
   60 CONTINUE
      WRITE(6,70)
   70 FORMAT('2',11X,'SSE1= ',10X,'SSE2= ',10X,'SSE3= ')
      WRITE(6,75)SSE1,SSE2,SSE3
   75 FORMAT(' ',5X,3(5X,F9.4))
      STOP
      END


C  PROGRAM:  EWMA FORECASTING FOR MONTHLY SEASONAL DATA
C
C  THIS PROGRAM CAN BE IMPLEMENTED ONLY WHEN N, THE
C  NUMBER OF MONTHLY DATA VALUES EXCEEDS 24.  INITIAL
C  ESTIMATES OF S, THE SMOOTHED AVERAGE; R, THE UPDATED
C  TREND GAIN; AND F, THE UPDATED SEASONAL FACTOR AT
C  TIMES T = 1,2,...,12 ARE OBTAINED.  THESE ESTIMATES
C  ARE THEN USED TO COMPUTE S, R, AND F FOR TIMES
C  T = 13,...,24.  BEGINNING WITH TIME PERIOD 25, THIS
C  PROGRAM PRODUCES THE ESTIMATES OF S, R, AND F, THE
C  ESTIMATE OF Y FOR T = 25,...,N, AND THE ERROR SUM
C  OF SQUARES IN FORECASTING THE (N-24) VALUES OF THE
C  TIME SERIES.
C
C  USER SPECIFICATIONS
C
C  THE USER MUST SPECIFY THE VALUES OF N, THE SIZE OF
C  THE DATA SET; A, B, AND C, THE SMOOTHING CONSTANTS
C  AND LT, THE FORECAST LEAD TIME.  THE TWO DIMENSION
C  STATEMENTS AND THE FIRST READ STATEMENT MUST BE
C  MODIFIED TO REFLECT THE SIZE OF THE DATA SET, N.
```

```
C   NOTE THAT THE DIMENSIONS OF THE VECTORS T, Z, AND
C   FF REMAIN CONSTANT AT 24, INDEPENDENT OF THE VALUE
C   OF N.
C
      DIMENSION T(24),Z(24),Y(60),YE(60),FF(24),S(60),R(60)
      DIMENSION F(60), ER(60)
      A=0.1
      B=0.1
      C=0.4
      LT=1
      READ(5,10) (Y(I),I=1,60)
   10 FORMAT(8F10.0)
      N=60
      YB=0.0
      B2=0.0
      DO 30 I=1,24
      T(I)=I*(1.0)
   30 CONTINUE
      DO 32 I=1,24
      B2=(T(I)-12.5)*Y(I)+B2
   32 CONTINUE
      B2=B2/(1150.0)
      DO 34 I=1,24
      YB=Y(I)+YB
   34 CONTINUE
      YB=YB/(24.0)
      B1=YB-(12.5)*B2
      DO 35 I=1,24
      Z(I)=B1+B2*T(I)
   35 CONTINUE
      SO=Z(1)
      RO=(Z(24)-Z(1))/(23.0)
      FF(I)=Y(I)/Z(I)
   37 CONTINUE
      S(1)=A*Y(1)/FF(1)+(1.0-A)*(SO+RO)
      R(1)=B*(S(1)-SO)+(1.0-B)*RO
      F(1)=C*Y(1)/S(1)+(1.0-C)*FF(1)
      DO 40 I=2,12
      S(I)=A*Y(I)/FF(I)+(1.0-A)*(S(I-1)+R(I-1))
      R(I)=B*(S(I)-S(I-1))+(1.0-B)*R(I-1)
      F(I)=C*Y(I)/S(I)+(1.0-C)*FF(I)
   40 CONTINUE
      DO 50 I=13,N
      S(I)=A*Y(I)/F(I-12)+(1.0-A)*(S(I-1)+R(I-1))
      R(I)=B*(S(I)-S(I-1))+(1.0-B)*R(I-1)
      F(I)=C*Y(I)/S(I)+(1.0-C)*F(I-12)
   50 CONTINUE
```

```
      DO 52 I=25,N
      YE(I)=(S(I-LT)+(LT)*(R(I-LT)))*F(I-12)
      ER(I)=(Y(I)-YE(I))**2
   52 CONTINUE
      DO 55 I=1,24
      YE(I)=0.0
      ER(I)=0.0
   55 CONTINUE
      SSE=0.0
      DO 60 I=25,N
      SSE=SSE+ER(I)
   60 CONTINUE
      WRITE(6,70)
   70 FORMAT('1',1X,'I= ',7X,'S= ',11X,'R= ',12X,'F= ',12X,
     1'Y= ',12X,'YE= ')
      DO 80 I=1,N
      WRITE(6,75)I,S(I),R(I),F(I),Y(I),YE(I)
   75 FORMAT(' ',I3,5(5X,F10.4))
   80 CONTINUE
      WRITE(6,85)
   85 FORMAT('2',11X,'SSE= ')
      WRITE(6,90)SSE
   90 FORMAT(' ',9X,F11.4)
      STOP
      END
```

SOLUTIONS TO SELF-CORRECTING EXERCISES

Set 2A

1. a. Range = 59 - 18 = 41

   b.-c. Each student will obtain slightly different results. Dividing the range by 10 produces intervals of length slightly more than 4. A more convenient choice is to use 11 intervals of length 4, beginning at 17.5.

Class	*Class Boundaries*	*Tally*	f_i
1	17.5 - 21.5	1111	4
2	21.5 - 25.5	1111	4
3	25.5 - 29.5	11111 1	6
4	29.5 - 33.5	11111 11	7
5	33.5 - 37.5	11111 1	6
6	37.5 - 41.5	1111	4
7	41.5 - 45.5	1111	4
8	45.5 - 49.5	11	2
9	49.5 - 53.5	111	3
10	53.5 - 57.5	1	1
11	57.5 - 61.5	1	1

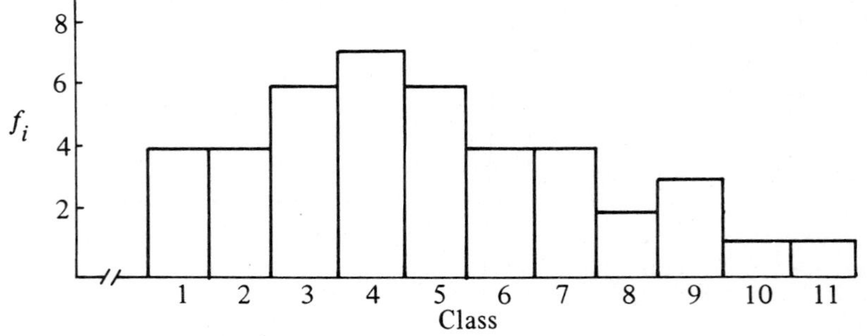

d. Dividing the range by 6, each interval must be of length 7.

Class	*Class Boundaries*	*Tally*	f_i
1	17.5 - 24.5	11111 11	7
2	24.5 - 31.5	11111 11111	10
3	31.5 - 38.5	11111 11111 1	11
4	38.5 - 45.5	11111 11	7
5	45.5 - 52.5	11111	5
6	52.5 - 59.5	11	2

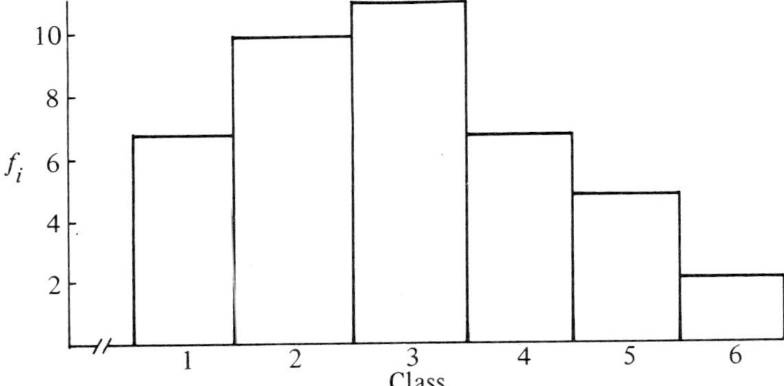

e. The second histogram is more informative, since it exhibits the piling up of the data in the middle classes. Using too many classes tends to flatten out the histogram, producing nearly equal frequencies in each class.

2. a. An extra column in the tabulation is used to calculate relative frequency.

Class	*Class Boundaries*	*Tally*	f_i	f_i/n
1	5.55 - 7.55	11111	5	5/32
2	7.55 - 9.55	11111	5	5/32
3	9.55 - 11.55	11111 11111 11	12	12/32
4	11.55 - 13.55	11111	5	5/32
5	13.55 - 15.55	111	3	3/32
6	15.55 - 17.55	1	1	1/32
7	17.55 - 19.55	1	1	1/32

b. $\frac{1}{32} + \frac{1}{32} = \frac{1}{16}$; c. $\frac{5}{32} + \frac{5}{32} = \frac{5}{16}$; d. $\frac{12}{32} + \frac{5}{32} + \frac{3}{32} = \frac{20}{32} = \frac{5}{8}$

Set 2B

1. a. The stems range from 1 to 5, and the leaves have been reordered in order of ascending magnitude.

1	8 9
2	1 1 3 3 3 5 6 7 7 8 8 9
3	0 0 1 2 2 2 3 4 4 5 5 6 7 8 9
4	1 1 2 3 4 4 6 9
5	0 1 2 5 9

The coding is LEAF DIGIT = 1.0, 1 8 REPRESENTS 18.0

b. Use the results of part a. Each stem is split into two, with (*) corresponding to leaf digits 0, 1, 2, 3, and 4, while (.) corresponds to leaf digits 5, 6, 7, 8, and 9.

1.	8 9
2*	1 1 3 3 3
2.	5 6 7 7 8 8 9
3*	0 0 1 2 2 2 3 4 4
3.	5 5 6 7 8 9
4*	1 1 2 3 4 4
4.	6 9
5*	0 1 2
5.	5 9

c. Part b provides a slightly better visual description, showing that the data are relatively mound-shaped.

2. a. The stems range from 3 to 16, and the stem and leaf display uses the coding LEAF DIGIT = 10, 13 2 REPRESENTS 1320. Notice that one extremely large measurement was placed in the HI category. Also, notice the clumsiness of the display, because of the 4 and 5 digit leaves.

3	5340
4	6750 7040 7580
5	3890 4810 5280 5800 6390 7000 8000 8480 8960
6	0060 0520 1030 1290 2760 3950 4430 4980 5020 5030
	5080 7240 8060 8100 8290 8530 9000
7	1260 4350 5270 5330 5720 5730
8	1570 3610 3730 5390 7930 9690
9	2190 3180 3210 4130
10	0140
11	0490
12	
13	
14	
15	
16	2240
HI	6316.40

b. The data is rounded to the nearest ten, and the digit in the tens place is used as the leaf. The display is much clearer, showing the mound-shaped distribution, with two unusually high measurements.

3	5
4	7 7 8
5	4 5 5 6 6 7 8 8 9
6	0 1 1 1 3 4 4 5 5 5 6 7 8 8 8 9 9
7	1 4 5 5 6 6
8	2 4 4 5 8
9	0 2 3 3 4
10	0
11	0
HI	1620, 6320

Set 2C

1. a. The height of each bar represents the total civilian labor force for the year of interest and the shaded area represents the proportion employed.

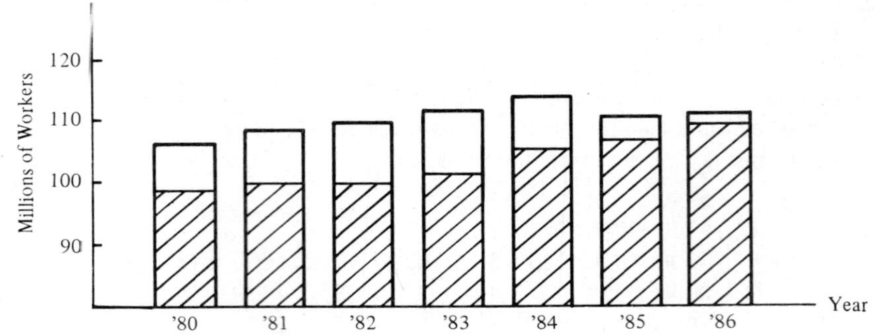

b. In order to make the drop in employment in 1982 look large, the vertical scale must be stretched and perhaps should begin at the point "85 million workers".

2. For each subdivision, the number of degrees in the central angle of its sector is given below.

Group	*Degrees*
1. Managerial, professional	26.6(360)/109.7 = 87
2. Technical, sales, administrative support	34.4(360)/109.7 = 113
3. Service occupations	14.7(360)/109.7 = 48
4. Precision production, craft and repair	13.4(360)/109.7 = 44
5. Operators, fabricators, laborers	17.2(360)/109.7 = 56
6. Farming, forestry, fishing	3.4(360)/109.7 = 11

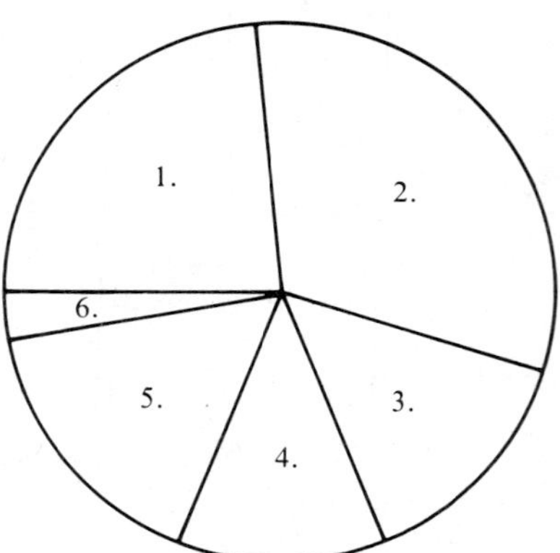

3. a. For each of the three years, a separate pie chart is constructed. Sector angles for the five subdivisions are given in the table below.

	Sector Angles		
	1984	*1985*	*1986*
USSR	77	76	75
U.S.	59	61	56
OPEC Nations	117	109	119
Other	106	113	109

b. Using a bar chart, countries are represented on the horizontal axis with each bar subdivided to show demands for 1984 (shaded) and 1986.

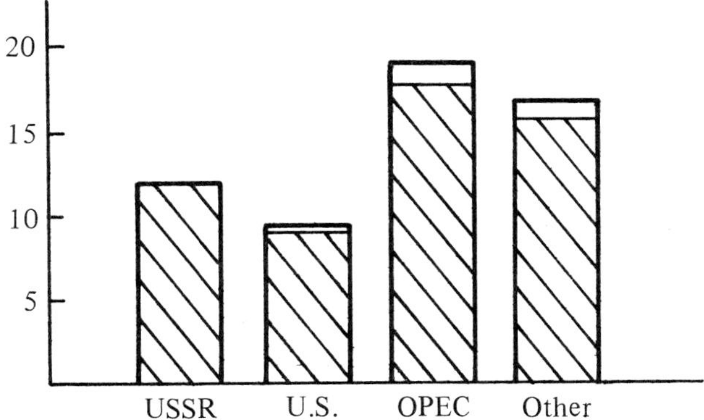

c. The bar chart seems more effective, clearly showing the increase in production for OPEC and Other oil, while the pie charts do, but not as dramatically.

Set 2D

1. a. Arrange the set of data in order of ascending magnitude.

6	9	11	13	16
8	10	12	13	17
9	10	12	15	19

median = 12 $\qquad \bar{x} = \dfrac{\sum_{i=1}^{n} x_i}{n} = \dfrac{180}{15} = 12$

b. There are 4 modes (9, 10, 12, 13) making it impossible to clearly locate the center of the data.

c. Range = 19 - 6 = 13

d.

x_i	$(x_i - \bar{x})$	$(x_i - \bar{x})^2$
6	-6	36
8	-4	16
9	-3	9
9	-3	9
10	-2	4
10	-2	4
11	-1	1
12	0	0
12	0	0
13	1	1
13	1	1
15	3	9
16	4	16
17	5	25
19	7	49
180	0	180

$$s^2 = \frac{\sum_{i=1}^{n} (x_i - \bar{x})^2}{n - 1}$$

$$= \frac{180}{14} = 12.8571$$

$$s = \sqrt{12.8571} = 3.59$$

2. a.

x_i	$(x_i - \bar{x})$	$(x_i - \bar{x})^2$
3	0	0
5	2	4
2	-1	1
7	4	16
2	-1	1
4	1	1
3	0	0
1	-2	4
0	-3	9
4	1	1
2	-1	1
33	0	38

$$\bar{x} = \frac{\sum_{i=1}^{n} x_i}{n} = \frac{33}{11} = 3$$

$$s^2 = \frac{\sum_{i=1}^{n} (x_i - \bar{x})^2}{n - 1} = \frac{38}{10} = 3.8$$

$$s = \sqrt{3.8} = 1.95$$

b. Arrange the data in order of ascending magnitude.

0	2	3	5
1	2	4	7
2	3	4	

median = 3 $\bar{x} = 3$

Set 2E

1. Display the data in a table as follows.

x_i	x_i^2
9	81
15	225
10	100
8	64
12	144
13	169
16	256
6	36
19	361
17	289
12	144
11	121
10	100
13	169
9	81
180	2340

$$s^2 = \frac{\Sigma x_i^2 - \frac{(\Sigma x_i)^2}{n}}{n-1}$$

$$= \frac{2340 - \frac{(180)^2}{15}}{14} = \frac{2340 - 2160}{14}$$

$$= \frac{180}{14} = 12.8571$$

2.

x_i	x_i^2
3	9
5	25
2	4
7	49
2	4
4	16
3	9
1	1
0	0
4	16
2	4
33	137

$$s^2 = \frac{\Sigma x_i^2 - \frac{(\Sigma x_i)^2}{n}}{n-1}$$

$$= \frac{137 - \frac{(33)^2}{11}}{10} = \frac{137 - \frac{1089}{11}}{10}$$

$$= \frac{137 - 99}{10} = \frac{38}{10} = 3.8$$

3. a. N: number of observations

MEAN: $\bar{x} = \Sigma x_i/n$

MEDIAN: Number in $.5(N + 1)$ position if N is odd; otherwise, the average of measurements on either side of the number in $.5(N + 1)$ position.

TMEAN: The upper and lower 5% of the observations are eliminated (in this case, 5% (32) = 1.6, so that one measurement is eliminated from the end of the ordered measurements). The mean is then calculated, based on 30 observations.

STDEV: $s = \sqrt{\dfrac{\Sigma x_i^2 - \dfrac{(\Sigma x_i)^2}{n}}{n - 1}}$ SEMEAN: $\dfrac{s}{\sqrt{n}}$

MAX: largest observation MIN: smallest observation

$Q3$: observation in position $.75(N + 1) = 24.75$

$Q1$: observation in position $.25(N + 1) = 8.25$

Hence Q_1 is $\frac{1}{4}$ the distance between observations 8 and 9, while Q_3 is $\frac{3}{4}$ the distance between observations 24 and 25.

Calculate the intervals for $k = 1, 2, 3$

k	$\bar{x} \pm ks$	*Interval*	*Percentage in Interval*
1	825 ± 817	8 to 1642	Approx. 68%
2	825 ± 1634	–809 to 2459	Approx. 95%
3	825 ± 2451	–1626 to 3276	Almost all

4. If $\bar{x}$ has been rounded off, then rounding error occurs each time $\bar{x}$ is subtracted from x_i in part a. Hence, there are n possible rounding errors. If part b is used, only one rounding error occurs when $(\Sigma x_i)^2$ is divided by n. Hence, part b is less subject to rounding errors and results in a more accurate computation.

Set 2F

1. The groupings used in this exercise are set up in this manner due to the fact that number of journeys can only be integer-valued. Hence, the group 1-3 would be equivalent to the group 0.5-3.5 if the methods of section 2.3 were used. The midpoint of this group, in either case, is 2. The data is displayed in the following table:

Class	Class Boundaries	f_i	m_i	$f_i m_i$	$f_i m_i^2$
1	1–3	6	2	12	24
2	4–6	8	5	40	200
3	7–9	4	8	32	256
4	10–12	2	11	22	242
		20		106	722

$$\bar{x}_g = \frac{\sum_{i=1}^{4} f_i m_i}{n} = \frac{106}{20} = 5.3$$

$$s_g^2 = \frac{\Sigma f_i m_i^2 - \frac{(\Sigma f_i m_i)^2}{n}}{n-1} = \frac{722 - \frac{(106)^2}{20}}{19} = \frac{722 - 561.8}{19}$$

$$= \frac{160.2}{19} = 8.4316$$

$$s_g = \sqrt{8.4316} = 2.90$$

2. In this case, each group consists of one and only one value of the measured variable, rather than a group of several measurements within each class. Hence, the class midpoint is simply that value.

m_i	f_i	$f_i m_i$	$f_i m_i^2$
0	10	0	0
1	18	18	18
2	13	26	52
3	6	18	54
4	2	8	32
5	1	5	25
	50	75	181

a. $$\bar{x} = \frac{\Sigma f_i m_i}{n} = \frac{75}{50} = 1.5 \qquad s^2 = \frac{\Sigma f_i m_i^2 - \frac{(\Sigma f_i m_i)^2}{n}}{n-1} = \frac{181 - \frac{(75)^2}{50}}{49}$$

$$= \frac{181 - 112.5}{49} = 1.3980$$

$$s = \sqrt{1.3980} = 1.18$$

b. Since each class midpoint is *exactly* the arithmetic mean of the measurements within each class, all of which are the same, there is no approximation necessary, and the formulas become exact.

Set 2G

1. Since $n = 42$, the median position is $.5(n + 1) = 21.5$ and $d(M) = 21$. Then $d(H) = \dfrac{d(M) + 1}{2} = 11$. Then

median = 33.5

upper hinge = 42

lower hinge = 27

H-spread = 42 - 27 = 15.

Since 1.5 H-spread = 22.5, the inner fences are

27 - 22.5 = 4.5 and 42 + 22.5 = 64.5

while the outer fences are

27 - 3(15) = -18 and 42 + 3(15) = 87

Adjacent values are 18 and 59. The box plot is shown below. There are no outliers.

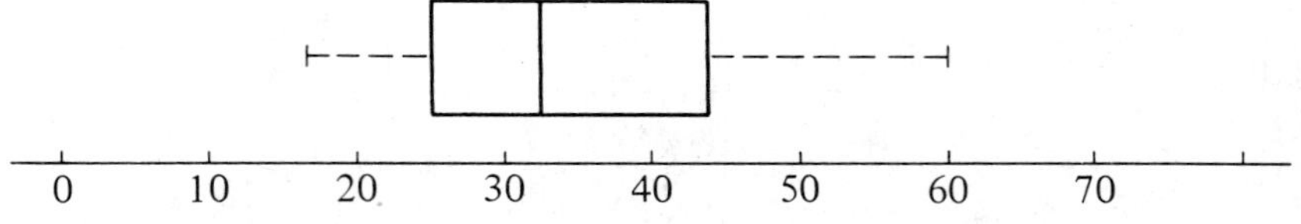

2. Since $n = 50$, the median position is $.5(n + 1) = 25.5$, $d(M) = 25$, $d(H) = (25 + 1)/2 = 13$. Then

$$\text{median} = \frac{672.4 + 680.6}{2} = 676.5 \qquad \text{lower hinge} = 589.6$$

upper hinge = 836.1 $\qquad$ H-spread = 246.5

The inner fences are 219.85 and 1205.85 while the outer fences are

$$589.6 - 3(246.5) = -149.9 \quad \text{and} \quad 836.1 + 3(246.5) = 1575.6$$

The box plot is shown below, with adjacent values 353.4 and 1104.9. The values 1622.4 and 6316.4 are extreme outliers.

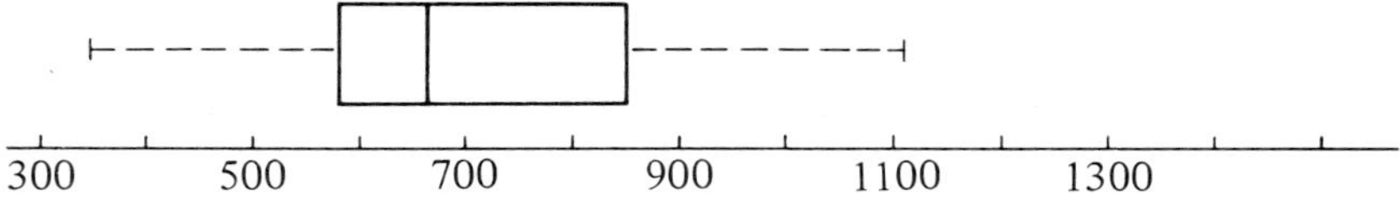

300 500 700 900 1100 1300

Set 3A

1. Denote the four good items as G_1, G_2, G_3, G_4, and the two defectives as D_1 and D_2.

   a. $E_1: G_1G_2$ $E_4: G_1D_1$ $E_7: G_2G_4$ $E_{10}: G_3G_4$ $E_{13}: G_4D_1$
      $E_2: G_1G_3$ $E_5: G_1D_2$ $E_8: G_2D_1$ $E_{11}: G_3D_1$ $E_{14}: G_4D_2$
      $E_3: G_1G_4$ $E_6: G_2G_3$ $E_9: G_2D_2$ $E_{12}: G_3D_2$ $E_{15}: D_1D_2$

   b. "At least one defective" implies one or two defectives, while "no more than one defective" implies zero or one defective.

      A: $\{E_4, E_5, E_8, E_9, E_{11}, E_{12}, E_{13}, E_{14}, E_{15}\}$;
      B: $\{E_4, E_5, E_8, E_9, E_{11}, E_{12}, E_{13}, E_{14}\}$;
      C: $\{E_1, E_2, E_3, E_4, E_5, E_6, E_7, E_8, E_9, E_{10}, E_{11}, E_{12}, E_{13}, E_{14}\}$

   c. Each sample point is assigned equal probability; that is, $P(E_i) = 1/15$.

      $P(A) = 9/15 = 3/5;\ P(B) = 8/15;\ P(C) = 14/15$

2. a. $E_1: FFFF$ $E_5: FFFM$ $E_9: MFFM$ $E_{13}: MFMM$
      $E_2: MFFF$ $E_6: FFMM$ $E_{10}: MFMF$ $E_{14}: MMFM$
      $E_3: FMFF$ $E_7: FMFM$ $E_{11}: MMFF$ $E_{15}: MMMF$
      $E_4: FFMF$ $E_8: FMMF$ $E_{12}: FMMM$ $E_{16}: MMMM$

   b. A: $\{E_6, E_7, E_8, E_9, E_{10}, E_{11}\}$; B: $\{E_1\}$;
      C: $\{E_2, E_3, E_4, E_5, E_6, E_7, E_8, E_9, E_{10}, E_{11}, E_{12}, E_{13}, E_{14}, E_{15}, E_{16}\}$;
      $D = A \cup B$: $\{E_1, E_6, E_7, E_8, E_9, E_{10}, E_{11}\}$; $E = BC$: no sample points;
      $F = A \cup C$: same as C.

c. Since each sample point is equally likely,

$$P(A) = \frac{6}{16} = \frac{3}{8};\quad P(B) = \frac{1}{16};\quad P(C) = \frac{15}{16};\quad P(D) = \frac{7}{16};\quad P(E) = 0;\ P(F) = \frac{15}{16}$$

Set 3B

1. a. $E_1: HH$ $\quad E_4: TT$ $\quad E_7: GT$

   $E_2: HT$ $\quad E_5: TG$ $\quad E_8: GH$

   $E_3: TH$ $\quad E_6: GG$ $\quad E_9: HG$

   b. $A: \{E_1, E_2, E_3, E_4\}$ $\quad B: \{E_1, E_2, E_3, E_8, E_9\}$

   $C: \{E_1, E_4, E_6\}$

   c. Since each sample point is equally likely,

   $$P(A) = \frac{4}{9};\quad P(B) = \frac{5}{9};\quad P(C) = \frac{3}{9} = \frac{1}{3};$$

   $$P(A \cup C) = \frac{5}{9};\quad P(BC) = \frac{1}{9}$$

   d.

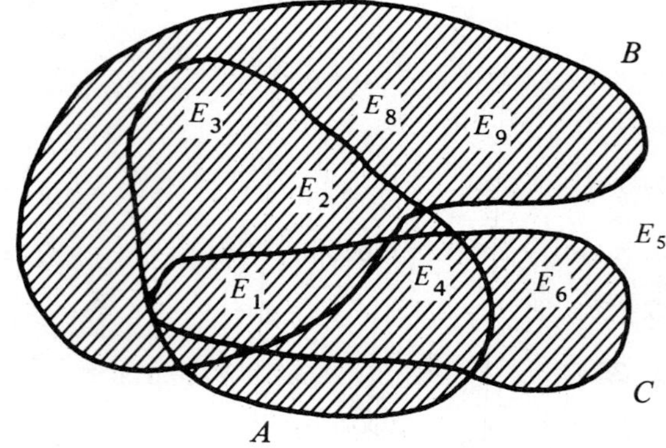

2. a. $E_1: HHH$ $\quad E_3: NHN$ $\quad E_5: HHN$ $\quad E_7: NHH$

   $E_2: HNN$ $\quad E_4: NNH$ $\quad E_6: HNH$ $\quad E_8: NNN$

   b. $P(A) = \frac{3}{8};\quad P(B) = \frac{4}{8} = \frac{1}{2};\quad P(C) = \frac{1}{8};\quad P(D) = \frac{4}{8} = \frac{1}{2}$

   c. $P(A \cup D) = \frac{4}{8} = \frac{1}{2};\quad P(BD) = \frac{3}{8}$

Set 3C

1. a. $D = A \cup B$; $E = BC$; $F = A \cup C$

   b. AB: no sample points; $B \cup C$: $\{E_1, E_2, \ldots, E_{16}\} = S$;

   $AC \cup BC$: $\{E_6, E_7, E_8, E_9, E_{10}, E_{11}\}$; $\bar{C}$: $\{E_1\}$;

   $\overline{AC}$: $\{E_1, E_2, \ldots, E_5, E_{12}, E_{13}, \ldots E_{16}\}$

   c. $P(A \cup B) = P(A) + P(B) - P(AB) = \frac{3}{8} + \frac{1}{16} - 0 = \frac{7}{16}$

   $P(\bar{C}) = 1 - P(C) = 1 - \frac{15}{16} = \frac{1}{16}$

   $P(\overline{BC}) = 1 - P(BC) = 1 - 0 = 1$

   d. $P(A/C) = P(AC)/P(C) = \frac{6}{16}\Big/\frac{15}{16} = \frac{6}{15}$ while $P(A) = \frac{3}{8}$

   A and C are dependent but are not mutually exclusive.

   e. $P(B/C) = P(BC)/P(C) = 0\Big/\frac{15}{16} = 0$ while $P(B) = \frac{1}{16}$ and $P(BC) = 0$

   B and C are dependent and mutually exclusive.

2. a. $P(A) = P$[the executive represents a small corporation] $= \frac{75}{200} = \frac{3}{8}$

   $P(F) = P$ [the executive favors gas rationing] $= \frac{15}{200} = \frac{3}{40}$

   $P(AF) = \frac{3}{200}$

   $P(A \cup G) = P$[executive favors conversion or represents a small corporation or both]

   $= P(A) + P(G) - P(AG) = \frac{75 + 22 - 10}{200} = \frac{87}{200}$

   $P(AD) = P$[executive represents a small corporation and favors car pooling]

   $= \frac{20}{200}$

   $P(\bar{F}) = 1 - P(F) = 1 - \frac{3}{40} = \frac{37}{40}$

b. $P(A|F) = P(AF)/P(F) = \dfrac{3/200}{15/200} = \dfrac{3}{15}$ $\quad P(A|D) = \dfrac{20/200}{55/200} = \dfrac{20}{55}$

Neither A and F nor A and D are mutually exclusive.
A and F and A and D are both dependent.

3. Let S represent a sale on a particular contact, and N represent no sale. There are 8 sample points in the experiment; however, they are not all equally likely.

SSS	*SNS*	*NNS*	*SNN*
SSN	*NSS*	*NSN*	*NNN*

The tree diagram consists of three steps, and the probabilities at each step are dependent on the step before.

Contact 1	*Contact 2*	*Contact 3*	*Outcome*	$P(E_i)$
S ($\frac{1}{2}$)	S ($\frac{3}{4}$)	S ($\frac{3}{4}$)	SSS	9/32
		N ($\frac{1}{4}$)	SSN	3/32
	N ($\frac{1}{4}$)	S ($\frac{1}{3}$)	SNS	1/24
		N ($\frac{2}{3}$)	SNN	2/24
N ($\frac{1}{2}$)	S ($\frac{1}{3}$)	S ($\frac{3}{4}$)	NSS	3/24
		N ($\frac{1}{4}$)	NSN	1/24
	N ($\frac{2}{3}$)	S ($\frac{1}{3}$)	NNS	2/18
		N ($\frac{2}{3}$)	NNN	4/18

Since $P(A) = P(\text{SSS}) + P(\text{SSN}) + P(\text{SNS}) + P(\text{NSS})$

We have $P(A) = \dfrac{9}{32} + \dfrac{3}{32} + \dfrac{1}{24} + \dfrac{3}{24} = \dfrac{13}{24}$

4. Define A: Company A shows an increase
B: Company B shows an increase
C: Company C shows an increase

It is given that $P(A) = .4$, $P(B) = .6$, $P(C) = .7$ and A, B, and C are independent events.

a. $P(ABC) = P(A)\,P(B)\,P(C) = (.4)\,(.6)\,(.7) = .168$

b. $P(\bar{A}\bar{B}\bar{C}) = P(\bar{A})\,P(\bar{B})\,P(\bar{C}) = [1 - P(A)]\;[1 - P(B)]\;[1 - P(C)]$
$= (.6)\,(.4)\,(.3) = .072$

c. $P[\text{at least one shows profit}] = 1 - P[\text{none show profit}]$
$= 1 - P(\bar{A}\bar{B}\bar{C}) = 1 - .072 = .928$

Set 3D

1. Define D: item is defective
   A: item supplied by company A
   B: item supplied by company B
   C: item supplied by company C

   It is given that $P(D|A) = .005$, $P(D|B) = .010$, $P(D|C) = .015$.

   a. Using Bayes' Law extended to three alternatives,

$$P(A|D) = \frac{P(A)P(D|A)}{P(A)P(D|A) + P(B)P(D|B) + P(C)P(D|C)}$$

$$= \frac{(.7)(.005)}{(.7)(.005) + (.2)(.010) + (.1)(.015)} = \frac{1}{2}$$

   b. Using the results of part a to find $P(B|D)$, we have

$$P(B|D) = \frac{P(B)P(D|B)}{P(A)P(D|A) + P(B)P(D|B) + P(C)P(D|C)}$$

$$= \frac{.002}{.007} = \frac{2}{7}$$

2. Define P: lie detector test is positive (guilty)
   I: a person is innocent

   It is given that $P(I) = .90$, $P(\bar{I}) = .10$; $P(P|I) = .08$, $P(\bar{P}|I) = .92$; and $P(P|\bar{I}) = .85$, $P(\bar{P}|\bar{I}) = .15$.

   Find: $$P(I|P) = \frac{P(IP)}{P(IP) + P(\bar{I}P)}$$

$$= \frac{P(I)P(P|I)}{P(I)P(P|I) + P(\bar{I})P(P|\bar{I})}$$

$$= \frac{(.90)(.08)}{(.90)(.08) + (.10)(.85)}$$

$$= \frac{.072}{.157} = .459$$

Set 3E

1. Since order is important, the number of distinct arrangements is

$$P_5^{13} = \frac{13!}{8!} = 13(12)(11)(10)(9) = 154{,}440$$

2. Using the *mn* rule, there are a total of 4(5)(3)(6) or 360 different systems which can be built. The total number of systems which do not include the one brand of receiver, the one brand of turntable, and so on, is (4–1)(5–1)(3–1)(6–1) = 120. Hence, the probability that the dealer will make a profit is

$$120/360 = \frac{1}{3}$$

3. Assuming that one account is assigned to each executive, order is important, and the total number of permutations is $P_6^6 = 6! = 720$.

4. There are two models to be selected from a total of four models (since two of the models have already been chosen to appear). The order of choice is unimportant, and the number of ways is

$$C_2^4 = \frac{4!}{2!2!} = \frac{4(3)}{2(1)} = 6$$

Set 4A

1. Each sample point consists of four elements, each representing the state of a particular component. Let S denote a successfully operating component and F denote a failure. Since components are independent, the Multiplicative Law of Probability can be used to find $P(E_i)$ with $P(S) = .99$ and $P(F) = .01$.

E_i	$P(E_i)$	x	E_i	$P(E_i)$	x
SSSS	.96059601	0	*FSSF*	.00009801	2
FSSS	.00970299	1	*FSFS*	.00009801	2
SFSS	.00970299	1	*FFSS*	.00009801	2
SSFS	.00970299	1	*SFFF*	.00000099	3
SSSF	.00970299	1	*FSFF*	.00000099	3
SSFF	.00009801	2	*FFSF*	.00000099	3
SFSF	.00009801	2	*FFFS*	.00000099	3
SFFS	.00009801	2	*FFFF*	.00000001	4

The probability distribution in compact form is

x	$p(x)$
0	.96059601
1	.03881196
2	.00058806
3	.00000396
4	.00000001

a. Reliability $= P[\text{system works}] = P[x = 0] = .9606$

b. Reliability $= P[\text{at least three components work}]$

$$= P[x \leqslant 1] = p(0) + p(1) = .9994$$

2. Let M represent a candidate with a masters degree and let C represent a candidate without such a degree. Define the following events:
CM: C ranked first, M ranked second
CC: C ranked first, C ranked second
MM: M ranked first, M ranked second
MC: M ranked first, C ranked second

$$p(0) = P[x = 0] = P(CC) = \frac{3}{5}\left(\frac{2}{4}\right) = \frac{6}{20};$$

$$p(1) = P[x = 1] = P(CM) + P(MC) = \frac{3}{5}\left(\frac{2}{4}\right) + \frac{2}{5}\left(\frac{3}{4}\right) = \frac{12}{20};$$

$$p(2) = P[x = 2] = P(MM) = \frac{2}{5}\left(\frac{1}{4}\right) = \frac{2}{20}$$

x	$p(x)$
0	3/10
1	6/10
2	1/10

3. Using the procedure in 2, define the event FC as "Ford Escort chosen first, Chevrolet Citation chosen second." Then

$$P[x = 0] = P(CC) = \frac{2}{5}\left(\frac{1}{4}\right) = \frac{1}{10};$$

$$P[x = 1] = P(CF) + P(FC) = \frac{2}{5}\left(\frac{3}{4}\right) + \frac{3}{5}\left(\frac{2}{4}\right) = \frac{6}{10};$$

$$P[x = 2] = P(FF) = \frac{3}{5}\left(\frac{2}{4}\right) = \frac{3}{10}$$

x	$p(x)$
0	.1
1	.6
2	.3

4. a. $p(0) = -2/10$ is not between 0 and 1.
b. $\sum_x p(x) = 7/10 \neq 1$.

5. Let U be the event that the primary wage earner is unemployed. There are 16 sample points with unequal probabilities.

$$p(0) = P[\bar{U}\bar{U}\bar{U}\bar{U}] = (.93)^4 = .748052$$

$$p(1) = 4P(\bar{U})^3 P(U) = 4(.93)^3(.07) = .225220$$

$$p(2) = 6P(\bar{U})^2 P(U)^2 = 6(.93)^2(.07)^2 = .025428$$

$$p(3) = 4P(\bar{U})P(U)^3 = 4(.93)(.07)^3 = .001276$$

$$p(4) = P(UUUU) = (.07)^4 = .000024$$

Set 4B

1. $\mu = E(x) = \sum_x x\,p(x) = 5000(.30) + 10000(.35) + 15000(.20)$

$$+ 20000(.10) + 25000(.05)$$

$$= 11250$$

$$\sigma^2 = E(x^2) - \mu^2 = (1000)^2\,[25(.3) + 100(.35) + 225(.20) + 400(.10) + 625(.05)] - (11250)^2$$

$$= 158750000 - 126562500 = 32187500$$

$$\sigma = \sqrt{32187500} = 5673.4$$

2. Note that $R = 20x$ so that, for example, $P[R = 100{,}000] = P[x = 5000] = .30$. The probability distribution for R is

R	$p(R)$
100,000	.30
200,000	.35
300,000	.20
400,000	.10
500,000	.05

$$E(R) = 20E(x) = 225{,}000$$

$$\sigma^2 = (20{,}000)^2\,[158.75] - (112500)^2$$

$$= 12{,}875{,}000{,}000$$

$$\sigma = 113{,}468$$

3. $P[R \leqslant 200{,}000] = .35 + .30 = .65$

4. Let x be the gain to the insurance company and let r be the premium charged by the company.

x	$p(x)$
r	.9900
$-40{,}000 + r$	.0075
$-80{,}000 + r$	.0025

In order to break even, $E(x) = 0$, or

$$E(x) = \sum_x x\,p(x) = .99r + .0075\,(-40{,}000 + r) + (-80{,}000 + r)\,(.0025) = 0$$

$r - 300 - 200 = 0$

$r = \$500$

Set 5A

1. Let x be the number of apartment dwellers who move within a year. Then $p = P$[move within a year] $= .2$ and $n = 7$.

   a. $P[x = 2] = C_2^7(.2)^2(.8)^5 = .27525$

   b. $P[x \leqslant 1] = C_0^7(.2)^0(.8)^7 + C_1^7(.2)^1(.8)^6 = .209715 + .367002$

   $= .576717$

2. Let x be the number of letters delivered within 4 days. Then $p = P$[letter delivered within 4 days] $= .7$ and $n = 20$.

   a. $P[x \geqslant 15] = 1 - P[x \leqslant 14] = 1 - .584 = .416$

   b. $P[x \geqslant 10] = 1 - P[x \leqslant 9] = 1 - .017 = .983$

   Notice that if 10 or fewer letters arrive later than 4 days then $20 - 10 = 10$ or more will arrive within 4 days.

3. Let x be the number of contracts awarded, so that $p = .6$ and $n = .5$.

   a. $P[x = 5] = P[x \leqslant 5] - P[x \leqslant 4] = 1 - .922 = .078$

   b. $P[x \geqslant 3] = 1 - P[x \leqslant 2] = 1 - .317 = .683$

4. Let x be the number of satisfactory pieces of lumber, so that $p = .6$ and $n = 10$.

   a. $P[x \leqslant 3] = .055$

   b. $P[x \geqslant 8] = 1 - P[x \leqslant 7] = 1 - .833 = .167$

   c. $P[x \geqslant 7] = 1 - P[x \leqslant 6] = 1 - .618 = .382$

Set 5B

1. x = number of stockholders favoring the proposal
   $p = P$[stockholder favors a proposal] = .3
   $n = 100$

   $\mu = np = 100(.3) = 30$; $\sigma^2 = npq = 100(.3)(.7) = 21$; $\sigma = \sqrt{21} = 4.58$

   Calculate $\mu \pm 2\sigma = 30 \pm 2(4.58) = 30 \pm 9.16$. We would expect between 20.84 and 39.16 (between 21 and 39) stockholders to favor the proposal.
2. x = number of registered voters belonging to a minority group
   $p = .2$
   $n = 80$

   $\mu = np = 80(.2) = 16$; $\sigma^2 = npq = 80(.2)(.8) = 12.8$; $\sigma = \sqrt{12.8} = 3.58$

   As in Exercise 1, calculate $\mu \pm 2\sigma = 16 \pm 2(3.58) = 16 \pm 7.16$ or 8.84 to 23.16. We would expect to see between 9 and 23 minority group members on the jury lists.
3. x = number watching the T.V. program
   $p = .4$
   $n = 400$

   $\mu = 400(.4) = 160$; $\sigma^2 = 400(.4)(.6) = 96$; $\sigma = \sqrt{96} = 9.80$

   Calculate $\mu \pm 2\sigma = 160 \pm 2(9.8) = 160 \pm 19.6$ or 140.4 to 179.6. Since we would expect the number watching the show to be between 141 and 179 with probability .95, it is highly unlikely that only 96 people would have watched the show *if* the 40% claim is correct. It is more likely that the percentage of viewers for this particular show is less than 40%.

Set 5C

1. Let x be the number of fires observed so that $p = P[\text{fire}] = .005$ and $n = 1000$. The random variable is binomial; however, since n is large and p is small with $\mu = np = 5$, the Poisson approximation is appropriate.

   a. $P[x = 0] = \dfrac{\mu^0 e^{-\mu}}{0!} = e^{-5} = .006738$

   b. $P[x \leqslant 3] = \dfrac{5^0 e^{-5}}{0!} + \dfrac{5^1 e^{-5}}{1!} + \dfrac{5^2 e^{-5}}{2!} + \dfrac{5^3 e^{-5}}{3!}$

   $= .006738\ (1 + 5 + 12.5 + 20.833) = .2650$

2. Let x be the number of defective panels with $\mu = 2$.

a. $P[x = 3] = \dfrac{2^3 e^{-2}}{3!} = 1.33(.135335) = .180$

b. $P[x \geqslant 2] = 1 - P[x \leqslant 1] = 1 - \dfrac{2^0 e^{-2}}{0!} - \dfrac{2^1 e^{-2}}{1!}$

$$= 1 - e^{-2}(1 + 2) = 1 - 3(.135335)$$

$$= .594$$

3. We are now concerned with the random variable x, the number of defective panels in a bundle of 200, with $\mu = 2(2) = 4$. Then

$$P[x \leqslant 4] = \frac{4^0 e^{-4}}{0!} + \frac{4^1 e^{-4}}{1!} + \frac{4^2 e^{-4}}{2!} + \frac{4^3 e^{-4}}{3!} + \frac{4^4 e^{-4}}{4!}$$

$$= .018316(1 + 4 + 8 + 10.67 + 10.67) = .629$$

4. Four employees will be chosen from 15, nine of whom are men and six of whom are women. Hence, $N = 15$, $k = 9$, $n = 4$, $N - k = 6$.

a. $P[\text{two or more men}] = P[x \geqslant 2] = \dfrac{C_2^9 C_2^6}{C_4^{15}} + \dfrac{C_3^9 C_1^6}{C_4^{15}} + \dfrac{C_4^9 C_0^6}{C_4^{15}}$

$$= \frac{36}{1365} + \frac{84(6)}{1365} + \frac{126}{1365} = \frac{666}{1365} = .488$$

b. $P[\text{exactly three women}] = P[\text{exactly one man}]$

$$= P[x = 1] = \frac{C_1^9 C_3^6}{C_4^{15}}$$

$$= \frac{9(20)}{1365} = .132$$

5. Define x to be the number of defective units chosen. Then $N = 50$, $k = 3$, $N - k = 47$, $n = 5$.

$$P[x = 0] = \frac{C_0^3 C_5^{47}}{C_5^{50}} = \frac{47!5!45!}{5!42!50!} = \frac{47(46)(45)(44)(43)}{50(49)(48)(47)(46)} = .724$$

Set 5D

1. Let x be the number of shirt sales of the new color, so that $p = P$[shirt sale will be of the new color] and $n = 25$. The hypothesis to be tested is

$$H_0: p = .4$$

$$H_a: p < .4$$

Small values of the test statistic, x, would favor rejection of H_0 in favor of H_a. Hence, we seek a rejection region of the form $x \leqslant a$ so that

$$\alpha = P[x \leqslant a \text{ when } p = .4] \leqslant .05$$

From Table 1, with $p = .4$, the rejection region is $x \leqslant 5$ with $\alpha = .029$.

Since the observed value of x ($x = 6$) does not fall in the rejection region, H_0 cannot be rejected. There is insufficient evidence to doubt the 40% figure. Note that we cannot "accept H_0" unless β, the probability of a Type II error, is assessed for meaningful alternative values of $p < .4$.

2. x = number of defectives
p = proportion defective
$n = 20$
Since the manufacturer claims that the proportion defective is at most .05, his claim will be rejected if it can be shown that the proportion defective is more than .05.

$$H_0: p = .05$$

$$H_a: p > .05$$

Large values of x suggest that H_a is true, and the rejection region must be of the form $x \geqslant a$, with

$$\alpha = P[x \geqslant a \text{ when } p = .05] \leqslant .05$$

$$1 - P[x \leqslant a - 1] \leqslant .05$$

$$P[x \leqslant a - 1] \geqslant .95$$

From Table 1, the necessary value of $a - 1$ is $a - 1 = 3$ and the rejection region will be $x \geqslant a$ or $x \geqslant 4$, with

$$\alpha = P[x \geqslant 4] = 1 - .984 = .016$$

The observed value of $x (x = 4)$ falls in the rejection region. Hence, H_0 is rejected and we conclude that $p > .05$. The manufacturer's claim is incorrect. The chance that this conclusion is incorrect is $\alpha = .016$.

3. x = number preferring Brand A
   $p = P$[person favors Brand A]
   $n = 15$
   If neither brand is preferred, then $p = .5$.

   $H_0: p = .5$

   $H_a: p \neq .5$

   Either large or small values of x will favor rejection of H_0, and the rejection region must be of the form

$$x \leqslant a \quad \text{or} \quad x \geqslant b \quad \text{with}$$

$$\alpha = P[x \leqslant a \text{ when } p = .5] + P[x \geqslant b \text{ when } p = .5] \leqslant .05$$

   Choosing the rejection region,

$$x \leqslant 3 \quad \text{or} \quad x \geqslant 12$$

   gives

$$\alpha = .018 + .018 = .036$$

   The student may verify by trial and error that this is the necessary region.
   Since the observed value is $x = 12$, the null hypothesis is rejected. There is a difference in preference for the two brands. The chance that this conclusion is incorrect is $\alpha = .036$.

Set 6A

Note: The student should illustrate each problem with a diagram and list all pertinent information before attempting the solution. Diagrams are omitted in order to conserve space.

1. a. $P[z > 2.1] = .5000 - A(2.1) = .5000 - .4821 = .0179$

   b. $P[z < -1.2] = .5000 - A(1.2) = .5000 - .3849 = .1151$

   c. $P[.5 < z < 1.5] = P[0 < z < 1.5] - P[0 < z < .5]$

$$= A(1.5) - A(.5) = .4332 - .1915 = .2417$$

   d. $P[-2.75 < z < -1.70] = A(2.75) - A(1.7) = .4970 - .4554 = .0416$

e. $P[-1.96 < z < 1.96] = A(1.96) + A(1.96) = 2(.4750) = .95$

f. $P[z > 1.645] = .5000 - A(1.645) = .5000 - .4500 = .05$

Notice that linear interpolation was used. That is, since the value $z = 1.645$ is halfway between two tabled values, $z = 1.64$ and $z = 1.65$, the appropriate area is taken to be halfway between the two tabled areas, $A(1.64) = .4495$ and $A(1.65) = .4505$. As a general rule, values of z will be rounded to two decimal places, except for this particular example, which will occur frequently in our calculations.

2. a. We know that $P[z > z_0] = .10$, or $.5000 - A(z_0) = .10$ which implies that

$$A(z_0) = .4000$$

The value of z_0 which satisfies this equation is $z_0 = 1.28$, so that $P[z > 1.28] = .10$

b. $P[z < z_0] = .01$ so that $.5000 - A(z_0) = .01$ and

$$A(z_0) = .4900$$

The value of z_0 which satisfies this equation is $z_0 = -2.33$ so that $P[z < -2.33] = .01$. The student who draws a diagram will see that z_0 must be negative, since it must be in the left-hand portion of the curve.

c. $P[-z_0 < z < z_0] = A(z_0) + A(z_0) = .95$ so that

$$A(z_0) = .4750$$

The necessary value of z_0 is $z_0 = 1.96$ and $P[-1.96 < z < 1.96] = .95$.

d. $P[-z_0 < z < z_0] = 2\,A(z_0) = .99$ so that

$$A(z_0) = .4950$$

The necessary value of z_0 is $z_0 = 2.58$ and $P[-2.58 < z < 2.58] = .99$.

3. The random variable of interest has a standard normal distribution and hence may be denoted as z.

a. $P[z > 1] = .5000 - A(1) = .5000 - .3413 = .1587$

b. $P[z > 1.5] = .5000 - A(1.5) = .5000 - .4332 = .0668$

c. $P[-1 < z < -.5] = A(1) - A(.5) = .3413 - .1915 = .1498$

d. The problem is to find a value of z, say z_0, such that

$$P[-z_0 < z < z_0] = .95$$

This was done in Exercise 2c and $z_0 = 1.96$. Hence, 95% of the billing errors will be between \$-1.96 and \$1.96.

e. Undercharges imply negative errors. Hence, the problem is to find z_0 such that

$$P[z < z_0] = .05$$

That is,

$$.5000 - A(z_0) = .05 \quad \text{or} \quad A(z_0) = .4500$$

The value of z_0 is $z_0 = -1.645$ (see Exercise 1f) and hence, 5% of the undercharges will be at least \$1.65.

Set 6B

1. We have $\mu = 10$, $\sigma = \sqrt{2.25} = 1.5$.

a. $P[x > 8.5] = P\left[\frac{x - \mu}{\sigma} > \frac{8.5 - 10}{1.5}\right] = P[z > -1]$

$$= .5000 + A(1) = .5000 + .3413 = .8413$$

b. $P[x < 12] = P\left[z < \frac{12 - 10}{1.5}\right] = P[z < 1.33] = .5000 + A(1.33)$

$$= .5000 + .4082 = .9082$$

c. $P[9.25 < x < 11.25] = P\left[\frac{9.25 - 10}{1.5} < z < \frac{11.25 - 10}{1.5}\right]$

$$= P[-.5 < z < .83] = .1915 + .2967 = .4882$$

d. $P[7.5 < x < 9.2] = P[-1.67 < z < -.53] = .4525 - .2019 = .2506$

e. $P[12.25 < x < 13.25] = P[1.5 < z < 2.17] = .4850 - .4332 = .0518$

2. The random variable of interest is x, the length of life for a standard household lightbulb. It is normally distributed with $\mu = 250$ and $\sigma = \sqrt{2500} = 50$.

a. $P[x > 300] = P\left[z > \dfrac{300 - 250}{50}\right] = P[z > 1] = .5000 - .3413 = .1587$

b. $P[190 < x < 270] = P[-1.2 < z < .4] = .3849 + .1554 = .5403$

c. $P[x < 260] = P[z < .2] = .5000 + .0793 = .5793$

d. It is necessary to find a value of x, say x_0, such that

$$P[x > x_0] = .90$$

Now,

$$P[x > x_0] = P\left[\frac{x - \mu}{\sigma} > \frac{x_0 - 250}{50}\right] = .90 \quad \text{so that}$$

$$P\left[z > \frac{x_0 - 250}{50}\right] = .5 + A\left(\frac{x_0 - 250}{50}\right) = .90 \quad \text{or}$$

$$A\left(\frac{x_0 - 250}{50}\right) = .40$$

By looking at a diagram, the student will notice that the value satisfying this equation must be negative. From Table 3, this value, $(x_0 - 250)/50$, is

$$\frac{x_0 - 250}{50} = -1.28$$

or $x_0 = -1.28(50) + 250 = 186$. Ninety percent of the bulbs have a useful life in excess of 186 hours.

e. Similar to part d. It is necessary to find x_0 such that $P[x < x_0] = .95$. Now,

$$P[x < x_0] = P\left[z < \frac{x_0 - 250}{50}\right] = .95$$

$$.5000 + A\left(\frac{x_0 - 250}{50}\right) = .95$$

$$A\left(\frac{x_0 - 250}{50}\right) = .45$$

Hence,

$$\frac{x_0 - 250}{50} = 1.645 \quad \text{or} \quad x_0 = 332.25$$

That is, 95% of all bulbs will burn out before 332.25 hours.

3. The random variable is x, scores on a personnel evaluation, and has a normal distribution with $\mu = 50$ and $\sigma = 5$.

   a. $P[x > 60] = P\left[z > \frac{60 - 50}{5}\right] = P[z > 2] = .5000 - .4772 = .0228$

   b. $P[x < 45] = P[z < -1] = .5000 - .3413 = .1587$

   c. $P[35 < x < 65] = P[-3 < z < 3] = .4987 + .4987 = .9974$

   d. It is necessary to find x_0 such that $P[x < x_0] = .95$. As in Exercise 2 e,

$$A\left(\frac{x_0 - 50}{5}\right) = .45$$

$$\frac{x_0 - 50}{5} = 1.645 \quad \text{or} \quad x_0 = 58.225$$

Set 6C

1. $n = 100, p = .15$, and the probability of interest is $P[x \geq 23]$. Since the probabilities associated with the values $x = 23, 24, \ldots, 100$ are needed, the area of interest is the area to the right of 22.5. Further, $\mu = np = 100(.15) = 15$, $\sigma^2 = npq = 100(.15)(.85) = 12.75$.

$$P[x \geq 23] \approx P[x > 22.5] = P\left[z > \frac{22.5 - 15}{\sqrt{12.75}}\right]$$

$$= P[z > 2.1] = .5000 - .4821 = .0179$$

   This event is one which we would expect to observe about two times in one hundred. It is a very unlikely event, given that $p = .15$. Perhaps the company is incorrect, and p is in fact greater than .15.

2. Let $p = P$[income is less than 22,000] = ½, since 22,000 is the median income. Also, $n = 100$, $\mu = np = 50$, $\sigma^2 = npq = 25$.

$$P[x \leq 37] \approx P[x < 37.5] = P\left[z < \frac{37.5 - 50}{5}\right]$$

$$= P[z < -2.5] = .5000 - .4938 = .0062$$

The observed event is highly unlikely under the assumption that \$22,000 is the median income. The \$22,000 figure does not seem reasonable.

3. $n = 100, p = .1, \mu = np = 10, \sigma^2 = npq = 9$. For a normal random variable, 95% of the measurements will be within the interval $\mu \pm 2\sigma$ and, using the normal approximation to the binomial, this should be true for the binomial random variable as well. Hence, $\mu \pm 2\sigma = 10 \pm 2(3)$ and the number of failures should lie between 4 and 16.

4. $n = 100, p = .25, \mu = 25, \sigma^2 = 18.75$.

$$P[x \geqslant 30] \approx P[x > 29.5] = P\left[z > \frac{29.5 - 25}{4.33}\right] = P[z > 1.04] = .1492$$

Set 6D

1. Since $b - a = .05 - (-.05) = .10$, $f(x) = 10$ for $-.05 \leqslant x \leqslant .05$.

   a. $P(x \geqslant .025) = (.05 - .025)/.10 = .25$

   b. $P(|x| \geqslant .025) = P(x \geqslant .025) + P(x \leqslant -.025)$

   $$= .25 + .25 = .50$$

   c. For the uniform distribution $\mu = \dfrac{-.05 + .05}{2} = 0$

   and $\sigma = .10/\sqrt{12} = .02887$

   so that $\mu \pm \sigma = 0 \pm .02887$ or $-.02887$ to $.02887$

   Then

   $$P(\mu - \sigma \leqslant x \leqslant \mu + \sigma) = \frac{2(.02887)}{.10} = .577$$

2. Since $\mu = 8$, $\lambda = 1/8$ and $f(x) = \frac{1}{8}e^{-x/8}$.

   a. $P(x < 8) = 1 - P(x \geqslant 8) = 1 - e^{-8/8} = 1 - e^{-1} = .63212$

   b. It is necessary to find x_0 such that

   $$P(x > x_0) = .05$$

   $$e^{-x_0/8} = .05$$

   Taking the natural logarithm of both sides,

   $$-x_0/8 = \ln .05$$

   $$x_0 = 8(2.9957) = 23.97$$

   c. It is necessary to find the median, m, such that

   $$P(x > m) = .5$$

   $$e^{-m/8} = .5$$

   $$\frac{m}{8} = -\ln .5$$

   $$m = 5.545$$

3. Since $\mu = 10$, $\lambda = 0.1$ and $f(x) = 0.1e^{-x/10}$

   a. $P(x > 15) = e^{-15/10} = e^{-1.5} = .223$

   b. $P(x < 5) + P(x > 15) = 1 - e^{-5/10} + e^{-1.5} = .616$

c. It is necessary to find x_0 such that

$$P(x < x_0) = .90 \quad \text{or} \quad P(x \geqslant x_0) = .10$$

Then $P(x \geqslant x_0) = e^{-x_0/10} = .10$

$$\frac{x_0}{10} = -\ln .10$$

$$x_0 = 23.03$$

4. a. $\mu = \dfrac{0+2}{2} = 1;\ \sigma = \dfrac{2-0}{\sqrt{12}} = .577$

b. $P(x \leqslant 1.5) = \dfrac{1.5}{2} = .75$

c. $P(.25 < x \leqslant 2) = (2 - .25)/2 = .875$

d. It is necessary to find x_0 such that

$$P(x \geqslant x_0) = .95$$

$$\frac{2 - x_0}{2} = .95$$

$x_0 = 2 - 2(.95) = .10$ hour or 6 minutes

Set 7A

1. Since there are $n = 2$ observations in each sample, the median will be the average of the two observations.

Sample #	1	2	3	4	5	6	7	8	9
Sample Median	3.25	3.25	3.5	3.5	4.5	3.5	3.75	3.75	4.75

Sample #	10	11	12	13	14	15
Sample Median	3.75	3.75	4.75	4.00	5.00	5.00

For $n = 2$, the sampling distribution of the median is identical to the sampling distribution of the mean.

m	$p(m)$
3.25	2/15
3.50	3/15
3.75	4/15
4.00	1/15
4.50	1/15
4.75	2/15
5.00	2/15

b. The sampling distribution is less variable than the original population.

c. For the population of size $N = 6$ the median is the measurement in the $.5(N + 1) = 3.5$ position, or $\frac{3.5 + 4}{2} = 3.75$. The expected value of the sample median is

$$E(m) = \Sigma mp(m) = 3.25\left(\frac{2}{15}\right) + \cdots + 5.00\left(\frac{2}{15}\right) = \frac{60}{15} = 4$$

which *does not* equal the population median.

2. When $n = 3$, there are $C_3^6 = 20$ possible samples, shown below with the corresponding value of $\bar{x}$.

Sample	*Sample Values*	$\bar{x}$	*Sample*	*Sample Values*	$\bar{x}$
1	3, 3.5, 3.5*	3.333	11	3.5, 3.5*, 4	3.667
2	3, 3.5, 4	3.500	12	3.5, 3.5*, 4*	3.667
3	3, 3.5, 4*	3.500	13	3.5, 3.5*, 6	4.333
4	3, 3.5, 6	4.167	14	3.5, 4, 4*	3.833
5	3, 3.5*, 4	3.500	15	3.5, 4, 6	4.500
6	3, 3.5*, 4*	3.500	16	3.5, 4*, 6	4.500
7	3, 3.5*, 6	4.167	17	3.5*, 4, 4*	3.833
8	3, 4, 4*	3.667	18	3.5*, 4, 6	4.500
9	3, 4, 6	4.333	19	3.5*, 4*, 6	4.500
10	3, 4*, 6	4.333	20	4, 4*, 6	4.667

The sampling distribution is shown below.

$\bar{x}$	$p(\bar{x})$
3.333	.05
3.500	.20
3.667	.15
3.833	.10
4.167	.10
4.333	.15
4.500	.20
4.667	.05

b. $E(\bar{x}) = 3.333(.05) + 3.500\,(.20) + \cdots + 4.667(.05) = 4.00$ which is the same as the population mean, $\mu = \frac{3 + 2(3.5) + 2(4) + 6}{6} = 4.$

c. $\sigma_{\bar{x}}^2 = \Sigma\bar{x}^2\,p(\bar{x}) - \mu_{\bar{x}}^2 = (3.333)^2(.05) + (3.500)^2(.20) + \cdots + (4.667)^2(.05) - 16 = .18333$ which is smaller than both σ_x^2 and $\sigma_{\bar{x}}^2$ for $n = 2$. As the sample size increases, the variability of $\bar{x}$ decreases.

3. With $n = 3$ and $N = 4$, there are $C_3^4 = 4$ samples, shown below with the associated values of s^2.

Sample	Sample Values	s^2
1	3, 4, 5	1.000
2	3, 4, 6	2.333
3	4, 5, 6	1.000
4	3, 5, 6	2.333

The probability distribution of s^2 is shown below.

s^2	$p(s^2)$
1	½
2.333	½

b. $E(s^2) = 1\left(\frac{1}{2}\right) + 2.333\left(\frac{1}{2}\right) = 1.6667$

c. $$\sigma^2 = \frac{\sum_{i=1}^{4}(x_i - \mu)^2}{N} = \frac{\Sigma x_i^2 - \frac{(\Sigma x_i)^2}{N}}{N} = \frac{86 - \frac{(18)^2}{4}}{4} = 1.25$$

For this finite population, $E(s^2) \neq \sigma^2$.

Set 7B

1. The weights of the rats will result from a combination of random factors, such as initial weight of the rat, genetic make-up of the rat, amount of food consumed, and so on. Hence the weights behave as a sum of independent random variables, and as such would be normally distributed according to the Central Limit Theorem.
2. Since $\bar{x}$ is normally distributed with mean $\mu = 60$ and with standard deviation $\sigma/\sqrt{n} = 10/\sqrt{30} = 1.8257$, the probability of interest is

$$P[\bar{x} > 65] = P\left[z > \frac{65 - 60}{1.8257}\right] = P[z > 2.74] = .5 - .4969 = .0031$$

3. a. $E(\bar{x}) = \mu = 4.0$

b. $\sigma_{\bar{x}}^2 = \frac{\sigma^2}{n}\left(\frac{N - n}{N - 1}\right) = \frac{.916667}{3}\left(\frac{6 - 3}{6 - 1}\right) = .18333$

c. Both results agree with those calculated directly in Exercise 2, SCE 7A.

Set 7C

1. a. $P(.8 \leqslant \hat{p} \leqslant .9) = P(16 \leqslant x \leqslant 18) = 1 - .994 = .006$ from Table 1.

b. Using the fact that $\mu_{\hat{p}} = p = .5$ and $\sigma_{\hat{p}} = \sqrt{\frac{pq}{n}} = \sqrt{\frac{.5(.5)}{20}} = .1118$,

$$P(.8 \leqslant \hat{p} \leqslant .9) = P\left(\frac{.8 - .5}{.1118} < z < \frac{.9 - .5}{.1118}\right) = P(2.68 < z < 3.58)$$

$$= .5 - .4963 = .0037$$

2. Let $p = P$[favor the canal]. Then $p = .3$ and $n = 50$, while $\mu_{\hat{p}} = p = .3$ and $\sigma_{\hat{p}} = \sqrt{\frac{pq}{n}} = \sqrt{\frac{.3(.7)}{50}} = .0648$. The probability of interest is

$$P(\hat{p} > .50) = P\left(z > \frac{.5 - .3}{.0648}\right) = P(z > 3.09) = .5 - .4990 = .001$$

Set 7D

1. The random variable $\bar{x}_1 - \bar{x}_2$ has an approximately normal distribution with mean $\mu_1 - \mu_2 = -5$ and variance $\frac{\sigma_1^2}{n_1} + \frac{\sigma_2^2}{n_2} = \frac{150}{35} + \frac{100}{35} = 7.14286$.

a. $P[\bar{x}_1 - \bar{x}_2 > 1] = P\left[z > \frac{1 - (-5)}{\sqrt{7.14286}}\right] = P[z > 2.24] = .5 - .4875 = .0125$

b. $P[0 \leqslant (\bar{x}_1 - \bar{x}_2) \leqslant 6] = P\left[\frac{0 - (-5)}{\sqrt{7.14286}} < z < \frac{6 - (-5)}{\sqrt{7.14286}}\right]$

$$= P[1.87 < z < 4.12] = .5 - .4693 = .0307$$

c. $P[(\bar{x}_1 - \bar{x}_2) > 2] + P[(\bar{x}_1 - \bar{x}_2) < -2] = P[z > 2.62] + P[z < 1.12]$

$$= .5 - .4956 + .5 + .3686 = .8730$$

2. The sampling distribution of $\hat{p}_1 - \hat{p}_2$ is approximately normal with mean $p_1 - p_2 = -.1$ and variance $\frac{p_1 q_1}{n_1} + \frac{p_2 q_2}{n_2} = \frac{.3(.7)}{100} + \frac{.4(.6)}{100} = .0045$.

a. $P[(\hat{p}_1 - \hat{p}_2) > .25] + P[(\hat{p}_1 - \hat{p}_2) < -.25] = P\left[z > \frac{.25 - (-.1)}{\sqrt{.0045}}\right]$

$$+ P\left[z > \frac{-.25 - (-.1)}{\sqrt{.0045}}\right] = P[z > 5.22]$$

$$+ P[z < -2.24] = .5 - .4875 = .0125$$

b. $P[\hat{p}_1 > \hat{p}_2] = P[\hat{p}_1 - \hat{p}_2 > 0] = P\left[z > \frac{0 - (-.1)}{\sqrt{.0045}}\right] = P[z > 1.49]$

$$= .5 - .4319 = .0681$$

Set 8A

1. $\hat{p} = \frac{x}{n} = \frac{25}{100} = .25$ with approximate bound on error $1.96\sqrt{\frac{\hat{p}\hat{q}}{n}} = 1.96\sqrt{\frac{.25(.75)}{100}}$

$= 1.96(.0433) = .085$

2. $\bar{x} = 89.50$ with approximate bound on error $1.96\frac{s}{\sqrt{n}} = 1.96\frac{(25.10)}{\sqrt{50}} = 6.96$

3. $\bar{x}_1 - \bar{x}_2 = 150.5 - 160.2 = -9.7$ with approximate bound on error

$$1.96\sqrt{\frac{s_1^2}{n_1} + \frac{s_2^2}{n_2}} = 1.96\sqrt{\frac{23.72}{35} + \frac{36.37}{35}} = 1.96\sqrt{1.7169} = 2.568$$

4. $\hat{p}_1 - \hat{p}_2 = \frac{x_1}{n_1} - \frac{x_2}{n_2} = \frac{31}{204} - \frac{41}{191} = .15 - .21 = -.06$

Approximate bound on error: $1.96\sqrt{\frac{\hat{p}_1\hat{q}_1}{n_1} + \frac{\hat{p}_2\hat{q}_2}{n_2}} = 1.96\sqrt{.000625 + .000869}$

$= 1.96(.039) = .076$

Set 8B

1. $\bar{x} \pm z_{\alpha/2}\frac{s}{\sqrt{n}}$; $18{,}750 \pm 1.96\frac{3050}{\sqrt{50}}$; $18{,}750 \pm 845.54$; or \$17,904.46 to \$19,595.54

2. a. $\hat{p} = \frac{x}{n} = \frac{86}{200} = .43$ with approximate bound on error,

$$1.96\sqrt{\frac{\hat{p}\,\hat{q}}{n}} = 1.96\sqrt{\frac{.43(.57)}{200}} = 1.96(.035) = .07$$

b. $\hat{p} \pm z_{\alpha/2}\sqrt{\frac{\hat{p}\,\hat{q}}{n}}$; $.43 \pm 1.645\sqrt{\frac{.43(.57)}{200}}$; $.43 \pm .058$; or $.372$ to $.488$

3. a. Of the total number of accidents (32 + 41 = 73), 23 involved injury and \$400 or more damage. Hence,

$$\hat{p} = \frac{x}{n} = \frac{23}{73} = .32$$

The 95% confidence interval is $\hat{p} \pm z_{\alpha/2}\sqrt{\dfrac{\hat{p}\,\hat{q}}{n}}$

$$.32 \pm 1.96\sqrt{\frac{.32(.68)}{73}}$$

$$.32 \pm .11 \quad \text{or} \quad .21 \text{ to } .43$$

b. $\hat{p}_1 = \dfrac{10}{32} = .31, \quad \hat{p}_2 = .56$

$$(\hat{p}_1 - \hat{p}_2) \pm 1.96\sqrt{\frac{\hat{p}_1\hat{q}_1}{n_1} + \frac{\hat{p}_2\hat{q}_2}{n_2}}$$

$$-.25 \pm 1.96\sqrt{\frac{.31(.69)}{32} + \frac{.56(.44)}{41}}$$

$$-.25 \pm .22 \quad \text{or} \quad -.47 \text{ to } -.03$$

4. a. $(\bar{x}_1 - \bar{x}_2) \pm z_{\alpha/2}\sqrt{\dfrac{s_1^2}{n_1} + \dfrac{s_2^2}{n_2}}$

$$(20520 - 19210) \pm 2.58\sqrt{\frac{(1510)^2}{90} + \frac{(950)^2}{60}}$$

$$1310 \pm 2.58\,(200.938)$$

$$1310 \pm 518.42 \quad \text{or} \quad 791.58 \text{ to } 1828.42$$

b. If the two plants belonged to populations having the same mean annual income, then $\mu_1 = \mu_2$, or $\mu_1 - \mu_2 = 0$. This value of $\mu_1 - \mu_2$ does not fall in the confidence interval obtained above. Hence, it is unlikely that the two plants belong to populations having the same mean annual income.

Set 8C

1. The estimator of μ is $\bar{x}$, with standard deviation $\sigma/\sqrt{n}$. Hence, solve

$$1.96\,\sigma/\sqrt{n} = B, \quad 1.96\,\frac{8}{\sqrt{n}} = 3, \quad \sqrt{n} = \frac{15.68}{3}, \quad n = 27.32$$

The experimenter should obtain $n = 28$ measurements.

Alternatively, using the sample size formula,

$$n = \frac{(1.96)^2(64)}{9} = 27.32$$

2. The estimator of p is $\hat{p} = x/n$ with standard deviation $\sqrt{pq/n}$. Since it is given that $0 \leqslant p \leqslant .1$, maximum variation will occur when $p = .1$ and the sample size must be large enough to account for this maximum variation. Hence, solve

$$1.96\sqrt{\frac{pq}{n}} = B, \quad 1.96\sqrt{\frac{.1(.9)}{n}} = .01, \quad \sqrt{n} = \frac{.588}{.01}, \quad n = 3457.44$$

or 3458 items should be sampled.

3. For each subsidiary, the range of overtime hours is 150, so that $\sigma_1 \approx \sigma_2 \approx \text{Range}/4 = 37.5$. Hence, assuming equal sample sizes are acceptable, solve

$$1.96\sqrt{\frac{\sigma_1^2}{n} + \frac{\sigma_2^2}{n}} = 10, \quad 1.96\sqrt{\frac{2(37.5)^2}{n}} = 10$$

$$\sqrt{n} = \frac{\sqrt{2812.5}}{5.102}, \quad n = 108.045$$

Hence, 109 weekly records from each subsidiary should be checked.

4. Maximum variation occurs when $p_1 = p_2 = .5$. Again assuming equal sample sizes, solve

$$n = \frac{z_{.025}^2(2)(.25)}{(.01)^2} = \frac{(1.96)^2(.5)}{.0001} = 19208$$

Set 8D

1. $H_0: p = .5 \quad H_a: p > .5$ Test statistic: $z = \dfrac{\hat{p} - p_0}{\sqrt{\dfrac{p_0 q_0}{n}}}$

With $\alpha = .05$, reject H_0 if $z > 1.645$. Since $\hat{p} = \frac{34}{65} = .52$,

$$z = \frac{.52 - .50}{\sqrt{\frac{.5(.5)}{65}}} = \frac{.02}{.062} = .32$$

H_0 is not rejected. There is insufficient evidence to conclude that the proportion favoring the merger is greater than .5.

2. $H_0: \mu_1 - \mu_2 = 0$ $H_a: \mu_1 - \mu_2 \neq 0$ Test statistic: $z = \dfrac{(\bar{x}_1 - \bar{x}_2) - 0}{\sqrt{\dfrac{s_1^2}{n_1} + \dfrac{s_2^2}{n_2}}}$

With $\alpha = .01$, reject H_0 if $|z| > 2.58$. Calculate

$$z = \frac{21.1 - 18.0}{\sqrt{\dfrac{(3.5)^2}{30} + \dfrac{(4.2)^2}{40}}} = \frac{3.1}{\sqrt{.8493}} = \frac{3.1}{.92} = 3.37$$

H_0 is rejected. There is a significant difference in the mean assembly times for these two methods.

3. $H_0: p_1 - p_2 = 0$ $H_a: p_1 - p_2 \neq 0$ Test statistic: $z = \dfrac{(\hat{p}_1 - \hat{p}_2) - 0}{\sqrt{\hat{p}\hat{q}\left(\dfrac{1}{n_1} + \dfrac{1}{n_2}\right)}}$

Note that if $p_1 = p_2$ as proposed under H_0, the best estimate of this common value of p is

$$\hat{p} = \frac{x_1 + x_2}{n_1 + n_2} = \frac{160 + 90}{400 + 250} = \frac{250}{650} = .38$$

With $\alpha = .05$, reject H_0 if $|z| > 1.96$. Calculate

$$z = \frac{\dfrac{160}{400} - \dfrac{90}{250}}{\sqrt{.38(.62)\left(\dfrac{1}{400} + \dfrac{1}{250}\right)}} = \frac{.04}{\sqrt{.0015314}} = \frac{.04}{.039} = 1.03$$

H_0 is not rejected. There is insufficient evidence to conclude that there is a difference in the proportions for Cities 1 and 2.

4. $H_0: \mu = 25$ $H_a: \mu > 25$ Test statistic: $z = \dfrac{\bar{x} - \mu_0}{\sigma/\sqrt{n}}$

With $\alpha = .01$, reject H_0 if $z > 2.33$. It is given that $\sigma = 3$ for the normal inspection procedure. Hence,

$$z = \frac{29 - 25}{3/\sqrt{30}} = \frac{4}{.548} = 7.30$$

H_0 is rejected. The first inspector is not working up to company standards.

Set 8E

1. p-value $= P[z > .32] = .5 - .1255 = .3745$. Since this is a relatively high value, it would probably be unacceptable as an α value. The researcher would probably not reject H_0.

2. p-value $= P[|z| > 3.37] = 2P[z > 3.37] \leqslant 2(.5 - .499) = .002$. This is a very small value. Hence, we reject H_0 for any α as small as .002.

3. Calculate $\Sigma x_i = 73$, $\Sigma x_i^2 = 235$, $\bar{x} = 2.433$, $s^2 = 1.978$.

$$H_0: \mu = 3.75; \quad H_a: \mu \neq 3.75$$

Test statistic:

$$z \approx \frac{\bar{x} - \mu}{s/\sqrt{n}} = \frac{2.433 - 3.75}{\sqrt{\dfrac{1.978}{30}}} = -5.13$$

p-value $= 2P[z > 5.13] < 2(.001) = .002$. Since this value is very small, we reject H_0 for any α as small as .002.

Set 9A

1. $\Sigma x_i = 131.8, \quad \Sigma x_i^2 = 2487.9, \quad \bar{x} = \dfrac{\Sigma x_i}{n} = \dfrac{131.8}{7} = 18.8$

$$s^2 = \frac{2487.9 - \dfrac{(131.8)^2}{7}}{6} = \frac{6.2943}{6} = 1.049 \qquad s = \sqrt{1.049} = 1.024$$

a. $\bar{x} \pm t_{.025}\dfrac{s}{\sqrt{n}}, \quad 18.8 \pm 2.447\dfrac{1.024}{\sqrt{7}}, \quad 18.8 \pm .95$ or 17.85 to 19.75

b. $H_0: \mu = 17.5 \quad H_a: \mu > 17.5$ Test statistic: $t = \dfrac{\bar{x} - \mu}{s/\sqrt{n}}$

With $\alpha = .05$ and $n - 1 = 6$ degrees of freedom, reject H_0 if $t > t_{.05} = 1.943$. Calculate

$$t = \frac{18.8 - 17.5}{1.024/\sqrt{7}} = \frac{1.3}{.39} = 3.33$$

H_0 is rejected. The modification has significantly increased the average number of miles per gallon at the $\alpha = .05$ level of significance. p-value = $P[t > 3.33] < .01$ but greater than .005. Hence, $.005 < (p\text{-value}) < .01$.

2. a. $H_0: \mu = .050 \quad H_a: \mu > .050$ Test statistic: $t = \dfrac{\bar{x} - \mu}{s/\sqrt{n}}$

With $\alpha = .01$ and $n - 1 = 24$ degrees of freedom, reject H_0 if $t > t_{.01} = 2.492$. Calculate

$$t = \frac{.057 - .050}{.008/\sqrt{25}} = \frac{.007\,(5)}{.008} = 4.375$$

H_0 is rejected. Wednesday's production has an excess amount of impurities.

b. $\bar{x} \pm t_{.025}\dfrac{s}{\sqrt{n}}, \quad .057 \pm 2.064\dfrac{.008}{5}, \quad .057 \pm .0033$ or .0537 to .0603

Set 9B

1. See Section 9.4, paragraph 1.

2. $H_0: \mu_1 - \mu_2 = 0 \quad H_a: \mu_1 - \mu_2 \neq 0$ Test statistic: $t = \dfrac{(\bar{x}_1 - \bar{x}_2) - D_0}{s\sqrt{\dfrac{1}{n_1} + \dfrac{1}{n_2}}}$

With $\alpha = .05$ and $n_1 + n_2 - 2 = 10 + 8 - 2 = 16$ degrees of freedom, reject H_0 if $|t| > t_{.025} = 2.120$. Calculate

$$s^2 = \frac{(n_1 - 1)s_1^2 + (n_2 - 1)s_2^2}{n_1 + n_2 - 2} = \frac{9(1.1)^2 + 7(2.2)^2}{16} = \frac{10.89 + 33.88}{16}$$

$$= 2.798$$

$$t = \frac{(6.3 - 7.2) - 0}{\sqrt{2.798\left(\dfrac{1}{10} + \dfrac{1}{8}\right)}} = \frac{-.9}{.793} = -1.13$$

Do not reject H_0. There is insufficient evidence to conclude that the two teams are significantly different.

3. a. $H_0: \mu_1 - \mu_2 = 0 \quad H_a: \mu_1 - \mu_2 \neq 0$ Test statistic: $t = \dfrac{(\bar{x}_1 - \bar{x}_2) - D_0}{s\sqrt{\dfrac{1}{n_1} + \dfrac{1}{n_2}}}$

With $\alpha = .05$ and $n_1 + n_2 - 2 = 28$ degrees of freedom, reject H_0 if $|t| > t_{.025} = 2.048$. Calculate

$$s^2 = \frac{14(6.2)^2 + 14(9.3)^2}{28} = 62.47$$

$$t = \frac{(80.3 - 68.7) - 0}{\sqrt{62.47\left(\frac{1}{15} + \frac{1}{15}\right)}} = \frac{11.6}{2.89} = 4.01$$

Reject H_0. There is a significant difference in mean scores for the two presentations.

b. $(\bar{x}_1 - \bar{x}_2) \pm t_{.025}\, s\sqrt{\frac{1}{n_1} + \frac{1}{n_2}}$, $11.6 \pm 2.048\,(2.89)$, 11.6 ± 5.92

or $5.68 < \mu_1 - \mu_2 < 17.52$. Since it is possible that $(\mu_1 - \mu_2) < 10$ according to the confidence interval, approval should not be given for campaign number one to proceed to the next stage.

c. $p\text{-value} = P[|t| > 4.01] = 2P[t > 4.01] < 2(.005) = .01$

Set 9C

1. $H_0: \mu_d = \mu_P - \mu_H = 0 \quad H_a: \mu_d = \mu_P - \mu_H < 0$ Test statistic: $t = \dfrac{\bar{d} - \mu_d}{s_d/\sqrt{n}}$

With $\alpha = .05$ and $n - 1 = 10 - 1 = 9$ degrees of freedom, reject H_0 if $t < -t_{.05} = -1.833$. The 10 differences and the calculation of the test statistic are given below.

d_i	d_i^2
-5	25
-2	4
4	16
-3	9
-3	9
1	1
-1	1
0	0
-5	25
1	1
-13	91

$$\bar{d} = \frac{-13}{10} = -1.3 \quad s_d^2 = \frac{91 - \frac{(-13)^2}{10}}{9} = \frac{74.1}{9} = 8.2333$$

$$s_d = \sqrt{8.2333} = 2.869$$

$$t = \frac{-1.3 - 0}{2.869/\sqrt{10}} = -1.43$$

Do not reject H_0.

2.

d_i	d_i^2
4.6	21.16
1.8	3.24
-1.0	1.00
2.2	13.84
1.0	1.00
1.2	1.44
2.6	6.76
2.8	7.84
2.0	4.00
3.0	9.00
20.2	69.28

$$\bar{d} = \frac{20.2}{10} = 2.02 \quad s_d^2 = \frac{69.28 - 40.804}{9} = \frac{28.476}{9} = 3.164$$

$s_d = 1.78$

a. $\bar{d} \pm t_{.025} \dfrac{s_d}{\sqrt{n}}$, $2.02 \pm 2.262 \dfrac{1.78}{\sqrt{10}}$,

2.02 ± 1.27 or $.75 < \mu_d < 3.29$

b. $H_0: \mu_P - \mu_H = 0 \quad H_a: \mu_P - \mu_H > 0$

Test statistic: $t = \dfrac{\bar{d} - \mu_d}{s_d/\sqrt{n}}$

With $\alpha = .05$ and $n - 1 = 10$ degrees of freedom, reject H_0 if $t > t_{.05} = 1.833$. Calculate

$$t = \frac{2.02}{.563} = 3.59$$

Reject H_0. Per-unit scale increases production.

Set 9D

1. $H_0: \sigma = 3(\sigma^2 = 9)$; $H_a: \sigma < 3(\sigma^2 < 9)$.

Test statistic: $\chi^2 = (n - 1)s^2/\sigma_0^2$

With $\alpha = .05$ and $n - 1 = 4$ degrees of freedom, reject H_0 if $\chi^2 < \chi^2_{.95} = .710721$. Calculate

$$s^2 = \frac{\Sigma x_i^2 - (\Sigma x_i)^2/n}{n - 1} = \frac{1{,}930.5 - 1{,}905.152}{4}$$

$$= 6.337$$

$\chi^2 = 25.348/9 = 2.816$. Do not reject H_0.

2. $H_0: \sigma^2 = 100$; $H_a: \sigma^2 < 100$.

Test statistic: $\chi^2 = (n - 1)s^2/\sigma_0^2$

With $\alpha = .05$ and $n - 1 = 29$ degrees of freedom, reject H_0 if $\chi^2 < \chi^2_{.95} = 17.7083$. Calculate

$$\chi^2 = 29(8.9)^2/100 = 22.97$$

Do not reject H_0. From Table 5 with 29 degrees of freedom, $\chi^2 = 22.97$ exceeds $\chi^2_{.90}$. Hence, p-value $> .10$.

3. a. $H_0: \sigma = 5$; $H_a: \sigma > 5$.

   Test statistic: $\chi^2 = (n-1)s^2/\sigma_0^2$

   With $\alpha = .05$, reject H_0 if $\chi^2 > 42.5569$. Since $\chi^2 = 29(7.3)^2/25 = 61.81$, reject H_0. The new technique is less sensitive.

   b. $$\frac{(n-1)s^2}{\chi^2_U} < \sigma^2 < \frac{(n-1)s^2}{\chi^2_L}$$

   $$\frac{29(7.3)^2}{45.7222} < \sigma^2 < \frac{29(7.3)^2}{16.0471}$$

   $$33.80 < \sigma^2 < 96.30, \quad 5.81 < \sigma < 9.81$$

Set 9E

1. $H_0: \sigma_1^2 = \sigma_2^2$; $H_a: \sigma_1^2 \neq \sigma_2^2$. Test statistic: $F = s_1^2/s_2^2$, where population 1 is the population of distances for people wanting the center closed. With $\alpha = .02$ and $\nu_1 = 8$, $\nu_2 = 15$, reject H_0 if $F > 4.00$ from Table 6.

   $$F = (5.3)^2/(2.8)^2 = 28.09/7.84 = 3.58$$

   Do not reject H_0.

2. $H_0: \sigma_1^2 = \sigma_2^2$; $H_a: \sigma_1^2 \neq \sigma_2^2$; Test statistic: $F = s_1^2/s_2^2$, where population 1 represent commodity 2. With $\alpha = .10$ and $\nu_1 = \nu_2 = 9$, reject H_0 if $F > 3.18$. Calculate

   $$F = \frac{(2.49)^2}{(1.59)^2} = 2.45$$

   Do not reject H_0. The commodities exhibit the same basic variation.

Set 10A

1. $CM = \dfrac{(93.8)^2}{15} = 586.5627$; Total $SS = 596.26 - CM = 9.6973$

   $$SST = \frac{32.3^2 + 28.2^2 + 33.3^2}{5} - CM = 589.484 - CM = 2.9213$$

$SSE = 9.6973 - 2.9213 = 6.7760$

ANOVA

Source	*d.f.*	*SS*	*MS*	*F*
Treatments	2	2.9213	1.4607	2.5867
Error	12	6.7760	.5647	
Total	14	9.6973		

a. $H_0: \mu_1 = \mu_2 = \mu_3$ Test statistic: $F = \dfrac{MST}{MSE}$

H_a: at least one of the equalities is incorrect.

With $\nu_1 = 2$ and $\nu_2 = 12$ degrees of freedom, reject H_0 if $F > F_{.05} = 3.89$. Since $F = 2.5867$, do not reject H_0. We cannot find a significant difference.

b. $$(\bar{T}_2 - \bar{T}_3) \pm t_{.025}\sqrt{MSE\left(\frac{1}{n_2} + \frac{1}{n_3}\right)} = (5.64 - 6.66) \pm 2.179\sqrt{\frac{2(.5647)}{5}}$$

$$= -1.02 \pm 2.179(.4753) = -1.02 \pm 1.04 \quad \text{or}$$

$$-2.06 < \mu_2 - \mu_3 < .02 \quad \text{with 95\% confidence.}$$

2. a. $F = 4.78 > F_{.05} = 3.71$. Reject H_0. There is a difference in mean time to assemble for the four lengths of time.

b. $$(\bar{T}_2 - \bar{T}_4) \pm t_{.025}\sqrt{MSE\left(\frac{1}{n_2} + \frac{1}{n_4}\right)} = (7 - 5.33) \pm 2.228\sqrt{4.4167\left(\frac{2}{3}\right)}$$

$$= 1.67 \pm 2.228(1.7159) = 1.67 \pm 3.82 \quad \text{or} \quad -2.15 < \mu_2 - \mu_4 < 5.49$$

c. $$(7 - 6.25) \pm 2.228\sqrt{4.4167\left(\frac{1}{3} + \frac{1}{4}\right)} = .75 \pm 2.228(1.6051) = .75 \pm 3.58$$

$$\text{or} \quad -2.83 < \mu_2 - \mu_3 < 4.33$$

Set 10B

1. a. $F = 7.82 > 3.44$. Reject H_0. There is a significant difference between conditions.

b. $F = 2.94 > F_{.05} = 2.27$. Reject H_0. There is a significant difference between employees. Blocking was effective.

c. $(\bar{T}_2 - \bar{T}_3) \pm t_{.025}\sqrt{MSE\left(\frac{2}{b}\right)} = (14.33 - 20.42) \pm 2.074\sqrt{14.7551\left(\frac{2}{12}\right)}$

$= -6.09 \pm 2.074(1.5682) = -6.09 \pm 3.25$ or

$-9.34 < \mu_2 - \mu_3 < 2.84$

2. $CM = \dfrac{(83.4)^2}{20} = 347.778$; Total $SS = 358.5 - CM = 10.722$

$$SST = \frac{(19.1)^2 + (21.9)^2 + (20.9)^2 + (21.5)^2}{5} - CM = 348.696 - CM = 0.918$$

$$SSB = \frac{(15.8)^2 + (18.3)^2 + (12.8)^2 + (20.9)^2 + (15.6)^2}{4} - CM$$

$= 357.135 - CM = 9.357$

$SSE = 10.722 - .918 - 9.357 = .447$

ANOVA

Source	*d.f.*	*SS*	*MS*	*F*
Brands	3	0.918	.306	8.215
Areas	4	9.357	2.339	62.799
Error	12	0.447	.037	
Total	19	10.722		

a. $F = \dfrac{MS \text{ Brands}}{MSE} = 8.215 > 3.49$ $\qquad F = \dfrac{MS \text{ Areas}}{MSE} = 62.799 > 3.26$

Both areas and brands are significant.

b. $(4.38 - 4.18) \pm 2.179\sqrt{\frac{2}{5}(.037)} = .20 \pm 2.179(.122) = .20 \pm .27$ or

$-.07 < \mu_2 - \mu_4 < .47$

c. $(3.95 - 5.23) \pm 2.179\sqrt{\frac{2}{4}(.037)} = -1.28 \pm 2.179(.136) = -1.28 \pm .30$

or $-1.58 < \mu_{A1} - \mu_{A4} < -.98$

Set 10C

1. a. The experiment is a 3 X 3 factorial, with 4 replicates per treatment combination, in a completely randomized experimental design.

   b. $CM = \dfrac{(2859)^2}{36} = 227{,}052.25$; $TSS = 229{,}557 - CM = 2504.75$

   $$SS\text{ (Fungicide)} = \frac{2{,}740{,}145}{12} - CM = 228{,}345.4167 - CM = 1293.1667$$

   $$SS\text{ (Variety)} = \frac{2{,}733{,}113}{12} - CM = 277{,}759.416 - CM = 707.1667$$

   $$SS\ (V \times F) = \frac{916{,}441}{4} - CM - SSF - SSV = 57.6667$$

   $$SSE = TSS - SSF - SSV - SS\ (VF) = 446.75$$

Source	*df*	*SS*	*MS*	*F*
V	2	707.1667	353.58	21.37
F	2	1293.1667	646.59	39.08
V × *F*	4	57.6667	14.4175	.8713
Error	27	446.7500	16.5462963	
Total	35	2504.7500		

   c. The test for interaction is $F = \dfrac{MS(VF)}{MSE} = .8713$, which is not significant ($F_{.05} = 2.73$). Hence, we can investigate the differences between treatments or between varieties separately.

   d. The test for differences between the three varieties is $F = \dfrac{MSV}{MSE} = 21.37$, while the test for differences between fungicide treatments is $F = \dfrac{MSF}{MSE} = 39.08$. Both are significant at $\alpha = .05$ ($F_{.05} = 3.35$). Hence, the germination rate is affected both by the type of bean and the type of fungicide treatment.

2. a. The experiment is a 3 X 2 factorial, with 5 replicates per treatment combination, in a completely randomized experimental design.

   b. $CM = \dfrac{(183)^2}{30} = 1116.3$; $TSS = 1179 - CM = 62.7$

   $$SS\text{ (HMO)} = \frac{16889}{15} - CM = 1125.9333 - CM = 9.6333$$

$$SS\text{ (Dept)} = \frac{11{,}309}{10} - CM = 1130.9 - CM = 14.6000$$

$$SS\ (H \times D) = \frac{5753}{5} - CM - SSH - SSD = 10.0667$$

$$SSE = TSS - SSH - SSD - SS(HD) = 28.4000$$

Source	*df*	*SS*	*MS*	*F*
H	1	9.6333	9.6333	8.138
D	2	14.6000	7.3000	6.17
$H \times D$	2	10.0667	5.0333	4.25
Error	24	28.4000	1.1833	
Total	29	62.7000		

c. The test for interaction is $F = \frac{MS(HD)}{MSE} = 4.25$, which is significant at $\alpha = .05$ ($F_{.05} = 3.40$).

d. Since the interaction is significant, the ratings for the three departments behave differently in one *HMO* than the other. Hence, main effects need not be considered. Attention should be focused on the mean ratings for the six treatment combinations.

e. *Pediatrics:* $(\bar{x}_1 - \bar{x}_2) \pm t_{.025}\sqrt{MSE}\sqrt{\frac{1}{5} + \frac{1}{5}}$

$$(5.8 - 8.2) \pm 2.064\sqrt{1.1833}\sqrt{\frac{2}{5}} = -2.4 \pm 1.42$$

OB/GYN: $(6.2 - 5.8) \pm 2.064\sqrt{1.1833}\sqrt{\frac{1}{5} + \frac{1}{5}} = 0.4 \pm 1.42$

Family Practice: $(4.6 - 6.0) \pm 2.064\sqrt{1.1833}\sqrt{\frac{1}{5} + \frac{1}{5}} = -1.4 \pm 1.42$

Set 11A

1. a.

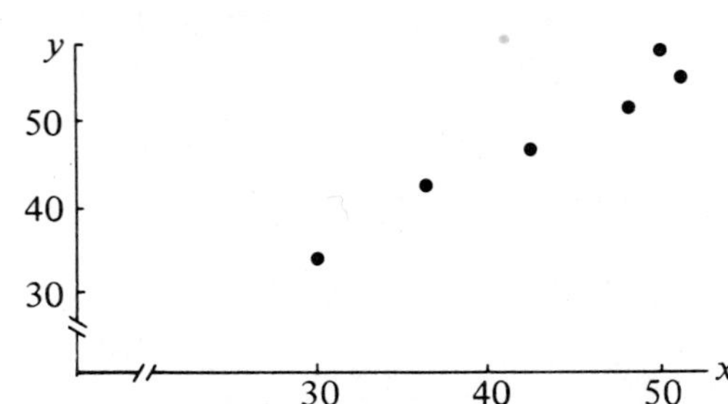

The trend appears to be linear.

b. $\Sigma x_i = 256$ $\quad \Sigma x_i y_i = 12608$

$\Sigma y_i = 286$ $\quad n = 6$

$\Sigma x_i^2 = 11294$ $\quad \Sigma y_i^2 = 14096$

$$S_{xy} = 12608 - 12202.667 = 405.333$$

$$S_{xx} = 11294 - 10922.667 = 371.333$$

$$\hat{\beta}_1 = \frac{S_{xy}}{S_{xx}} = \frac{405.333}{371.333} = 1.09$$

$$\hat{\beta}_0 = \frac{286}{6} - 1.09\left(\frac{256}{6}\right) = 47.6667 - 46.5067 = 1.16$$

$$\hat{y} = 1.16 + 1.09x$$

c. $\hat{y} = 1.16 + 1.09(50) = 55.66$ or 5566 students.

2. a. $\Sigma x_i = 31.6$ $\quad \Sigma x_i y_i = 624.6$ $\quad S_{xy} = 624.6 - 609.429 = 15.171$

$\Sigma y_i = 135$ $\quad n = 7$ $\quad S_{xx} = 149.82 - 142.651 = 7.169$

$\Sigma x_i^2 = 149.82$ $\quad \Sigma y_i^2 = 2645$

$$\hat{\beta}_1 = \frac{15.171}{7.169} = 2.12$$

$$\hat{\beta}_0 = 19.29 - 2.12(4.51) = 9.73$$

$$\hat{y} = 9.73 + 2.12x$$

b.

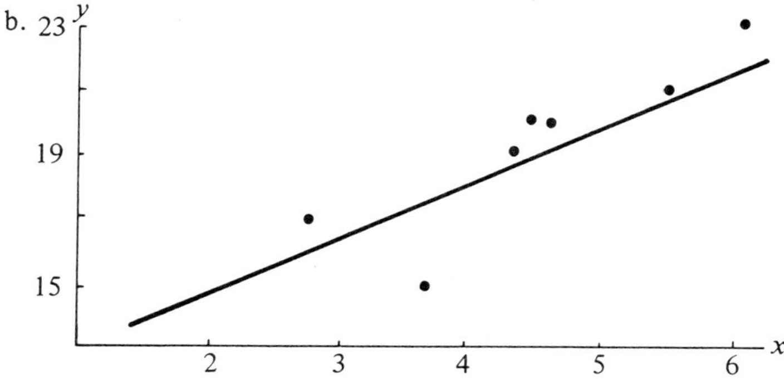

3. a. $\Sigma x_i = 96$ $\quad \Sigma x_i y_i = 1799$ $\quad S_{xy} = 1799 - 1851.429 = -52.429$

$\Sigma y_i = 135$ $\quad n = 7$ $\quad S_{xx} = 1402 - 1316.571 = 85.429$

$\Sigma x_i^2 = 1402$ $\quad \Sigma y_i^2 = 2645$ $\quad \hat{\beta}_1 = -0.61$

$\hat{\beta}_0 = 19.29 - (-.61)(13.71) = 27.65$

$\hat{y} = 27.65 - .61x$

b.

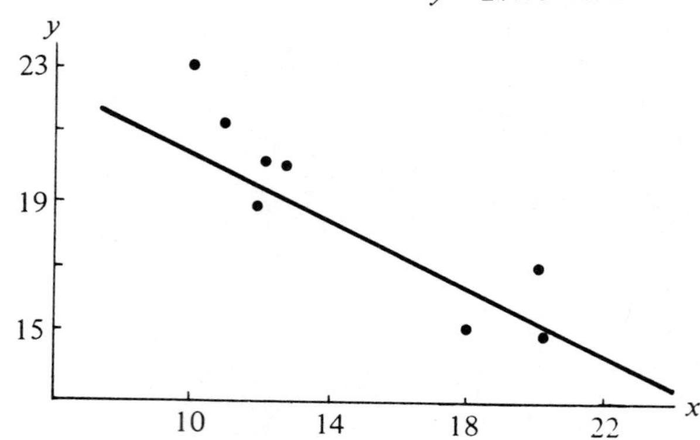

Set 11B

1. $S_{yy} = 14096 - 13632.667 = 463.333$

$SSE = S_{yy} - \hat{\beta}_1 S_{xy} = 463.333 - (1.09)(405.333) = 20.87$

Note that the unrounded value of $\hat{\beta}_1$ has been used for the sake of accuracy.

$s^2 = \dfrac{20.87}{4} = 5.22 \quad s = \sqrt{5.22} = 2.28$

a. $H_0: \beta_1 = 0 \qquad H_a: \beta_1 \neq 0 \qquad$ Reject H_0 if $|t| > t_{.025,4} = 2.776$

Test statistic: $t = \dfrac{\hat{\beta}_1 - \beta_1}{s/\sqrt{S_{xx}}} = \dfrac{1.09}{\sqrt{\dfrac{5.22}{371.33}}} = \dfrac{1.09}{.12} = 9.08$. Reject H_0.

b. $\hat{\beta}_1 \pm t_{.025} \dfrac{s}{\sqrt{S_{xx}}} = 1.09 \pm 2.776(.12) = 1.09 \pm .33$

or $\quad .76 < \beta_1 < 1.42$

2. $S_{yy} = 2645 - 2603.571 = 41.429$

$SSE = 41.429 - 2.12(15.171) = 9.33$

$s^2 = \dfrac{9.33}{5} = 1.87 \qquad s = \sqrt{1.87} = 1.37$

$H_0: \beta_1 = 0 \qquad H_a: \beta_1 \neq 0$

Rejection region: With 5 degrees of freedom and $\alpha = .05$, reject H_0 if $|t| > t_{.025} = 2.571$

Test statistic: $t = \dfrac{\hat{\beta}_1 - 0}{s/\sqrt{S_{xx}}} = \dfrac{2.12}{\sqrt{\dfrac{1.87}{7.17}}} = \dfrac{2.12}{.51} = 4.16$

Reject H_0.

3. $S_{yy} = 2645 - 2603.571 = 41.429$

$SSE = 41.429 - (-0.61)(-52.429) = 9.25$

$s^2 = \dfrac{9.25}{5} = 1.85 \qquad s = 1.36$

$H_0: \beta_1 = 0 \qquad H_a: \beta_1 \neq 0$

Reject H_0 if $|t| > t_{.025,5} = 2.571$

$t = \dfrac{-.61 - 0}{\sqrt{\dfrac{1.85}{85.43}}} = \dfrac{-.61}{.15} = -4.067 \qquad$ Reject H_0.

Set 11C

1. $H_0: E(y \text{ when } x = 0) = 0$ Test statistic: $t = \dfrac{\hat{y} - E_0}{s\sqrt{\dfrac{1}{n} + \dfrac{(x_p - \bar{x})^2}{S_{xx}}}}$

$H_a: E(y \text{ when } x = 0) \neq 0$

Rejection region: With $\alpha = .05$, reject H_0 if $|t| > t_{.025} = 2.776$. Calculate:

$\hat{y} = 1.16 + 1.09(0) = 1.16$

$t = \dfrac{1.16 - 0}{\sqrt{5.22\left\{\dfrac{1}{7} + \dfrac{(42.67)^2}{371.33}\right\}}} = \dfrac{1.16}{\sqrt{26.34}} = \dfrac{1.16}{5.13} = .226$

Do not reject H_0. Note that $\hat{y} = 1.16 + 1.09x$ does not pass through the origin, even though we could not reject the hypothesis, $H_0: E(y \text{ when } x = 0) = \beta_0 = 0$. We would not expect that it would though, with only 6 observations, due to random variation.

2. $(\hat{y} \text{ when } x = 4.5) = 9.73 + 2.12(4.5) = 9.73 + 9.54 = 19.27$

$$\hat{\sigma}^2_{\hat{y}} = 1.87\left\{\frac{1}{7} + \frac{(4.50 - 4.51)^2}{7.17}\right\}$$

$$= 1.87(.14) = .2618$$

The 90% confidence interval is $\hat{y} \pm t_{.05}\sqrt{\hat{\sigma}^2_{\hat{y}}}$

$$= 19.27 \pm 2.015\sqrt{.2618}$$

$$= 19.27 \pm 1.03$$

or $18.24 < E(y \text{ when } x = 4.5) < 20.30$.
Since $x = 250$ is outside the limits for the observed x, one should not predict for that value.

3. If $x = 12$, $\hat{y} = 27.65 - .61(12) = 20.33$;

$$\hat{\sigma}^2_{\hat{y}} = 1.85\left[\frac{1}{7} + \frac{(12 - 13.71)^2}{85.43}\right] = 1.85(.18) = .33$$

The 90% confidence interval is

$$20.33 \pm 2.015\sqrt{.33} = 20.33 \pm 2.015(.57) = 20.33 \pm 1.15 \quad \text{or}$$

$$19.18 < E(y \mid x = 0) < 21.48$$

Note that this interval predicts a slightly higher expected yield.

4. If $x = 40$, $\hat{y} = 1.16 + 1.09(40) = 44.76$;

$$\hat{\sigma}^2_{\hat{y}} = 5.22\left[\frac{1}{6} + \frac{(40 - 42.67)^2}{371.33}\right] = 5.22(.19) = .99$$

The 95% confidence interval is

$$44.76 \pm 2.776\sqrt{.99} = 44.76 \pm 2.776 \quad \text{or}$$

$$41.98 < E(y \text{ when } x = 40) < 47.54$$

Enrollment will be between 4198 and 4754 with 95% confidence.

Set 11D

1. a. Total $SS = \Sigma y_i^2 - \dfrac{(\Sigma y_i)^2}{n} = 41.43$; $SSE = 9.33$; therefore,

$$SSR = 41.43 - 9.33 = 32.10$$

b. $r^2 = \dfrac{SSR}{\text{Total } SS} = \dfrac{32.10}{41.43} = .7748$; c. $r = \sqrt{.7748} = .88$

2. a. $SSR = 41.43 - 9.25 = 32.18$; $r^2 = \dfrac{32.18}{41.43} = .7767$ while

$r = -\sqrt{.7767} = -.88$. Total variation is reduced by 77.67% by using number of damaging insects to aid in prediction.

b. The predictors are equally effective.

3.

x_1 (Bolls)	x_2 (Insects)
5.5	11
2.8	20
4.7	13
4.3	12
3.7	18
6.1	10
4.5	12

$\Sigma x_1 = 31.6$ $\Sigma x_2 = 96$

$\Sigma x_1^2 = 149.82$ $\Sigma x_2^2 = 1402$

$n = 7$ $\Sigma x_1 x_2 = 410.80$

$$r = \frac{410.80 - (31.6)(96)/7}{\sqrt{[149.82 - (31.6)^2/7]\,[1402 - (96)^2/7]}}$$

$$= \frac{-22.571}{\sqrt{7.169\,(85.429)}} = -.91$$

High correlation explains the fact that either variable is equally effective in predicting cotton yield.

Set 12A

1.

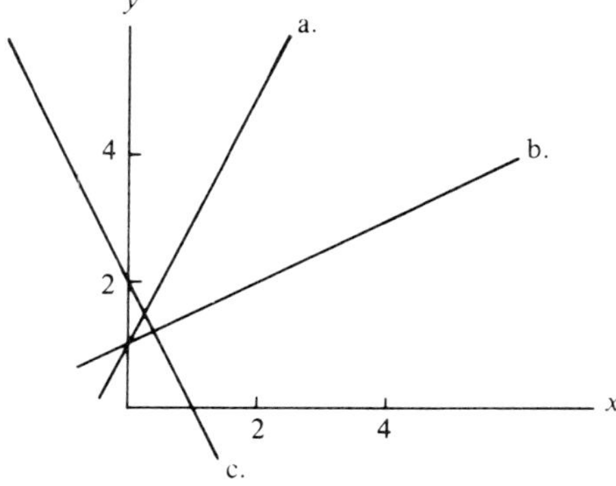

2.

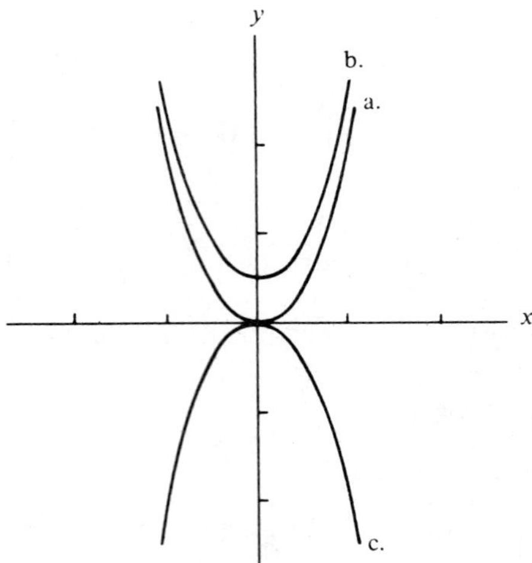

3.

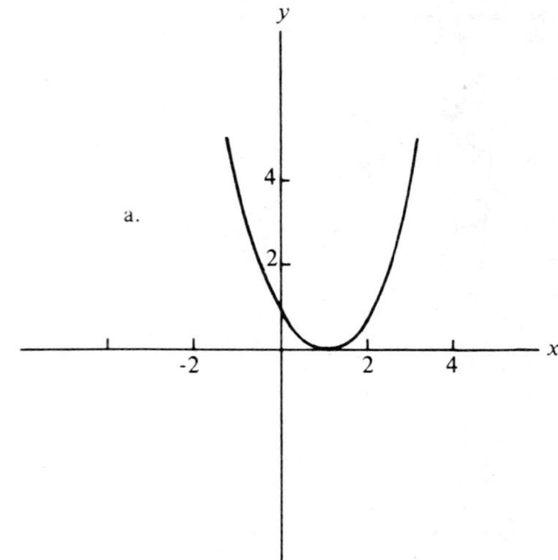

b. The addition of $-2x$ to the equation has the effect of moving the parabola one unit to the right along the x-axis.
c. If the term $2x$ were added to the equation, the parabola would be moved one unit to the left along the x-axis.

4. a. When $x_2 = 0$, $E(y) = 2 + 3x_1$. When $x_2 = 1$, $E(y) = 1 + 3x_1$ and when $x_2 = 2$, $E(y) = 3x_1$.
   b. The three lines are parallel.

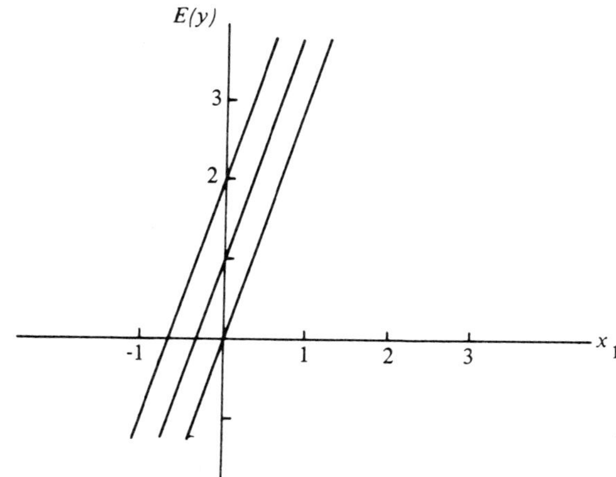

   c. When $x_1 = 0$, $E(y) = 2 - x_2$. When $x_1 = 1$, $E(y) = 5 - x_2$ and when $x_1 = 2$, $E(y) = 8 - x_2$.
   d. The lines are again parallel.

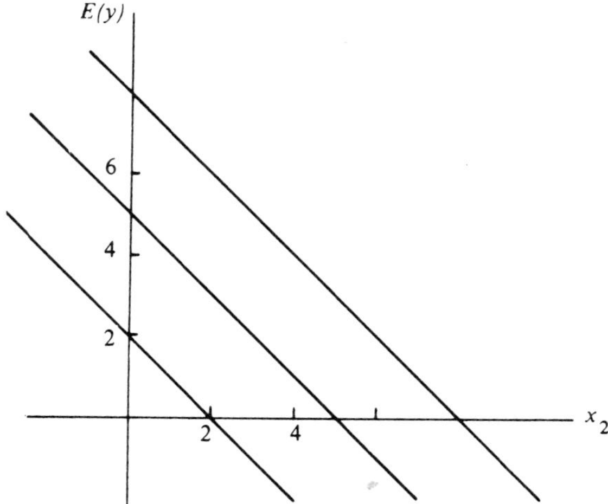

Set 12B

1. a. Refer to the section labeled "INDIVIDUAL ANALYSIS OF VARIABLES." In the column labeled "COEFFICIENT," find $\hat{\beta}_0 = 11.43463$, $\hat{\beta}_1 = .34$, $\hat{\beta}_2 = -.20519$. Then

$$\hat{y} = 11.43463 + .34x - .20519x^2$$

b. From a, $\hat{\beta}_1 = .34$ and $s_{\hat{\beta}_1} = .09539$ from the column labeled "STD ERROR." The 90% confidence interval for β_1 is

$$\hat{\beta}_1 \pm t_{.05}\, s_{\hat{\beta}_1}$$

$$.34 \pm 1.943(.09539)$$

$$.34 \pm .19 \quad \text{or} \quad .15 < \beta_1 < .53$$

c. $H_0: \beta_2 = 0$; $H_a: \beta_2 \neq 0$.

Test statistic: $t = \dfrac{\hat{\beta}_2}{s_{\hat{\beta}_2}} = -4.87$

with level of significance .0028. Reject H_0. There is significant curvature.

d. When $x = 1$, $\hat{y} = 11.43463 + .34 - .20519 = 11.56944$.

2. a. The least squares estimates are found in the column labeled "COEFFICIENT," and the prediction equation is

$$\hat{y} = 10.98293 + 4.43713x_1 + .64905x_2 - .35151x_1x_2$$

b. When $x_1 = 4.4$ and $x_2 = 16$,

$$\hat{y} = 10.98293 + 19.23372 + 10.3848 - 24.746304 = 15.855$$

c. $H_0: \beta_1 = 0$; $H_a: \beta_1 \neq 0$

Test statistic: $t = \dfrac{\hat{\beta}_1}{s_{\hat{\beta}_1}} = 2.74$ with a p-value of .0713.

Reject H_0 for $\alpha \geqslant .0713$. Otherwise, do not reject H_0. The variable x_1 is not significant in the presence of x_2.

d. $H_0: \beta_2 = 0$; $H_a: \beta_2 \neq 0$

Test statistic: $t = \dfrac{\hat{\beta}_2}{s_{\hat{\beta}_2}} = 1.38$ with a p-value of .2619.

Do not reject H_0. The variable x_2 is not significant in the presence of x_1.

e. $\hat{\beta}_1 \pm t_{.025}\, s_{\hat{\beta}_1} = 4.43713 \pm 3.182\,(1.61861)$ or 4.44 ± 5.15.

Set 12C

1. a. $H_0: \beta_1 = \beta_2 = 0$; H_a: at least one of β_1 or β_2 is nonzero

   Test statistic: $F = \dfrac{MSR}{MSE} = 18.23$ with p-value of .0028.

   Reject H_0. The regression is significant.

   b. $R^2 = .8587$ or 85.87% of the variation in y is accounted for by x and x^2.

   c. $R_a^2 = 1 - \dfrac{.54595}{23.18/8} = 1 - .1884 = .8116$
   which is not too different from R^2.

2. a. $R^2 = .9365$ or 93.65% of the variation in y is accounted for by the model.

   b. $R_a^2 = 1 - \dfrac{.87693}{41.42857/6} = .8730$ which is much smaller than R^2.
   We would suspect that at least one x_i is not contributing information for prediction in the presence of the other x_i.

   c. $H_0: \beta_1 = \beta_2 = \beta_3 = 0$; H_a: at least one β_i is nonzero.

   Test statistic: $F = \dfrac{MSR}{MSE} = 14.75$ with p-value of .0311.

   Reject H_0. The regression is significant.

   d. From Exercise 1, Self-Correcting Exercises 11D, $r^2 = .7748$. Hence, the additional percentage is $100(.9365 - .7748) = 16.17\%$.

   e. Each variable, x_1 or x_2, adds very little to the model (given that the other is already present) because of their high correlation. Hence, each partial regression is non-significant. Together however, much of the variation in y is explained by x_1, x_2 and their interaction; hence, the significant multiple regression.

Set 12D (Optional)

1.

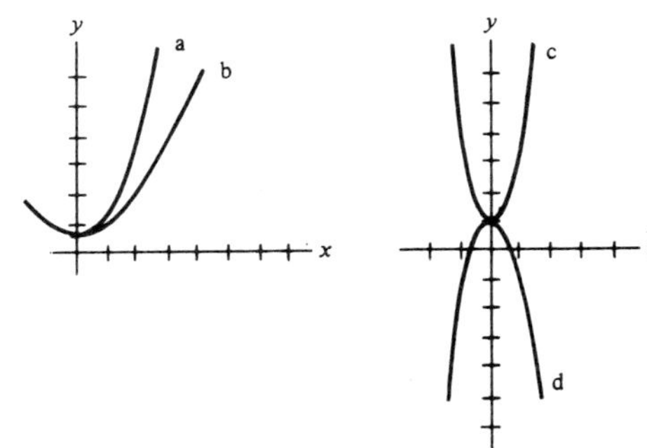

2. $y = \beta_0 + \beta_1 x_1 + \beta_2 x_2 + \beta_3 x_1 x_2 + \epsilon$

3. $y = \beta_0 + \beta_1 x_1 + \beta_2 x_2 + \beta_3 x_1 x_2 + \beta_4 x_3 + \beta_5 x_1 x_3 + \epsilon$

4. The three lines corresponding to areas 1, 2, and 3 are

Area 1: $\hat{y} = 2 + x_1$

Area 2: $\hat{y} = 2 + x_1 + 1 + 3x_1 = 4x_1 + 3$

Area 3: $\hat{y} = 2 + x_1 + 2 + x_1 = 2x_1 + 4$

The graphs are omitted, but the student is referred to Chapter 11, where the graph of a straight line is discussed.

Set 12E

1. a. $H_0: \beta_1 = \beta_2 = \beta_3 = 0$ $\quad H_a$: at least one of the β_i is non-zero.

Test statistic: $F = \dfrac{MSR}{MSE} = \dfrac{85.5402}{3.59657} = 23.78$

Reject H_0 if $F > F_{3,6} = 4.76$. There is a significant regression of y on x_1, x_2 and x_3 since H_0 is rejected.

b. $H_0: \beta_2 = \beta_3 = 0$ $\quad H_a$: at least one of β_2 or β_3 is non-zero.

Test statistic: $F = \dfrac{MS(\text{Drop})}{MSE_2} = \dfrac{(SSE_1 - SSE_2)/(k - g)}{MSE_2}$

Calculate $MSE_2 = \dfrac{SSE_2}{6} = 3.59657$

$MS(\text{Drop}) = \dfrac{(49.08683 - 21.57941)}{3 - 1} = 13.75371$

Then $F = \dfrac{13.75371}{3.59657} = 3.82$

Reject H_0 if $F > F_{2,6} = 5.14$. Do not reject H_0. The variables x_2 and x_3 contribute no significant additional information.

c. $H_0: \beta_1 = 0$ $\quad H_a: \beta_1 \neq 0$

Test statistic: $F = \dfrac{MS(\text{Drop})}{MSE_2}$

$$\text{where } MS(\text{Drop}) = \frac{176.3438 - 21.57941}{3 - 2} = 154.76439$$

$$\text{Then } F = \frac{154.76439}{3.59657} = 43.03$$

Reject H_0 if $F > F_{1,6} = 5.99$. Reject H_0. The variable x_1 contributes significant information. Note that this test is equivalent to the test presented in Section 12.3, and that the F-value appears in the printout.

d. Number in family unit and area are not relevant to predicting amount of money in a savings account, but income is.

Set 13A

1. a.

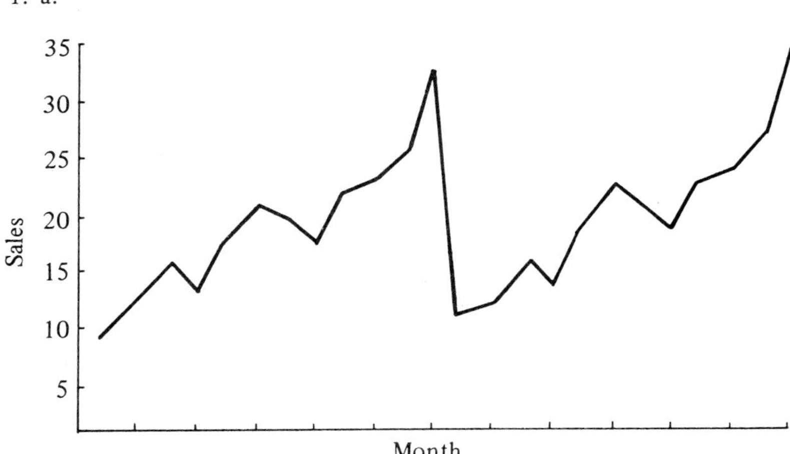

b. The seasonal component, with a period of 12 months.

c. Calculate:

$$\bar{y}_2 = \frac{y_1 + y_2 + y_3}{3} = \frac{37.5}{3} = 12.5 \qquad \bar{y}_3 = \frac{y_2 + y_3 + y_4}{3} = \frac{41.5}{3} = 13.8$$

The 22 averages are given below.

12.5, 13.8, 15.8, 17.5, 19.5, 19.5, 19.8, 20.9, 23.6, 27.3, 23.4,
19.1, 13.3, 14.3, 16.1, 18.5, 20.5, 20.7, 20.8, 22.0, 25.0, 28.9

The centered moving-average smoothed series is the series connected with the dotted line below.

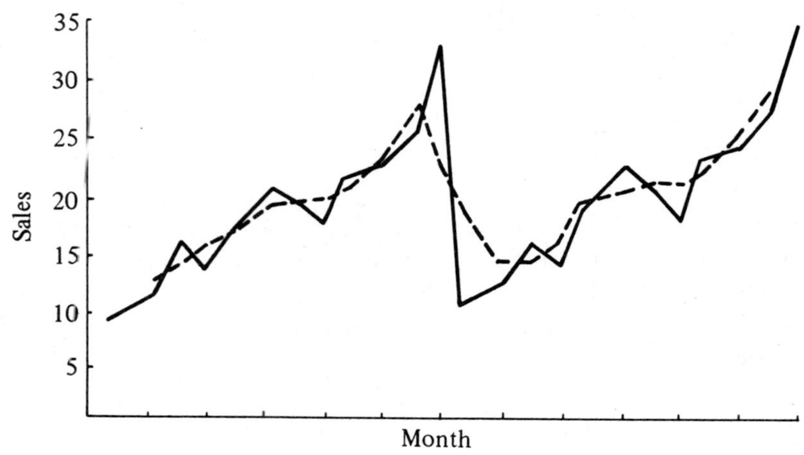

The seasonal component is even more apparent in the smoothed series since some random variation has been eliminated.

d. Let $S_1 = y_1 = 9.5$. Then calculate:

$$S_2 = .1y_2 + .9S_1 = .1(11.6) + .9(9.5) = 9.71$$

Similarly,

$$S_3 = .1(16.4) + .9(9.71) = 10.38$$

$$S_4 = .1(13.5) + .9(10.38) = 10.69$$

The 23 exponentially smoothed values are given below.

9.50, 9.71, 10.38, 10.69, 11.38, 12.37, 13.10, 13.54, 14.40, 15.26, 16.31, 18.00, 17.33, 16.87, 16.77, 16.52, 16.67, 17.31, 17.61, 17.71, 18.28, 18.86, 19.73, 21.26.

e. Let $S_1 = 9.5$. Then $S_2 = .5y_2 + .5S_1 = 10.55$, $S_3 = .5(16.4) + .5(10.55) = 13.48$. The 23 exponentially smoothed values follow.

9.50, 10.55, 13.48, 13.49, 15.55, 18.43, 19.07, 18.29, 20.20, 21.60, 23.70, 28.45, 19.88, 16.29, 16.10, 15.20, 16.60, 19.85, 20.08, 19.34, 21.37, 22.74, 25.17, 30.09

f. The original series is the dotted line in the graph below.

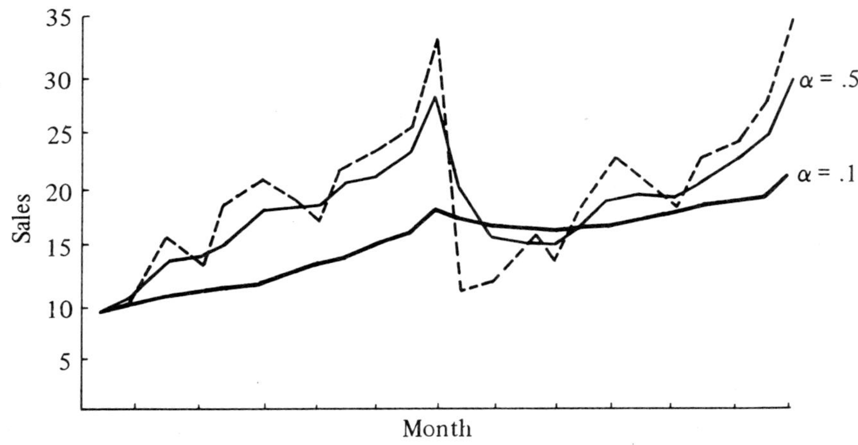

g. The smaller constant smooths the series too much, leaving little information, while the larger constant removes random variation, leaving the seasonal trend visible.

2. The original series is smoothed using a centered moving average with $M = 4$ and adjusted by averaging adjacent centered moving averages. The results are shown below.

Quarter	y_t	*MA (4)*	*Adjusted MA*	*Quarter*	y_t	*MA (4)*	*Adjusted MA*
1	.13	*		11	.30	.2200	.21750
2	.21	.1800		12	.16	.2250	.22250
3	.26	.1850	.18250	13	.18	.2325	.22875
4	.12	.1850	.18500	14	.26	.2375	.23500
5	.15	.1875	.18625	15	.33	.2475	.24250
6	.21	.1925	.19000	16	.18	.2600	.25375
7	.27	.1950	.19375	17	.22	.2750	.26750
8	.14	.2025	.19875	18	.31	.2850	.28000
9	.16	.2100	.20625	19	.39	*	
10	.24	.2150	.21250	20	.22		

The specific seasonal indexes are shown below. The four seasonal indexes are found as the average of the specific seasonal indexes.

Q_1	Q_2	Q_3	Q_4
*	*	1.425	.649
.805	1.105	1.394	.704
.776	1.129	1.379	.719
.787	1.106	1.361	.709
.822	1.107	*	*
.798	1.112	1.390	.695

Since the sum of the seasonal indexes is 3.995, the normalized indexes are

$S_1 = 4(.798)/3.995 = .799$ $\qquad$ $S_3 = 4(1.390)/3.995 = 1.392$

$S_2 = 4(1.112)/3.995 = 1.113$ $\qquad$ $S_4 = 4(.695)/3.995 = .696$

The deseasonalized series is shown below.

Q_1	Q_2	Q_3	Q_4
.16	.19	.19	.17
.19	.19	.19	.20
.20	.22	.22	.23
.23	.23	.24	.26
.28	.28	.28	.32

The long-term trend is now clearly evident. The graph is omitted.

Set 13B

1. Let $I_k = \dfrac{\text{price in year } k}{\text{price in 1983}}(100)$. Then

$$I_{1984} = \frac{325}{340}(100) = 95.6;\ I_{1985} = \frac{350}{340}(100) = 102.9;\ I_{1986} = \frac{380}{340}(100)$$
$$= 111.8$$

$$I_{1987} = \frac{400}{340}(100) = 117.6;\ I_{1988} = \frac{410}{340}(100) = 120.6$$

2. Compute adjusted wages using the wage indices for the three years.

$$A_{1986} = \frac{100(17880)}{121.4} = 14728.17;\ A_{1987} = \frac{100(18400)}{125.2} = 14696.49$$

$$A_{1988} = \frac{100(18850)}{129.0} = 14612.40$$

Thus, the real wages, A_{1986}, A_{1987}, A_{1988} have *decreased* over the three-year period.

3. $I_k = \dfrac{\Sigma p_{ki}}{\Sigma p_{oi}}(100) = \dfrac{1.10 + 1.35 + 7.25}{.35 + .75 + 4.25}(100) = \dfrac{970}{5.35} = 181.31$

4. $I_k = \frac{\Sigma p_{ki} q_{ki}}{\Sigma p_{oi} q_{oi}}(100) = \frac{1.10(700) + 1.35(40) + 7.25(11)}{.35(500) + .75(50) + 4.25(8)}(100) = \frac{90375}{246.5}$

$= 366.63$

Gasoline and mechanic's time increased both in quantity and in price; an average priced item (oil) decreased only slightly; hence the index increased.

5. $I_L = \frac{\Sigma p_{ki} q_{oi}}{\Sigma p_{oi} q_{oi}}(100) = \frac{1.10(500) + 1.35(50) + 7.25(8)}{246.5}(100) = \frac{67550}{246.5}$

$= 274.04$

Comparisons made per given number of units sold; increase in mechanic's time and gasoline are not considered. Hence, index is lower.

6. $I_P = \frac{\Sigma p_{ki} q_{ki}}{\Sigma p_{oi} q_{ki}}(100) = \frac{90375}{.35(700) + .75(40) + 4.25(11)} = \frac{90375}{321.75} = 280.89$

Slightly different from I_L in 5 due to different weights.

7. $I_F = \sqrt{I_P I_L} = \sqrt{76975.096} = 277.44$

Set 14A

1.

t	$\frac{2\pi t}{12}$	$\cos \frac{2\pi t}{12}$	$11.5 \cos \frac{2\pi t}{12}$	$\hat{y}_t$
1	$\pi/6$	$\sqrt{3}/2$	9.96	43.46
2	$\pi/3$	1/2	5.75	39.75
3	$\pi/2$	0	0	34.50
4	$2\pi/3$	-1/2	-5.75	29.25
5	$5\pi/6$	$-\sqrt{3}/2$	-9.96	25.54
6	π	-1	-11.5	24.50
7	$7\pi/6$	$-\sqrt{3}/2$	-9.96	26.54
8	$4\pi/3$	-1/2	-5.75	31.25
9	$3\pi/2$	0	0	37.50
10	$5\pi/3$	1/2	5.75	43.75
11	$11\pi/3$	$\sqrt{3}/2$	9.96	48.46
12	2π	1	11.50	50.50

2. For $t = 1$, $\hat{y}_1 = 10.29 + .13(1) = 10.42$. For $t = 2$ to $t = 12$, calculations are similar.

t	y_t	$\hat{y}_t$	$y_t - \hat{y}_t$
1	10.0	10.42	-.42
2	10.6	10.55	.05
3	10.9	10.68	.22
4	10.8	10.81	-.01
5	11.1	10.94	.06
6	11.3	11.07	.23
7	11.0	11.20	-.20
8	11.5	11.33	.17
9	11.6	11.46	.14
10	11.2	11.59	-.39
11	11.7	11.72	-.02
12	11.8	11.85	-.05

Then $MSE = \sum_{t=1}^{12} (y_t - \hat{y}_t)^2/12$

$= [(-.42)^2 + \cdots + (-.05)^2]/12$

$= .5274/12 = .04395$

3.

b. The values for y, x_1, x_2, x_3 and x_4 are shown below, and entered into the computer program.

y_t	$x_1 = t$	x_2	x_3	x_4
10.0	1	0	0	0
10.6	2	0	0	0
10.9	3	0	0	0
10.8	4	1	0	0
11.1	5	1	0	0
11.3	6	1	0	0
11.0	7	0	1	0
11.5	8	0	1	0
11.6	9	0	1	0
11.2	10	0	0	1
11.7	11	0	0	1
11.8	12	0	0	1

The prediction equation is

$$\hat{y}_t = 9.85 + .325t - .40833x_2$$
$$-1.08333x_2 - 1.85833x_3,$$

as shown in the computer printout following.

RSQ = .96037898
SEY = .12817399

	COEFF	S.E.	F
INTERCEPT	9.85000	0.11701	7086.86 ***
VAR 1	0.32500	0.04532	51.43 ***
VAR 2	−0.40833	0.17156	5.66 *
VAR 3	−1.08333	0.29134	13.83 **
VAR 4	−1.85833	0.42106	19.48 **

ANALYSIS OF VARIANCE

SOURCE	DF	SS	MS	F
REGRESSION	4	2.78750	0.69687	42.42 ***
RESIDUAL	7	0.11500	0.01643	
TOTAL	11	2.90250		

PRINT RESIDUAL? Y

	OBS Y	PRED Y	RES Y	N D
1	10.00000	10.17500	−0.17500	−1.37
2	10.60000	10.50000	0.10000	0.78
3	10.90000	10.82500	0.07500	0.59
4	10.80000	10.74167	0.05833	0.46
5	11.10000	11.06667	0.03333	0.26
6	11.30000	11.39167	−0.09167	−0.72
7	11.00000	11.04167	−0.04167	−0.33
8	11.50000	11.36667	0.13333	1.04
9	11.60000	11.69167	−0.09167	−0.72
10	11.20000	11.24167	−0.04167	−0.33
11	11.70000	11.56667	0.13333	1.04
12	11.80000	11.89167	−0.09167	−0.72

c.-d. The forecasts for January through December are shown in the column labeled PRED Y and $MSE = .01643$ from the analysis of variance table. The model is more accurate than that given in Exercise 2.

Set 14B

1. A simple moving average forecast will be appropriate when there is no pronounced linear trend.
2. If the trend is positive, a simple moving average forecast will tend to underestimate the actual series values.

3. The first-order difference transformation filters out the linear trend component, and is used when in fact this linear trend exists in the series.
4. The second-order difference transformation filters out a quadratic or other non-linear trend when it exists in the time series. A plot of the second differences should fluctuate randomly about $\nabla^2 y_t = 0$ if the second differencing has been effective.
5. a. Let $t = 1$ for January. Then for July, the one-month ahead forecast is

$$\hat{y}_7 = \frac{y_6 + y_5 + y_4}{3} = \frac{14.6 + 15.1 + 14.1}{3} = 14.6$$

   b. For August, the two-month ahead forecast is the same as the one-month ahead forecast for July, or

$$\hat{y}_8 = 14.6$$

6. a.

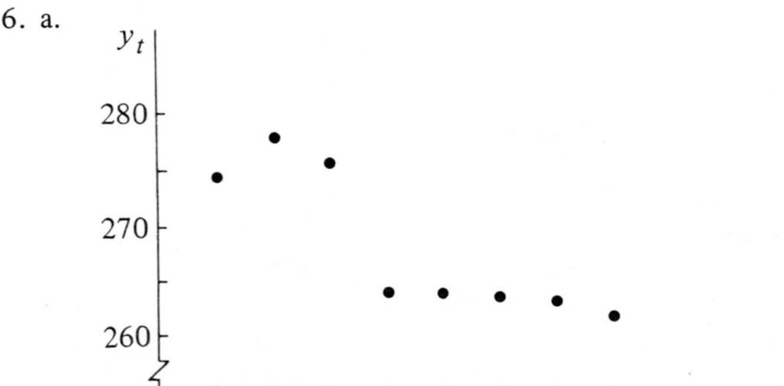

There does not appear to be a significant trend.

b.–c.

t	y_t	$\hat{y}_t$(b)	∇y_t	3-MA Forecast of ∇y_t	$\hat{y}_t$(c)
1	274.7		–	–	
2	277.6		2.9	–	
3	276.4		–1.2	–	
4	264.6		–11.8	–	
5	264.3	272.867	–0.3	–3.367	261.233
6	264.1	268.433	–0.2	–4.433	259.867
7	264.0	264.333	–0.1	–4.100	260.000
8	263.4	264.133	–0.6	–0.200	263.800
9		263.833		–0.300	263.100

d. For (b), $MAD = \dfrac{\Sigma|y_t - \hat{y}_t|}{4} = \dfrac{13.966}{4} = 3.4915$

For (c), $MAD = \dfrac{11.7}{4} = 2.925$

The first-difference forecasts appear slightly more accurate.

7. a.

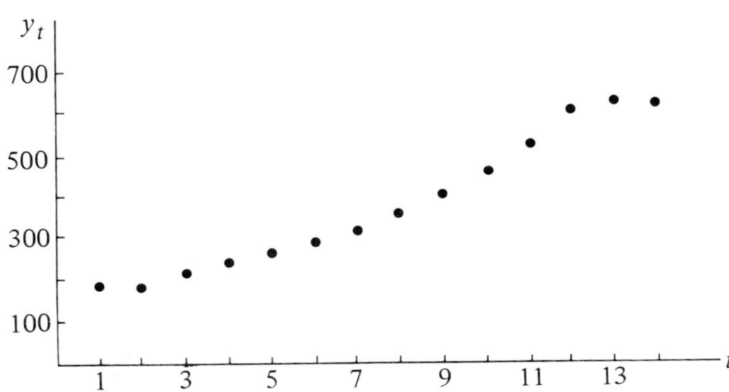

There is a nonlinear trend; second differencing should be used for predicting future values.

b.–d.

t	y_t	∇y_t	$\nabla^2 y_t$	MA(4) Forecast of ∇y_t	$\hat{y}_t$(c)	MA(4) Forecast of $\nabla^2 y_t$	$\hat{y}_t$(d)
1	196	–	–				
2	192	-4	–				
3	210	18	22				
4	238	28	10				
5	269	31	3				
6	294	25	-6				
7	303	9	-16				
8	358	55	46				
9	400	42	-13				
10	460	60	18				
11	520	60	0	41.50	501.50	8.75	528.75
12	602	82	22	54.25	574.25	12.75	592.75
13	618	16	-66	61.00	663.00	6.75	690.75
14	601	-17	-33	54.50	672.50	-6.50	627.50
15				35.25	636.25	-19.25	564.75

For (c), $MAD = \frac{(520 - 501.5) + \cdots + |601 - 672.5|}{4} = \frac{162.75}{4} = 40.6875$

For (d), $MAD = \frac{117.25}{4} = 29.3125$

Second differencing provides the more accurate forecast.

Set 14C

1. Since $T = 1$, $\alpha = .1$, the forecasting equation will be identical to that given in Example 14.3; namely,

$$\hat{y}_{t+1} = 2.11S_t - 1.11S_t(2)$$

with $S_t = .1y_t + .9S_{t-1}$ and $S_t(2) = .1S_t + .9S_{t-1}(2)$

The smoothed statistics and the appropriate forecasts are given below.

t	y_t	S_t	$S_t(2)$	$\hat{y}_t$
1	10.0	10.000000	10.000000	–
2	10.6	10.060000	10.006000	10.00
3	10.9	10.144000	10.019800	10.12
4	10.8	10.209600	10.038780	10.28
5	11.1	10.298640	10.064766	10.40
6	11.3	10.398776	10.098166	10.56
7	11.0	10.458898	10.134238	10.73
8	11.5	10.563008	10.177114	10.82
9	11.6	10.666707	10.226072	10.99
10	11.2	10.720036	10.275467	11.16
11	11.7	10.818032	10.329723	11.21
12	11.5	10.886228	10.385372	11.36

2. Similar to Example 14.6. Given that $S_0 = 18.0$ and $R_0 = .20$, the necessary formulas are:

$$S_t = .1\frac{y_t}{F_{t-L}} + .9(S_{t-1} + R_{t-1});\ F_t = .4\frac{y_t}{S_t} + .6F_{t-L}$$

$$R_t = .1(S_t - S_{t-1}) + .9R_{t-1};\ \hat{y}_{t+1} = (S_t + R_t)F_{t-L+1}$$

The calculations are shown in the table on the following page:

t	y_t	S_t	R_t	F_t	$\hat{y}_t$
1	9.5	1.7925 + 16.38 = 18.17	.017 + .18 = .197	.2091 + .318 = .53	18.200(.53) = 9.65
2	11.6	1.9016 + 16.5303 = 18.43	.026 + .177 = .203	.2518 + .366 = .62	18.367(.61) = 11.20
3	16.4	1.8427 + 16.7697 = 18.61	.018 + .183 = .201	.3525 + .534 = .89	18.633(.89) = 16.58
4	13.5	1.8750 + 16.9299 = 18.80	.019 + .181 = .200	.2872 + .432 = .72	18.811(.72) = 13.54
5	17.6	1.9130 + 17.1000 = 19.01	.021 + .180 = .201	.3703 + .552 = .92	19.000(.92) = 17.48
6	21.3	1.9189 + 17.2899 = 19.21	.020 + .181 = .201	.4435 + .666 = 1.11	19.211(1.11) = 21.32
7	19.7	1.9314 + 17.4699 = 19.40	.019 + .181 = .200	.4062 + .612 = 1.02	19.411(1.02) = 19.80
8	17.5	1.9444 + 17.6400 = 19.58	.018 + .180 = .198	.3575 + .540 = .90	19.600(.90) = 17.64
9	22.1	1.9732 + 17.8902 = 19.86	.028 + .178 = .206	.4451 + .672 = 1.12	19.878(1.12) = 22.26
10	23.0	1.9828 + 18.0594 = 20.04	.018 + .185 = .203	.4591 + .696 = 1.16	20.066(1.16) = 23.28
11	25.8	1.9846 + 18.2187 = 20.20	.016 + .183 = .199	.5109 + .780 = 1.29	20.243(1.30) = 26.32
12	33.2	2.0000 + 18.3591 = 20.36	.016 + .179 = .195	.6523 + .996 = 1.65	20.399(1.66) = 33.86
13	11.3	2.1321 + 18.4995 = 20.63	.027 + .176 = .203		20.555(.53) = 10.89
14	12.7	2.0484 + 18.7497 = 20.80	.017 + .183 = .200		20.833(.62) = 12.92
15	15.9	1.7865 + 18.9000 = 20.69	.011 + .180 = .169		21.000(.89) = 18.69
16	14.3	1.9861 + 18.7731 = 20.76	.007 + .152 = .159		20.859(.72) = 15.02
17	18.0	1.9565 + 18.8271 = 20.78	.002 + .143 = .145		20.919(.92) = 19.25
18	23.1	2.0811 + 18.8325 = 20.91	.013 + .131 = .144		20.925(1.11) = 23.23
19	20.3	1.9902 + 18.9486 = 20.94	.003 + .130 = .133		21.054(1.02) = 21.48
20	18.6	2.0667 + 18.9657 = 21.03	.009 + .120 = .129		21.073(.90) = 18.97
21	23.4	2.0893 + 19.0431 = 21.13	.010 + .116 = .126		21.159(1.12) = 23.70
22	24.1	2.0776 + 19.1304 = 21.21	.008 + .113 = .121		21.256(1.16) = 24.66
23	27.6	2.1395 + 19.1979 = 21.34	.013 + .109 = .122		21.331(1.29) = 27.52
24	35.0				21.462(1.65) = 35.41

Set 15A

1. a. Using Table 12 with $n = 10$, we have $A_2 = .308$. Then

$$LCL = \bar{\bar{x}} - A_2\bar{R} = 67.54 - .308(.12) = 67.503$$

$$UCL = \bar{\bar{x}} + A_2\bar{R} = 67.54 + .308(.12) = 67.577$$

Observations falling outside the interval (LCL, UCL) should cause close examination of the production process.

b. From Table 12, $D_3 = .223$ and $D_4 = 1.777$. Then

$$LCL = D_3\bar{R} = .223(.12) = .027$$

$$UCL = D_4\bar{R} = 1.777(.12) = .213$$

c. The probability of interest is $P(67.4 < x < 67.8)$. Estimating σ as $\hat{\sigma} \cong \bar{R}/d_2 = .12/3.078 = .03899$, the probability is

$$P(67.4 < x < 67.8) = P\left(\frac{-.2}{.03899} < z < \frac{.2}{.03899}\right)$$

$$= P(-5.13 < z < 5.13) \cong 1$$

The process is quite capable of meeting the specification limits.

2. The process means are outside of the control limits on all five days. The process must be examined and adjusted.
3. The means and ranges for the 16 samples are shown below. Then

$$\bar{\bar{x}} = \frac{287.89}{16} = 17.9931$$

$$\bar{R} = .05125$$

Sample	$\bar{x}$	R	Sample	$\bar{x}$	R
1	17.9925	.09	9	17.9975	.02
2	17.9800	.04	10	18.0125	.04
3	18.0150	.05	11	17.9850	.06
4	17.9950	.05	12	17.9825	.05
5	17.9900	.04	13	17.9900	.06
6	17.9975	.05	14	17.9775	.04
7	17.9800	.04	15	18.0025	.08
8	17.9875	.06	16	18.0050	.05

a. From Table 12, $A_2 = .729$. Then

$$LCL = \bar{\bar{x}} - A_2\bar{R} = 17.9931 - .729(.05125) = 17.9557$$

$$UCL = \bar{\bar{x}} + A_2\bar{R} = 17.9931 + .729(.05125) = 18.0305$$

b. From Table 12, $D_3 = 0$ and $D_4 = 2.282$. Then

$$LCL = D_3\bar{R} = 0 \quad \text{and} \quad UCL = D_4\bar{R} = 2.282(.05125) = .117$$

Observations falling outside the control limits imply that the process should be examined and/or adjusted.

Set 15B

1. From Exercise 1, Set 15A we have $\hat{\sigma} = .03899$, and USL - LSL = 67.8 - 67.4 = .4. Then $C_p = \dfrac{.4}{6(.03899)} = 1.7098$. The process is capable of meeting specification limits.
2. $C_{pk} = \min\left(\dfrac{67.8 - 67.54}{3(.03899)}, \dfrac{67.54 - 67.4}{3(.03899)}\right) = \min(2.223, 1.197) = 1.197$. The process is capable of meeting specifications.
3. a. From Exercise 3, Set 15A, we can calculate

$$\hat{\sigma} = \bar{R}/d_2 = .05125/2.059 = .02489$$

while an estimate of σ^2 based on the entire set of 4(16) = 64 measurements is

$$s^2 = \frac{20720.2004 - \dfrac{(1151.56)^2}{64}}{63} = \frac{.037375}{63} = .0005933$$

and $\hat{\sigma} = s = .0244$.

b. Since USL - LSL = .04, $C_p = \dfrac{.04}{6(.02489)} = .268$ using the first estimate, or

$$C_p = \frac{.04}{6(.0244)} = .273 \quad \text{using the second estimate.}$$

The process is *not* capable of meeting specifications.

Set 15C

1. $\bar{p} = .0554$ and $3\sqrt{\dfrac{\bar{p}(1-\bar{p})}{700}} = 3(.0086) = .02594$. Hence,

$$\text{LCL} = .0554 - .02594 = .02948$$

$$\text{UCL} = .0554 + .02594 = .08137$$

2. The sample proportions are $25/700 = .0357$, $37/700 = .0529$, $42/700 = .06$, $47/700 = .0671$, $55/700 = .0786$. The proportion defective shows a steady increase, and the process will soon be out of statistical control. The process should be carefully checked for sources contributing to the observed increase.
3. a. $\bar{c} = 8.75$ and $3\sqrt{\bar{c}} = 8.87$. Then

$$\text{UCL} = 8.75 + 8.87 = 17.62 \quad \text{and} \quad \text{LCL} = 8.75 - 8.87 = -.12 \text{ (or zero)}$$

   b. The number of defects is steadily rising toward the UCL; the process should be inspected for possible causes in the increase before the process is out of statistical control.

Set 15D

1. a. $P(\text{acceptance}) = C_0^4 p^0 q^4 + C_1^4 p^1 q^3$ for various values of p.
   When $p = 0$, $P(\text{acceptance}) = 1$; $p = .3$, $P(\text{acceptance}) = (.7)^4 + 4(.3)(.7)^3$

$$= .2401 + .4116$$

$$= .6517$$

   When $p = 1$, $P(\text{acceptance}) = 0$. The graph follows the procedures used in Section 15.9 and is omitted here.
   b. Keep $n = 4$, take $a > 1$; keep $a = 1$, take $n < 4$.
2. a.

p	0	.1	.3	.5	1.0
$n = 10, a = 1$	1	.736	.149	.011	0
$n = 25, a = 1$	1	.271	.002	.000	0

   c. If the student will graph the 3 OC curves as given in part a and problem 1, he will see that increasing n has the effect of decreasing the probability of acceptance.

3. a.

p	0	.1	.3	.5	1.0
$n = 25, a = 3$	1	.764	.033	.000	0
$n = 25, a = 5$	1	.967	.193	.002	0

   c. Increasing a has the effect of increasing the probability of acceptance.

Set 16A

1. Assign random numbers 01 through 99 to accounts no. 1 through no. 99 and assign random number 00 to account no. 100. Randomly select 20 random numbers and sample the associated accounts.
2. a. Using three digit numbers 001 through 250 to identify the $N = 250$ workers, we could use the random digits 001 through 250 to identify the workers to be included in the sample, and for any three digit random number in the range 251 through 999 use its remainder upon division by 250. For example, worker number 200 would be associated with the random numbers 200, 450, 700 and 950. Worker number 250 would be associated with the random digits 250, 500, 750 and 000.
   b. Suppose a random starting point was determined as line 66, column 5 of the random number table in your text. The first three digits of lines 66–70 in columns 5–10 are

294	218	150	345	333	061
173	376	470	420	974	486
058	248	869	603	164	032
844	605	793	934	688	254
379	610	439	152	806	439

   The remainders after division by 250 are

44	218	150	95	83	61
173	126	220	170	224	236
58	248	119	103	164	32
94	105	43	184	188	4
129	110	189	152	56	189

   Since 189 appeared twice, the next 3 digit number, 952, which reduces to 202, is included. Therefore, the 30 workers associated with the above numbers are to be included in the sample.

Set 16B

1. a. The estimate of average assessed value with bound on error is

$$\bar{x} \pm 1.96\sqrt{\left(\frac{N-n}{N}\right)\left(\frac{s^2}{n}\right)}$$

$$\$86500 \pm 1.96\sqrt{\left(\frac{975}{1000}\right)\left(\frac{8600^2}{25}\right)}$$

$$\$86500 \pm \$3329$$

b. The estimate of total assessed value is

$$\hat{\tau} = N\bar{x} = 1000(86500) = 86{,}500{,}000$$

with

$$\sigma_{\hat{\tau}} = \sqrt{N^2\hat{\sigma}^2_{\bar{x}}} = 1000\sqrt{\frac{(8600)^2}{25}\left(\frac{975}{1000}\right)} = 1{,}698{,}364$$

The estimate of τ with bound on error is

$$\$86{,}500{,}000 \pm 1.96(1{,}698{,}364)$$

$$\$86{,}500{,}000 \pm \$3{,}328{,}793$$

2. Calculate $\hat{p} = \dfrac{x}{n} = \dfrac{8}{50} = .16$. Then

$$.16 \pm 1.96\sqrt{\left(\frac{N-n}{N}\right)\frac{\hat{p}\hat{q}}{n-1}}$$

$$\hat{p} \pm 1.96\sqrt{\left(\frac{950}{1000}\right)\frac{.16(.84)}{49}}$$

$$.16 \pm 1.96(.0510)$$

$$.16 \pm .1001$$

Set 16C

1. Calculate $N = \sum_{i=1}^{L} N_i = 3000$. Then

$$n_1 = n\left(\frac{N_1}{N}\right) = 60\left(\frac{1100}{3000}\right) = 22$$

$$n_2 = n\left(\frac{N_2}{N}\right) = 60\left(\frac{600}{3000}\right) = 12$$

$$n_3 = n\left(\frac{N_3}{N}\right) = 60\left(\frac{800}{3000}\right) = 16$$

$$n_4 = n\left(\frac{N_4}{N}\right) = 60\left(\frac{500}{3000}\right) = 10$$

2. a. Calculate $\bar{x}_{st} = \frac{\Sigma N_i \bar{x}_i}{N} = \frac{1100(1050) + 600(820) + 800(990) + 500(1280)}{3000}$

$$= \frac{3{,}079{,}000}{3000} = \$1026.33$$

Since $(N_i - n_i)/N_i = .98$ for $i = 1, 2, 3, 4$

$$\hat{\sigma}^2_{\bar{x}_{st}} = \frac{.98}{N^2} \Sigma \frac{N_i^2 s_i^2}{n_i}$$

$$= \frac{.98}{(3000)^2}\left[\frac{(1100)^2(1210)}{22} + \frac{(600)^2(930)}{12} + \frac{(800)^2(1080)}{16} + \frac{(500)^2(1510)}{10}\right]$$

$$= \frac{.98}{(3000)^2}(175{,}400{,}000)$$

$$= 19.0991$$

Then

$$\bar{x}_{st} \pm 1.96\hat{\sigma}_{\bar{x}_{st}} = \$1026.33 \pm 1.96(4.37)$$

$$= \$1026.33 \pm 8.57$$

b. $N\bar{x}_{st} \pm 1.96 N\hat{\sigma}_{\bar{x}_{st}}$

$3000(1026.33) \pm 1.96(3000)(4.37)$

$\$3{,}079{,}000 \pm \$25{,}697.09$

c. For stratum 1,

$$\bar{x}_1 \pm 1.96\sqrt{\left(\frac{N_1 - n_1}{N_1}\right)\frac{s_1^2}{n_1}}$$

$$\$1050 \pm 1.96\sqrt{.98\left(\frac{1210}{22}\right)}$$

$\$1050 \pm 1.96(7.34)$

$\$1050 \pm \$14.39$

3. Calculate $\hat{p}_1 = \frac{12}{22} = .5454, \hat{p}_2 = \frac{5}{12} = .4167, \hat{p}_3 = \frac{6}{16} = .3750, \hat{p}_4 = \frac{3}{10}$ $= .3000$. Then

$$\hat{p}_{st} = \frac{1}{N} \Sigma N_i \hat{p}_i$$

$$= \frac{1}{3000} [1100(.5454) + 600(.4167) + 800(.3750) + 500(.3000)]$$

$$= \frac{1300}{3000} = .4333$$

$$\hat{\sigma}^2_{\hat{p}_{st}} = \frac{.98}{(3000)^2} \Sigma N_i^2 \left(\frac{\hat{p}_i \hat{q}_i}{n_i - 1}\right)$$

$$= \frac{.98}{(3000)^2} (38{,}074.0604)$$

$$= .00415$$

and

$$\hat{p}_{st} \pm 1.96 \hat{\sigma}_{\hat{p}_{st}}$$

$$.4333 \pm 1.96 \sqrt{.00415}$$

$$.43 \pm .13$$

Set 16D

1. a. Calculate $\Sigma t_i = 137{,}090$ $\qquad \Sigma n_i = 156$

$\Sigma t_i^2 = 2{,}045{,}261{,}700$ $\qquad \Sigma n_i^2 = 2790$

$\Sigma t_i n_i = 2{,}341{,}180$

Then

$$\bar{x}_{cl} = \frac{\Sigma t_i}{\Sigma n_i} = \frac{137{,}090}{156} = \$878.78$$

Also,

$$\Sigma(t_i - \bar{x}_{cl}n_i)^2 = 2{,}045{,}261{,}700 - 2(878.78)(2{,}341{,}180)$$

$$+ (878.78)^2(2790)$$

$$= 85{,}086{,}843.84$$

and $\bar{n} = \frac{1}{m}\,\Sigma n_i = \frac{1}{10}\,(156) = 15.6$

With $M = 200$,

$$\hat{\sigma}^2_{\bar{x}_{cl}} = \frac{(M-m)}{Mm\bar{n}^2}\left(\frac{\Sigma(t_i - \bar{x}_{cl}n_i)^2}{m-1}\right)$$

$$= \frac{(200-10)}{200(10)(15.6)^2}\left(\frac{85{,}086{,}843.84}{9}\right)$$

$$= 3690.5774$$

and $\hat{\sigma}_{\bar{x}_{cl}} = \sqrt{3690.5774} = 60.75$

Therefore, $\bar{x}_{cl} \pm 1.96\hat{\sigma}_{\bar{x}_{cl}}$

$$\$878.78 \pm 1.96(60.75)$$

$$\$878.78 \pm \$119.07$$

b. $\hat{\tau} = \frac{M}{m}\Sigma t_i = \frac{200}{10}(137{,}090) = \$2{,}741{,}800$

Calculate

$$\Sigma(t_i - \bar{t})^2 = \Sigma t_i^2 - \frac{(\Sigma t_i)^2}{m}$$

$$= 2{,}045{,}261{,}700 - 1{,}879{,}366{,}810$$

$$= 165{,}894{,}890$$

Then

$$\hat{\sigma}^2_{\hat{\tau}} = M^2\left(\frac{M-m}{Mn}\right)\left(\frac{\Sigma(t_i - \bar{t})^2}{m-1}\right)$$

$$= (200)^2\left(\frac{190}{2000}\right)\left(\frac{165{,}894{,}890}{9}\right)$$

$$= 70{,}044{,}509{,}110$$

and $\hat{\sigma}_{\hat{\tau}} = 264{,}659.23$.

Therefore, $\hat{\tau} \pm 1.96\hat{\sigma}_{\tau} = \$2{,}741{,}800 \pm 1.96(264{,}659.23)$

$\$2{,}741{,}800 \pm \$518{,}732.09$

2. Calculate $\Sigma a_i = 126$ $\quad \Sigma n_i = 258$

$\Sigma a_i^2 = 2608$ $\quad \Sigma n_i^2 = 9526$

$\Sigma a_i n_i = 4903$

Then $\hat{p}_{cl} = \dfrac{\Sigma a_i}{\Sigma n_i} = \dfrac{126}{258} = .4883$

To determine the value for $\hat{\sigma}^2_{\hat{p}_{cl}}$, calculate

$$\Sigma(a_i - \hat{p}_{cl}n_i)^2 = \Sigma a_i^2 - 2\hat{p}_{cl}\Sigma n_i a_i + \hat{p}_{cl}^2\Sigma n_i^2$$

$$= 2608 - 2(.4883)(4903) + (.4883)^2(9526)$$

$$= 91.08001414$$

and $\bar{n} = \dfrac{1}{m}\Sigma n_i = \dfrac{258}{10} = 25.8$

Then

$$\hat{\sigma}^2_{\hat{p}_{cl}} = \left(\frac{M - m}{Mm\bar{n}^2}\right)\frac{\Sigma(a_i - \hat{p}_{cl}n_i)^2}{m - 1}$$

$$= \left(\frac{(75 - 10)}{750(25.8)^2}\right)\frac{91.08001414}{9}$$

$$= .001317629$$

and $\hat{\sigma}_{\hat{p}_{cl}} = \sqrt{.001317629} = .0363$

Therefore,

$$\hat{p}_{cl} \pm 1.96\sigma_{\hat{p}_{cl}}$$

$$.4883 \pm 1.96(.0363)$$

or $$.49 \pm .07$$

Set 15E

1. With $B = .05$, and $\sigma^2 = pq \approx (.5)(.5) = .25$, and $D = \dfrac{B^2}{(1.96)^2} = .000651$,

$$n = \frac{N\sigma^2}{(N-1)D + \sigma^2} = \frac{12000(.25)}{11999(.000651) + .25}$$

$$= \frac{300}{8.061349} = 37.21 \text{ or } 38 \text{ members}$$

2. a. Calculate

$$D = \frac{B^2}{(1.96)^2} = \frac{.0025}{(1.96)^2} = .000651$$

$$\Sigma N_i\sigma_i^2 = 6000(.7)(.3) + 4000(.6)(.4) + 2000(.5)(.5)$$

$$= 2720$$

Then

$$n = \frac{\Sigma N_i\sigma_i^2}{ND + \dfrac{1}{N}\Sigma N_i\sigma_i^2}$$

$$= \frac{2720}{12000(.000651) + (2720/12000)}$$

$$= \frac{2720}{8.0387} = 338.36 \text{ or } 339 \text{ members}$$

b. $n_1 = 339\left(\dfrac{6000}{12000}\right) = 169.18$ or $n_1 = 170$

$n_2 = 339\left(\dfrac{4000}{12000}\right) = 113$ or $n_2 = 113$

$$n_3 = 339\left(\frac{2000}{12000}\right) = 56.5 \quad \text{or} \quad n_3 = 57$$

c. If $p_1 = p_2 = p_3 = .5$,

$$n \approx \frac{N}{NB^2 + 1} = \frac{12000}{12000(.0025) + 1} = 387.10$$

or $\quad n = 388$ members

3. Calculate

$$\sigma_1 \approx \frac{(500 - 25)}{4} = 118.75, \ \sigma_2 \approx \frac{(1500 - 300)}{4} = 300$$

Then

$$\Sigma N_i \sigma_i^2 = (10000)(118.75)^2 + (5000)(300)^2$$
$$= 591{,}015{,}625$$

and

$$n = \frac{\Sigma N_i \sigma_i^2}{ND + \frac{1}{N}\Sigma N_i \sigma_i^2}$$

$$= \frac{591{,}015{,}625}{15000(30)^2/4 + (591{,}015{,}625/15000)}$$

$$= \frac{591{,}015{,}625}{3{,}414{,}401.042} = 173.09 \text{ or } n = 174$$

The proportional allocation is

$$n_1 = 174\left(\frac{10000}{15000}\right) = 116 \text{ and } n_2 = 174\left(\frac{5000}{15000}\right) = 58$$

Set 17A

1. $H_0: p_1 = p_2 = p_3 = p_4 = p_5 = \frac{1}{5}$

H_a: at least one of the above equalities is incorrect.

$$E(n_i) = np_i = 250\left(\frac{1}{5}\right) = 50 \quad \text{for} \quad i = 1, 2, \ldots, 5$$

With $k - 1 = 5 - 1 = 4$ degrees of freedom, reject H_0 if $X^2 > \chi^2_{.05} = 9.49$.
Test statistic:

$$X^2 = \Sigma \frac{[n_i - E(n_i)]^2}{E(n_i)}$$

$$= \frac{(62 - 50)^2 + (48 - 50)^2 + (56 - 50)^2 + (39 - 50)^2 + (45 - 50)^2}{50}$$

$$= \frac{144 + 4 + 36 + 121 + 25}{50} = 6.6$$

Do not reject H_0. We cannot say there is a preference for color.

2. $H_0: p_1 = .41, \quad p_2 = .12, \quad p_3 = .03, \quad p_4 = .44$

H_a: at least one equality is incorrect.

	Blood Type			
	A	*B*	*AB*	*O*
Observed n_i	90	16	10	84
Expected $E(n_i)$	82	24	6	88

With $k - 1 = 3$ degrees of freedom, reject H_0 if $X^2 > \chi^2_{.05} = 7.81$.
Test statistic:

$$X^2 = \frac{(90 - 82)^2}{82} + \frac{(16 - 24)^2}{24} + \frac{(10 - 6)^2}{6} + \frac{(84 - 88)^2}{88}$$

$$= .7805 + 2.6667 + 2.6667 + .1818 = 6.30$$

Do not reject H_0. There is insufficient evidence to refute the given proportions.

Set 17B

1. H_0: independence of classifications.
   H_a: classifications are not independent.
   Expected and observed cell counts are:

Party Affiliation	*Income*			*Totals*
	Low	*Average*	*High*	
Republican	33(30.57)	85(74.77)	27(39.66)	145
Democrat	19(30.78)	71(75.29)	56(39.93)	146
Other	22(12.65)	25(30.94)	13(16.41)	60
Totals	74	181	96	351

With $(r - 1)(c - 1) = 2(2) = 4$ degrees of freedom, reject H_0 if $X^2 > \chi^2_{.05} = 9.49$.

Test statistic:

$$X^2 = \frac{(2.43)^2}{30.57} + \frac{(10.23)^2}{74.77} + \ldots + \frac{(-3.41)^2}{16.41} = 25.61$$

Reject H_0. There is a significant relationship between income levels and political party affiliation.

2. H_0: opinion independent of sex.
   H_a: opinion dependent upon sex.
   Expected and observed cell counts are:

Sex	*Opinion*		*Totals*
	For	*Against*	
Male	114(116.58)	60(57.42)	174
Female	87(84.42)	39(41.58)	126
Totals	201	99	300

With $(r - 1)(c - 1) = 1$ degree of freedom and $\alpha = .05$, reject H_0 if $X^2 > \chi^2_{.05} = 3.84$. Test statistic is

$$X^2 = \frac{(-2.58)^2}{116.58} + \frac{(2.58)^2}{57.42} + \frac{(2.58)^2}{84.42} + \frac{(-2.58)^2}{41.58} = .4119$$

Do not reject H_0. There is insufficient evidence to show that opinion is dependent upon sex.

Set 17C

1. $H_0: p_1 = p_2 = p_3 = p_4 = p$
   $H_a: p_i \neq p$ for at least one $i = 1, 2, 3, 4$.

	Ward				
	1	*2*	*3*	*4*	*Totals*
Favor	75(66.25)	63(66.25)	69(66.25)	58(66.25)	265
Against	125(133.75)	137(133.75)	131(133.75)	142(133.75)	535
Totals	200	200	200	200	800

With $(r-1)(c-1)=3$ degrees of freedom and $\alpha = .05$, reject H_0 if $X^2 > \chi^2_{.05} = 7.81$.
Test statistic:

$$X^2 = \frac{(8.75)^2}{66.25} + \frac{(-3.25)^2}{66.25} + \ldots + \frac{(8.25)^2}{133.75} = \frac{162.75}{66.25} + \frac{162.75}{133.75} = 3.673$$

Do not reject H_0. There is insufficient evidence to suggest a difference from ward to ward.

2. H_0: independence of classifications
   H_a: dependence of classifications

	Categories			
Satisfaction	*I*	*II*	*III*	*IV*
High	40(50)	60(50)	52(50)	48(50)
Medium	103(90)	87(90)	82(90)	88(90)
Low	57(60)	53(60)	66(60)	64(60)

With $(r-1)(c-1) = 6$ degrees of freedom, reject H_0 if $X^2 > \chi^2_{.05} = 12.59$.
Test statistic:

$$X^2 = \frac{(-10)^2}{50} + \frac{10^2}{50} + \ldots + \frac{4^2}{60} = 8.727$$

Do not reject H_0.

Set 17D

1. With $e^{-2} = .135335$, $p(0) = .135335$, $p(1) = 2e^{-2} = .270670$, $p(2) = 2e^{-2} = .270670$, and $P[x \geqslant 3] = 1 - p(0) - p(1) - p(2) = .323325$. The observed and expected cell counts are shown below.

n_i	4	15	16	15
$E(n_i)$	6.77	13.53	13.53	16.17

With $k - 1 = 3$ degrees of freedom, reject H_0 if $X^2 > \chi^2_{.05} = 7.81$.
Test statistic:

$$X^2 = \frac{(-2.77)^2}{6.77} + \frac{(1.47)^2 + (2.47)^2}{13.53} + \frac{(-1.17)^2}{16.17}$$

$$= 1.133 + .611 + .085 = 1.829$$

Do not reject the model.

2. Expected numbers are $E(n_i) = np_i = 100p_i$, where $p_i = P$[observation falls in cell i when score drawn from the standard normal distribution]. Hence, using Table 3,

$$p_1 = P[z < -1.5] = .0668$$

$$p_2 = P[-1.5 < z < -0.5] = .2417$$

$$p_3 = P[-0.5 < z < 0.5] = 2(.1915) = .3830$$

$$p_4 = .2417$$

$$p_5 = .0668$$

Observed and expected cell counts are shown below.

n_i	8	20	40	29	3
$E(n_i)$	6.68	24.17	38.30	24.17	6.68

With $k - 1 = 4$ degrees of freedom, reject H_0 if $X^2 > \chi^2_{.05} = 9.49$.
Test statistic:

$$X^2 = \frac{1.32^2}{6.68} + \frac{(-4.17)^2}{24.17} + \ldots + \frac{(-3.68)^2}{6.68}$$

$$= .2608 + .7194 + .0755 + .9635 + 2.0273 = 4.047$$

Do not reject the model.

Set 18A

1. Let $p = P$[paint A shows less wear] and x = number of locations where paint A shows less wear. Since no numerical measure of a response is given, the sign test is appropriate.

$$H_0: p = ½$$

$$H_a: p < ½$$

Rejection region: With $n = 25, p = ½$, reject H_0 iif $x \leq 8$ with $\alpha = .054$. See Table 1(e).

Observe $x = 8$; therefore, reject H_0. Paint B is more durable.

2. Let $p = P$[dye 1 measurement exceeds dye 2 measurement]

$H_0: p = ½$

$H_a: p > ½$

Rejection region: Using $n = 8$ (since there is one tie), the rejection region is $x = 7, 8$ with $\alpha = 1/256 + 8/256 = .035$. From Chapter 9, Exercise 15, $x = 6$. Therefore, do not reject H_0.

3. Rank from smallest to largest and give solvent businesses the top 6 ranks (or equivalently, the average of the top 6 ranks).

With (1)	*Without (2)*
4	1
7	2
10	3
13	5
15	6
16	8
17	9
18	11
19	12
20	14

H_0: no difference between the two states.

H_a: businesses in state with strict requirements are more likely to succeed.

Rejection region: State with strict regulations should have higher ranks if H_a is true, making $U = n_1 n_2 + \frac{1}{2} n_1(n_1 + 1) - T_1$, small.

With $\alpha = .056$, using Table 7, reject H_0 if $U \leqslant 28$.

Calculate $U = 10(10) + \frac{1}{2}(10)(11) - 139 = 16$. Reject H_0.

4. Rank the scores from low to high. Note $n_1 = 7$, $n_2 = 8$.

Executives (1)	*Administrators(2)*
6(10)	3(6)
10(15)	5(9)
3(6)	2(4)
8(12.5)	0(1.5)
8(12.5)	3(6)
7(11)	1(3)
9(14)	0(1.5)
	4(8)

H_0: no difference in the distributions.

H_a: scores are higher for executives.

Rejection region: Executives should have higher ranks if H_a is true, making $U = n_1 n_2 + \frac{1}{2} n_1(n_1 + 1) - T_1$ small.

Using Table 7, reject H_0 if $U \leqslant 13$ with $\alpha = .0469$.

Calculate $U = 7(8) + \frac{1}{2}(7)(8) - 81 = 3$. Reject H_0.

Set 18B

1. The data are ranked according tc magnitude.

1	*2*	*3*
7.1 (13.5)	4.9 (2)	6.7 (10)
6.2 (6.5)	6.6 (9)	6.0 (5)
7.0 (12)	6.8 (11)	7.3 (15)
5.6 (4)	4.6 (1)	6.2 (6.5)
6.4 (8)	5.3 (3)	7.1 (13.5)
$R_1 = 44$	$R_2 = 26$	$R_3 = 50$

Test statistic:

$$H = \frac{12}{15(16)}\left(\frac{44^2 + 26^2 + 50^2}{5}\right) - 3(16) = 51.12 - 48 = 3.12$$

Rejection region: With $\alpha = .05$ and $\nu = t - 1 = 2$, reject H_0 if $H \geqslant \chi^2_{.05} = 5.99$. Do not reject H_0. There is insufficient evidence to indicate a difference between rations.

2. The data are ranked according to magnitude.

0.5	*1.0*	*1.5*	*2.0*
8 (9.5)	9 (11.5)	4 (1.5)	4 (1.5)
14 (14)	7 (7)	6 (5)	7 (7)
9 (11.5)	5 (3.5)	7 (7)	5 (3.5)
12 (13)		8 (9.5)	
$R_1 = 48$	$R_2 = 22$	$R_3 = 23$	$R_4 = 12$

Test statistic:

$$H = \frac{12}{14(15)}\left(\frac{48^2}{4} + \frac{22^2}{3} + \frac{23^2}{4} + \frac{12^2}{3}\right) - 3(15)$$

$$= 52.4333 - 45 = 7.4333$$

Rejection region: With $\alpha = .01$ and $\nu = t - 1 = 3$ degrees of freedom, reject H_0 if $H \geqslant 11.3449$.
Do not reject H_0. There is insufficient evidence to indicate a difference in the four lengths of instructional time.

Set 18C

1. $H_0: p = 1/2$ where $p = P[\text{Appr. A exceeds Appr. B}]$.

   $H_a: p \neq 1/2$

   With $\alpha = .022$ from Table 1, reject H_0 if $x = 0, 1, 9, 10$. Since x = number of plus signs = 8, do not reject H_0. We cannot detect a difference between appraisers A and B.
2. H_0: no difference in distributions of appraisals for A and B.
   H_a: appraisals different for appraisers A and B.

Rank the absolute differences from smallest to largest and calculate T, the smaller of the two (positive and negative) rank sums.

Property	1	2	3	4	5	6	7	8	9	10
d_i	1860	1380	3490	1200	-80	920	2190	390	-320	520
Rank $\lvert d_i \rvert$	8	7	10	6	1	5	9	3	2	4

Rejection region: With $\alpha = .02$ and a two-sided test, reject H_0 if $T \leqslant 5$. Since $T = 1 + 2 = 3$, reject H_0, there is a difference between A and B.

3.

Sample	d_i	*Rank* $\lvert d_i \rvert$
1	2	6.5
2	1	2
3	-1	2
4	2	6.5
5	3	8
6	-1	2
7	0	*
8	2	6.5
9	2	6.5

H_0: no difference in brightness scores.

H_a: difference in brightness scores.

Rejection region: With $\alpha = .05$ and a two-sided test, reject H_0 if $T \leqslant 4$ ($n = 8$, Table 9)

Since $T = 2 + 2 = 4$, H_0 is rejected. There is a difference in mean brightness scores for the two dyes.

4. $H_0: p = ½$ where $p = P$[positive difference] and $n = 24$.

$H_a: p > ½$

Using $\alpha = .05$ and the normal approximation, H_0 will be rejected if

$$\frac{x - .5n}{.5\sqrt{n}} > +1.645$$

where x = number of positive differences. Calculate

$$z = \frac{x - 12}{.5\sqrt{24}} = \frac{16 - 12}{2.45} = 1.63. \text{ Do not reject } H_0.$$

5. The ranks of the absolute differences are given below along with their corresponding signs.

-12, 13, 6, -4, -10, 3, 14.5, 20, 8, 16, -9, -1, 22, 17, 11, 18, 19, 24, -5, 21, -7, 14.5, -2, 23

With $\alpha = .05$ and a one-sided test, reject H_0 if $T \leqslant 92$. Since $T = 50$, reject H_0. Note that the sign test is computationally simple, but the Wilcoxon signed rank test is more efficient since it allows us to reject H_0 while the sign test did not.

Set 18D

1. The responses within readers are ranked from 1 to 4.

	Reader	*1*	*2*	*3*	*4*	*5*	
Type Style	1	3	1.5	2	2.5	2.5	$R_1 = 11.5$
	2	4	3	4	4	2.5	$R_2 = 17.5$
	3	2	4	3	2.5	4	$R_3 = 15.5$
	4	1	1.5	1	1	1	$R_4 = 5.5$

Test statistic:

$$X^2 = \frac{12}{5(4)(5)}(11.5^2 + 17.5^2 + 15.5^2 + 5.5^2) - 3(5)(5) = 85.08 - 75$$
$$= 10.08$$

Rejection region: With $\alpha = .01$ and $\nu = t - 1 = 3$, reject H_0 if $X^2 \geqslant \chi^2_{.01} = 11.3449$.
Do not reject H_0. There is insufficient evidence to indicate a difference due to type styles.

2. The data are ranked within areas from 1 to 4.

	Brands	*1*	*2*	*3*	*4*
Areas	1	1	2	4	3
	2	1	4	2	3
	3	1	4	2	3
	4	1.5	3	1.5	4
	5	1	4	3	2
		$R_1 = 5.5$	$R_2 = 17$	$R_3 = 12.5$	$R_4 = 15$

Test statistic:

$$X^2 = \frac{12}{5(4)(5)}(5.5^2 + 17^2 + 12.5^2 + 15^2) - 3(5)(5)$$
$$= 84.06 - 75 = 9.06$$

Rejection region: With $\alpha = .05$ and $\nu = t - 1 = 3$, reject H_0 if $X^2 \geqslant 7.81$.
Reject H_0. There is a difference among the four brands.

Set 18E

1. H_0: advertising has no effect on sales.
   H_a: advertising increases sales of advertised model.
   Rejection region: With $n_1 = 13, n_2 = 14$ the normal approximation is used and H_0 is rejected if

$$z = \frac{R - E(R)}{\sigma_R} < -1.645$$

   Calculate

$$E(R) = 1 + \frac{2(13)(14)}{27} = 14.48$$

$$\sigma_R^2 = \frac{364(337)}{27^2(26)} = \frac{122668}{18963} = 6.4688$$

$$z = \frac{9 - 14.48}{\sqrt{6.4688}} = \frac{-5.48}{2.54} = -2.16 \qquad \text{Reject } H_0.$$

2. The sequence of runs is AAAAAAEAAEEEEEE or AAAAEAAAAEEEEEE or AAAAAEAAAEEEEEE, depending on how the three observations with rank 6 are arranged. In any case, $R = 4$. The rejecton region, with $n_1 = 7, n_2 = 8$ and $\alpha = .051$ is to reject H_0 if $R \leqslant 5$. Hence, H_0 is rejected and we conclude that status-frustration scores are higher among corporate executives.
3. Rank the examination scores, and note that the interview scores are already in rank order.

Interview Rank (x_i)	*Exam Rank* (y_i)
4	3
7	2
5	5
3	4
6	1
2	6
1	7

$n = 7$ $\qquad \Sigma x_i^2 = 140$

$\Sigma x_i = 28$ $\qquad \Sigma y_i^2 = 140$

$\Sigma y_i = 28$ $\qquad \Sigma x_i y_i = 88$

$$r_s = \frac{88 - \dfrac{(28)^2}{7}}{140 - \dfrac{(28)^2}{7}} = \frac{88 - 112}{140 - 112} = -.857$$

To test $H_0: \rho_s = 0$; $H_a: \rho_s < 0$, the rejection region is $r_s < -.714$. Hence, H_0 is rejected with $\alpha = .05$.

4. $n = 9$

$\Sigma x_i = \Sigma y_i = 45$

$\Sigma x_i^2 = \Sigma y_i^2 = 285$

$\Sigma x_i y_i = 173$

$H_0: \rho_s = 0$

$H_a: \rho_s < 0$

$$r_s = \frac{173 - \dfrac{45^2}{9}}{285 - \dfrac{45^2}{9}} = \frac{-52}{60} = -.87$$

With $\alpha = .05$, reject H_0 if $r_s < -.600$. Reject H_0.

Set 19A

1. For each truck purchased, the company will incur a loss of 250 + 500 = 750, whether or not the truck is in service. If the truck is in service, it will earn 1250 - 150 = \$1100, so that the total profit will be 1100 - 750 = 350.

Profit Table

		Number in Service		
		1	*2*	*3*
Number of trucks bought	1	350	350	350
	2	-400	700	700
	3	-1150	-50	1050

Opportunity Loss Table

		Number in Service		
		1	*2*	*3*
Number of trucks bought	1	0	350	700
	2	750	0	350
	3	1500	750	0

2. If one bid is submitted, he spends \$85,000 and earns \$100,000 for a profit of \$15,000. If two bids are submitted, he initially spends \$10,000; if one bid is awarded he earns \$20,000 - 10,000, while if two bids are awarded he earns \$200,000 - 155,000 - 10,000 = \$35,000. Similarly, the profits for three bids may be calculated.

Profit Table

		Number of Contracts Awarded			
		0	*1*	*2*	*3*
No. of Bids Submitted	1	- 5,000	15,000	15,000	15,000
	2	-10,000	10,000	35,000	35,000
	3	-15,000	5,000	30,000	60,000

Opportunity Loss Table

		Number of Contracts Awarded			
		0	*1*	*2*	*3*
No. of Bids Submitted	1	0	0	20,000	45,000
	2	5,000	5,000	0	25,000
	3	10,000	10,000	5,000	0

Set 19B

1.

s_j	$p(s_j)$
1	.3
2	.6
3	.1

a. $E(L_1) = 0(.3) + 350(.6) + 700(.1) = 280$
$E(L_2) = 750(.3) + 350(.1) = 260$
$E(L_3) = 1500(.3) + 750(.6) = 900$
To minimize $E(L_i)$, purchase two trucks.

b. Cost of uncertainty is $E(L_2) = \$260$

2. a. Profit = (Price per unit) × (No. of units) = \$60.

Profit Table

Crop	Weather: Dry	Avg.	Excess
1	165	390	465
2	240	440	240
3	290	240	140

Opportunity Loss Table

Crop	Weather: Dry	Avg.	Excess
1	125	50	0
2	50	0	225
3	0	200	325

b. $E(L_1) = 125(.2) + 50(.7) = \$60$
$E(L_2) = 50(.2) + 225(.1) = \$32.50$
$E(L_3) = 200(.7) + 325(.1) = \$172.50$
To minimize $E(L_i)$, plant crop 2.

c. Cost of uncertainty is $E(L_2) = \$32.50$

Set 19C

1. a. **Profit Table**

Available Equipment	Demand: 0	1	2	3
1	-50	450	450	450
2	-100	400	900	900
3	-150	350	850	1350

Note: We assume that if a contractor demands more equipment than is available, he will rent the available equipment, and go elsewhere for the rest.

b. **Opportunity Loss Table**

Available Equipment	Demand: 0	1	2	3
1	0	0	450	900
2	50	50	0	450
3	100	100	50	0

Available	Max. Opp. Loss
1	900
2	450
3	100

The minimax decision is to keep 3 large pieces of equipment.

2.

No. Bought	*Max. Opp. Loss*
1	700
2	750
3	1500

Referring to Exercise 1, Self-Correcting Exercises 19A, the maximum opportunity losses are shown at the left. The minimax decision is to buy 1 truck.

3.

Crop	*Max. Opp. Loss*
1	125
2	225
3	325

Referring to Exercise 2, Self-Correcting Exercises 19B, the minimax decision is to plant crop 1.

4. Substitute utility values for monetary values in Exercise 1, Self-Correcting Exercises 19A.

$$E(U_1) = .30(.3) + .30(.6) + .30(.1) = .30$$

$$E(U_2) = .05(.3) + .60(.6) + .60(.1) = .435$$

$$E(U_3) = 0(.3) + .05(.6) + 1.00(.1) = .13$$

5. In order to maximize the expected utility, two trucks should be bought.

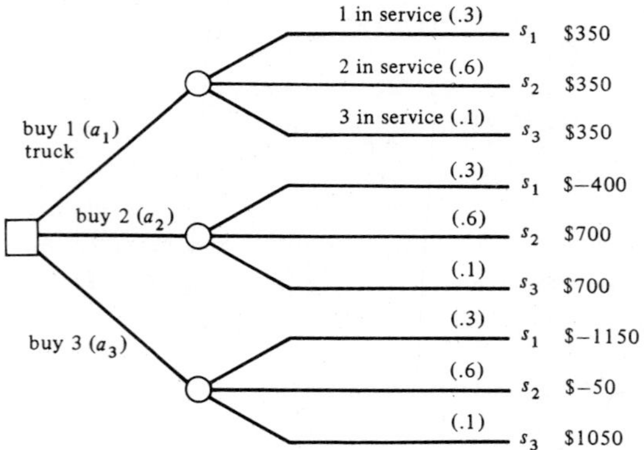

ANSWERS TO EXERCISES

Chapter 2 Answers

1. a. Range = 6.8; c. 80; 55; e. median = 19.5; f. 10; g. 75 (upper quartile); h. $\bar{x}$ = 19.03; s^2 = 2.7937; s = 1.67; i. Yes, since 70%, 95% and 100% of the measurements lie in the intervals $\bar{x} \pm ks$, k = 1, 2, 3, respectively; j. Yes (see i).
2. Outer fences: 11.85 and 26.20; no outliers; data roughly symmetric
3. a. Range = 7; b. 2; c. bimodal (0 and 2); d. $\bar{x}$ = 1.96; s^2 = 3.1233; s = 1.77; f. .44; .32; g. No, not bell-shaped.
4. Bar heights for each year represent total sales volume (cash + credit).
5. *Receipts chart:* Individual income taxes – 137 degrees; Corporation income taxes – 40 degrees; Social insurance receipts – 119 degrees; Excise taxes – 11 degrees; Other – 54 degrees.
   Expenditures chart: Income security – 151 degrees; National defense – 104 degrees; Net interest – 50 degrees; Other – 54 degrees.
6. *1978 chart:* Common stock – 180 degrees; Preferred stock – 36 degrees; Industrial bonds – 36 degrees; Government bonds – 90 degrees; Mortgages – 18 degrees.
   1988 chart: Common stock – 118 degrees; Preferred stock – 18 degrees; Industrial bonds – 54 degrees; Government bonds – 118 degrees; Mortgages – 72 degrees.
7. Bar height for each year represents total dollar volume (Australia and Great Britain and W. Germany).
8. a. At least zero, 3/4 and 8/9 of the measurements lie in the intervals 41.7 to 43.3, 40.9 to 44.1, 40.1 to 44.9, respectively.
   b. Approximately 68%, 95%, and 99.7% of the measurements lie in the intervals 41.7 to 43.3, 40.9 to 44.1, 40.1 to 44.9, respectively.

9. a. 16%; b. 81.5%
10. a. 4; b. 4; c. 1.7, 1.0, 1.25; e. $s = 1.58$ and is approximated as $\frac{6-2}{2.5} = 1.6$.
11. a. 8; b. 8.45 to 9.05; 12.05 to 12.45
12. $\mu = 6.6$ oz
13. a. s is approximated as 16.
    b. $\bar{x} = 136.07$; $s^2 = 292.4952$; $s = 17.1$
    c. $a = 101.82$; $b = 170.27$
    d. Yes, for *approximate* calculations.
    e. No.
14. s is approximated as .8; $\bar{x} = 5$; $s^2 = .5$; $s = .71$
16. Inner fences 96.25 and 174.25; no outliers; data roughly symmetric
17. $\bar{x} = 1.4$; $s^2 = 2.27$; $s = 1.5$
    At least zero, 3/4 and 8/9 of the measurements lie in the intervals -1 to 2.9, -1.6 to 4.4, and -3.1 to 5.9, respectively.
18. a. At least zero.
    b. Approximately .95 (95%).
19. a. Approximately 97.4%.
    b. Approximately 16.0%.
20. Approximately .025.
21. $\bar{x} = 14.9$; $s^2 = 5.88$; $s = 2.42$

Chapter 3 Answers

1. Sum of the probabilities for all sample points in A.
2. $0 \leqslant P(E_i) \leqslant 1$; $\Sigma P(E_i) = 1$
3. a. Independent if and only if $P(A|B) = P(A)$.
   b. Mutually exclusive if and only if $P(AB) = 0$.
4. a. ABC; ACB b. CAB; ACB;
   c. ABC; ACB; CAB; d. ACB;
   e. $P(A) = 1/3$; $P(A|B) = 1/2$; dependent.
5. a. .12; b. .38; c. .88
6. .77
7. a. 1/5; b. 2/5; c. No
8. a. 1/8; b. 0
9. 11/24
10. If independent, $P(AB) > 0$; if disjoint, $P(AB) = 0$.
11. a. 1/2; b. 1/2; c. 5/6
12.

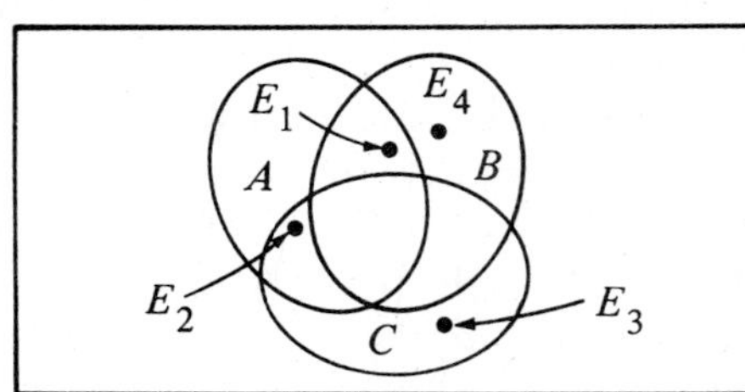

13. a. $\frac{1}{6}$; b. $\frac{2}{3}$; $\frac{1}{3}$; c. $\frac{2}{3}$; $\frac{2}{3}$; d. $\frac{5}{6}$; $\frac{5}{6}$

14. a. *B* and *C*; b. *A* and *B*; *A* and *C*

15. a. .25; b. .383; c. .617; d. .558; e. .692; f. .058; g. .13; h. .80; i. .583

16. 1 - .59 = .41

17. No, .5563 is the correct answer.

18. a. $\frac{1}{720}$; b. $\frac{17}{24}$

19. a. .328; b. .263

20. .0256

21. a. .128; b. .488

22. a. .2; b. .4

23. a. *P*[erroneous indication of tuberculosis]; b. .01089; c. Approximately 8% of those with positive x-rays have tuberculosis.

24. 59/64

25. 15/24

Chapter 4 Answers

1.

x	$p(x)$
0	1/6
1	2/3
2	1/6

3. The histogram would approach the probability histogram of Exercise 2.

4. $0 \leqslant p(x) \leqslant 1$, $x = 0, 1, 2$; $\Sigma_{x=0}^{2} p(x) = 1$.

5.

x	$p(x)$
0	1/27
1	6/27
2	12/27
3	8/27

6. $0 \leqslant p(x) \leqslant 1$, $x = 0, 1, 2, 3$; $\sum_{x=0}^{3} p(x) = 1$.

7.

x	$p(x)$
0	.2
1	.6
2	.2

8. a. $\frac{1}{4}$; b. $\frac{3}{16}$; c. $\frac{9}{64}$; d. $p(x) = \left(\frac{3}{4}\right)^{x-1}\left(\frac{1}{4}\right)$; e. Yes.

9. The mean is approximately 2; Range/4 = (3 - 1)/4 approximates σ; $\sigma \approx .5$
10. $E(x) = \frac{17}{8}$; $\sigma = .60$
11. $E(x) = 2$; $\sigma^2 = 5$
12. $E(x) = 2$
13.

x	$p(x)$
0	8/27
1	4/9
2	2/9
3	1/27

14. $E(x) = 1$; $\sigma^2 = \frac{2}{3}$
15. $E(x) = \$2800$
16. Premium = \$6.50
18. $E(x) = 1$; $\sigma^2 = \frac{1}{3}$; $\sigma = .58$
19. $E(x) = 1.3$; $\sigma^2 = .61$
20. .3
21. \$2.70
22. No, since the probability that the boy has randomly selected the 3 balls is .0006.
23. No

Chapter 5 Answers

2. $C_x^n p^x q^{n-x}$, $x = 0, 1, \ldots, n$
3. a. Not binomial. The number of trials is a random variable and x is not the number of successes.
   b. $C_x^5 (1/15)^x (14/15)^{5-x}$, $x = 0, 1, \ldots, 5$
   c. Not binomial. p is not a constant and the trials are dependent.
   d. $C_x^5 (.6)^x (.4)^{5-x}$, $x = 0, 1, \ldots, 5$
4. a.

x	$p(x)$
0	q
1	p

   b. $\mu = \sum_{x=0}^{1} x\, C_x^1 p^x q^{1-x} = p$;

$$\sigma^2 = \sum_{x=0}^{1} (x-p)^2 C_x^1 p^x q^{1-x} = pq$$

5. a. $p(x) = C_x^4 (1/2)^4, \quad x = 0, 1, \ldots, 4$
   b.

x	$p(x)$
0	1/16
1	4/16
2	6/16
3	4/16
4	1/16

   c. 2; d. 1; e. $np = 2$; $npq = 1$
6. $A = 81$; $B = 99$
7. 130; 170
8. 1202; 1246
9. a. 5/32; b. 31/32
10. a. .328; b. .942
11. a. 1/32; b. .812
12. a. .122; b. .957
13. a. 82; b. 76
14. .083
15. a. .214; .214
    b. .316; .211
16. $\alpha = .001$; $\beta = .05$
17. a. $H_0: p = .4$; b. .166; c. $H_a: p > .4$; d. .367
18. a. Declaration that the cheeses differ when they are equally desirable.
    b. Failure to declare that a difference exists when one of the cheeses is more desirable.
    c. .022; d. .952; e. .264; f. .004; g. When p is close to the value specified in H_0.
19. a. .629; b. 6
20. a. .110803; b. .012; c. .119
21. a. \$44; b. \$2200
22. .0758
23. a. 2 to 12; b. unemployment rate is higher than the national rate.
24. a. .794; b. .056

Chapter 6 Answers

1. a. .9713; b. .1009; c. .7257; d. .9706; e. .8925; f. .5917
2. a. $z_0 = 0.7$; b. $z_0 = -1.5$; c. $z_0 = 1.55$; d. $z_0 = -1.1$

3. a. $z_0 = 2.13$; b. $z_0 = 1.645$
4. a. .8413; b. .8944; c. .9876; d. .0401
5. a. .2743; b. .9452
6. a. .0475; b. .0475; c. .5788
7. a. .0139; b. .0668; c. .5764
8. a. .876; b. .875
9. a. .608; b. .595
10. a. .9838; b. .0000; c. .8686
11. a. .1635; b. .0192; c. Yes, since $P[x \leqslant 60 \text{ when } p = .2] = .0192$
12. a. .6826; b. .1574
13. $\mu = 10.071$
14. .0548
15. .3520
16. 87.48
17. .0516
18. a. $H_0: p = .2$; $H_a: p < .2$; b. $\alpha = .1292$; c. $\beta = .0336$
19. a. .0548; b. $(.0548)^3 = .0002$
20. a. .833; b. 1/3
21. a. .135; b. .471; c. 5991.46
22. a. 1; 1; b. .135; c. .693

Chapter 7 Answers

1. .9623
2. .3413
3. .0409
4. a. \$65,000 b. \$1980.097 c. \$2000
5. .9876
6. .0032
7. .0049
8. .0062
9. a. 110 ± 2(.99) or 108 to 112 b. Approximately 0
10. .0091

Chapter 8 Answers

1. The inference; measure of goodness.
2. Unbiasedness; minimum variance.
3. 61.23 ± 1.50
4. .06 ± .07
5. .030 ± .033
6. 2.705 ± .012
7. 38 ± 25
8. 22 ± 1
9. Approximately 246
10. Approximately 97
11. Approximately 97
12. Approximately 40

13. .1151 (use correction for continuity).
15. $z = 2.5$; yes.
16. $z = .65$; no
17. $z = -3.40$; yes
18. p-value $< .001$
19. a. $z = 5.8$; yes. b. $3.0 \pm .85$
20. a. $(\hat{p} - .2)\Big/\sqrt{\dfrac{(.2)(.8)}{400}}$; b. $z > 2.33$; c. $|z| > 2.58$; d. $.20 \pm .03$
21. Approximately 3458
22. $z = 1.25$; no.
23. $19.1 \pm .64$
24. $z = 5$; yes.
25. $.06 \pm .04$
26. $z = -1.67$; no.
27. $.07 \pm .08$
28. $z = -2.67$; yes.
29. .99
30. $z = .91$; no.
31. Approximately 38416
32. Approximately 385

Chapter 9 Answers

1. According to the Central Limit Theorem, these statistics will be approximately normally distributed for large n.
2. i. The parent population has a normal distribution.
   ii. The sample is a random sample.
3. The number of degrees of freedom associated with a t-statistic is the denominator of the estimator of σ^2.
4. a. 2.365; b. 2.947; c. 2.920; d. 1.315; e. 1.796
5. Do not reject H_0, since $t = -.6$.
6. $2.48 < \mu < 4.92$
7. Reject H_0, since $t = 3.2$.
8. $12.70 < \mu < 13.70$
9. Reject H_0, since $t = -2.12$.
10. Do not reject H_0, since $t = 1.09$.
11. i. The parent populations have normal distributions.
    ii. The population variances are equal.
    iii. The samples are independent random samples.
12. Reject H_0, since $t = 3.68$.
13. $.86 < \mu_1 - \mu_2 < 2.34$
14. Reject H_0, since $t = 2.92$.
15. Do not reject H_0, since $t = 2.29$.
16. Do not reject H_0, since $t = 1.03$.

17. a. 24.7690; b. 10.8649; c. 20.2777; d. 16.0471; e. 45.7222
18. Do not reject H_0, since $\chi^2 = 8.19$.
19. $.214 < \sigma^2 < 4.387$
20. Do not reject H_0, since $\chi^2 = 2.816$.
21. $2.275 < \sigma^2 < 52.326$
22. a. 2.23; b. 2.34; c. 3.43; d. 6.63
23. Do not reject H_0, since $F = 1.796$.
24. a. Yes, since the variances have not been shown to be significantly different.
    b. Do not reject H_0, since $t = 2.65$.
25. Reject H_0, since $F = 2.06$.

Chapter 10 Answers

1. a. Completely randomized design.
   b.

ANOVA

Source	*d.f.*	*SS*	*MS*	*F*
Chemicals	2	25.1667	12.5834	2.59
Error	9	43.75	4.8611	
Total	11	68.9167		

   c. no; d. -2.25 ± 3.53; e. 39; f. 43.75; g. 11 ± 2.02
2. a. Randomized block design.
   b.

ANOVA

Source	*d.f.*	*SS*	*MS*	*F*
Applications	3	18.9167	6.3056	9.87
Chemicals	2	62.1667	31.0833	48.65
Error	6	3.8333	0.6388	
Total	11	84.9167		

   c. $F = 48.65$; reject H_0; yes; d. 5.25 ± 1.38; e. 21; f. Yes.
3. a. 3×3 factorial experiment; two replications per treatment combination (in a completely randomized pattern)
   b.

ANOVA

Source	*d.f.*	*SS*	*MS*	*F*
A	2	48.7778	24.3889	10.21
C	2	98.1111	49.0556	20.53
AC	4	35.8889	8.9722	3.76
Error	9	21.5000	2.3889	
Total	17	204.2778		

   c. Yes; $F = 3.76$

4. a. Randomized block design.
   b.

ANOVA

Source	d.f.	SS	MS	F
Lines	2	102.2	51.1	11.53
Days	9	474.3	52.7	11.89
Error	18	79.8	4.43	
Total	29	656.3		

   c. $F = 11.5$; yes. d. $F = 11.9$; yes. e. 4.4 ± 1.98

5. a. Completely randomized design.
   b.

ANOVA

Source	d.f.	SS	MS	F
Treatments	3	1052.68	350.89	1.76
Error	15	2997.95	199.86	
Total	18	4050.63		

   c. $F = 1.76$; no.
   d. -12.6 ± 19.06
   e. i. If possible, form five blocks based upon academic achievement as measured by college grade point average, whereby those five graduates within each block would have similar GPA's.
      ii. When there is no effect of GPA upon performance measured by the examination.

6. a.

ANOVA

Source	d.f.	SS	MS	F
Programs	2	25817.49	12908.74	4.43
Error	13	37851.51	2911.65	
Total	15			

   $F = 4.43$; yes.
   b. -63.1 ± 59.9

7. a.

ANOVA

Source	d.f.	SS	MS	F
Autos	4	489.80	122.45	7.55
Additive	3	154.15	51.38	3.17
Error	12	194.60	16.22	
Total	19	838.55		

   b. $F = 3.17$; no. c. $F = 7.55$; yes; yes.

Chapter 11 Answers

1.

	y-intercept	slope
a.	-2	3
b.	0	2
c.	-0.5	-1
d.	2.5	-1.5
e.	2	0

2. a. $\hat{y} = .86 + .71x$
   c. $SSE = 4/7 = .5714$; $s^2 = .1143$;
   SSE will be zero only if all of the observed points were to lie on the fitted line.
   d. Reject $H_0: \beta_1 = 0$, since $t = 11.11$.
   e. $.56 < \beta_1 < .86$
   f. $r = .98$
   g. Since $r^2 = .96$, the use of the linear model rather than $\bar{y}$ as a predictor for y reduced the sum of squares for error by 96%.
   h. $.82 < y_p < 2.32$
   i. Reject $H_0: \beta_0 = 0$, since $t = 6.7$.
3. a. $\hat{y} = 8.86 - 1.27x$
   c. $SSE = 2.34$; $s^2 = .5857$; $s = .76$
   d. Reject $H_0: \beta_1 = 0$, since $t = -13.9$.
   e. $r^2 = .98$; see problem 2g.
   f. 2.51 ± 1.27; $1.24 < y_p < 3.78$
   g. $2.51 \pm .48$; $2.03 < E(y|x = 5) < 2.99$
4. If $r = 1$, the observed points all lie on the fitted line having a positive slope and if $r = -1$, the observed points all lie on the fitted line having a negative slope.
5. a. $\hat{y} = 2 - .875x$.
   c. $SSE = .25$; $s^2 = .0833$; $s = .289$
   d. Reject $H_0: \beta_1 = 0$, since $t = 12.12$.
   e. $2.525 < E(y|x = -1) < 3.225$
   f. $r^2 = .98$; see problem 2g.
   g. $-.345 < y_p < 2.595$
   h. $\bar{x}$.
6. The fitted line may not adequately describe the relationship between x and y outside the experimental region.
7. The error will be a maximum for the values of x at the extremes of the experimental region.
8. a. $\hat{y} = 7.0 + 15.4x$.
   b. $SSE = 50.4$; $s^2 = 8.4$.
   c. Reject $H_0: \beta_1 = 0$, since $t = 16.7$.
   d. $43.0 < E(y|x = 2.5) < 48.0$.
   e. $13.6 < \beta_1 < 17.2$.
   f. $r^2 = .979$; see problem 2g.

9. a. $\hat{y} = 6.96 + 2.31x$
   c. $SSE = .9751$; $s^2 = .1219$
   d. Reject $H_0: \beta_1 = 0$, since $t = 19.25$.
   e. $r = .99$
   f. $r^2 = .979$
   g. Do not reject H_0; $t = 1.67$.
   h. $9.27 \pm .69$; $8.58 < y_p < 9.96$
10. a. $\hat{y} = 20.47 - .758x$
   b. $SSE = 4.66$; $s^2 = .58$
   c. Reject $H_0: \beta_1 = 0$, since $t = -22.21$
   d. $-.84 < \beta_1 < -.66$
   e. $9.86 \pm .56$; $9.30 < E(y|x = 14) < 10.42$
   f. $r^2 = .984$; see problem 2g.

Chapter 12 Answers

1. a. .9976
   b. Yes; $F = 1470.84$
   c. $\hat{y} = -13.01227 + 1.46306x_1$
   d. $\hat{y} = 23.56$
2. a. 99.85%
   b. Yes; $F = 1676.61$
   c. Yes, $t = -2.65$
   d. Yes, $t = 15.14$
   e. 0.3% of the total variation is explained by the linear term.
3. The contributions of x_1 and x_2 are minimal in the presence of x_3 and x_4.
5. Do not reject H_0. $F = .904$
6. Reject H_0. $F = 11.739$. Variables x_3 and x_4 contribute significant information.

Chapter 13 Answers

1. 94.42; 111.56; 126.26; 134.83
2. a. 203.89; b. 212.24; c. 206.71
3. a. 102.44; b. 136.65

Chapter 15 Answers

3. $\bar{x}$ chart: LCL = 31.423; UCL = 31.977
   R chart: LCL = 0; UCL = 1.0152
4. mean too large at hours 2, 3 and 4; range too large at hours 2, 3, 4 and 6.
5. $C_p = 1.211$; $C_{pk} = 1.131$; process is capable of meeting specification limits.

6. a. $\bar{p} = .052$; UCL = .188, LCL = 0
   b. Fourth sample indicates p is too large
7. .3085
8. .5330
9. a. $\bar{c} = 3.25$, UCL = 9.65, LCL = 0
   b. Third sample indicates that c is too large.
10. a. $P(\text{accept when } p = .3) = .65$
    b. Keep n at 4, take $a > 1$; keep a at 1, take $n < 4$.
11. a.

p	0	.10	.30	.50	1
$n = 10$ $a = 1$	1.00	.74	.15	.01	.00
$n = 25$ $a = 1$	1.00	.27	.00	.00	.00

    c. Probability of acceptance decreased
12. a.

p	0	.10	.30	.50	1
$n = 25$ $a = 3$	1.00	.76	.03	.00	.00
$n = 25$ $a = 5$	1.00	.97	.19	.00	.00

    c. Probability of acceptance increased
13. a. 1.0, 1.0 b. .914, .873 c. .736, .537 d. .376, .092 e. .011, .000
    f. .000, .000

Chapter 16 Answers

4. a. $130.25 ± $6.00
   b. $13,025 ± $599.76
5. .15 ± .14
6. 15 ± 14.36
7. $n = 168$
8. .68 ± .05
9. $n = 182$
10. a. 37.9 ± 5.1 miles
    b. .29 ± .07
11. a. $\hat{R} = .8925$
    b. $\hat{\tau}_y = \hat{R}\tau_x = \$31{,}166.10$
    c. $\tau_y = N_{\bar{y}} = \$32{,}364$
12. a. $n = 100$
    b. Select a number between 1 and 100 at random. The sample will include the account corresponding to that random number and every 100th account on the list thereafter.

Chapter 17 Answers

2. a. Yes.
   b. No. Since p_i, $i = 1, 2, 3$ changes from trial to trial.
   c. Yes.
3. a. 8.4; b. 18.0; c. 75.6
4. Reject H_0, $X^2 = 16.535$.
5. Do not reject H_0, $X^2 = 2.300$
6. Reject H_0, $X^2 = 7.97$.
7. Do not reject $H_0: p_1 = p_2 = p_3 = p_4$, $X^2 = 1.709$.
8. Reject H_0, $X^2 = 9.333$.
9. Do not reject the model, $X^2 = 6.156$.

Chapter 18 Answers

1. Sign test: both; Mann-Whitney U test: independent; Wilcoxon signed rank test: related; runs test: independent.
2. $z = -2.54 < -1.645$. Reject H_0.
3. Reject H_0 when $R \leqslant 7$. For $R = 10$, do not reject H_0. The runs test is less efficient for detecting a difference in population means.
4. Reject H_0 when $T \leqslant 8$. For $T = 11$, do not reject H_0.
5. Reject H_0 if $x \leqslant 2$ with $\alpha = .055$. When $x = 1$, reject H_0.
6. $r_s = 1$. While $r = 1$ only when the data points all lie on the same straight line, r_s will be 1 whenever y increases steadily with x.
7. a. .738; b. $.738 \geqslant .643$; reject H_0.
8. With $\alpha = .032$, reject H_0 when $R \geqslant 13$. Observe $R = 13$; reject H_0.
9. a. randomized block design b. $X^2 = 12.95$, reject H_0; there is a difference in the three production lines.
10. a. completely randomized design b. $H = 4.86$; do not reject H_0.

Chapter 19 Answers

2. a. **Profit Table**

	Demand			
Inventory	*27*	*28*	*29*	*30*
27	5.40	5.40	5.40	5.40
28	5.10	5.60	5.60	5.60
29	4.80	5.30	5.80	5.80
30	4.50	5.00	5.50	6.00

b. **Opportunity Loss Table**

	Demand			
Inventory	*27*	*28*	*29*	*30*
27	0.00	0.20	0.40	0.60
28	0.30	0.00	0.20	0.40
29	0.60	0.30	0.00	0.20
30	0.90	0.60	0.30	0.00

c. Minimax level is 28.

d. 28 with expected opportunity loss of $0.17.

3. Invest in the savings account; expected return for drilling = $0; expected return for savings = $120.
4. Greater than .212.
5. a. **Profit Table**

	Rain	*No Rain*
Insurance	-2000	18,000
No Insurance	-5000	20,000

b. Do not buy insurance; expected profit for insuring = $13,000; expected profit for not insuring = $13,750.

6. Up to $1250.
7. a. p = .1429; b. $0.
8. Expected return given A = $9400; expected return given B = $11,000.
   a. Contract B; b. Contract B
9. a.

Cakes Pre-pared	Demand				
	0	*1*	*2*	*3*	*4*
0	0	2	4	6	8
1	2	0	2	4	6
2	4	2	0	2	4
3	6	4	2	0	2
4	8	6	4	2	0

b. Minimax decision = 2; c. 2 cakes

10. a.

	Alternative		
Sales volume	*Do not manufacture*	*Buy $1000 machine*	*Buy $2000 machine*
1000	0	0	500
2000	0	1000	1000
5000	0	4000	5500

b. Buy the $2000 machine; c. Buy the $2000 machine.

11. a. $9000. b. 5/41. c. 0

12. a. $E(L_{acc}) = \$4.00$; $E(L_{rej}) = \$9.20$; accept the lot.
    b. $E(L_{acc}) = \$12.25$; $E(L_{rej}) = \$2.57$; reject the lot.
    Revised probabilities are .02, .33, .40, .25.
    c. $E(L_{acc}) = \$15.60$; $E(L_{rej}) = \$2.06$; reject the lot.
    Revised probabilities are .04, .22, .29, .45.
    d. $1.43; e. $1.94
13. a. Let x be the basic cost of the domestic lot.
    E(domestic cost) = $100 + x
    E(foreign cost) = $120 + x; buy domestic lot.
    b. E(domestic cost) = $100
    E(foreign cost) = $128.60 + x; buy domestic lot.
    Revised probabilities are .297, .553, .151.
14. Contract B.